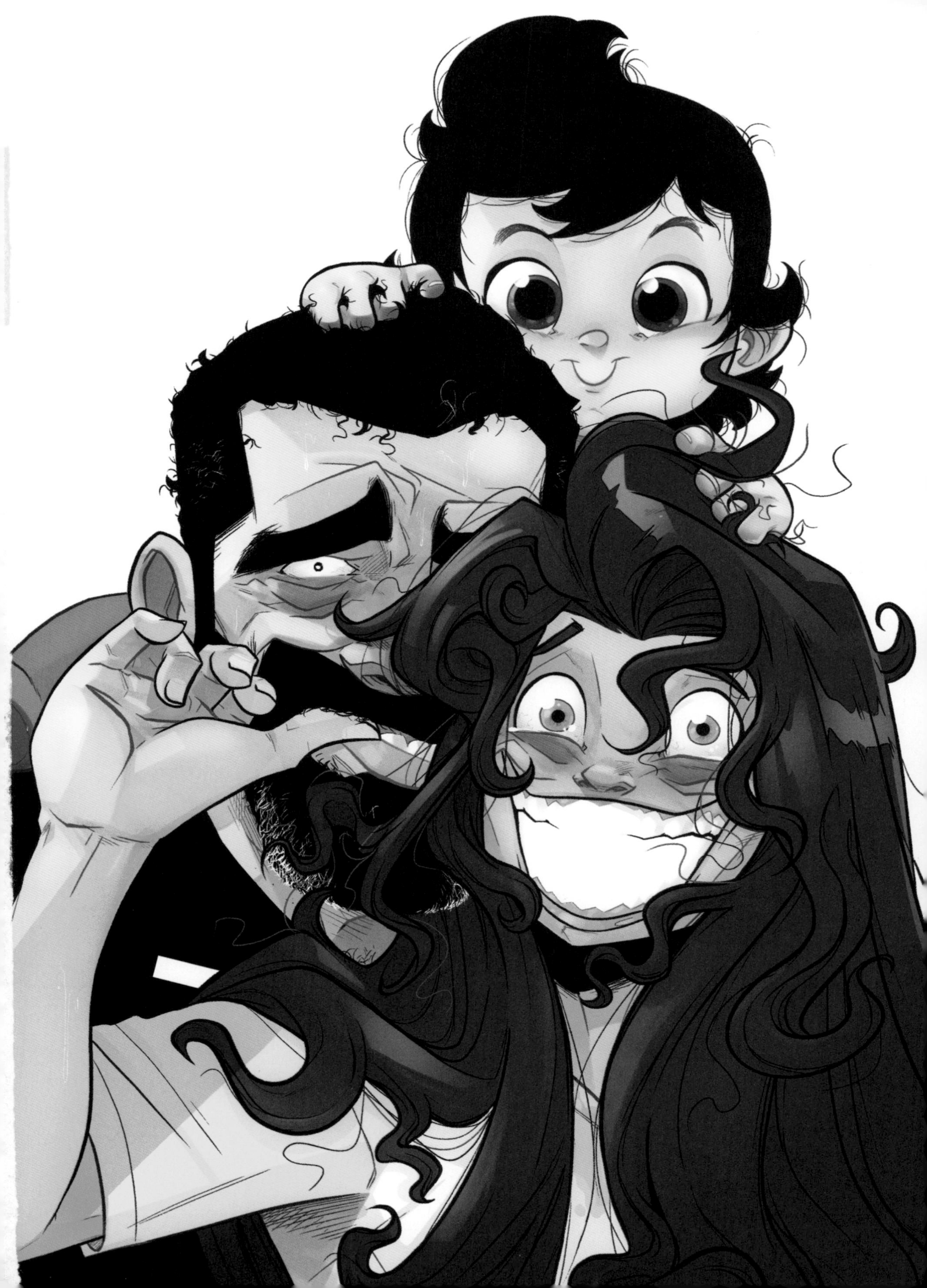

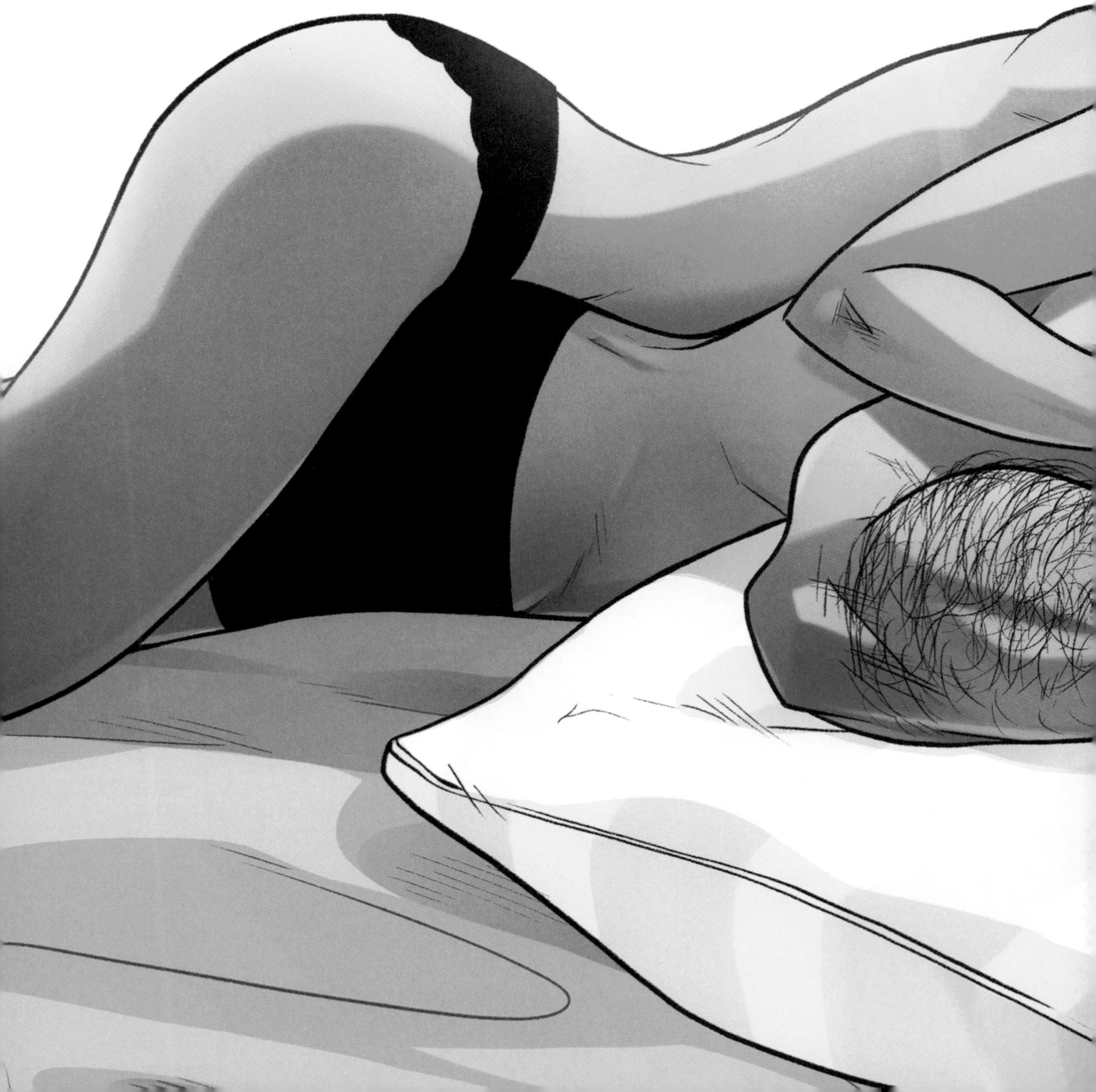

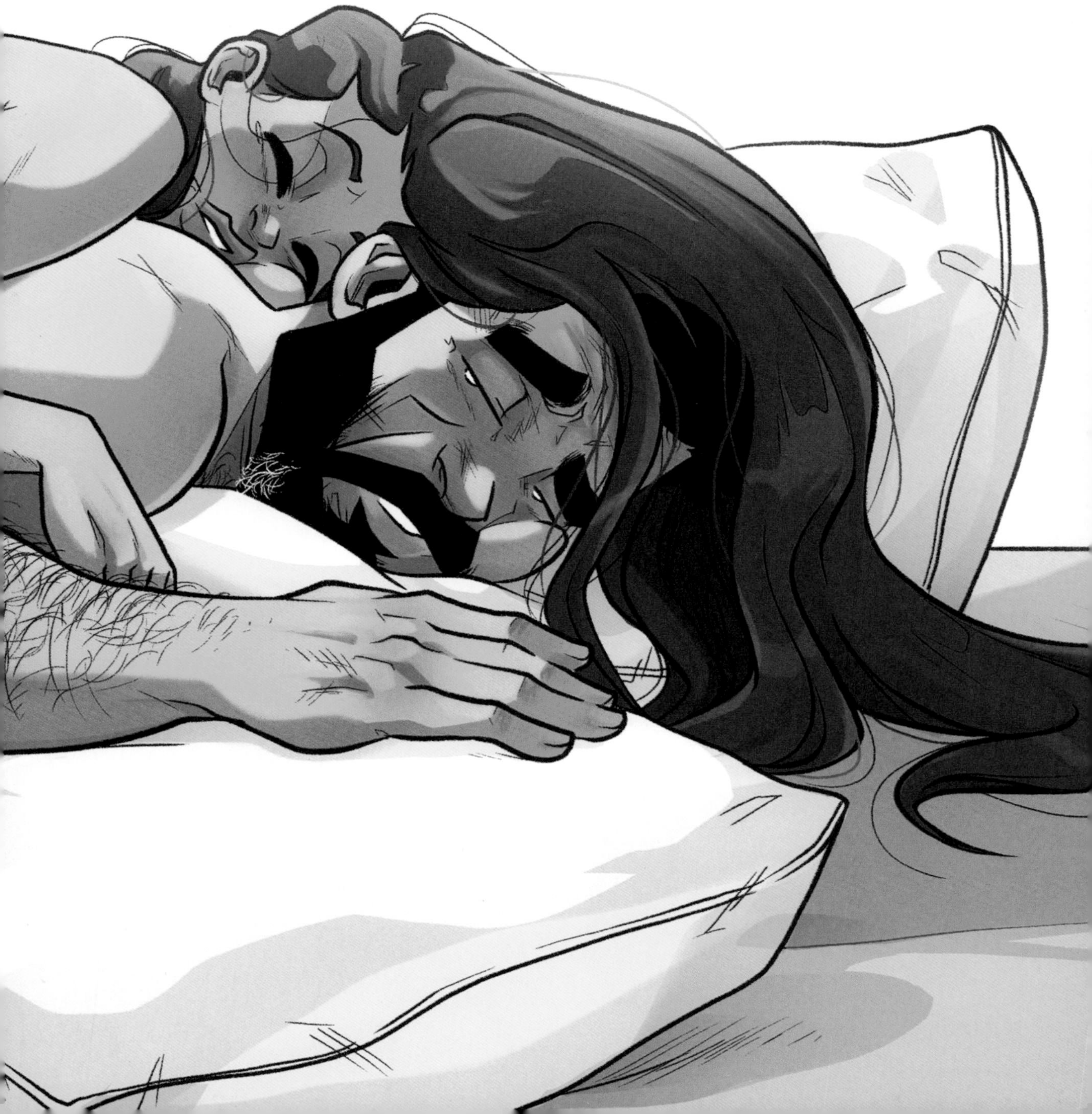

ONE OF THOSE DAYS

YEHUDA & MAYA DEVIR

Random House
New York

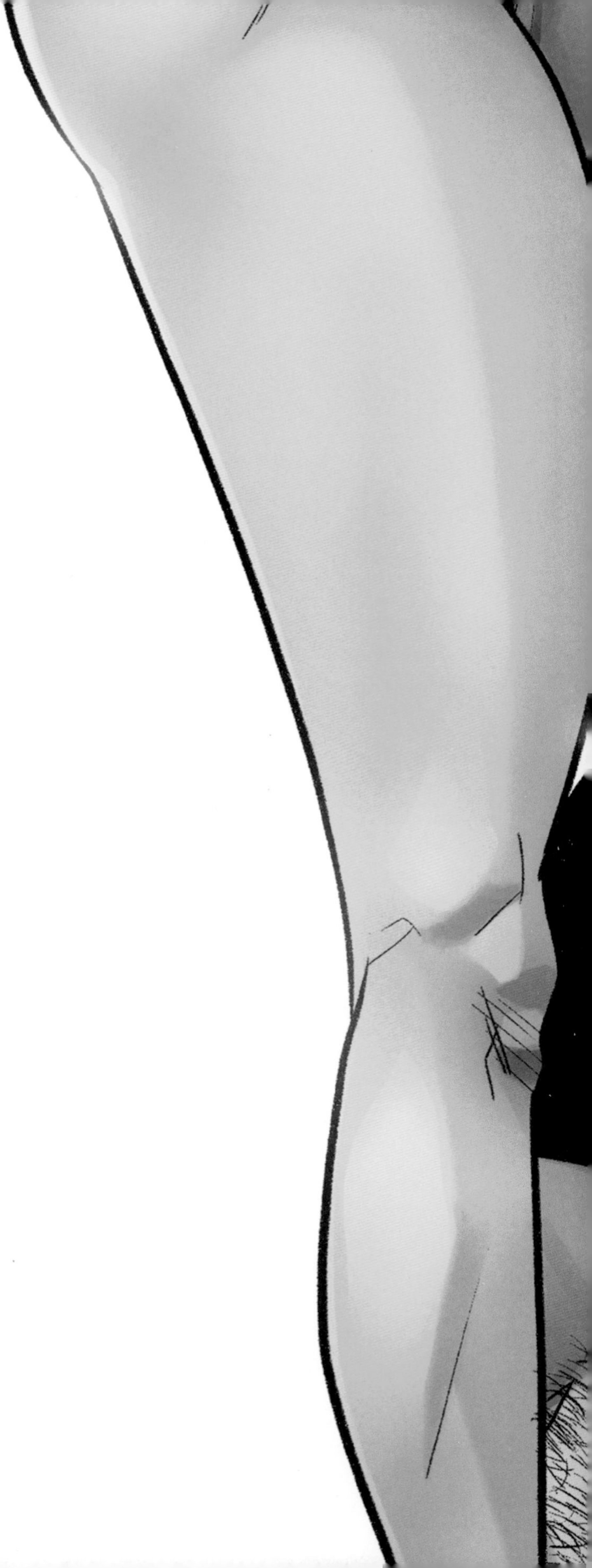

Published in the United States by Random House, an imprint and division of Penguin Random House LLC, New York.

Random House and the House colophon are registered trademarks of Penguin Random House LLC.

This edition collects material originally published weekly in "One of Those Days" web comics 2016–2019. It was subsequently privately published in three separate volumes as *One of Those Days,* vols. 1, 2, 3, by Yehuda and Maya Devir in Israel, copyright © 2017, 2018, 2019 by Yehuda Devir and Maya Devir.

Hardback ISBN 9780593231432
Ebook ISBN 9780593231456

Printed in China on acid-free paper

yehudadevir.com

randomhousebooks.com

9 8 7 6 5 4 3 2 1

First Edition

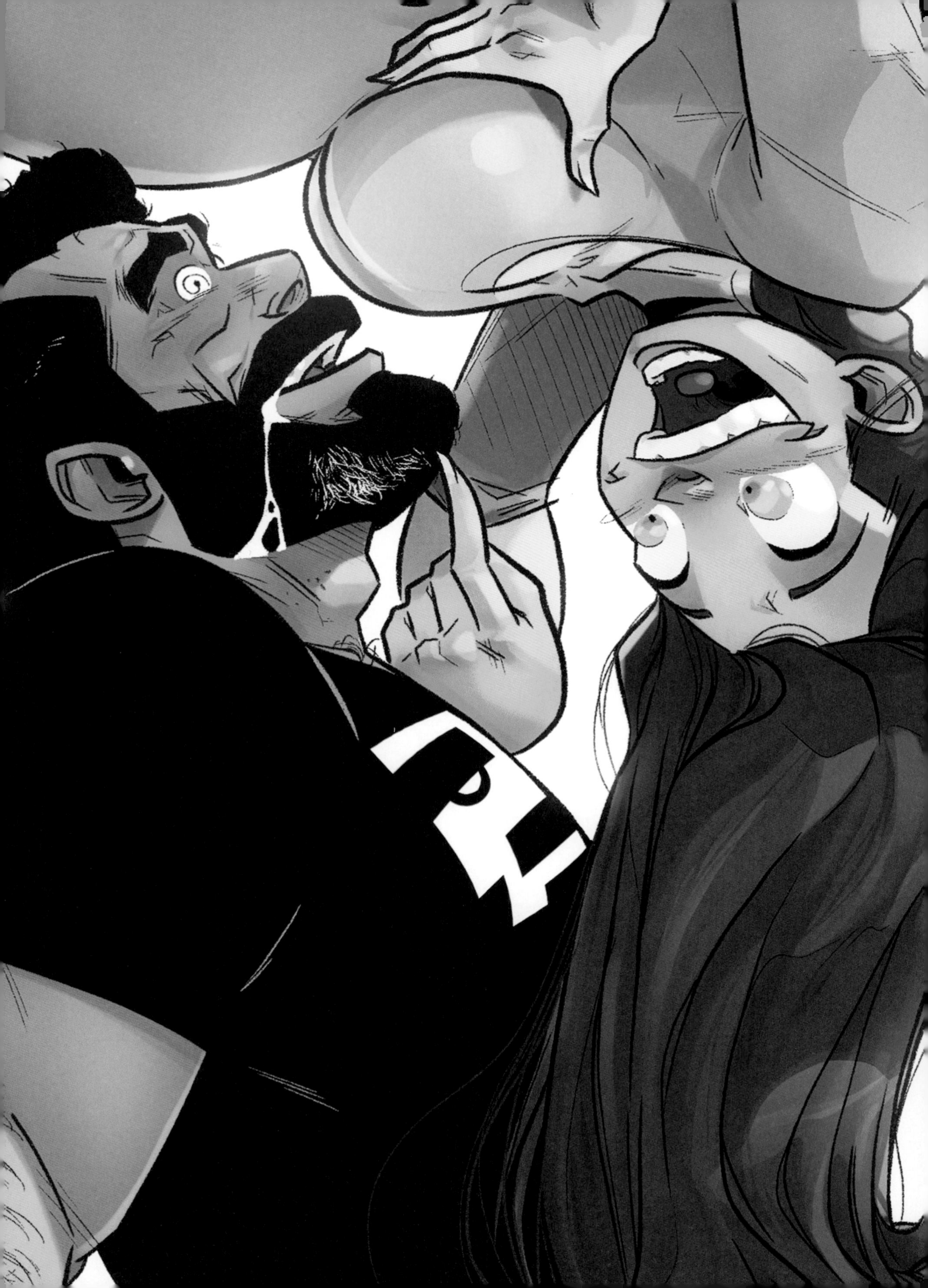

INTRODUCTION

To tell you the truth, *One of Those Days* wasn't planned at all. It began as a few illustrations we made to show our daily lives in the style of a superhero comic. They were meant to be a personal blog, or Yehuda's blog, to be exact, where he described what it was like to live with Maya. And, as an art director, Maya couldn't resist overseeing character design and joined the team immediately.

We quickly realized that these comics could have power and impact when we created an illustration where we share a boiling-hot shower—perfection to Maya's taste, while Yehuda is burning alive. That illustration went viral on social media, with millions of shares on different pages. And so we focused our energy on creating more, and *One of Those Days* was born.

The ability to share our private life in front of the whole world has not come easily to us. In the comics, we reveal a lot of non-photogenic moments and real struggles that we face on a daily basis, such as the difficulty we had getting pregnant. Maybe *One of Those Days* started from a naïve place in which we didn't understand the exposure potential of social media. But we started to grow more comfortable with it when we saw the power it can hold and the happiness it can bring to readers.

This book is a collection of all of those relatable everyday-life moments from marriage and parenthood.

We hope you can find yourself in them.

- Maya & Yehuda Devir -

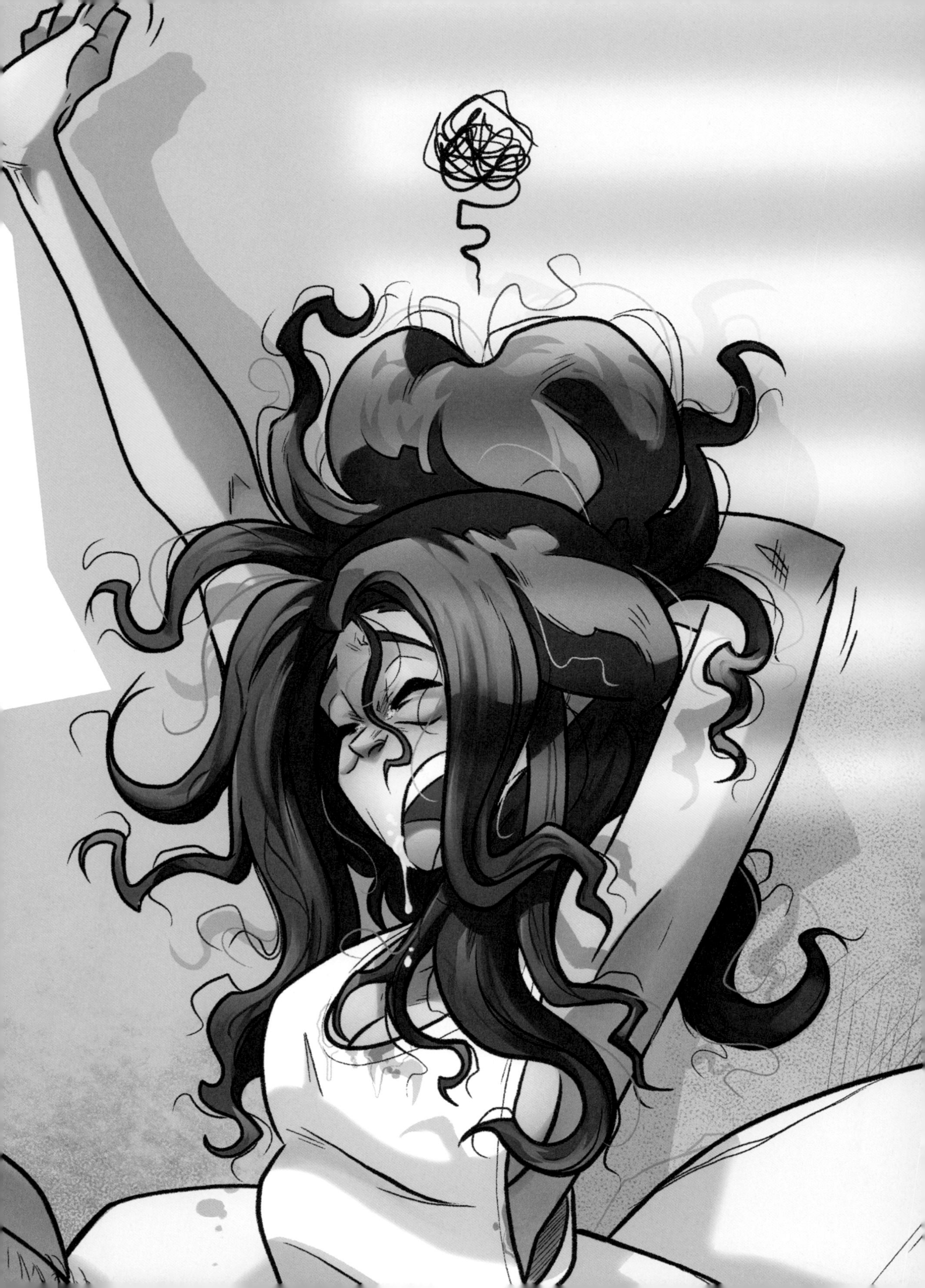

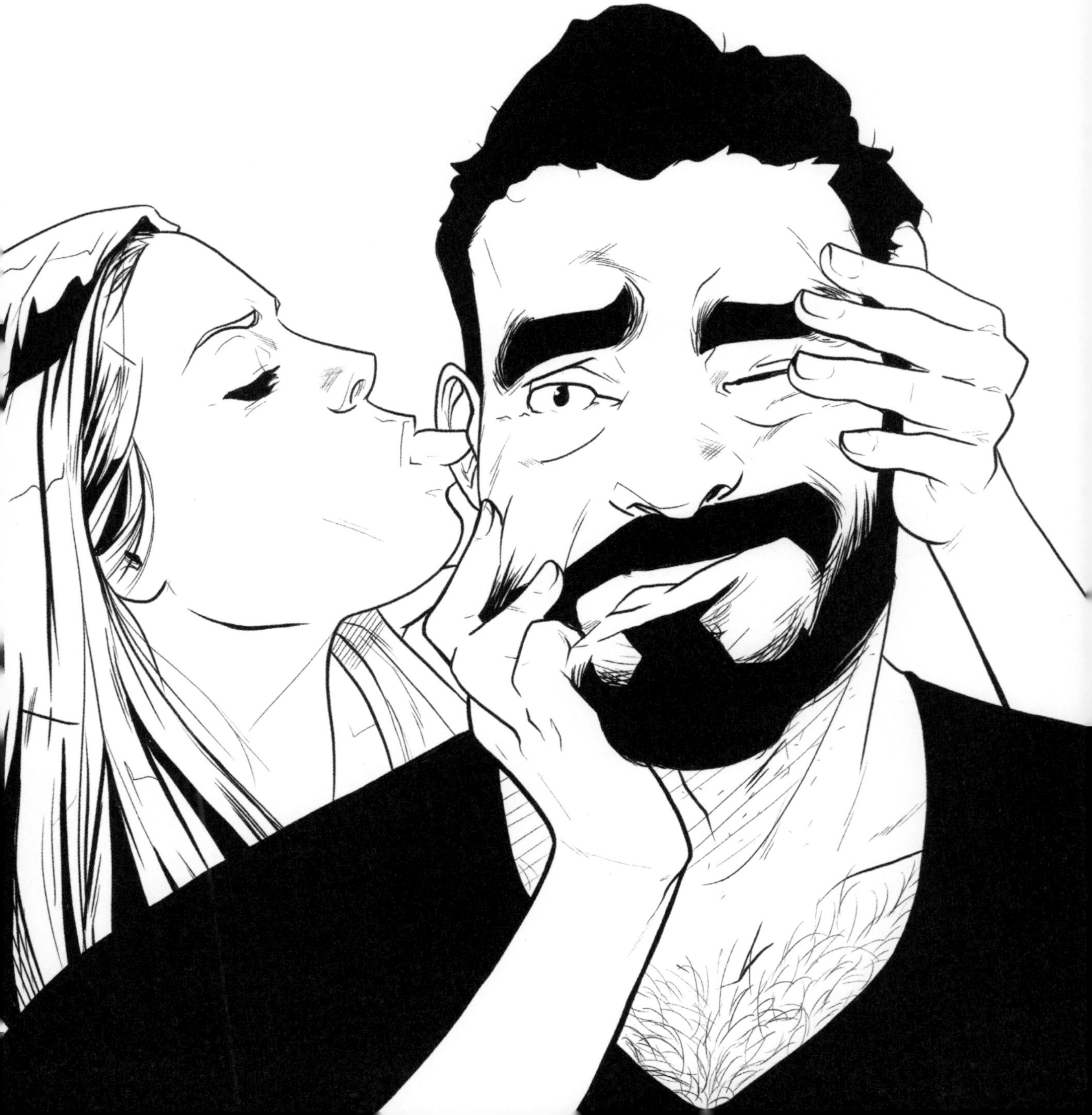

CHAPTER
ONE

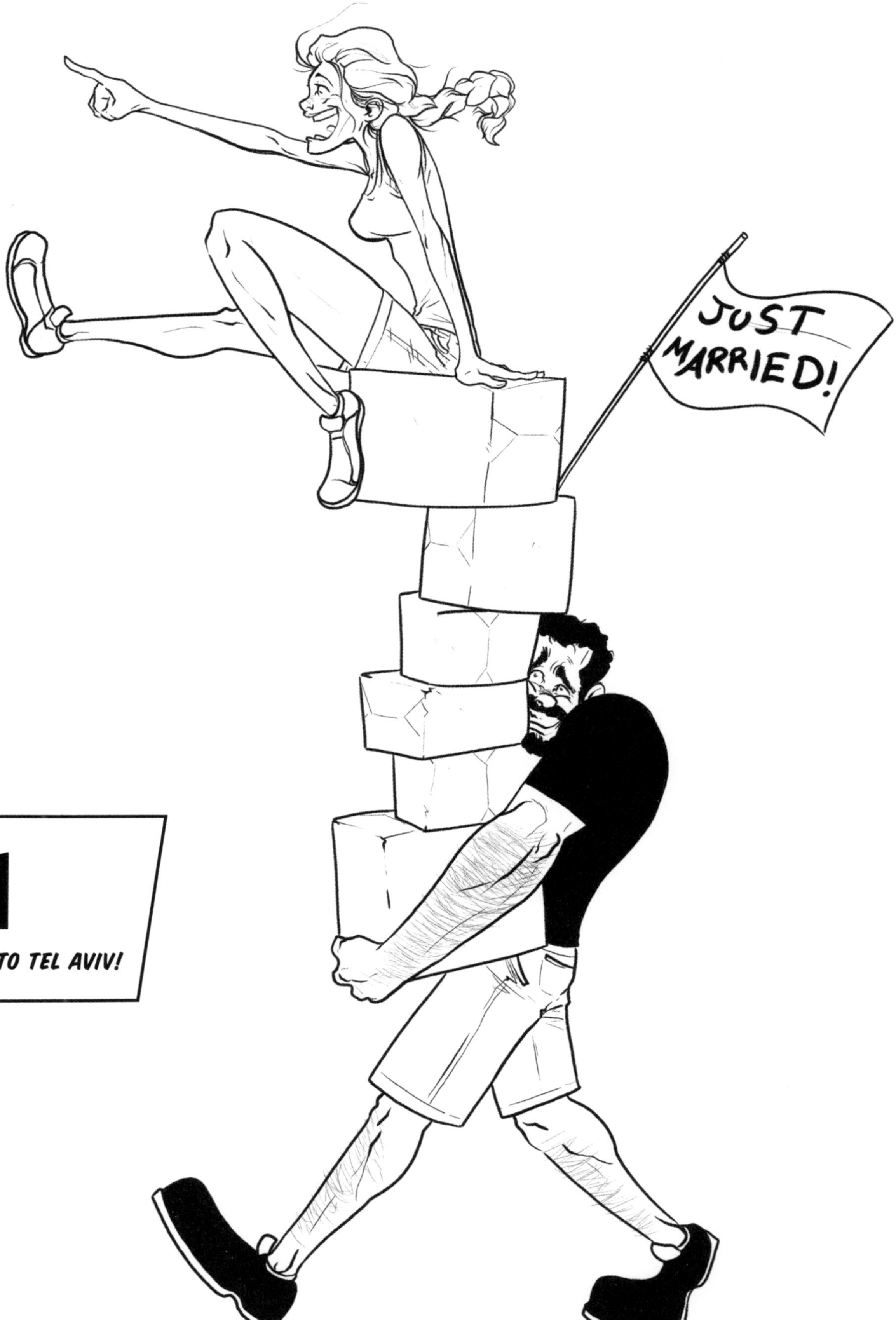
JUST MARRIED!

01

MOVING TO TEL AVIV!

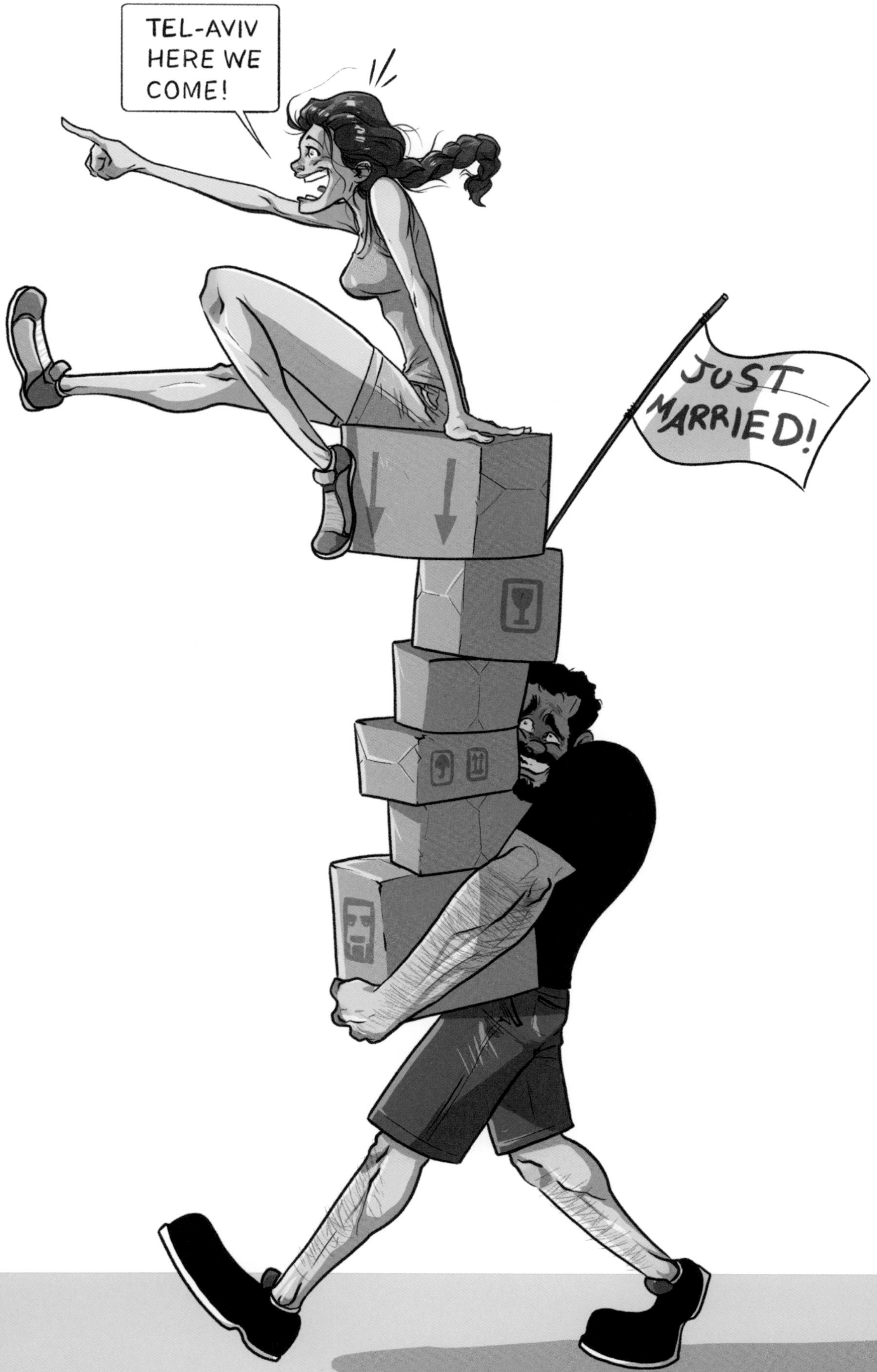
TEL-AVIV HERE WE COME!
JUST MARRIED!

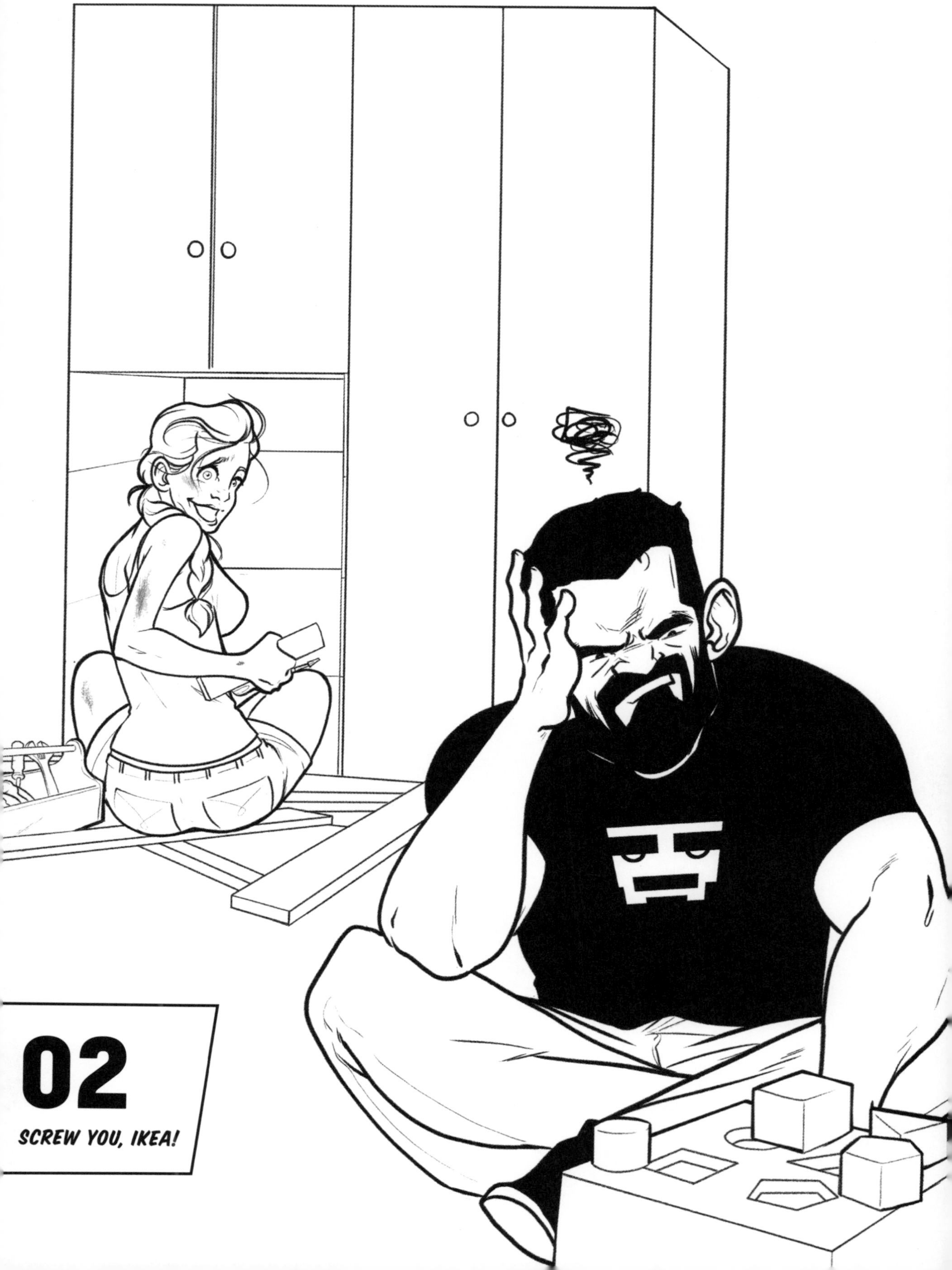

02

SCREW YOU, IKEA!

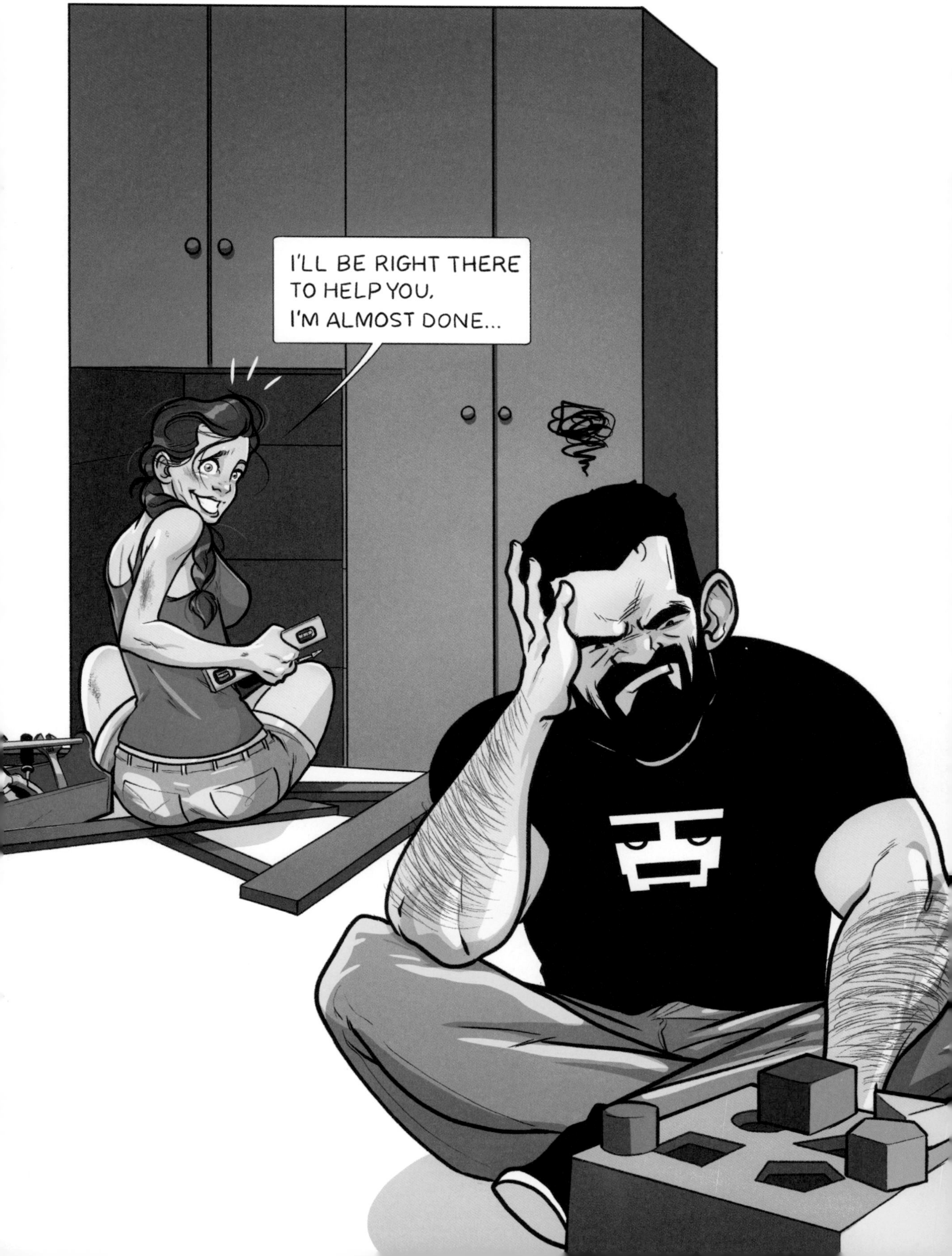
I'LL BE RIGHT THERE
TO HELP YOU,
I'M ALMOST DONE...

03

TEL AVIV BEACH!

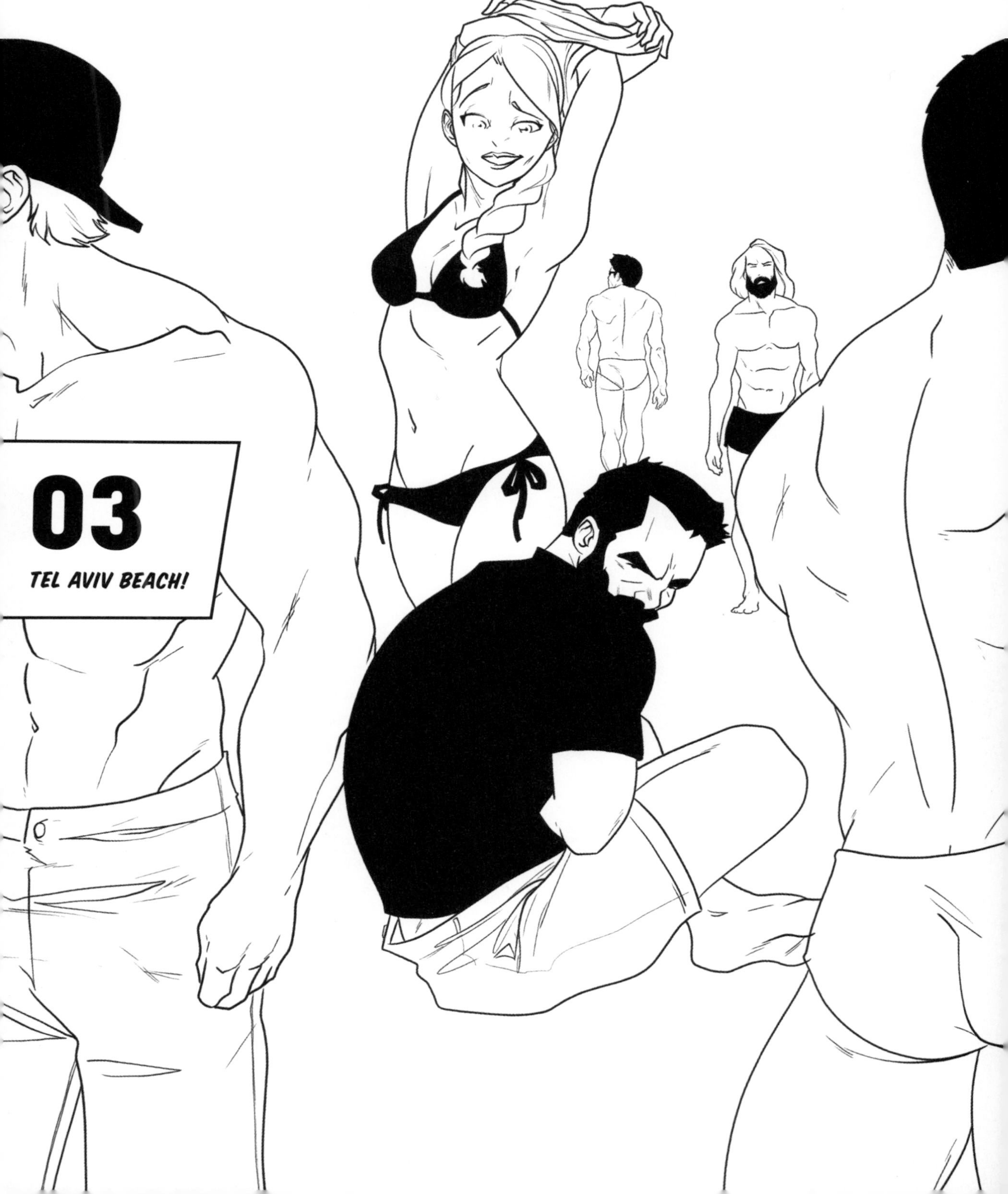

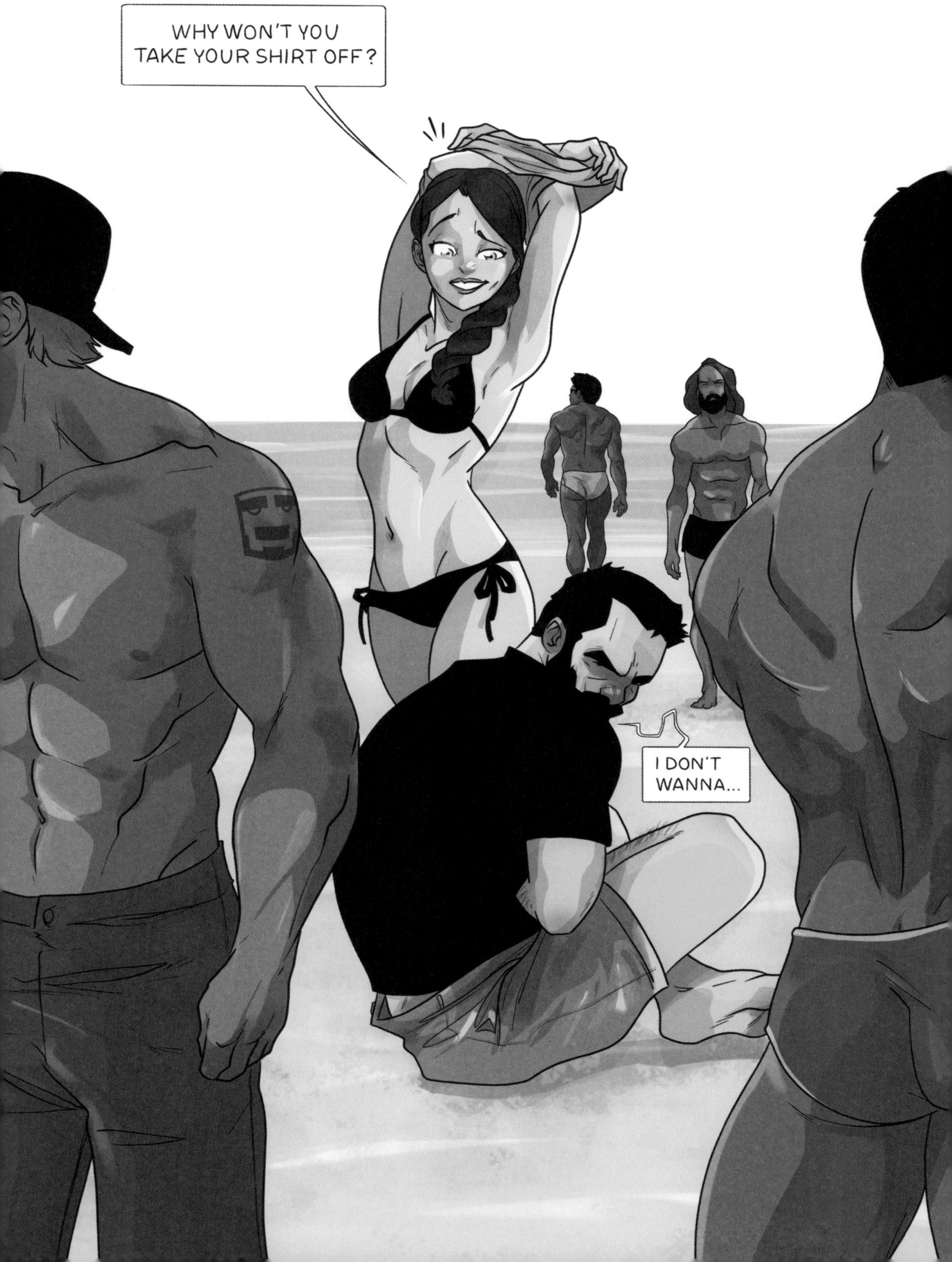
WHY WON'T YOU TAKE YOUR SHIRT OFF?
I DON'T WANNA...

04

WINTER IS HERE

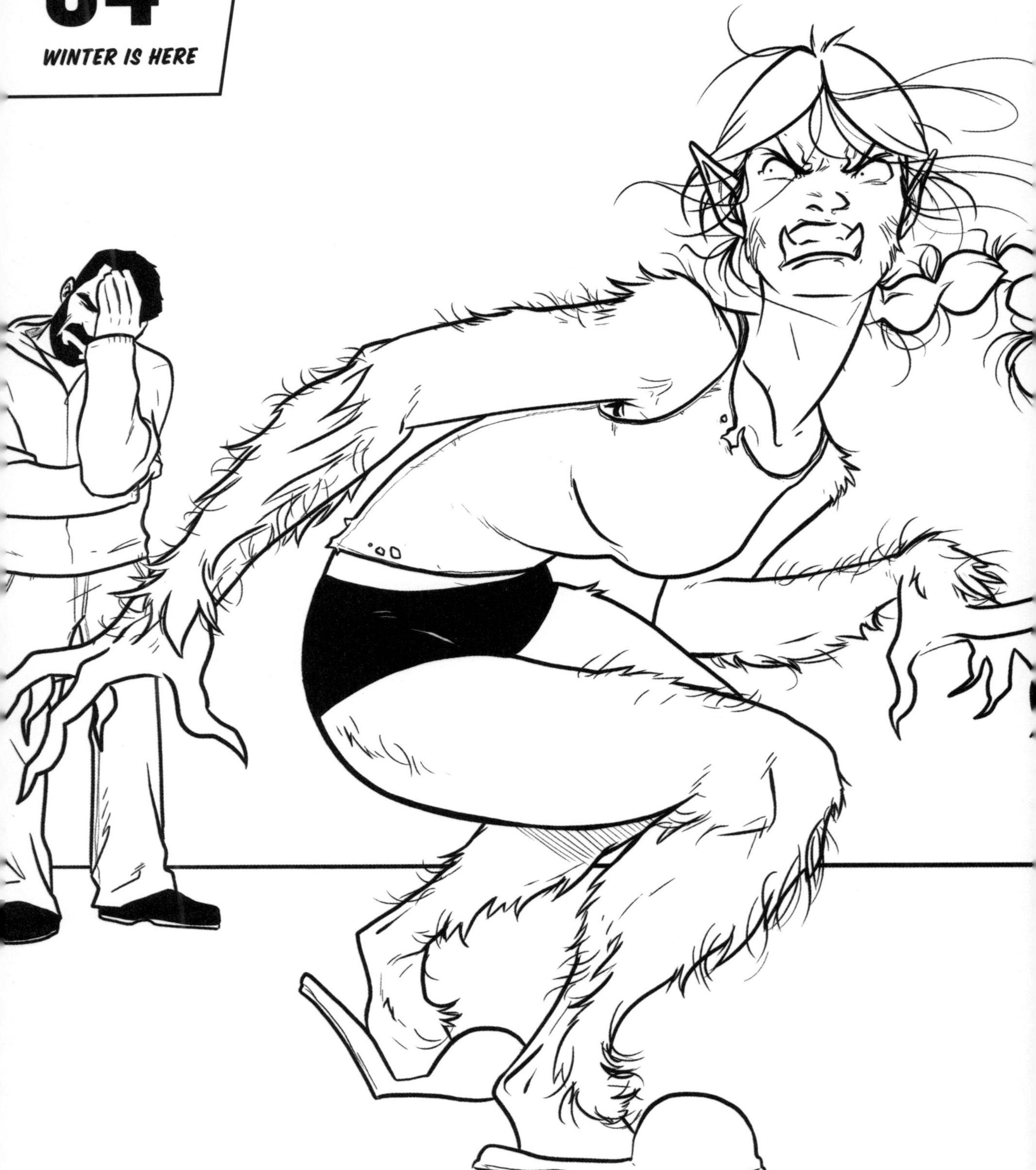

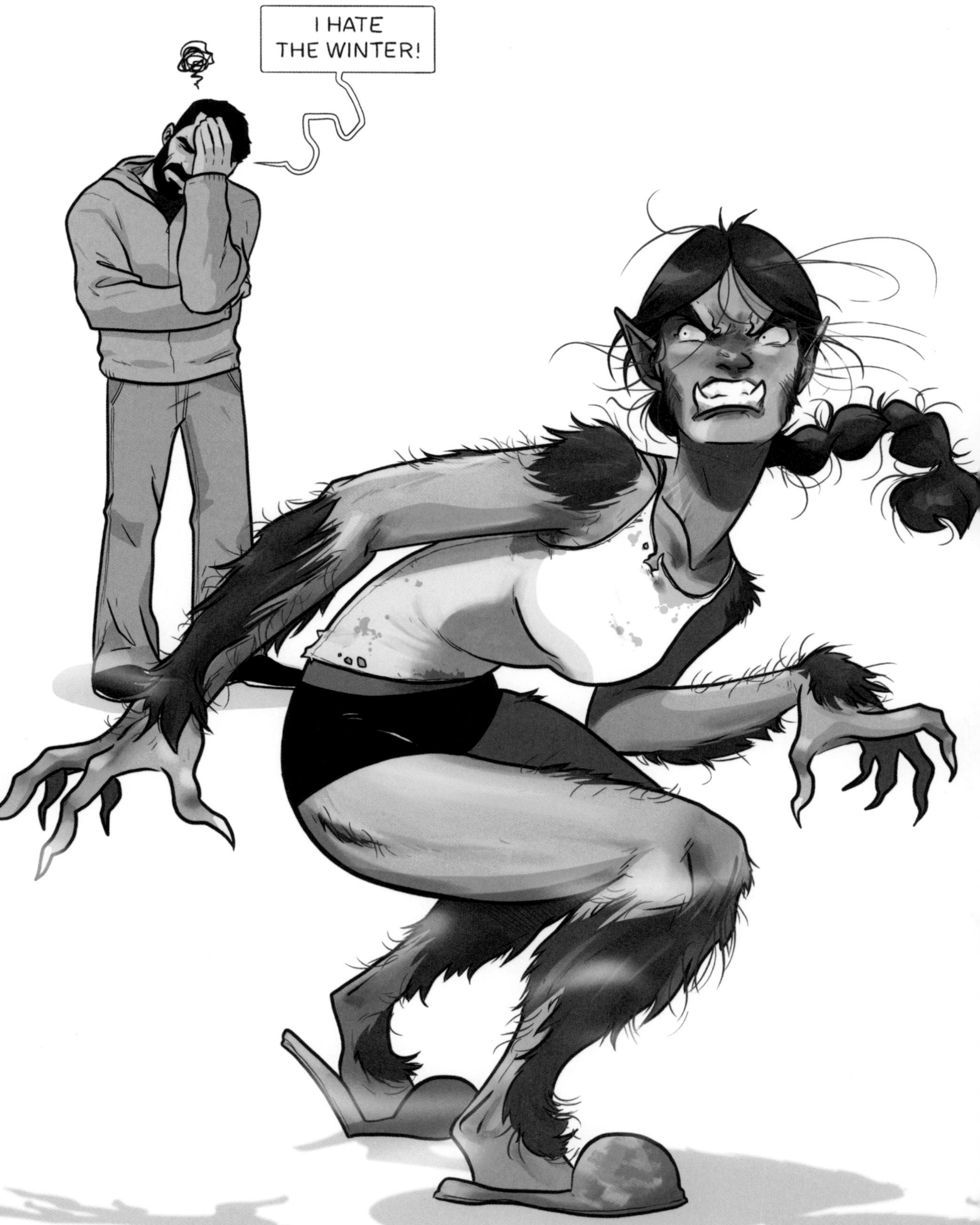
I HATE THE WINTER!

05

EVERY TIME I THINK ABOUT SHAVING

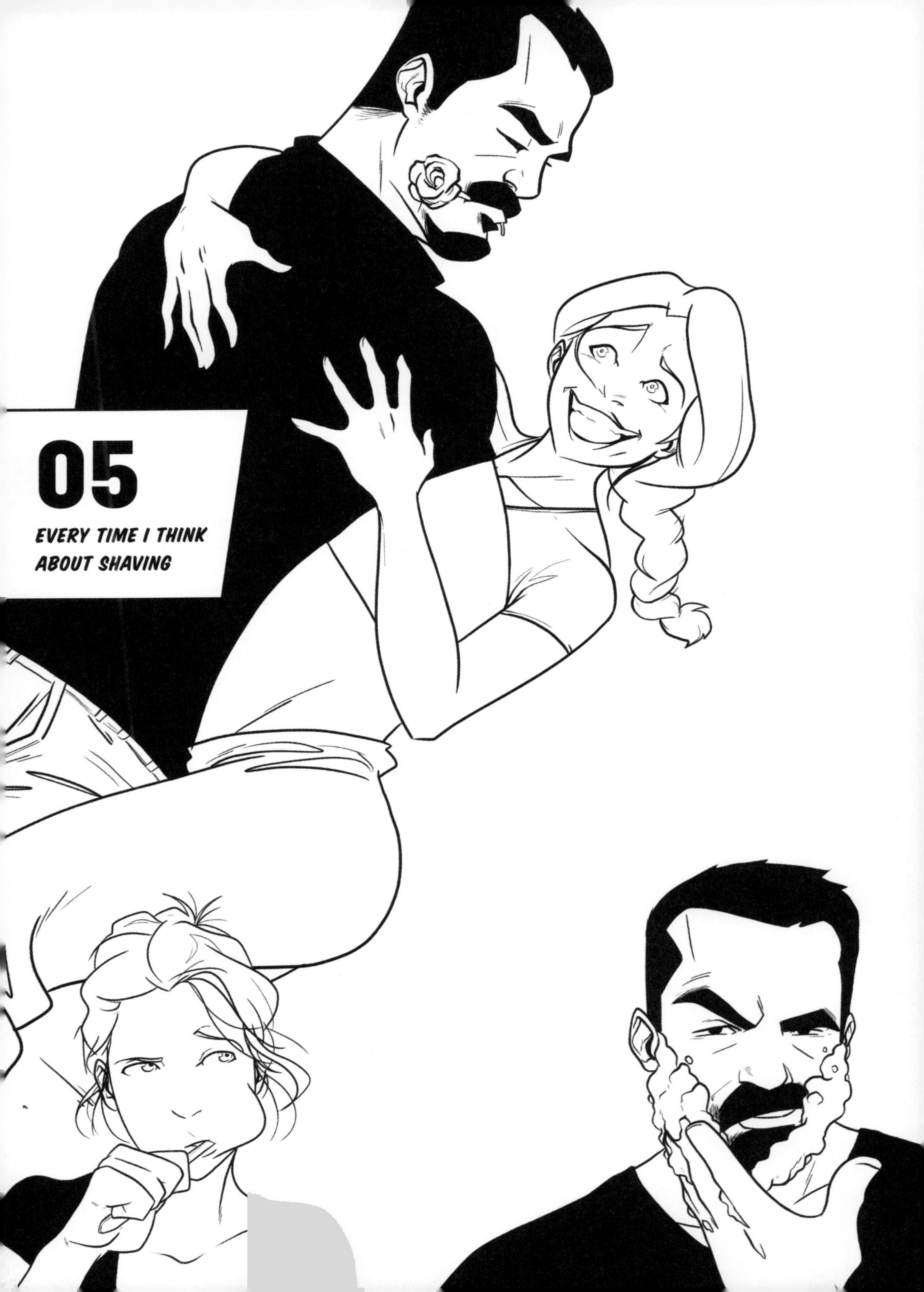

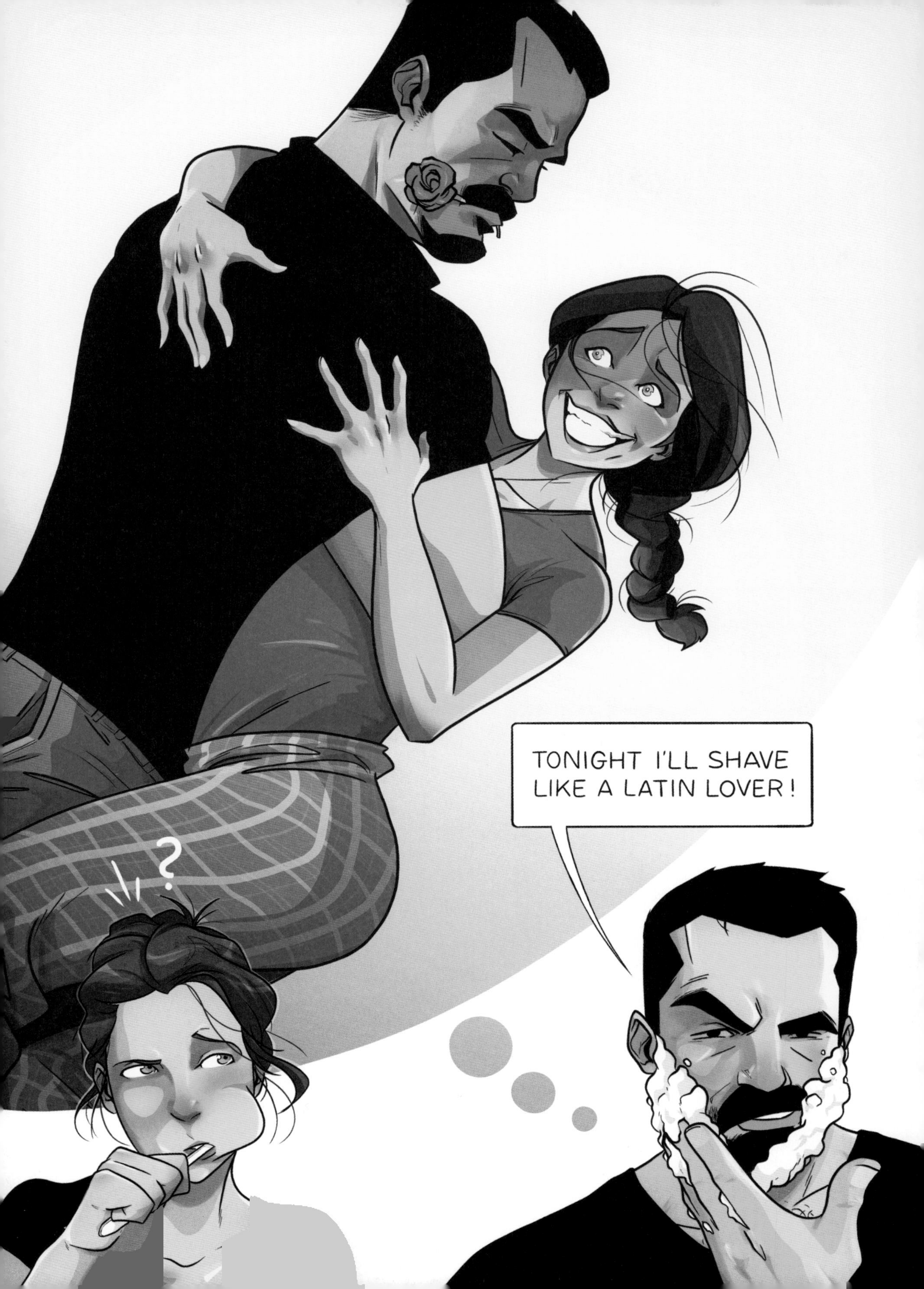
?
TONIGHT I'LL SHAVE LIKE A LATIN LOVER!

06

HAPPY FEET

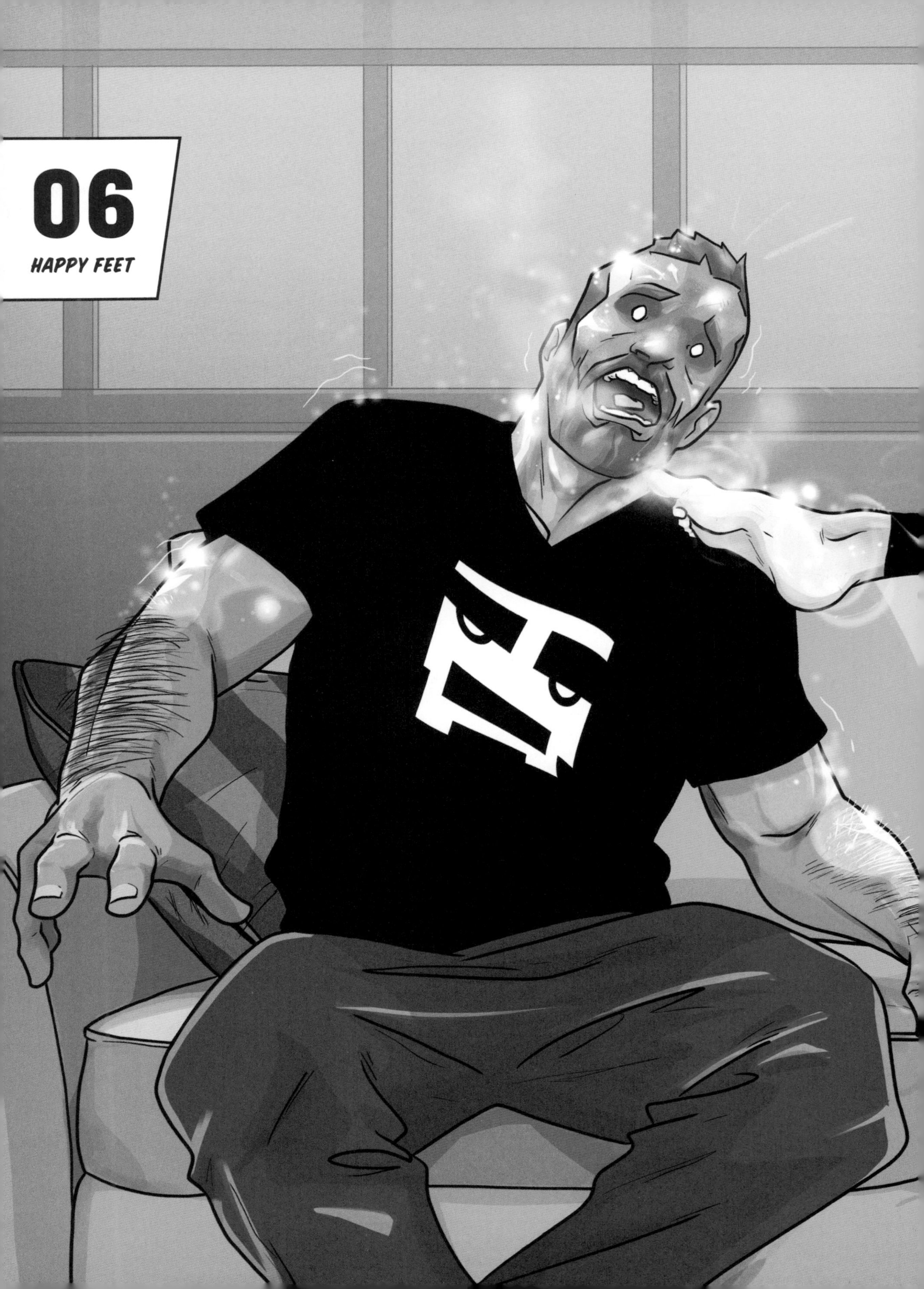

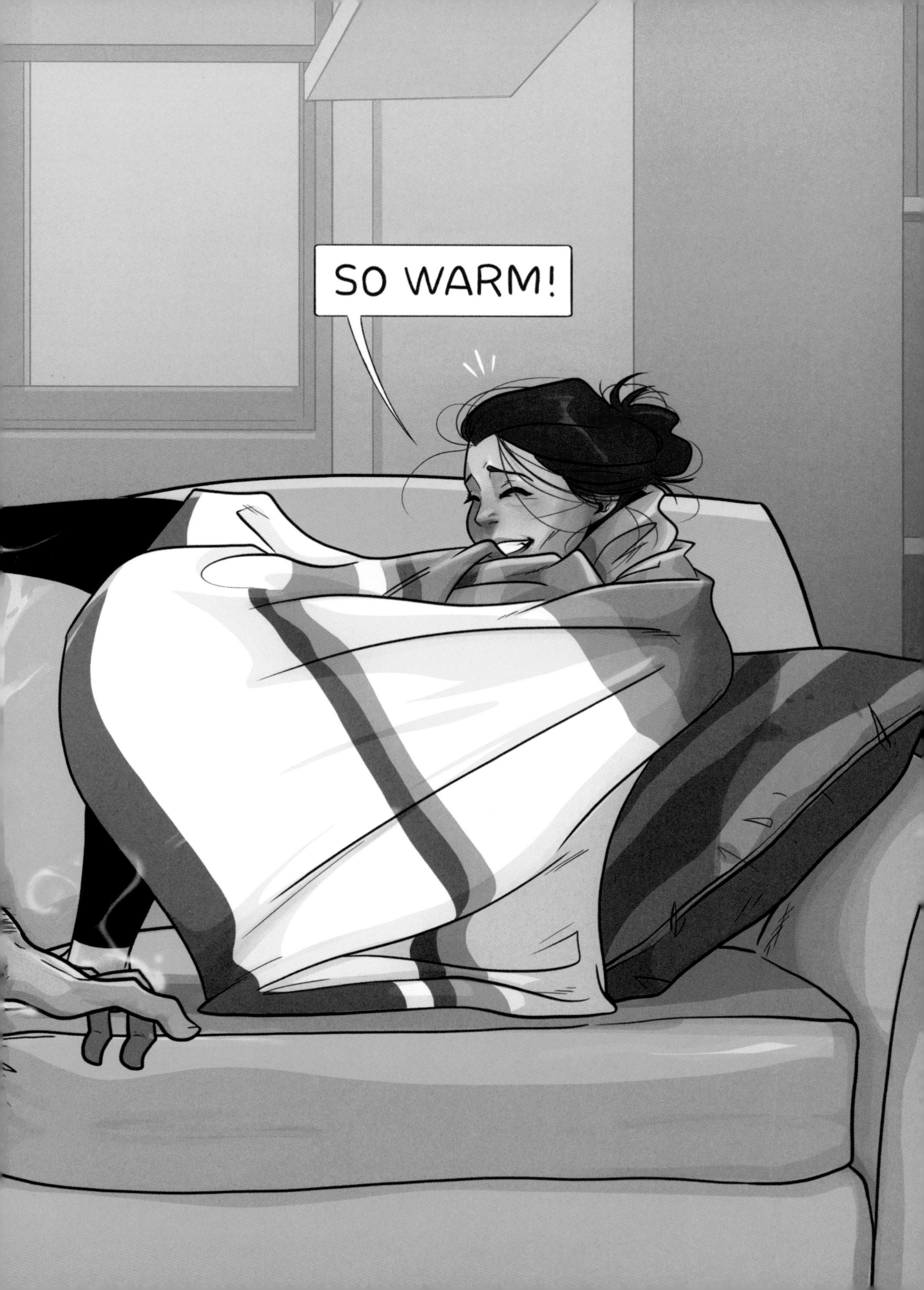
SO WARM!

07

THE SCARF

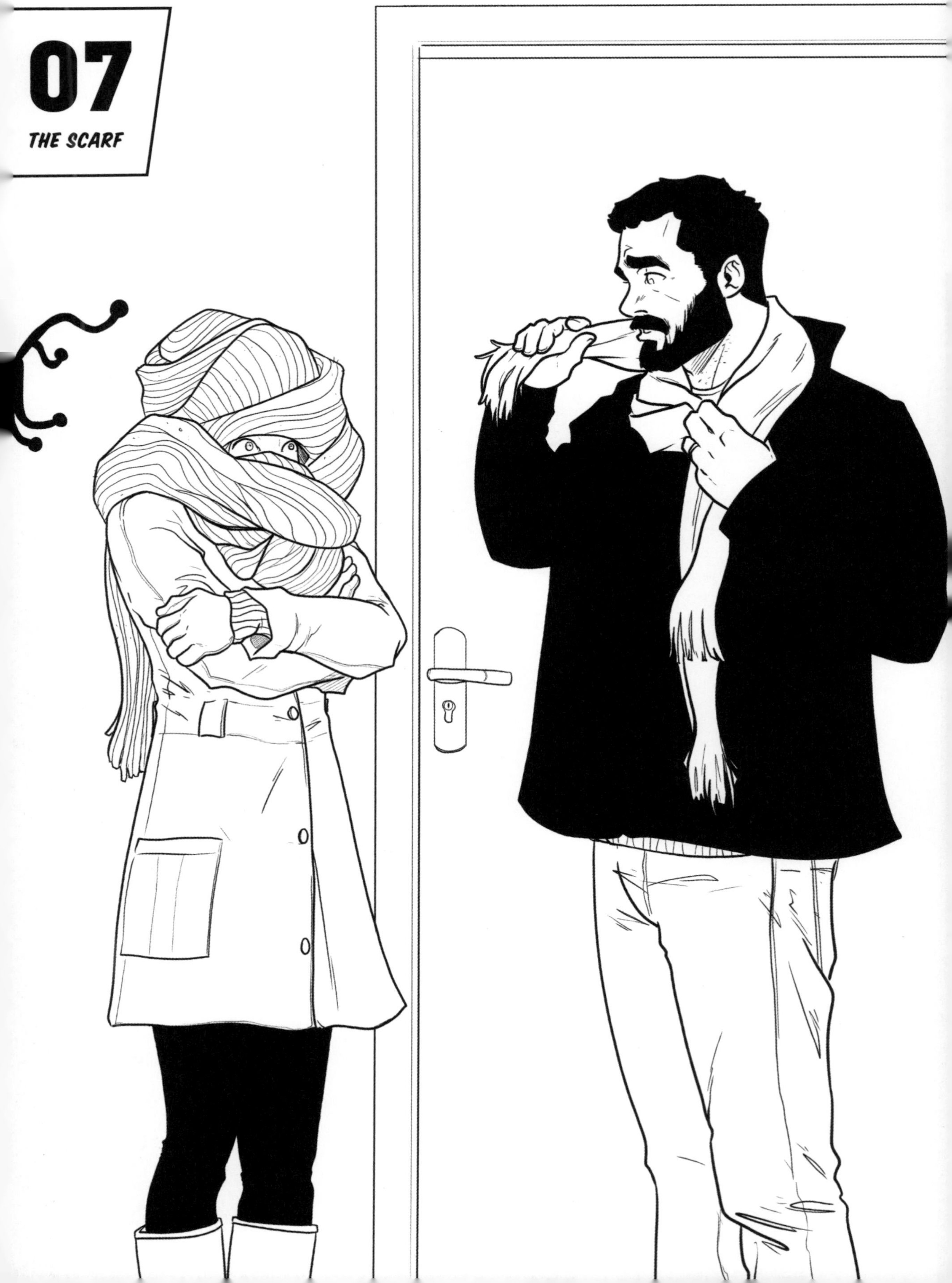

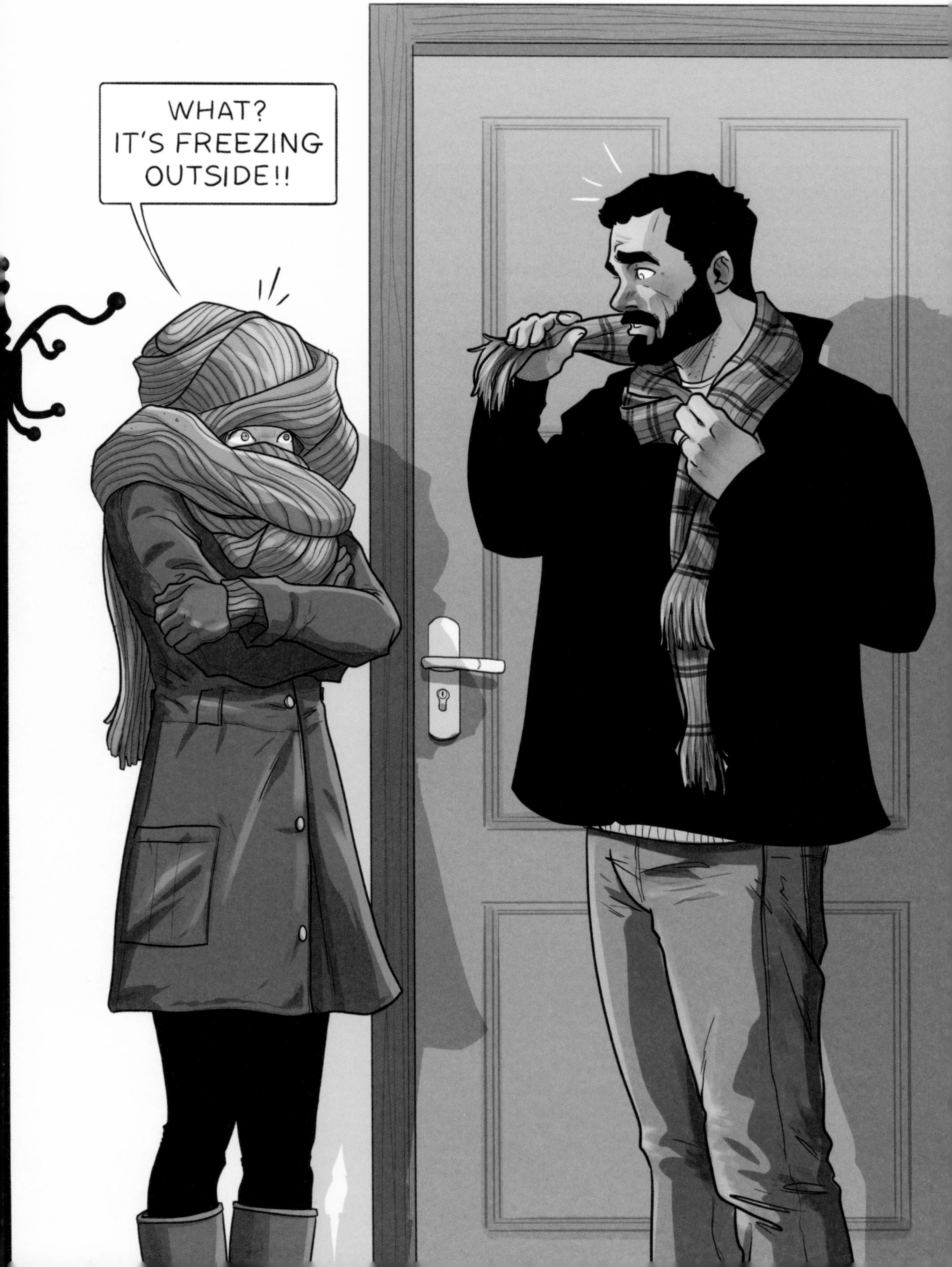
WHAT? IT'S FREEZING OUTSIDE!!

08

MY HOT WIFE

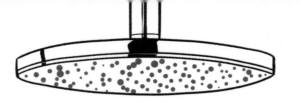

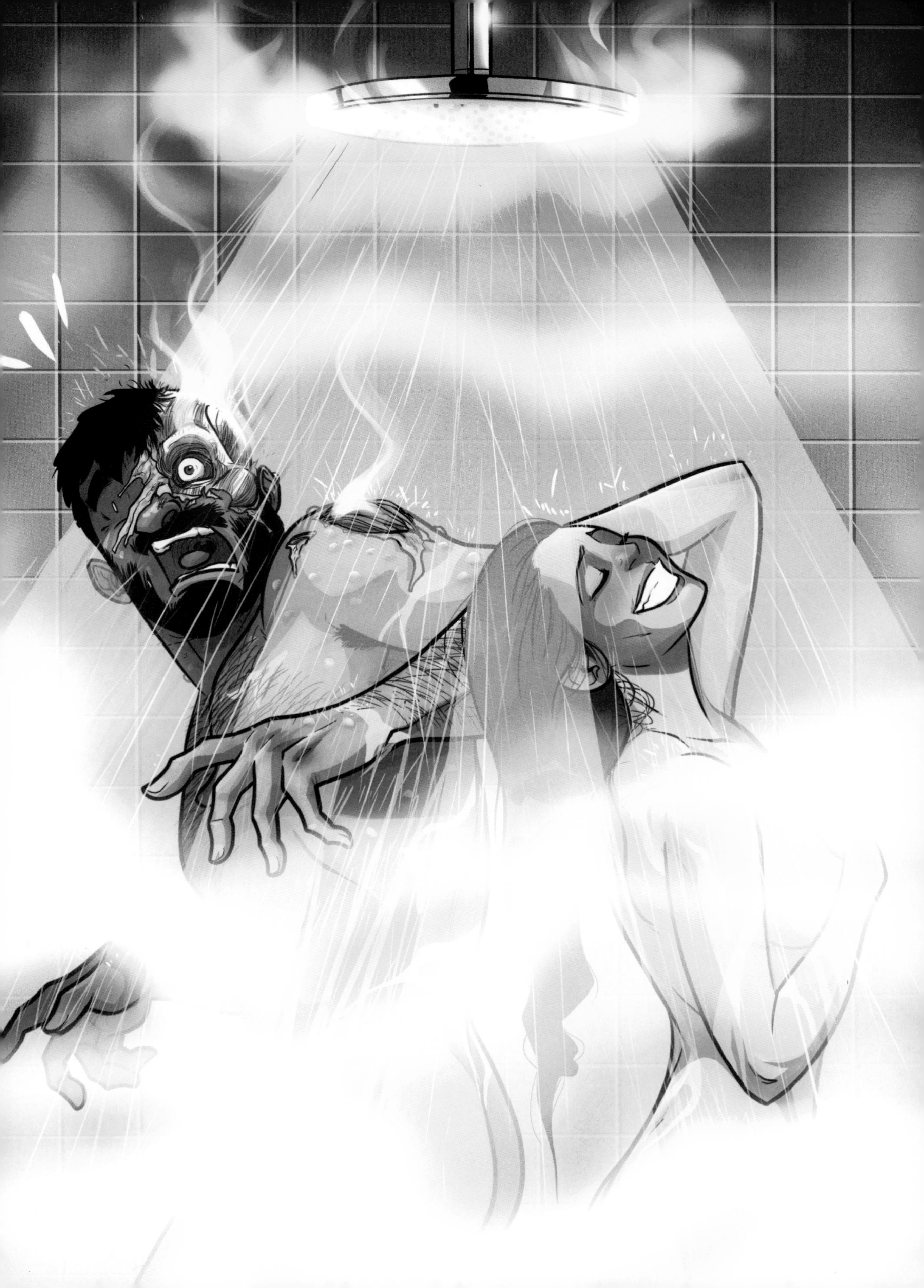

09

LET'S TAKE A SELFIE!

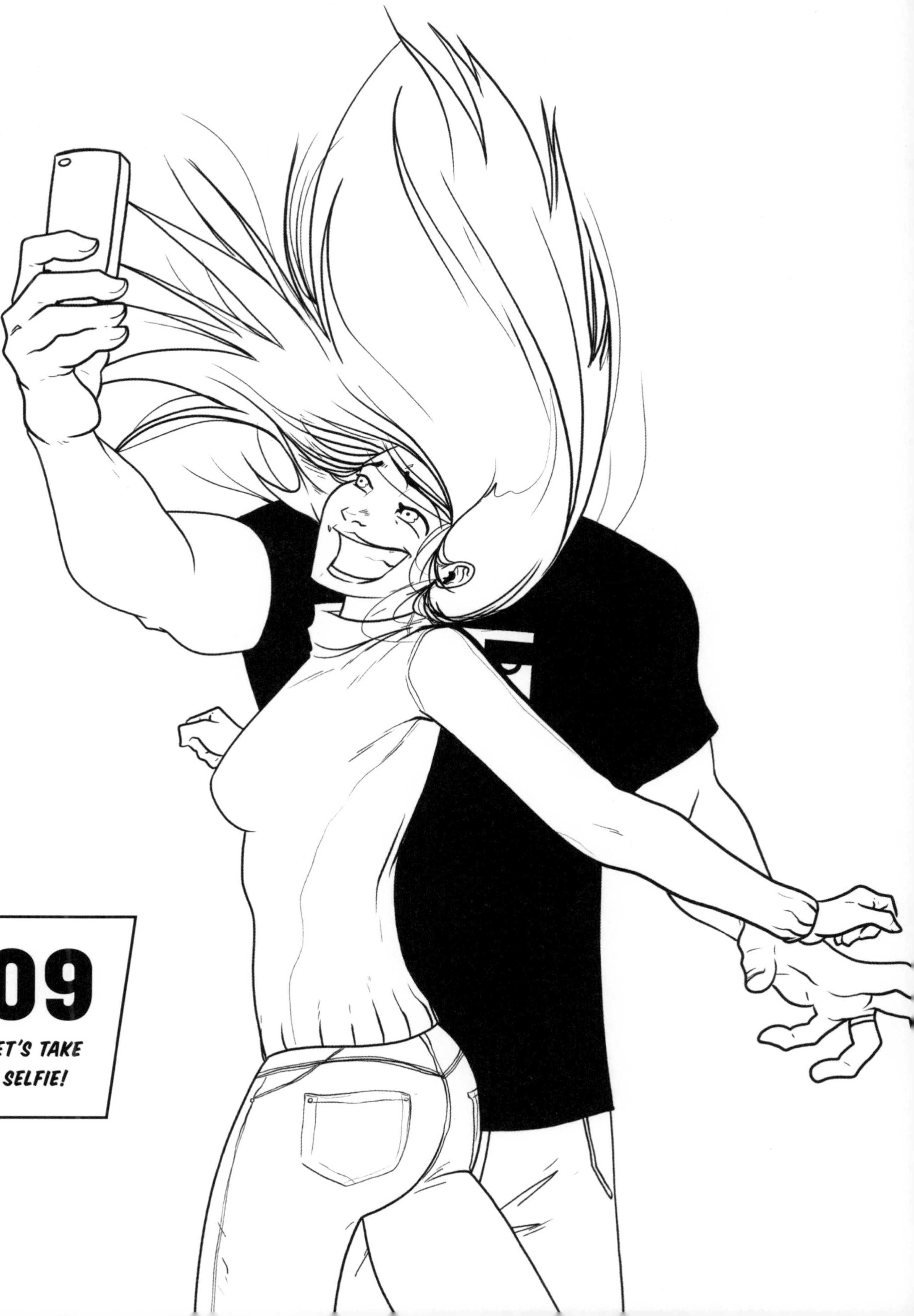

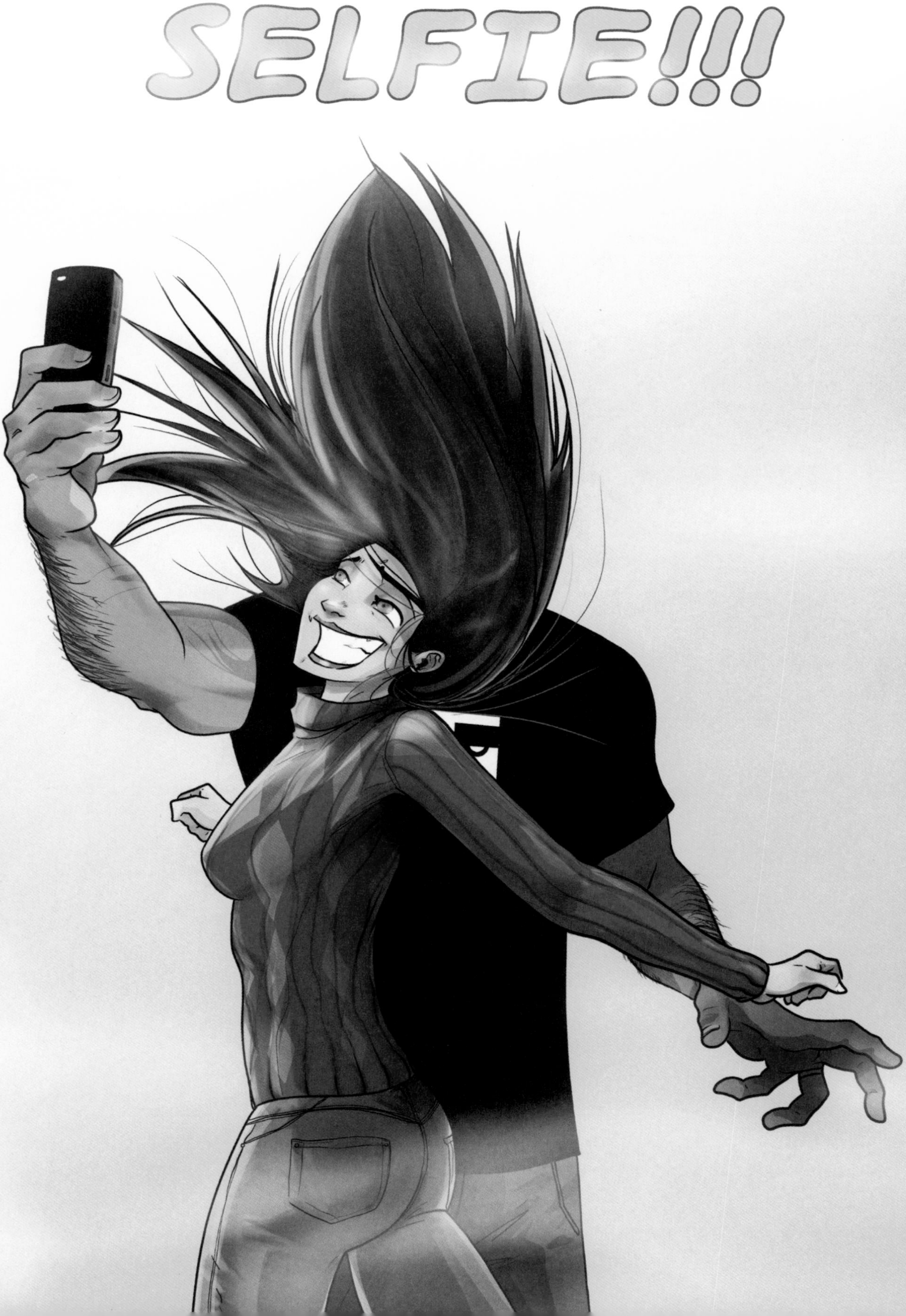
SELFIE!!!

10

MY WIFEINATOR!

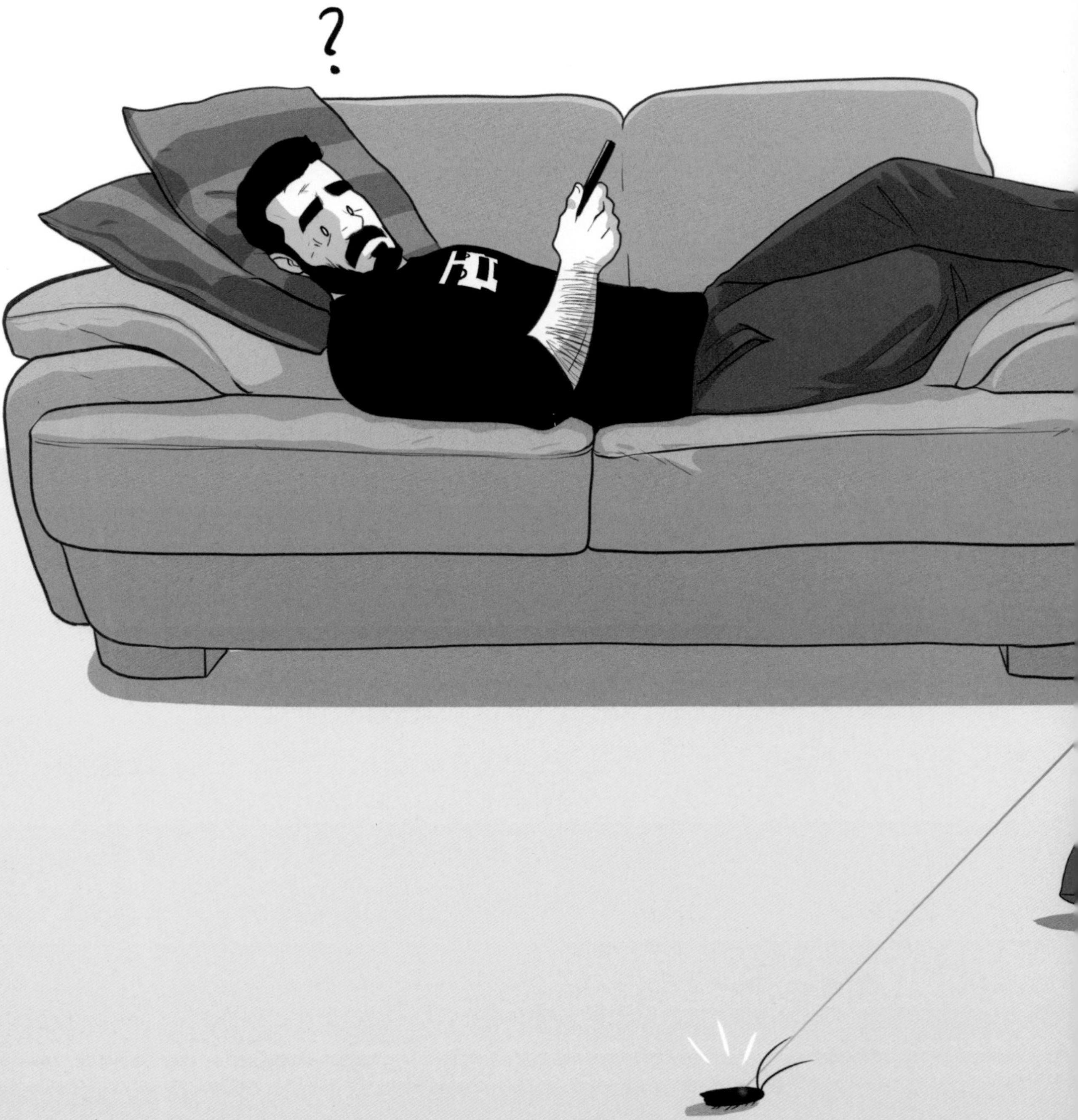
?

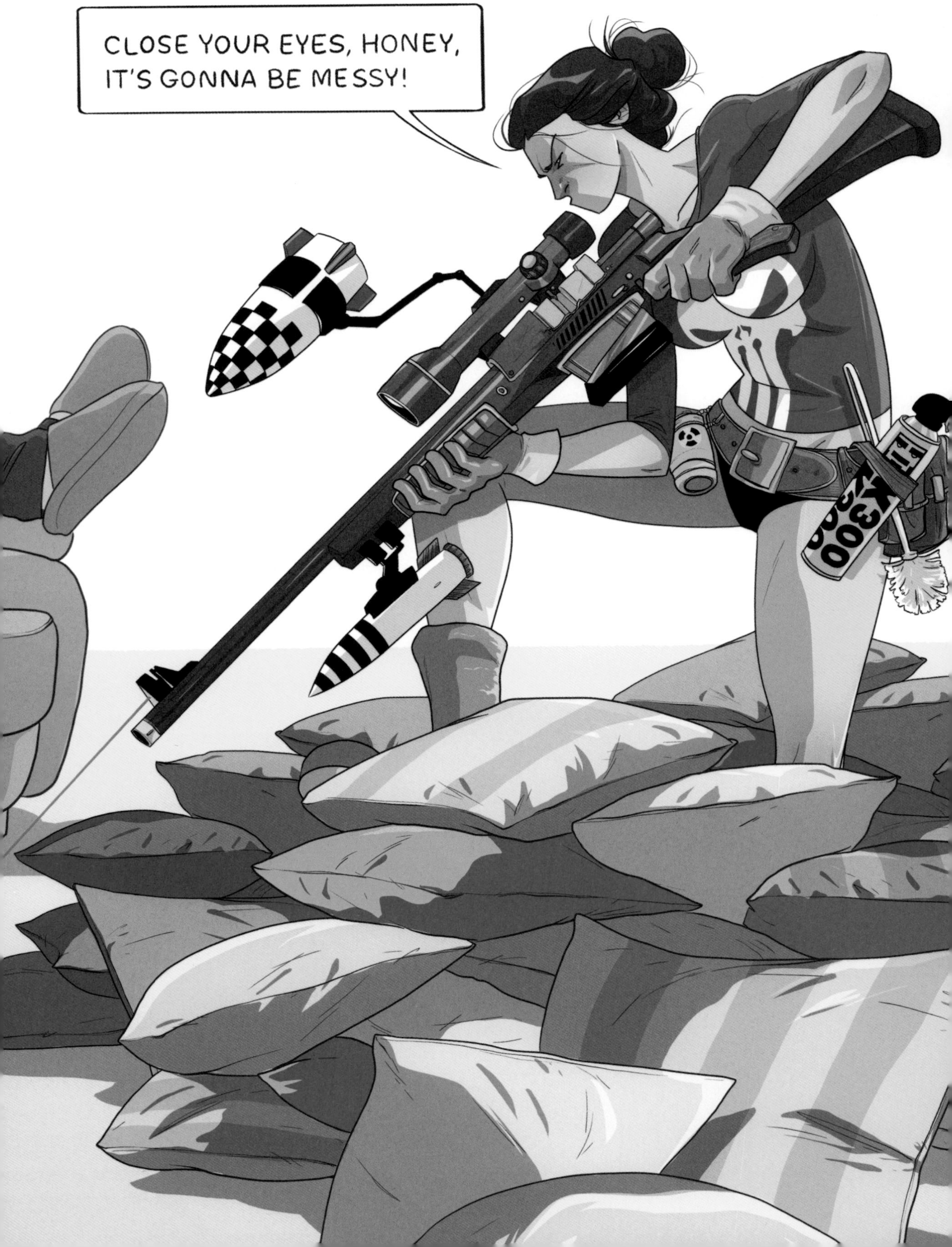
CLOSE YOUR EYES, HONEY,
IT'S GONNA BE MESSY!

11

VALENTINE'S DAY

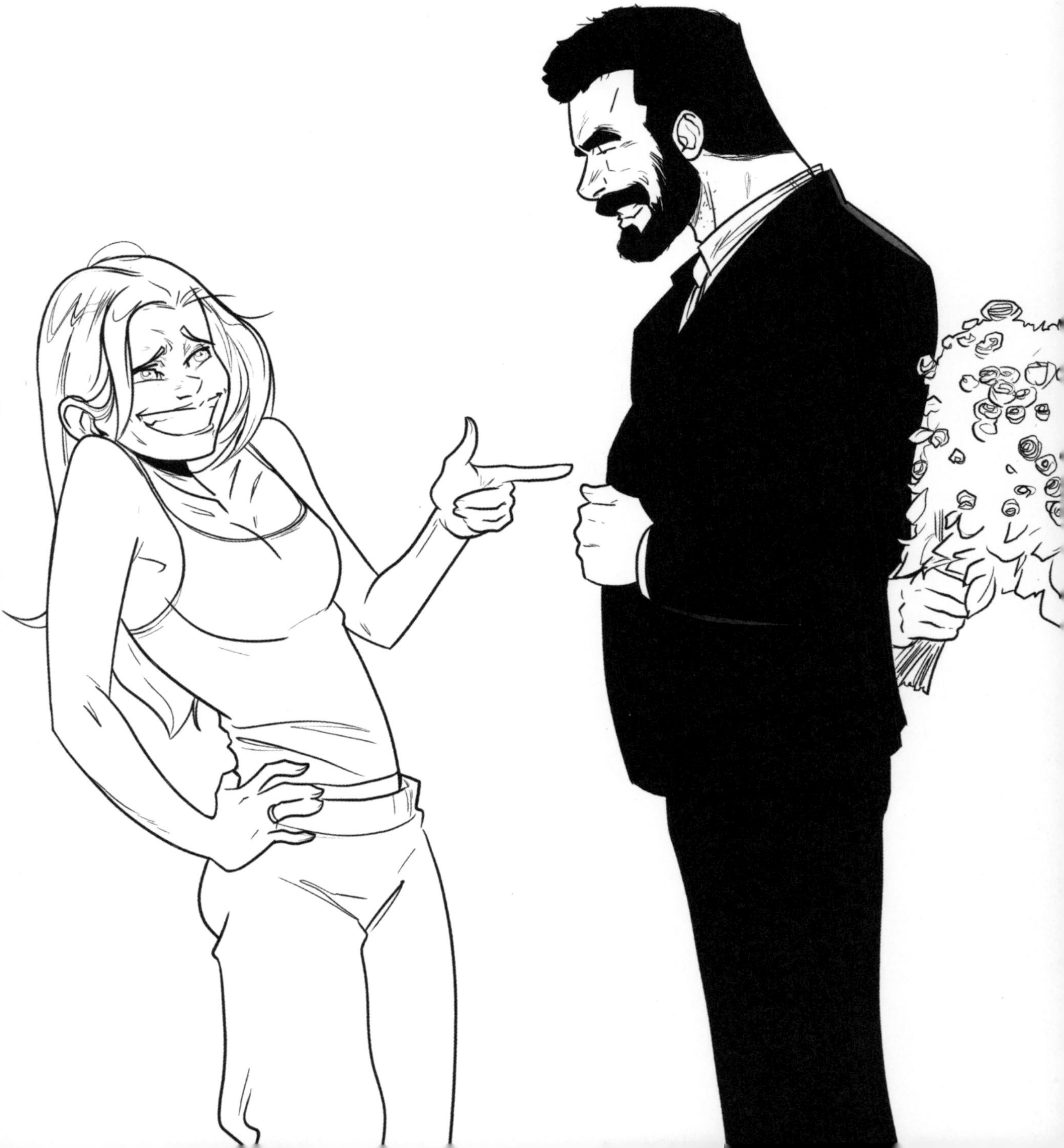

HAPPY VALENTINE'S DAY!

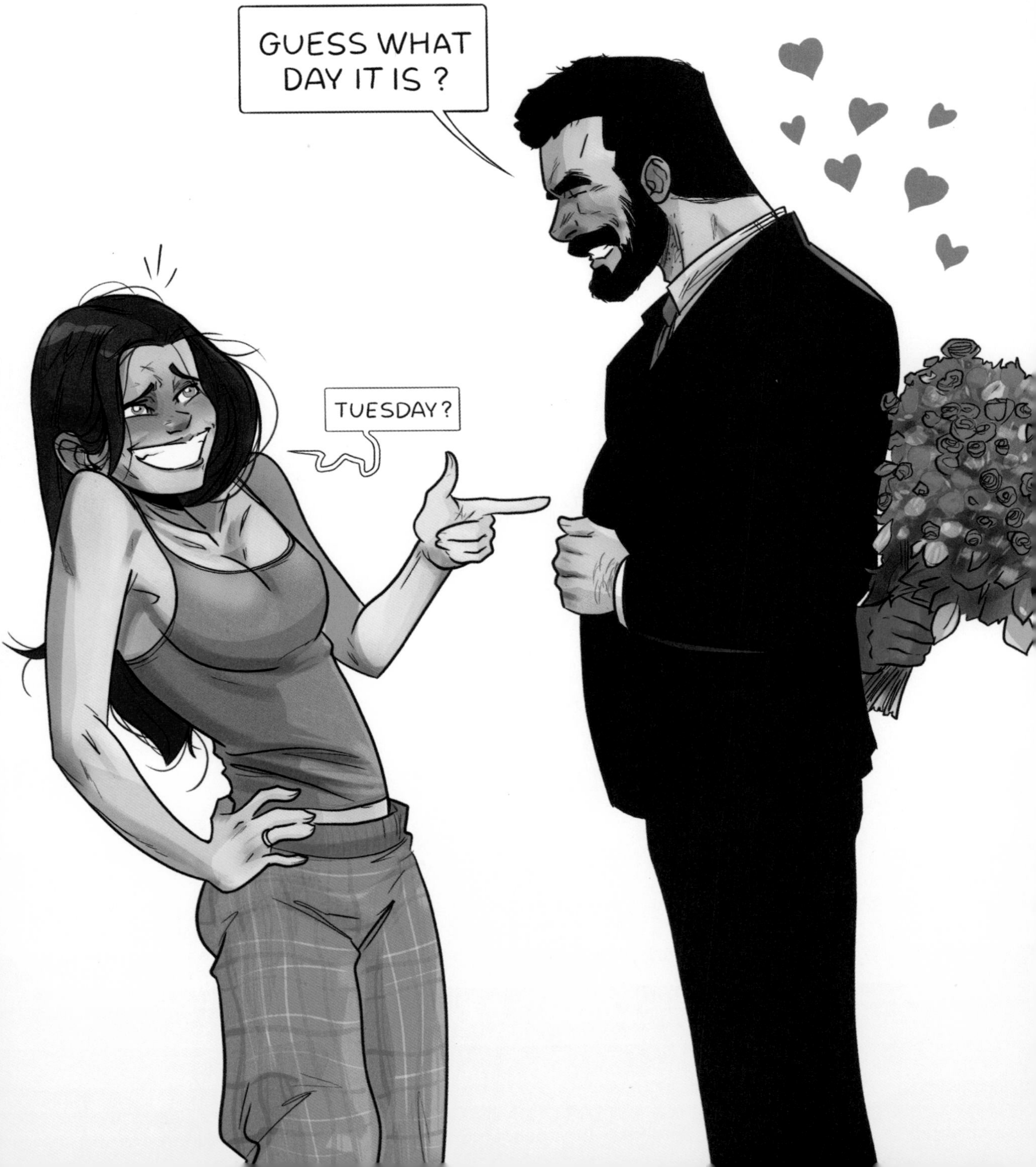
GUESS WHAT DAY IT IS ?
TUESDAY?

12

WE SAW JOHN WICK 2

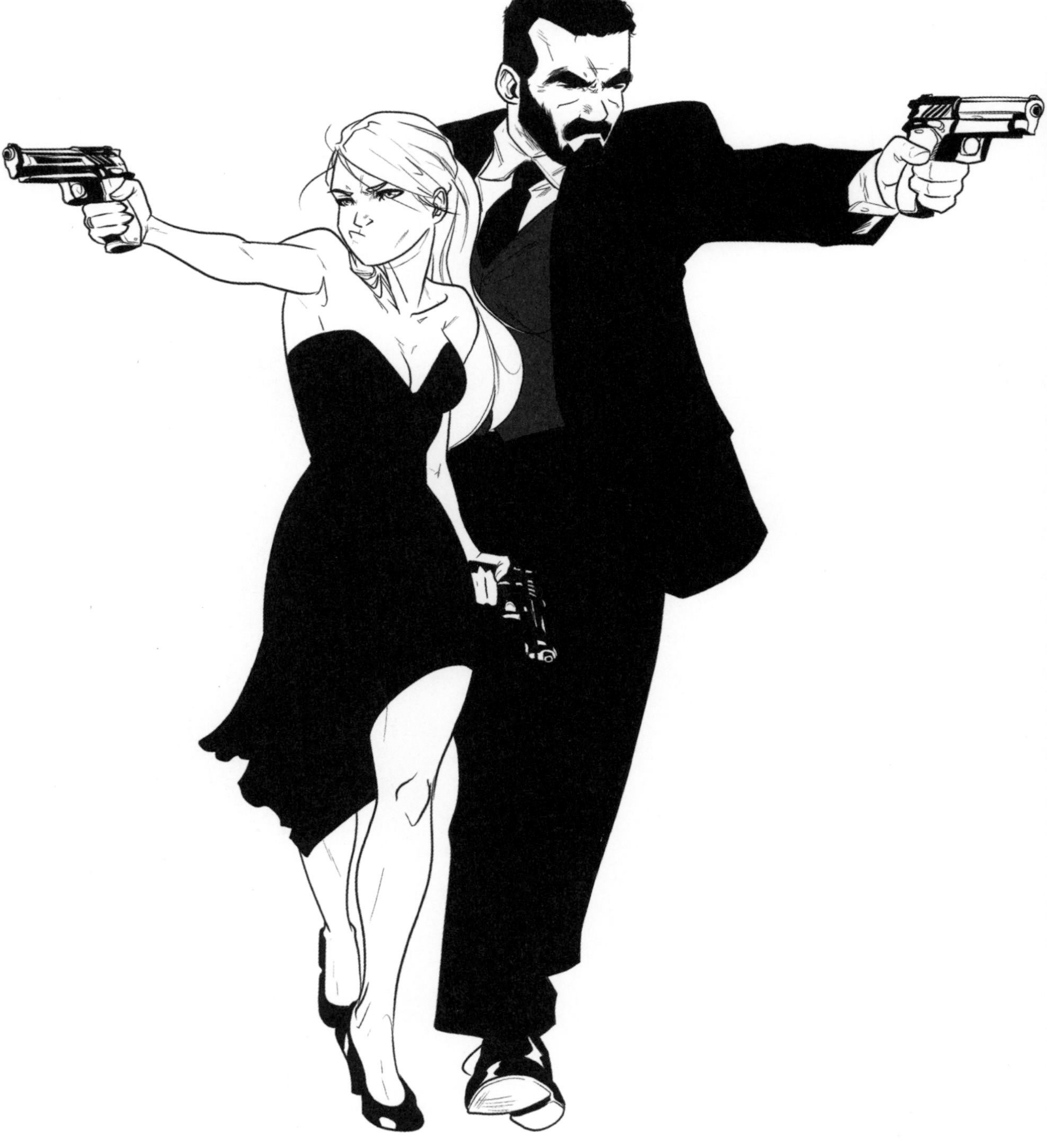

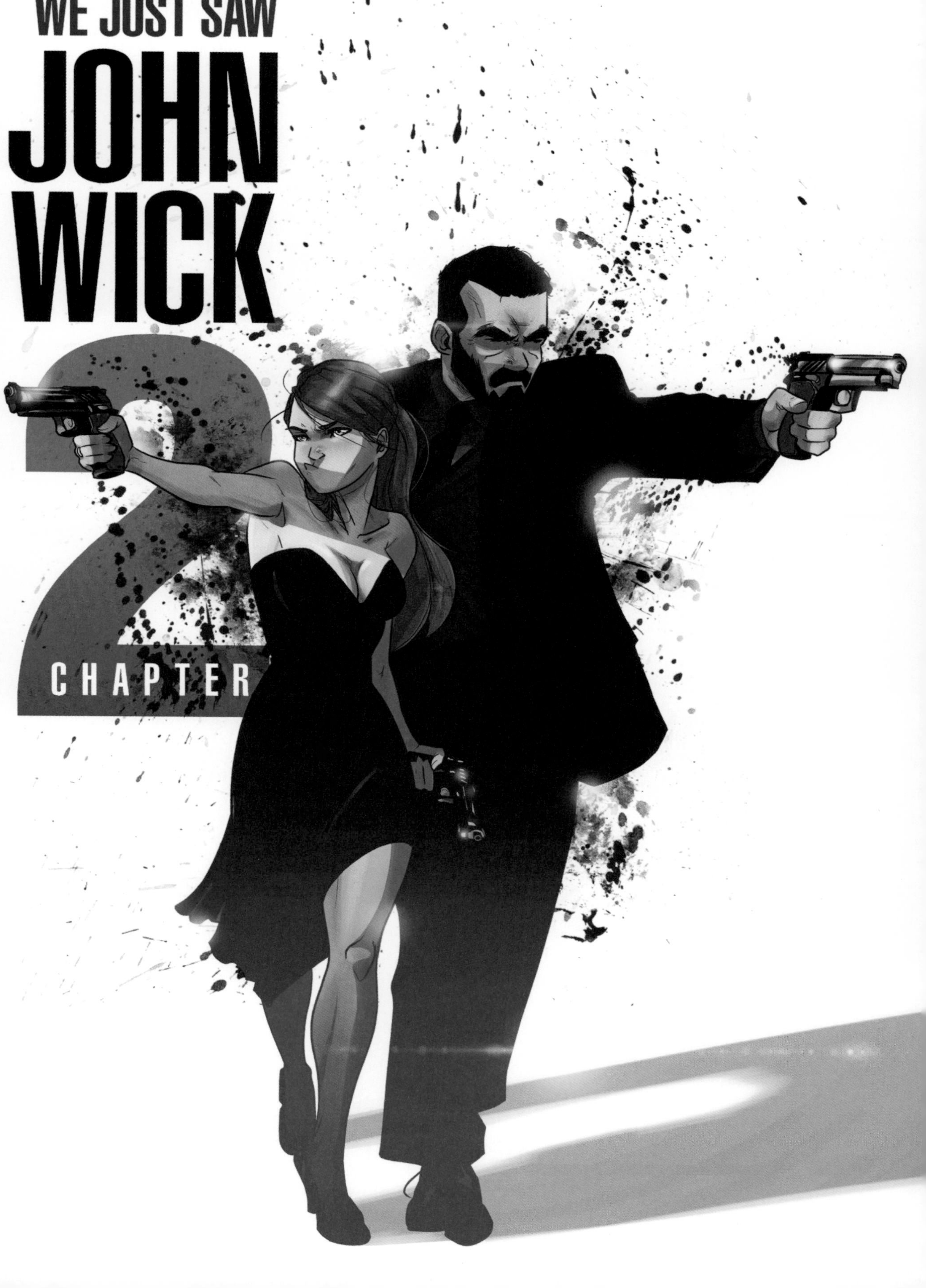
WE JUST SAW
JOHN
WICK
2
CHAPTER

13

EVERY MORNING

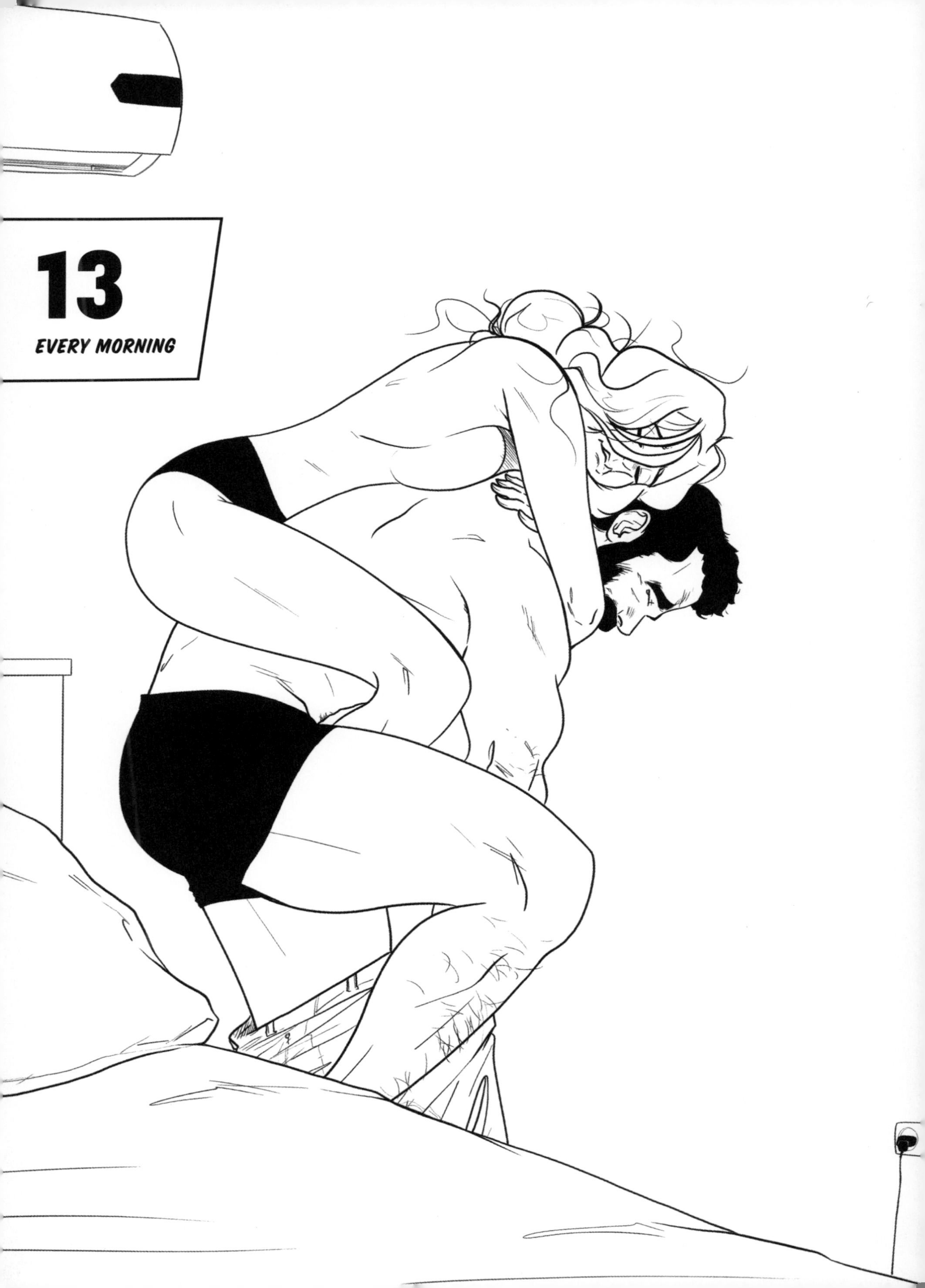

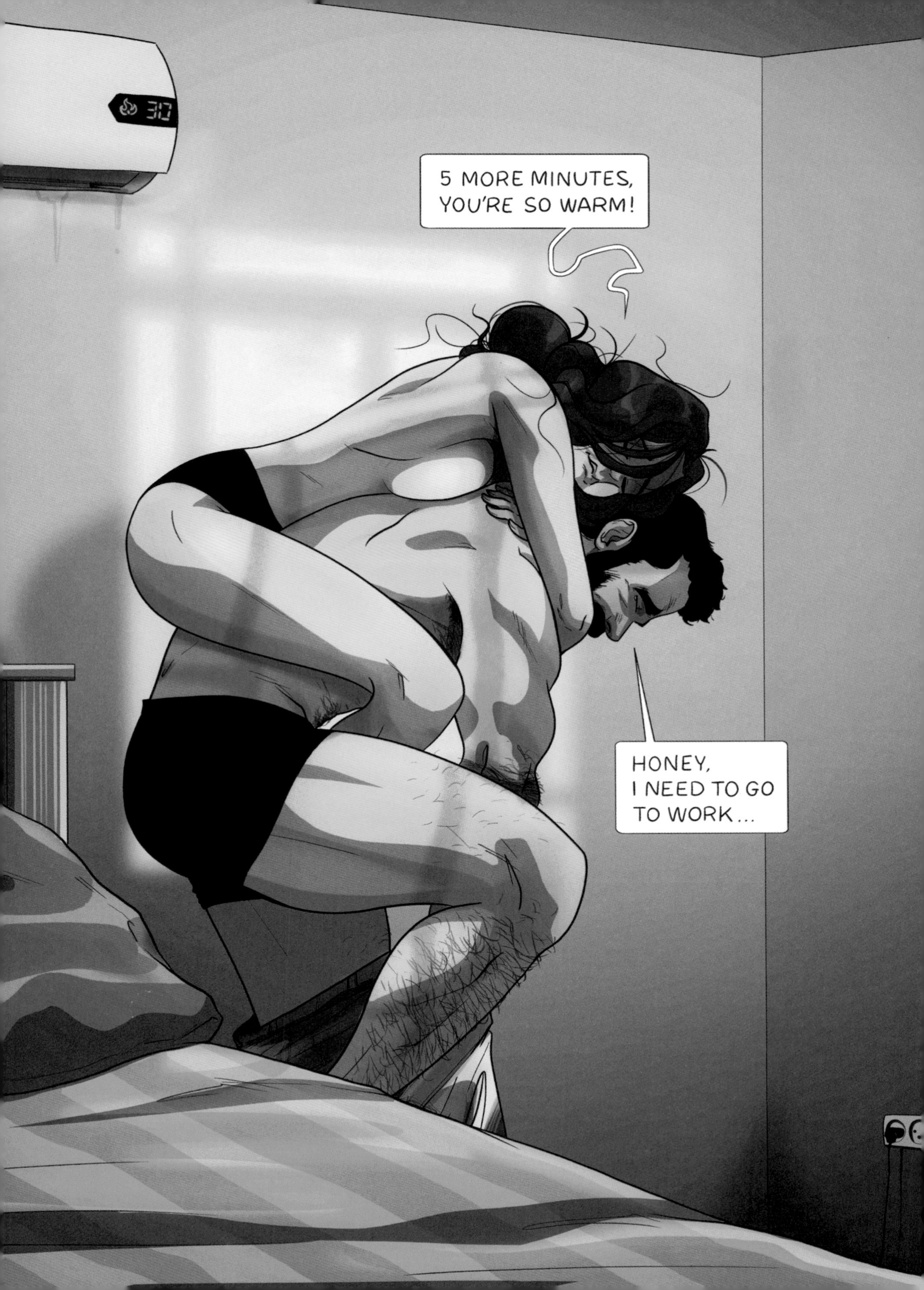
30
5 MORE MINUTES, YOU'RE SO WARM!
HONEY, I NEED TO GO TO WORK...

14

WATCHING WWE WITH MY WIFE

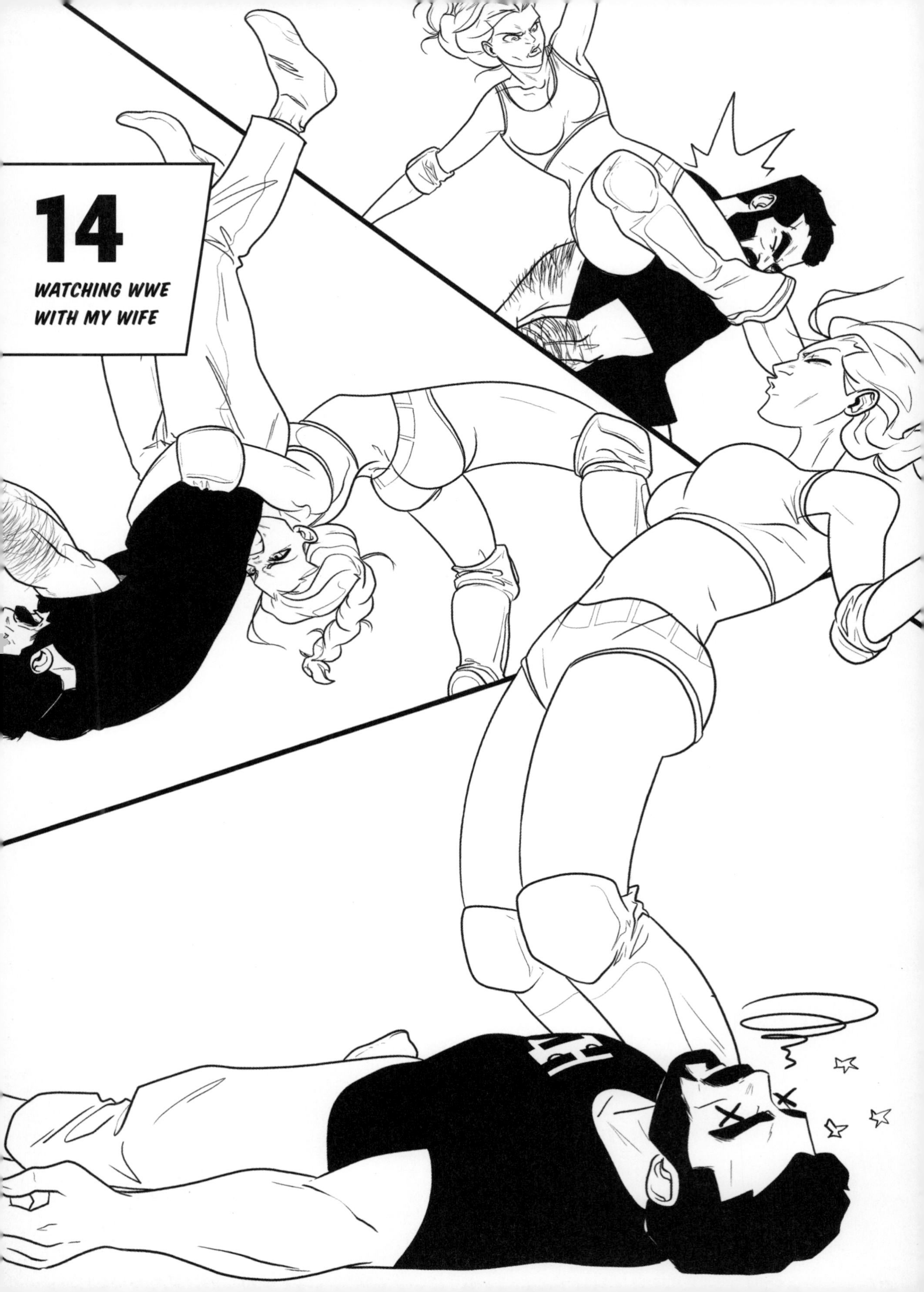

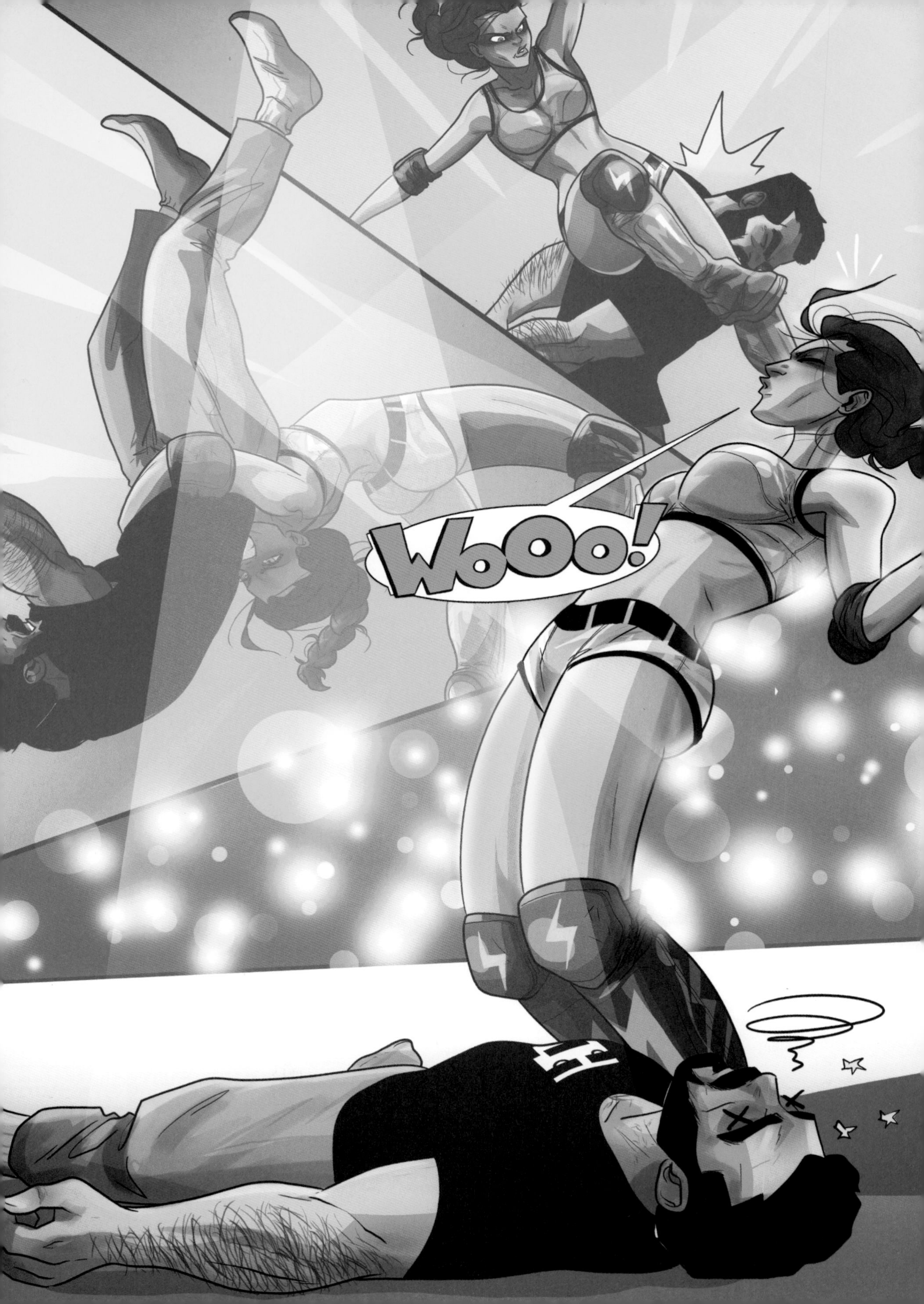
WoOo!

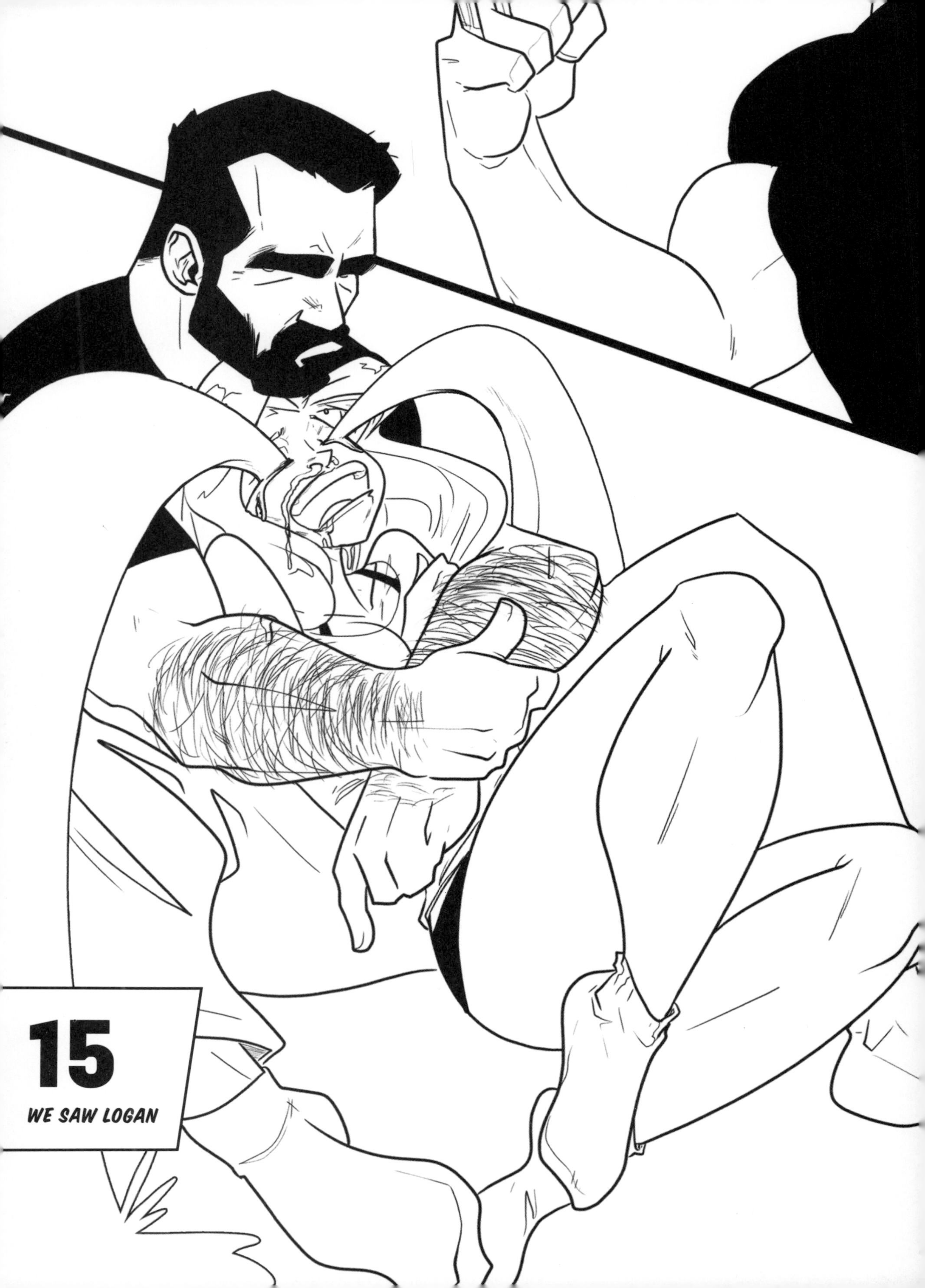

15

WE SAW LOGAN

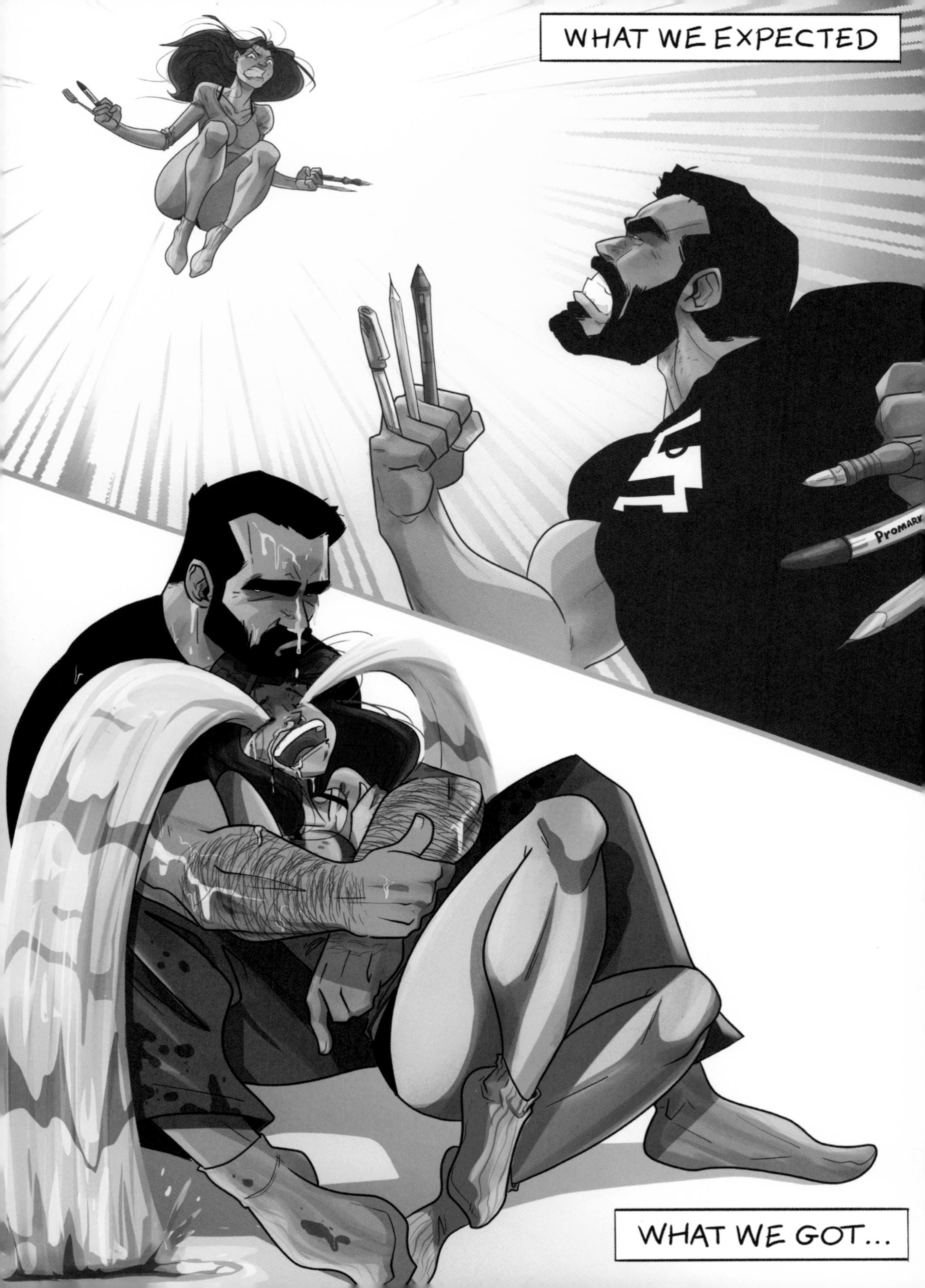
WHAT WE EXPECTED
Promark
WHAT WE GOT...

16

TRAVEL PILLOW

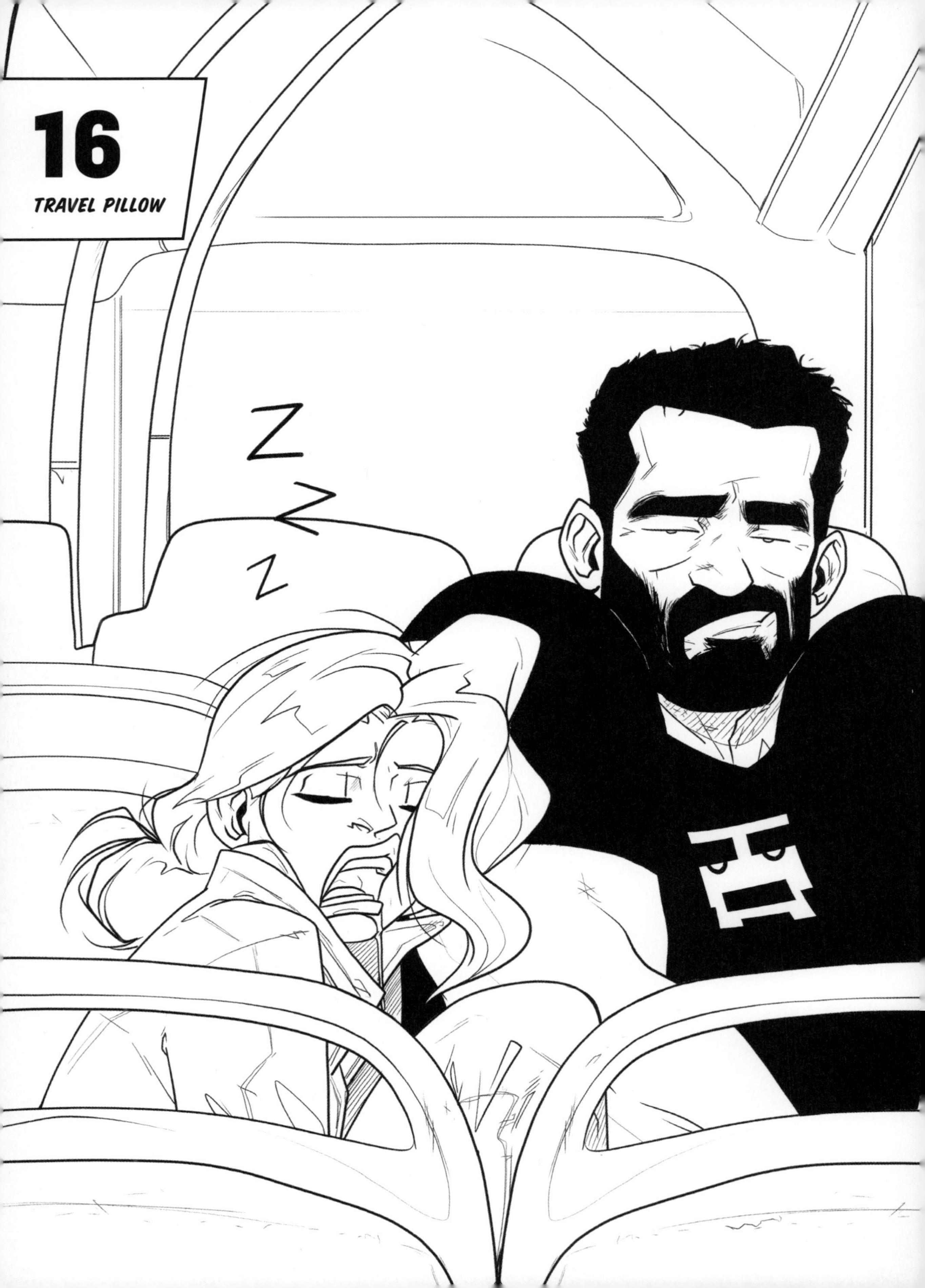
Z
Z
Z

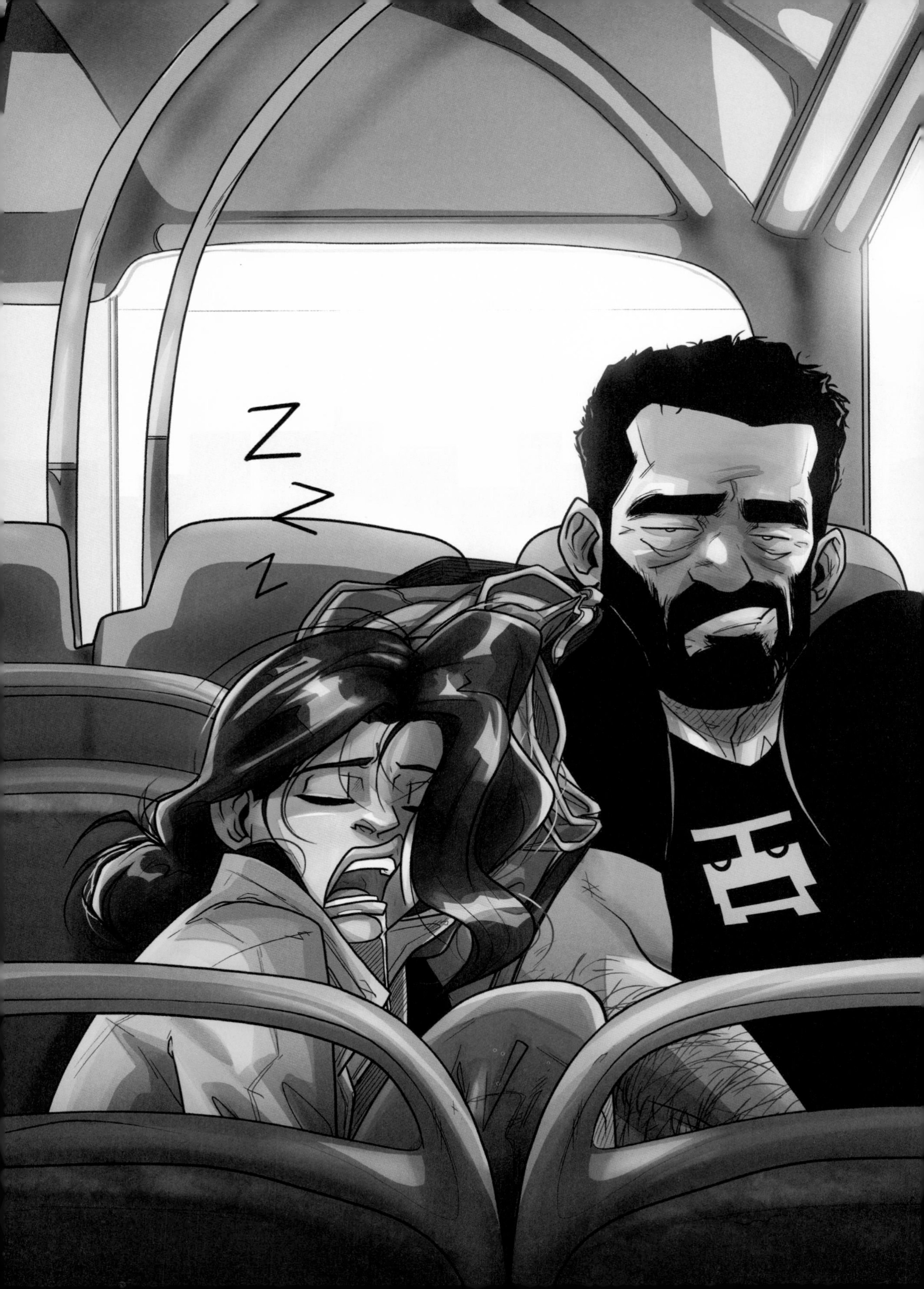
Z
Z
Z

17

WOMEN KNOW BEST

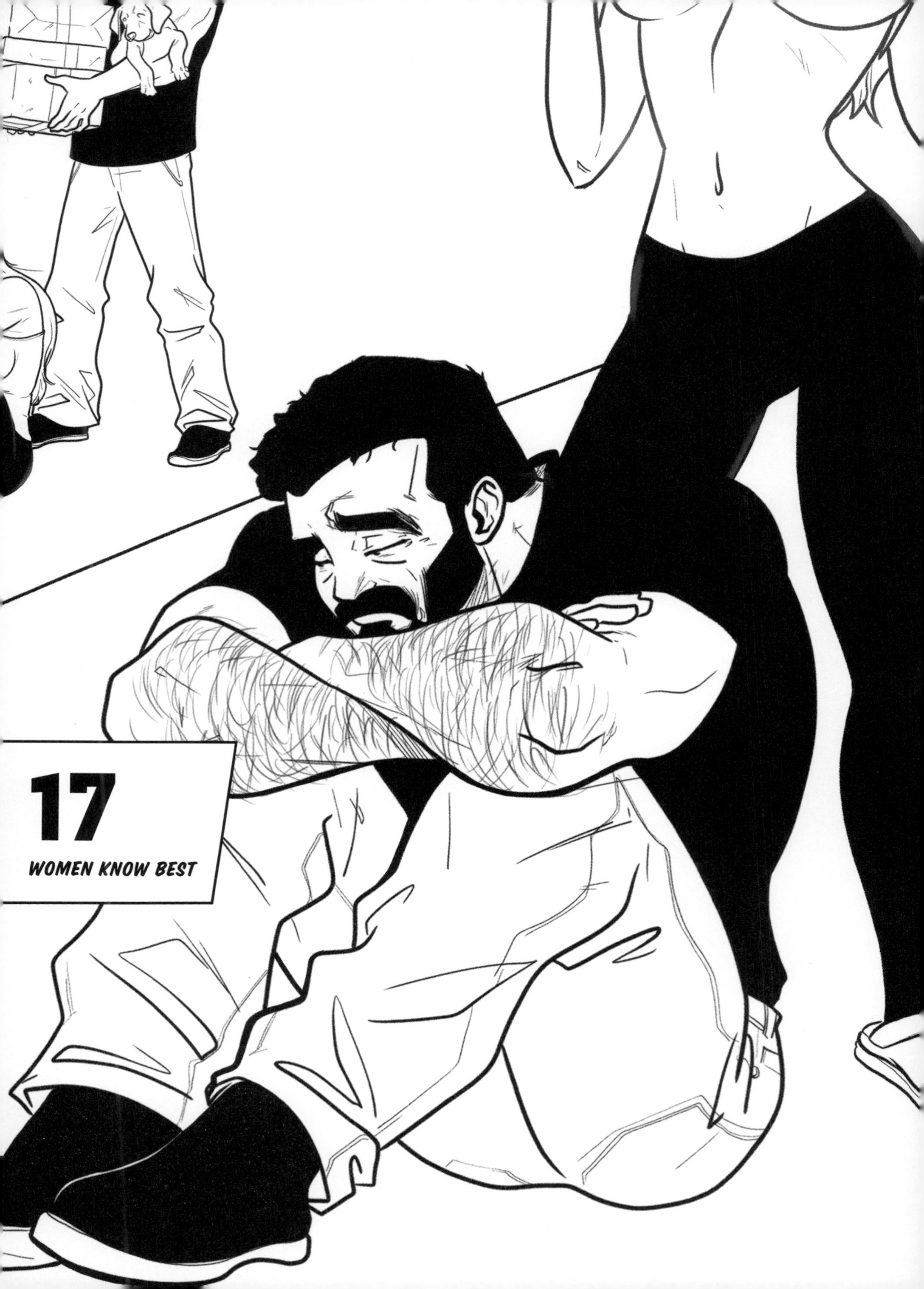

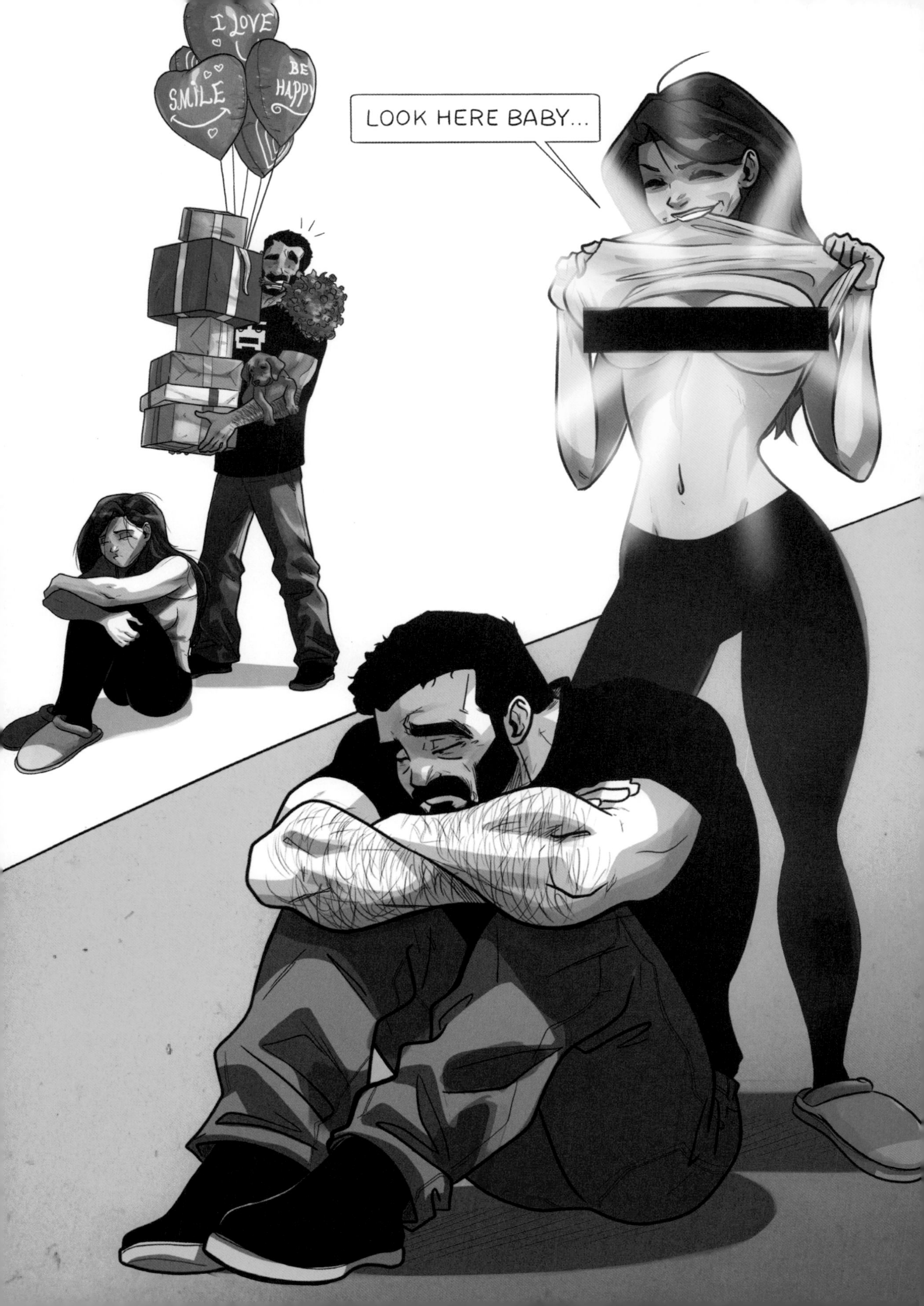
I LOVE
SMILE
BE HAPPY
LOOK HERE BABY...

18

MY WIFE'S CONCEPT OF WORKING OUT TOGETHER

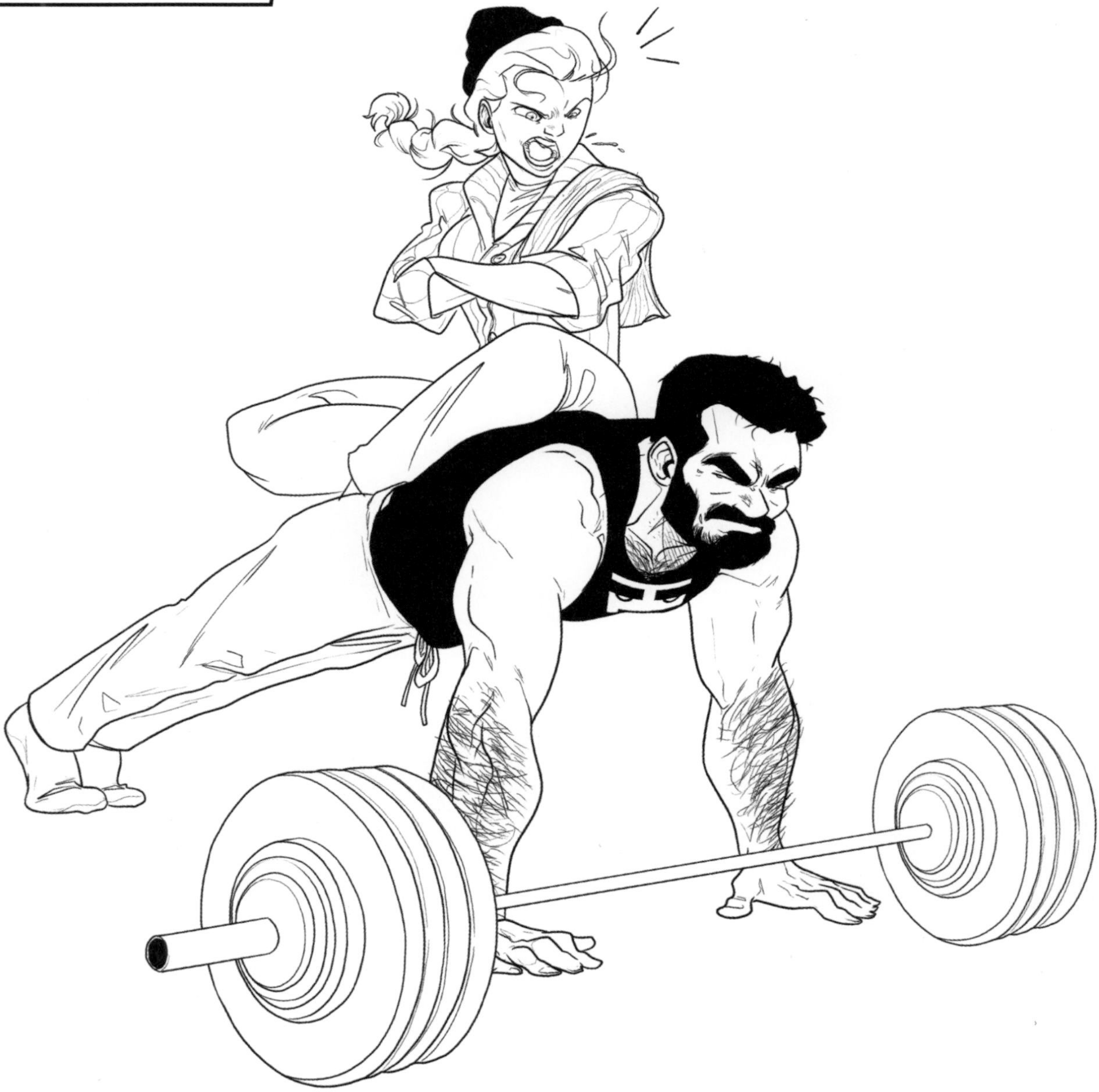

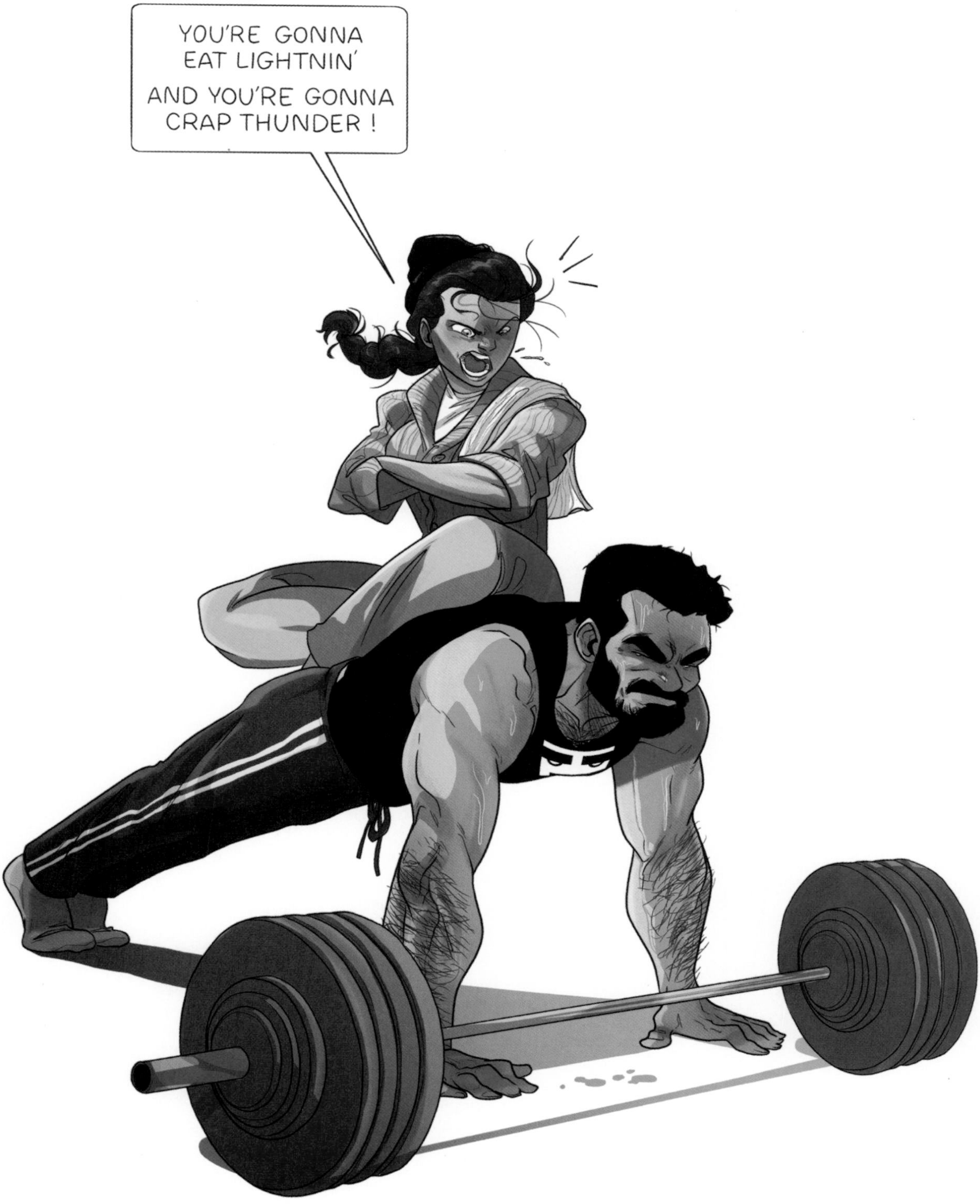
YOU'RE GONNA EAT LIGHTNIN' AND YOU'RE GONNA CRAP THUNDER !

19

SWEET DREAMS

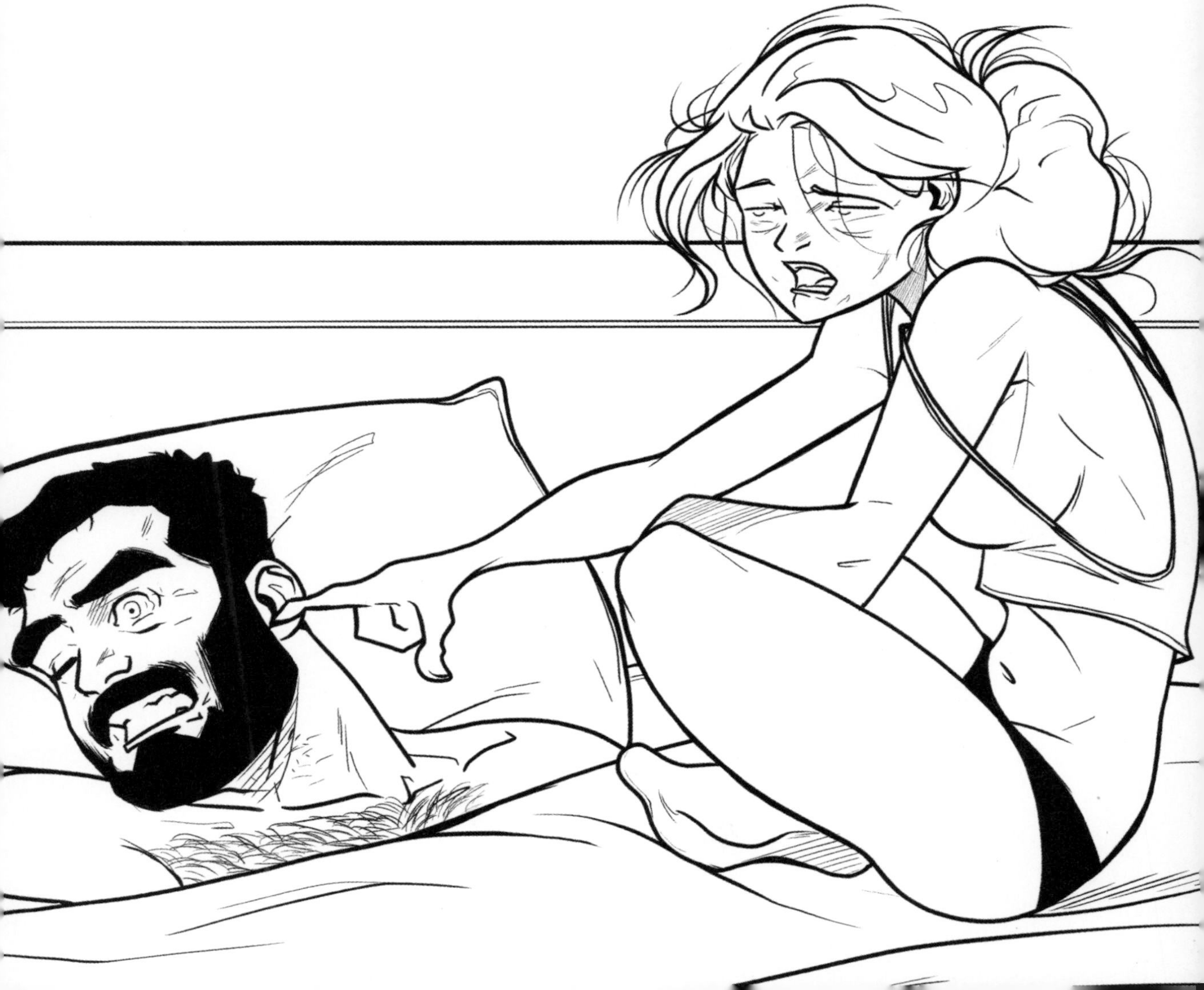

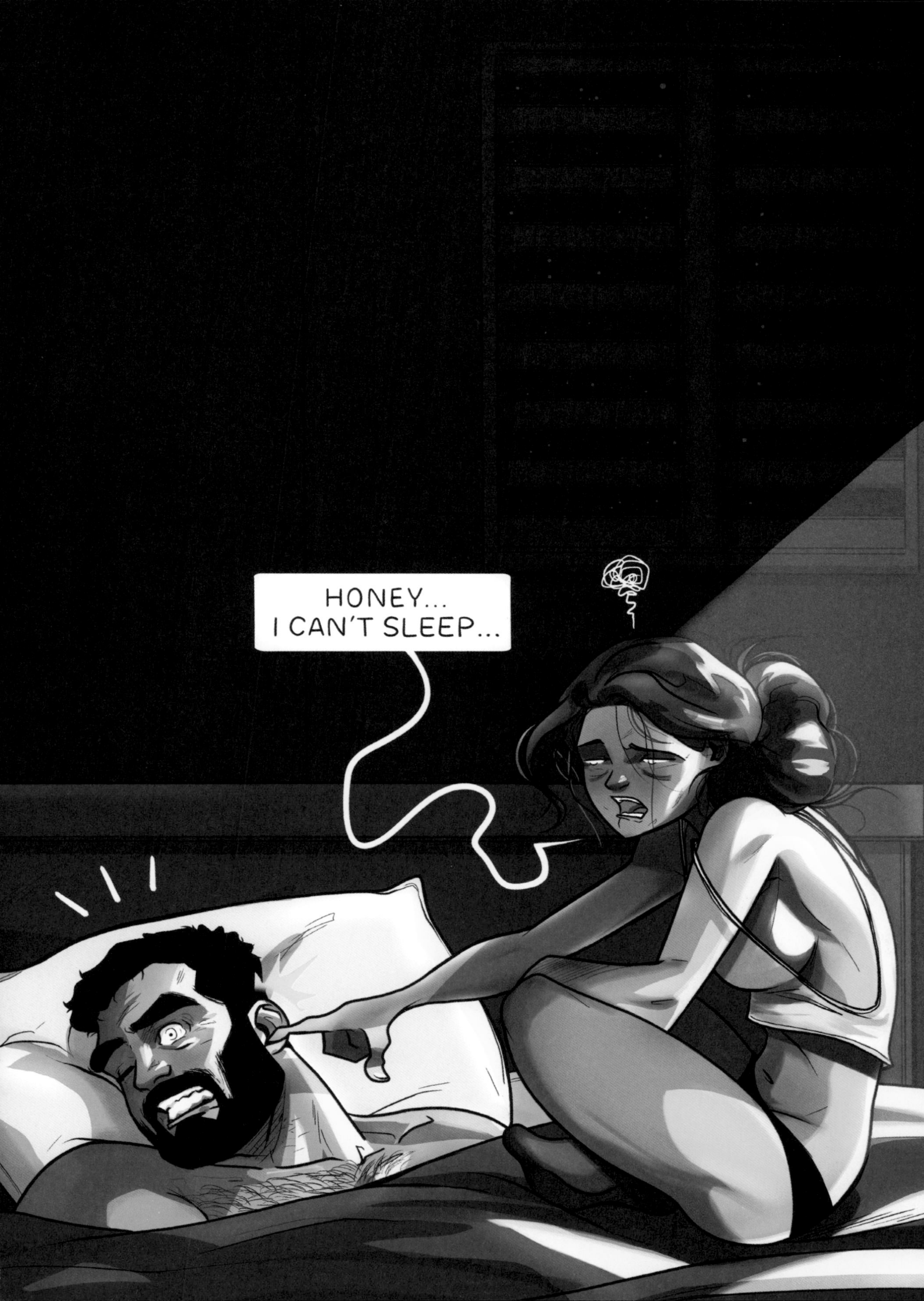
HONEY...
I CAN'T SLEEP...

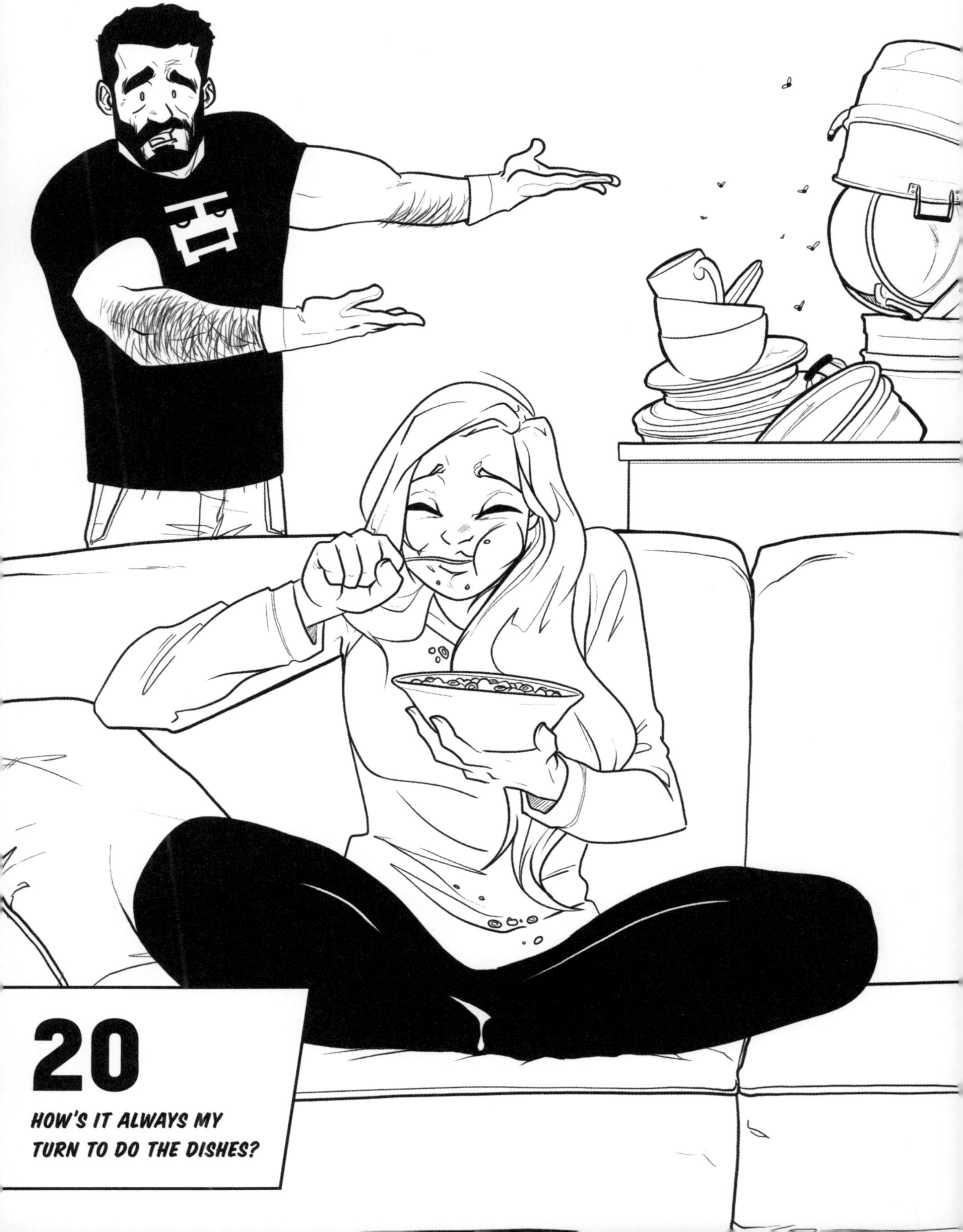

20

HOW'S IT ALWAYS MY TURN TO DO THE DISHES?

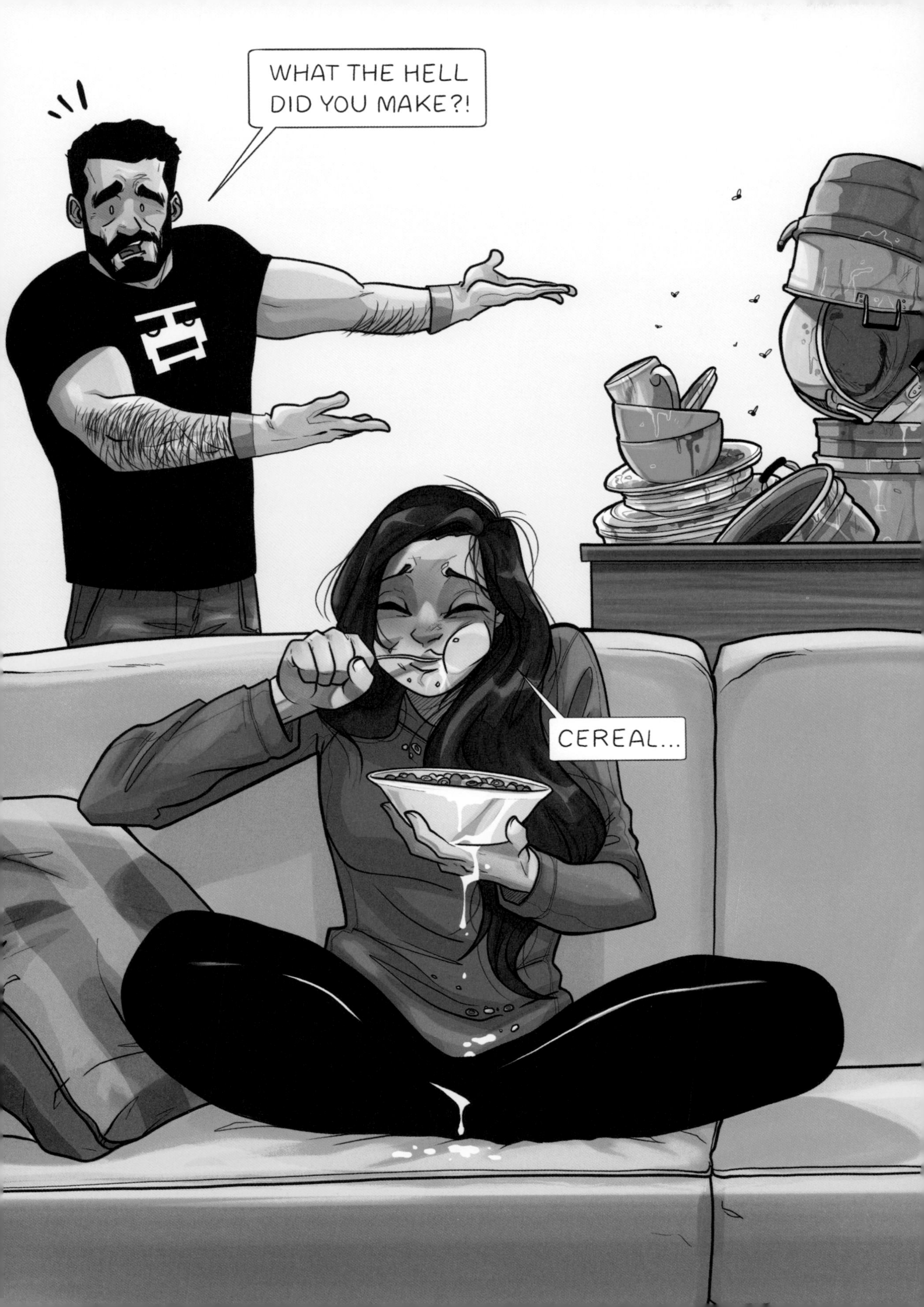
WHAT THE HELL
DID YOU MAKE?!
CEREAL...

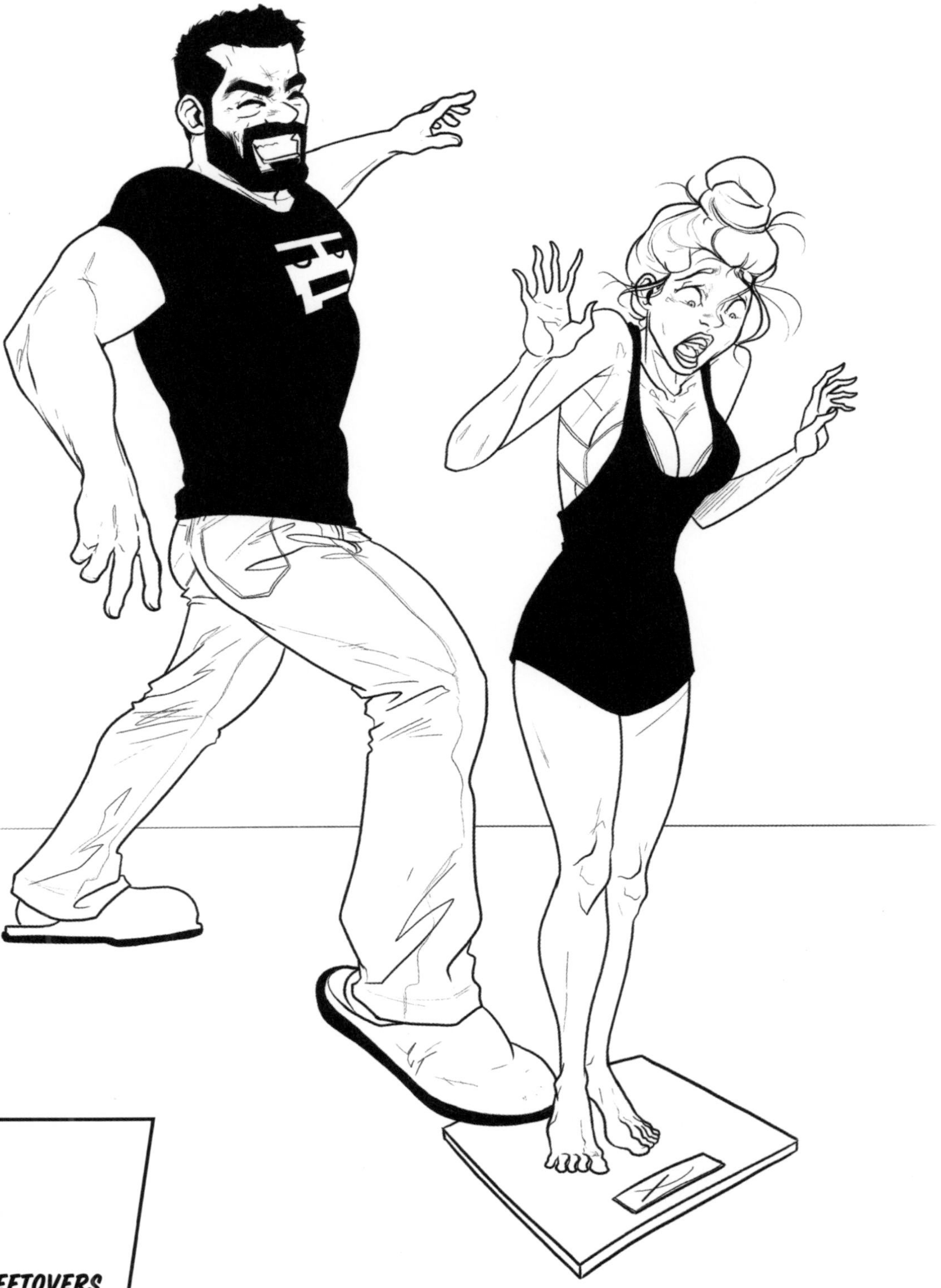

21

HOLIDAY LEFTOVERS

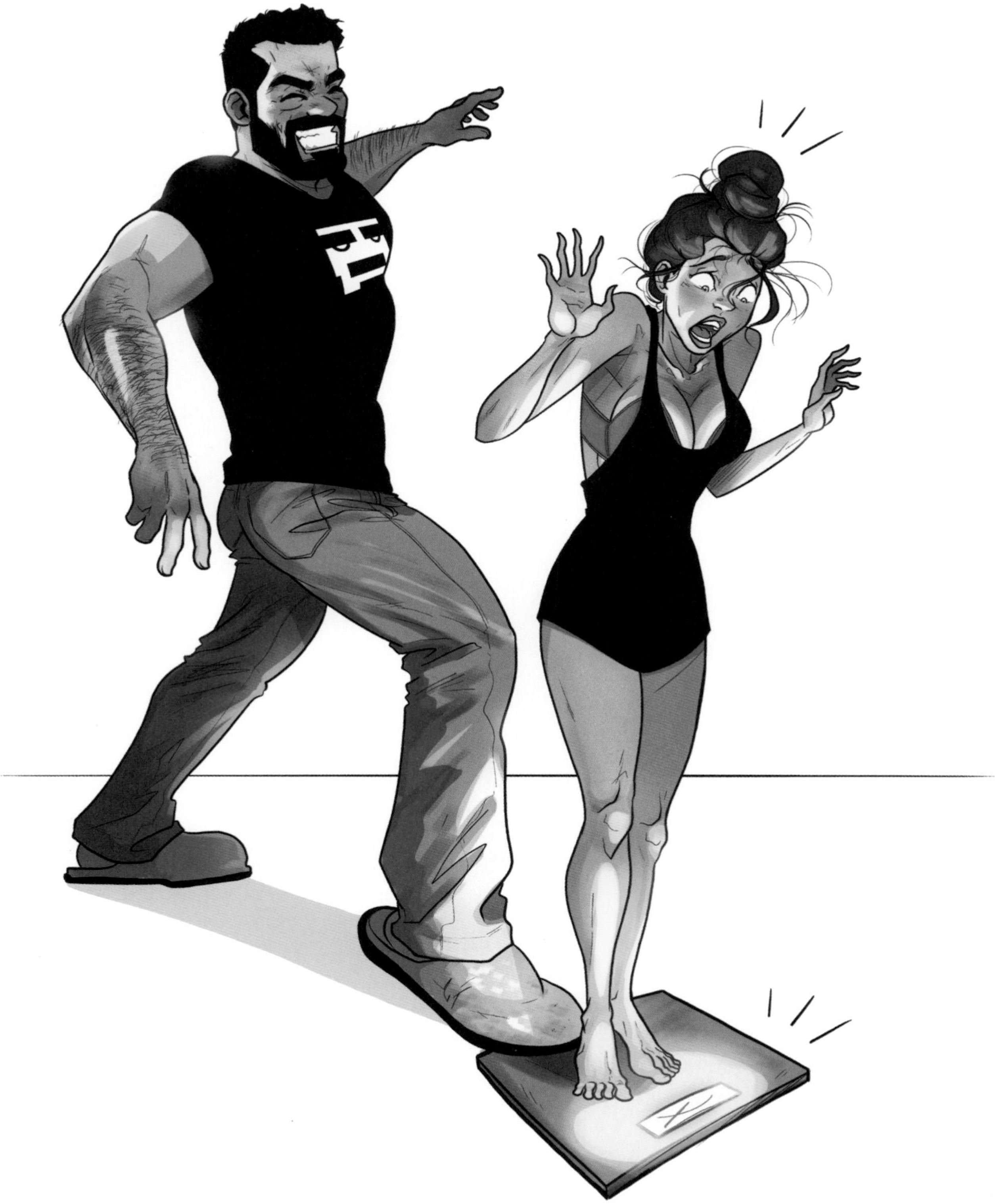

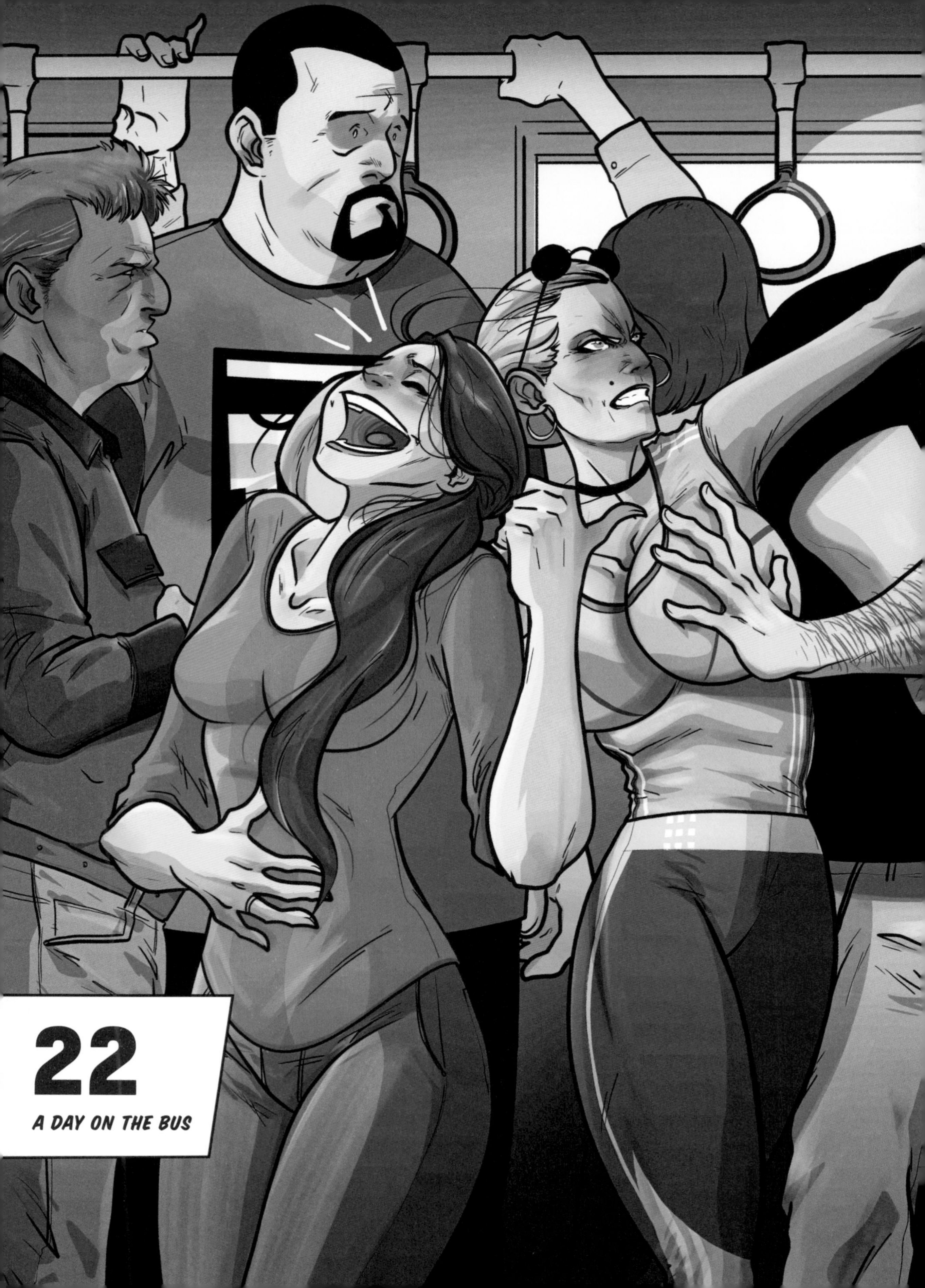

22

A DAY ON THE BUS

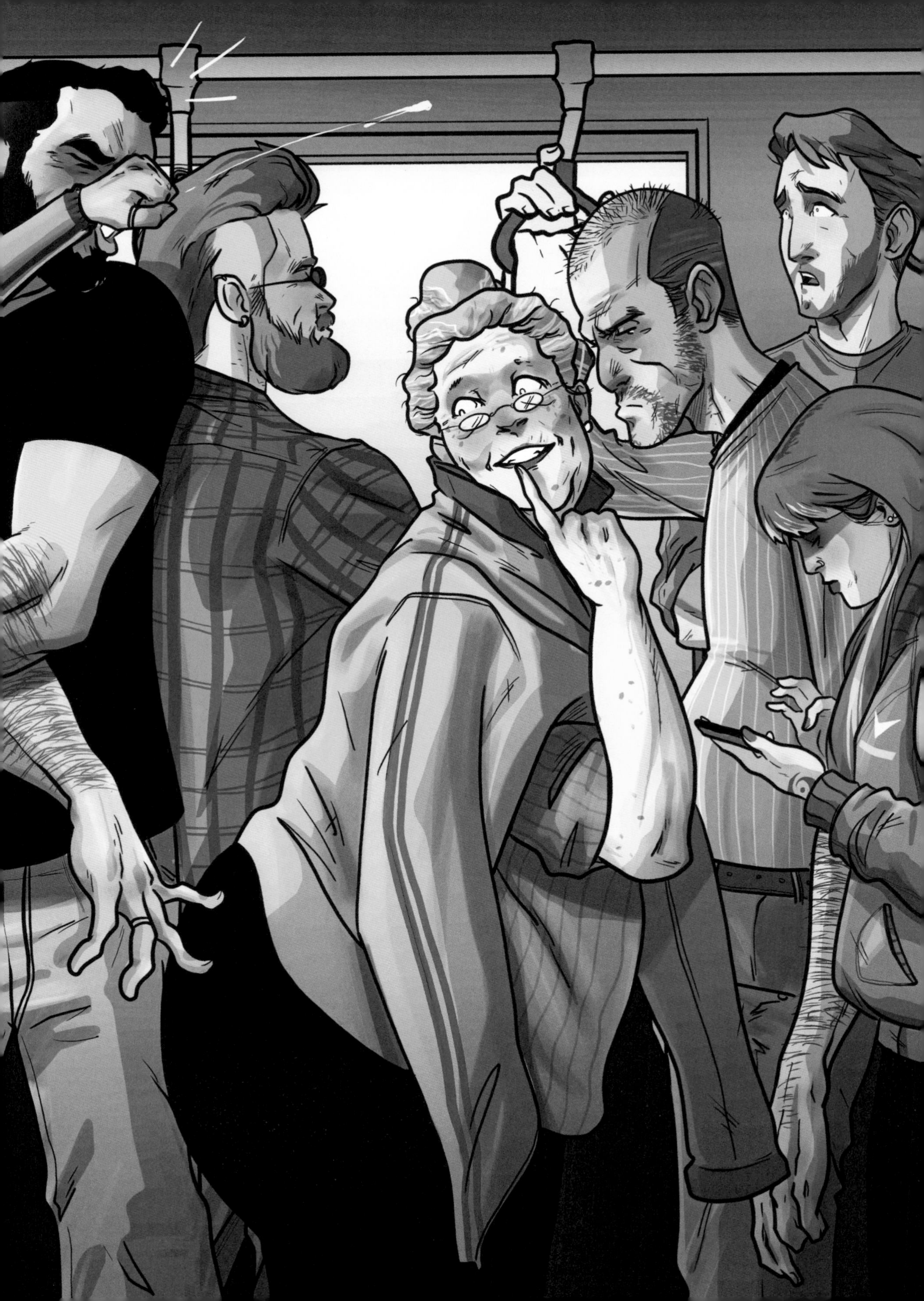

23

TYPICAL NIGHT OUT

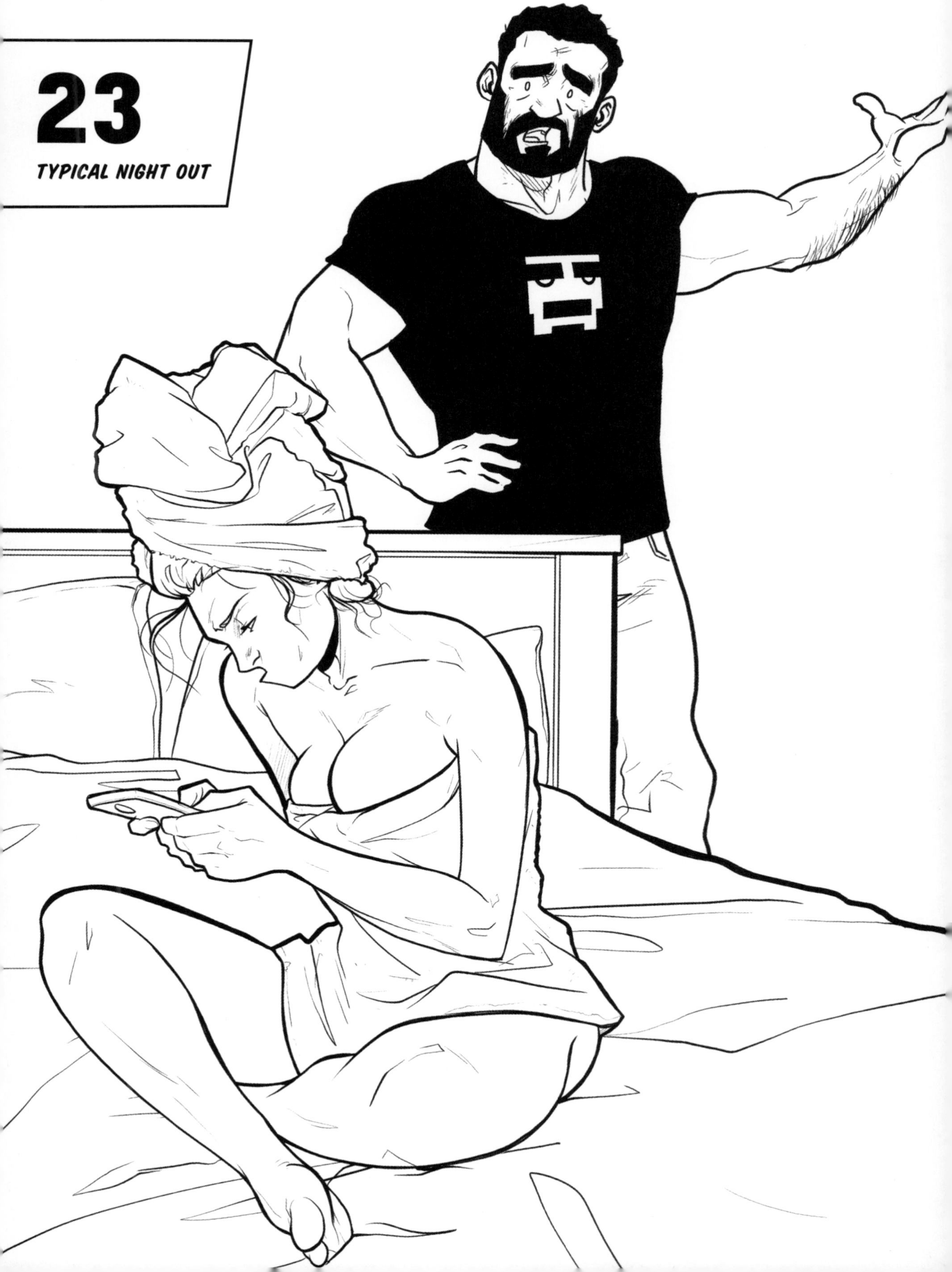

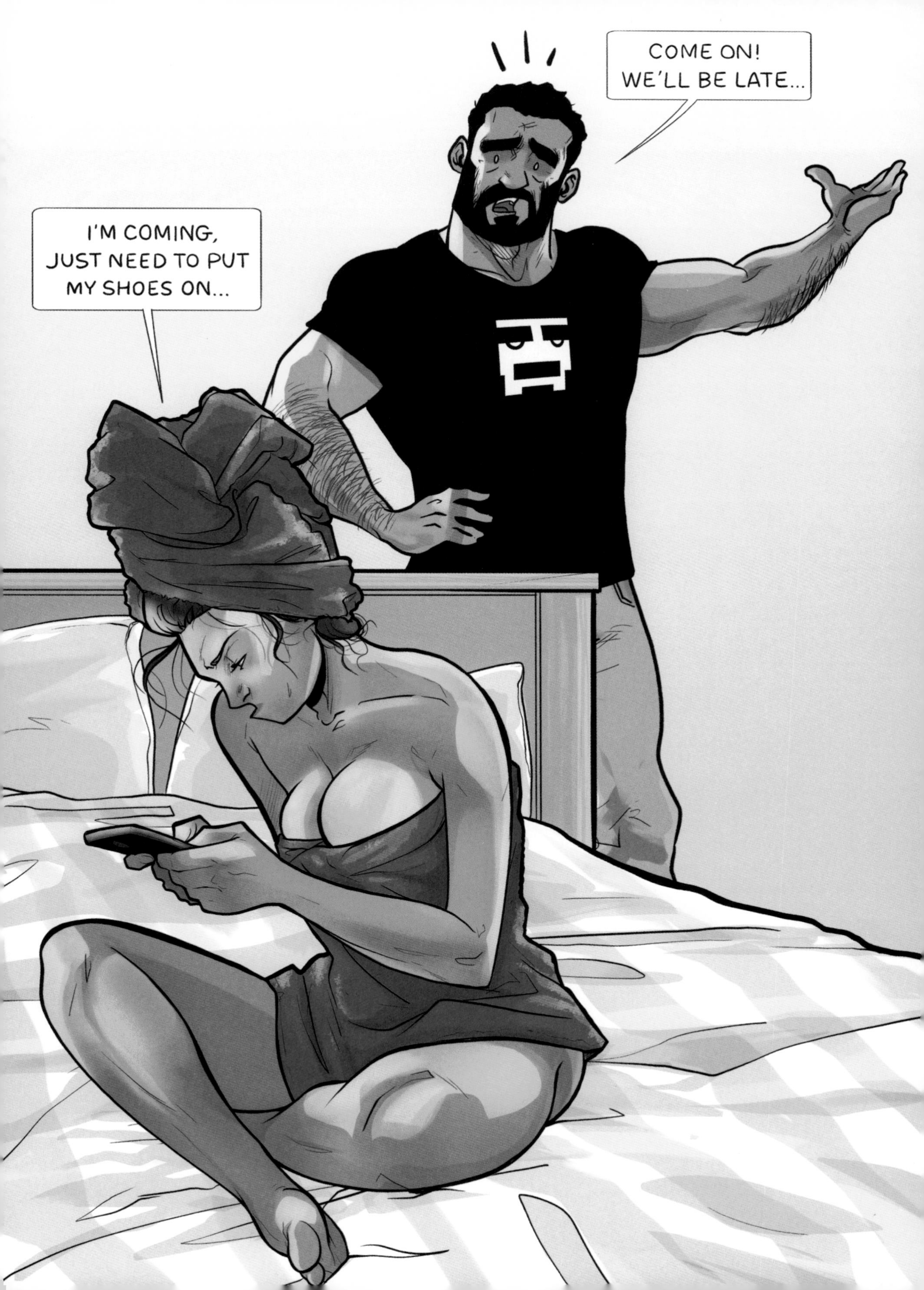
I'M COMING, JUST NEED TO PUT MY SHOES ON...
COME ON! WE'LL BE LATE...

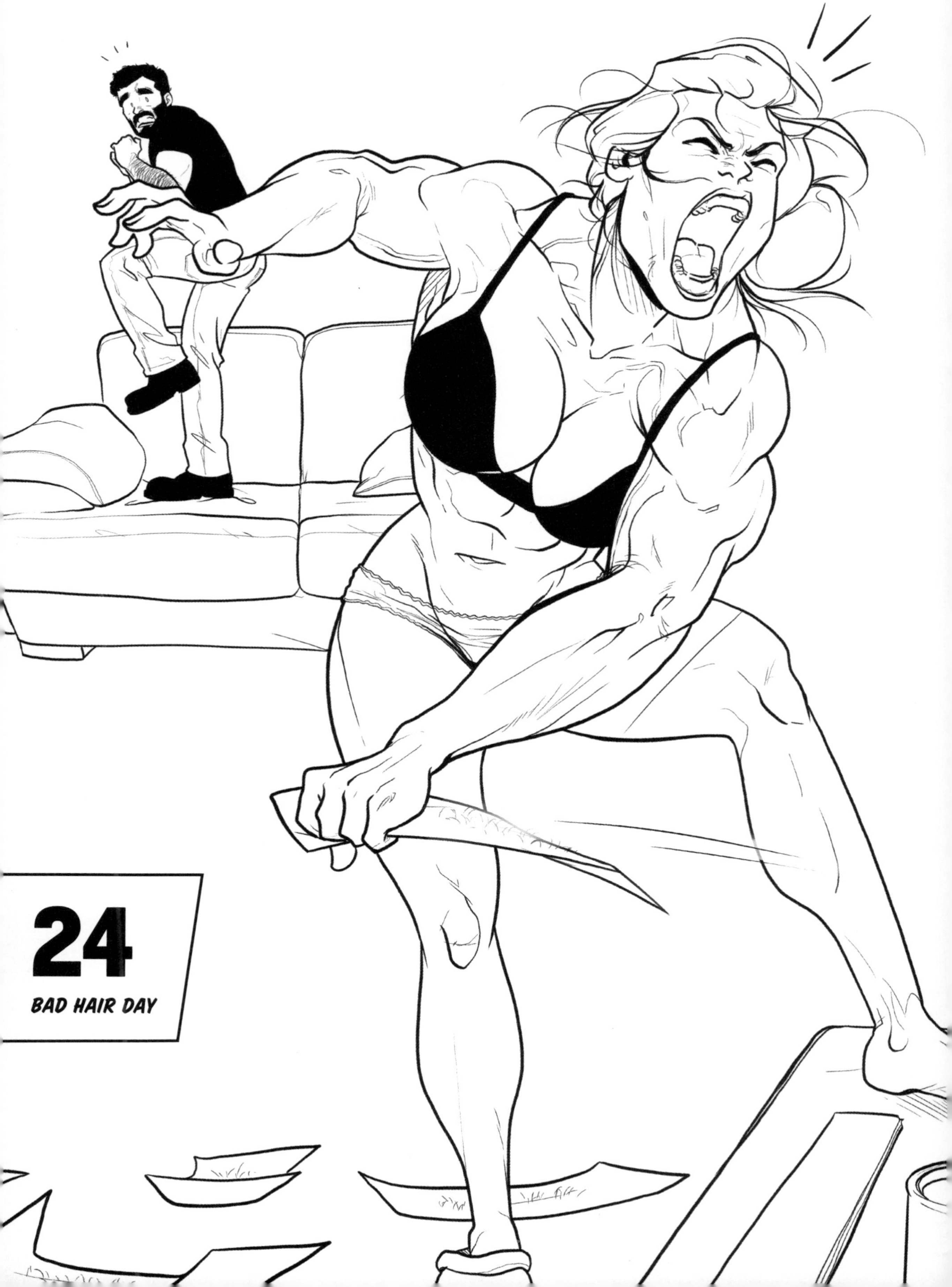

24

BAD HAIR DAY

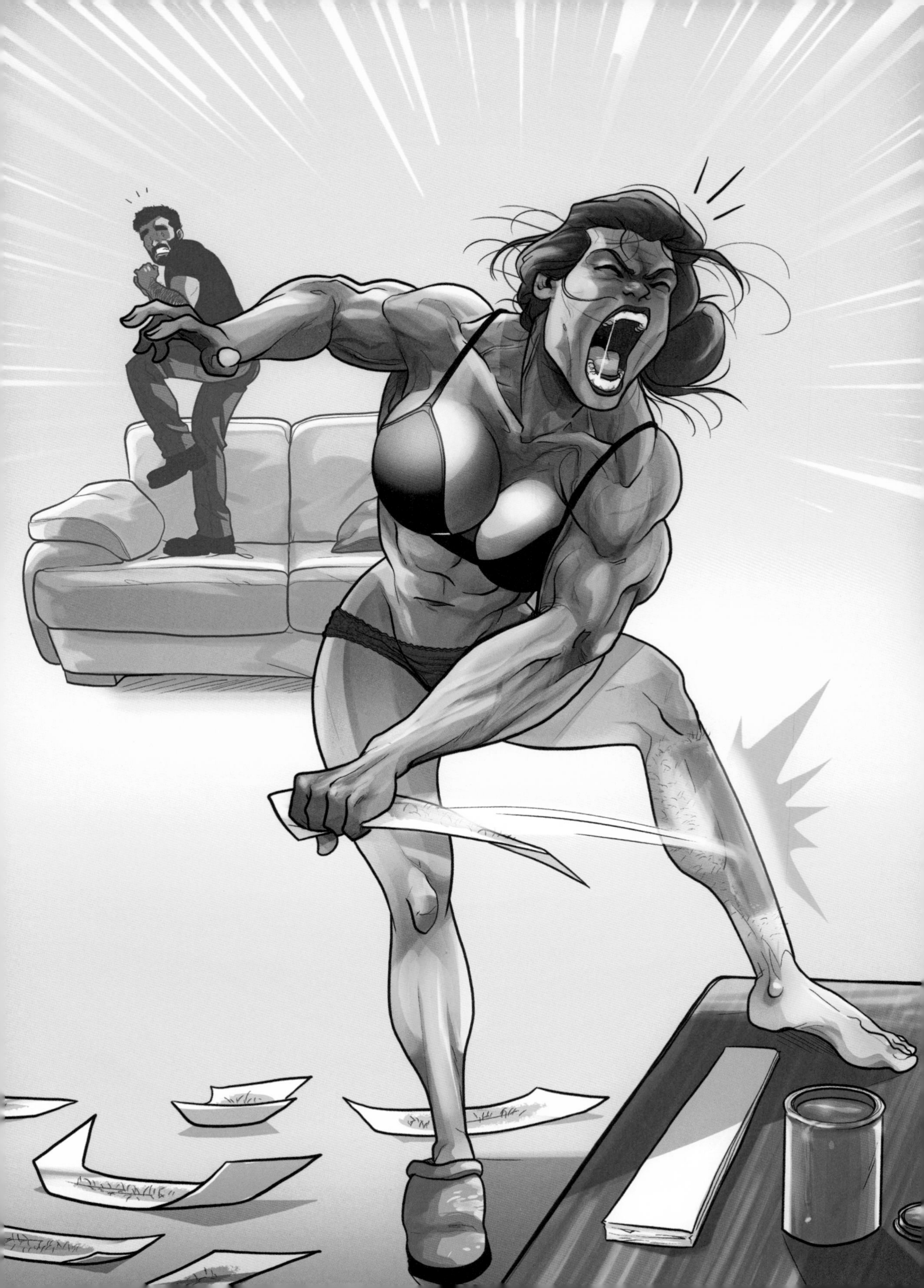

25
HER MAGIC TOUCH

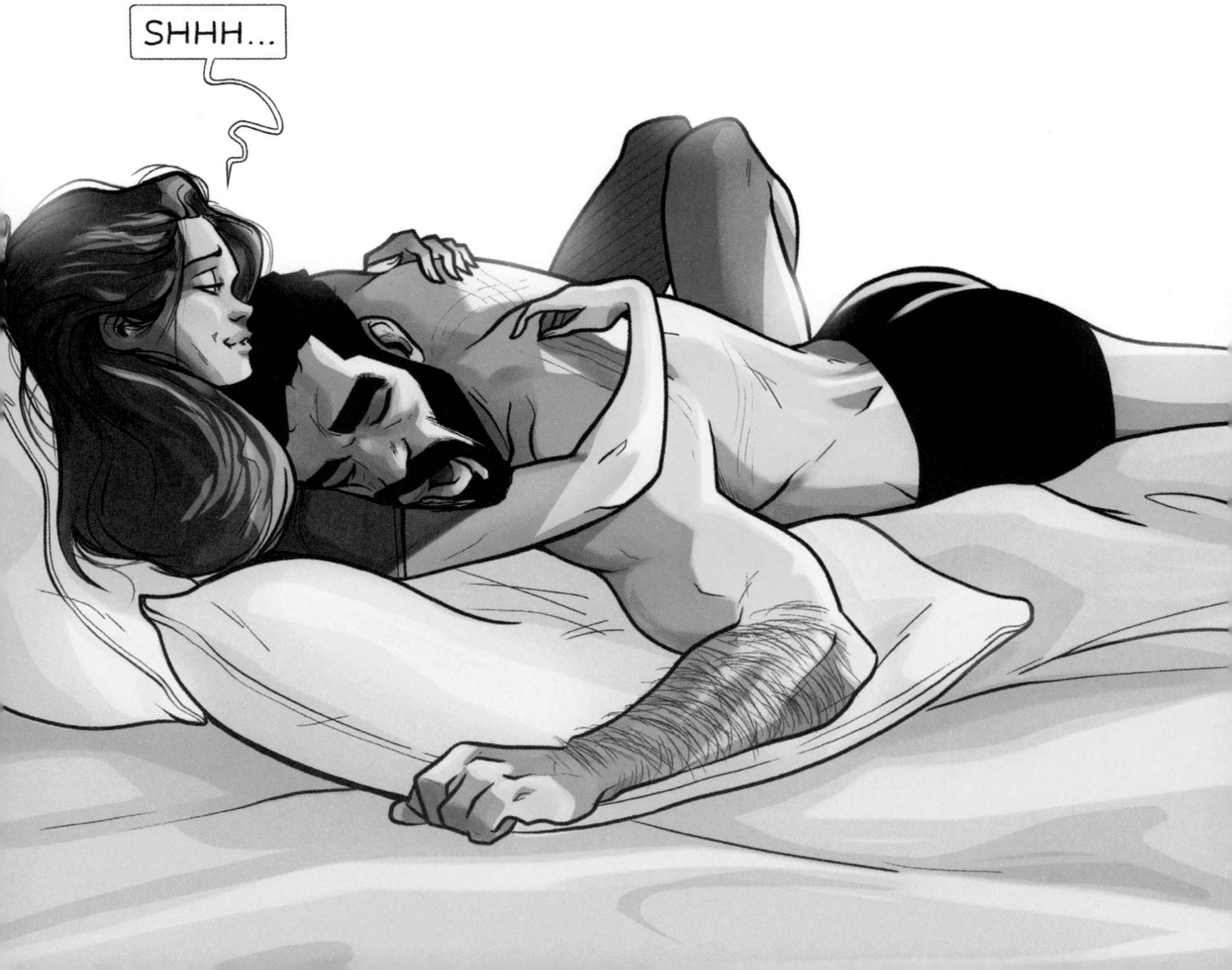
SHHH...

26

SMELL CHECK

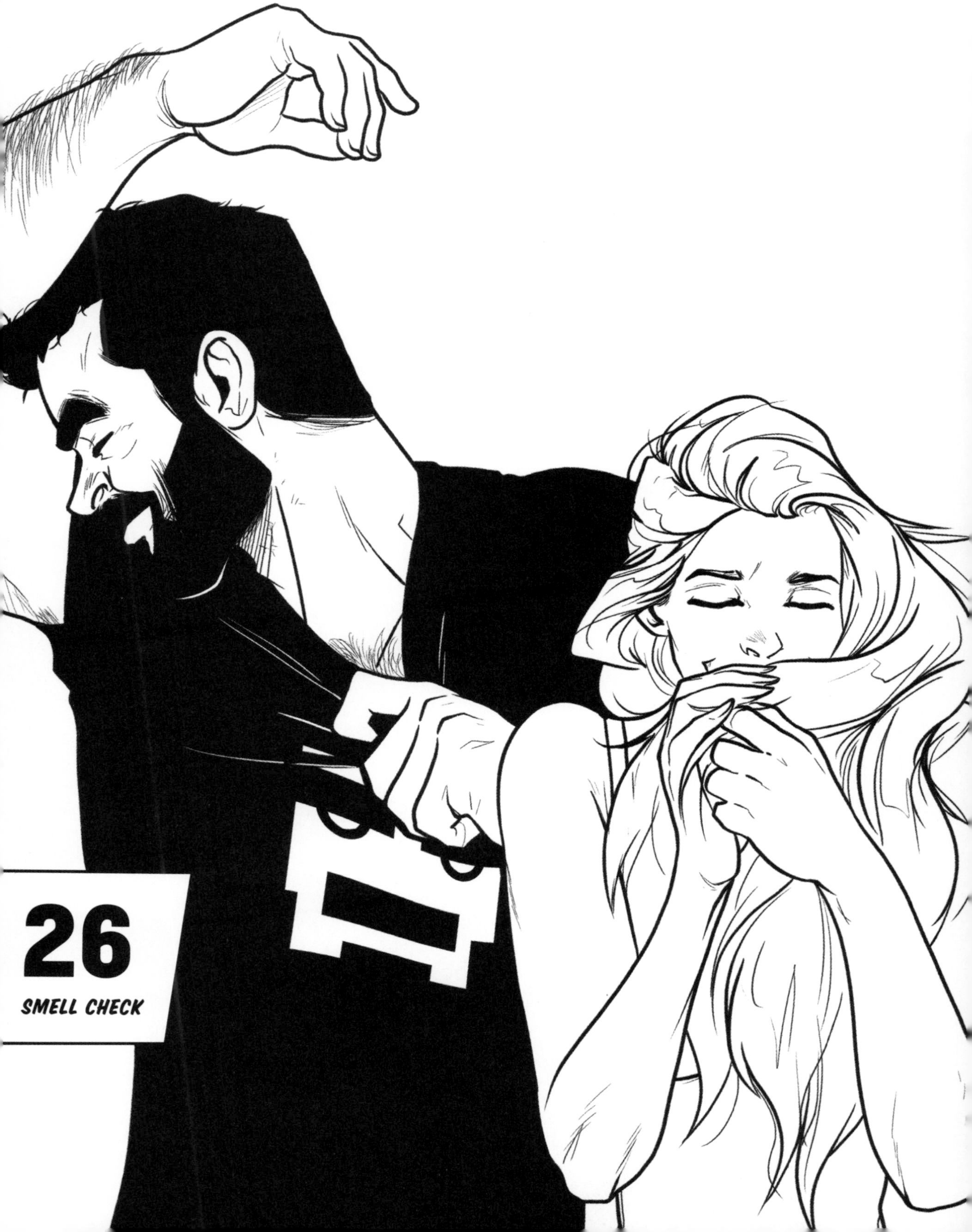

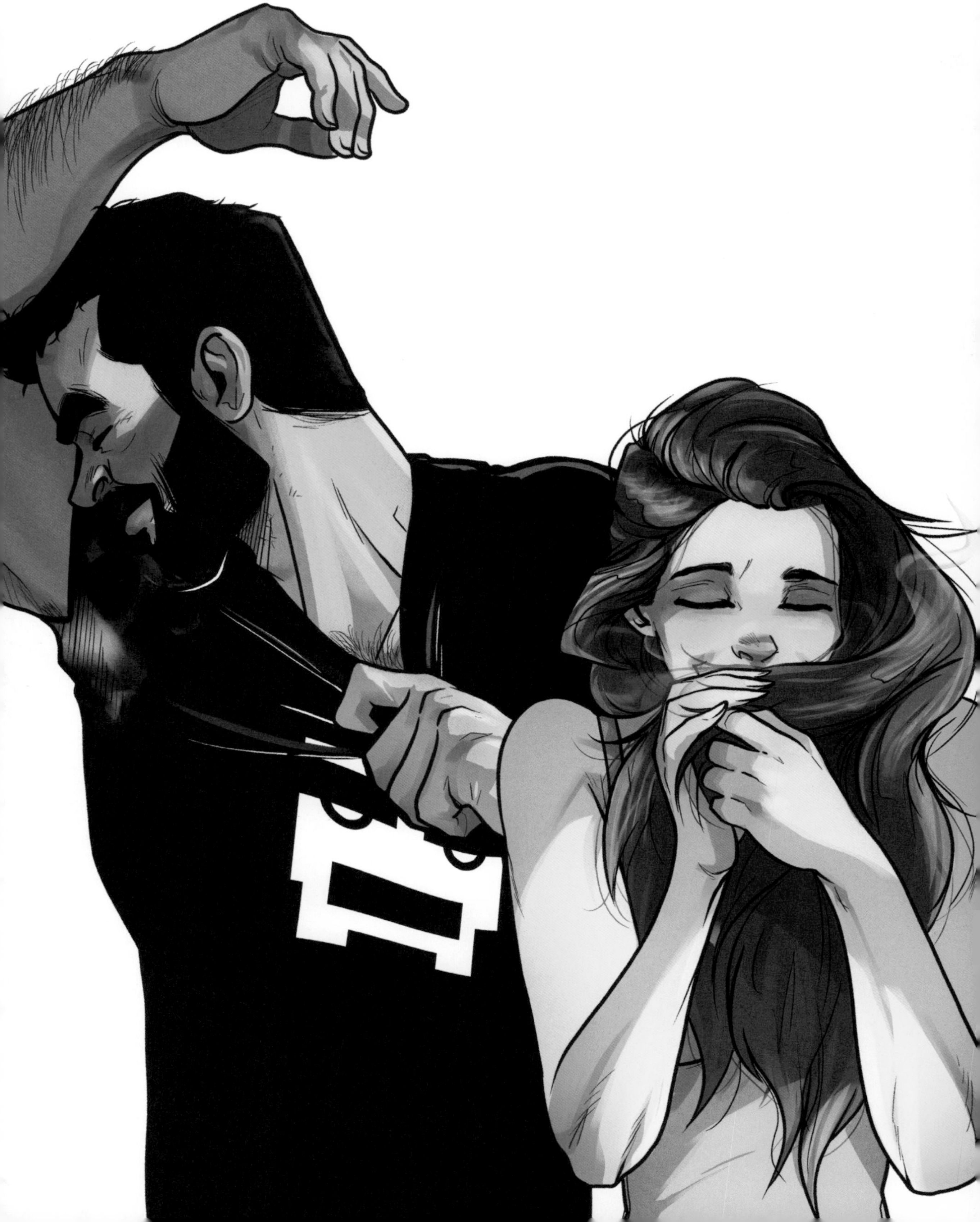

27

WE BOUGHT AN ELLIPTICAL

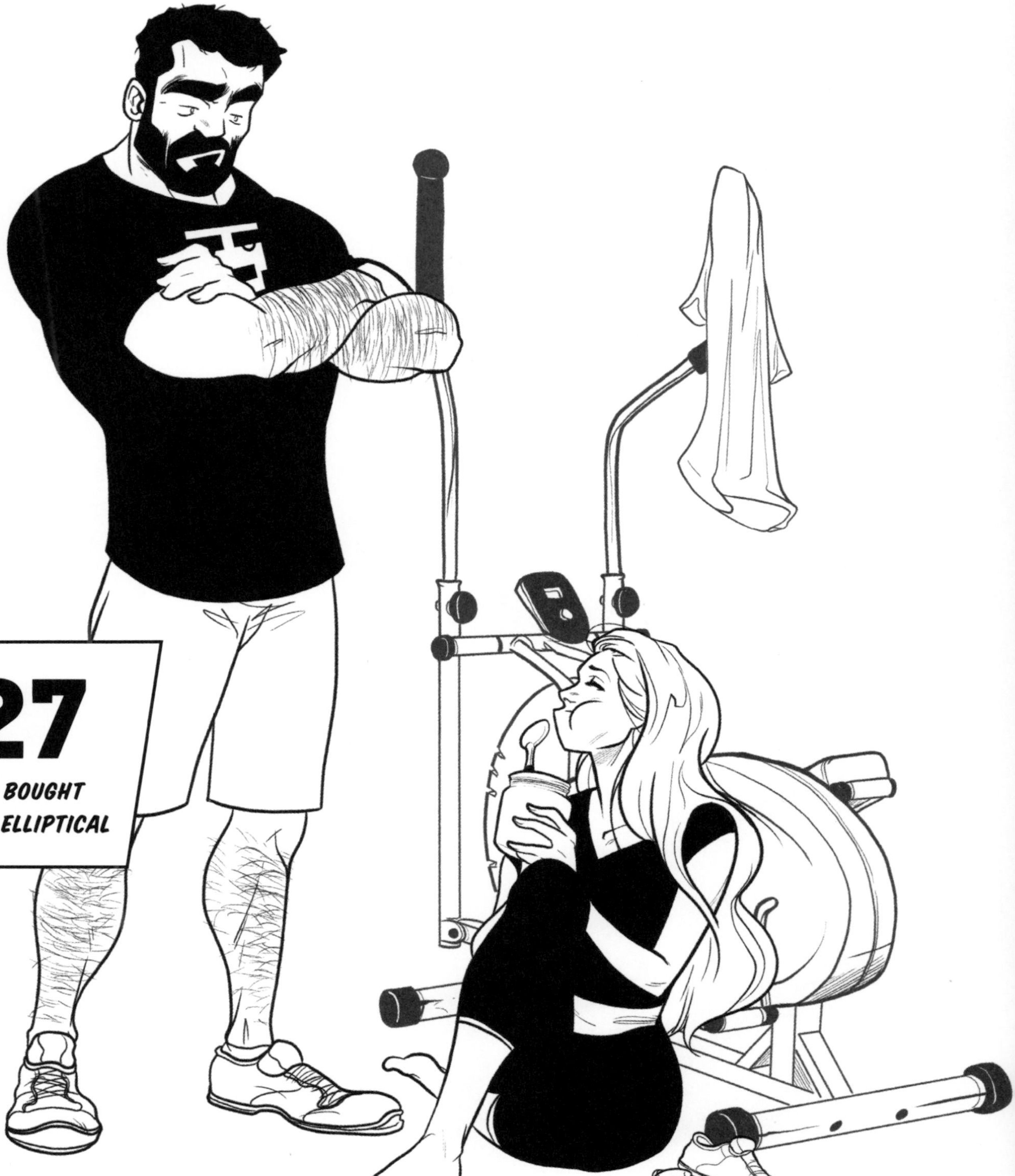

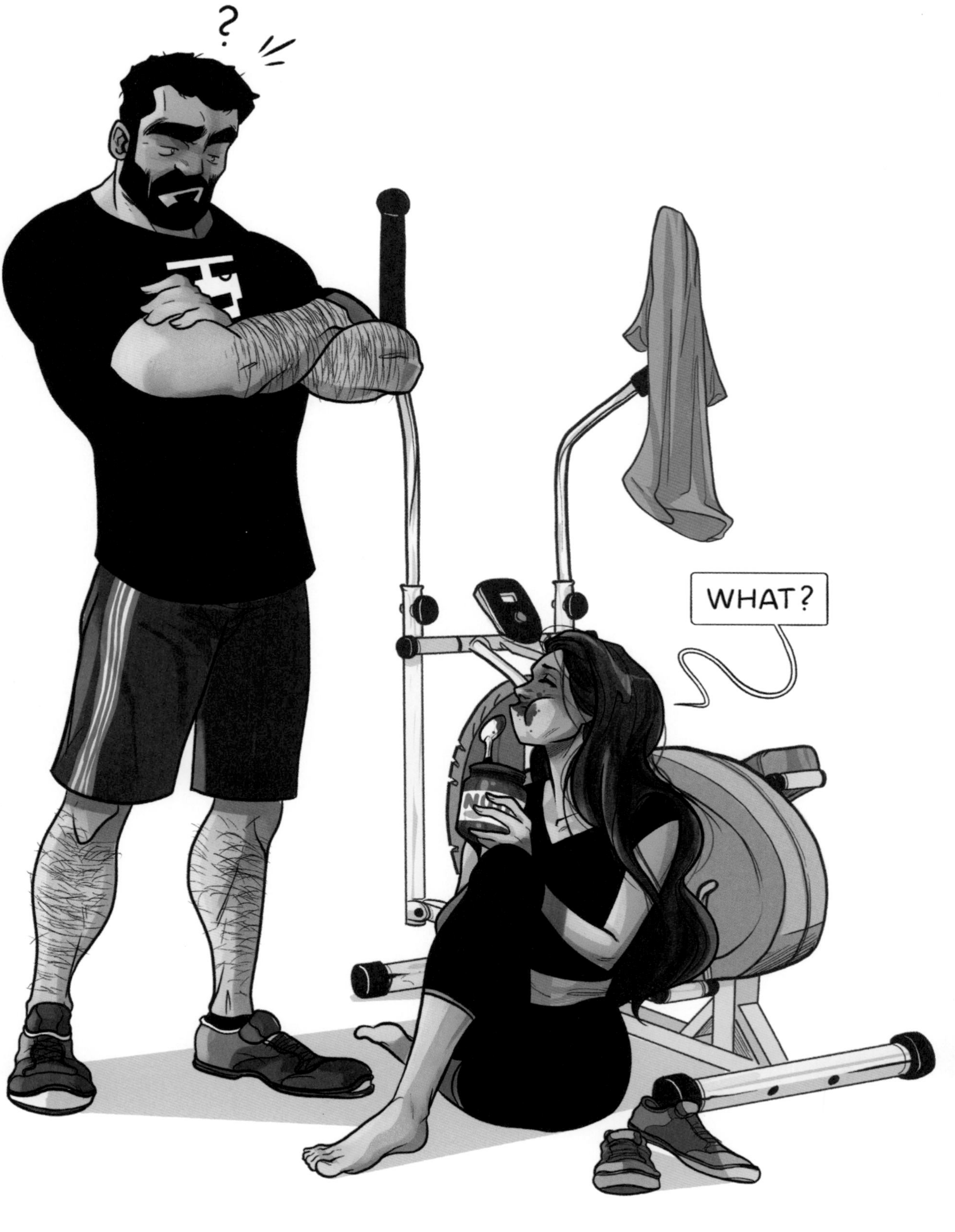
?
WHAT?

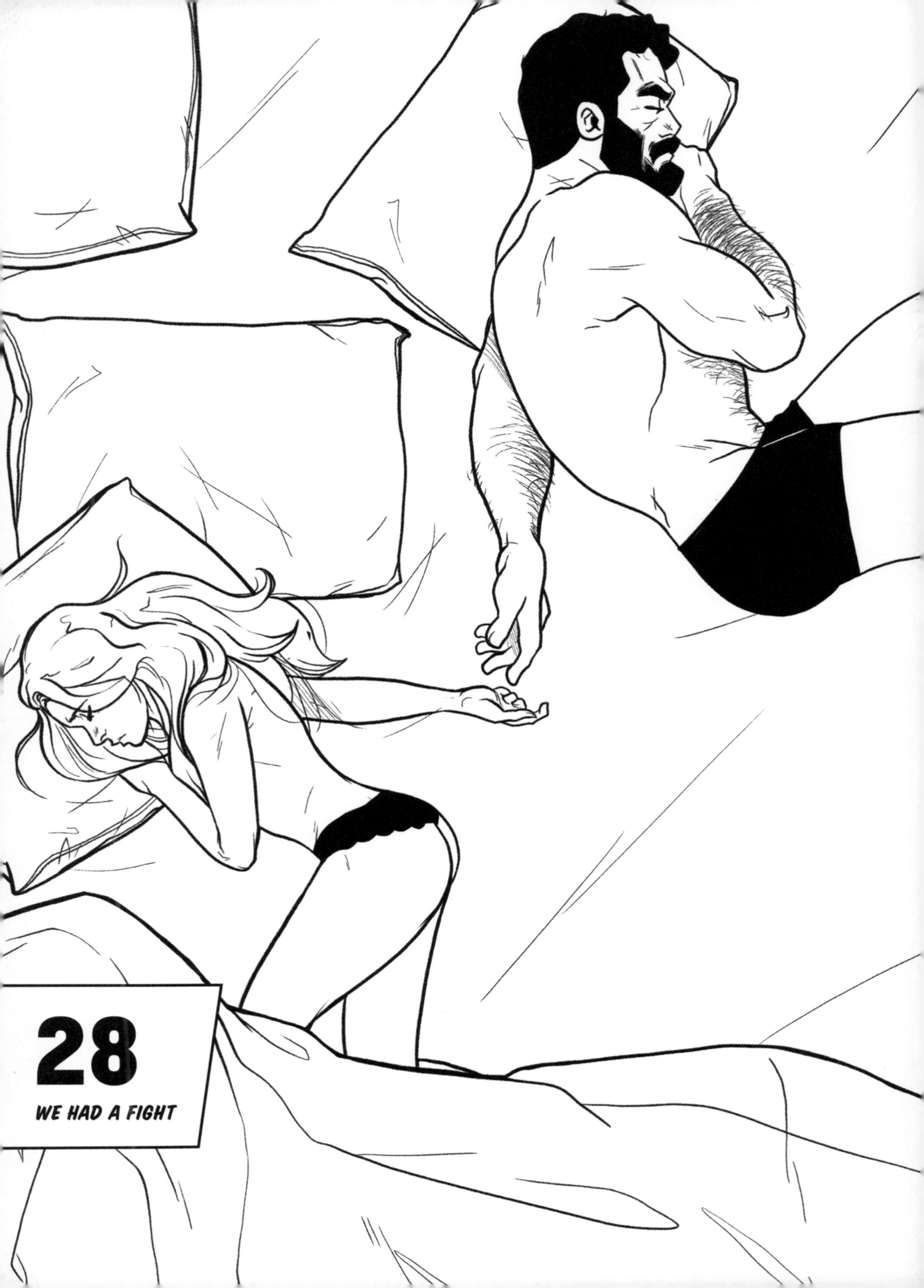

28

WE HAD A FIGHT

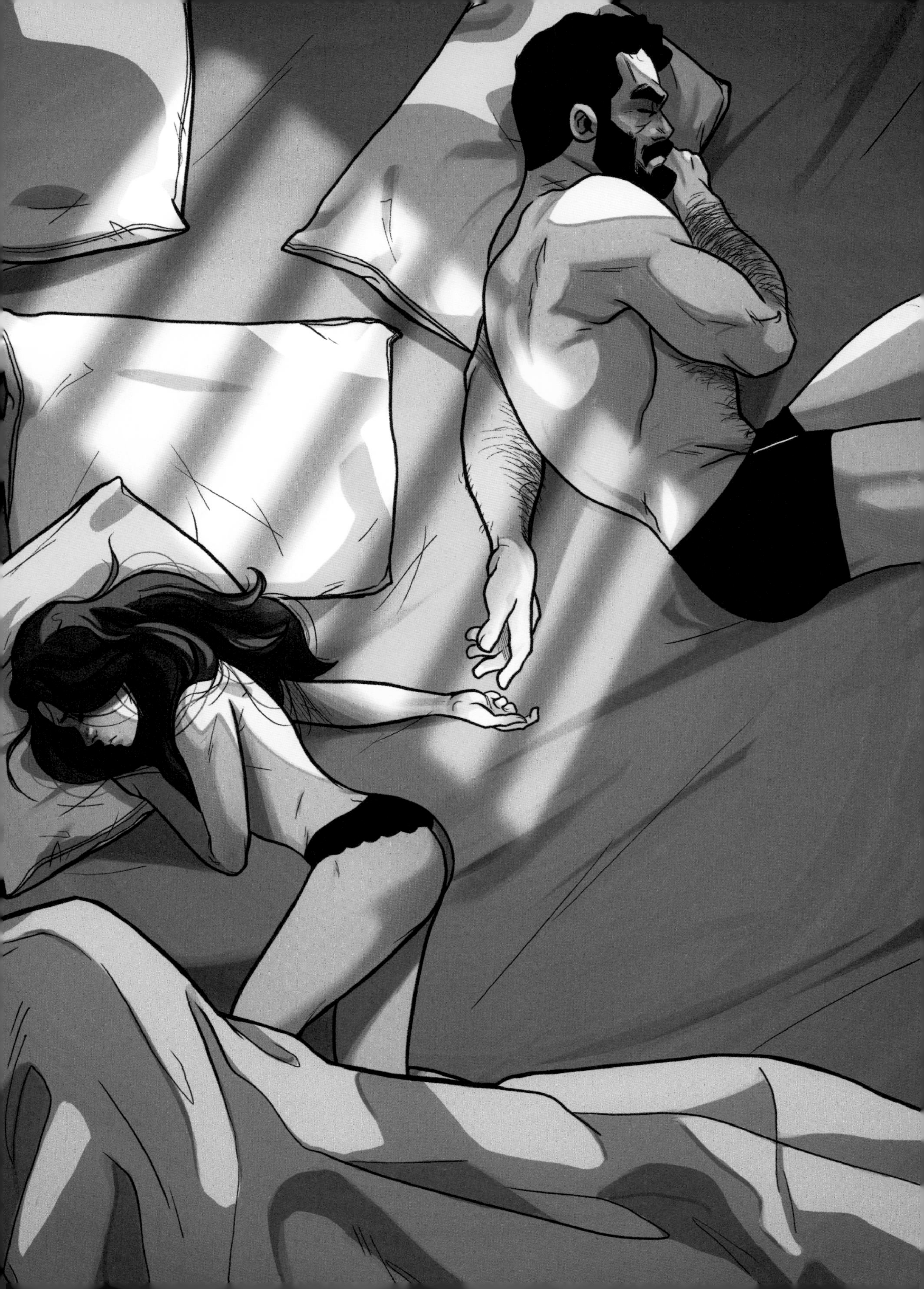

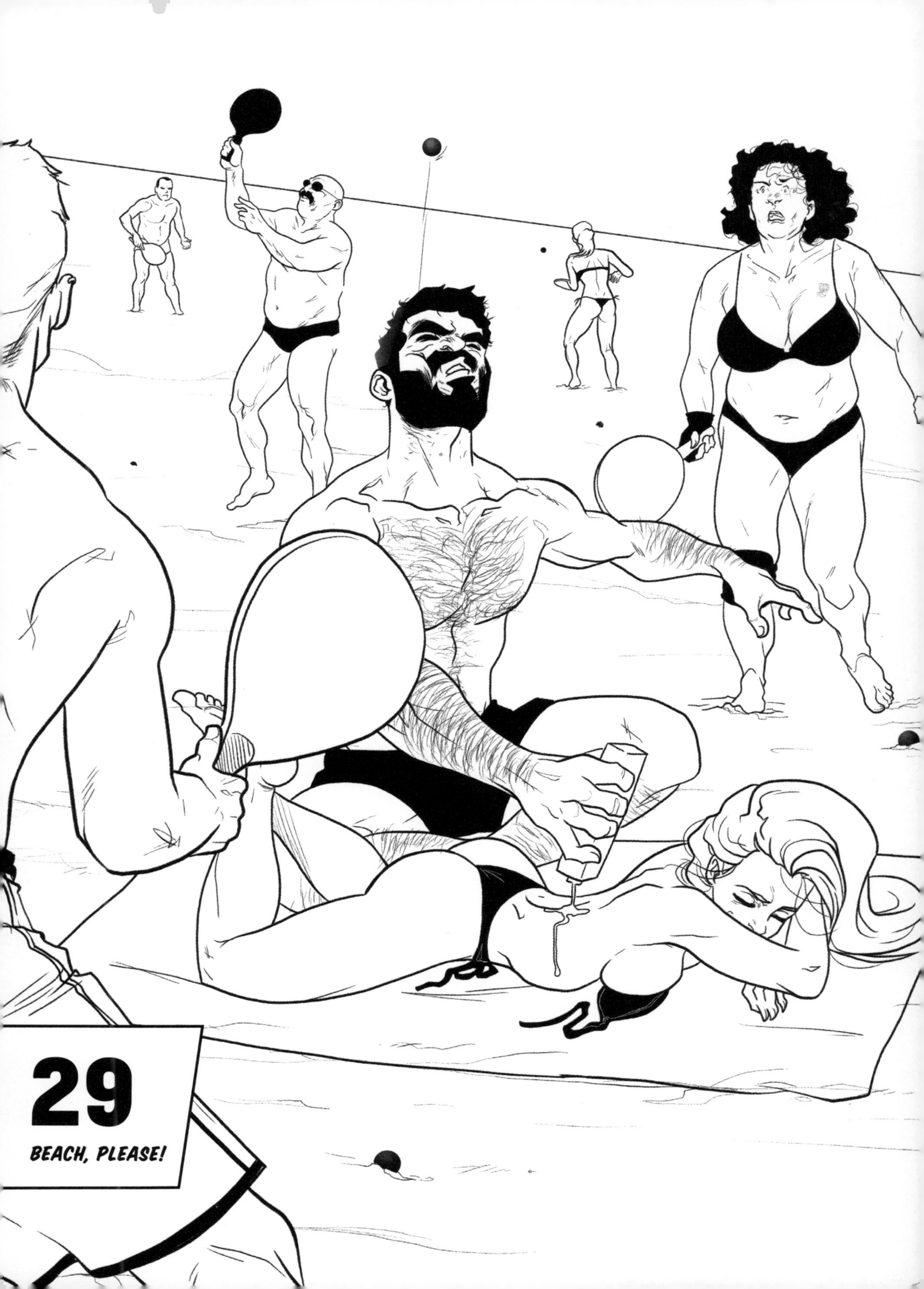

29

BEACH, PLEASE!

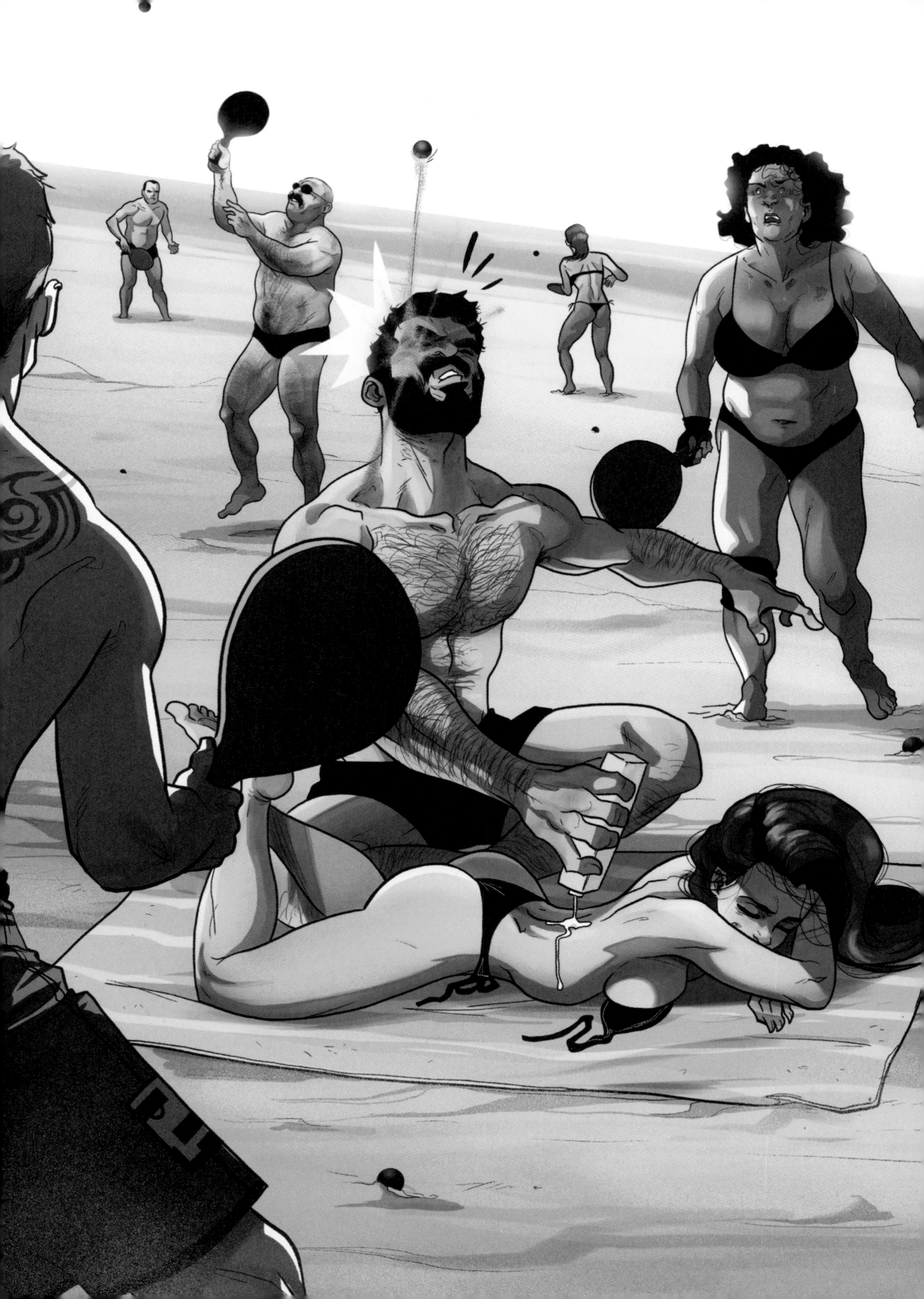

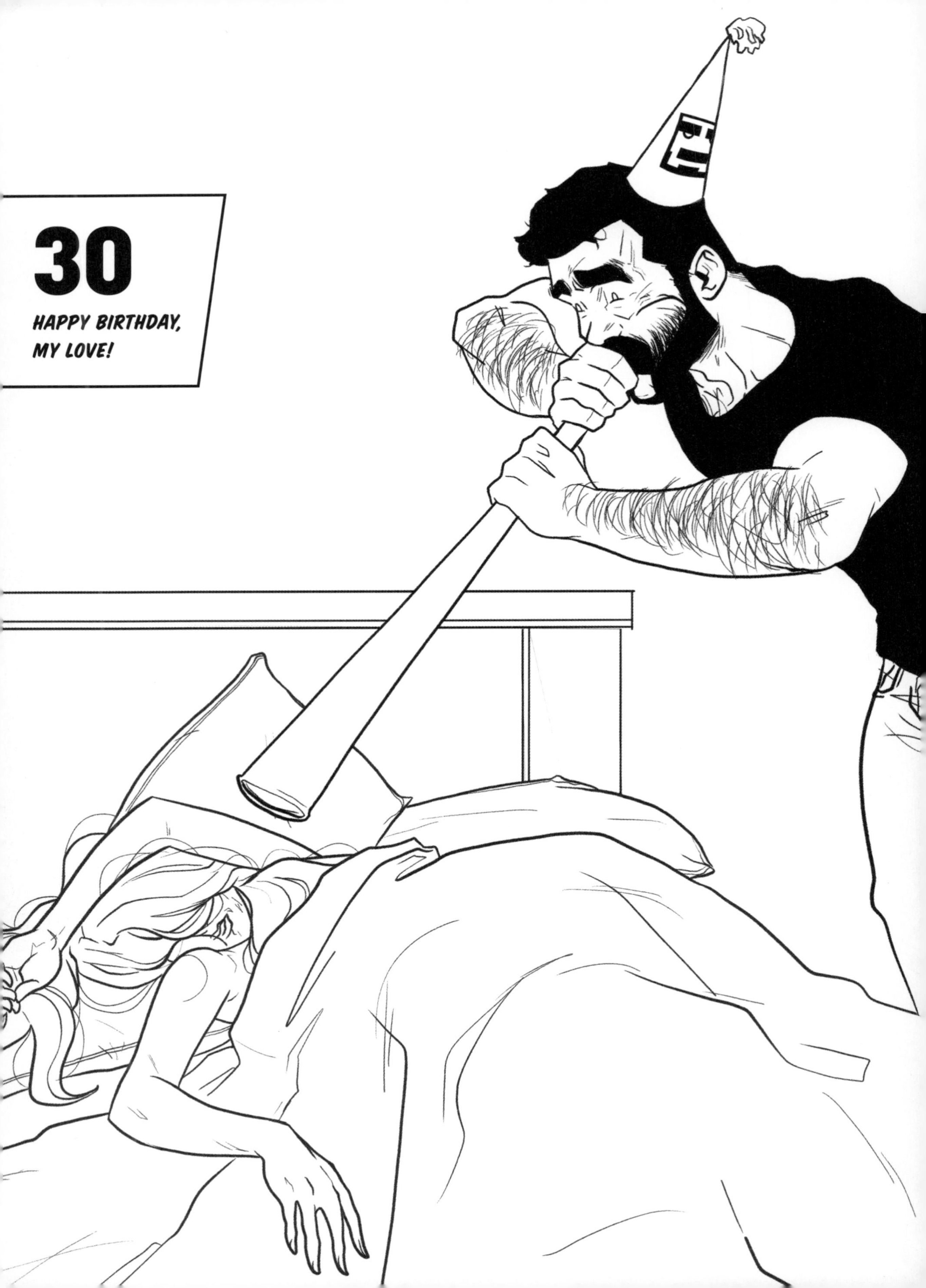
30
HAPPY BIRTHDAY,
MY LOVE!

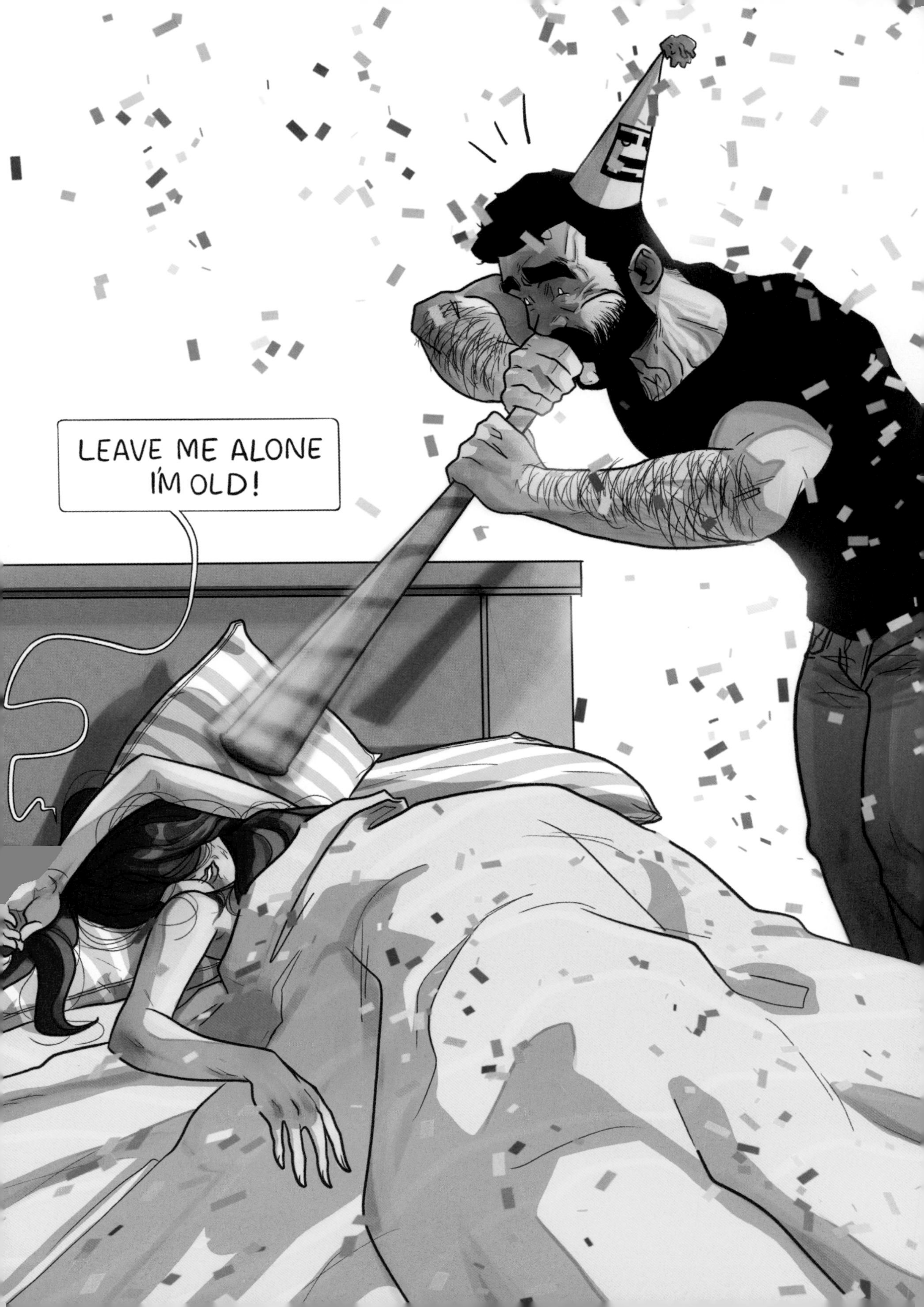
LEAVE ME ALONE I'M OLD!

31

SAFETY FIRST!

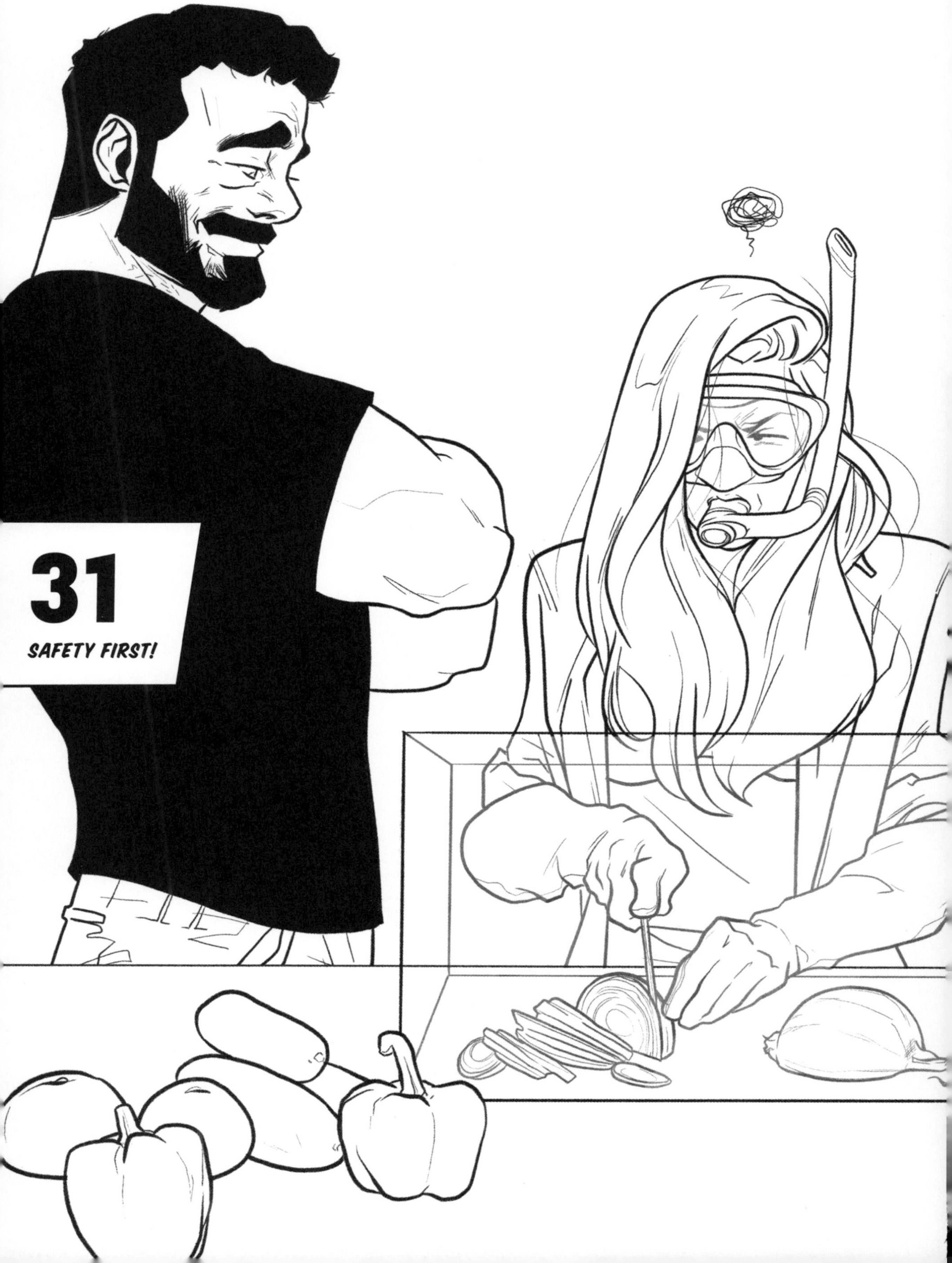

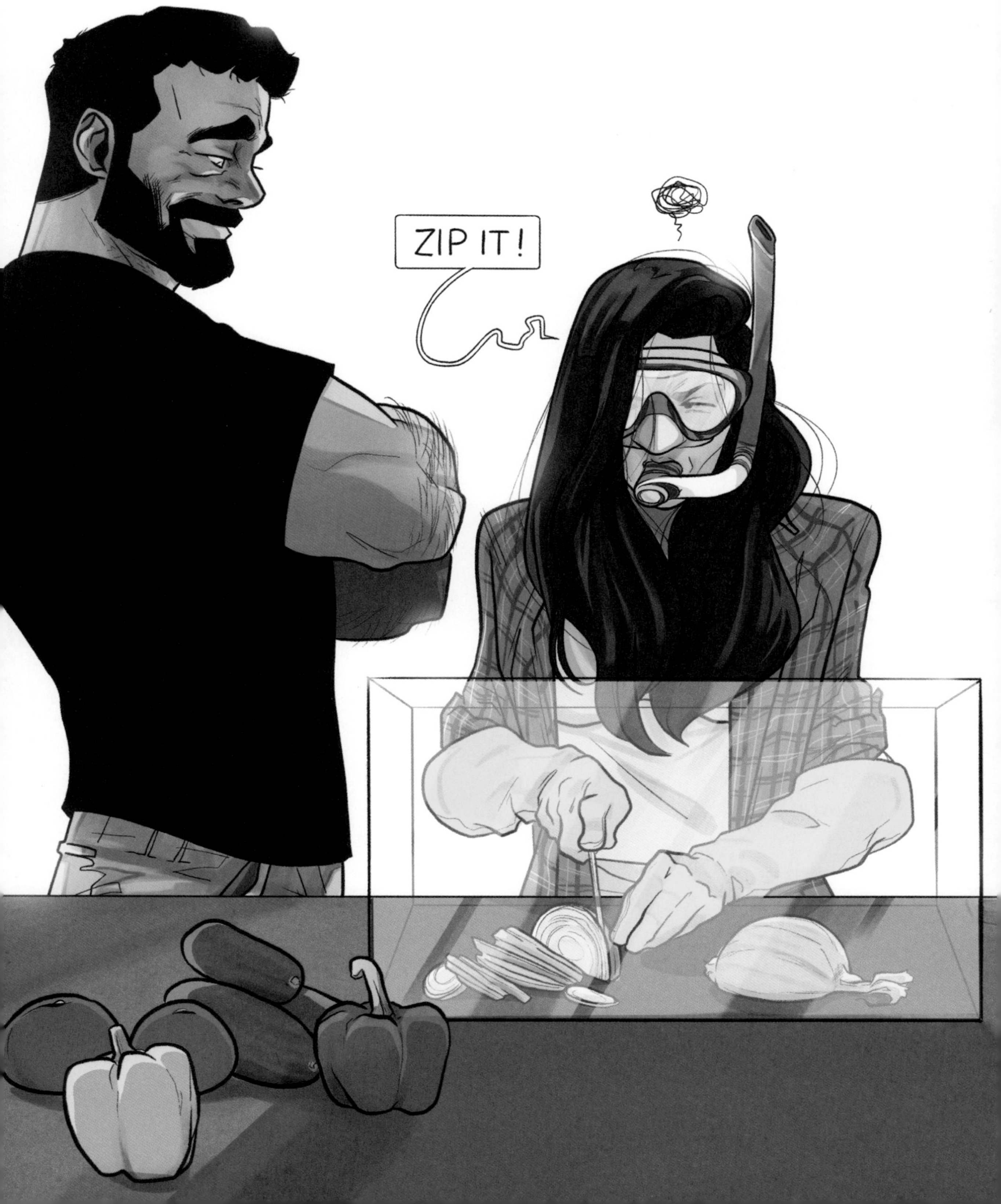
ZIP IT!

32

A WALK IN THE PARK

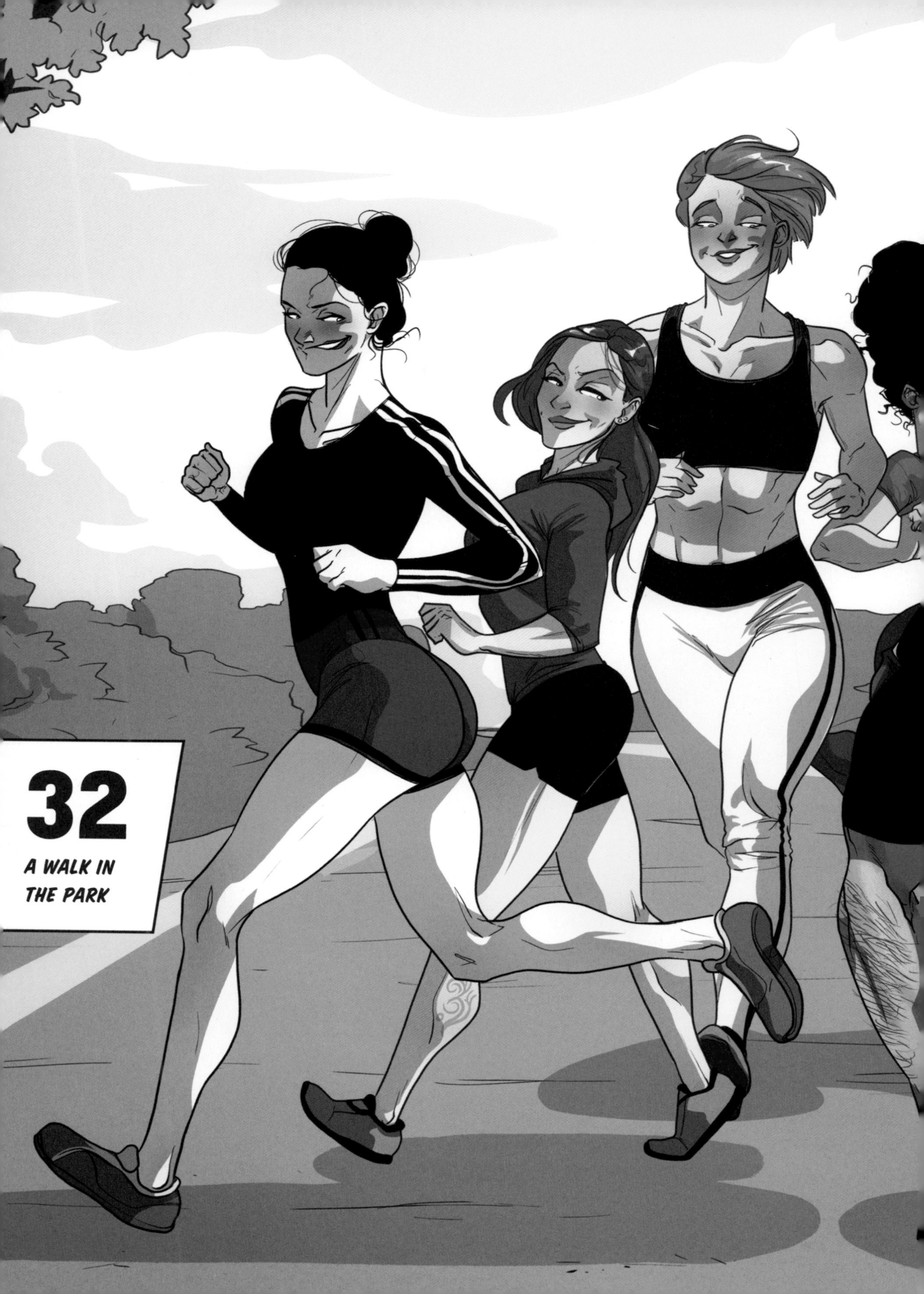

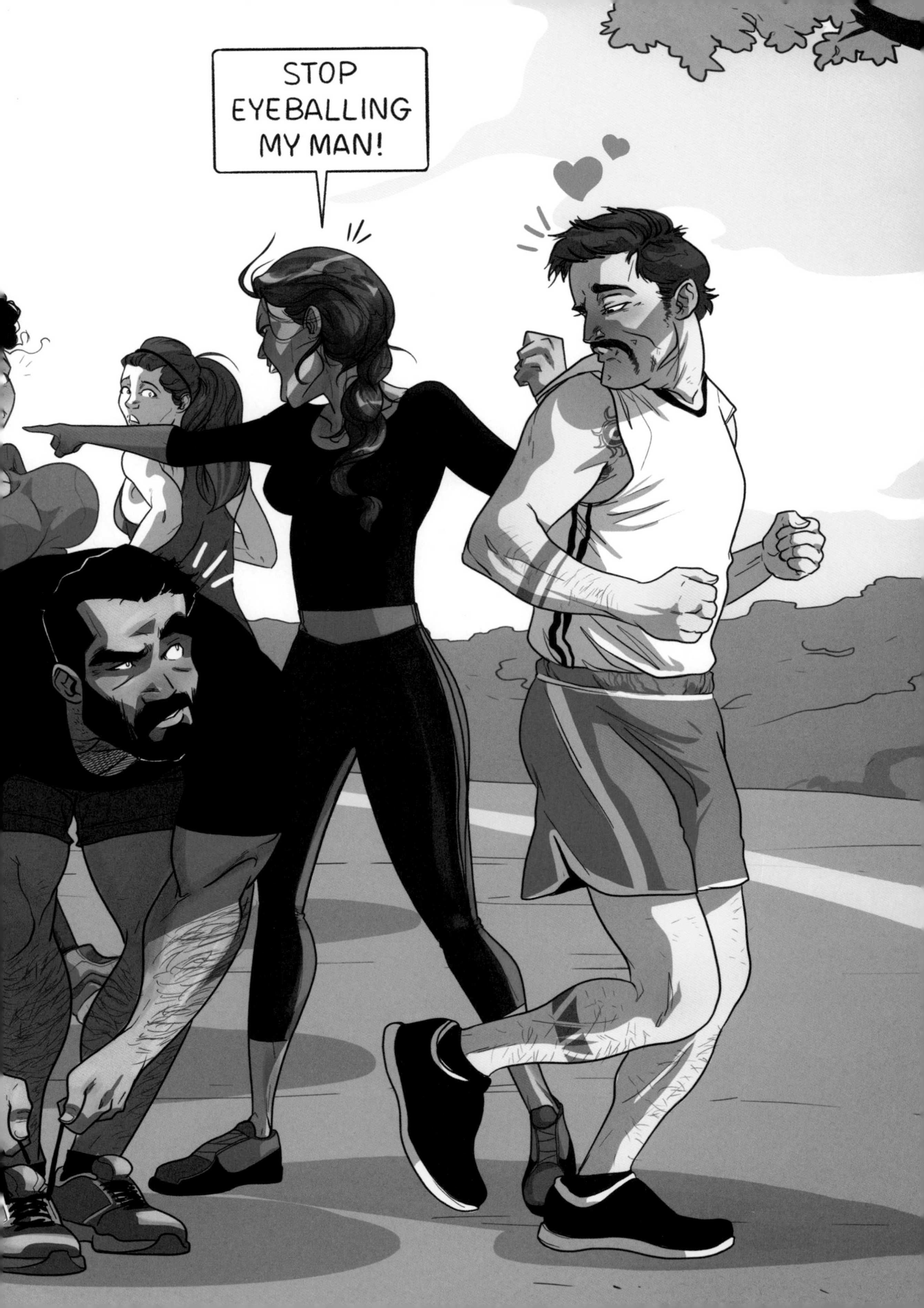
STOP EYEBALLING MY MAN!

33

MIRROR MIRROR

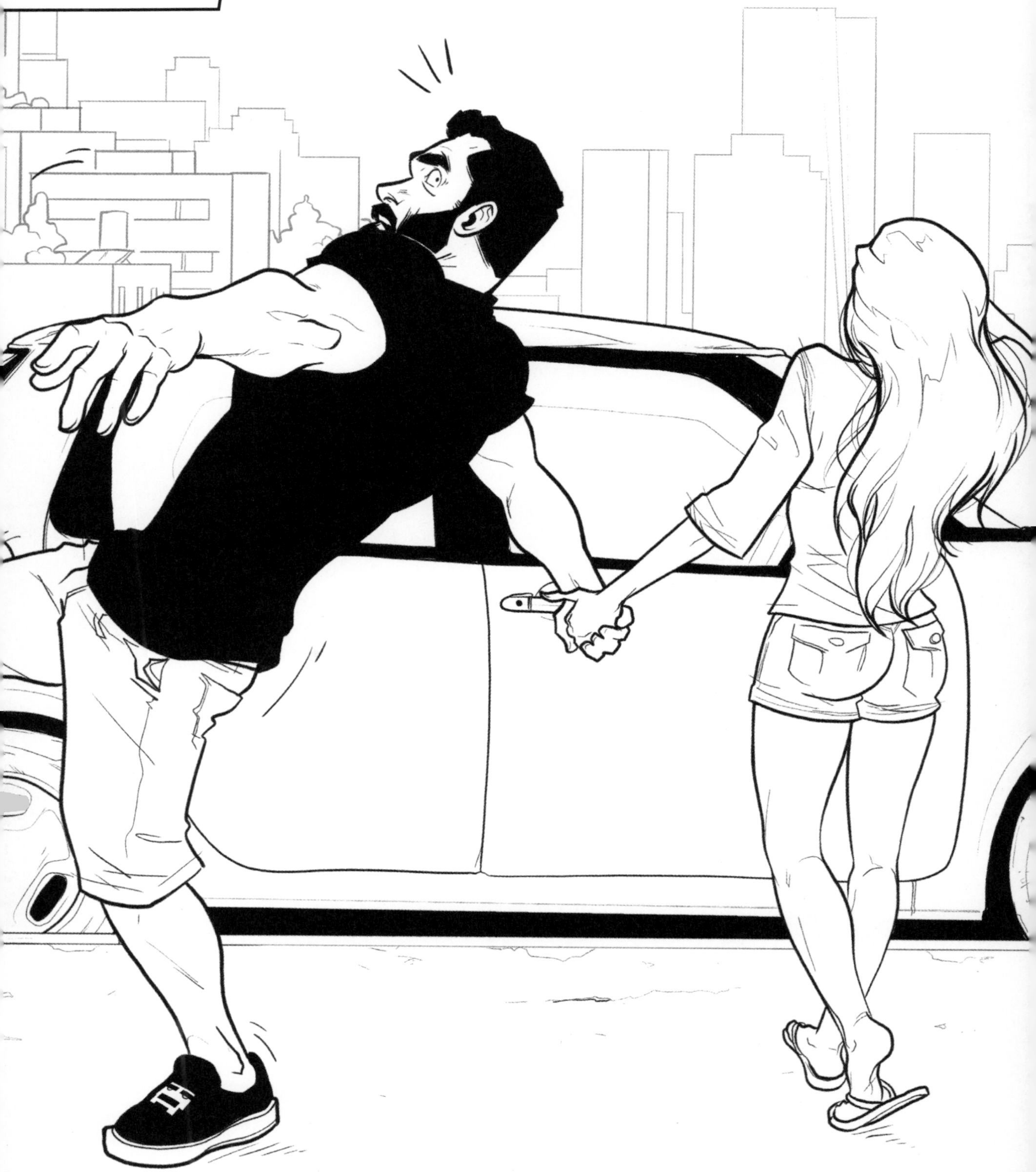

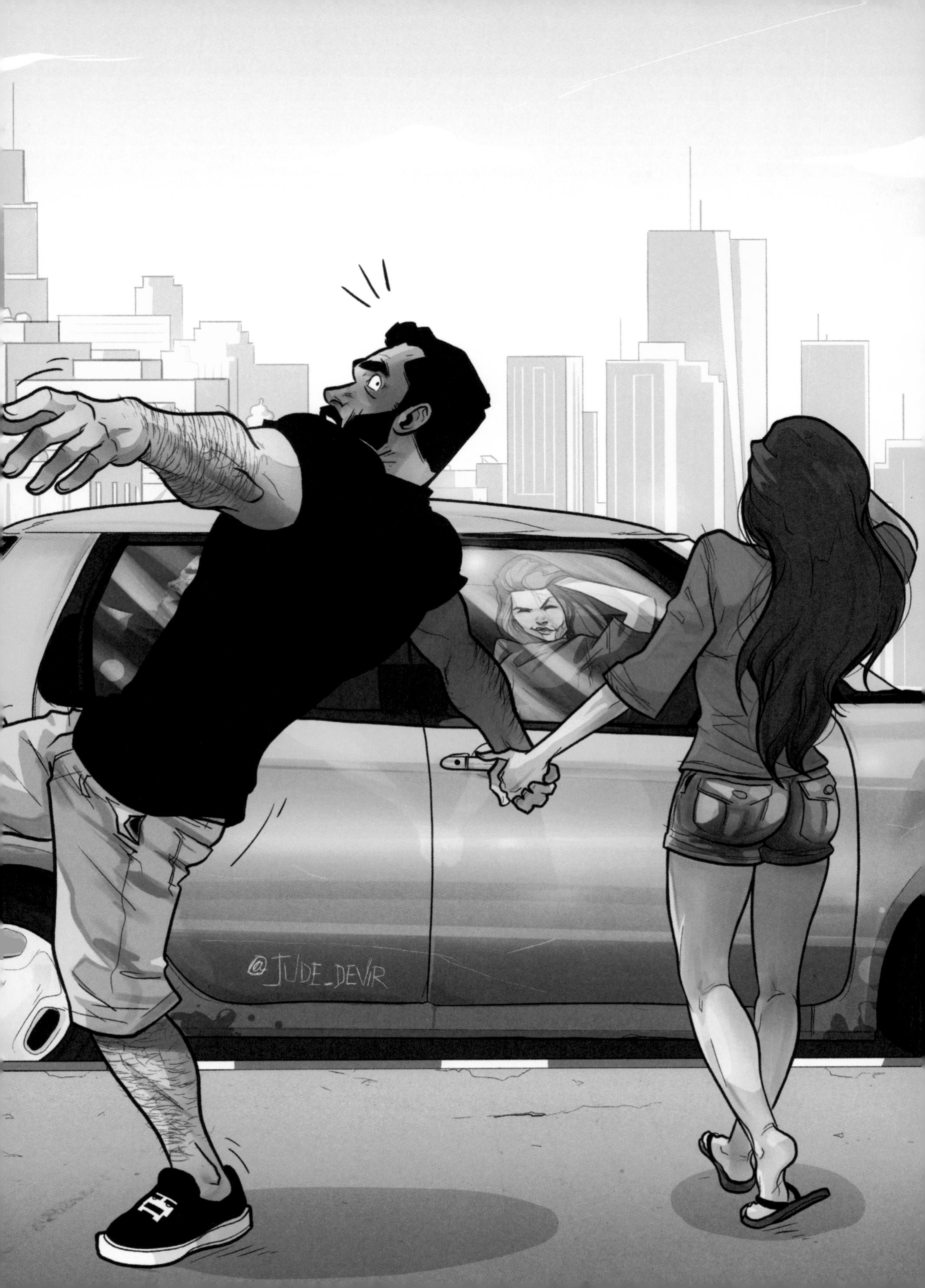
@JUDE_DEVIR

34

STREET BITERS

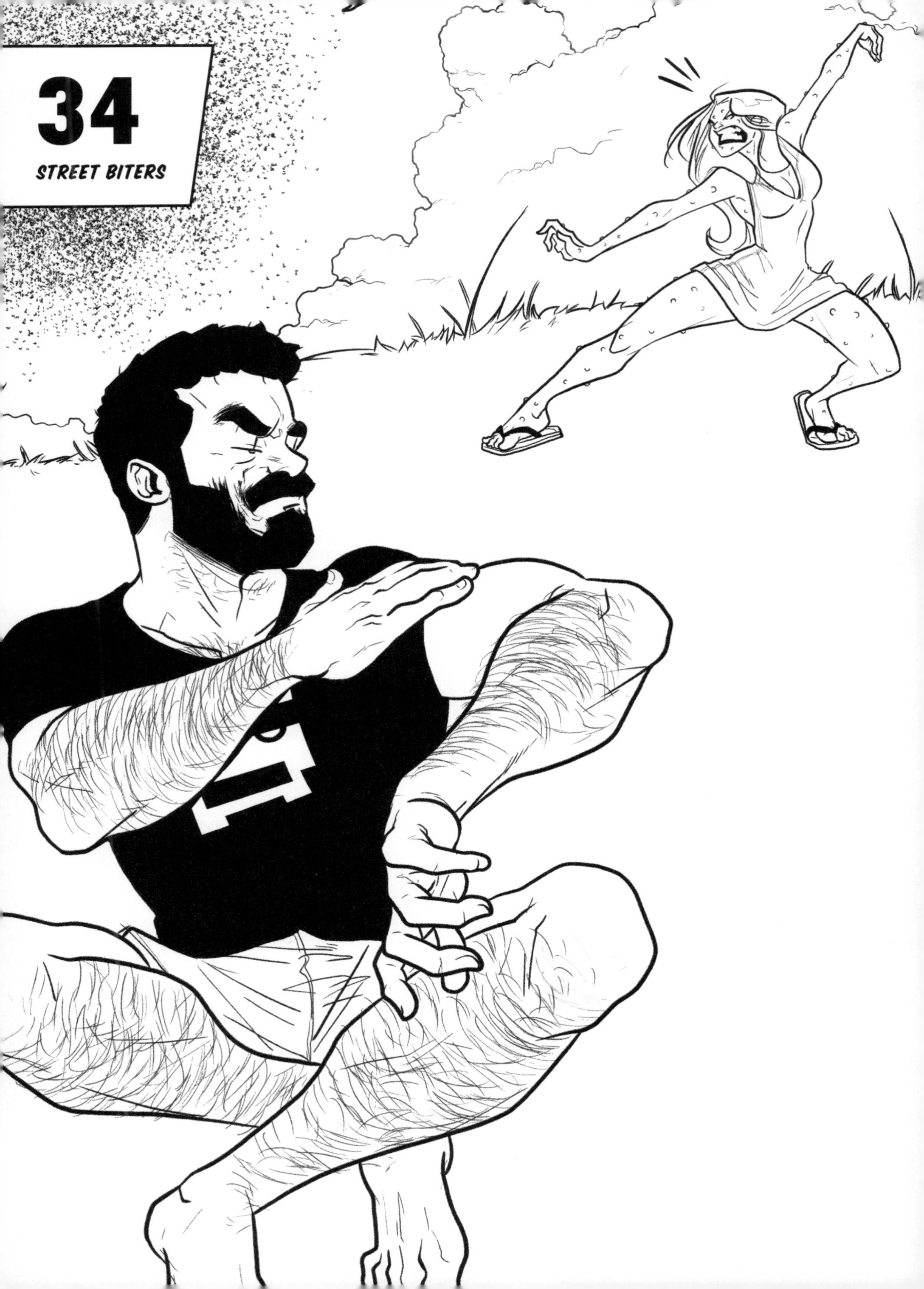

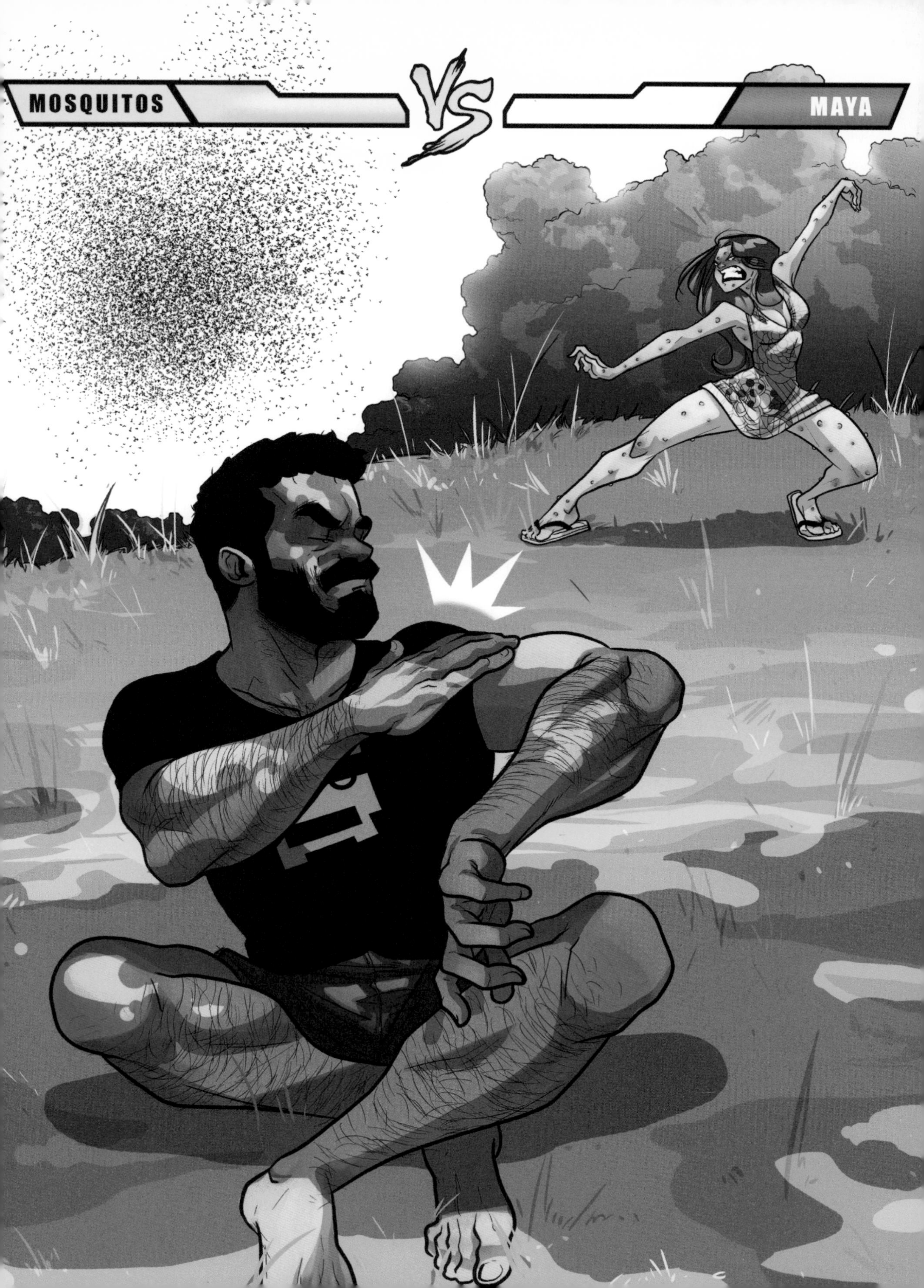
MOSQUITOS
VS
MAYA

35

HAPPY ANNIVERSARY, MY LOVE!

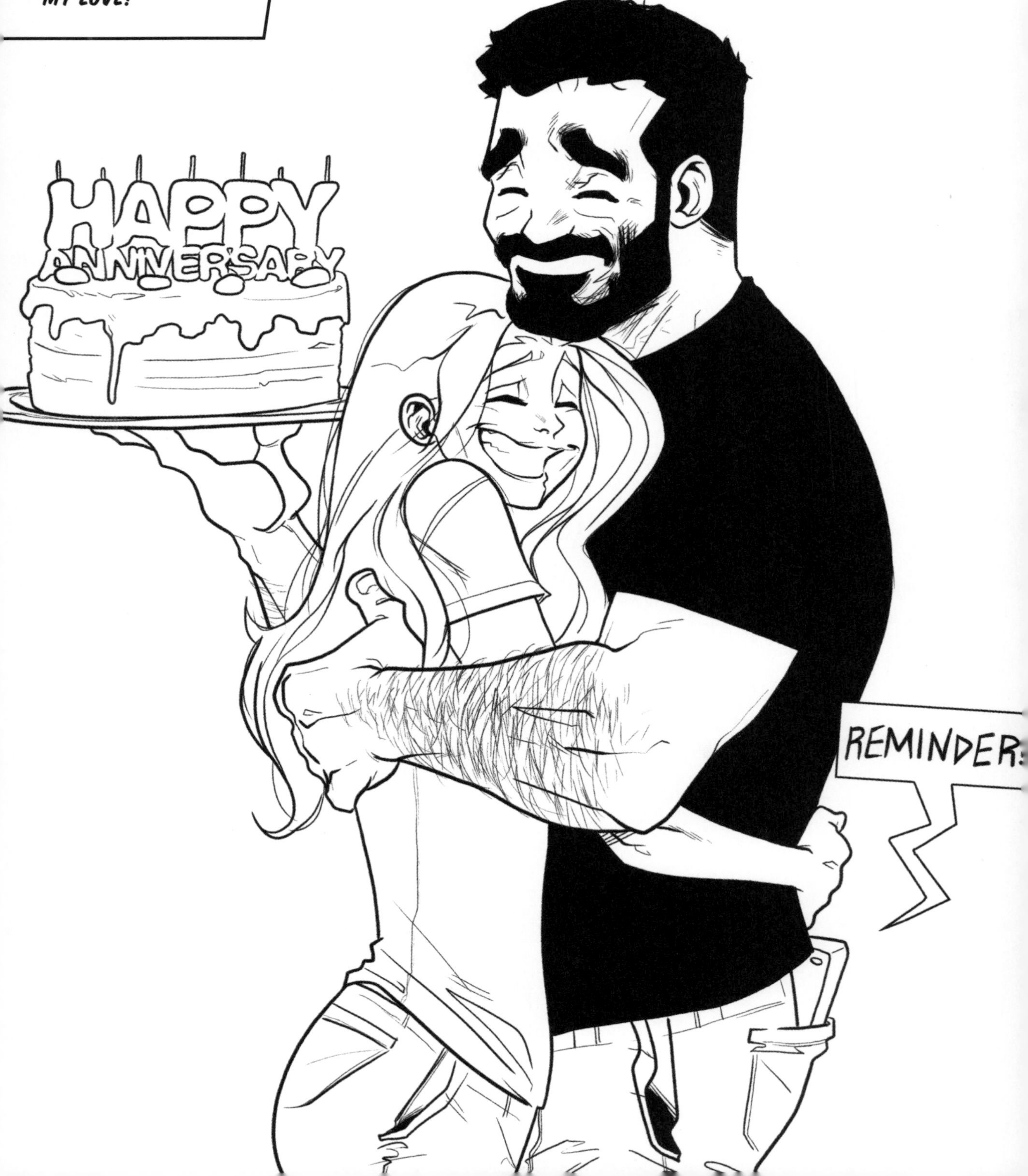

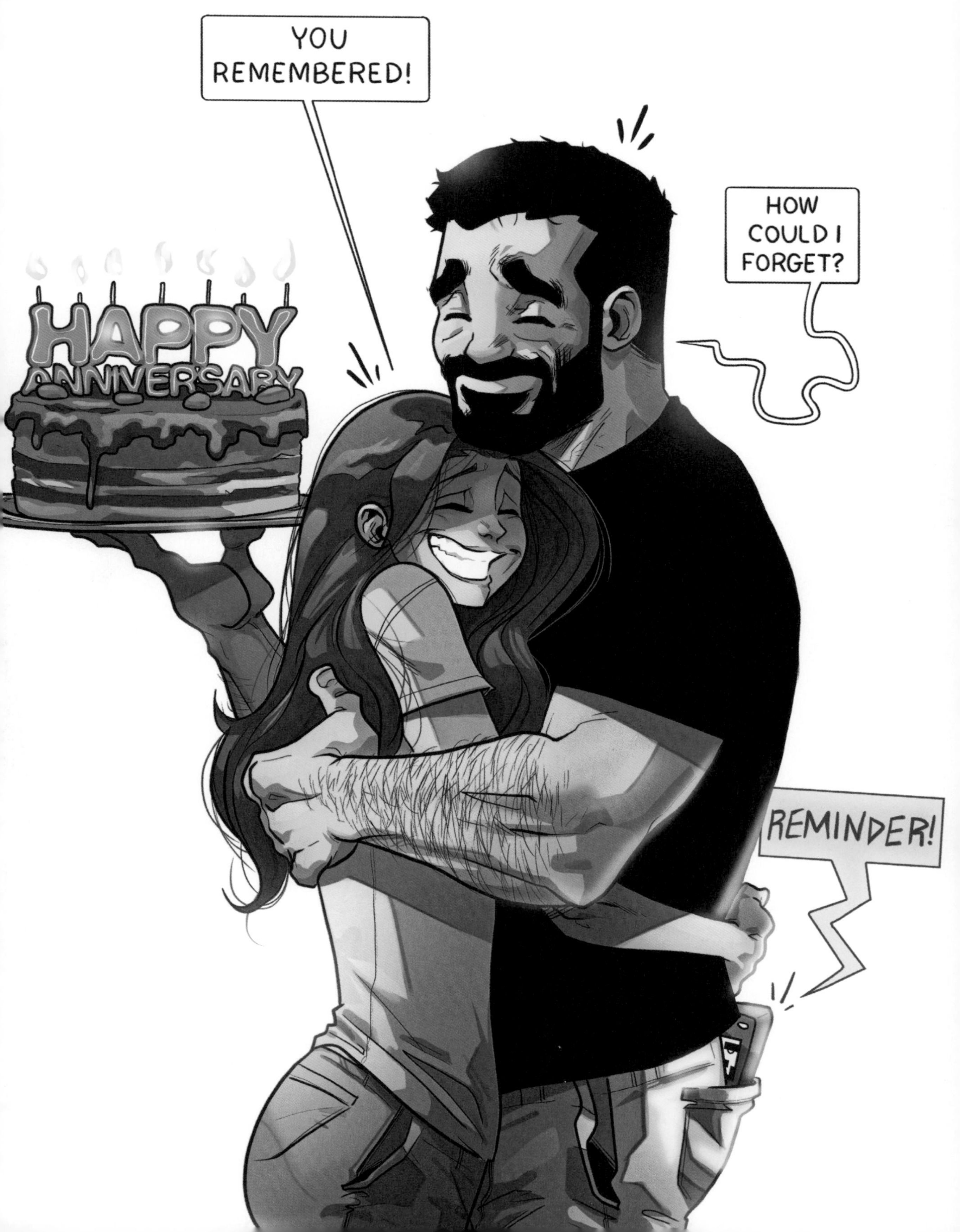

HAPPY ANNIVERSARY
YOU REMEMBERED!
HOW COULD I FORGET?
REMINDER!

36

WE OPENED A PATREON PAGE

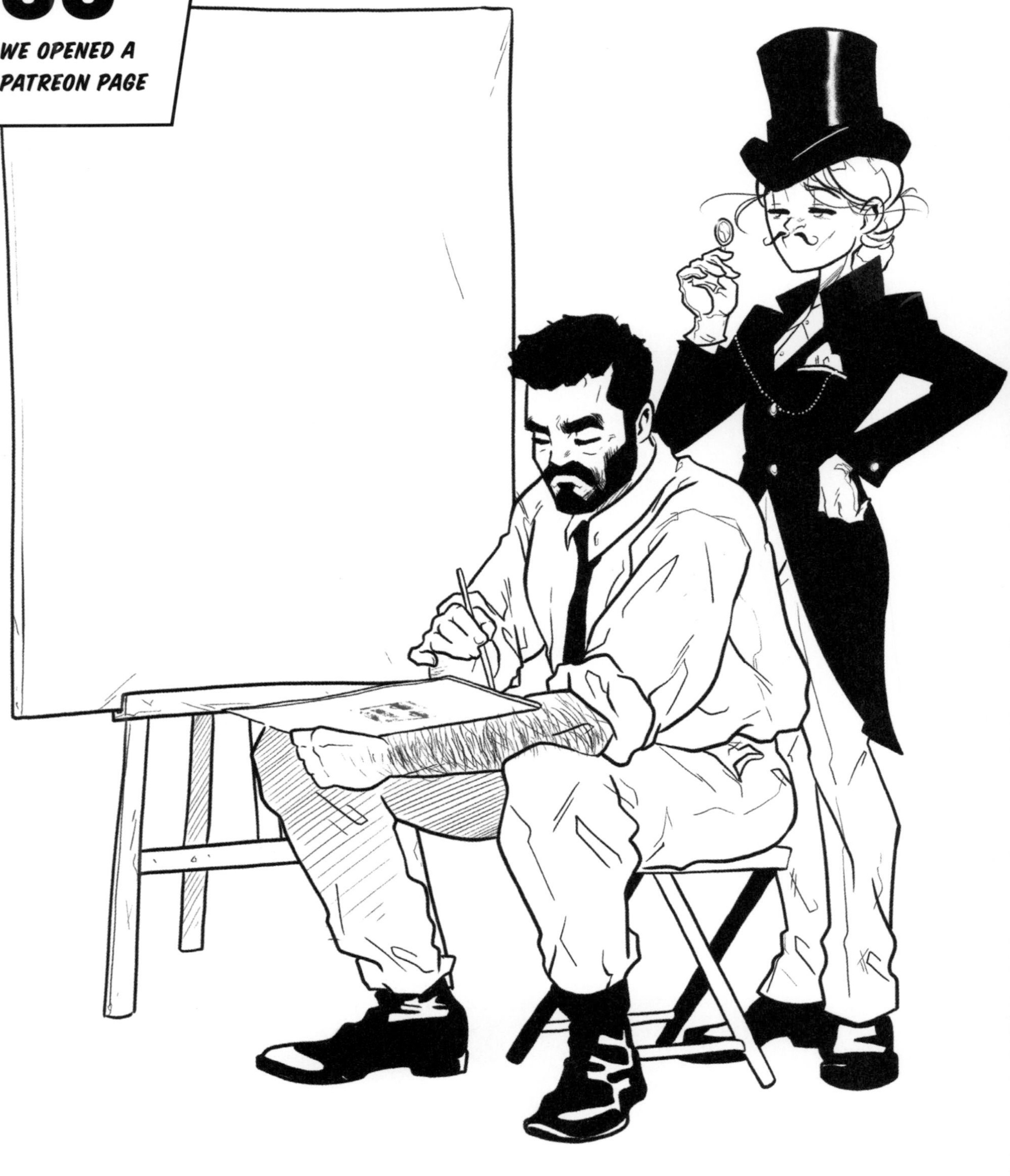

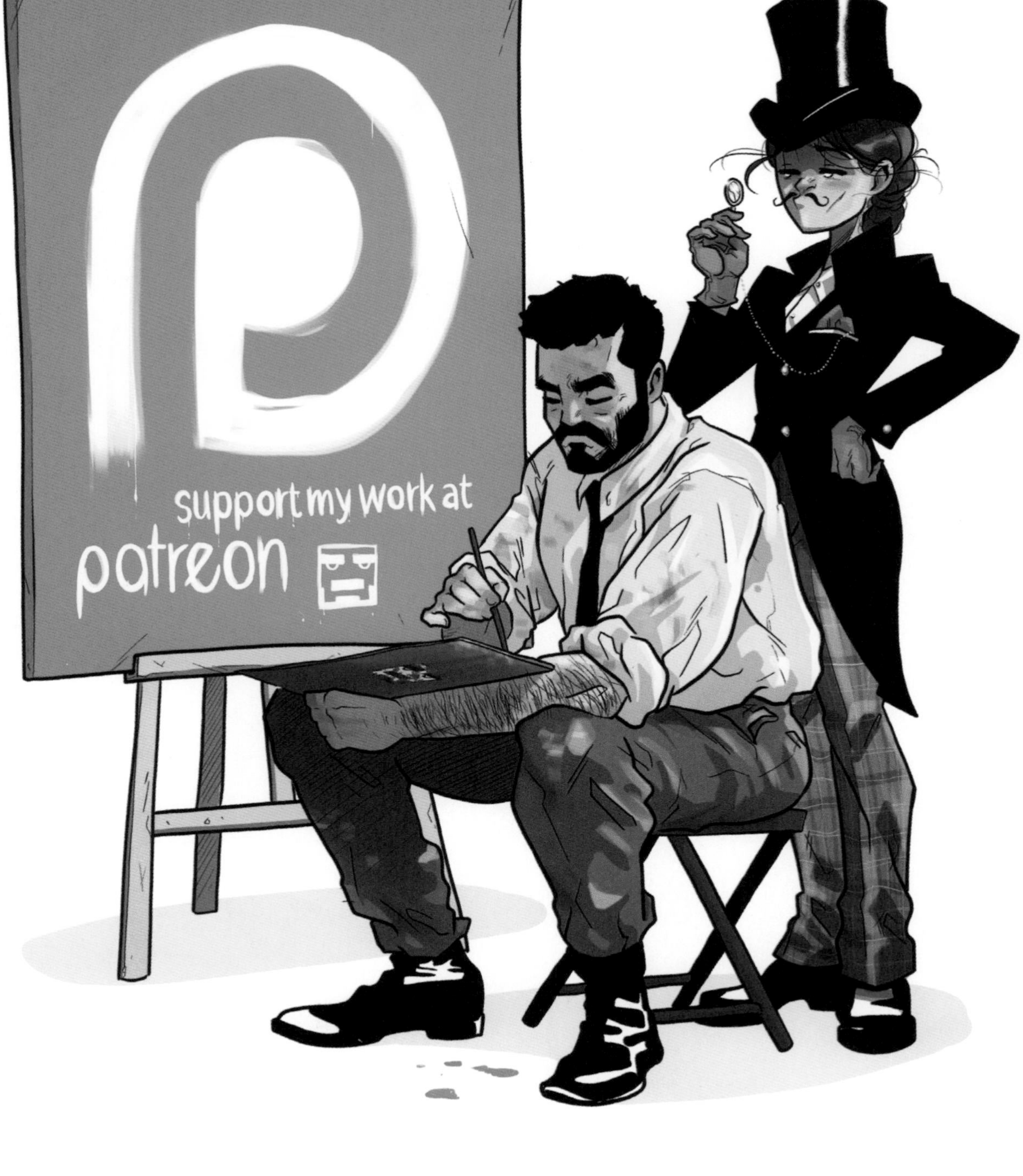
support my work at
patreon

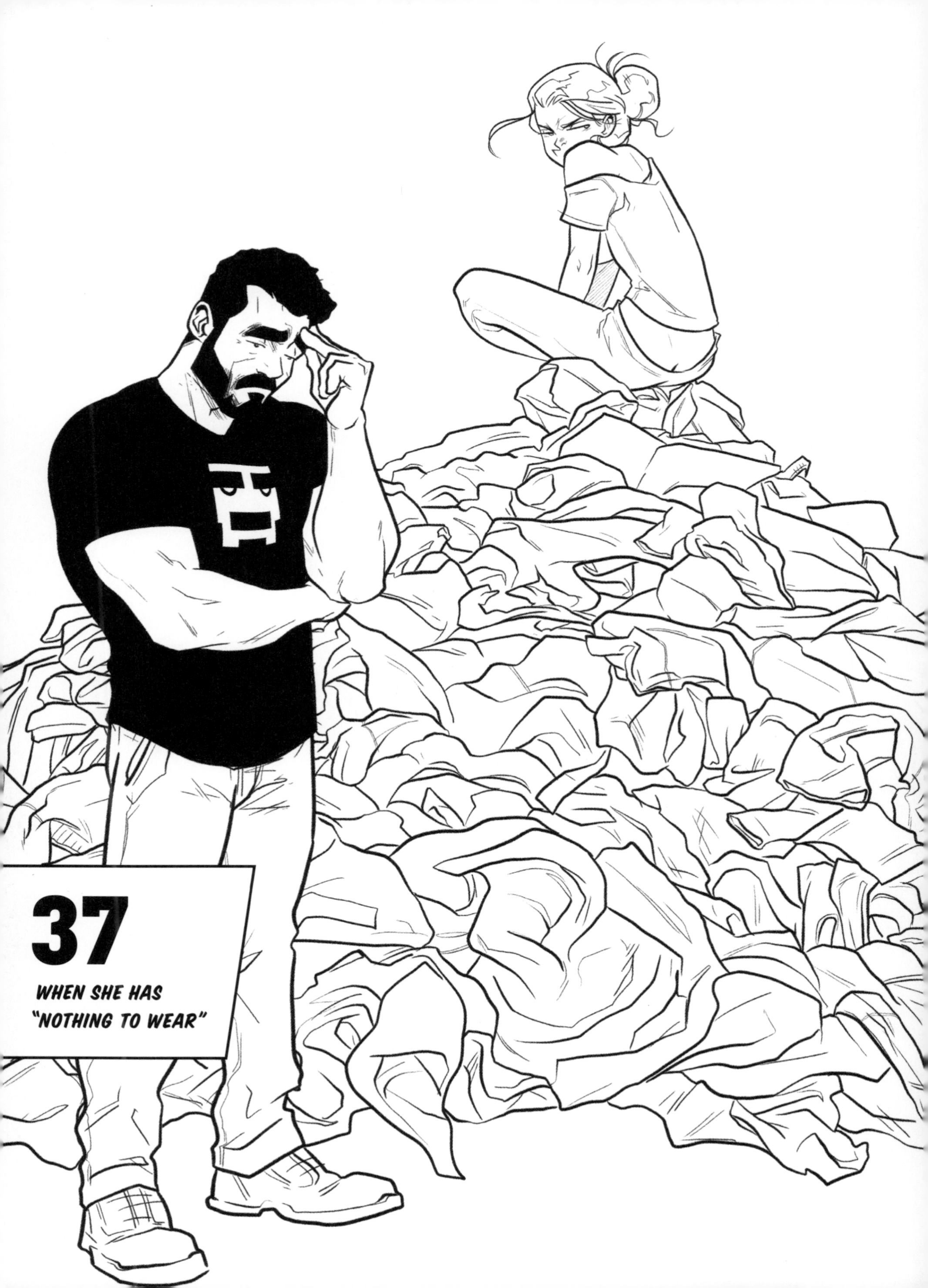

37

WHEN SHE HAS "NOTHING TO WEAR"

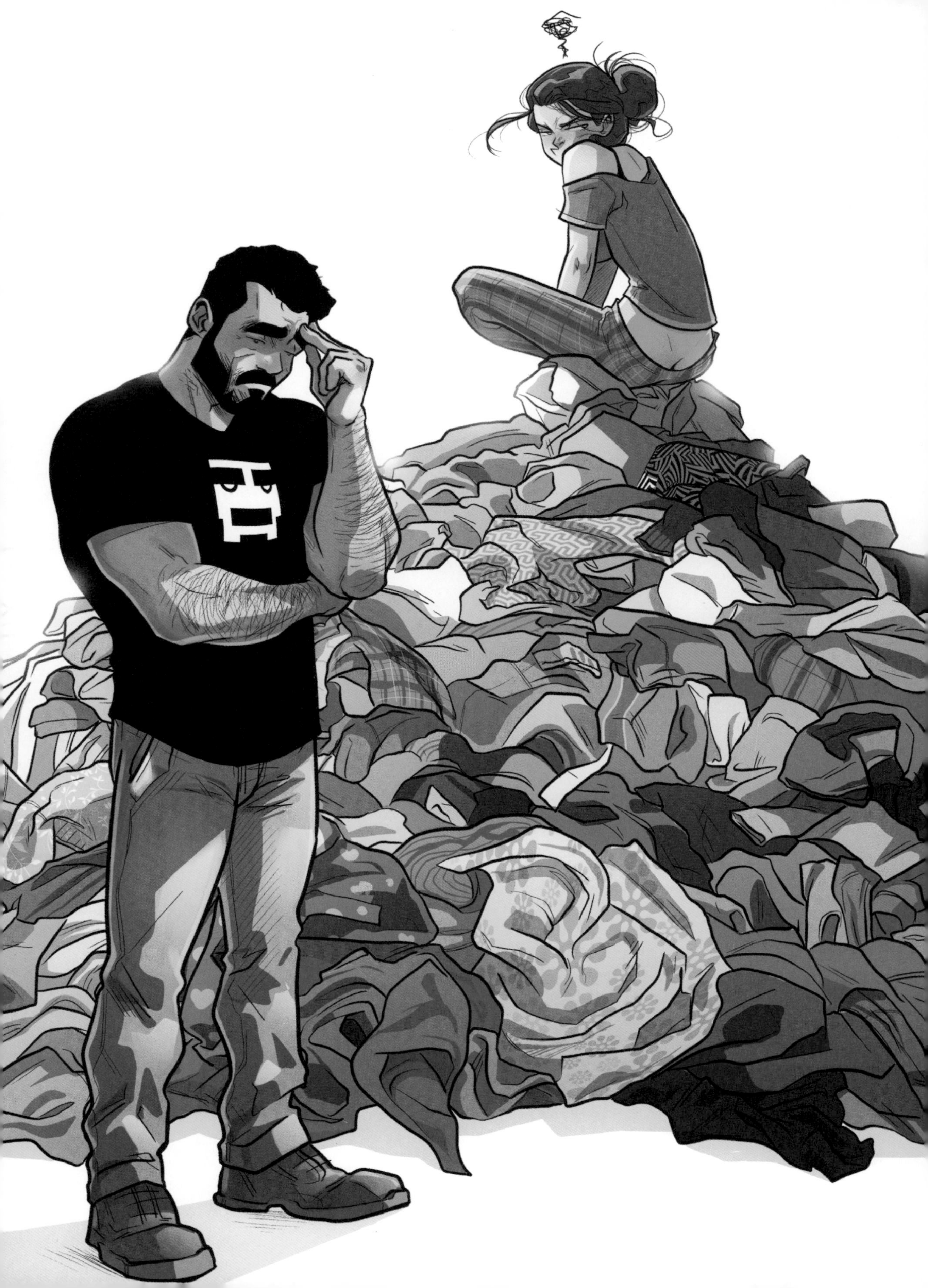

38

I UPGRADED MYSELF

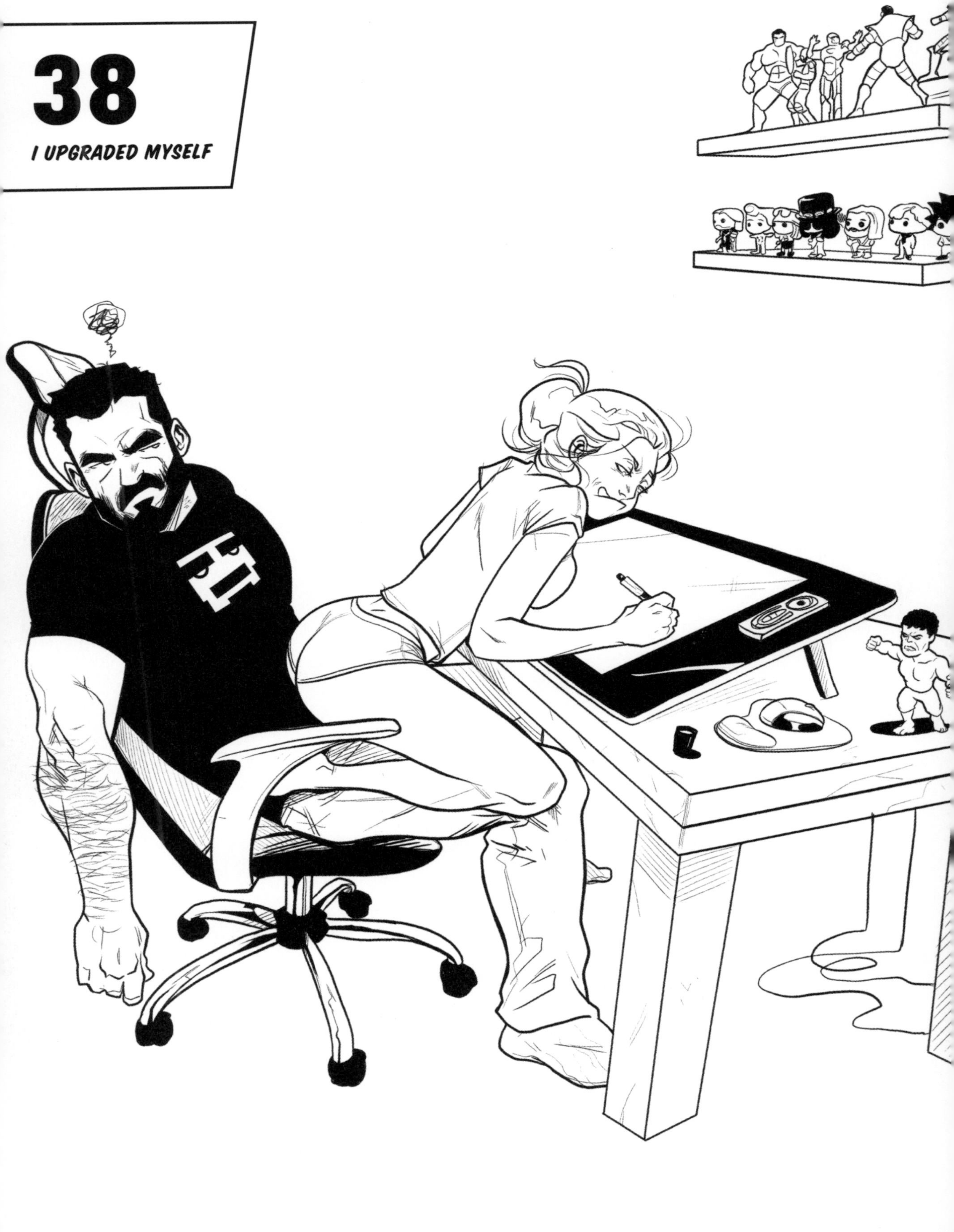

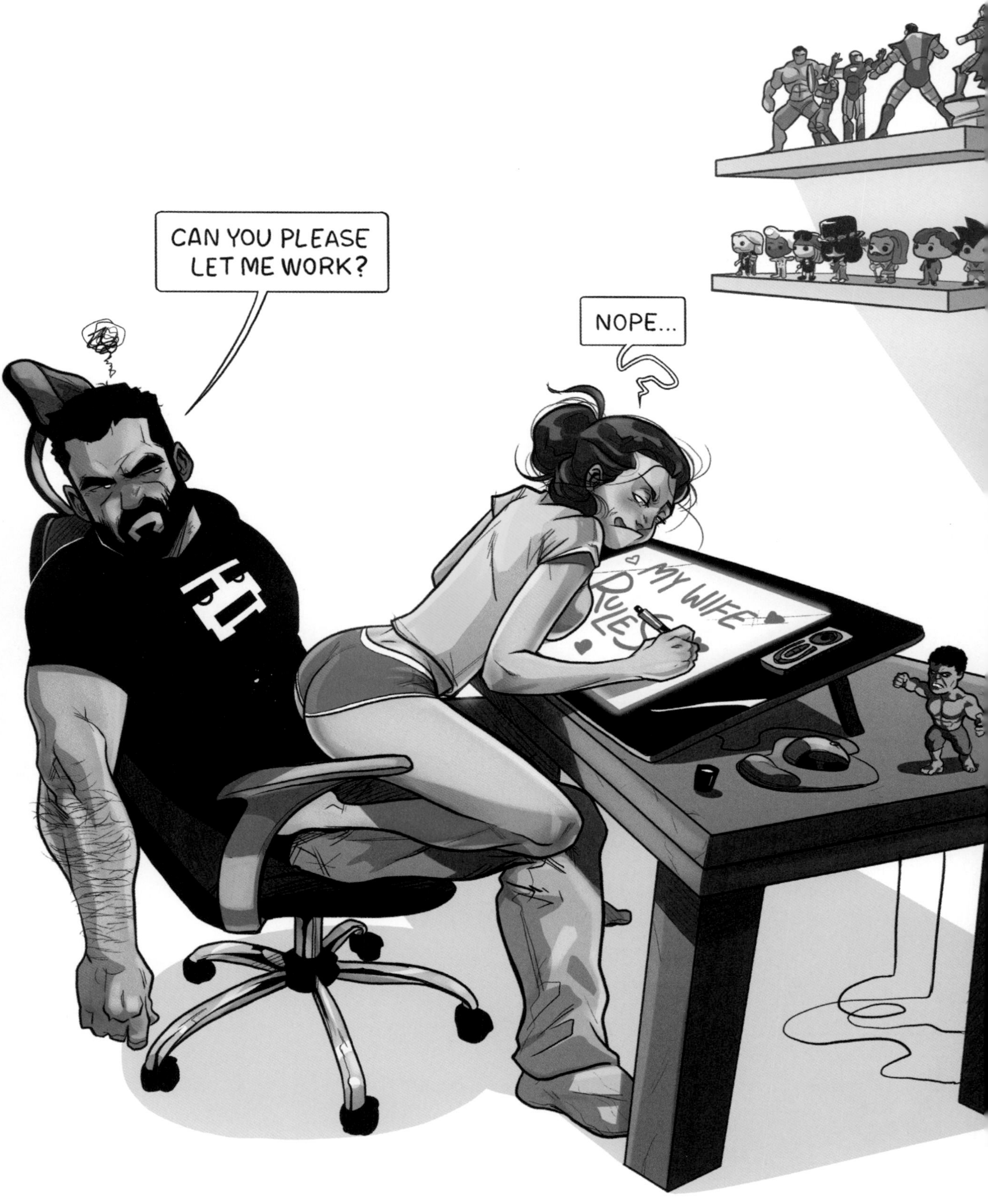
CAN YOU PLEASE LET ME WORK?
NOPE...
MY WIFE RULES

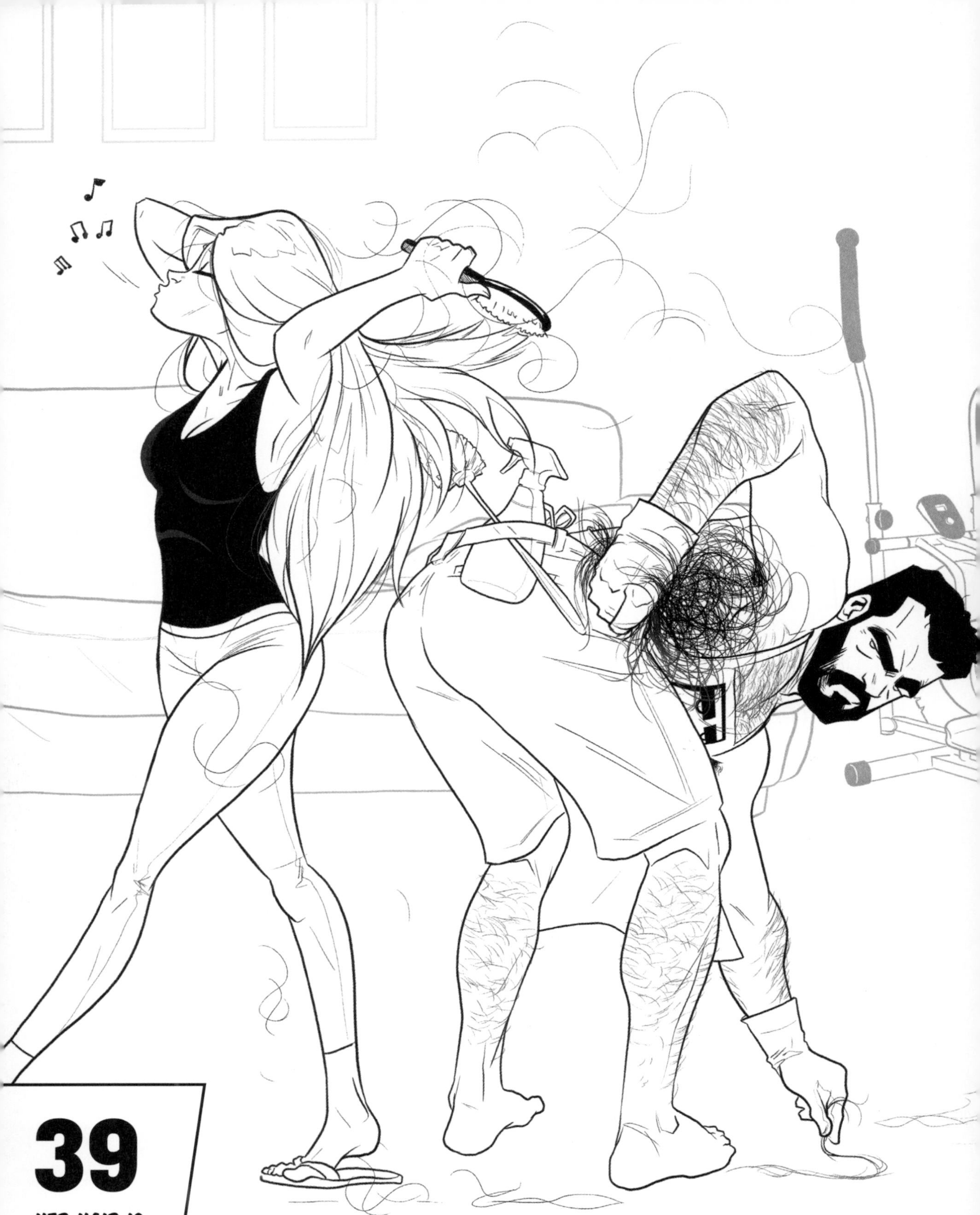

39

HER HAIR IS EVERYWHERE

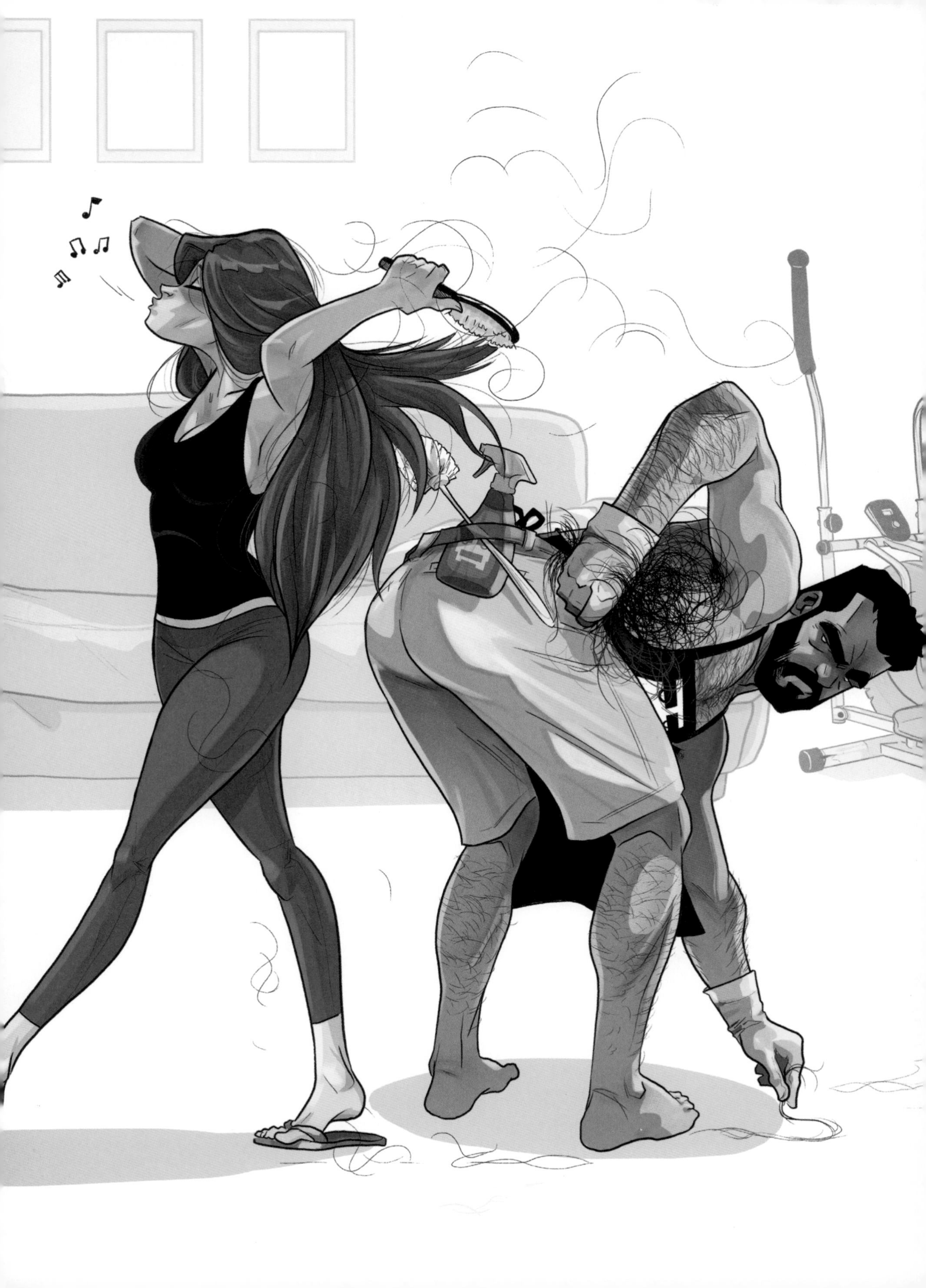

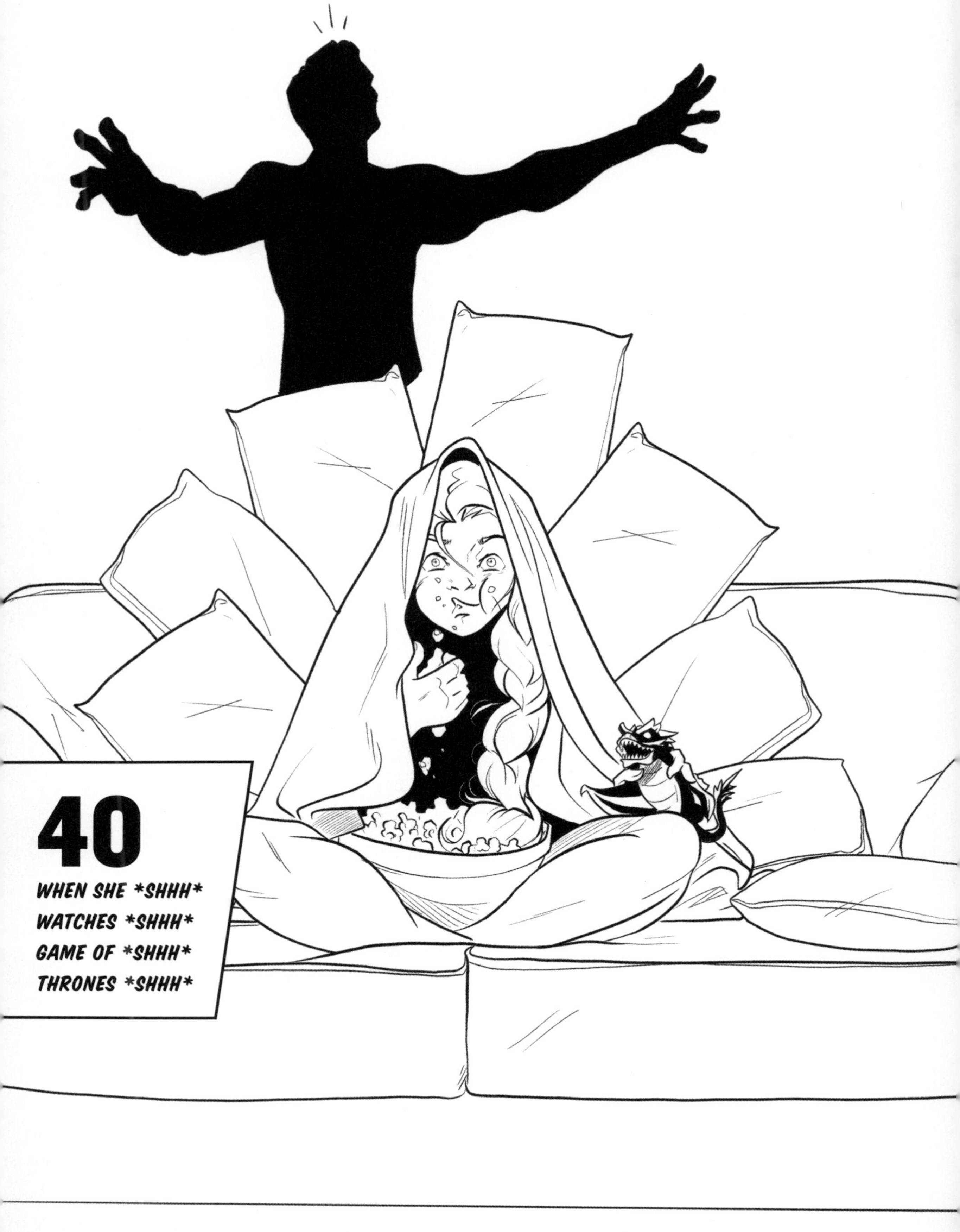

40

*WHEN SHE *SHHH* WATCHES *SHHH* GAME OF *SHHH* THRONES *SHHH**

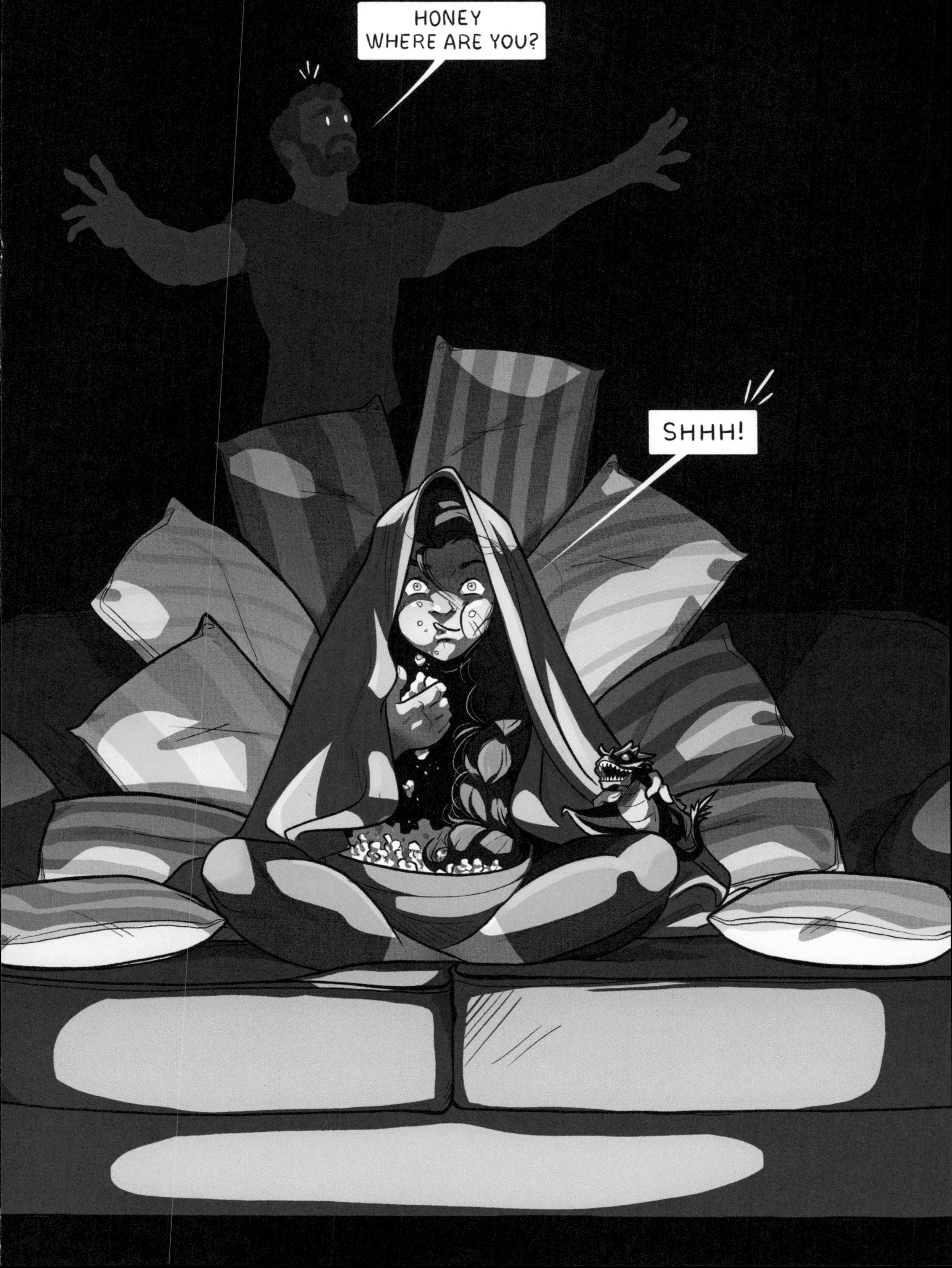
HONEY
WHERE ARE YOU?
SHHH!

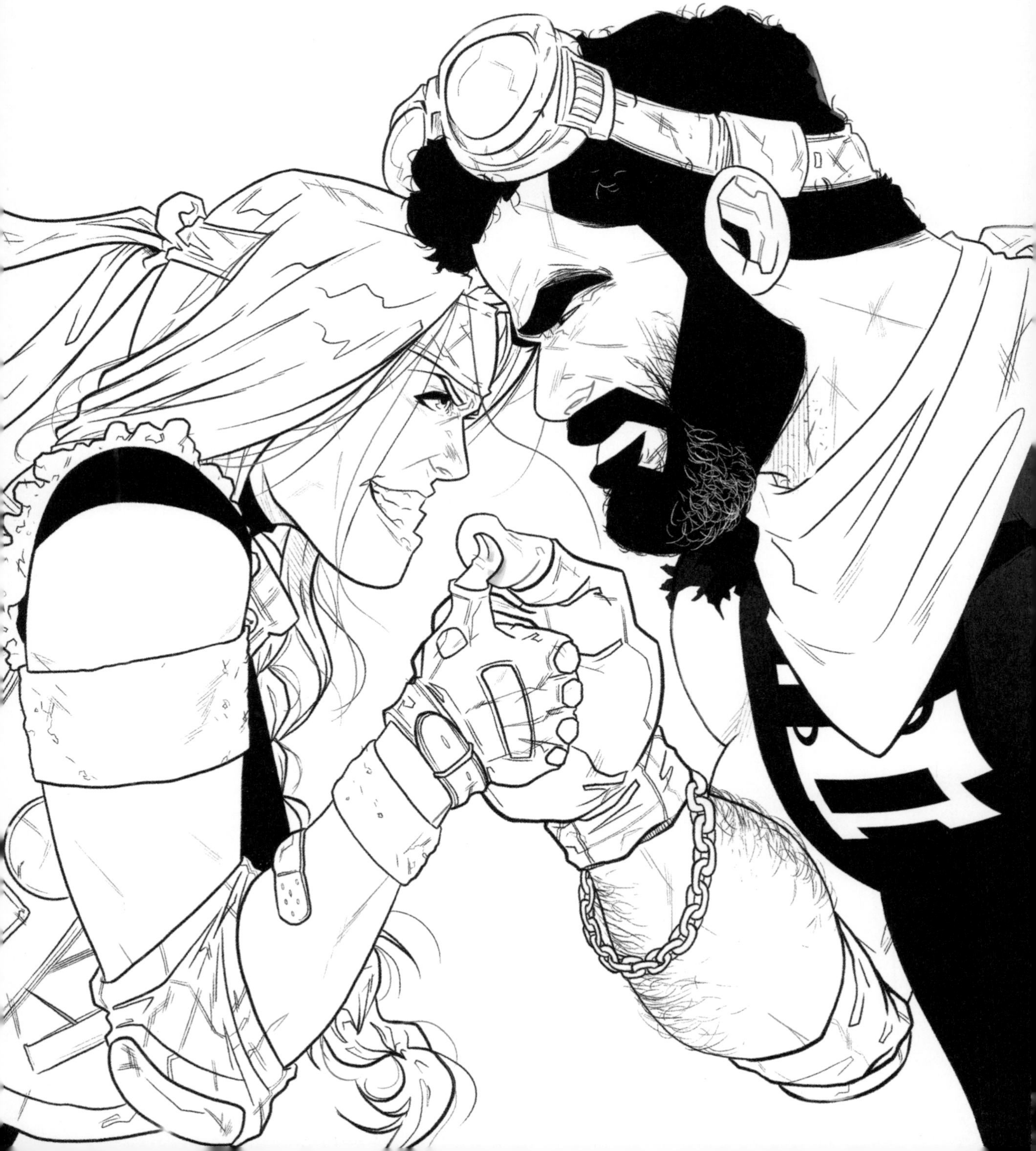

CHAPTER
TWO

41

THE PROPOSAL

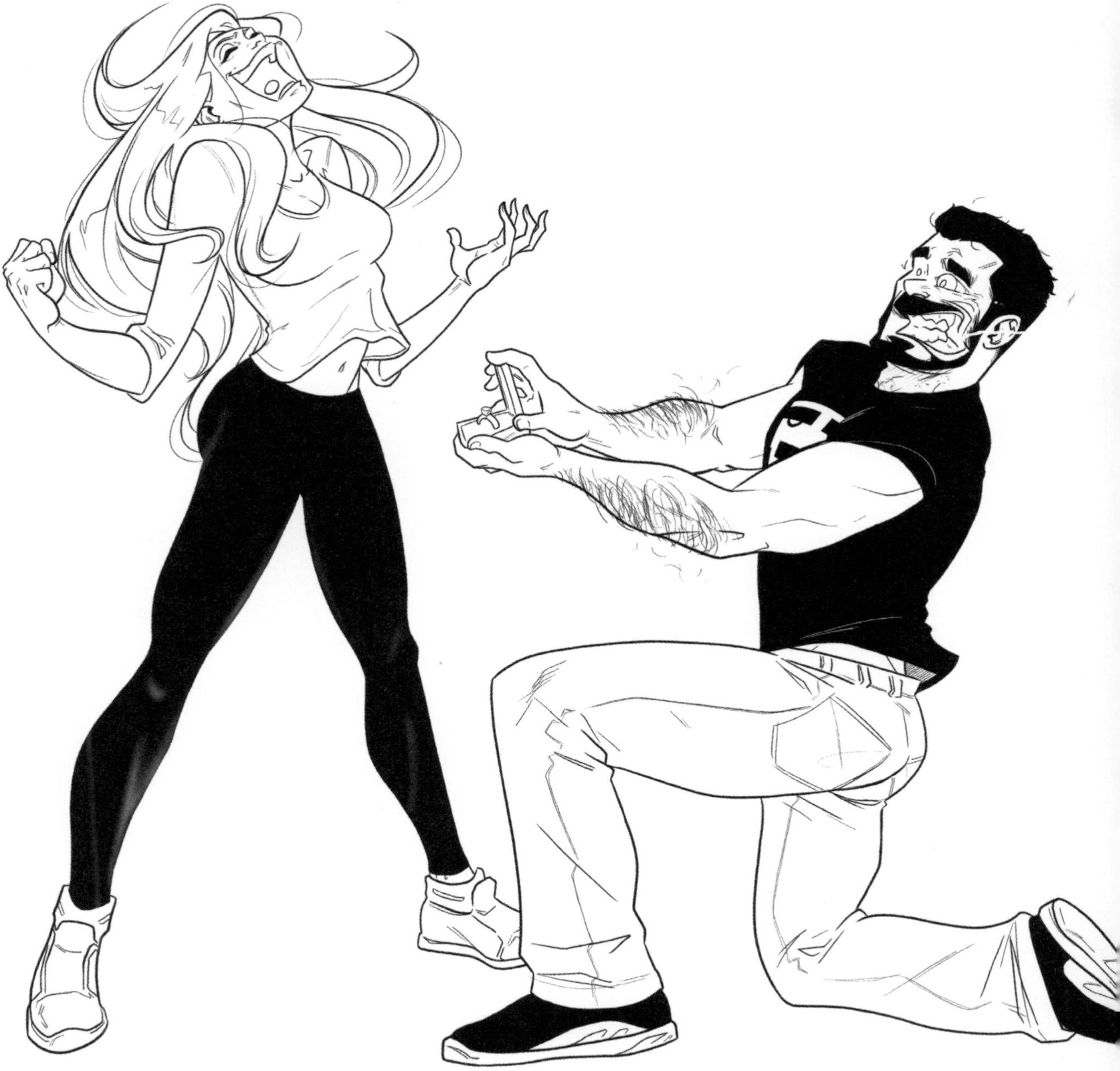

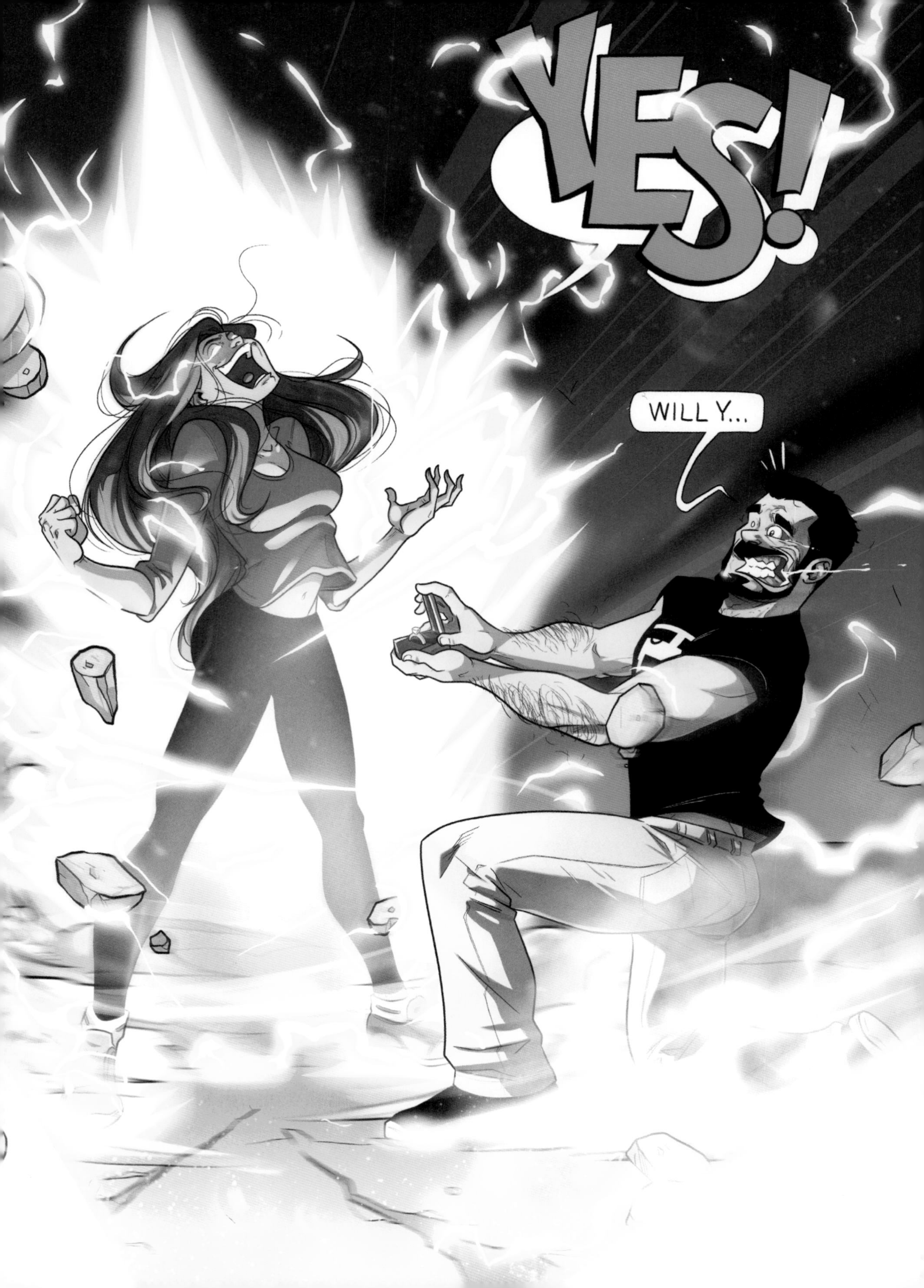
WILL Y...
YES!

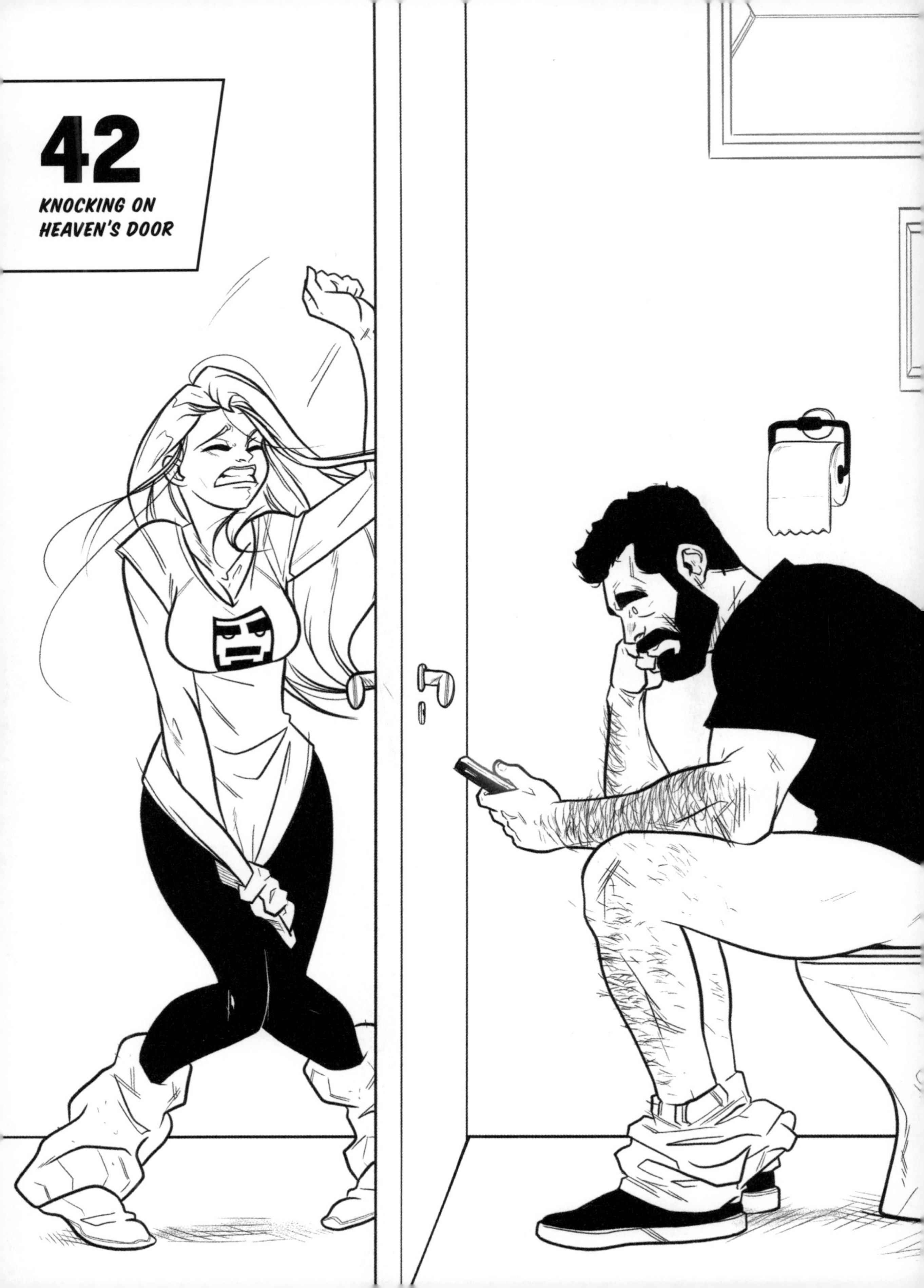
42
KNOCKING ON
HEAVEN'S DOOR

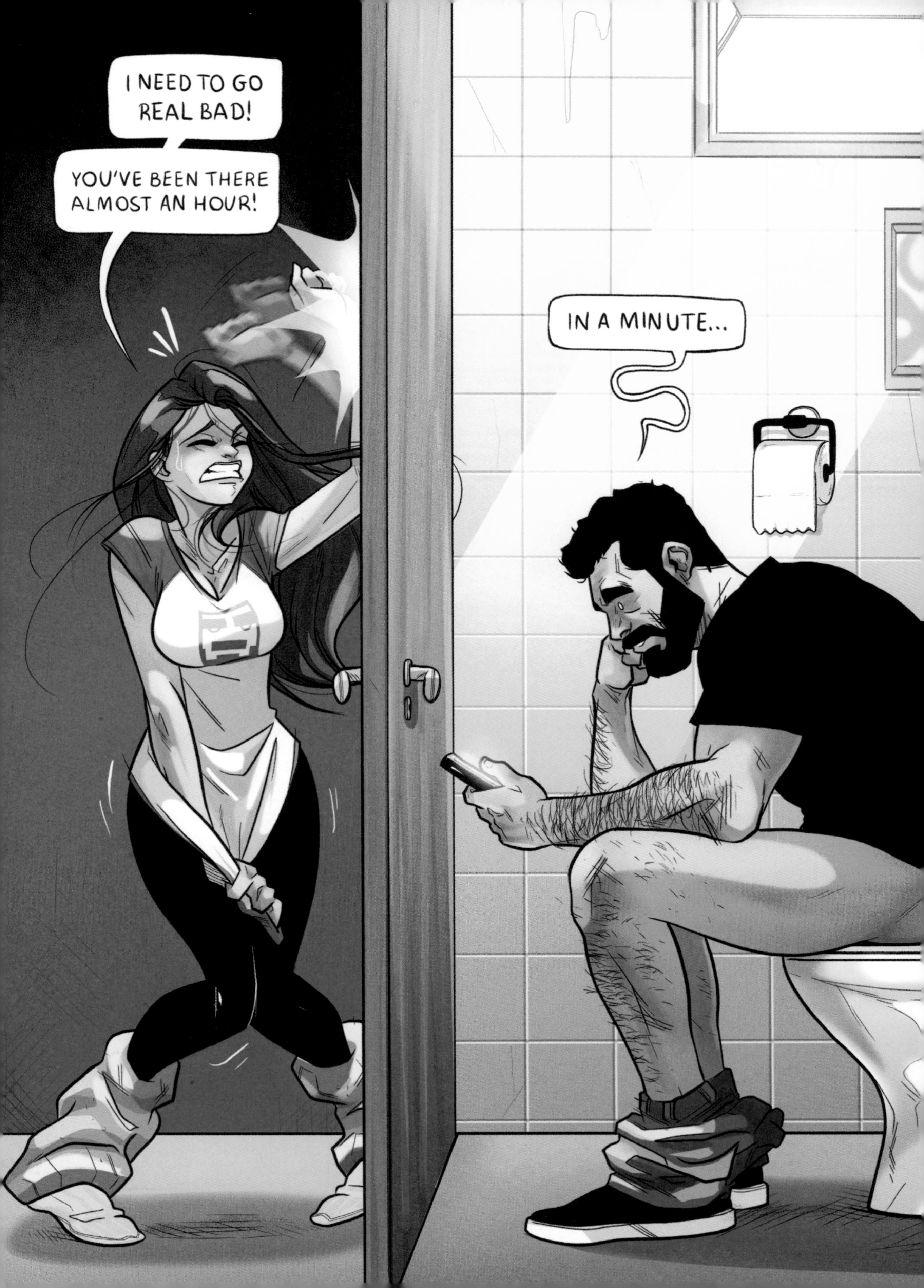
I NEED TO GO REAL BAD!
YOU'VE BEEN THERE ALMOST AN HOUR!
IN A MINUTE...

43

LOVE HURTS!

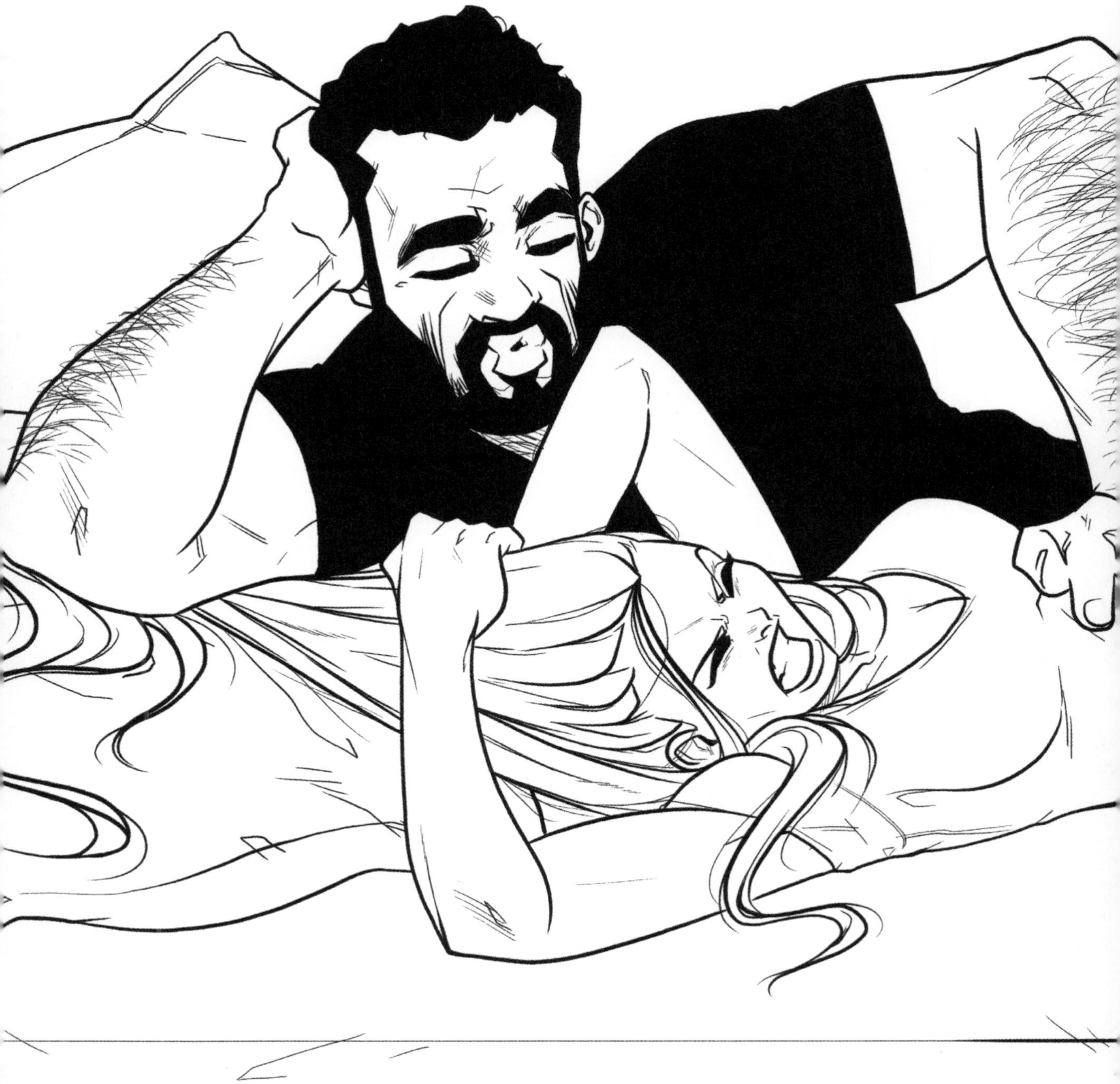

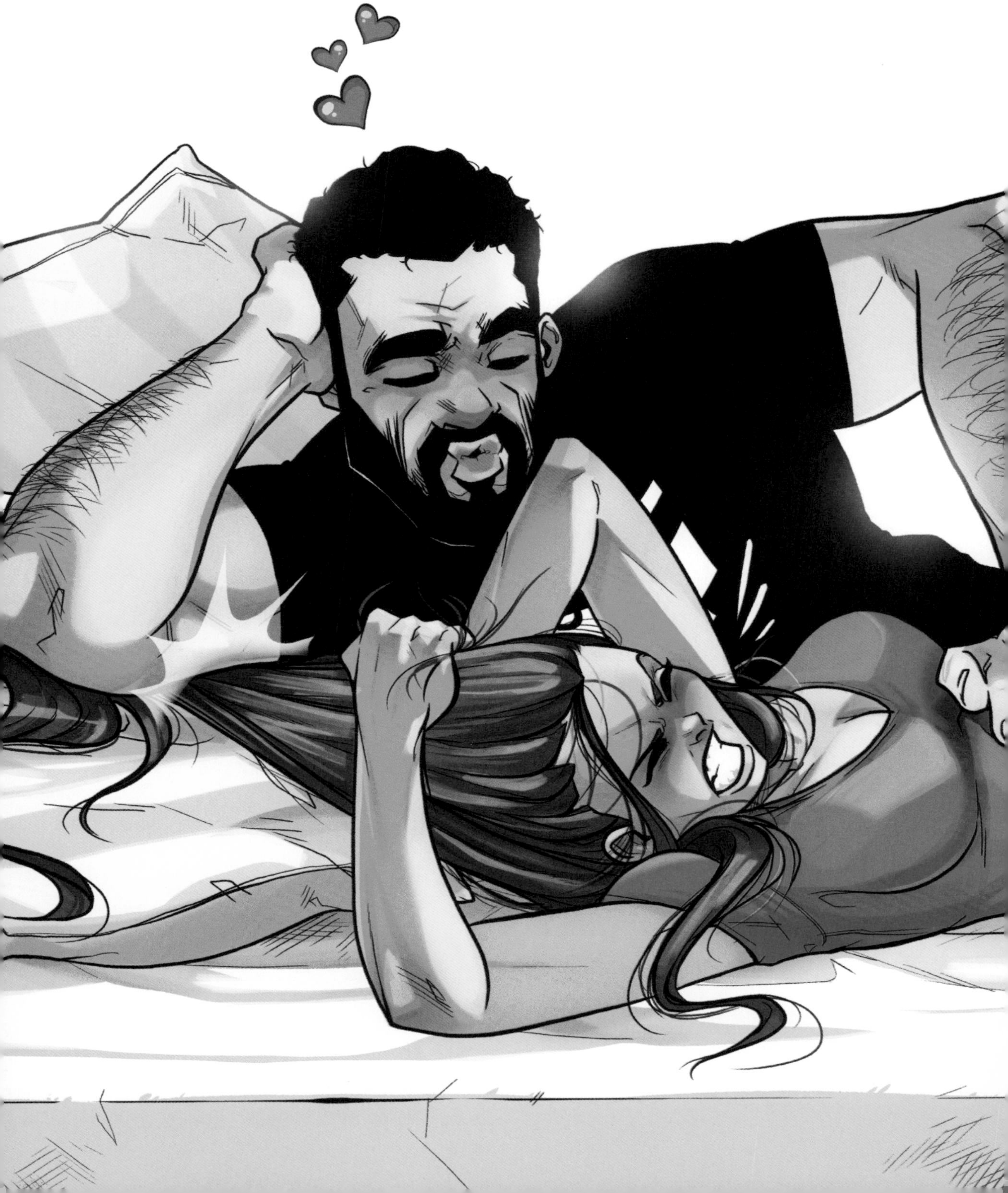

44

HAPPY ROSH HASHANAH!

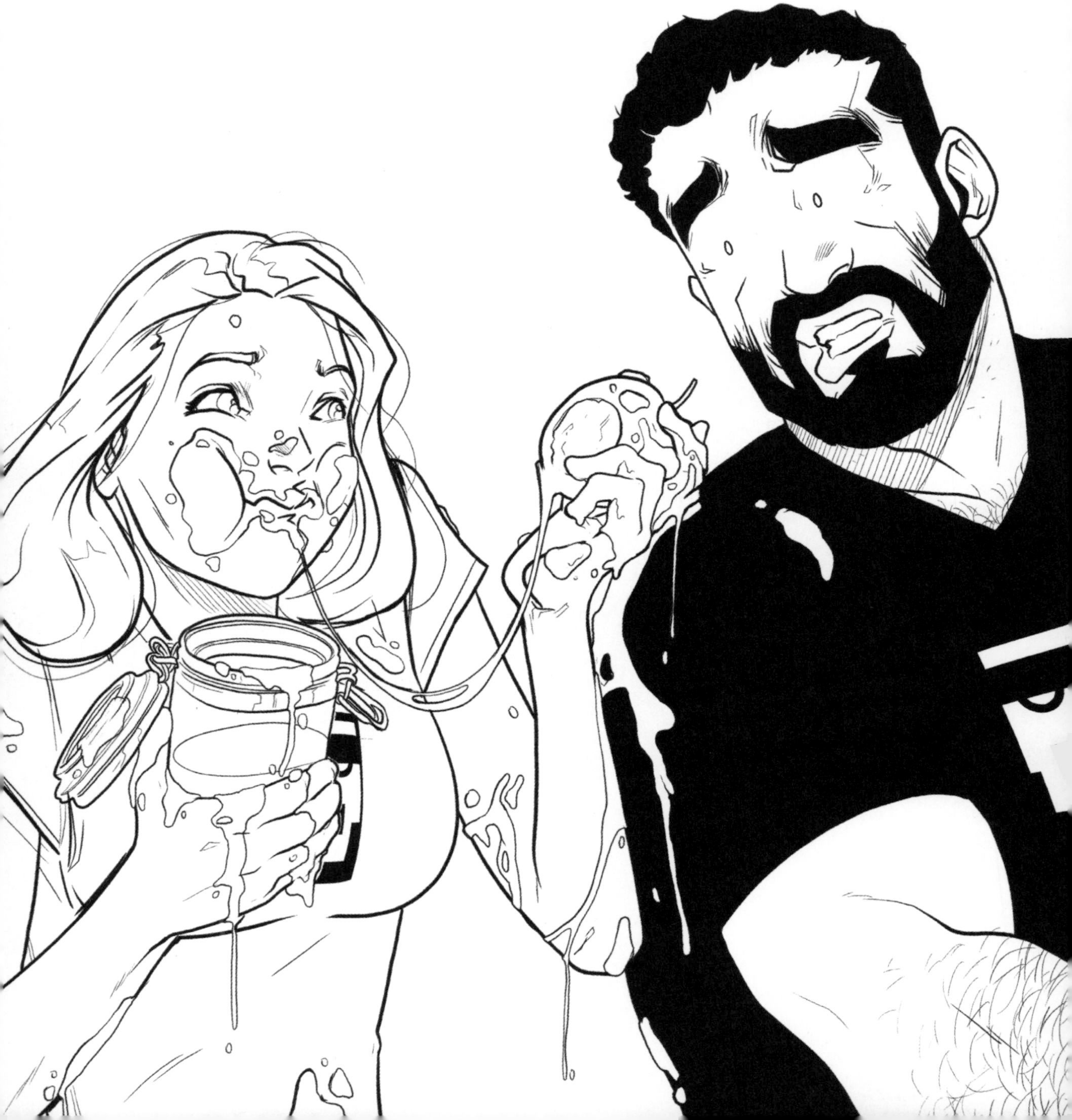

HAPPY ROSH HASHANAH!

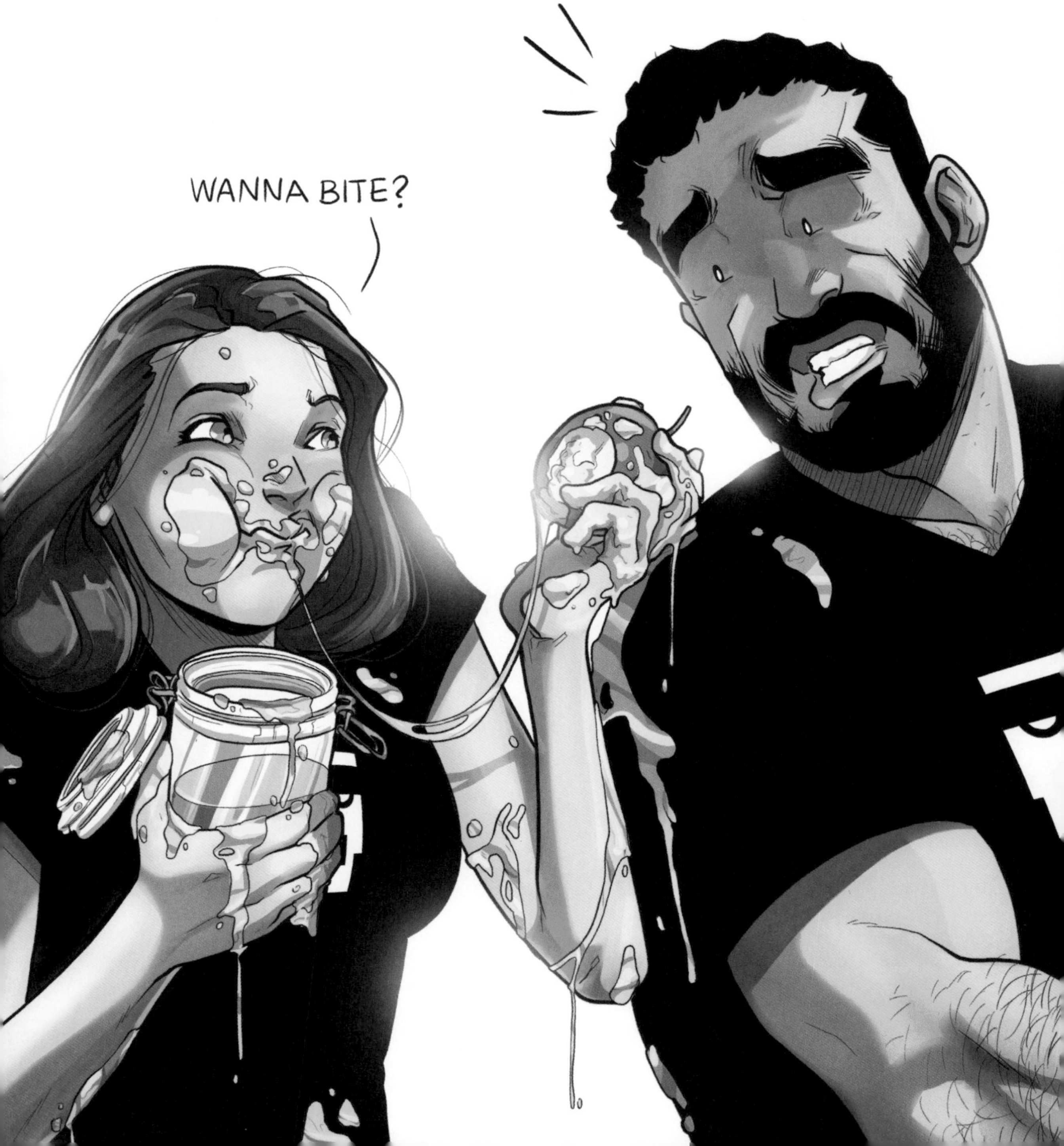
WANNA BITE?

45
EXHAUSTION

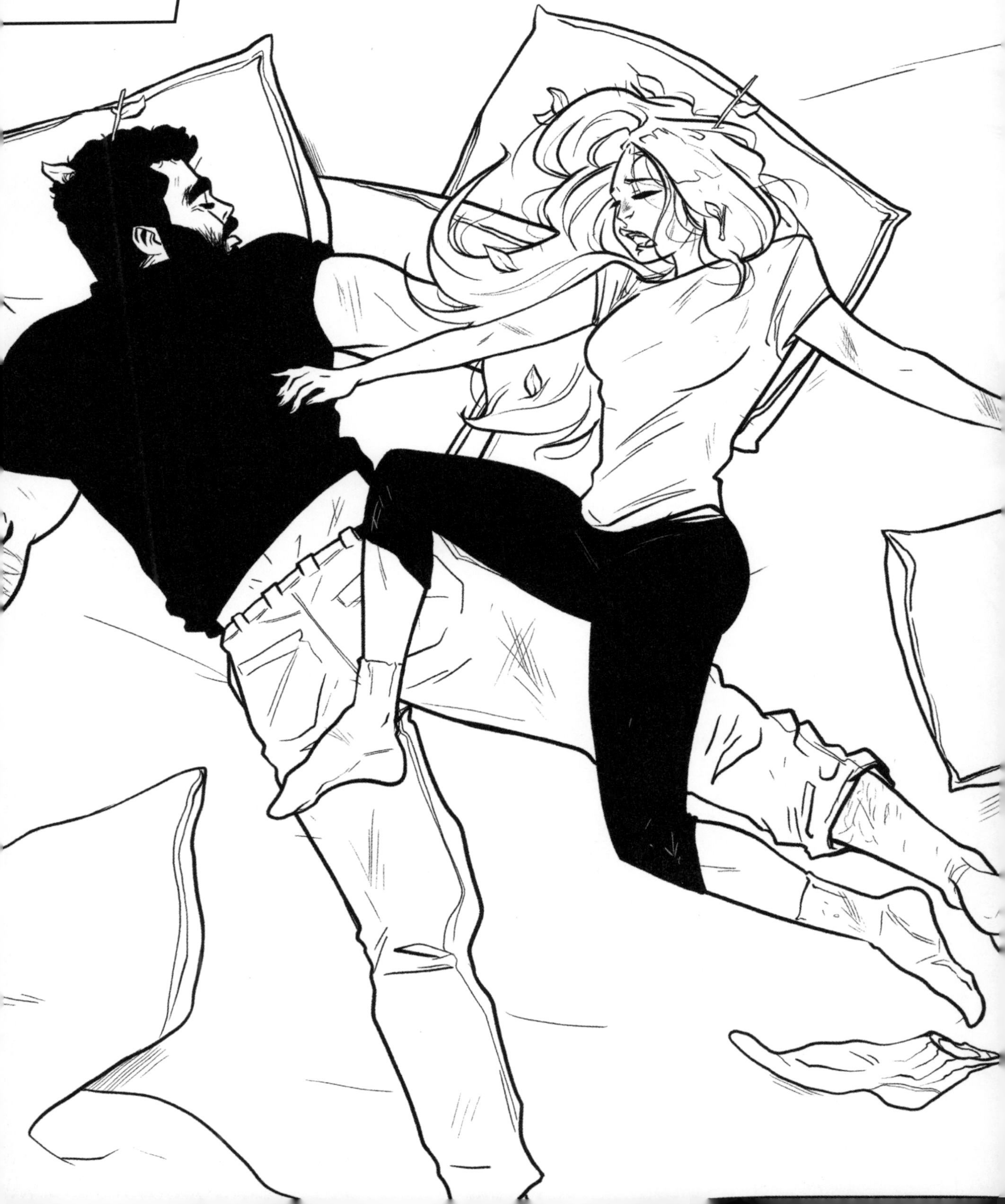

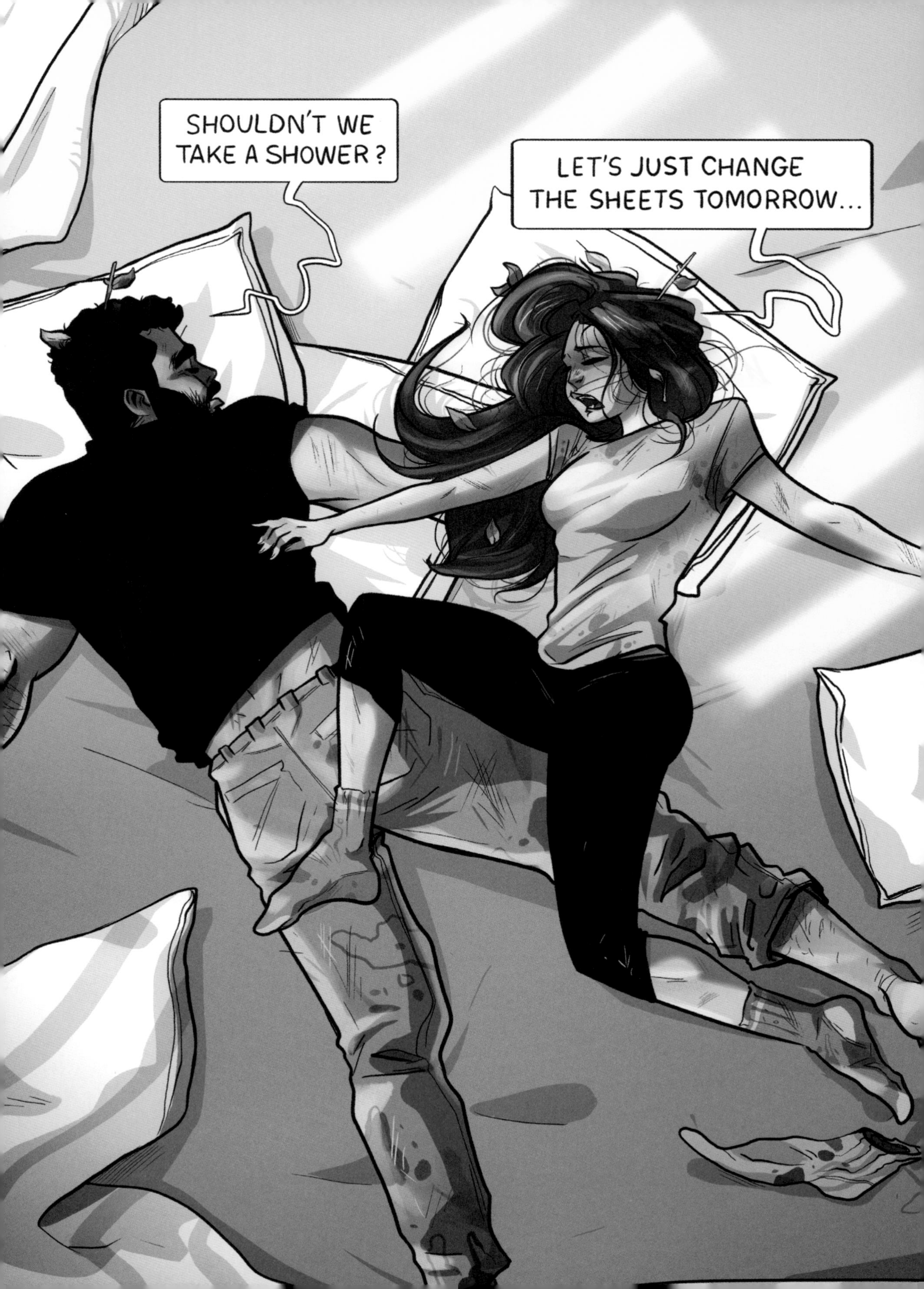
SHOULDN'T WE TAKE A SHOWER?
LET'S JUST CHANGE THE SHEETS TOMORROW...

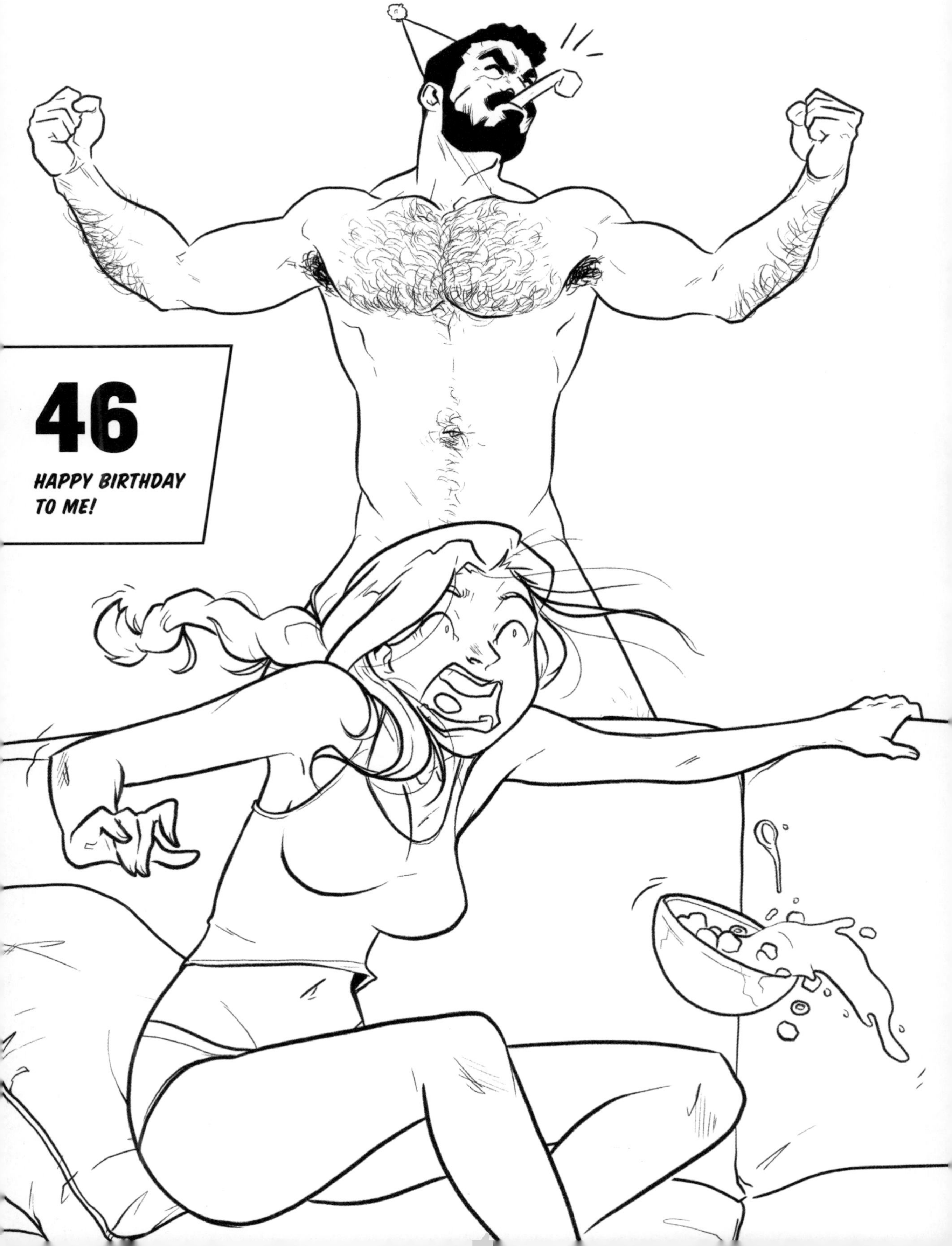
46
HAPPY BIRTHDAY
TO ME!

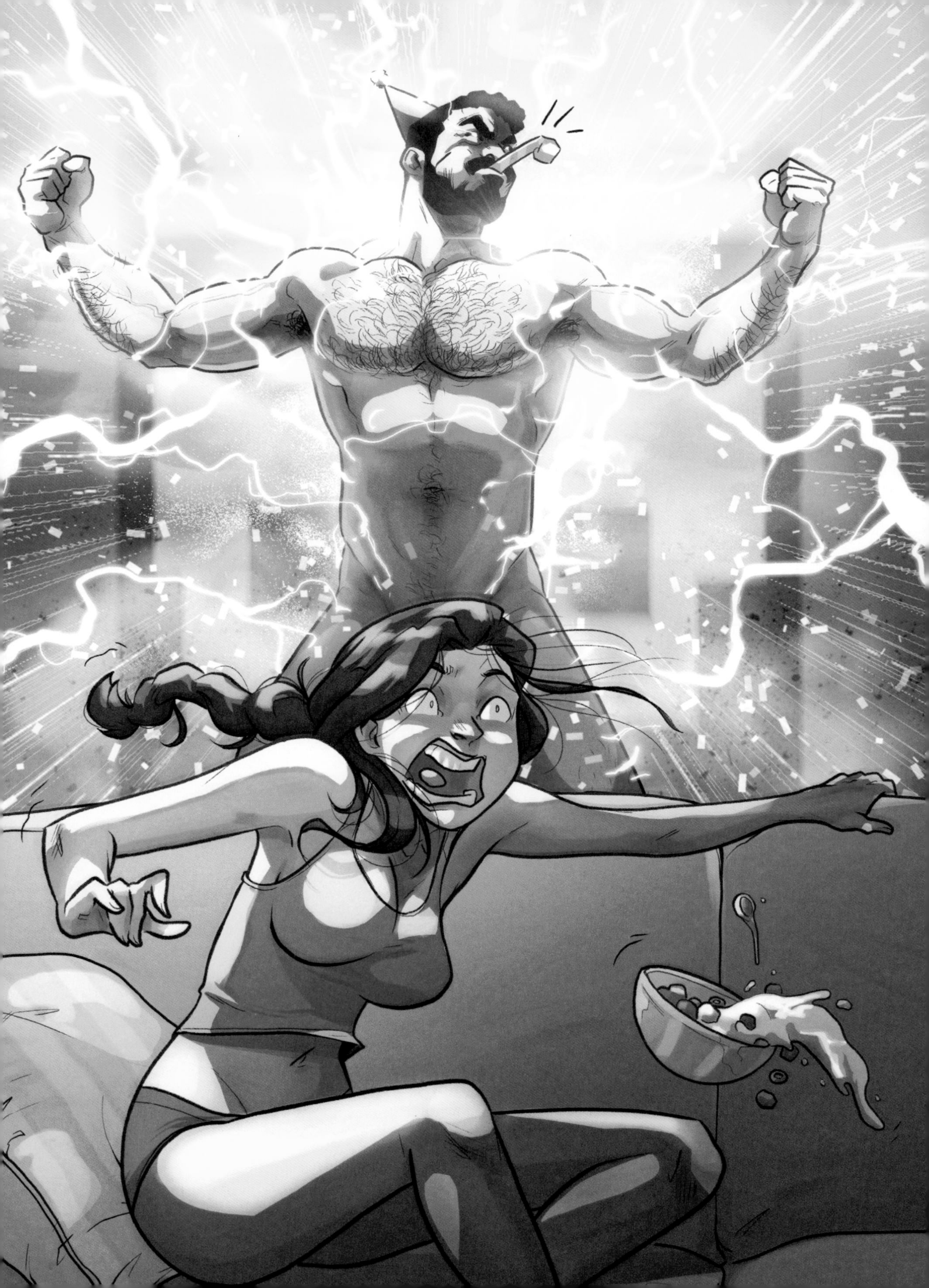

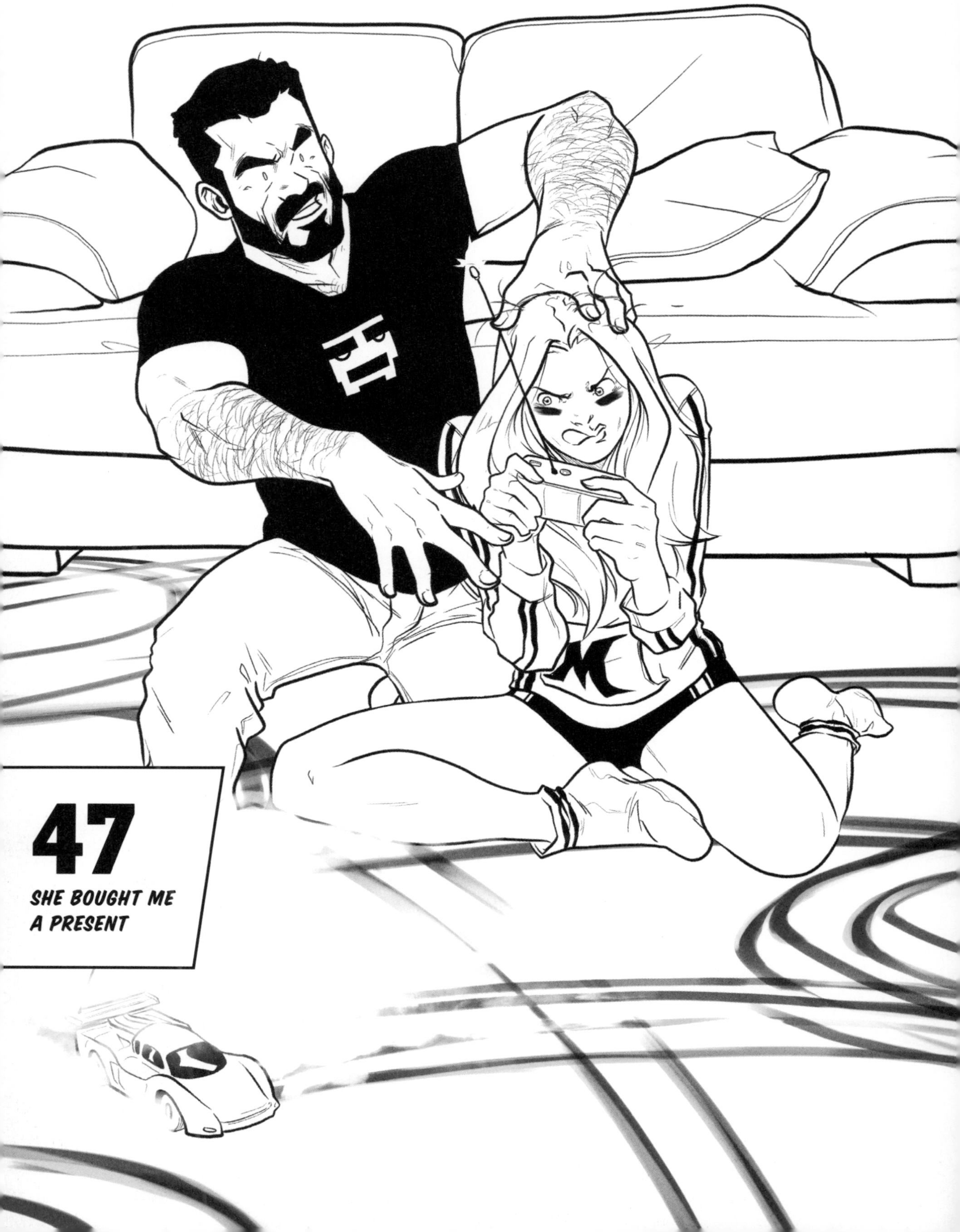

47

SHE BOUGHT ME A PRESENT

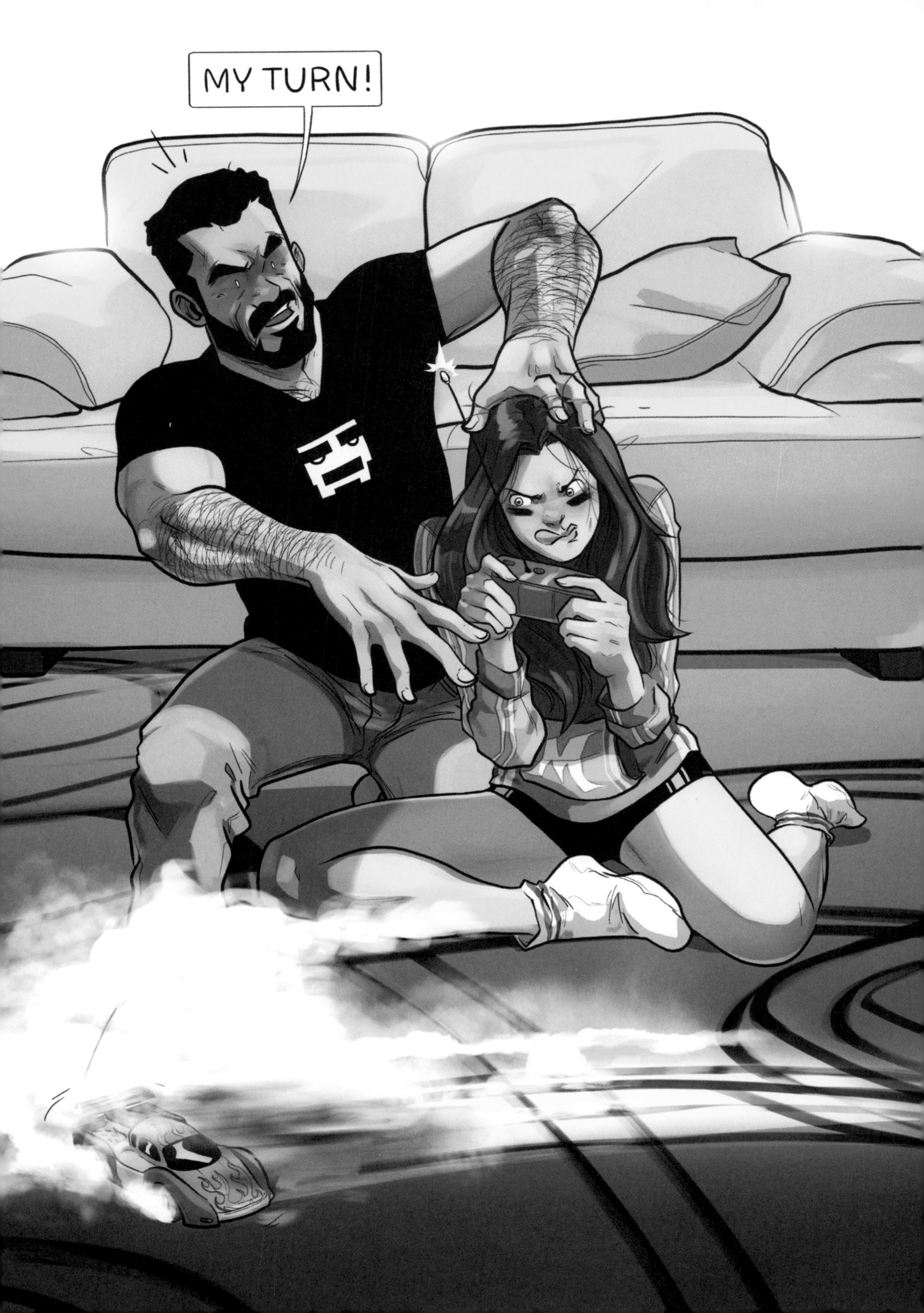
MY TURN!

48

OLD MAN YEHUDA

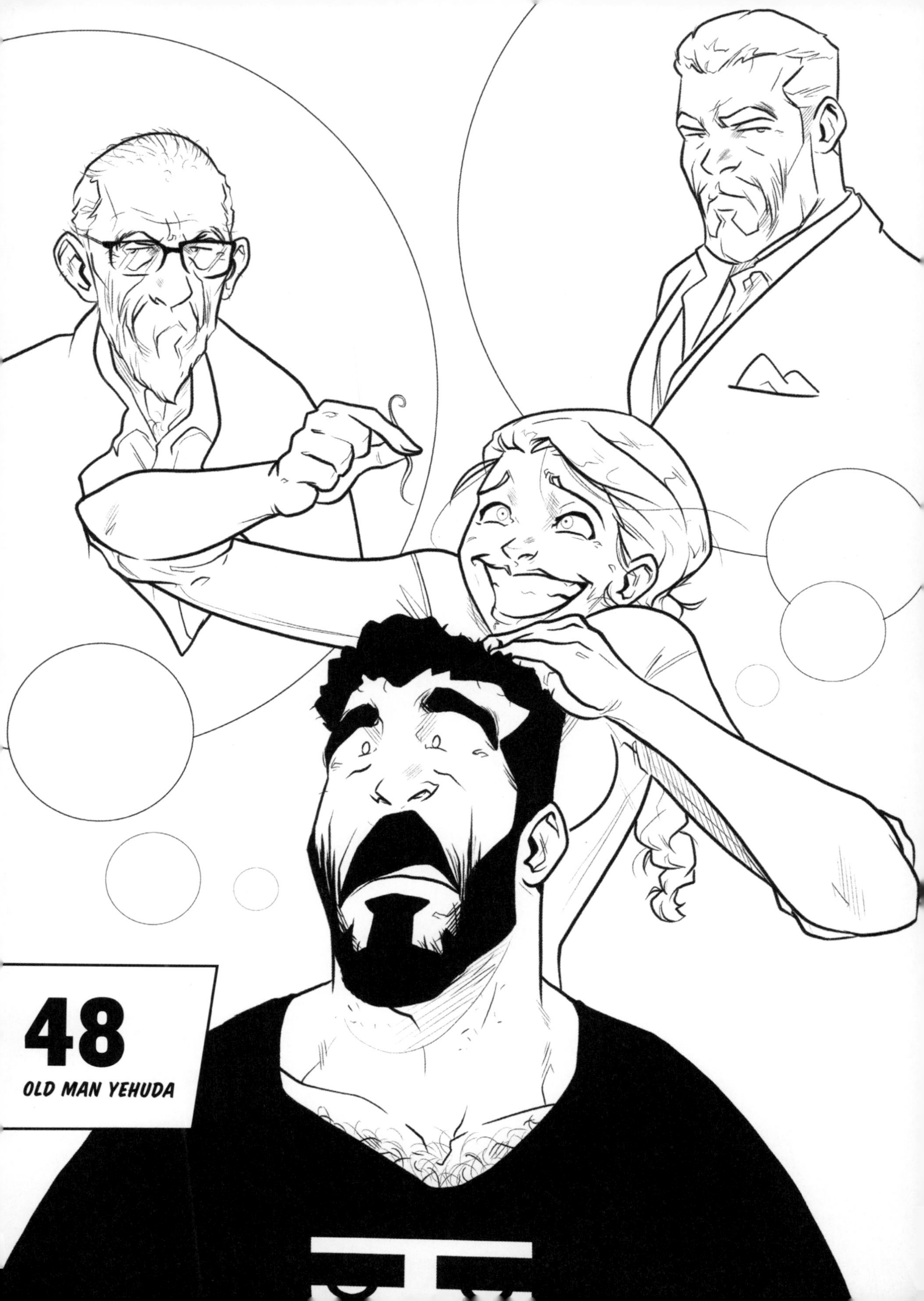

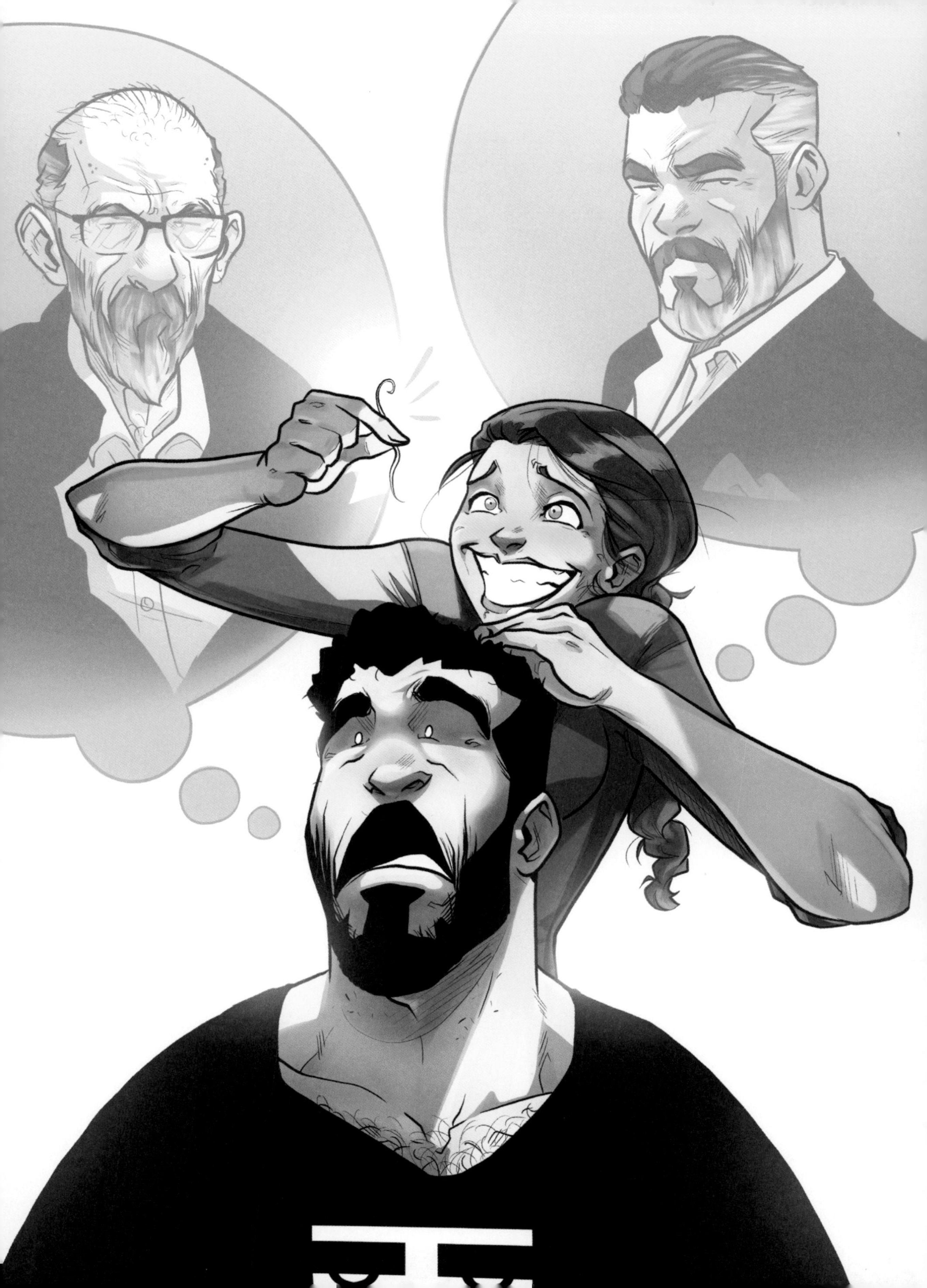

49

L'CHAIM!
SALUTE!
CHEERS!

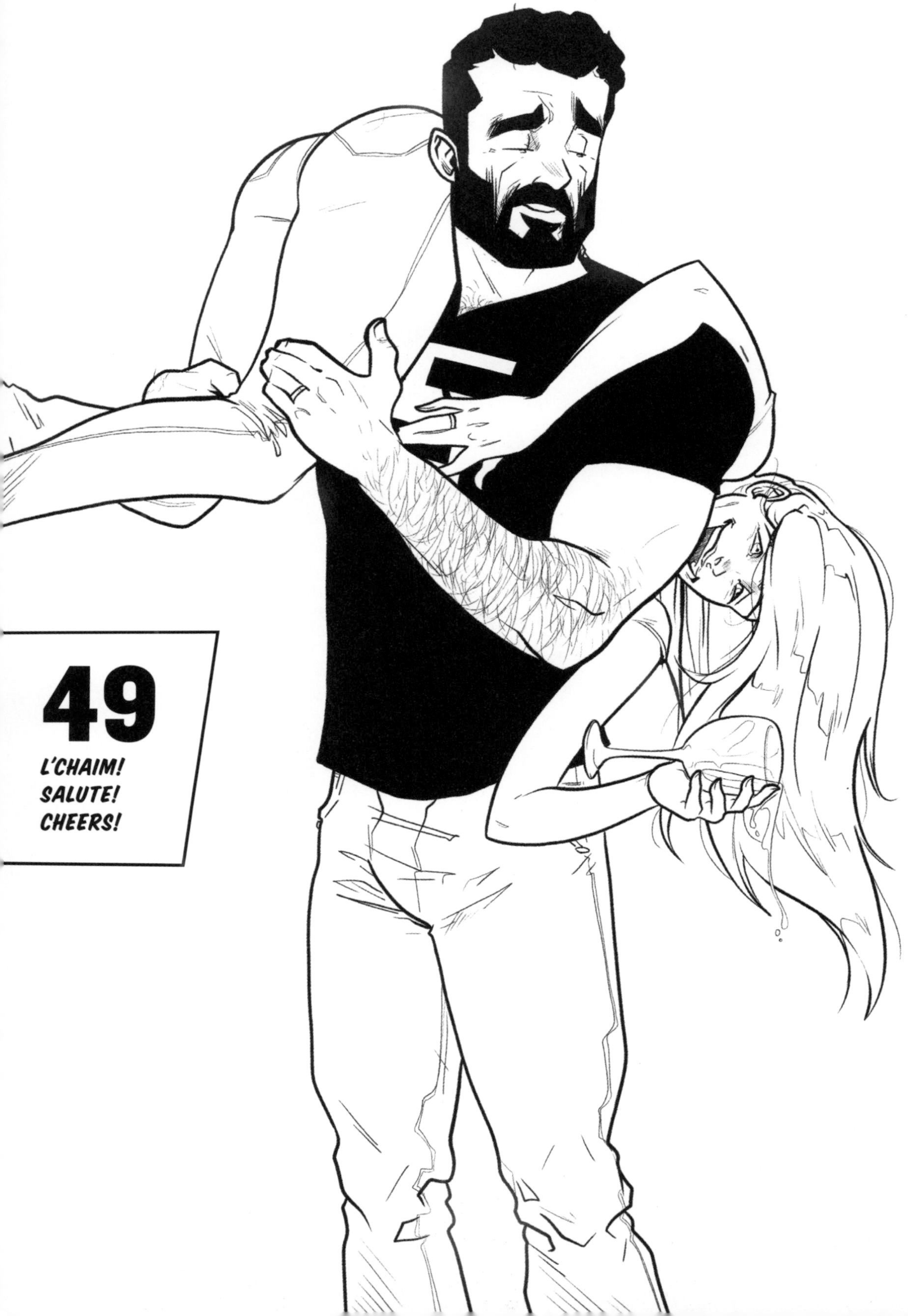

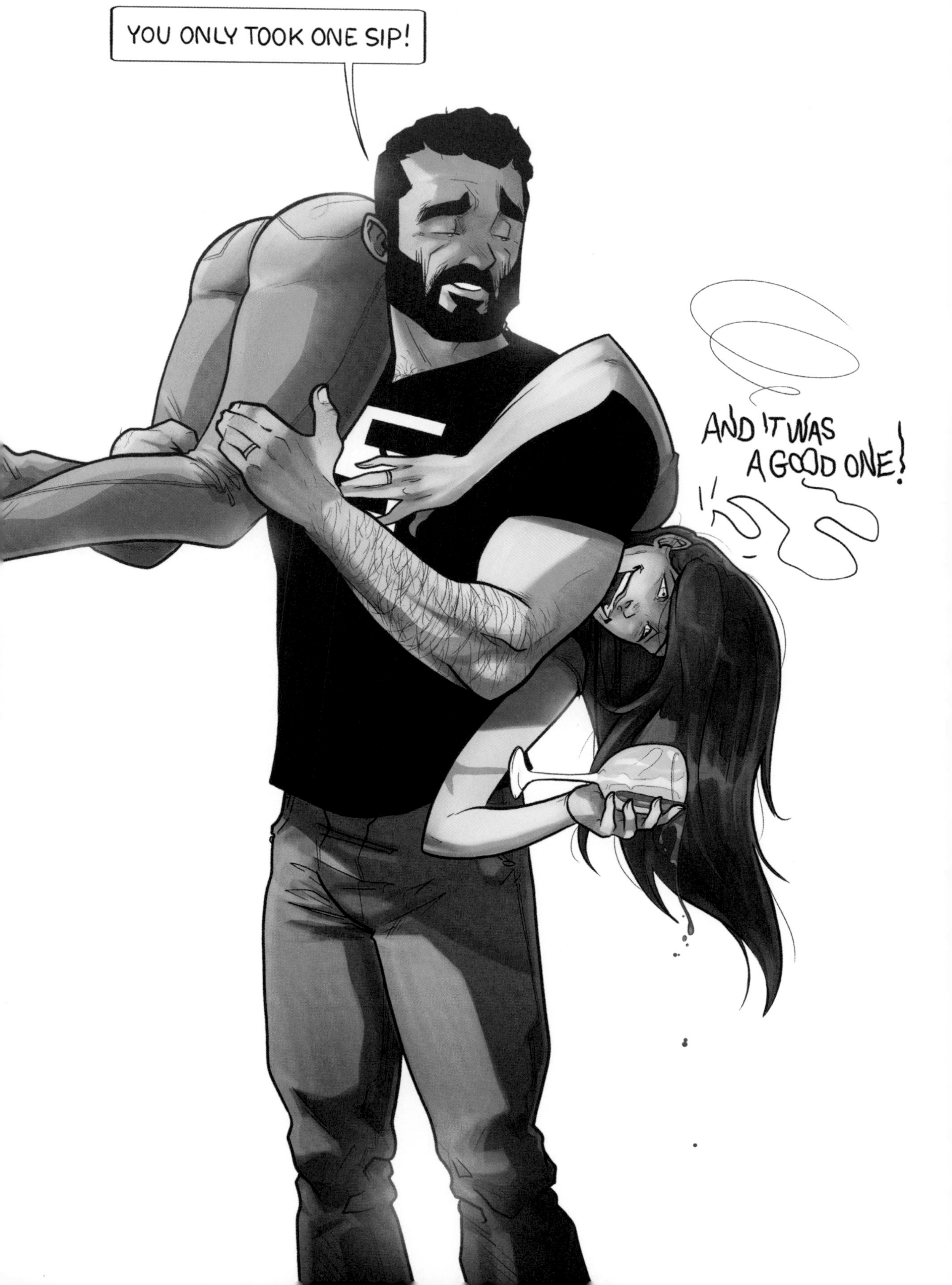
YOU ONLY TOOK ONE SIP!
AND IT WAS A GOOD ONE!

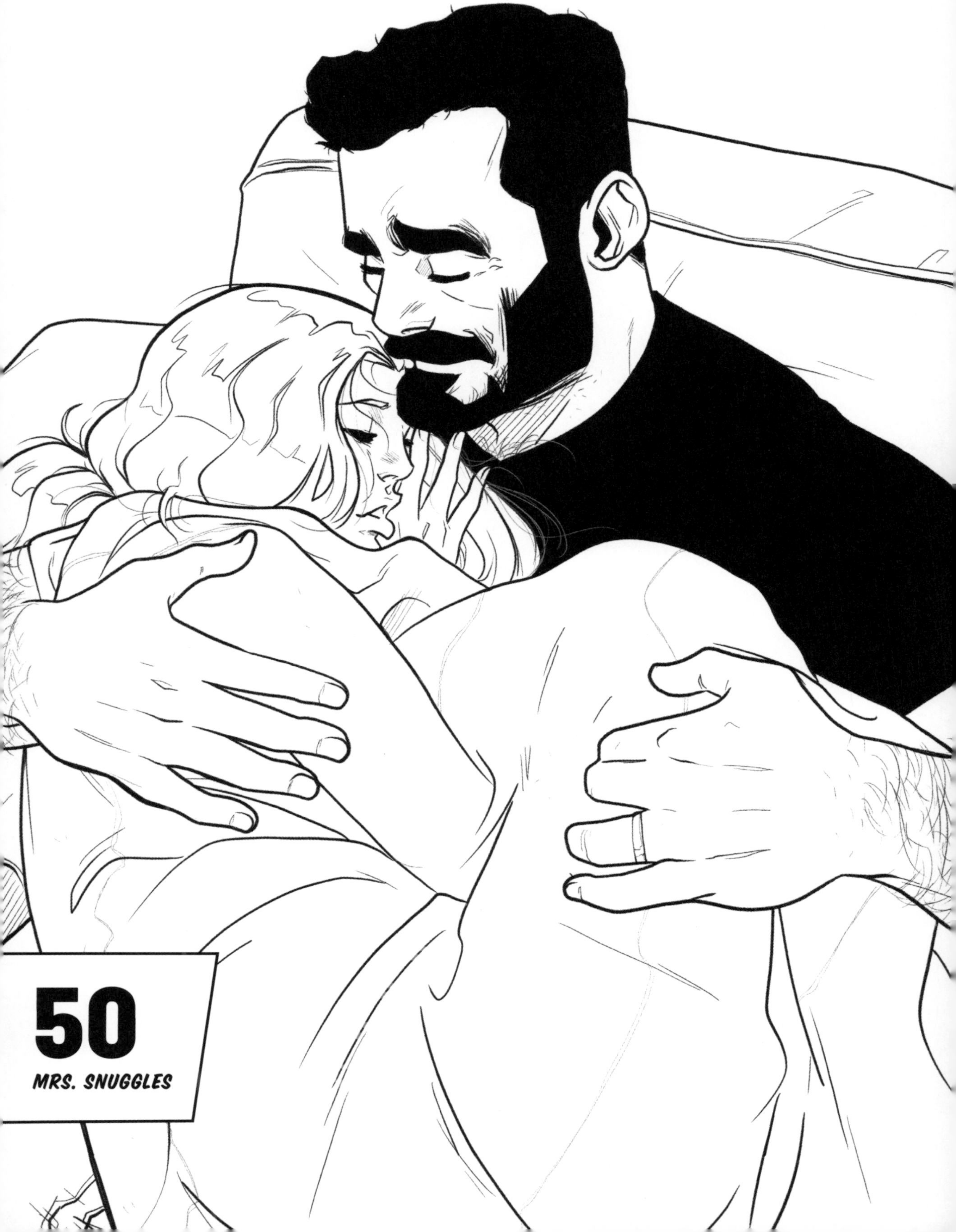

50

MRS. SNUGGLES

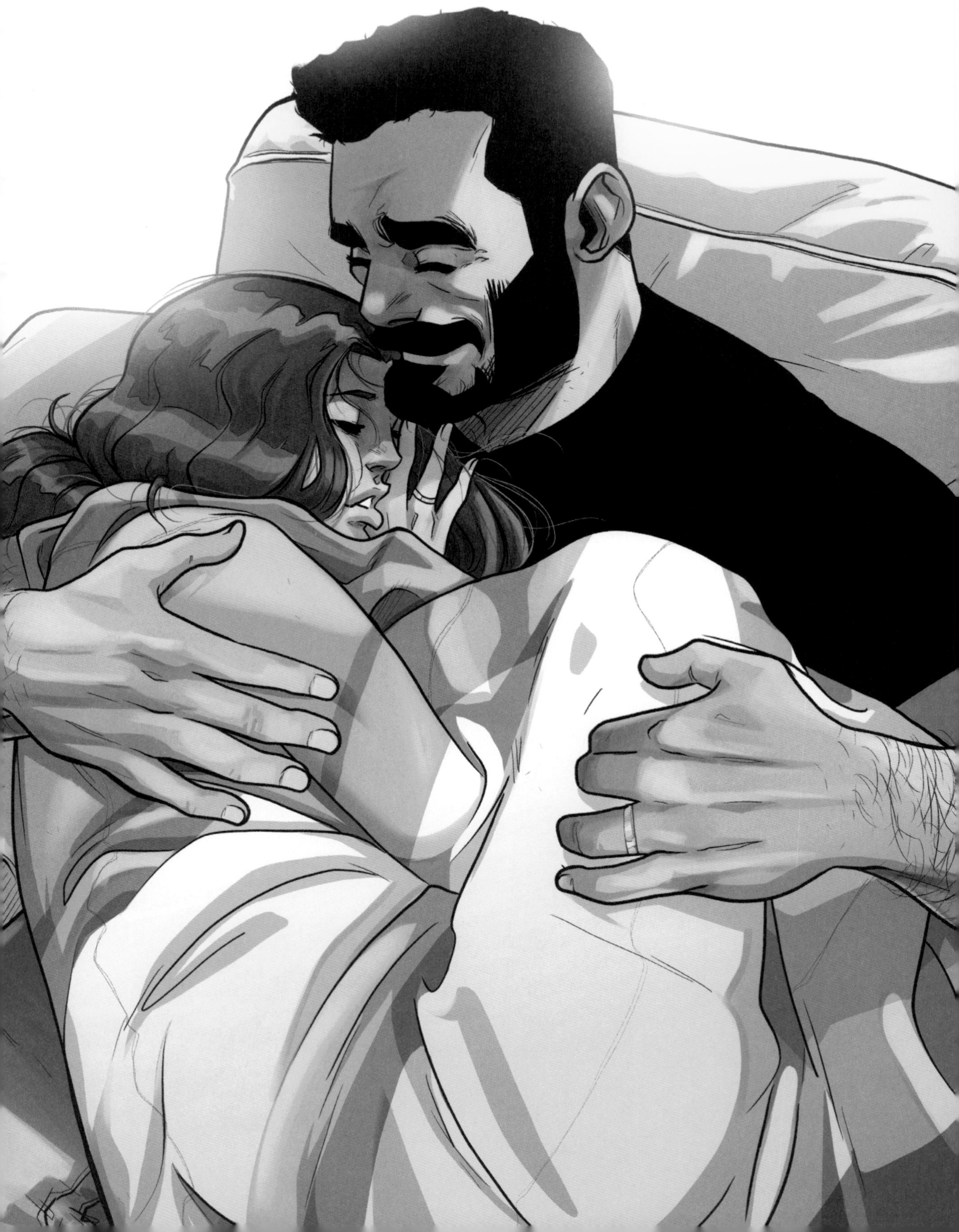

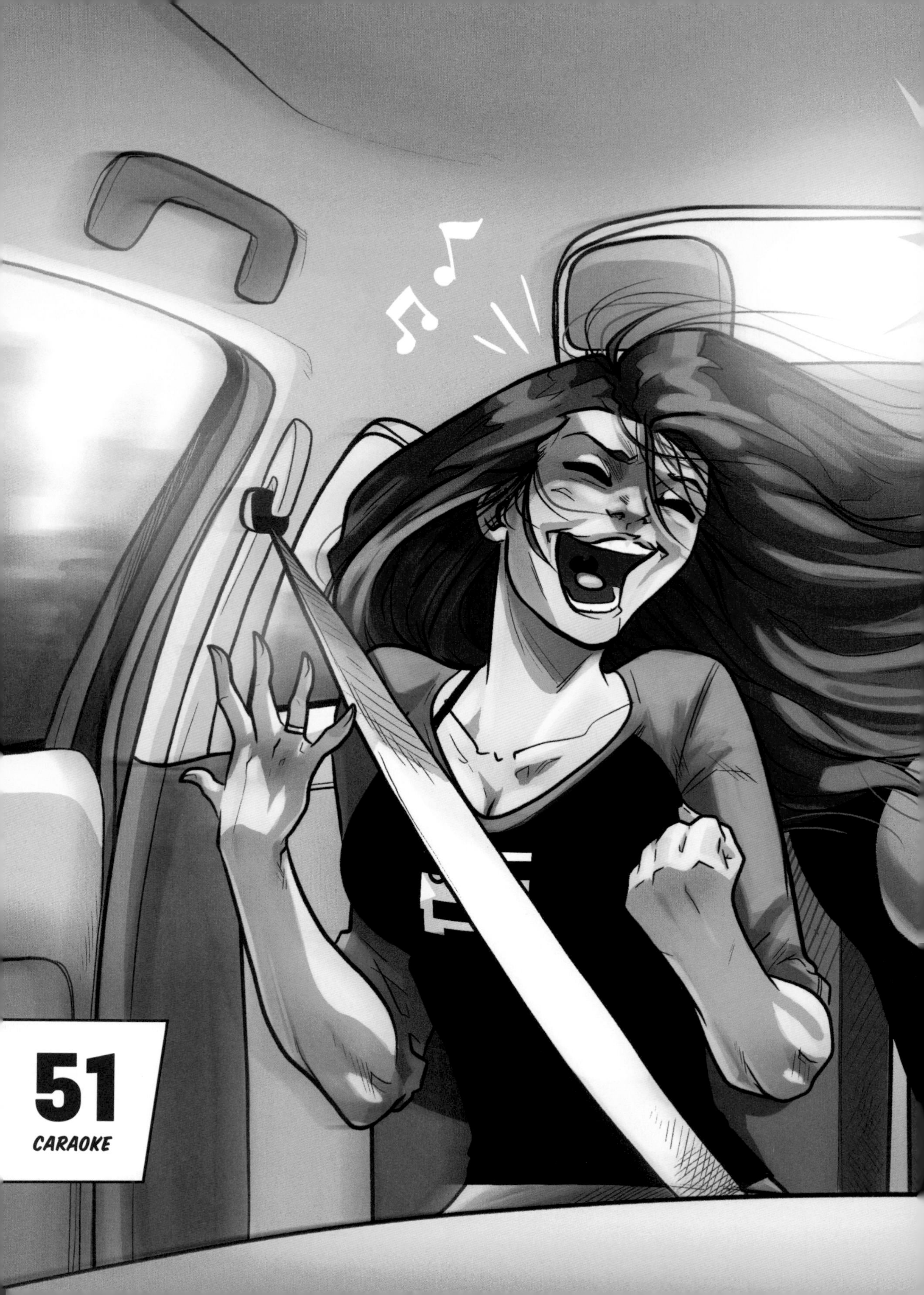

51
CARAOKE

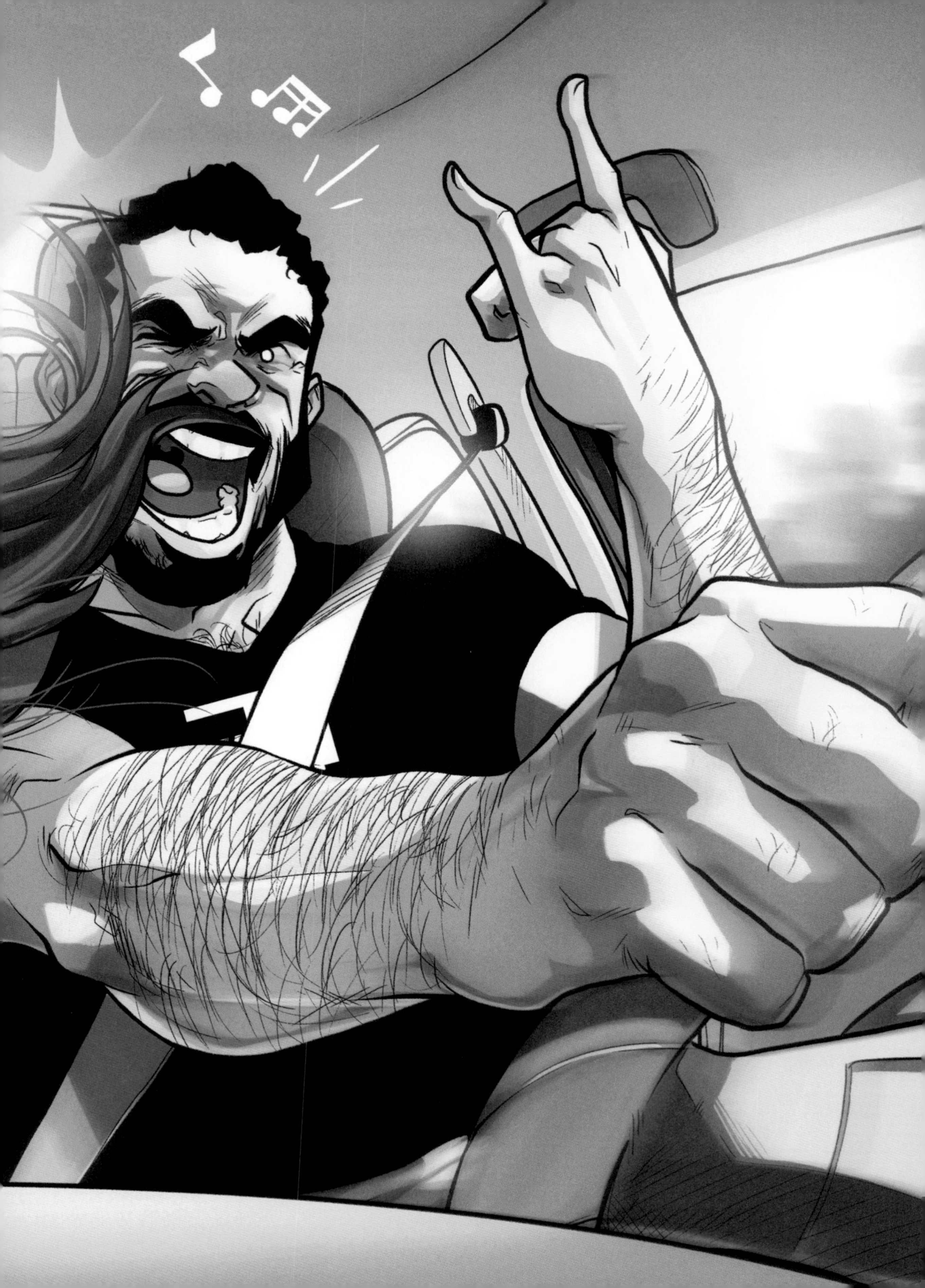

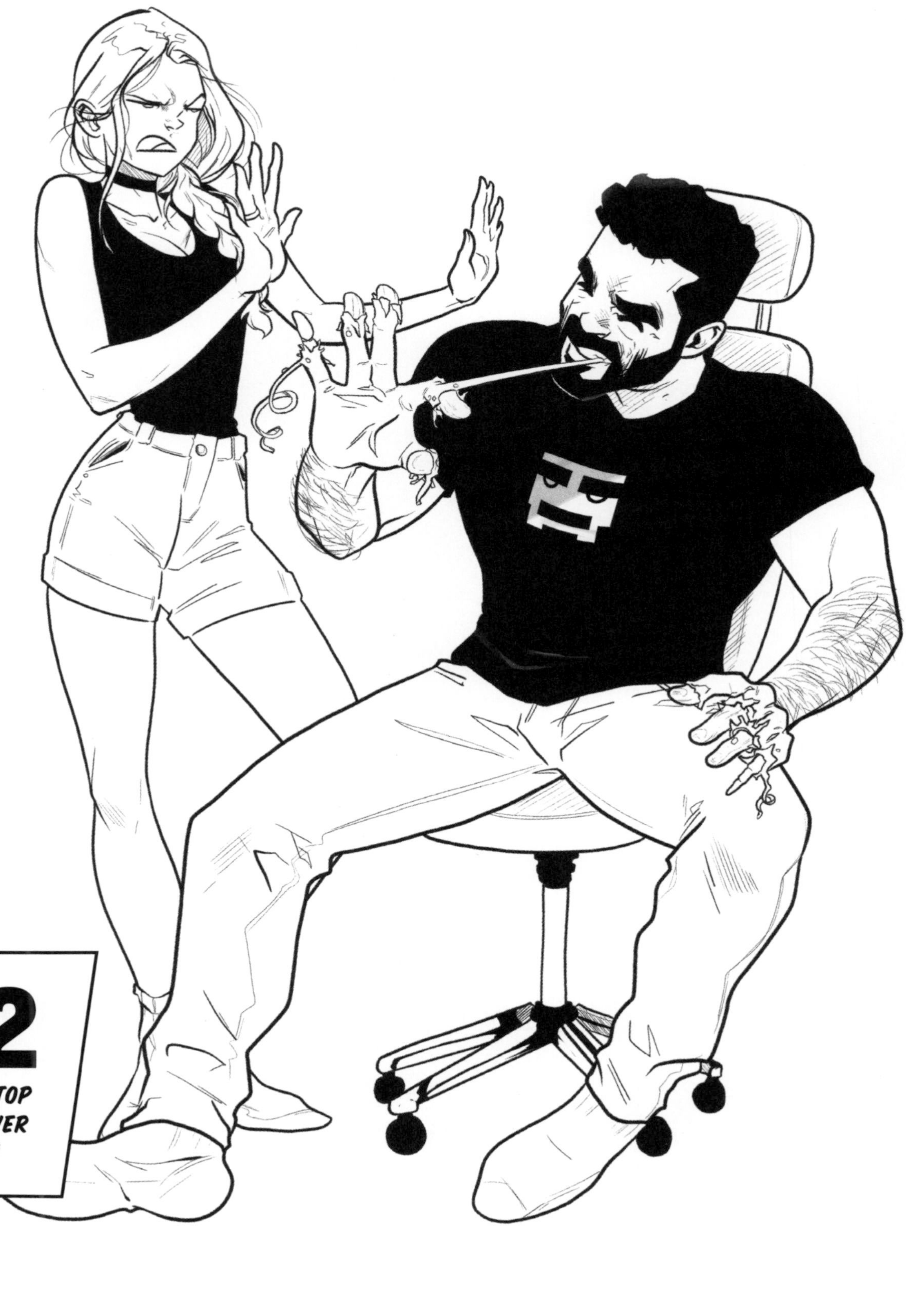

52

I CAN STOP WHENEVER I WANT!

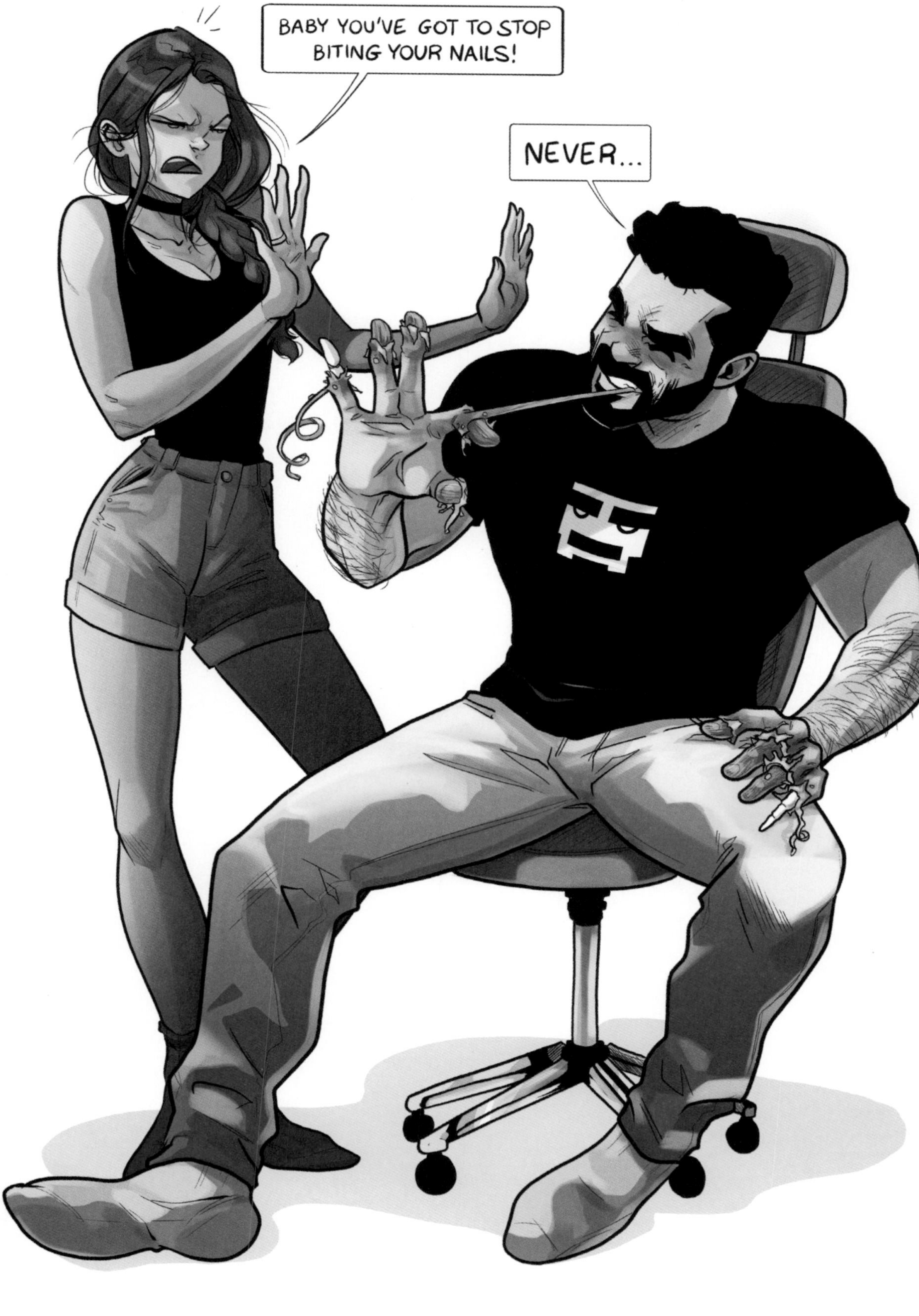
BABY YOU'VE GOT TO STOP BITING YOUR NAILS!
NEVER...

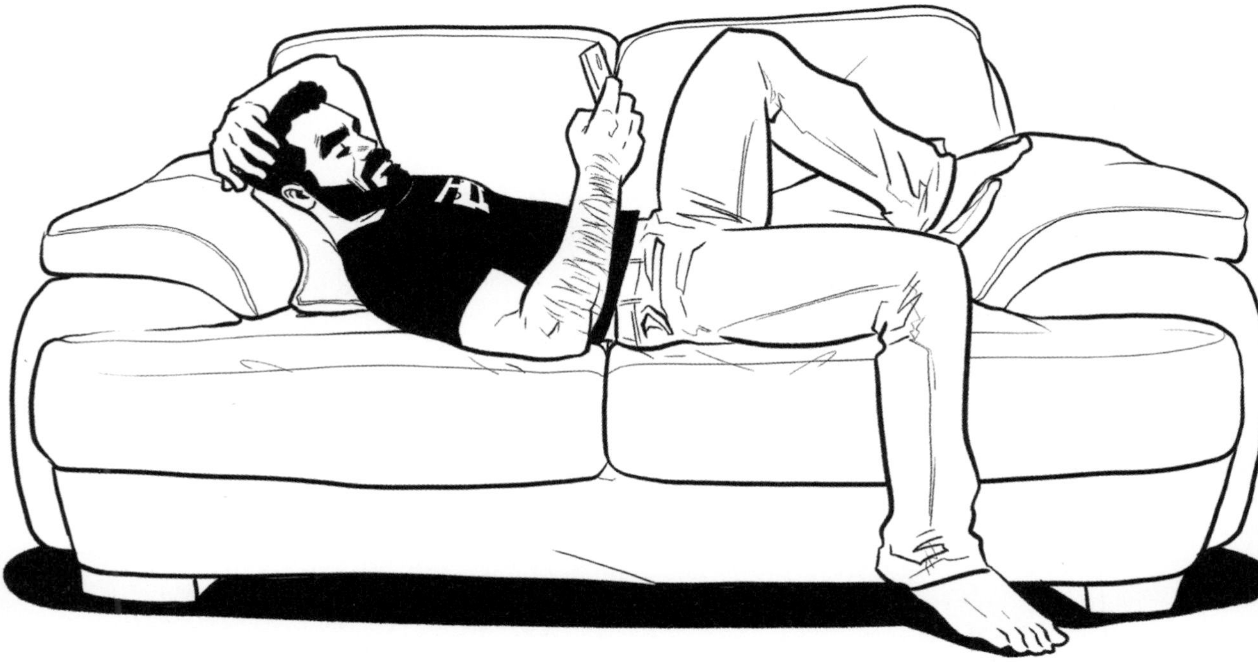

53

SAME HAIRCUT
SAME STORY

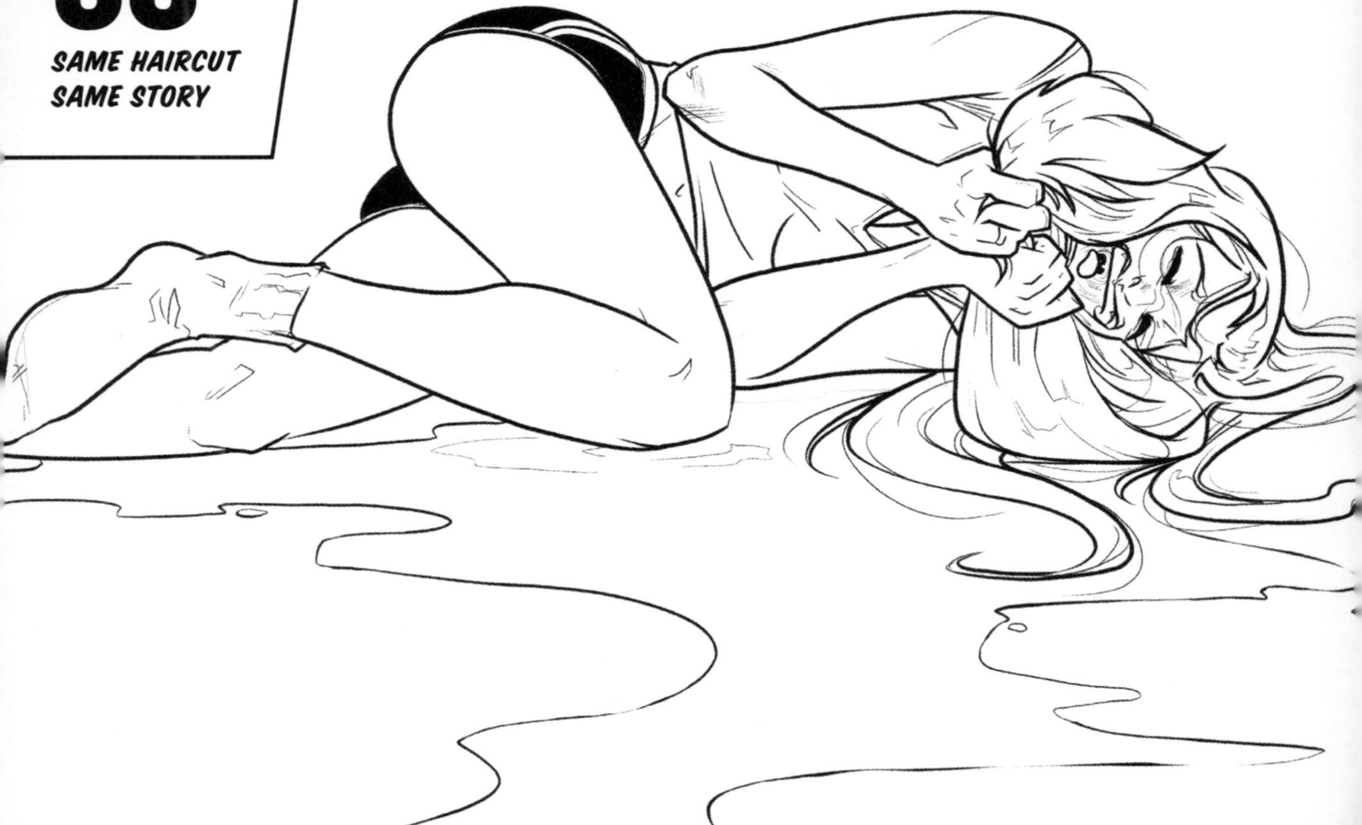

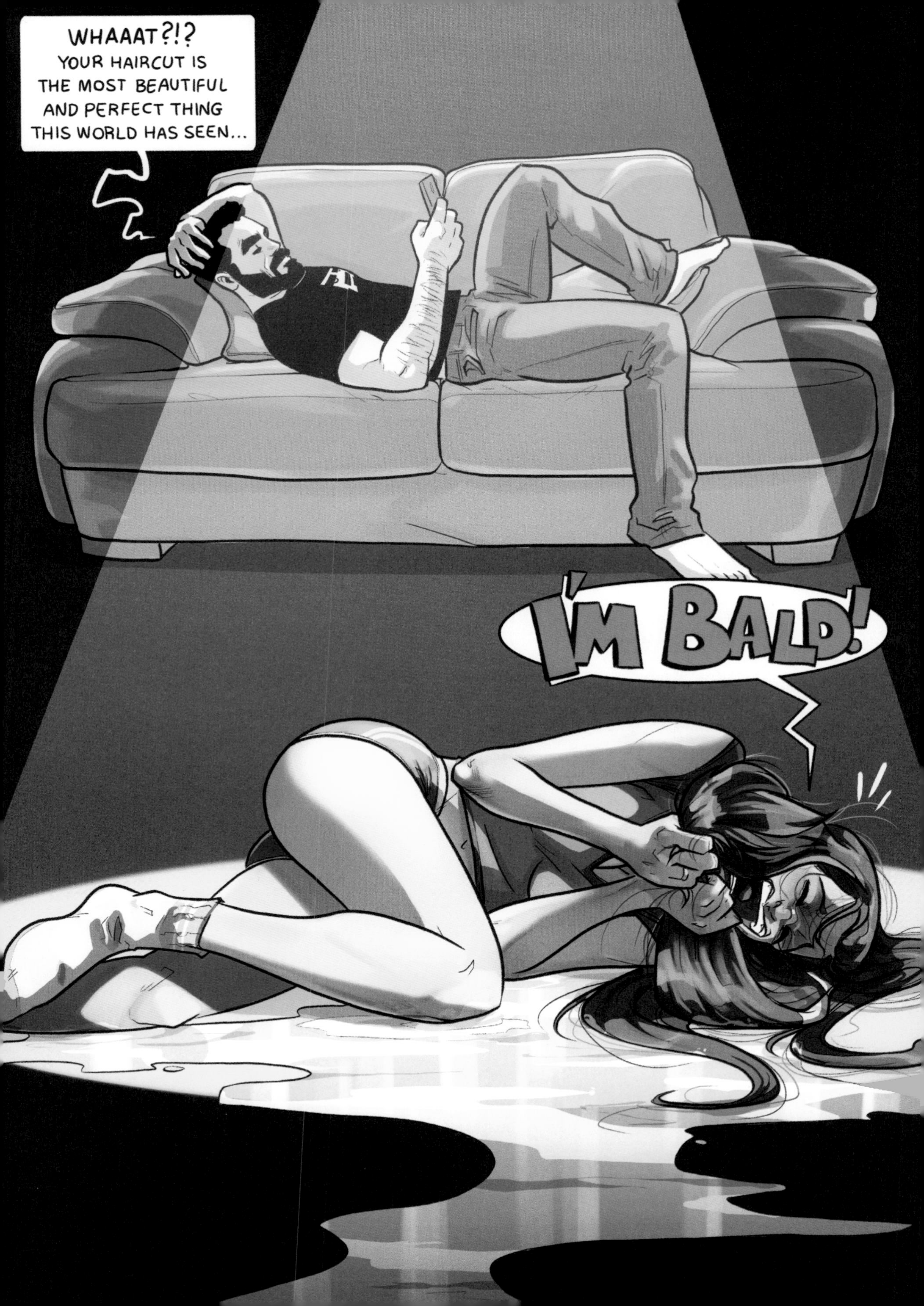
WHAAAT?!? YOUR HAIRCUT IS THE MOST BEAUTIFUL AND PERFECT THING THIS WORLD HAS SEEN...
I'M BALD!

54
WORKAHOLIC

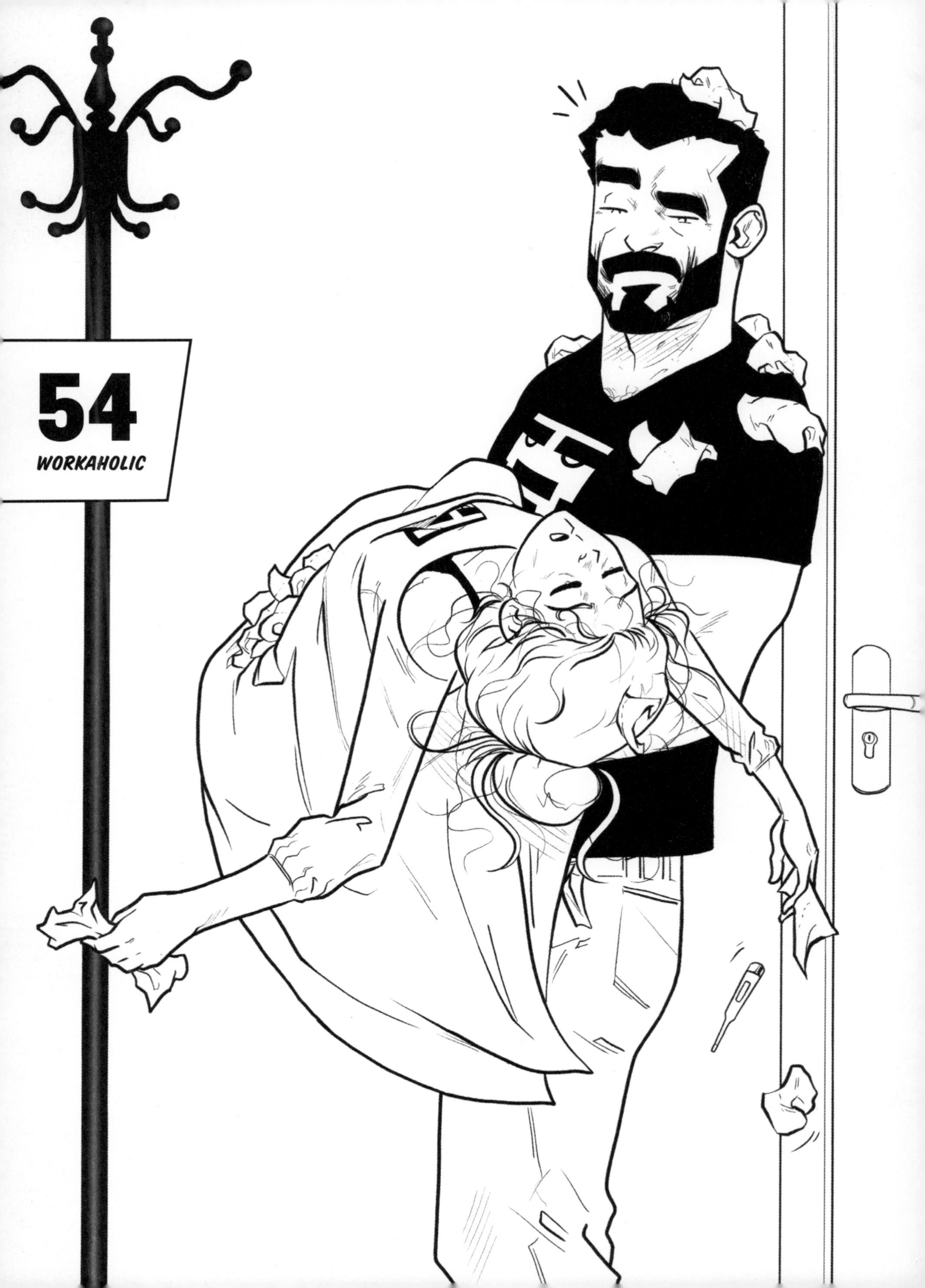

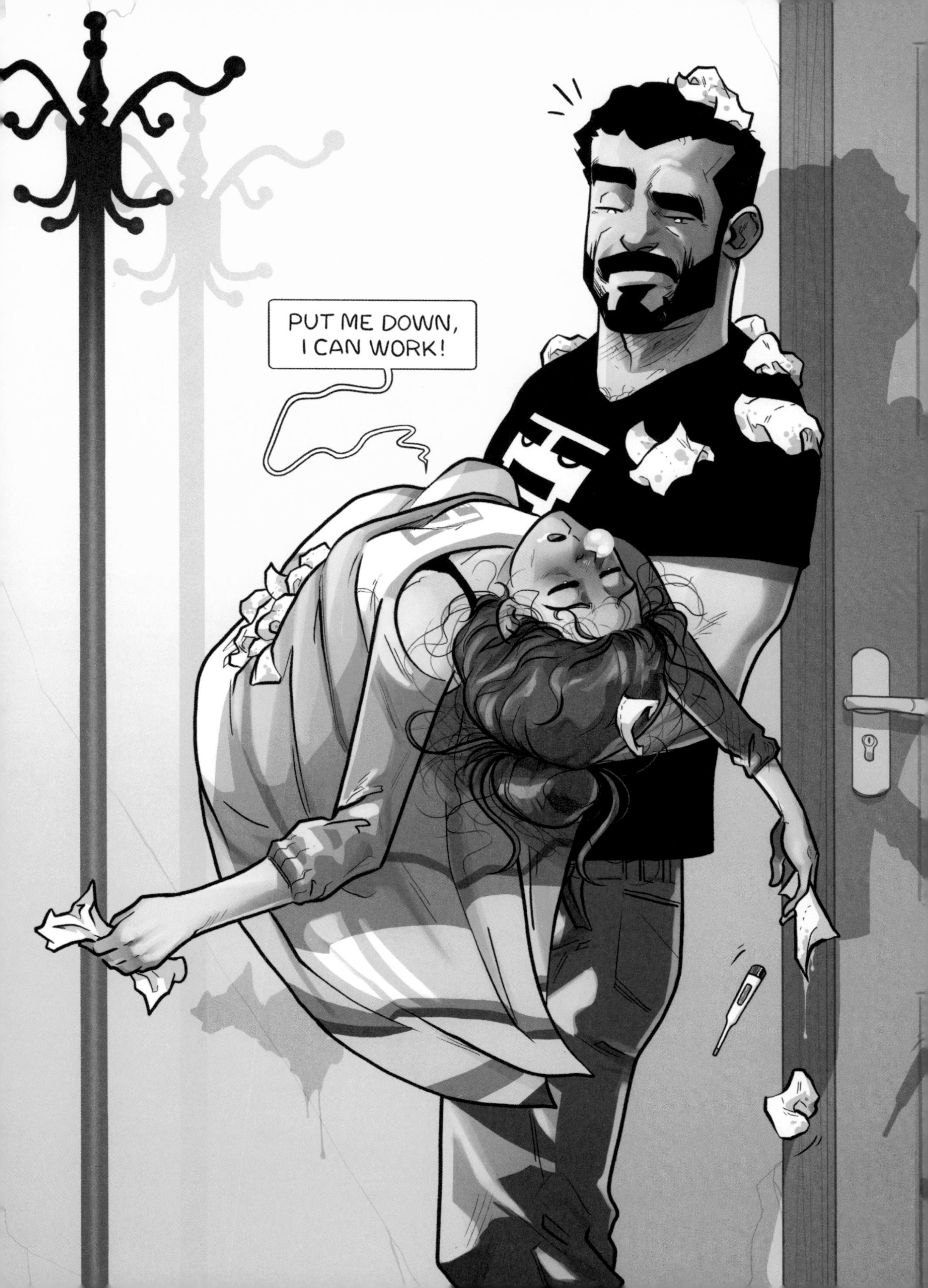
PUT ME DOWN, I CAN WORK!

55

1,000,000 FOLLOWERS

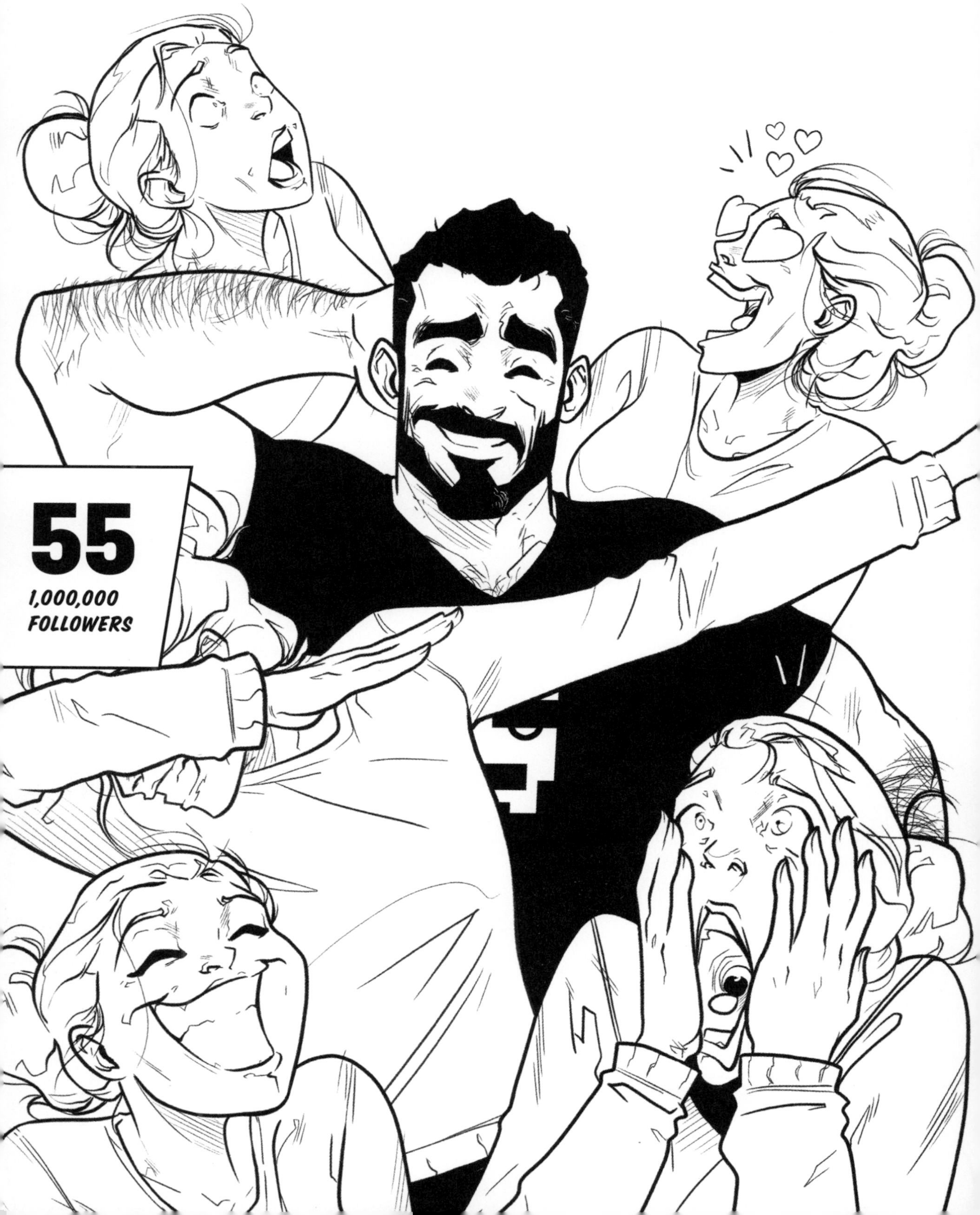

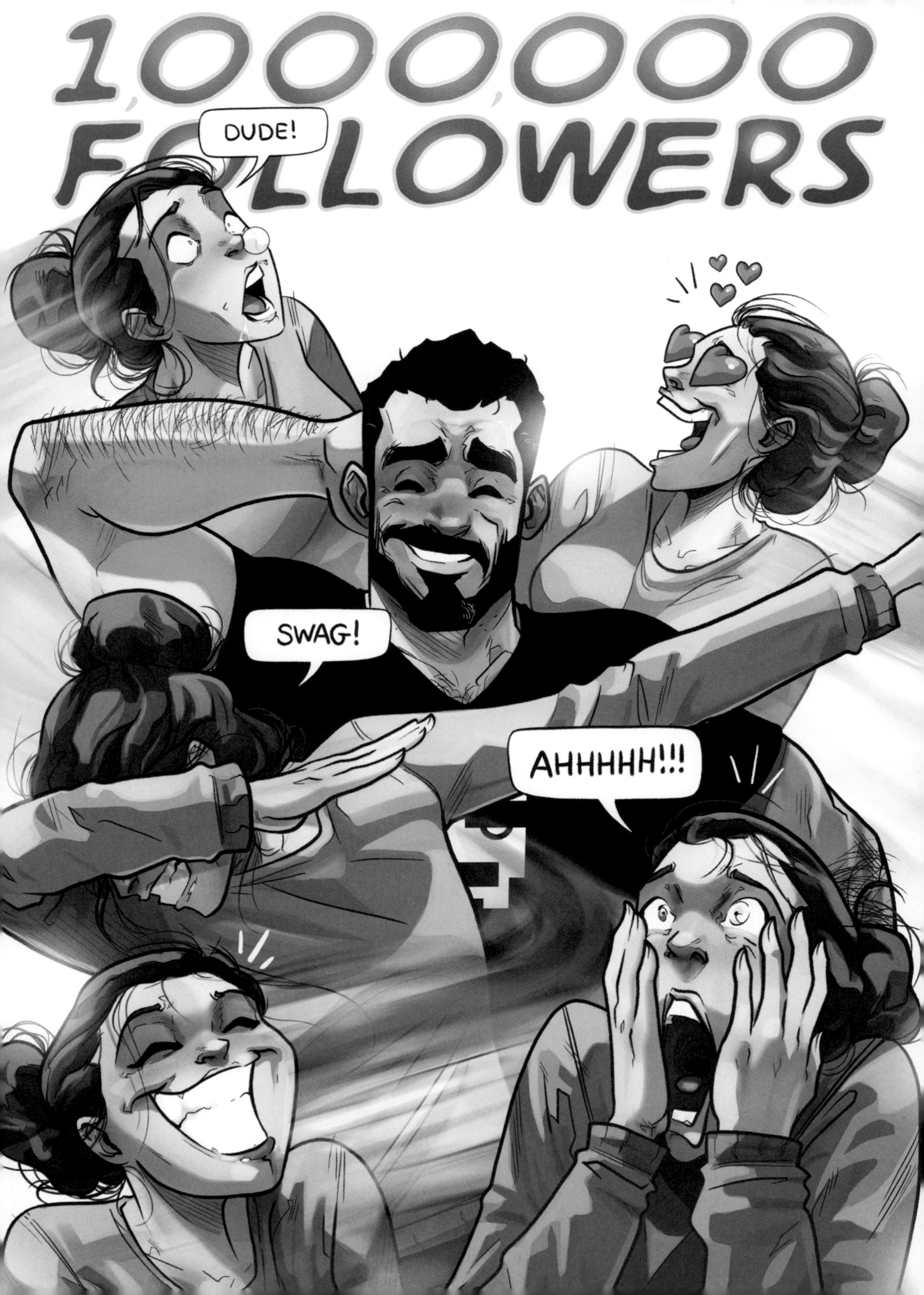
1,000,000
FOLLOWERS
DUDE!
SWAG!
AHHHHH!!!

56

JUICERSTEIN

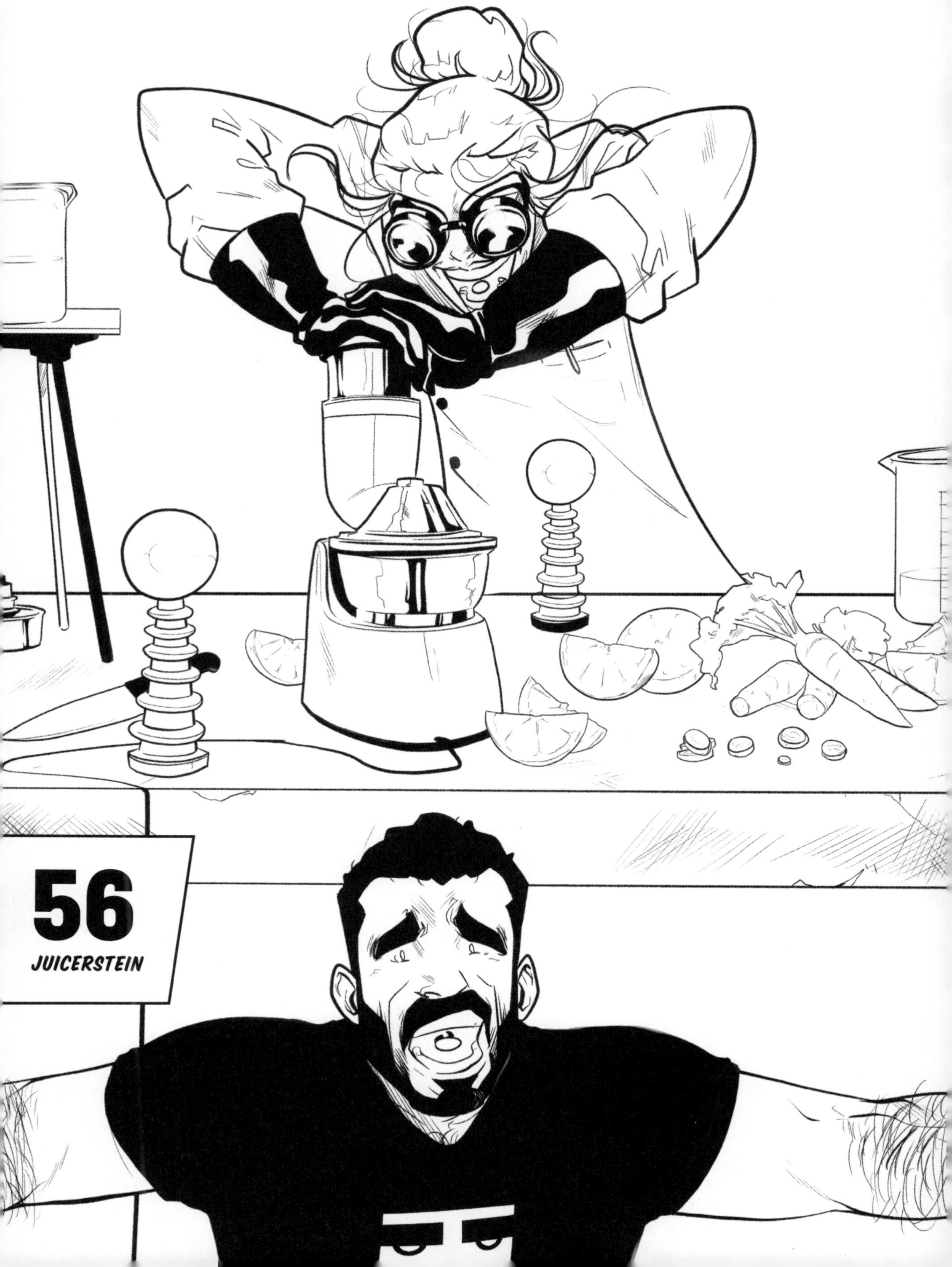

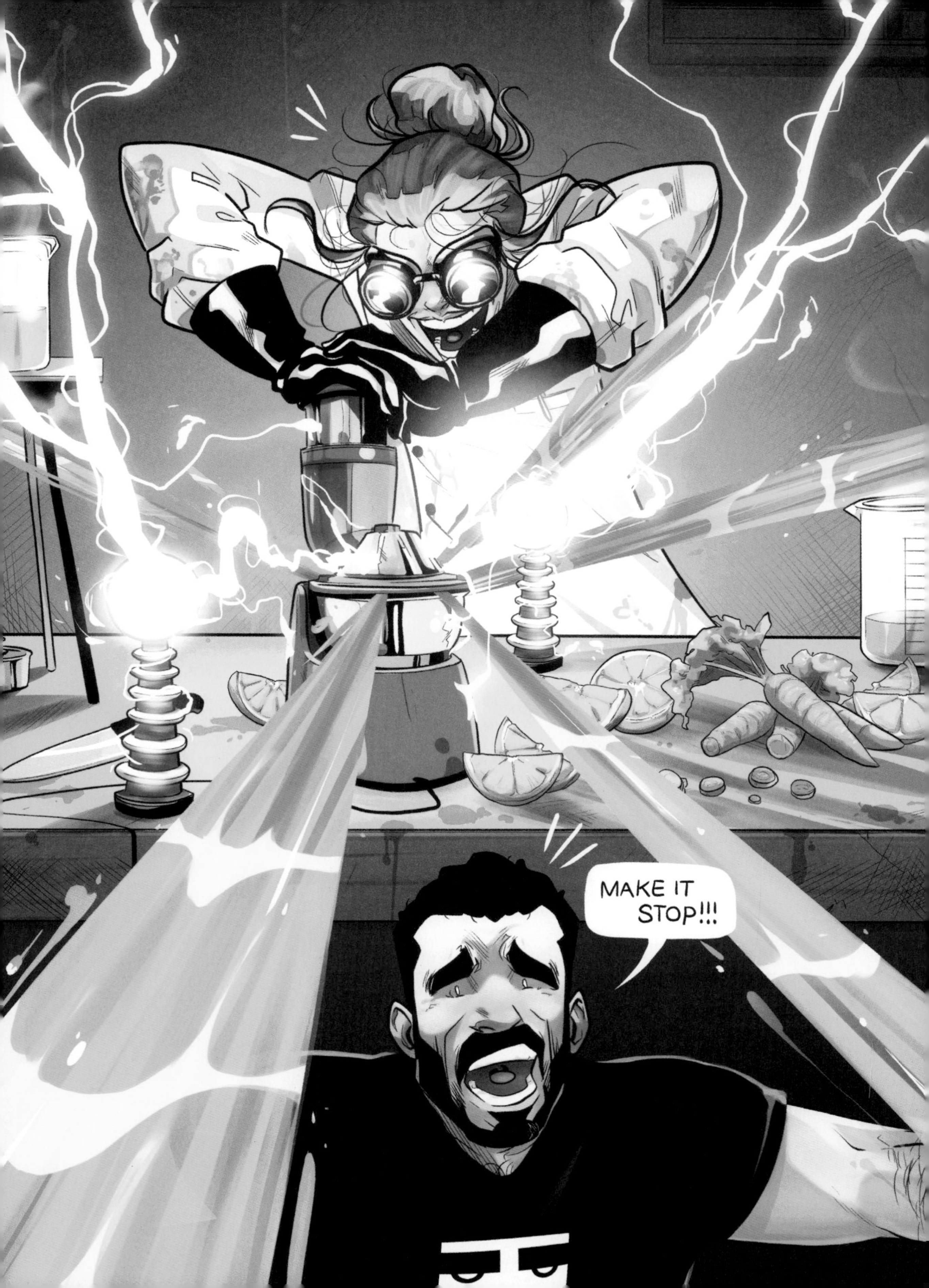
MAKE IT STOP!!!

57

BLACK FRIDAY

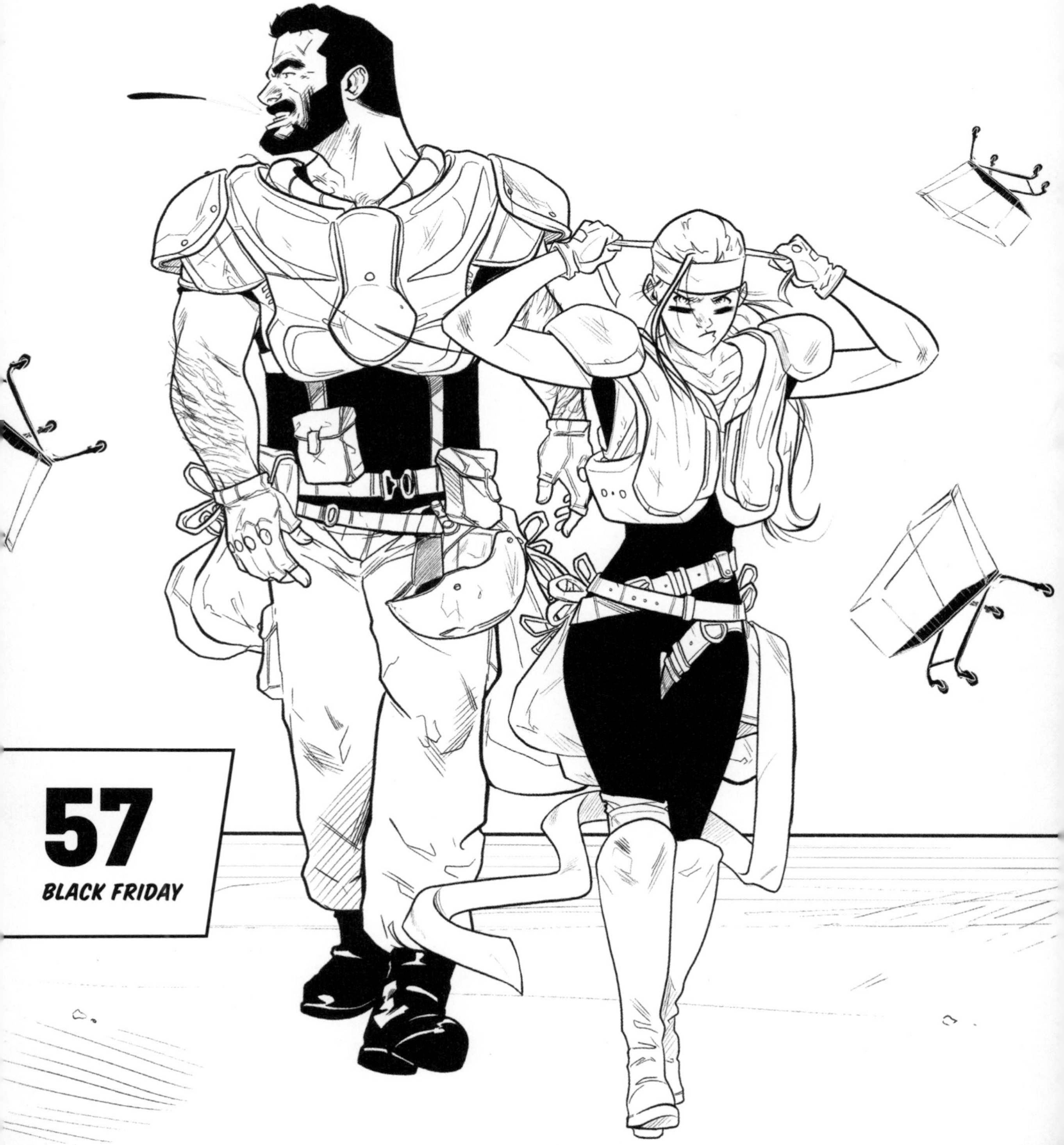

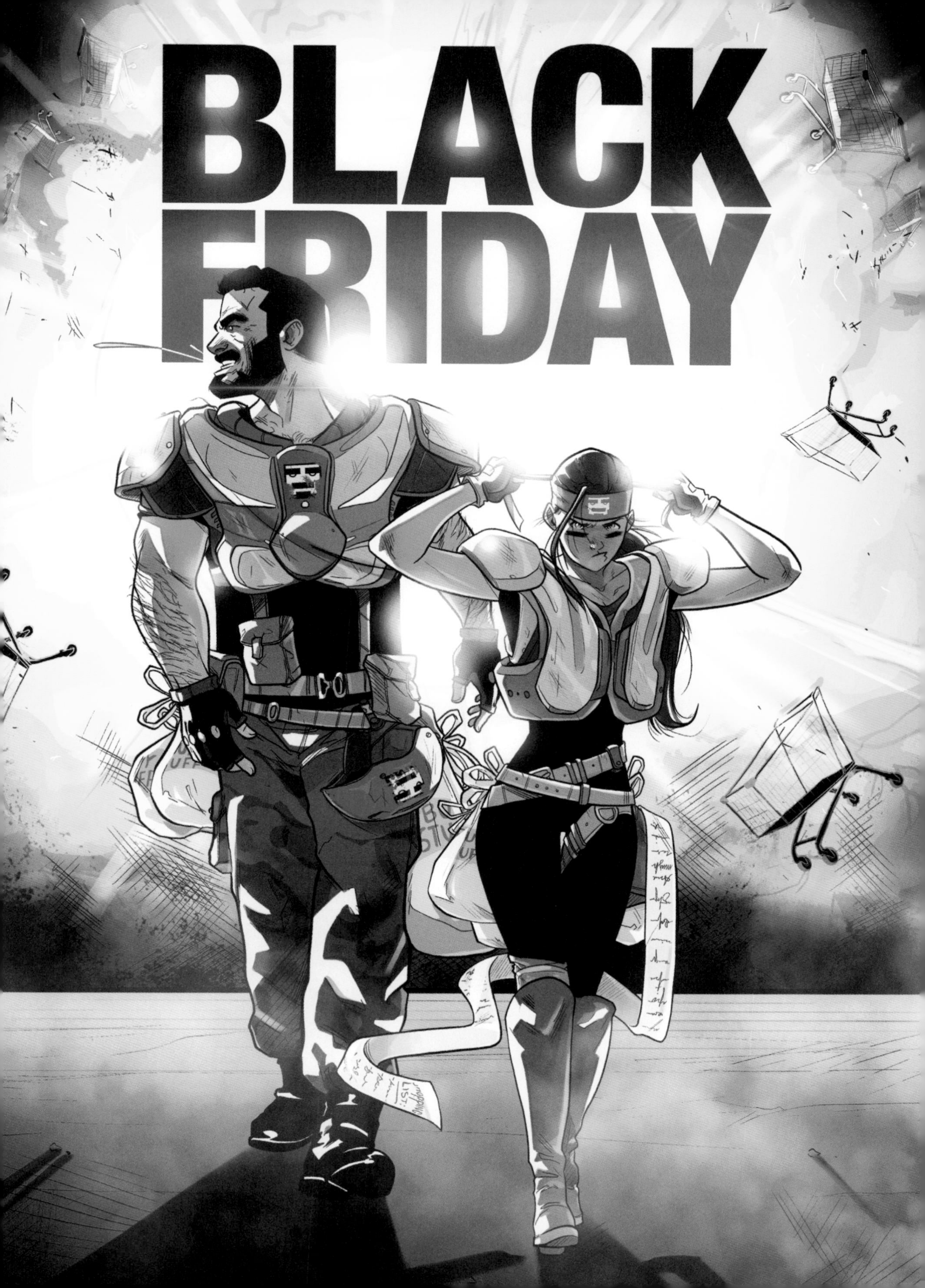
BLACK
FRIDAY

58

MY OTHER HALF

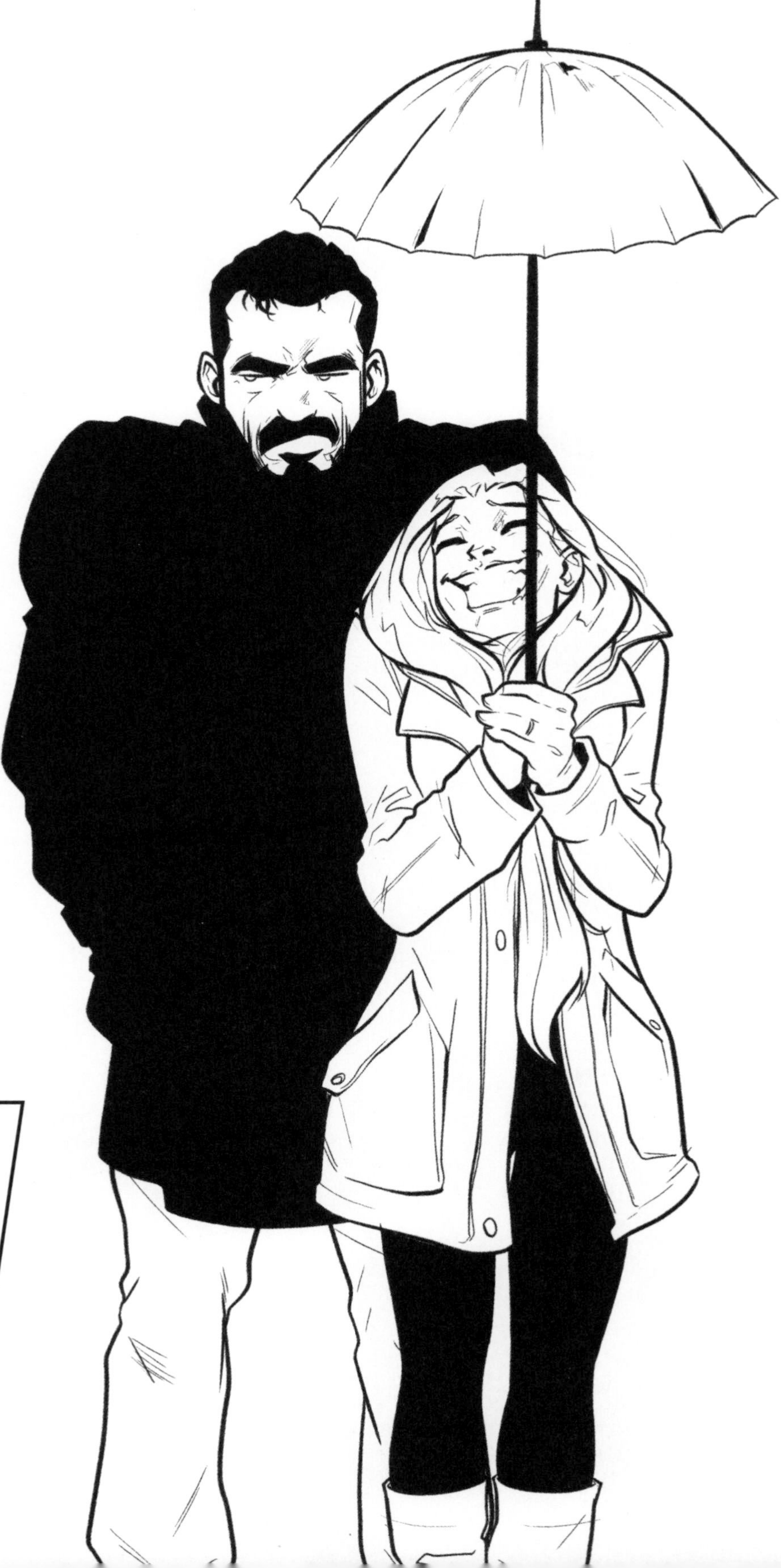

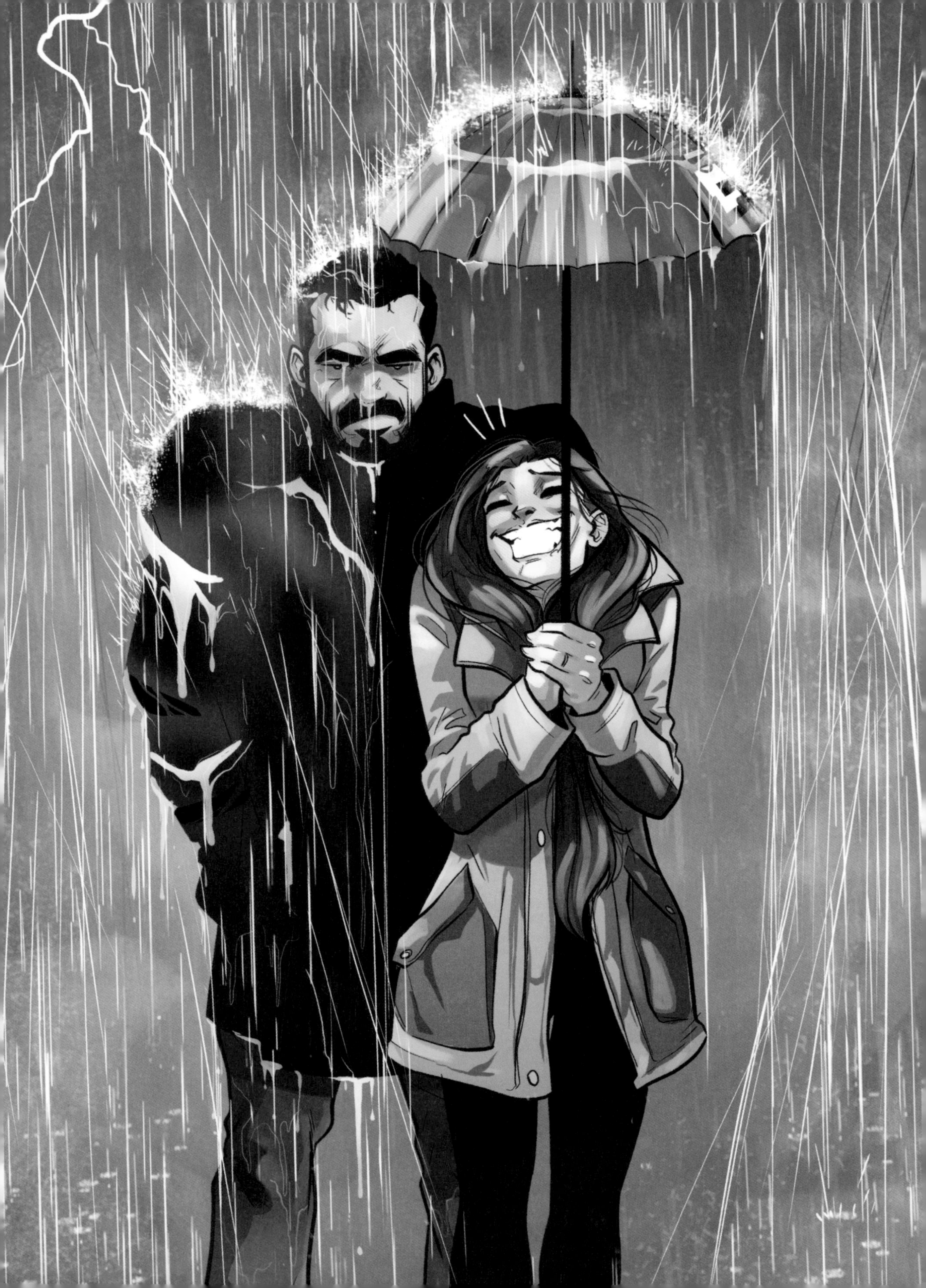

59

EVERYTHING I CAN DO SHE CAN DO BETTER!

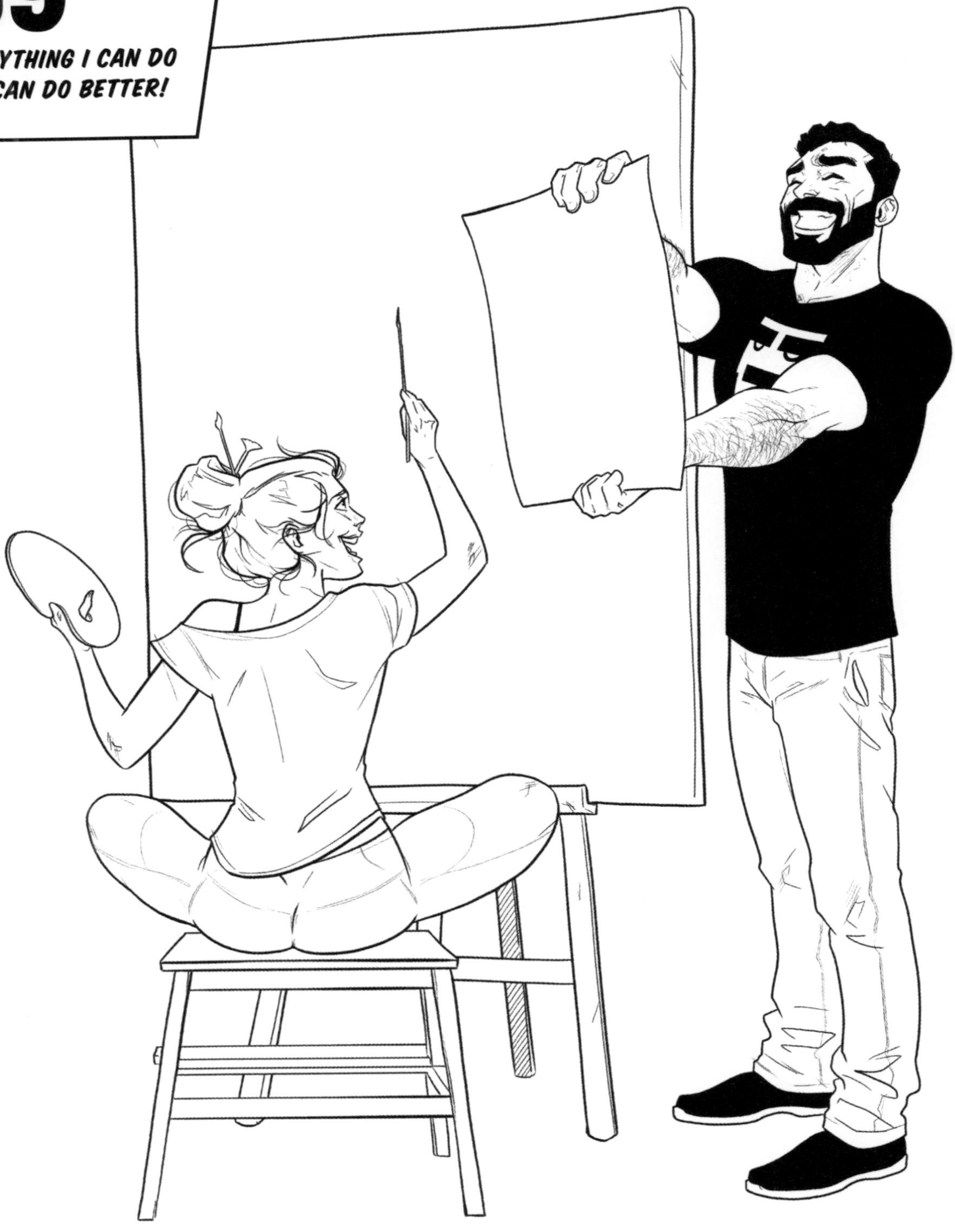

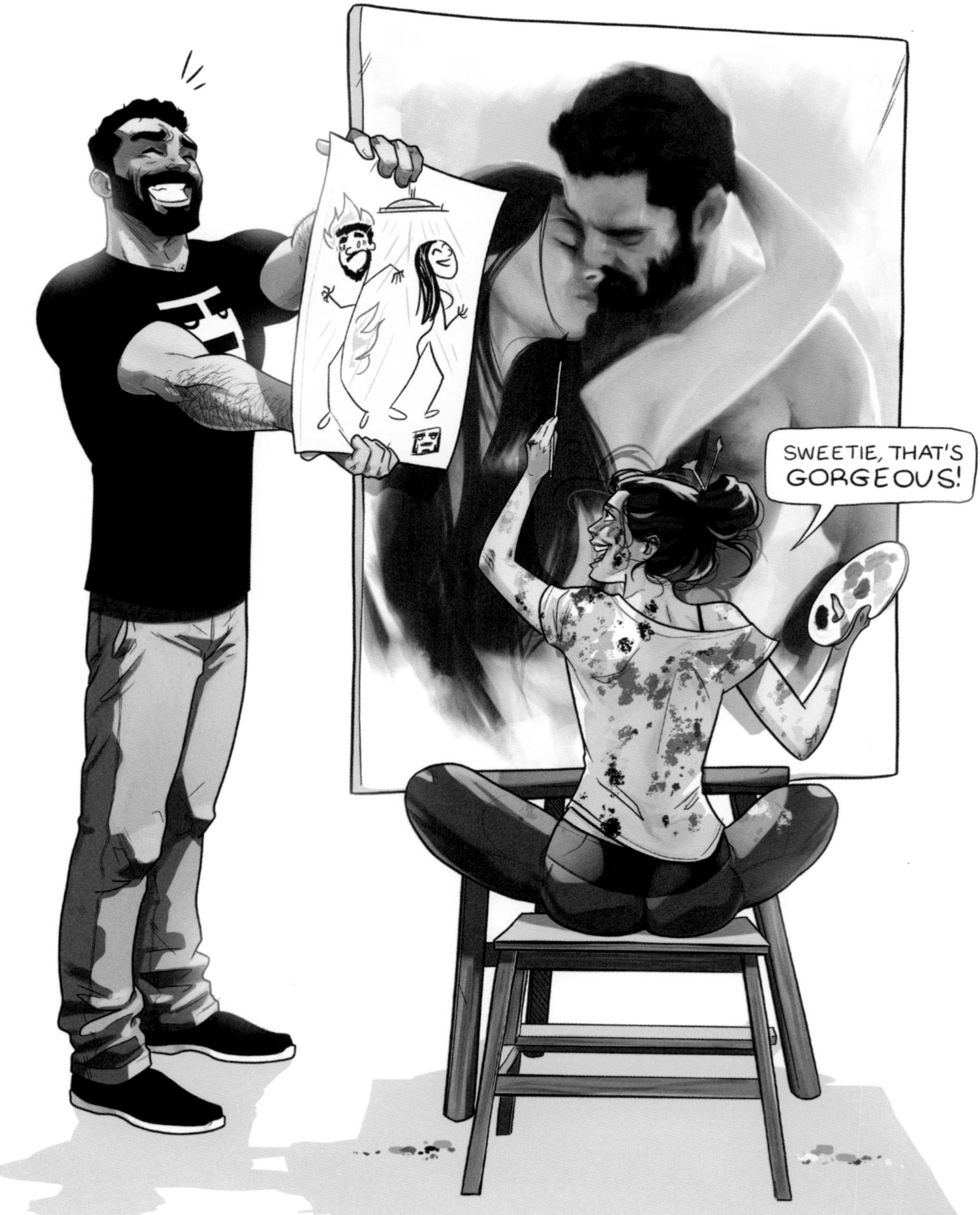
SWEETIE, THAT'S GORGEOUS!

60

NEW YEARZ-Z-Z EVE

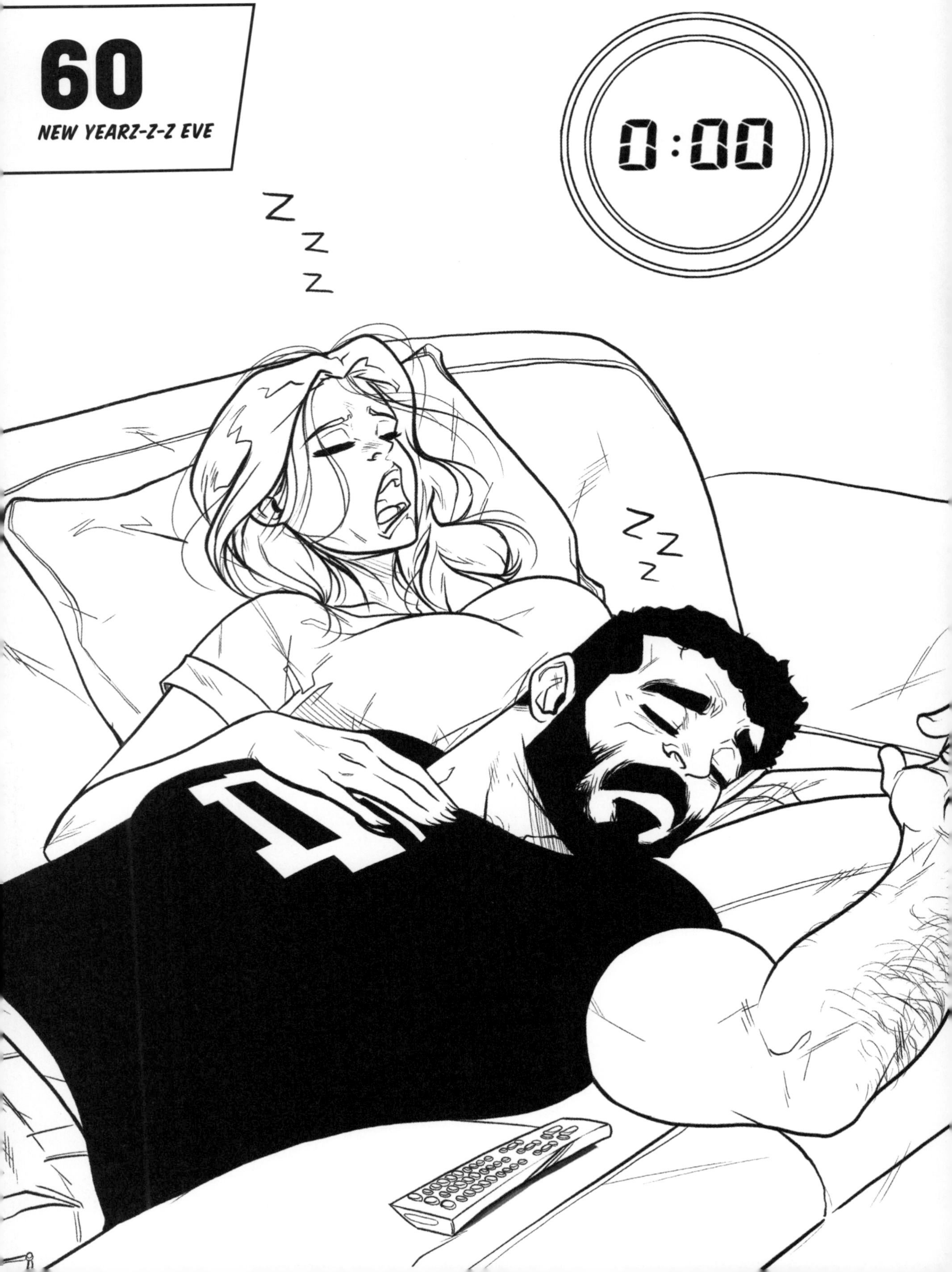
0:00
Z Z Z
Z Z Z

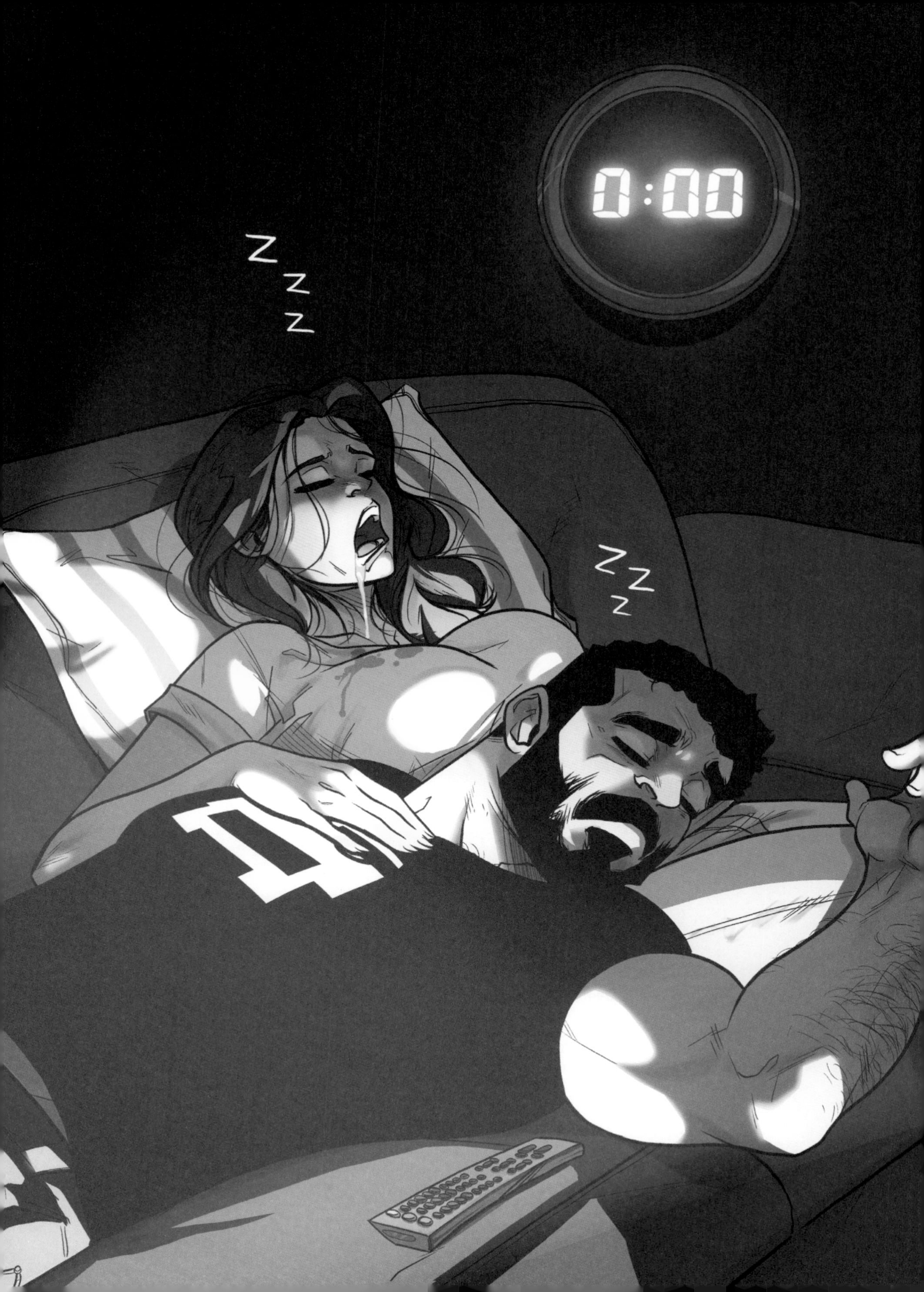
0:00
Z Z Z
Z Z Z

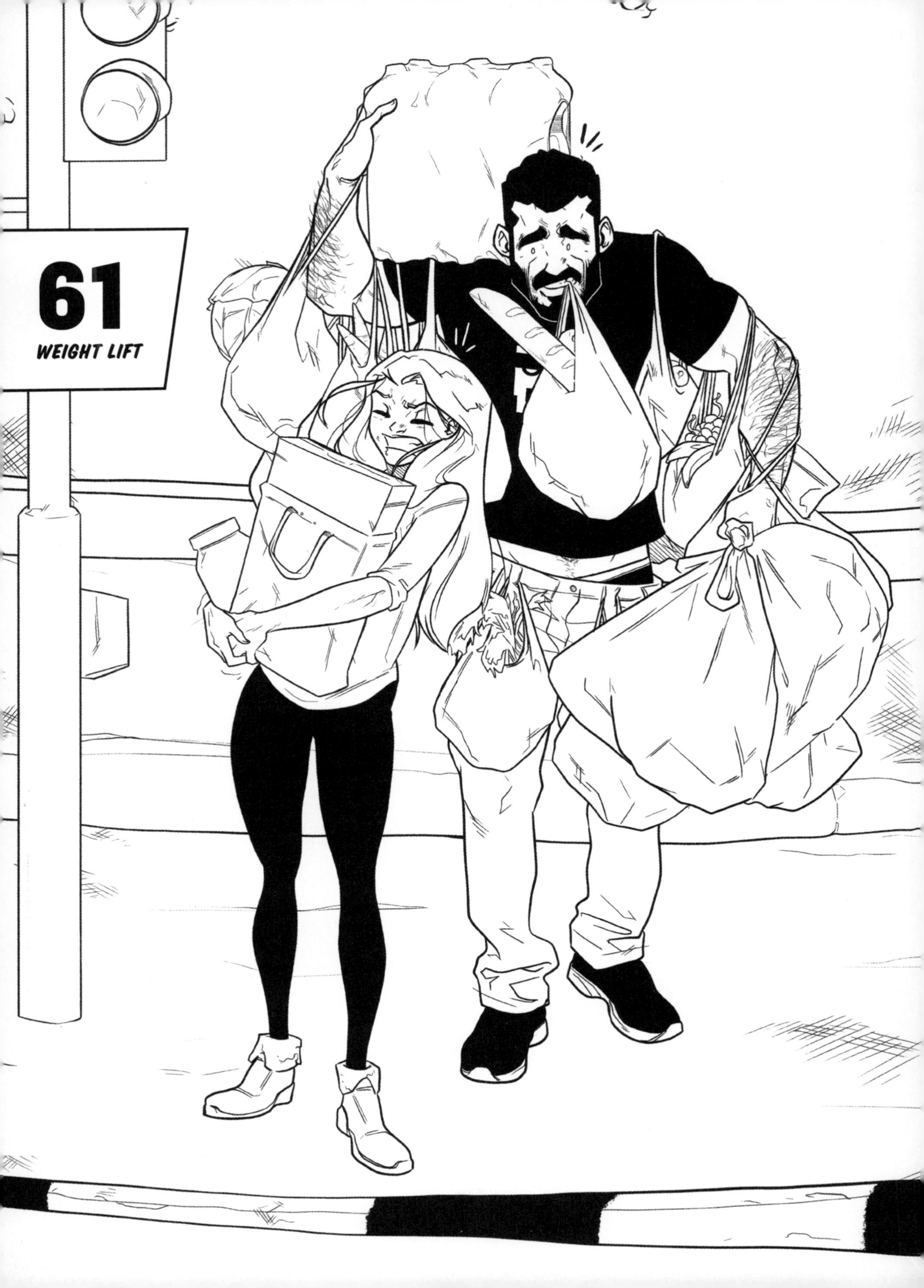
61
WEIGHT LIFT

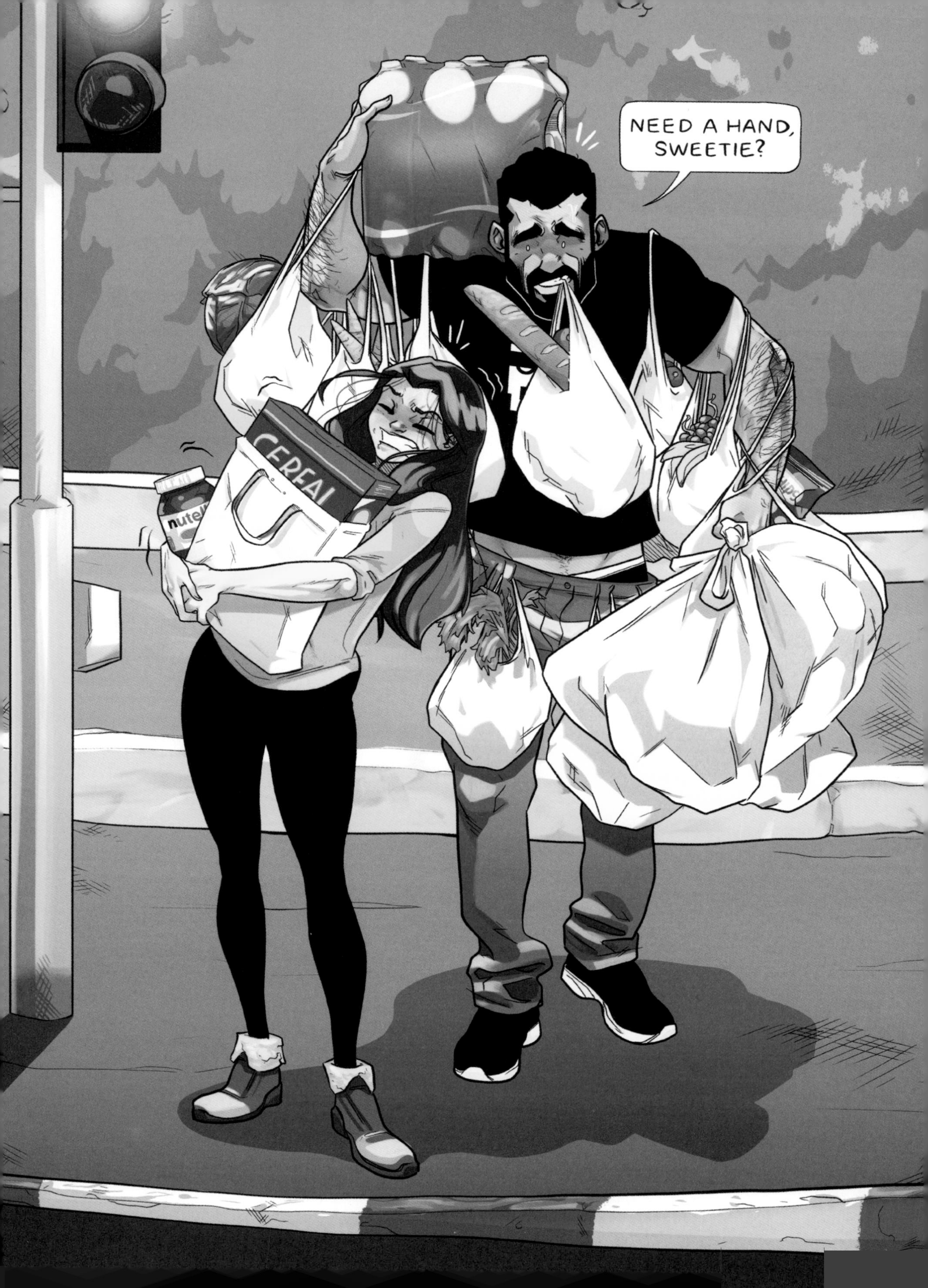
NEED A HAND, SWEETIE?
CEREAL
nutella

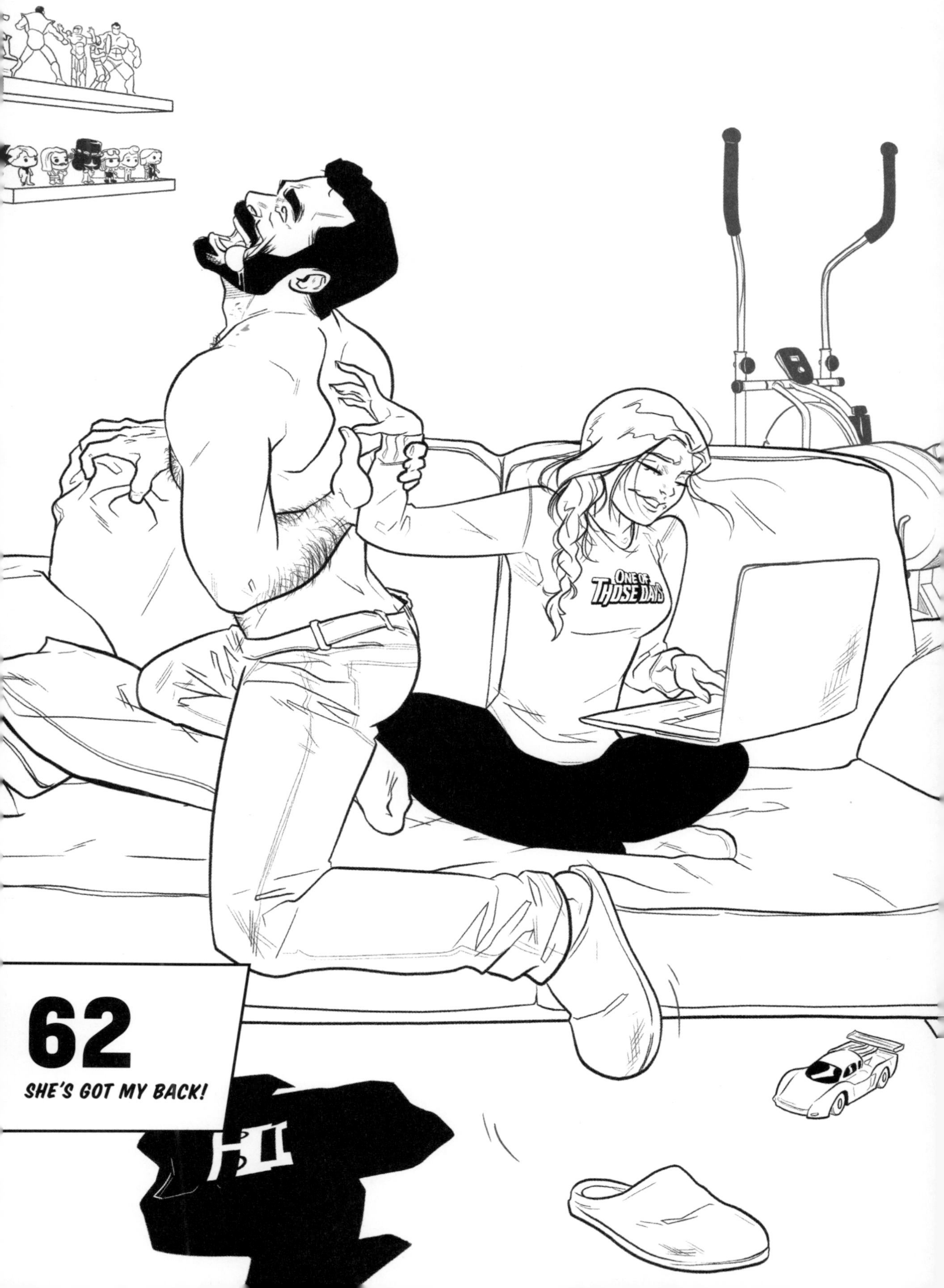
ONE OF
THOSE DAYS

62

SHE'S GOT MY BACK!

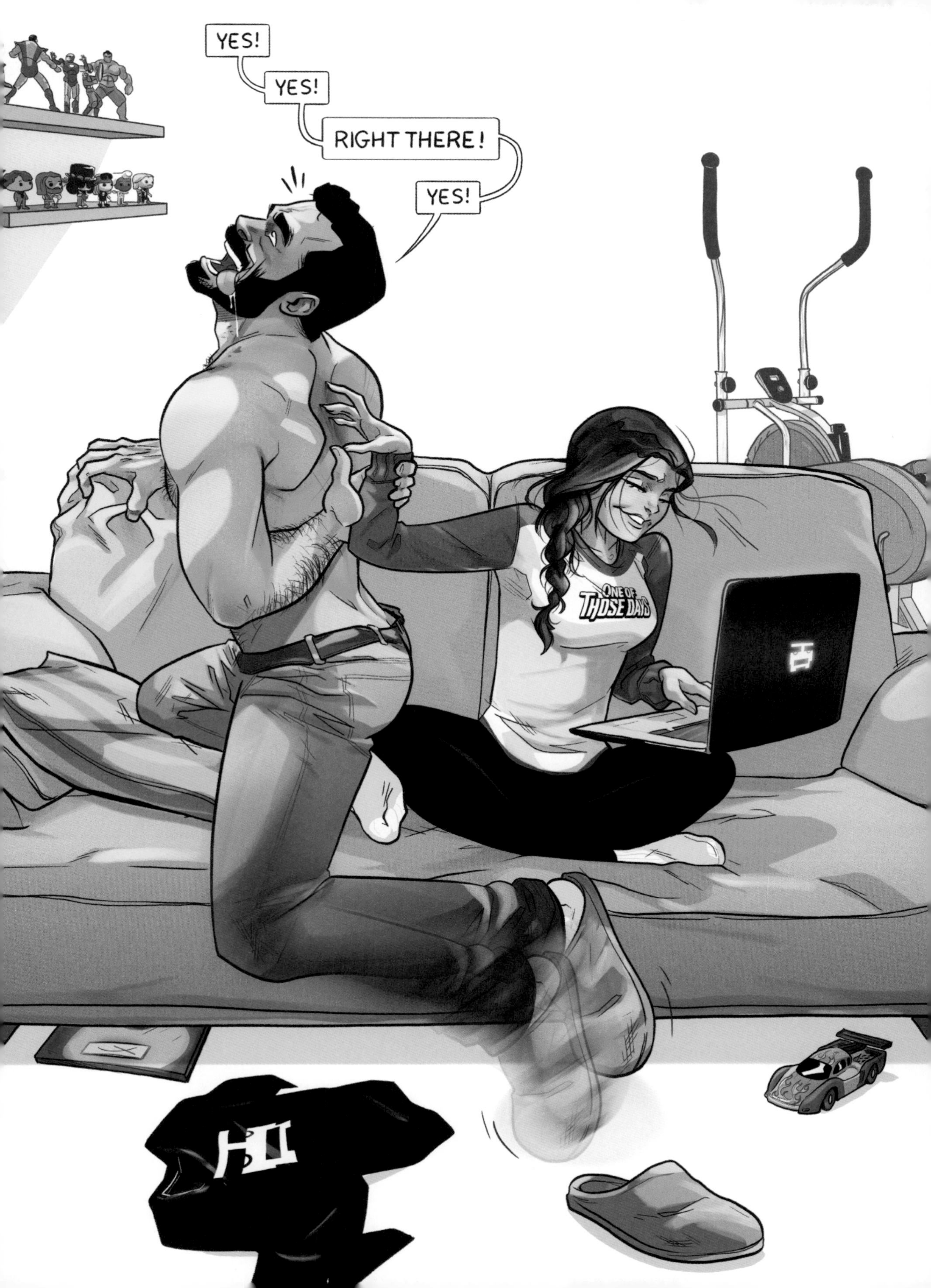
YES!
YES!
RIGHT THERE!
YES!
ONE OF THOSE DAYS

63

SERIES KILLER

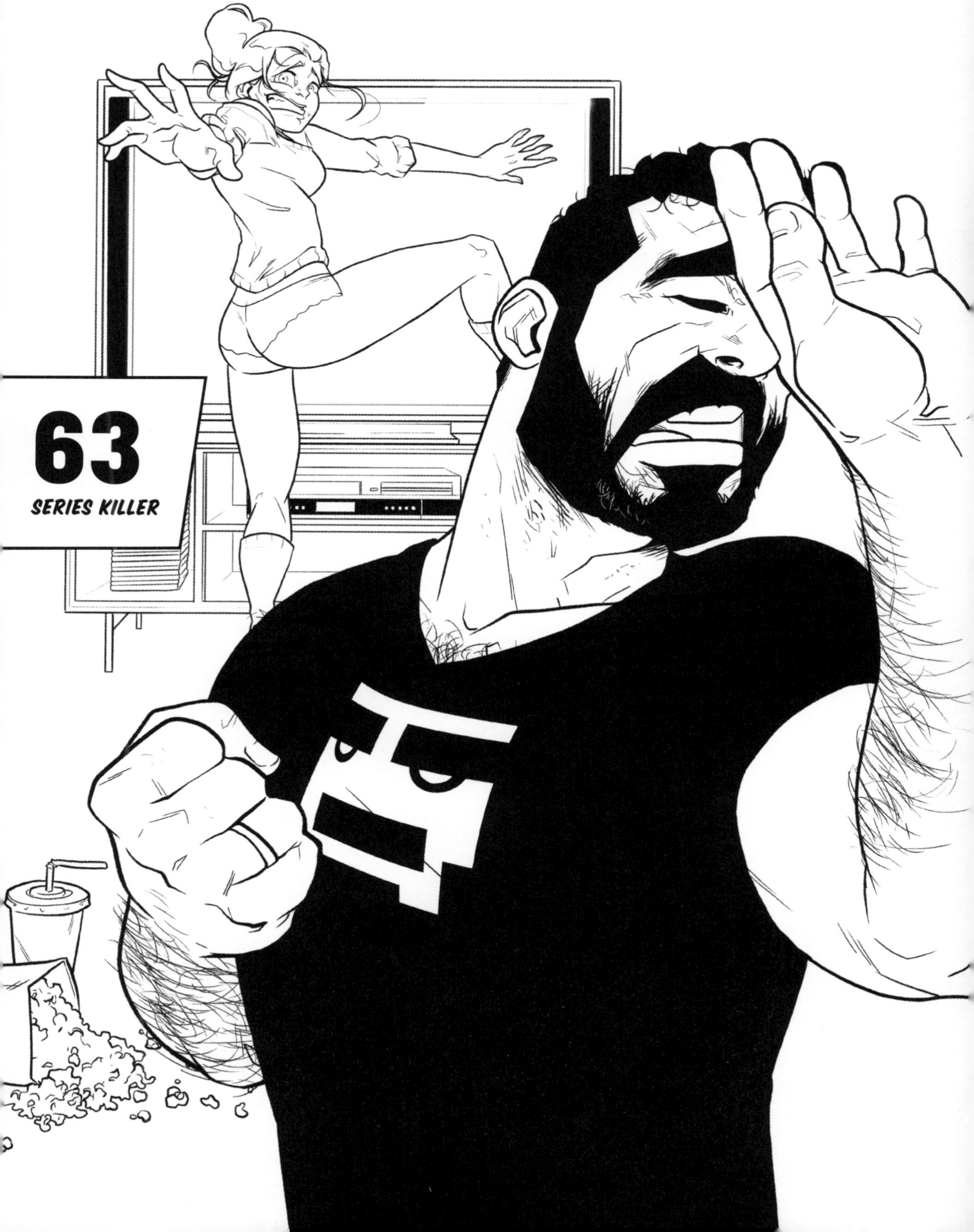

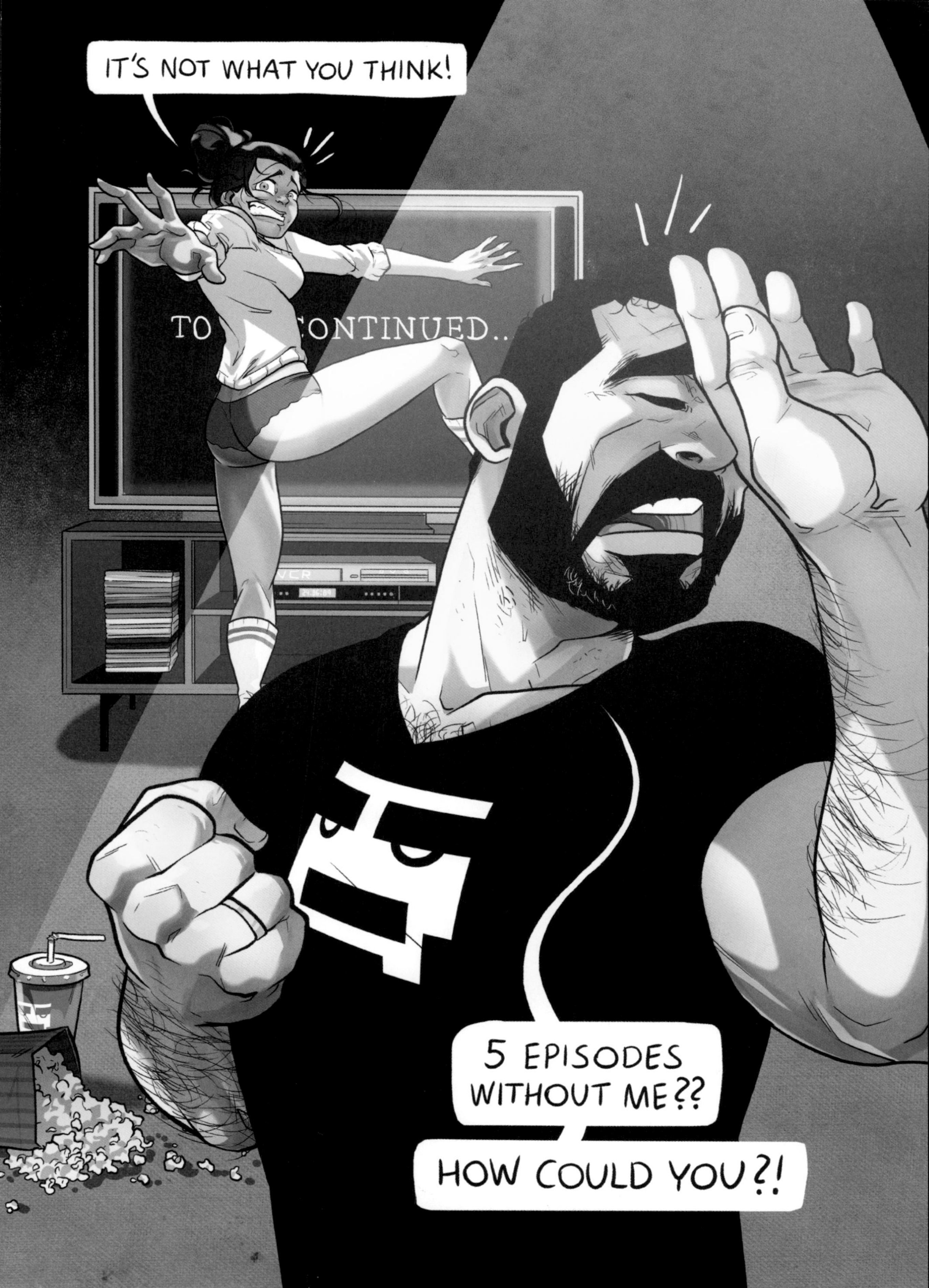
IT'S NOT WHAT YOU THINK!
5 EPISODES WITHOUT ME??
HOW COULD YOU?!

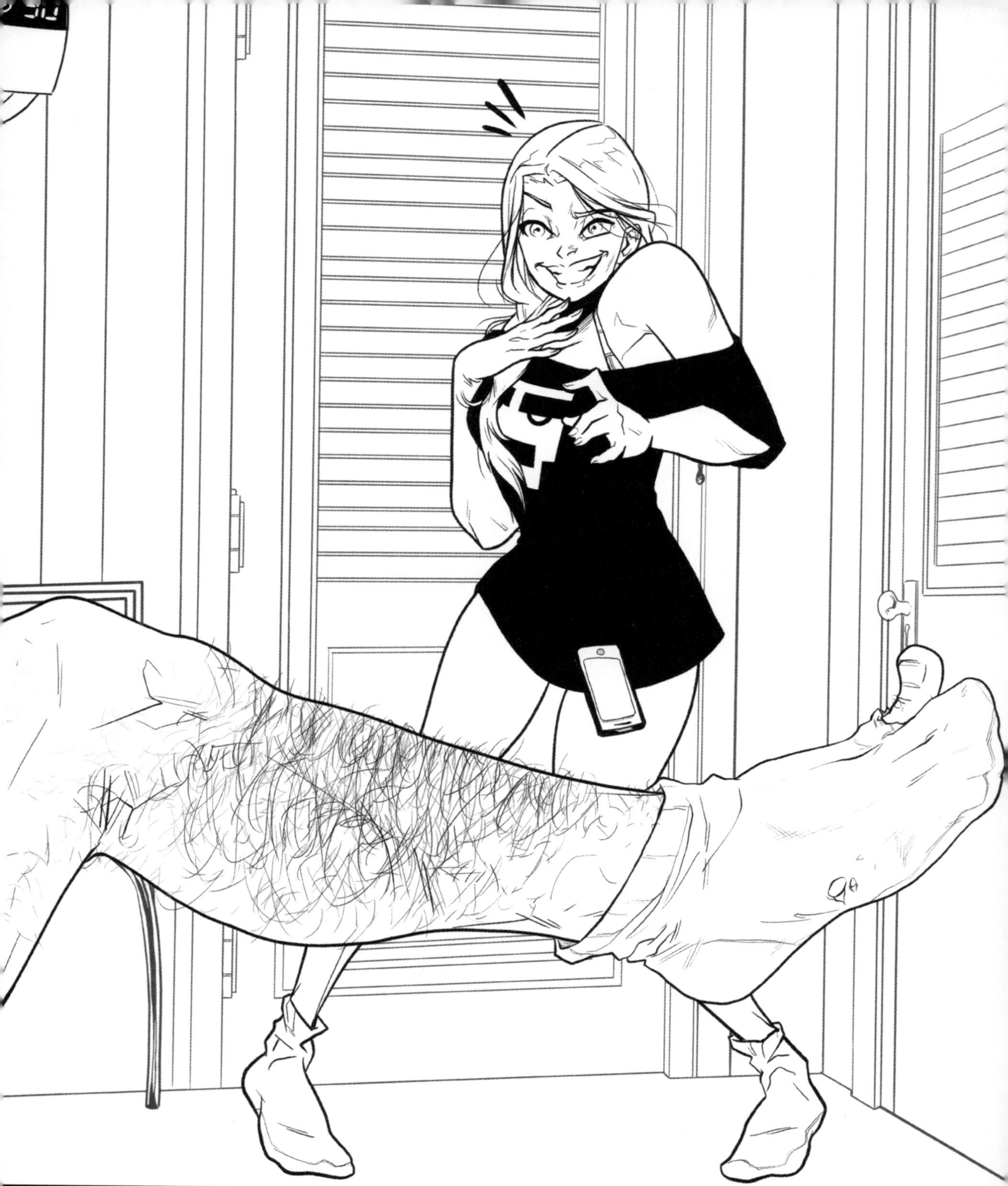

64

THE VALENTINE'S

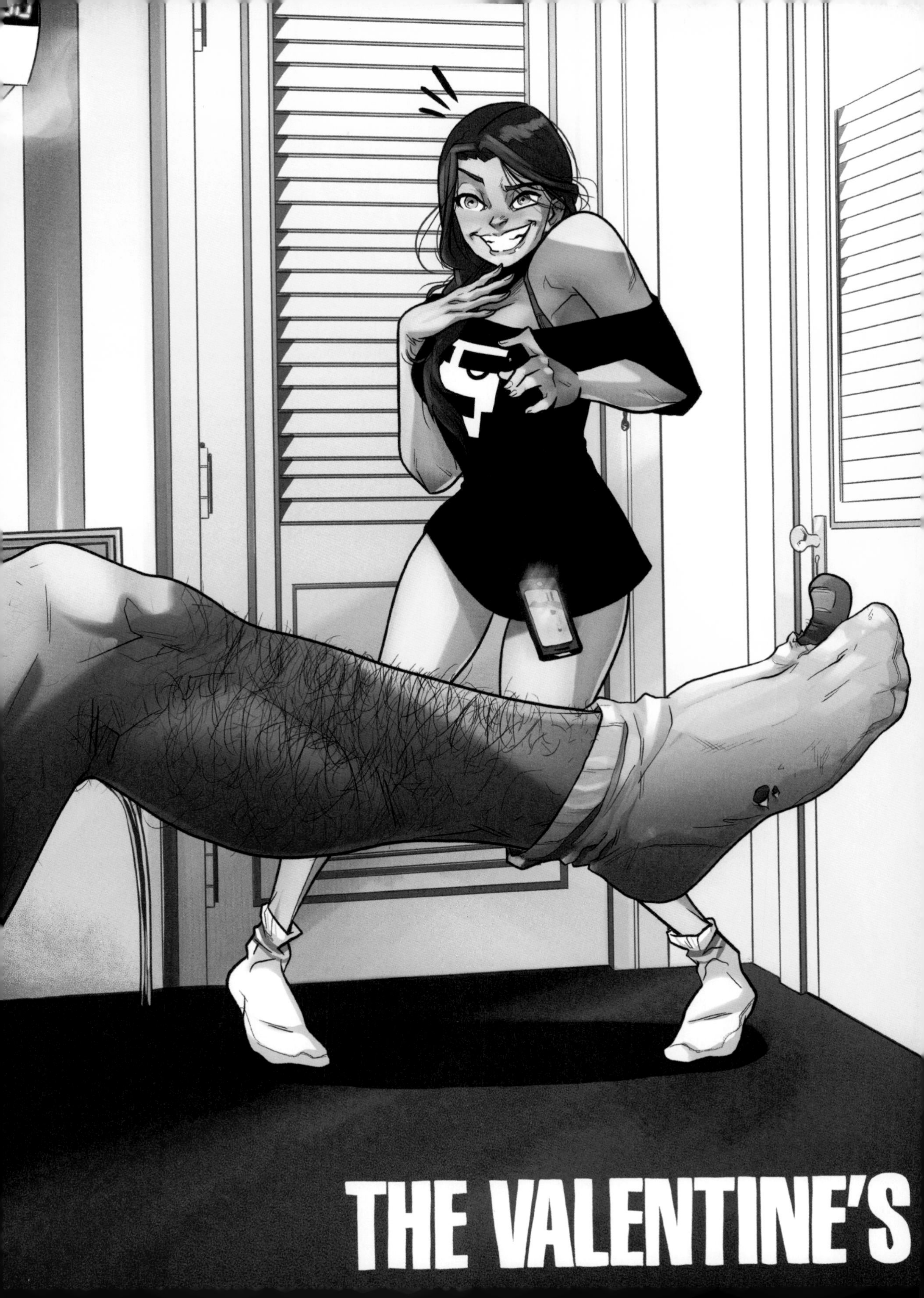
THE VALENTINE'S

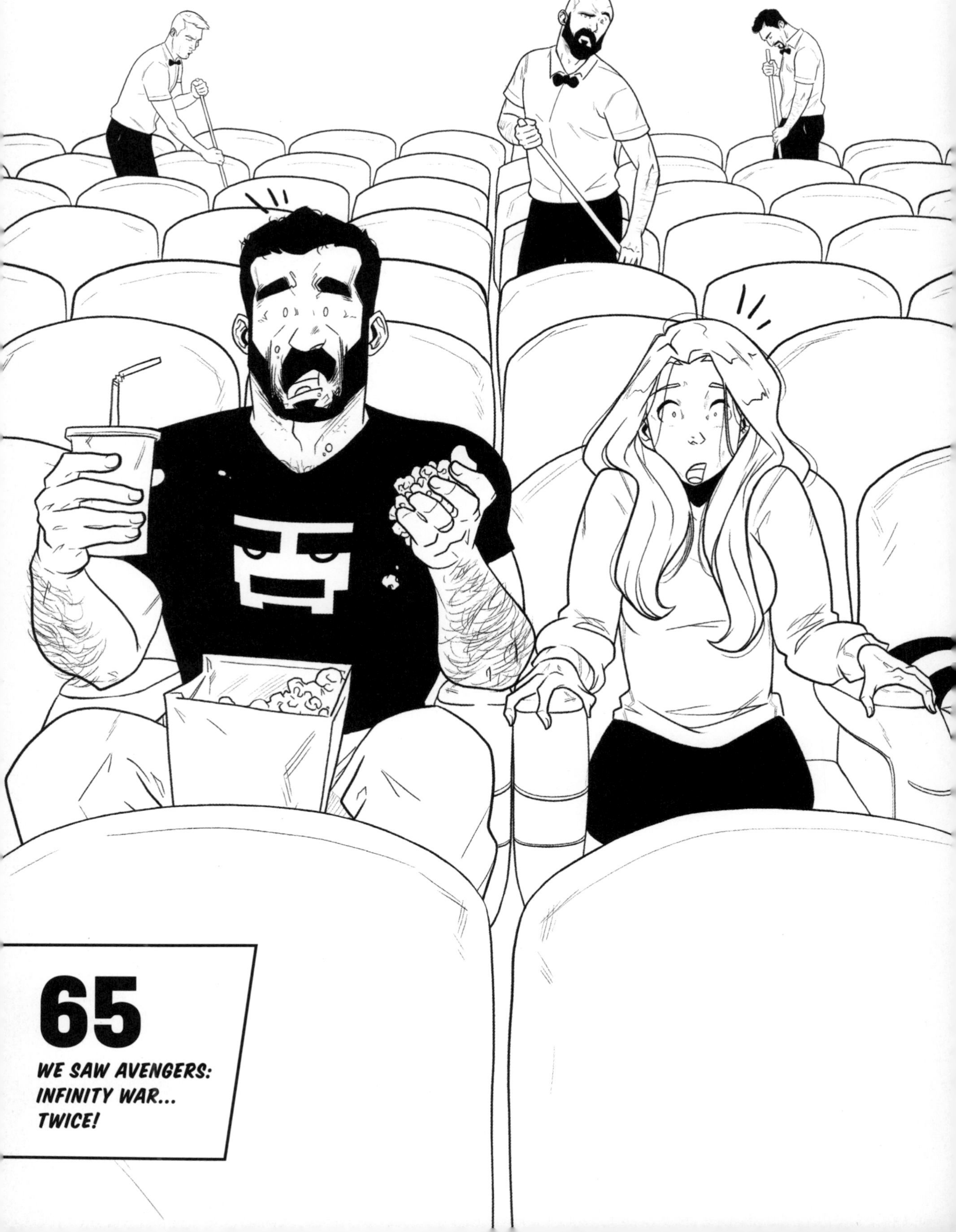

65

WE SAW AVENGERS: INFINITY WAR... TWICE!

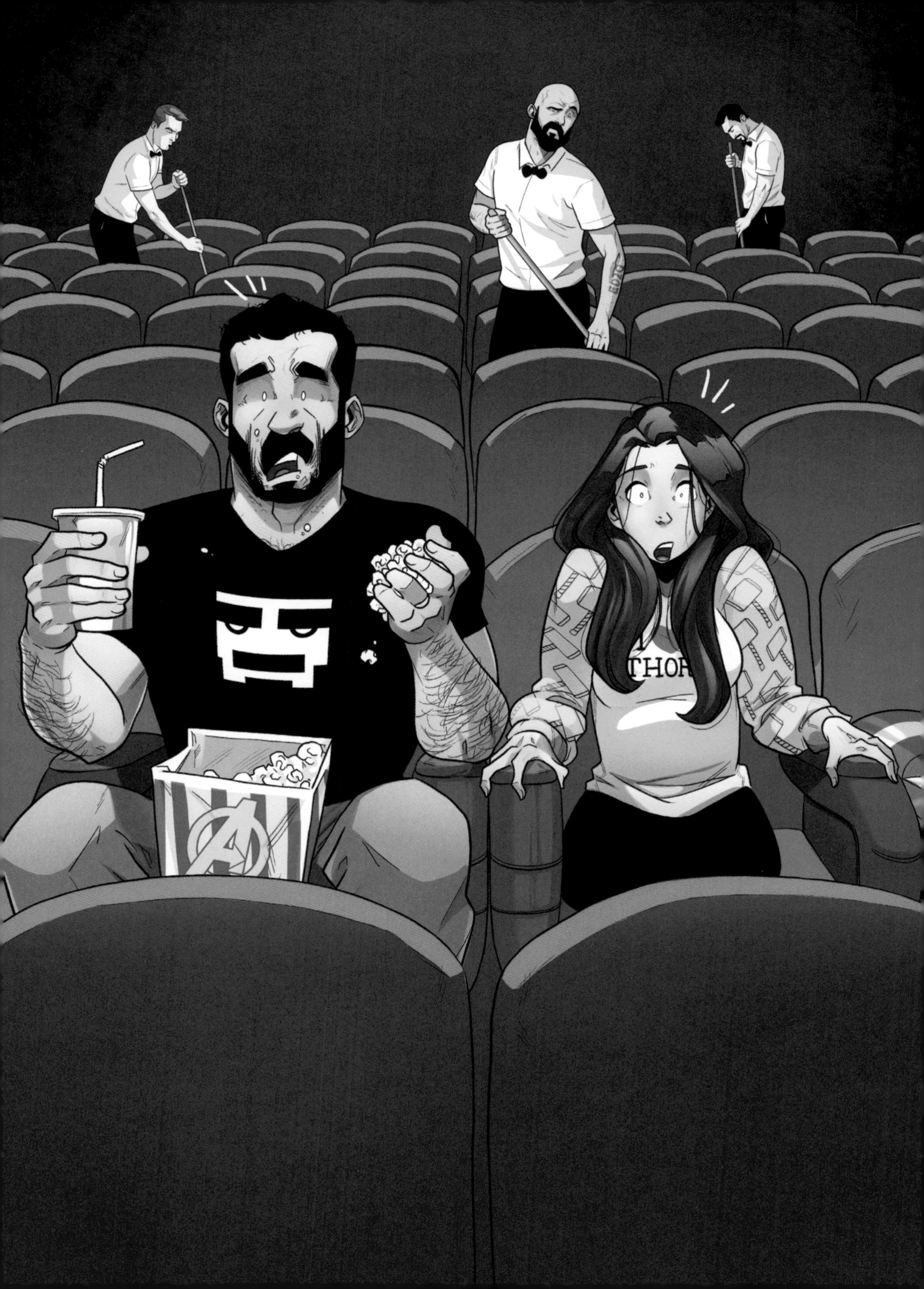
THOR

66

BABY FACE

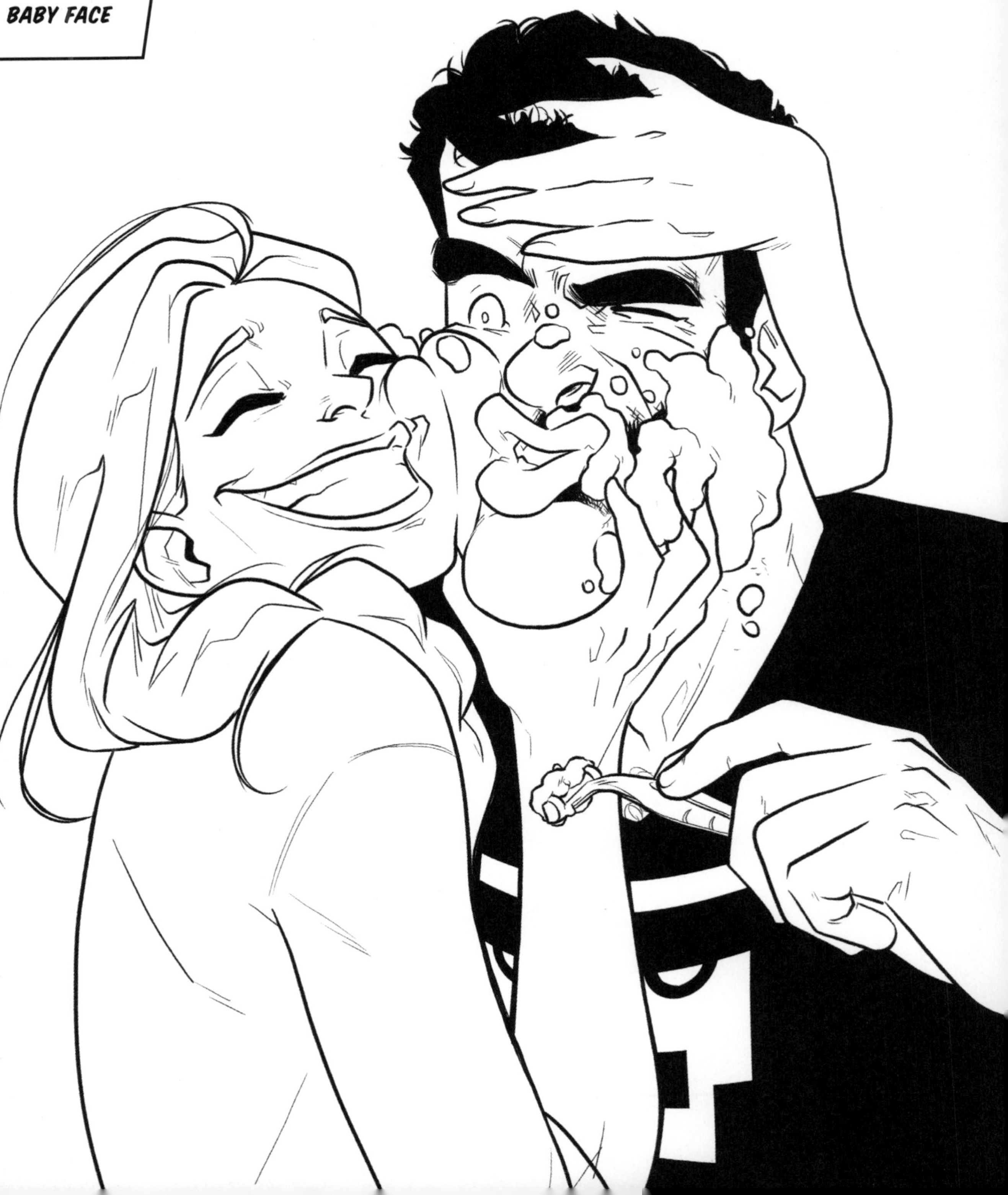

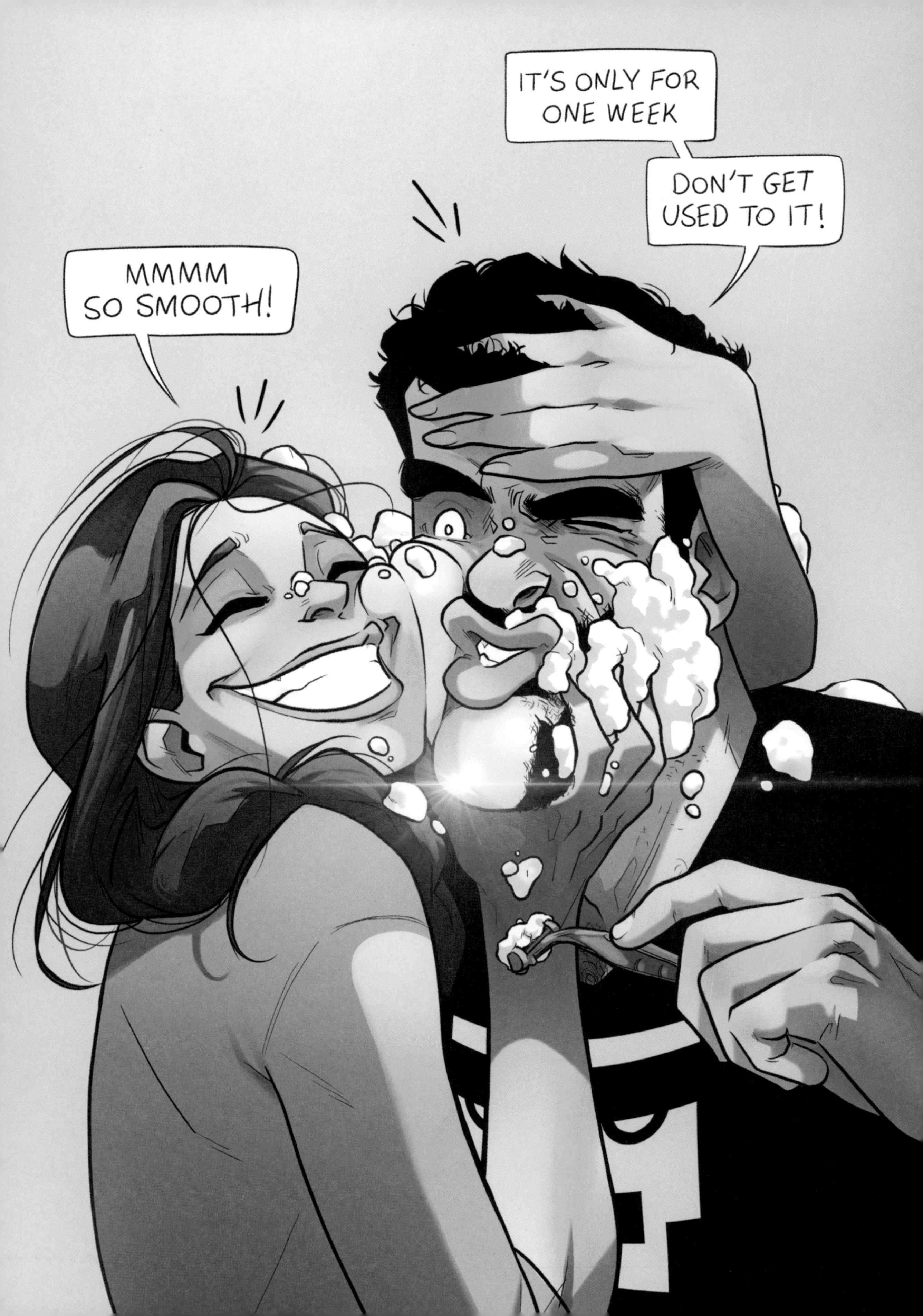
MMMM
SO SMOOTH!
IT'S ONLY FOR
ONE WEEK
DON'T GET
USED TO IT!

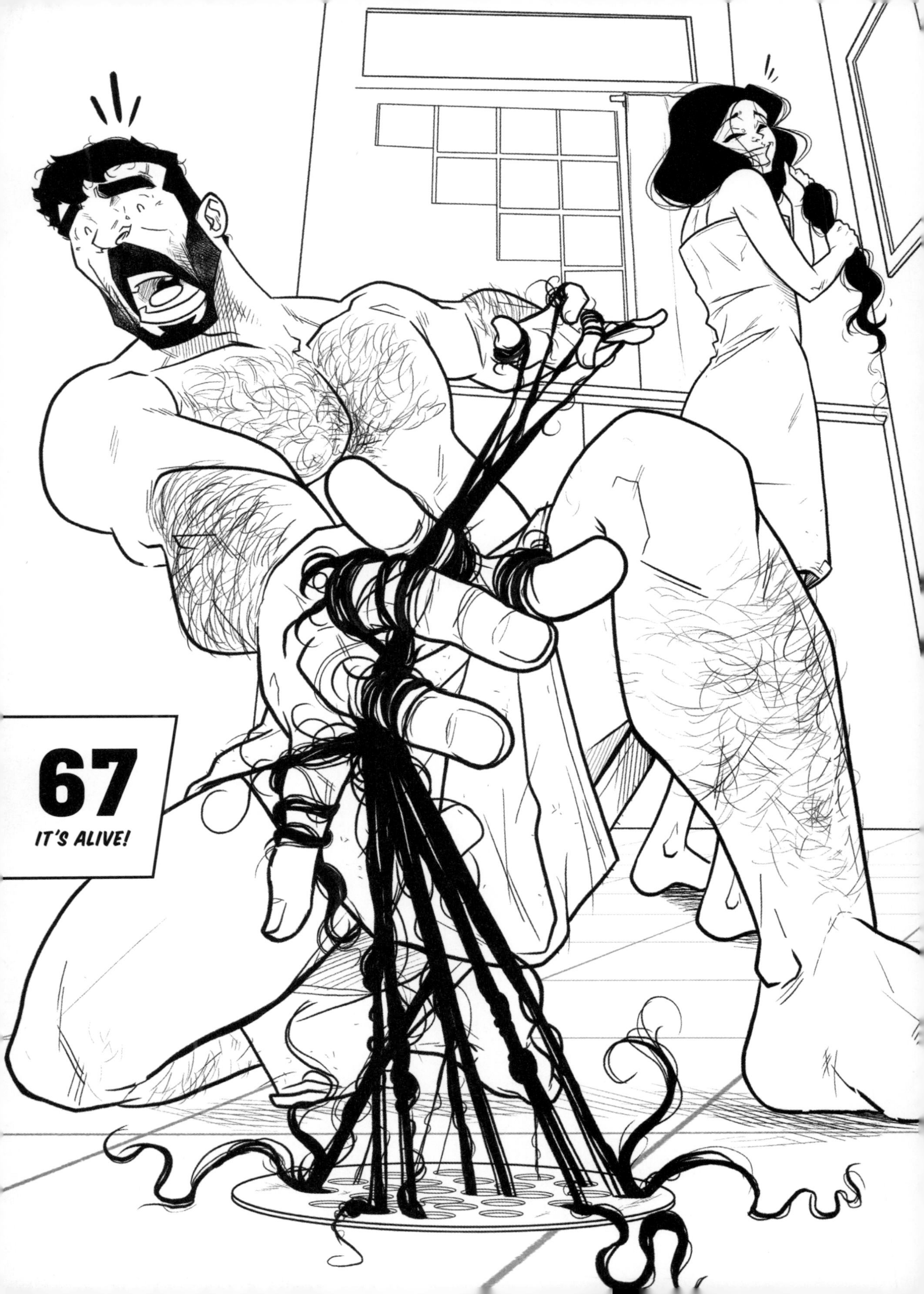

67

IT'S ALIVE!

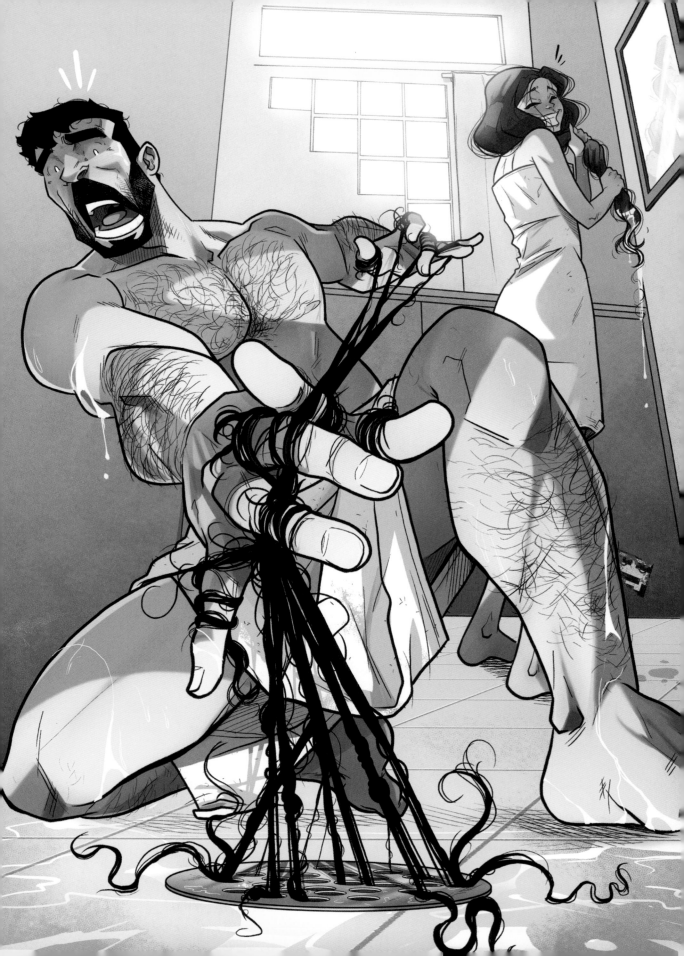

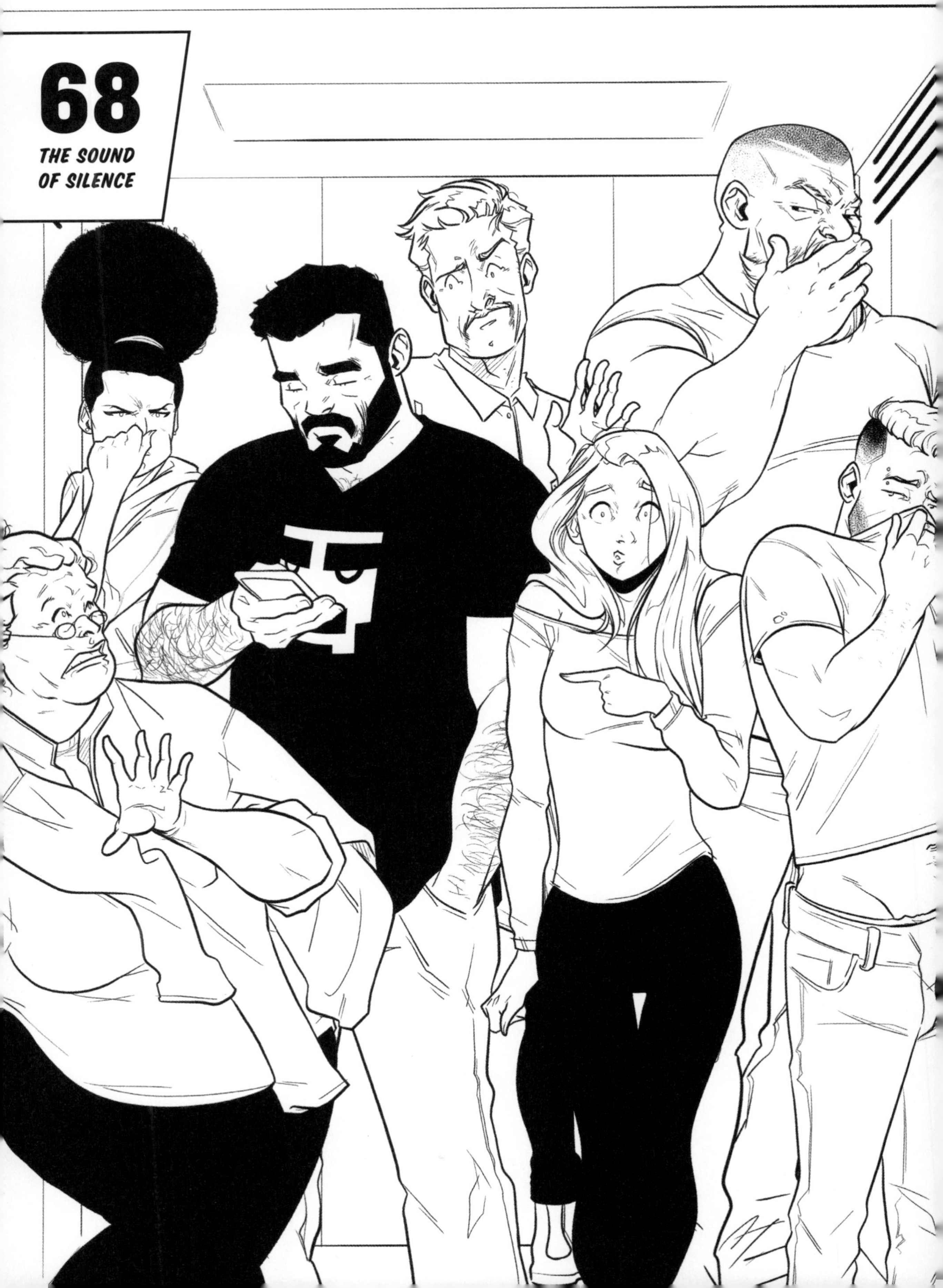
68
THE SOUND
OF SILENCE

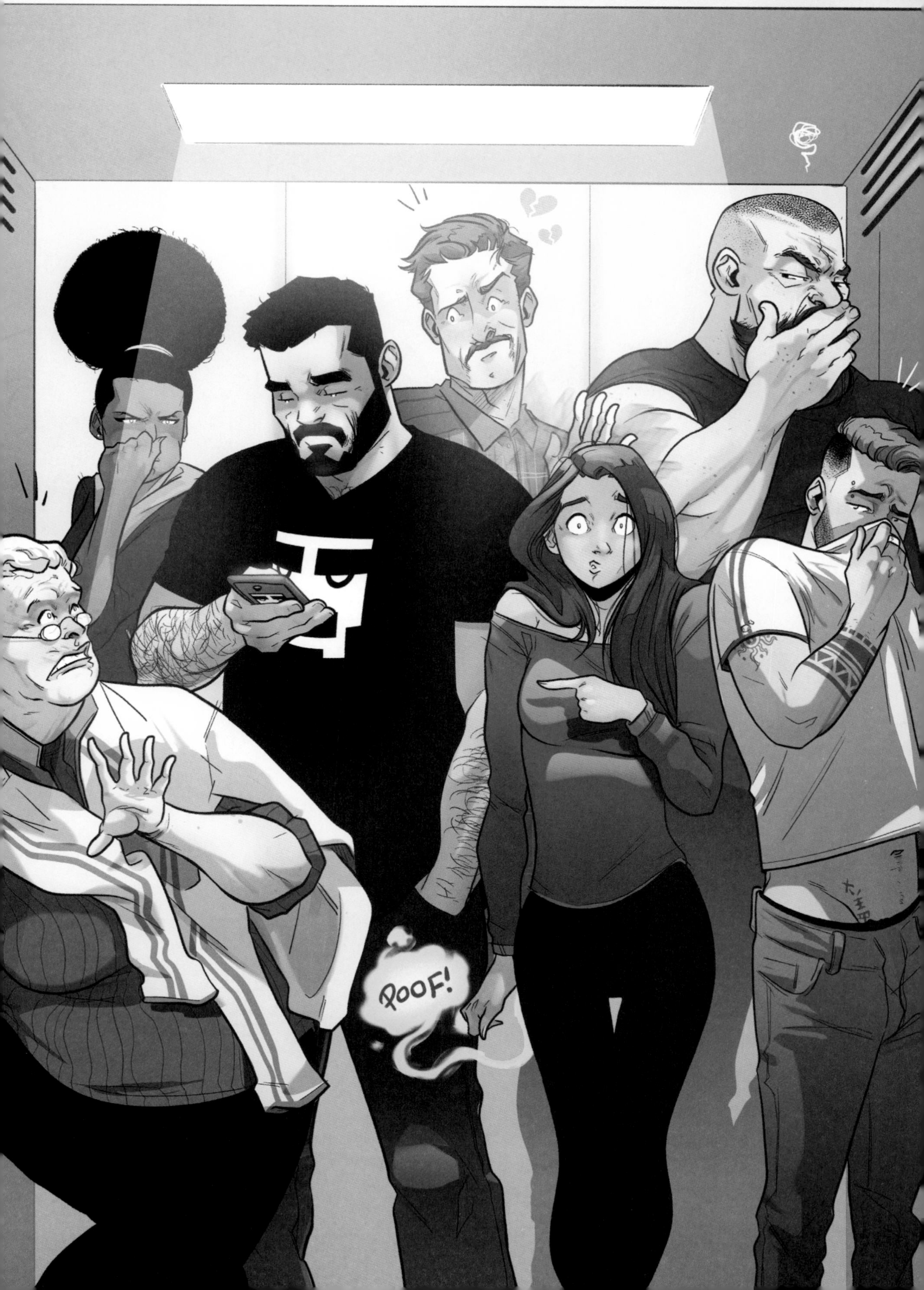
POOF!

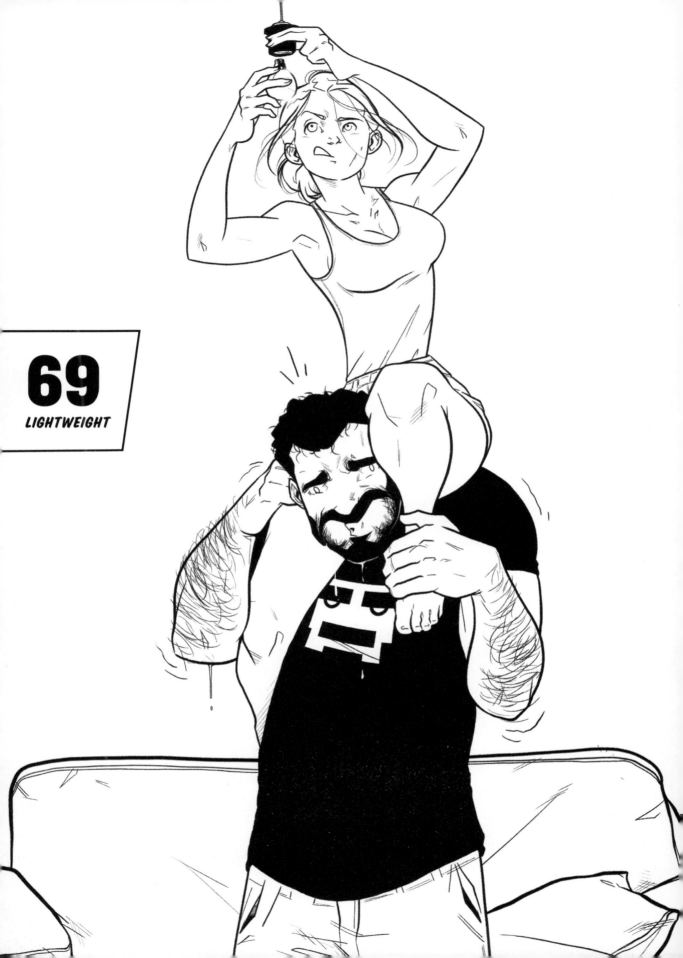

69

LIGHTWEIGHT

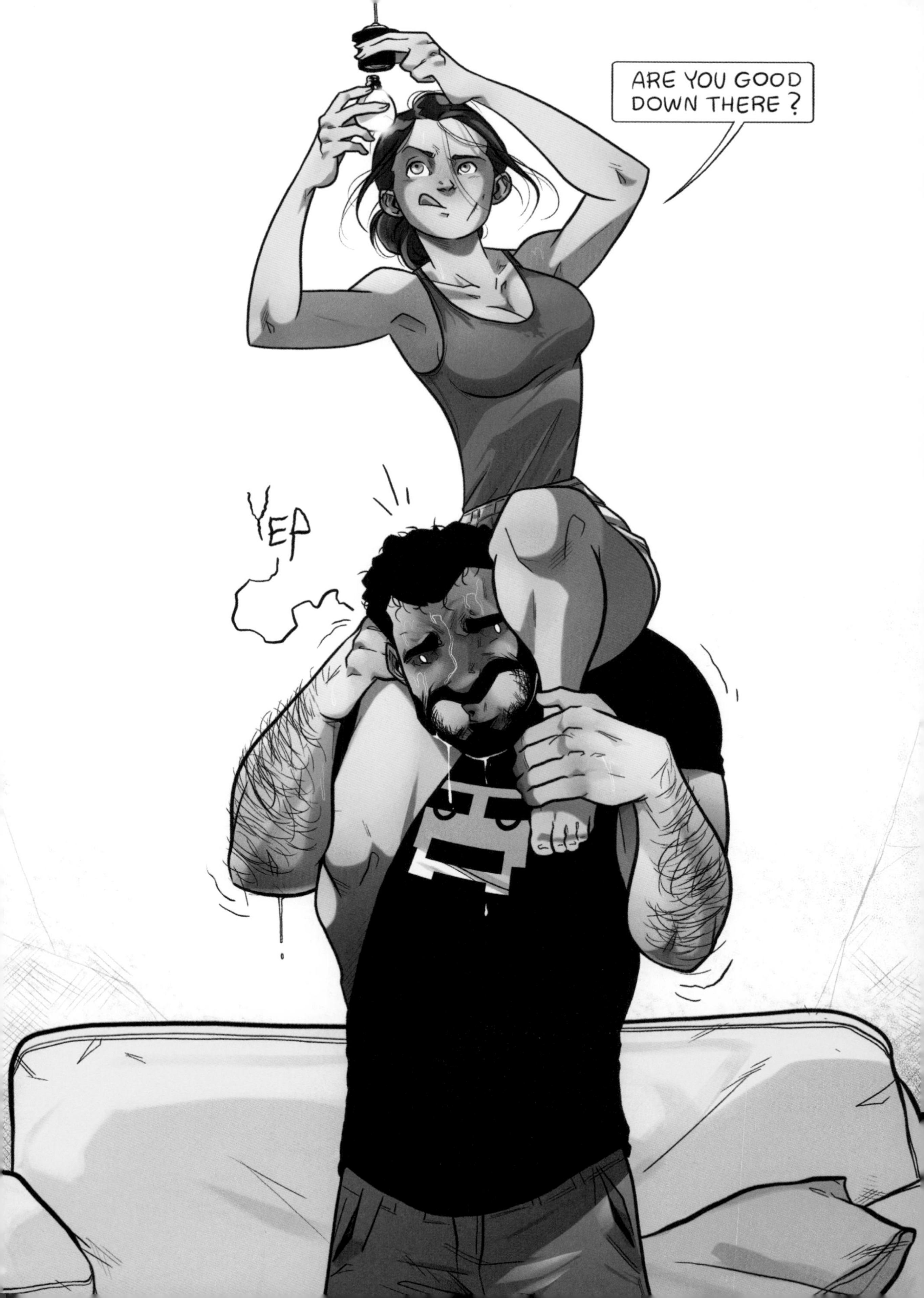
ARE YOU GOOD DOWN THERE?
YEP

70

UNHAPPY ENDING

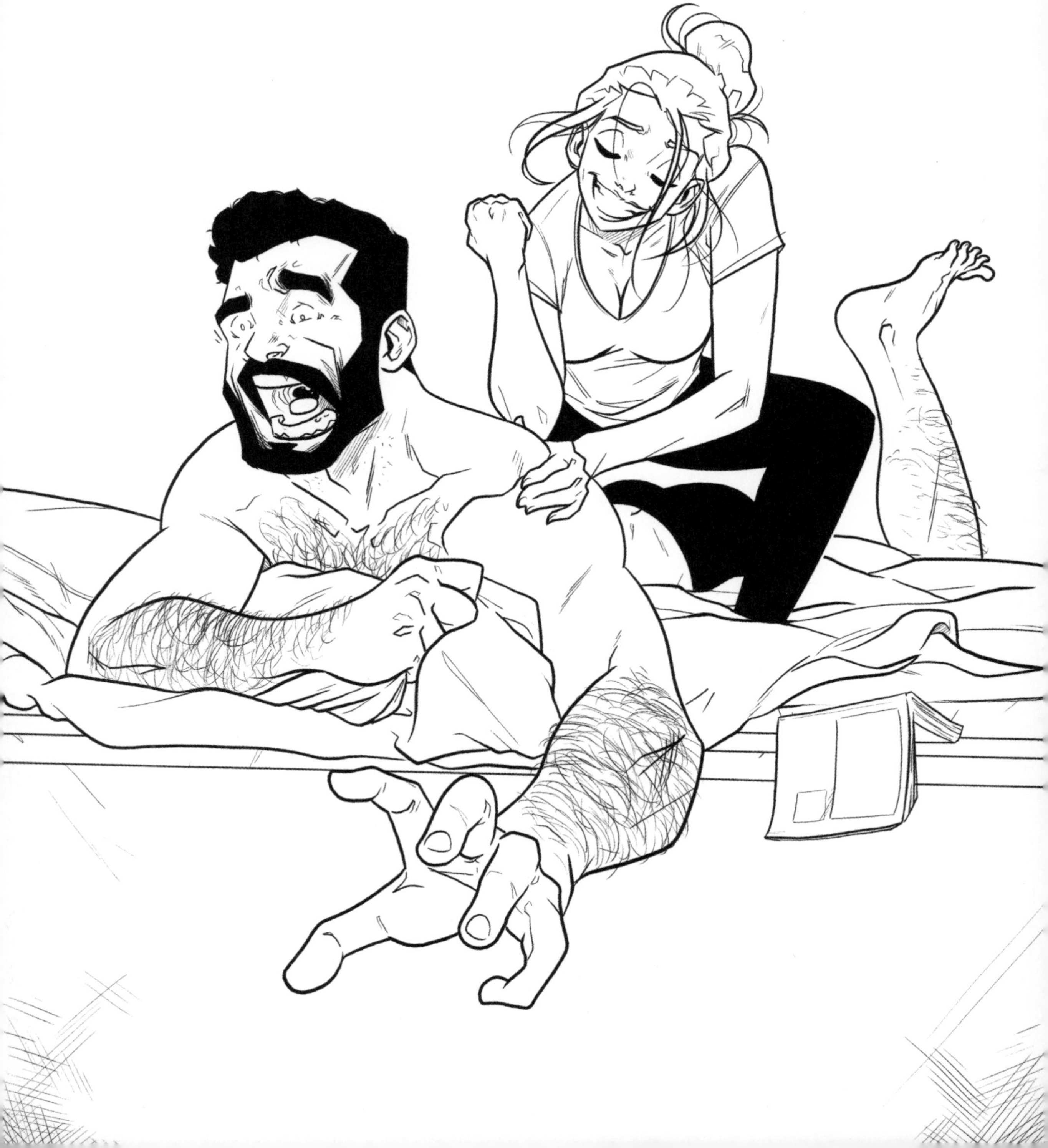

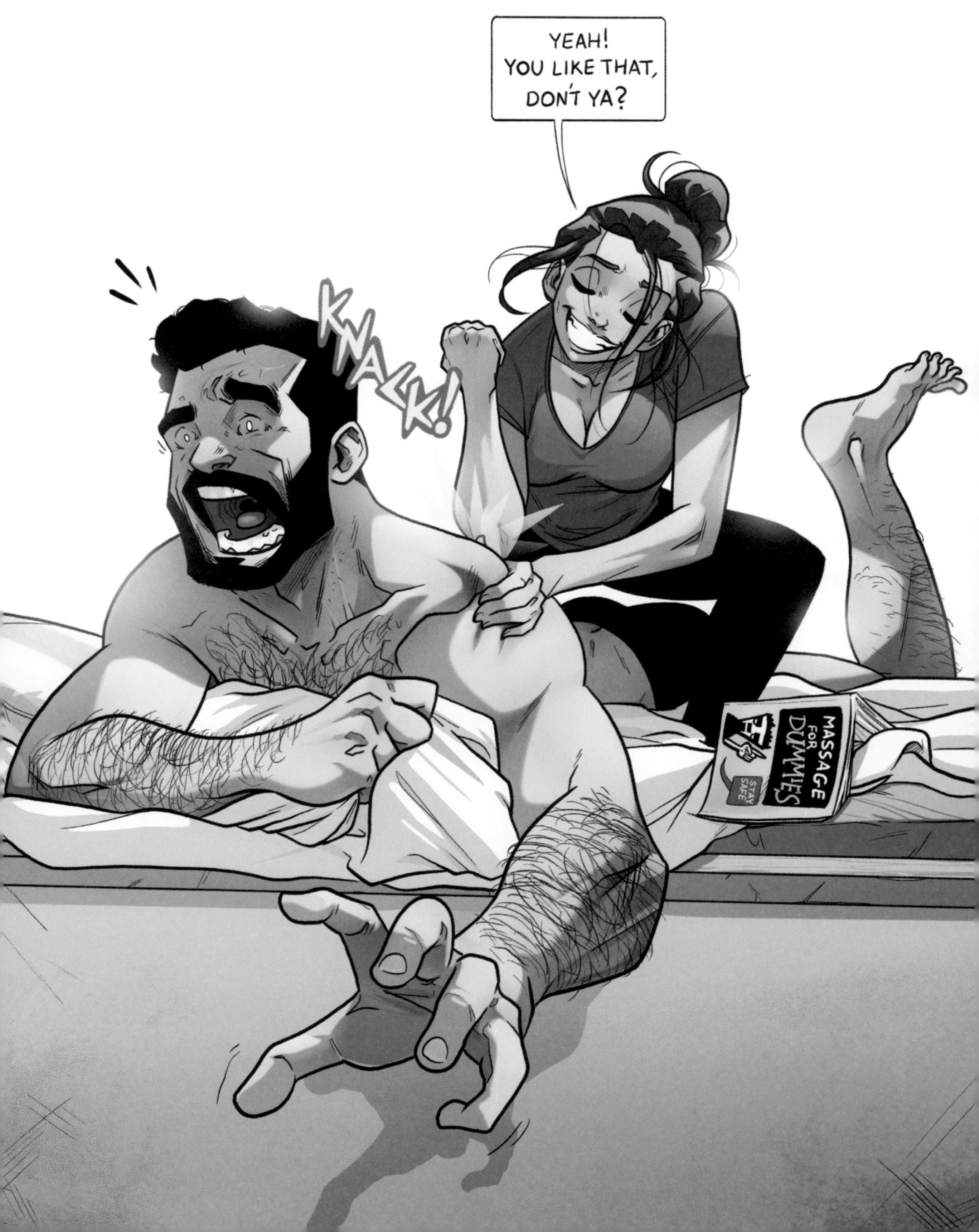
YEAH! YOU LIKE THAT, DON'T YA?
KNACK!
MASSAGE FOR DUMMIES
STAY SAFE

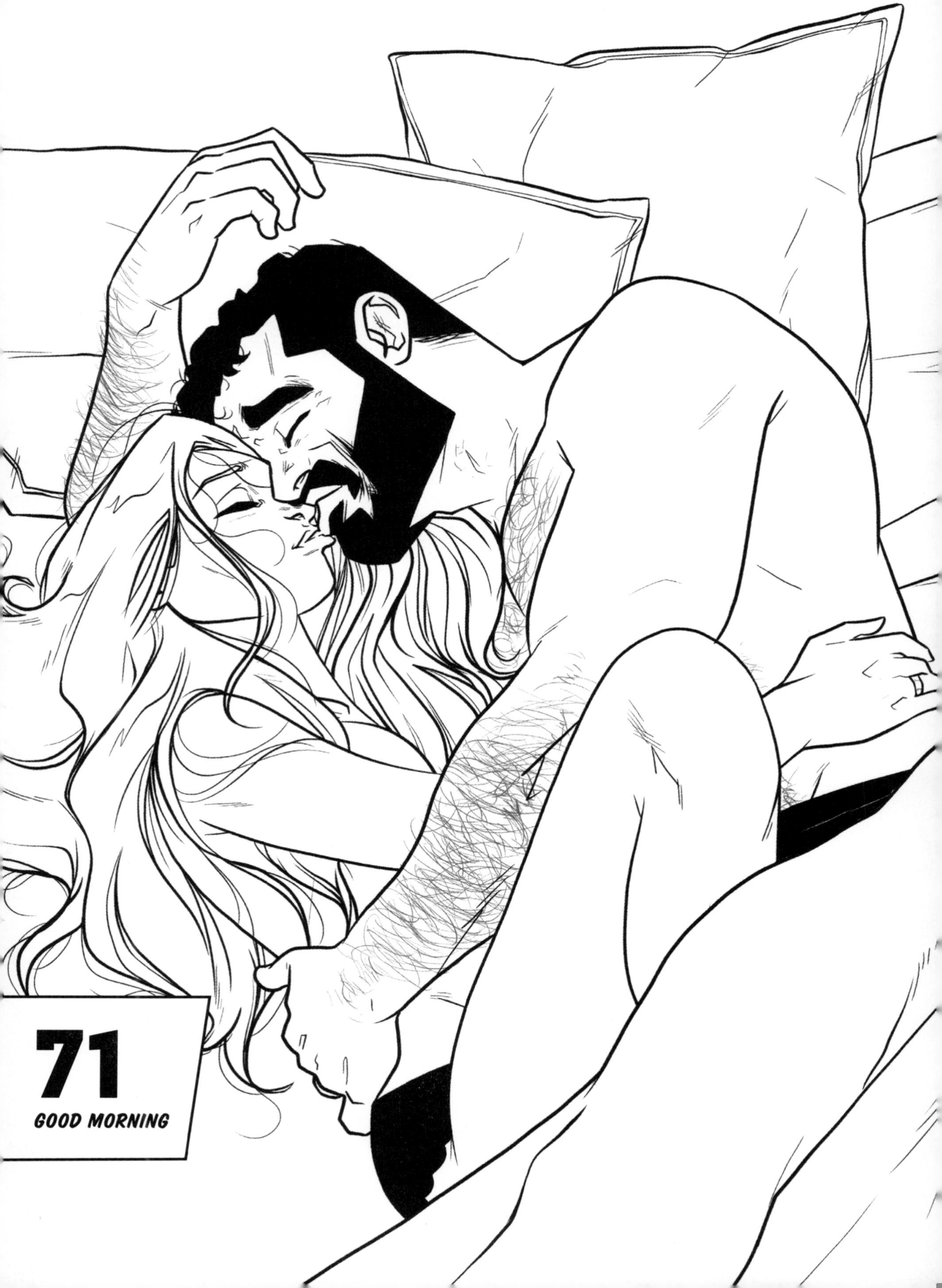

71

GOOD MORNING

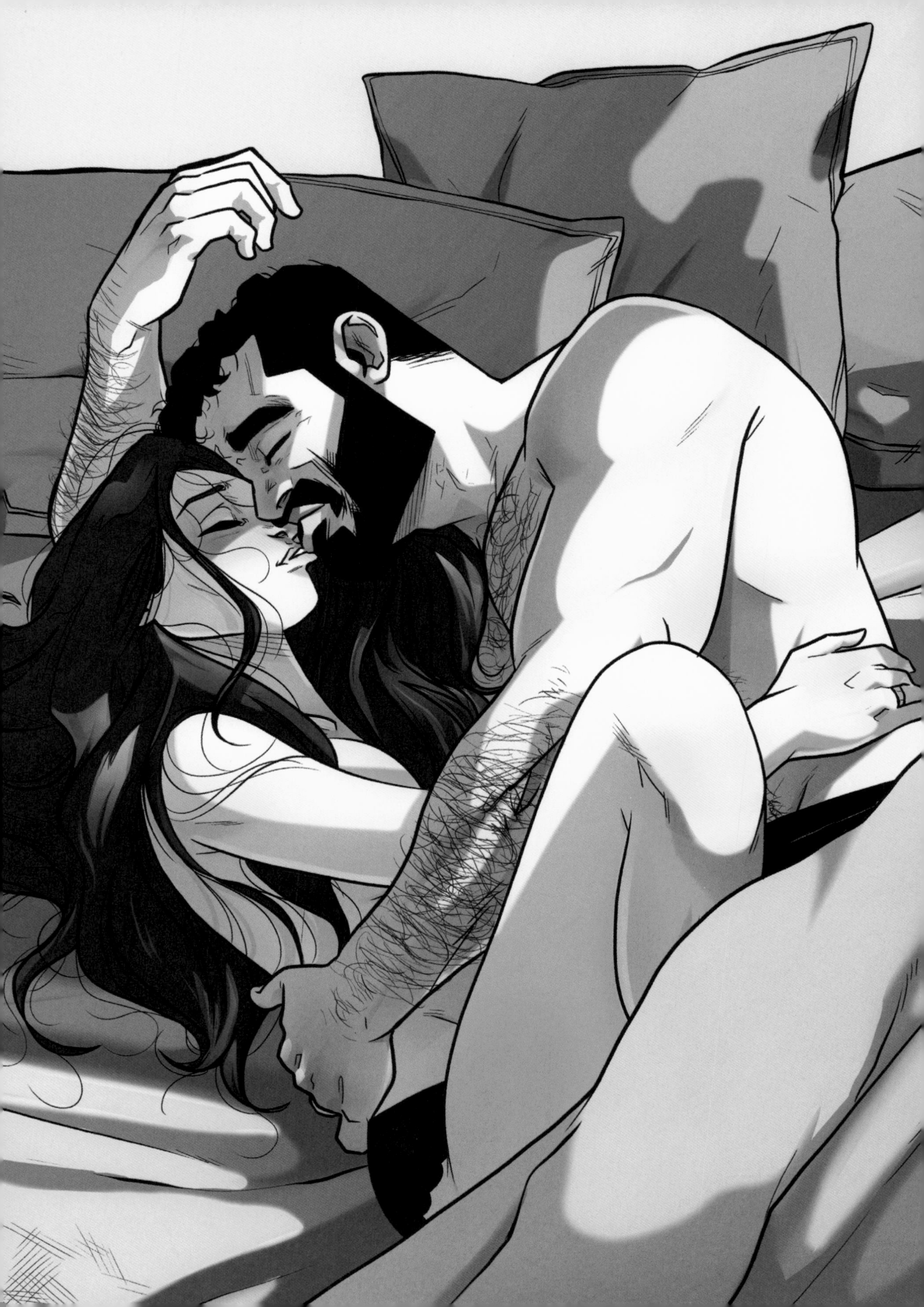

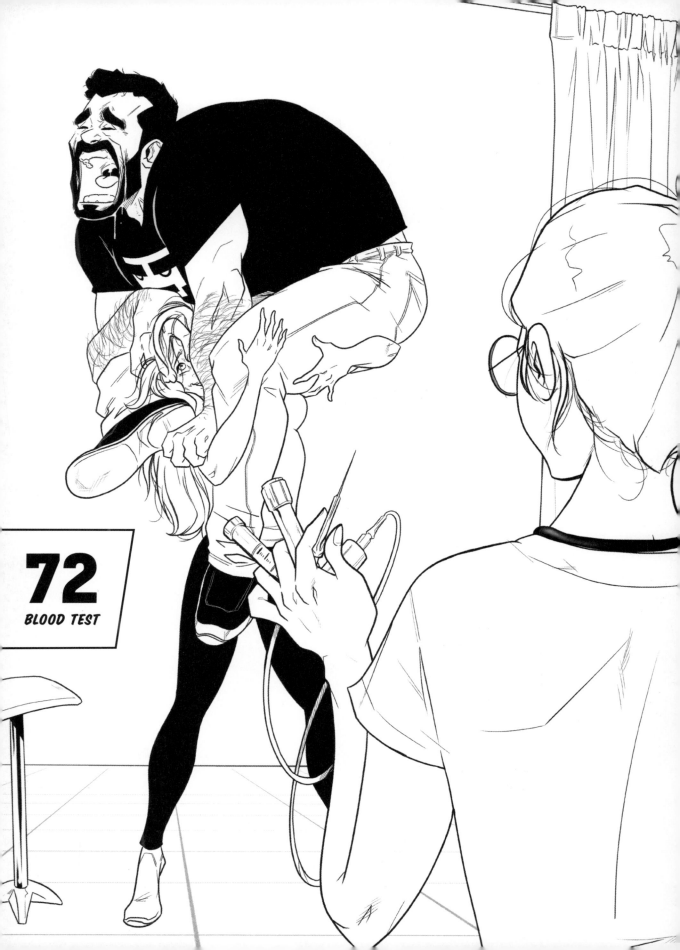

72
BLOOD TEST

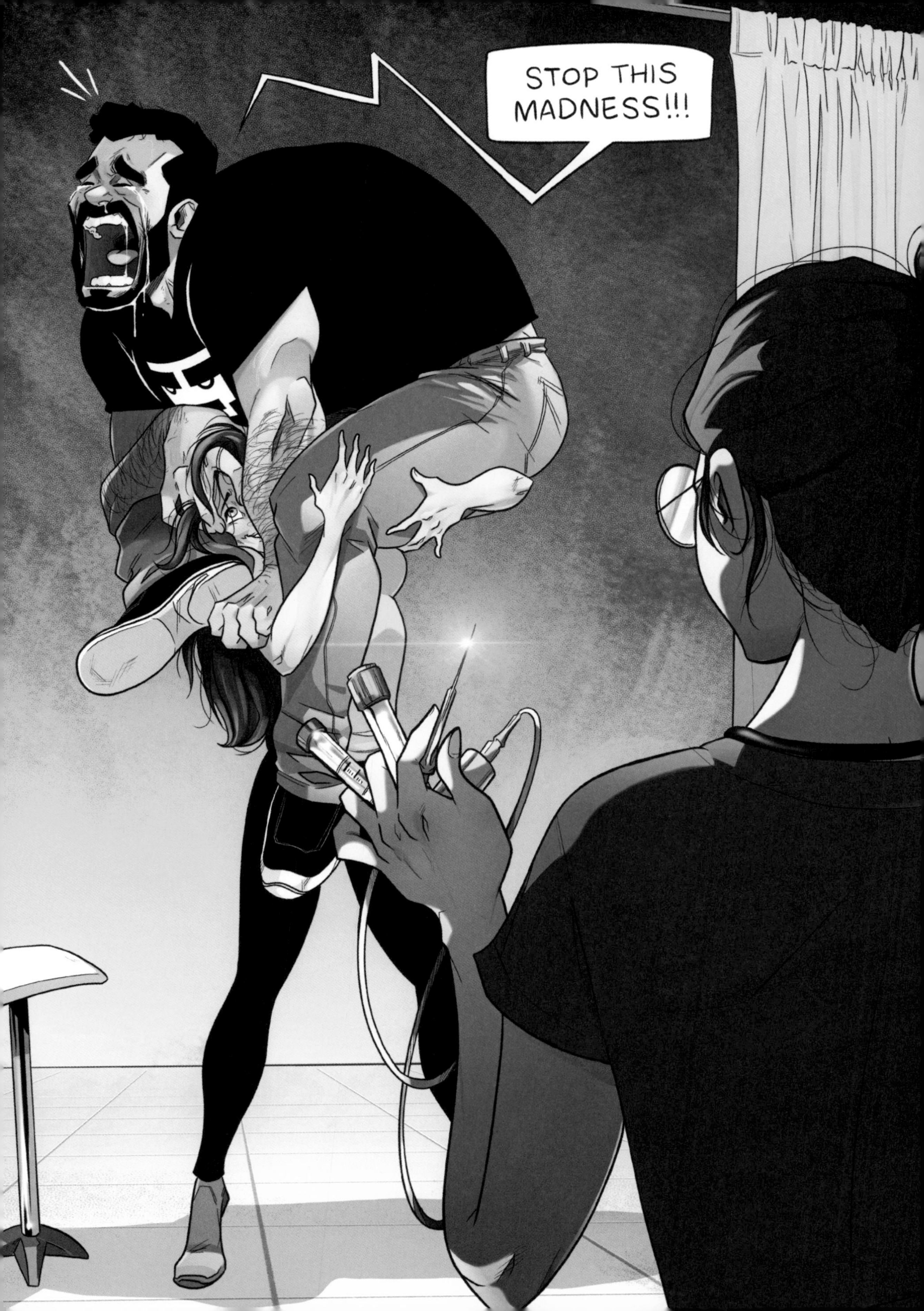
STOP THIS MADNESS!!!

73

HANGING BY A THREAD

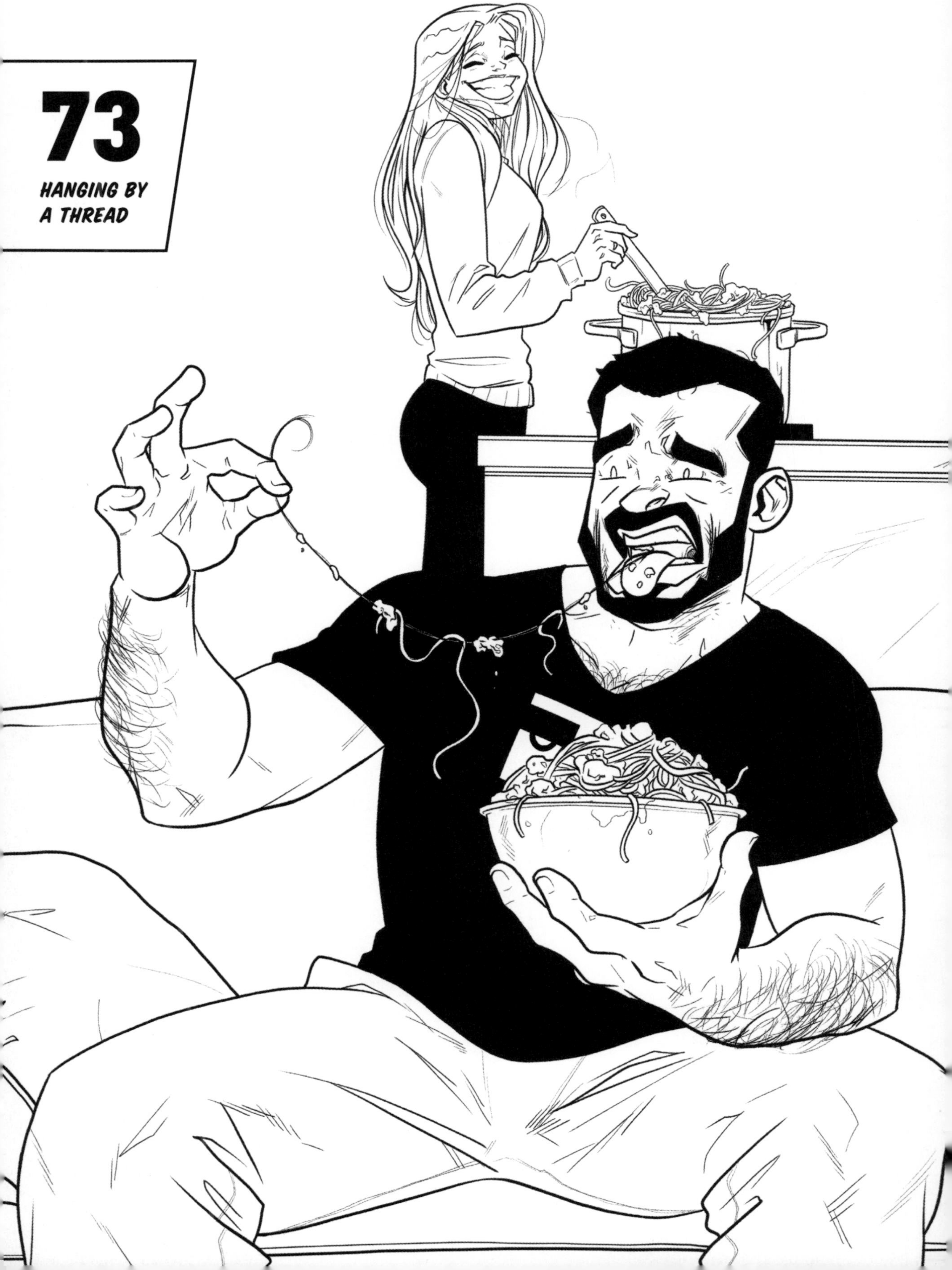

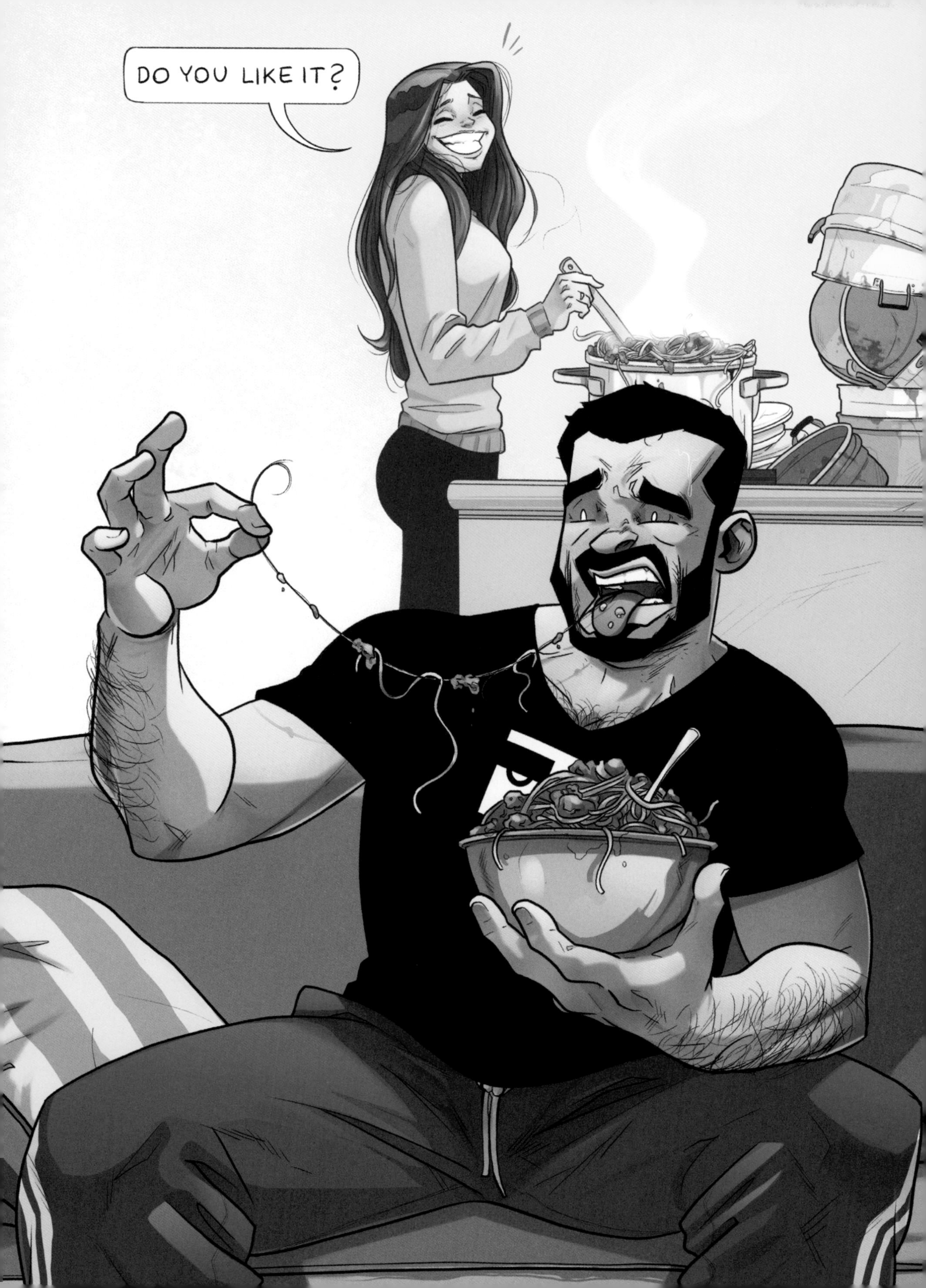
DO YOU LIKE IT?

74

NOBODY IS PERFECT

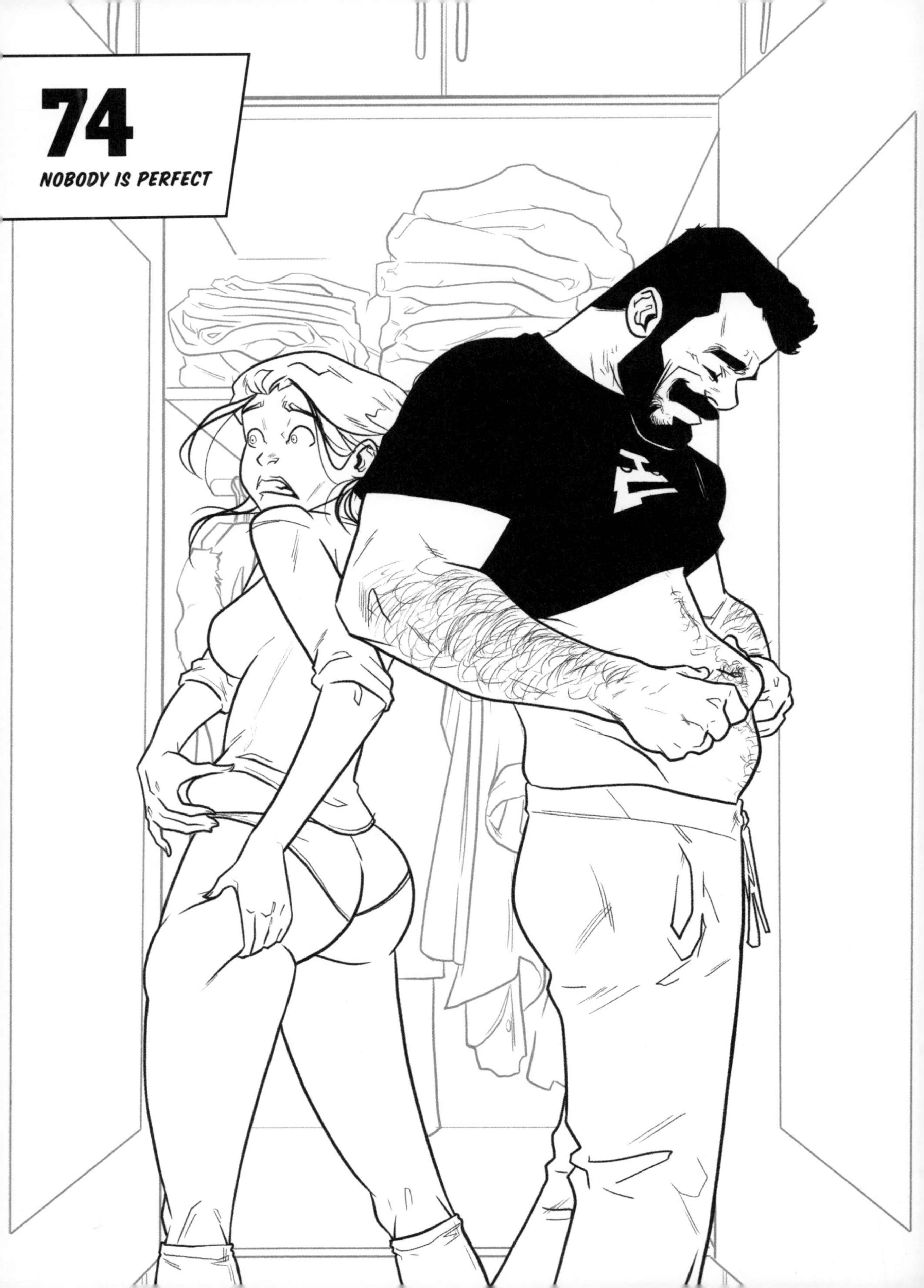

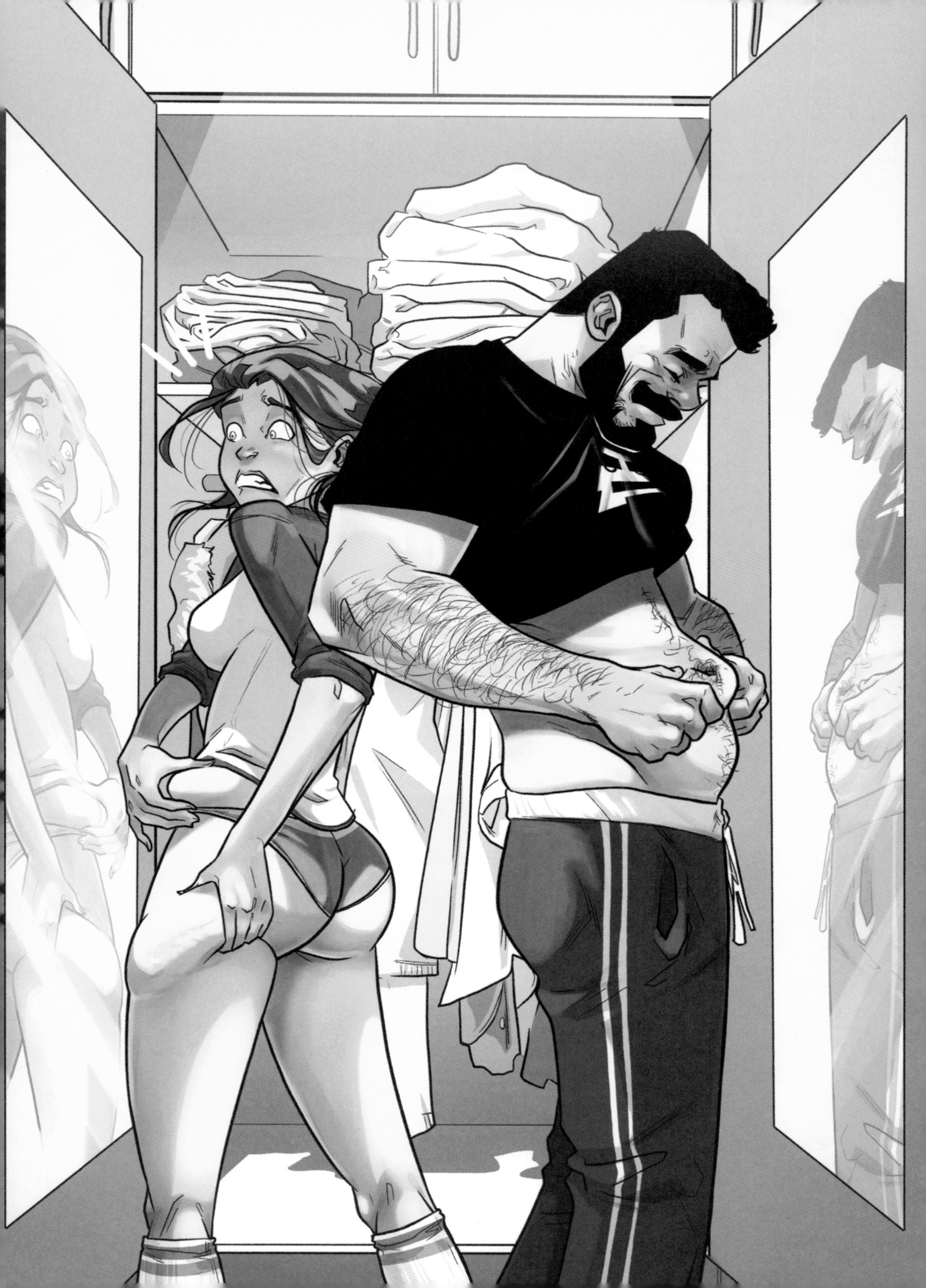

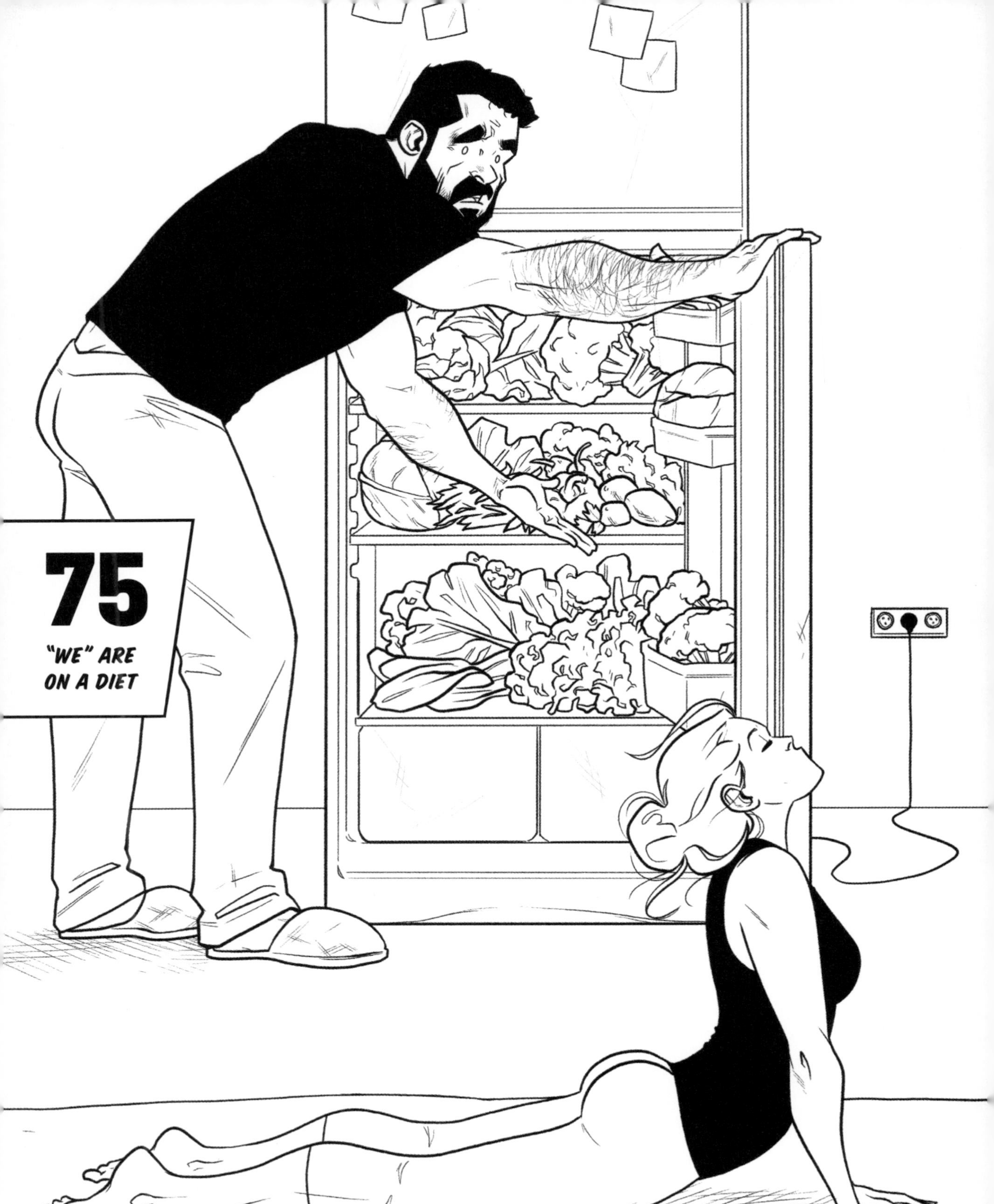

75

"WE" ARE ON A DIET

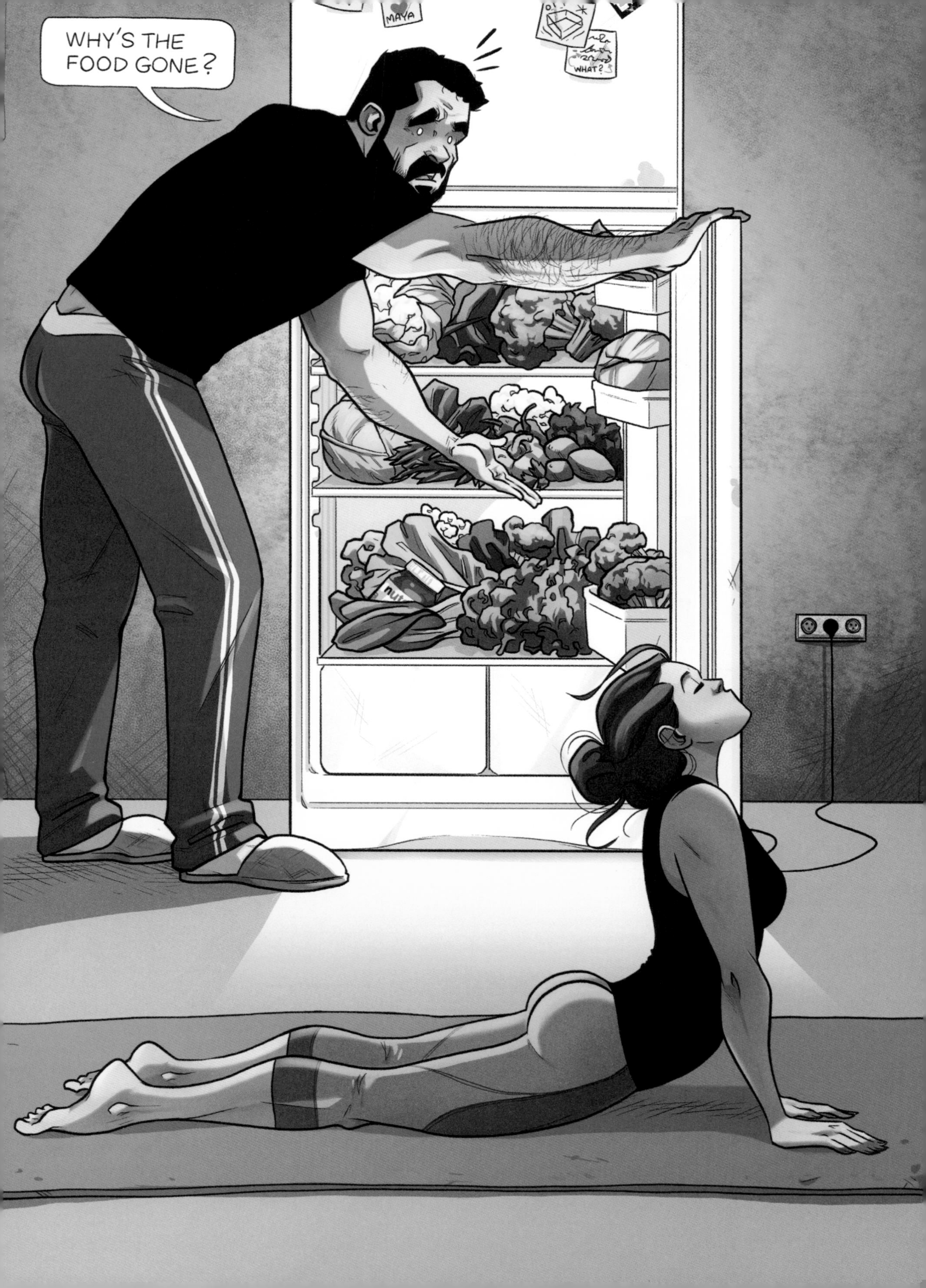
WHY'S THE FOOD GONE?
MAYA
WHAT?

76

MY QUEEN!
MY WIFE!
MY LOVE!

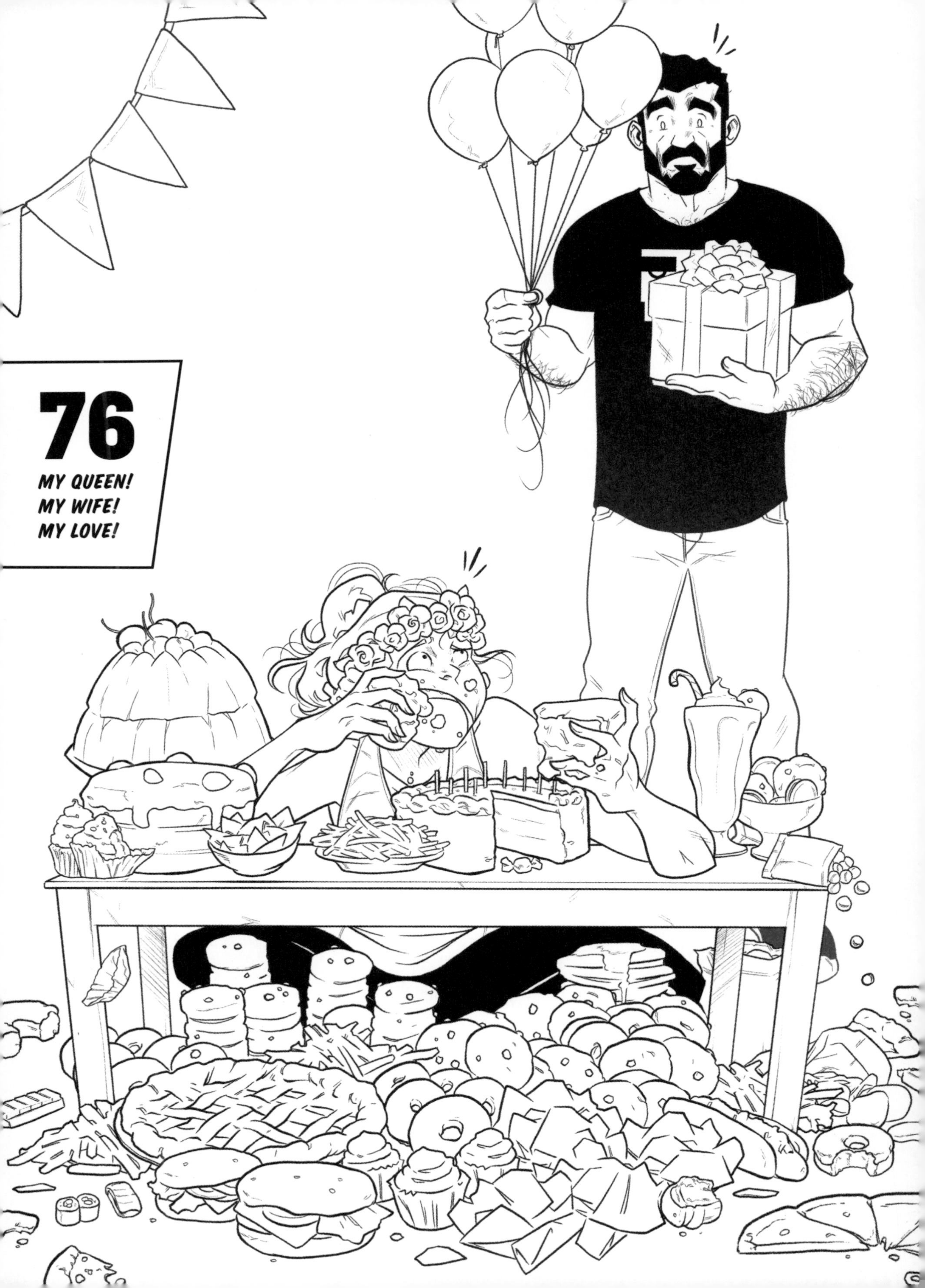

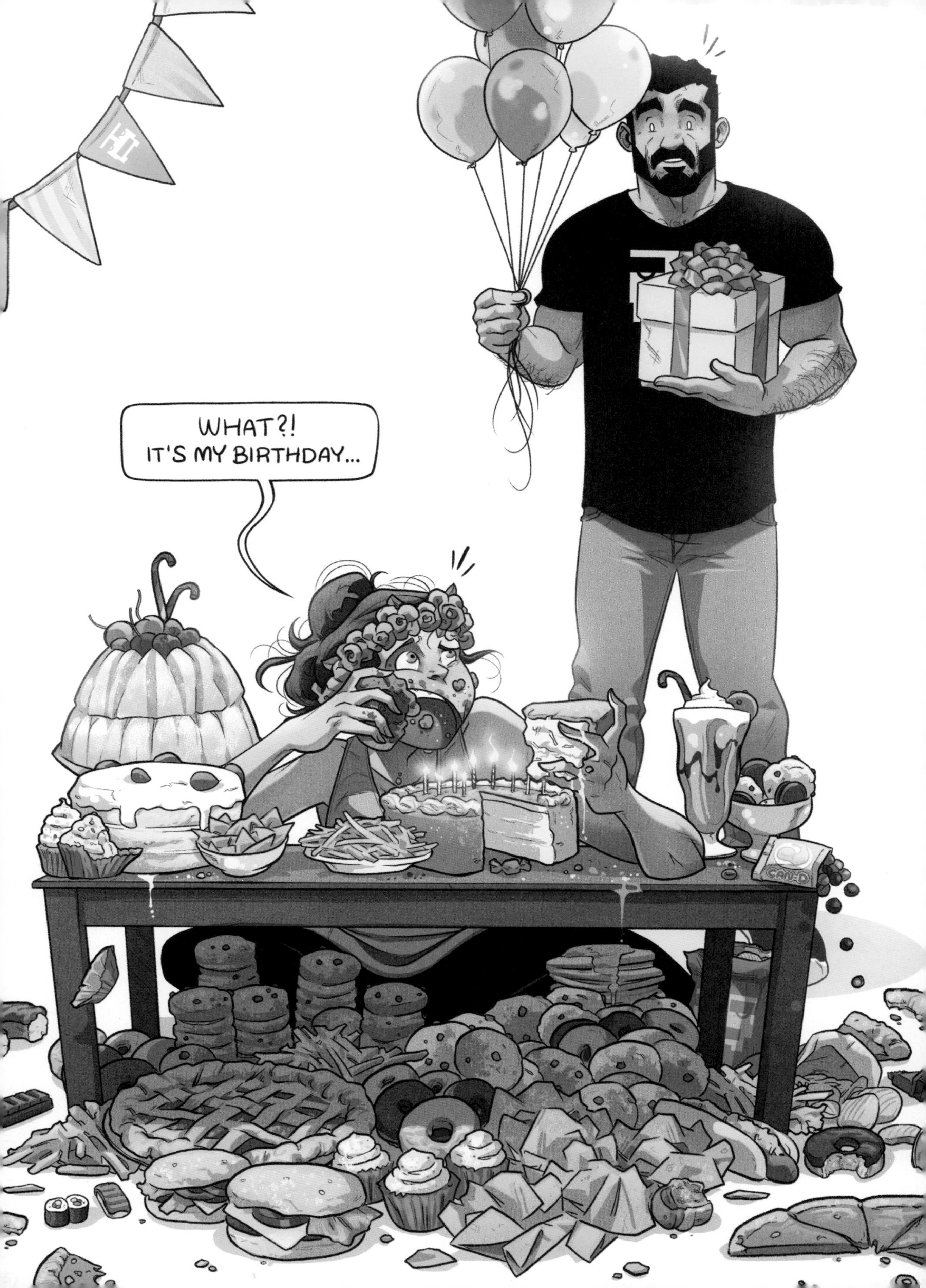
WHAT?! IT'S MY BIRTHDAY...
CAN-D

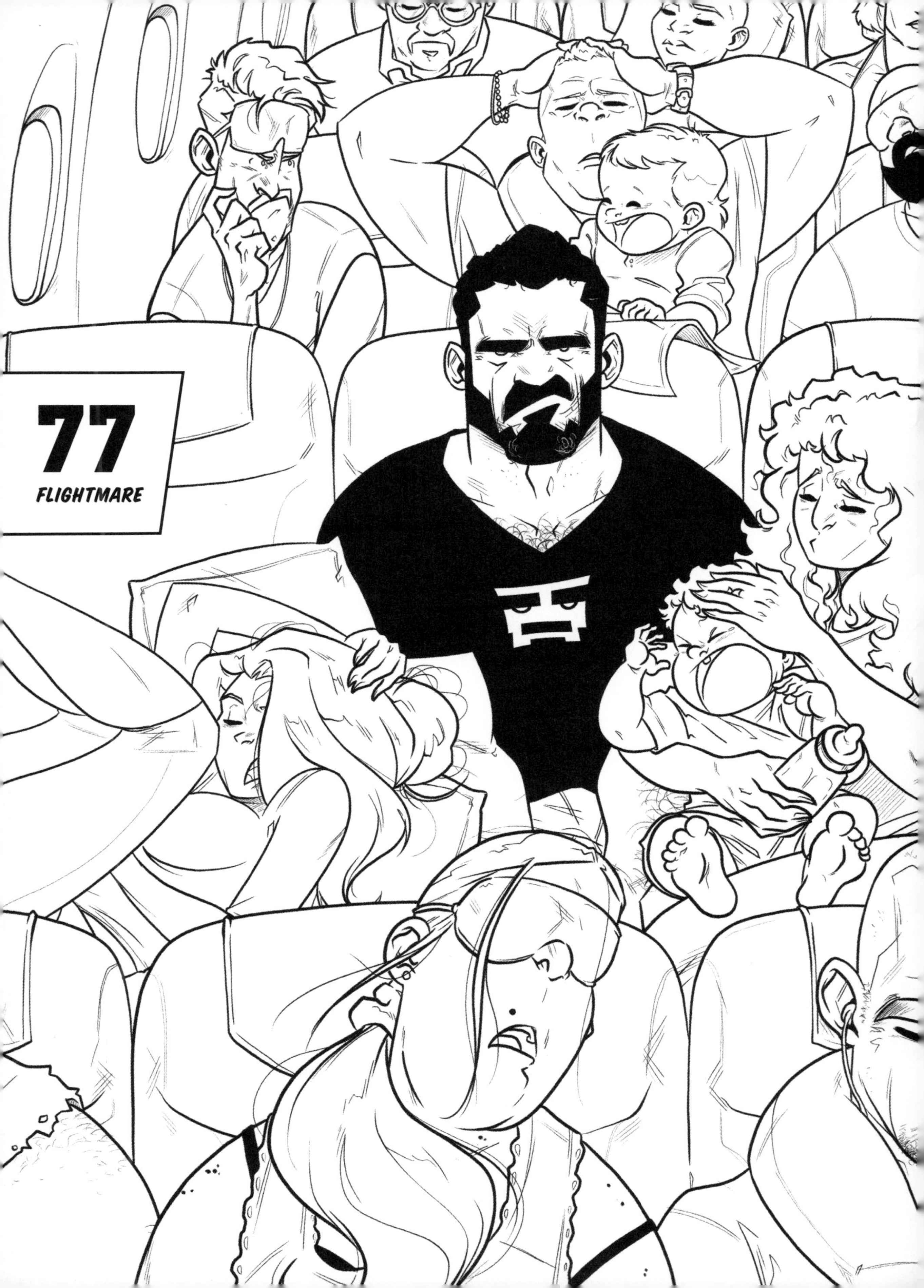
77
FLIGHTMARE

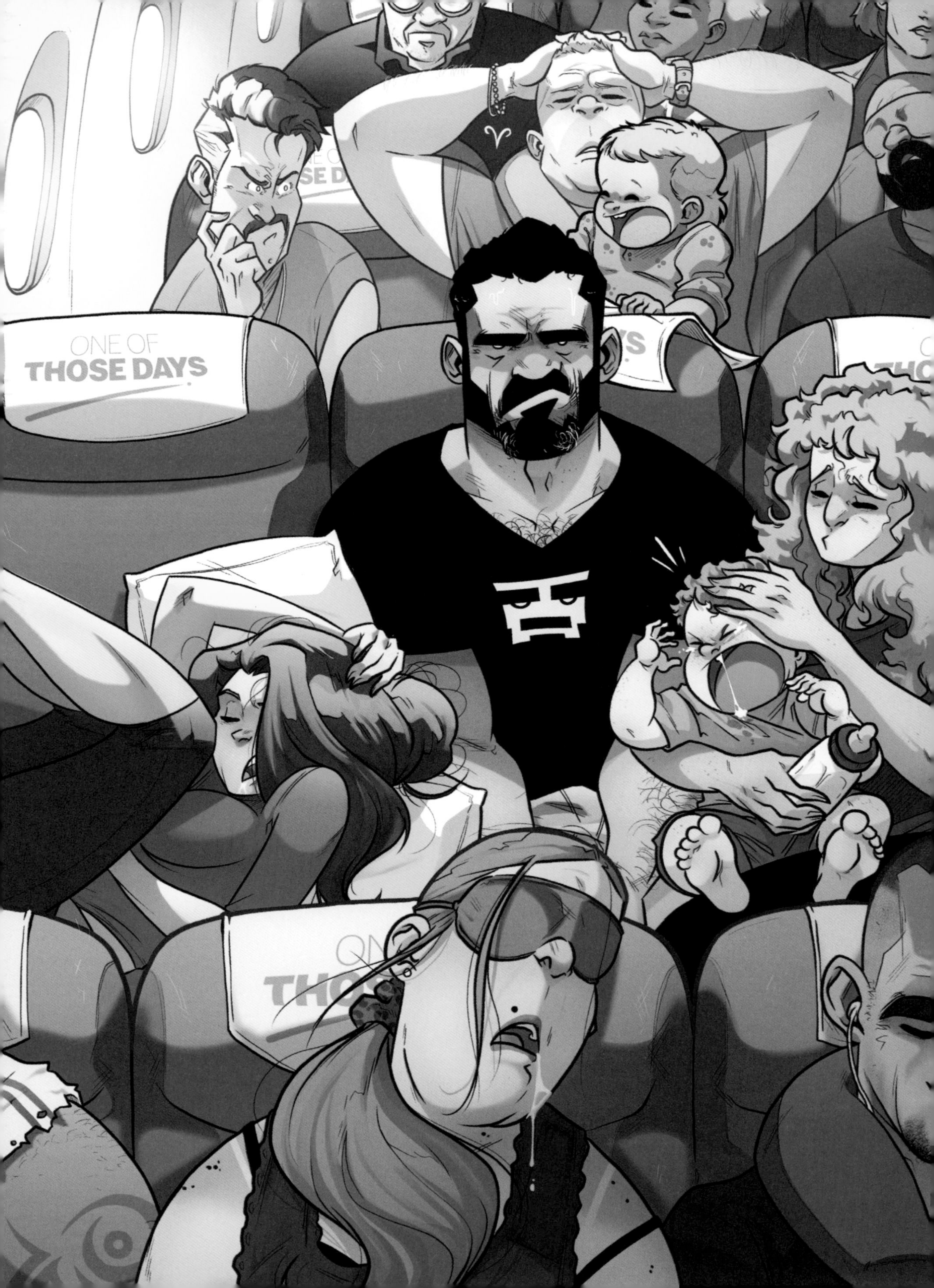
ONE OF
THOSE DAYS

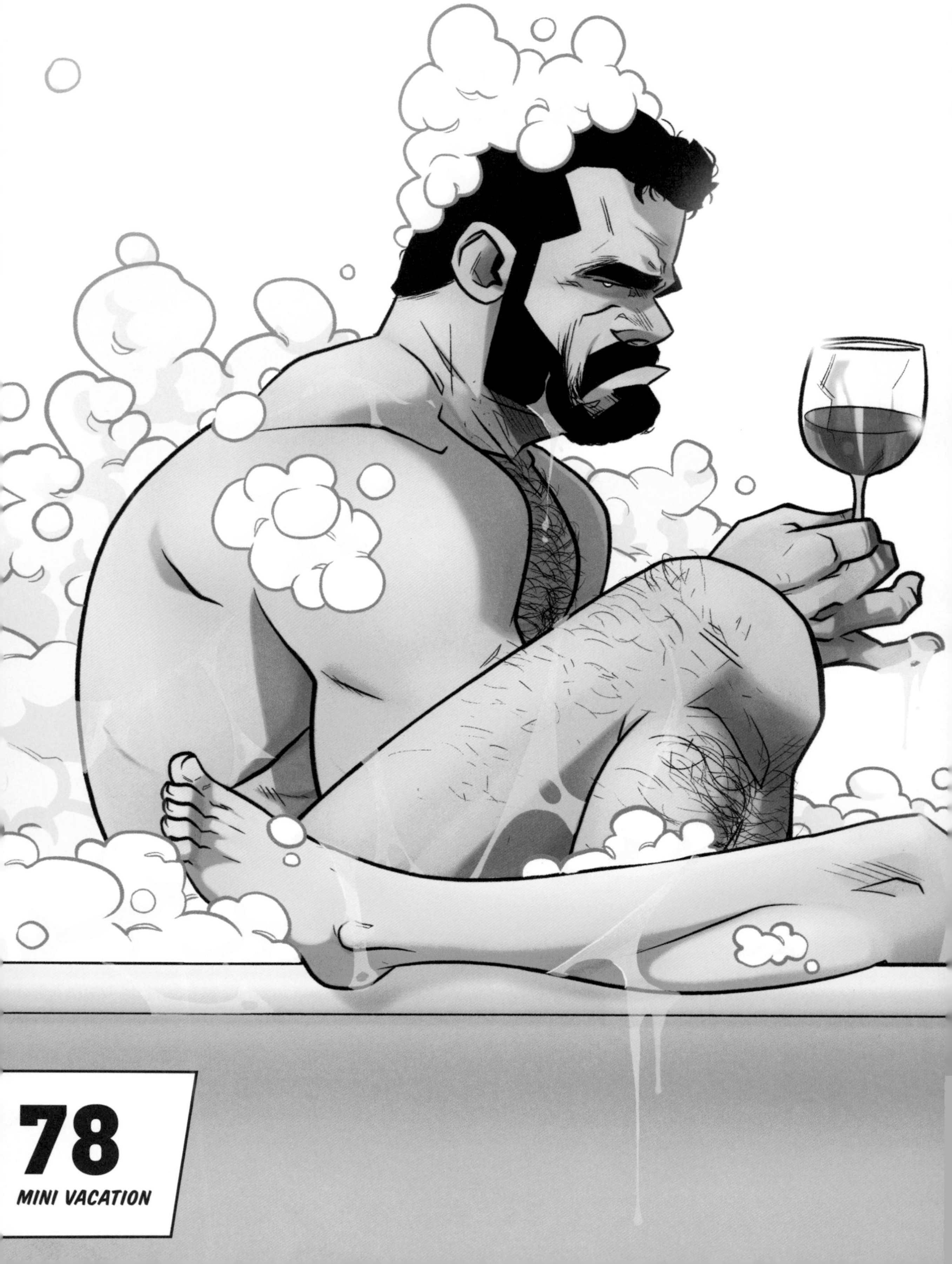

78

MINI VACATION

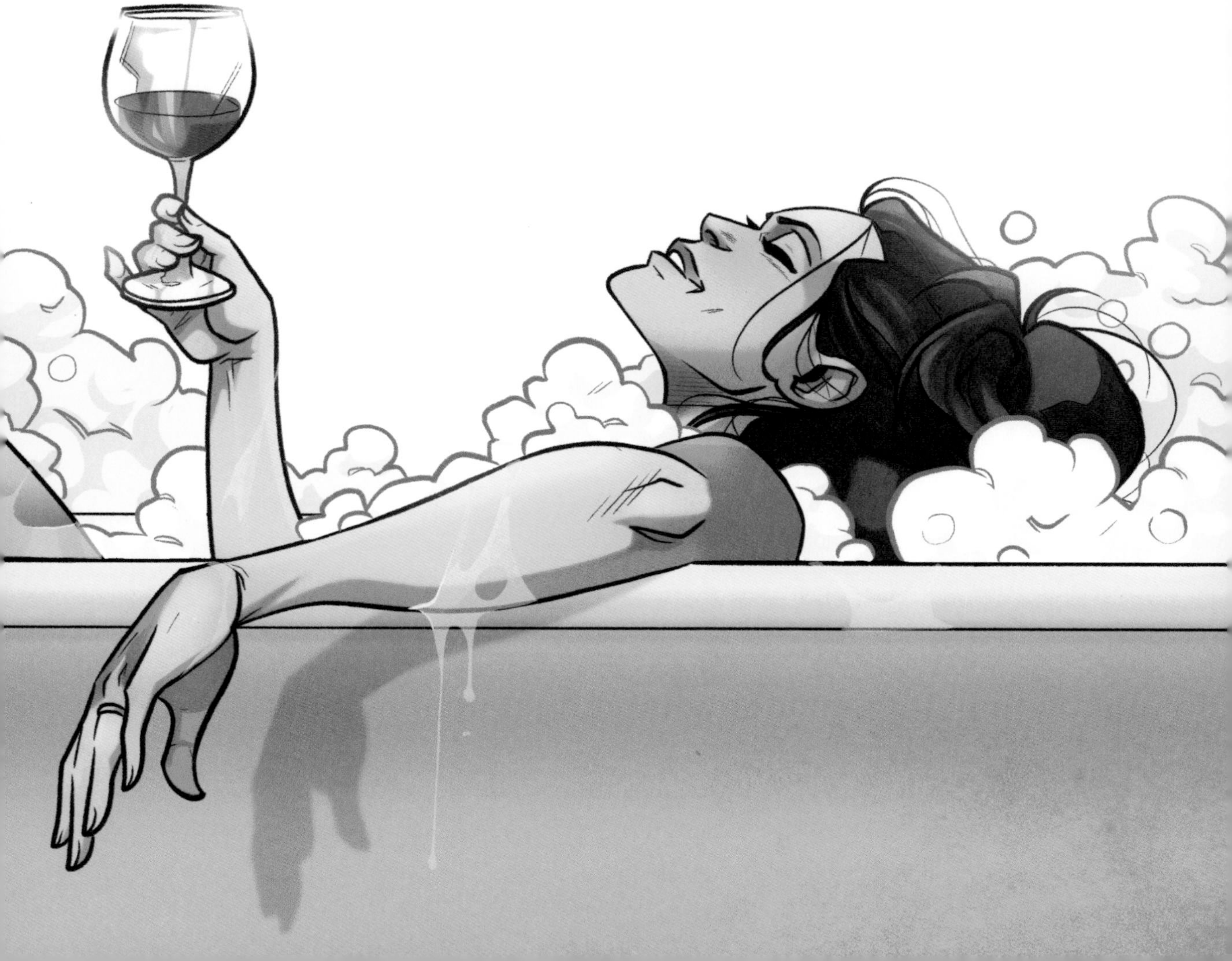

79

THE COLD NEVER BOTHERED ME ANYWAY

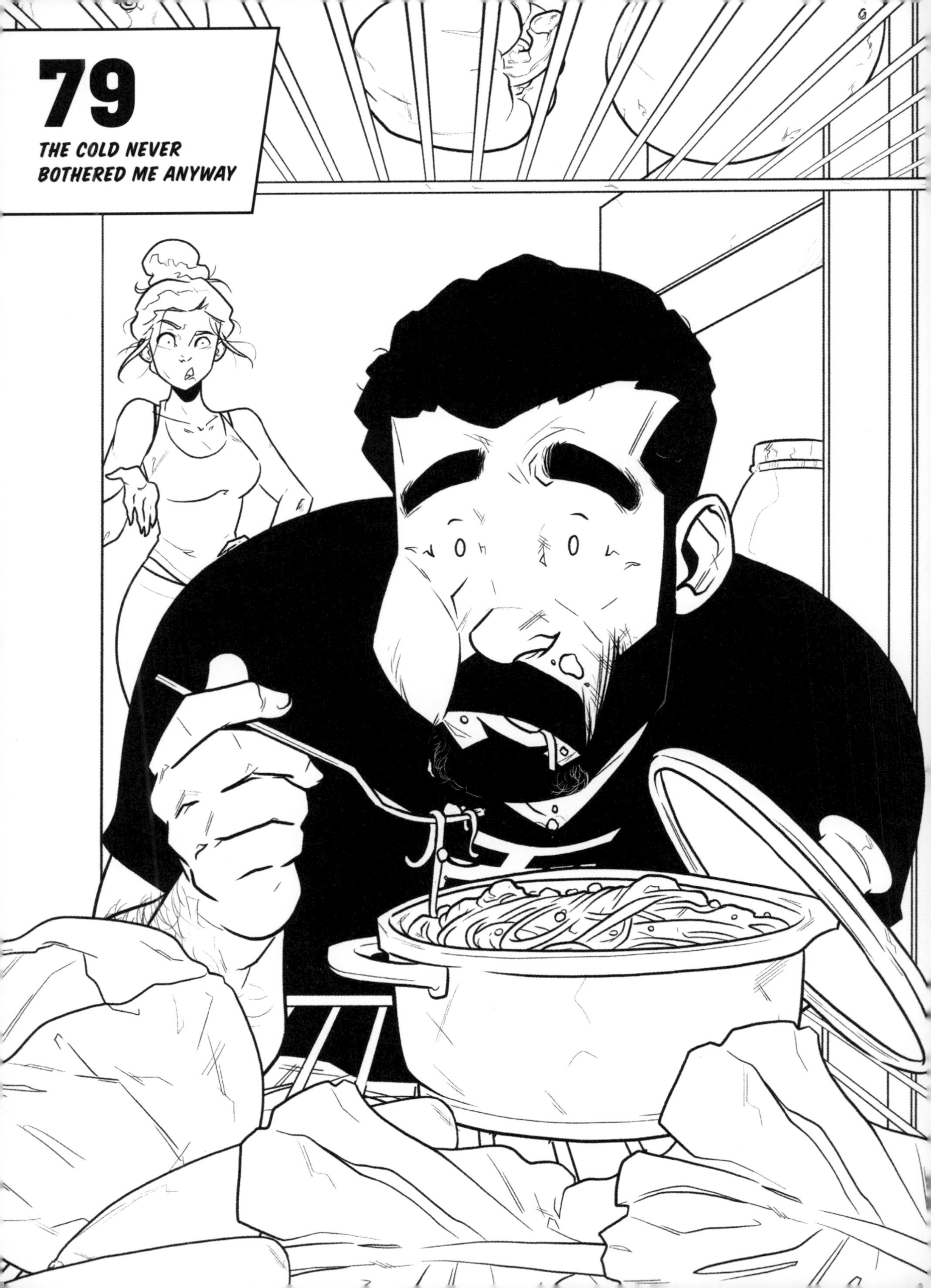

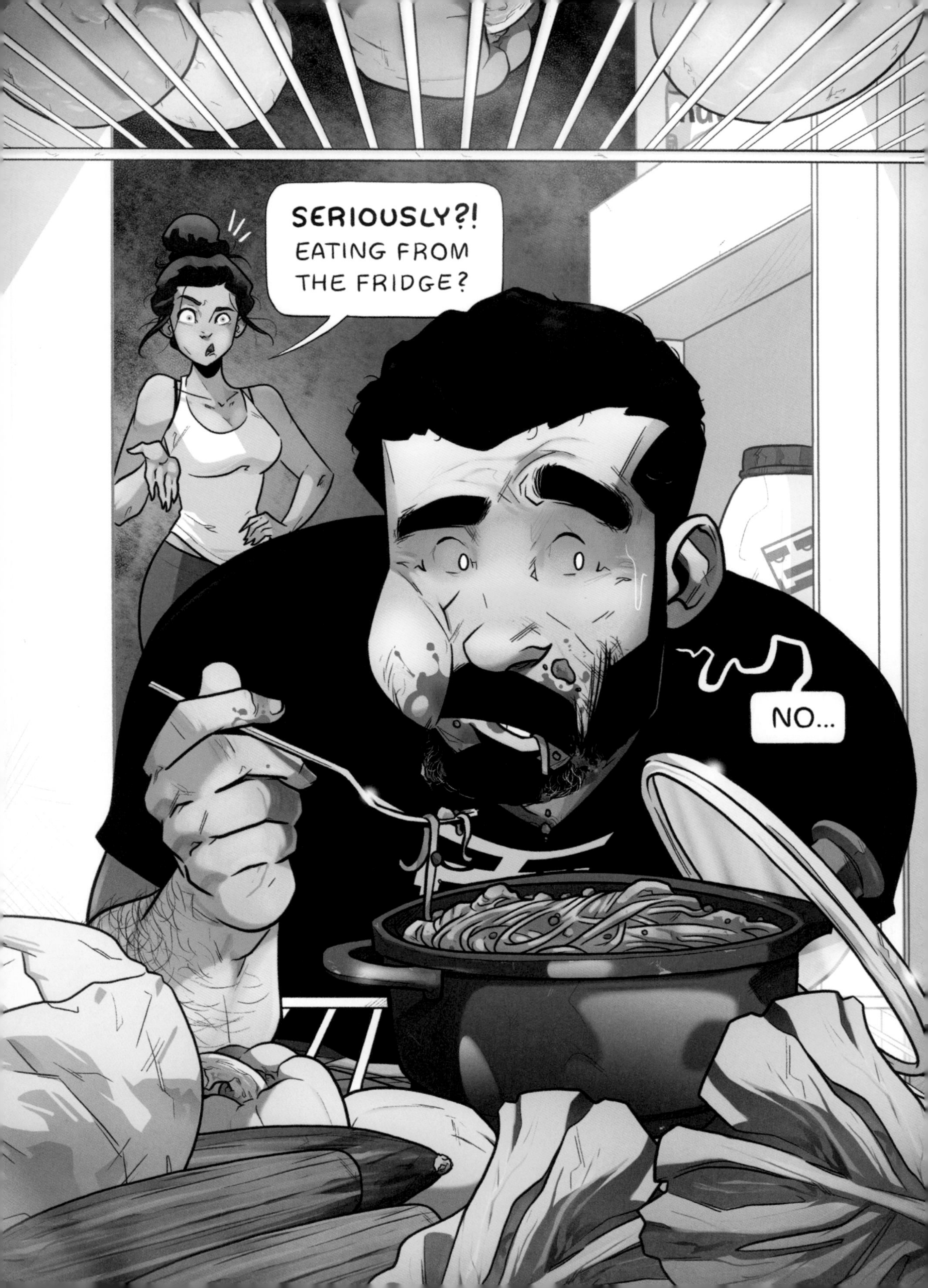
SERIOUSLY?! EATING FROM THE FRIDGE?
NO...

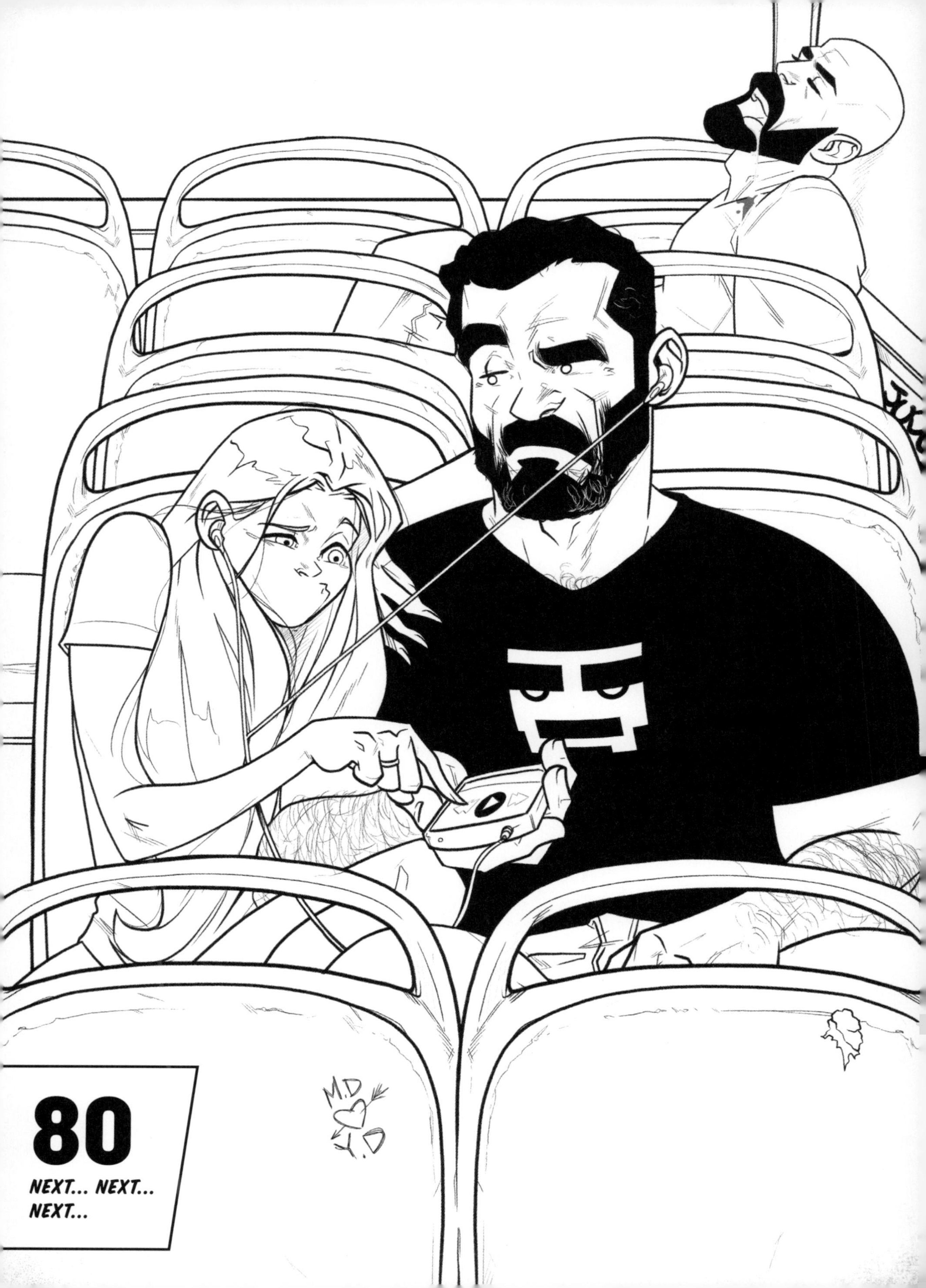
M.D
Y.D

80

NEXT... NEXT... NEXT...

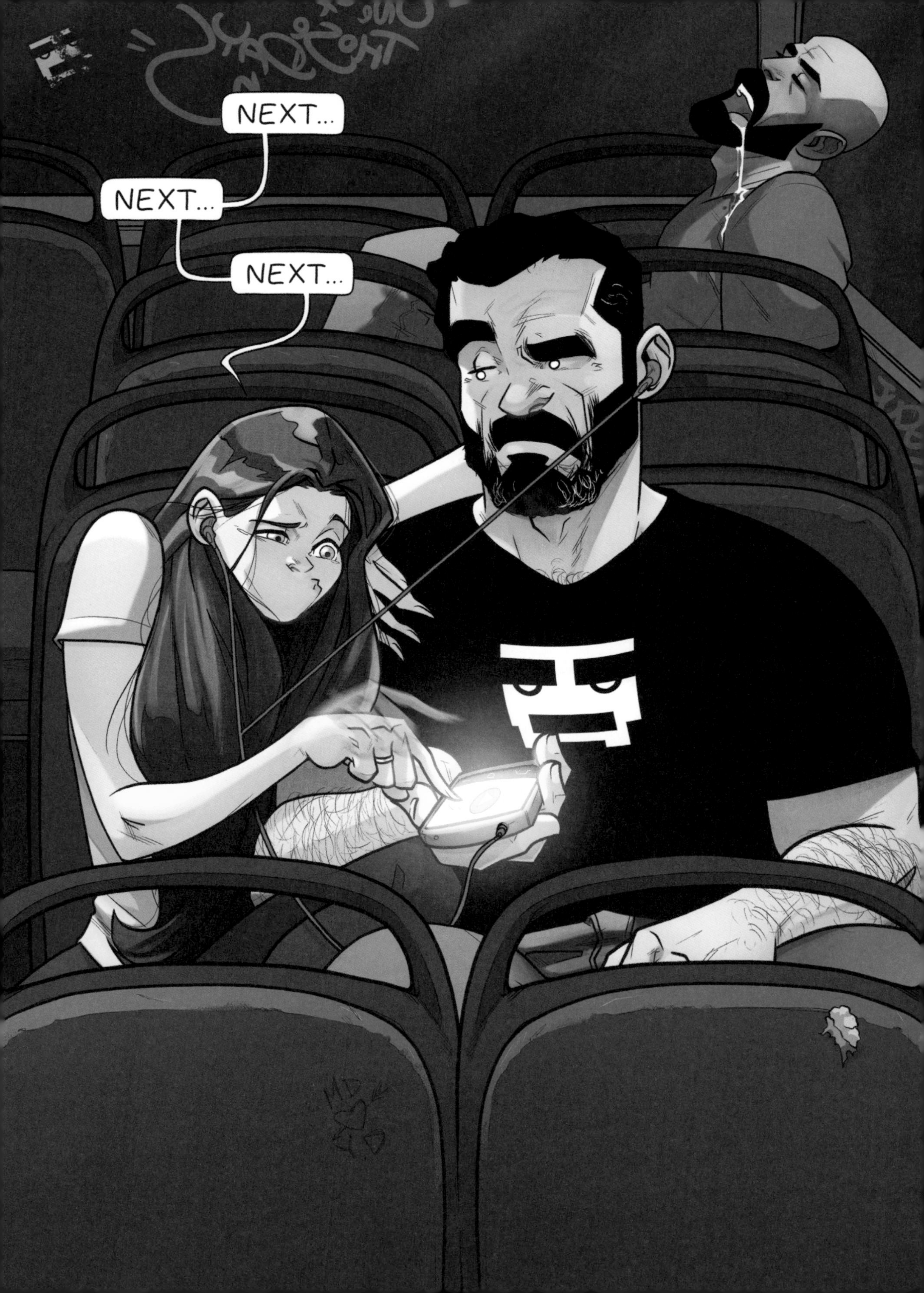
NEXT...
NEXT...
NEXT...

81

DIE, DEVIL BIRD!

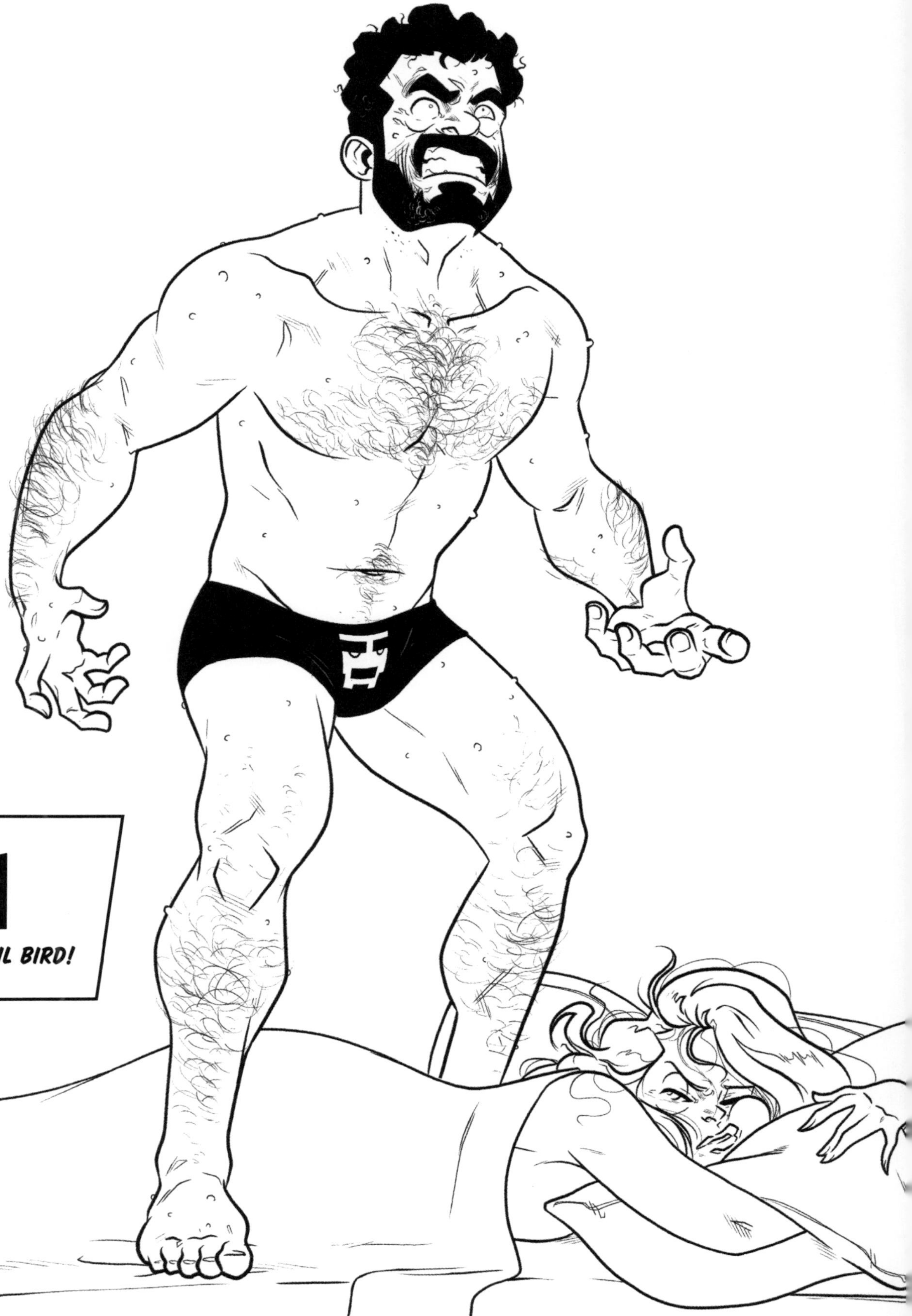

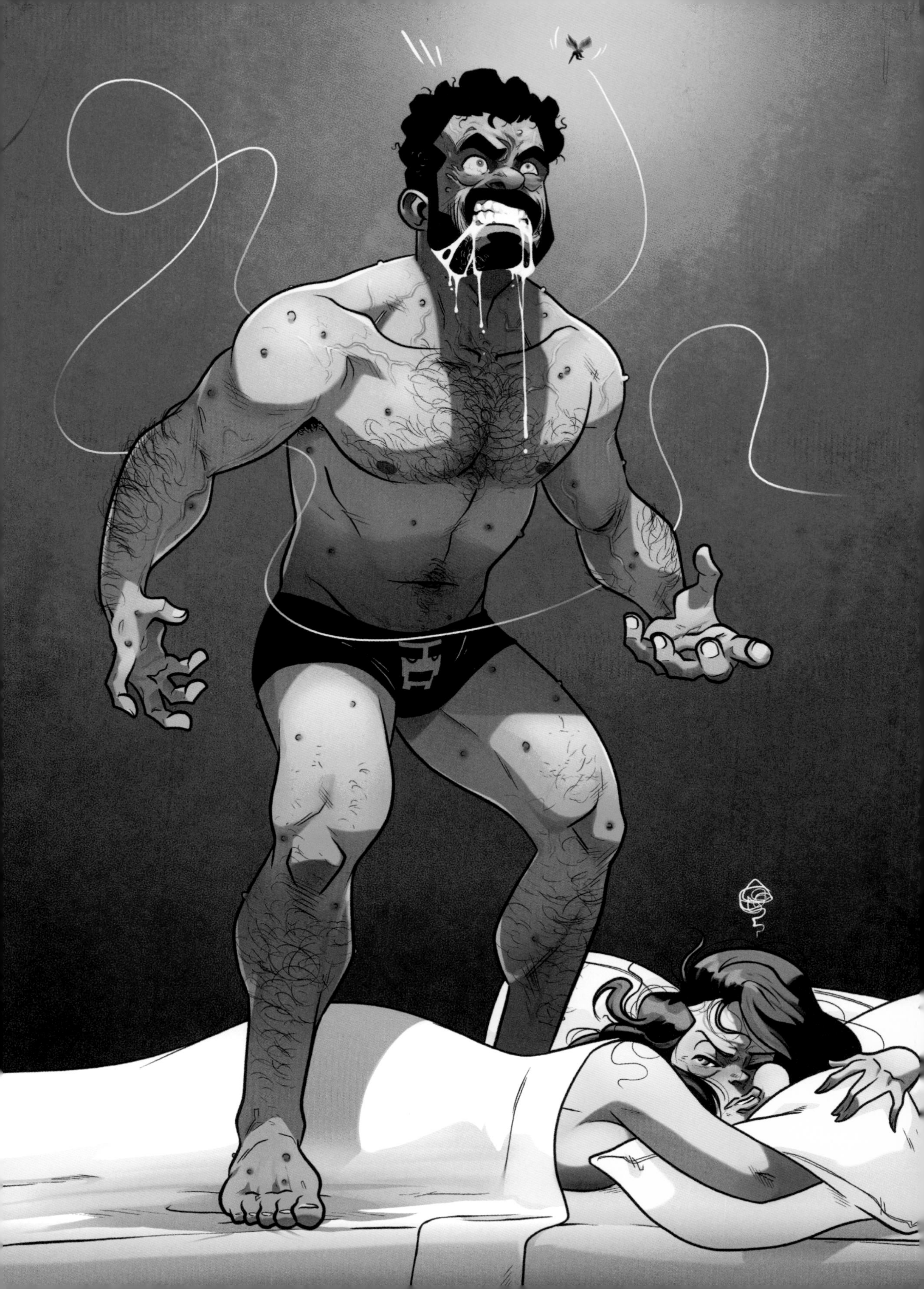

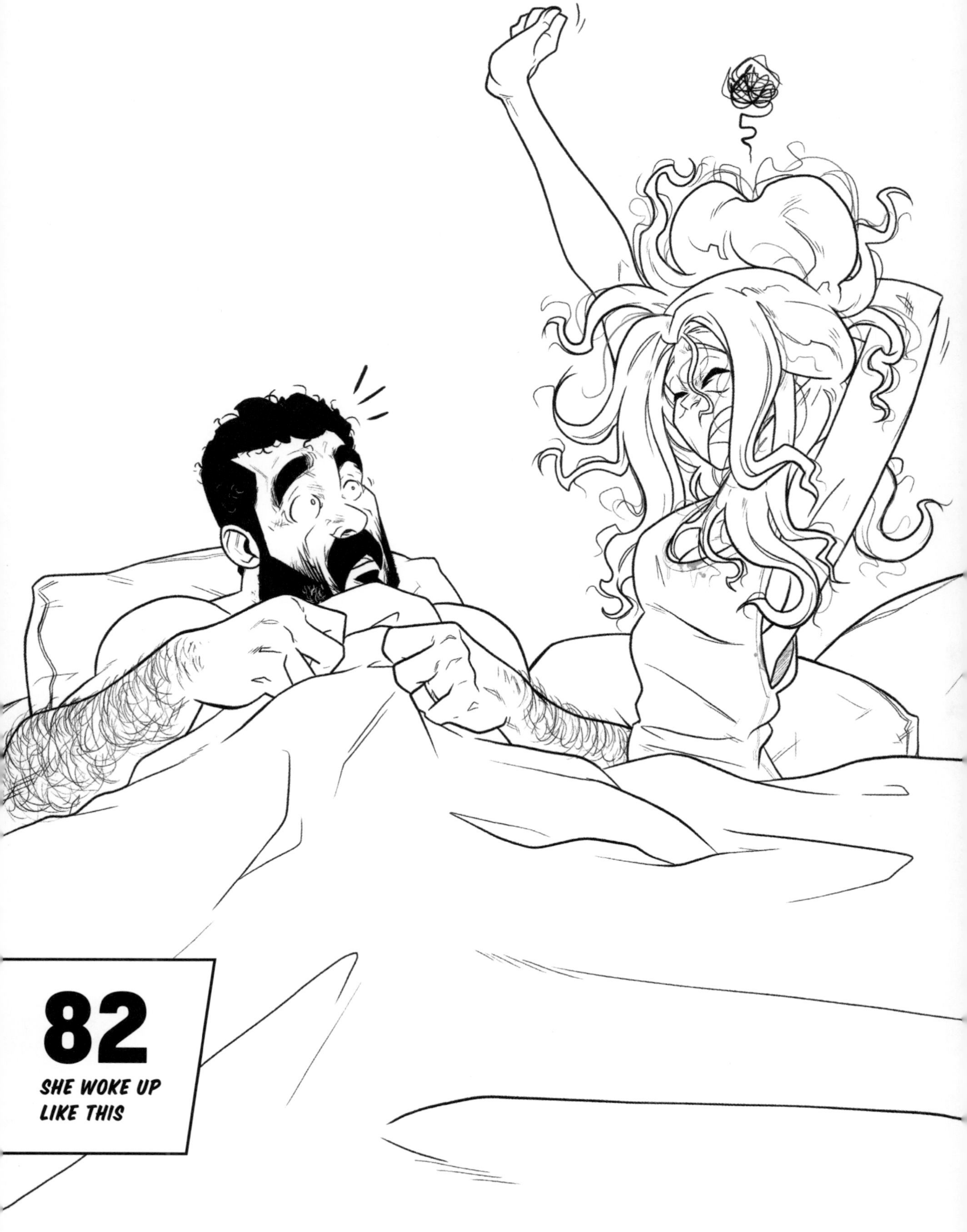

82

SHE WOKE UP LIKE THIS

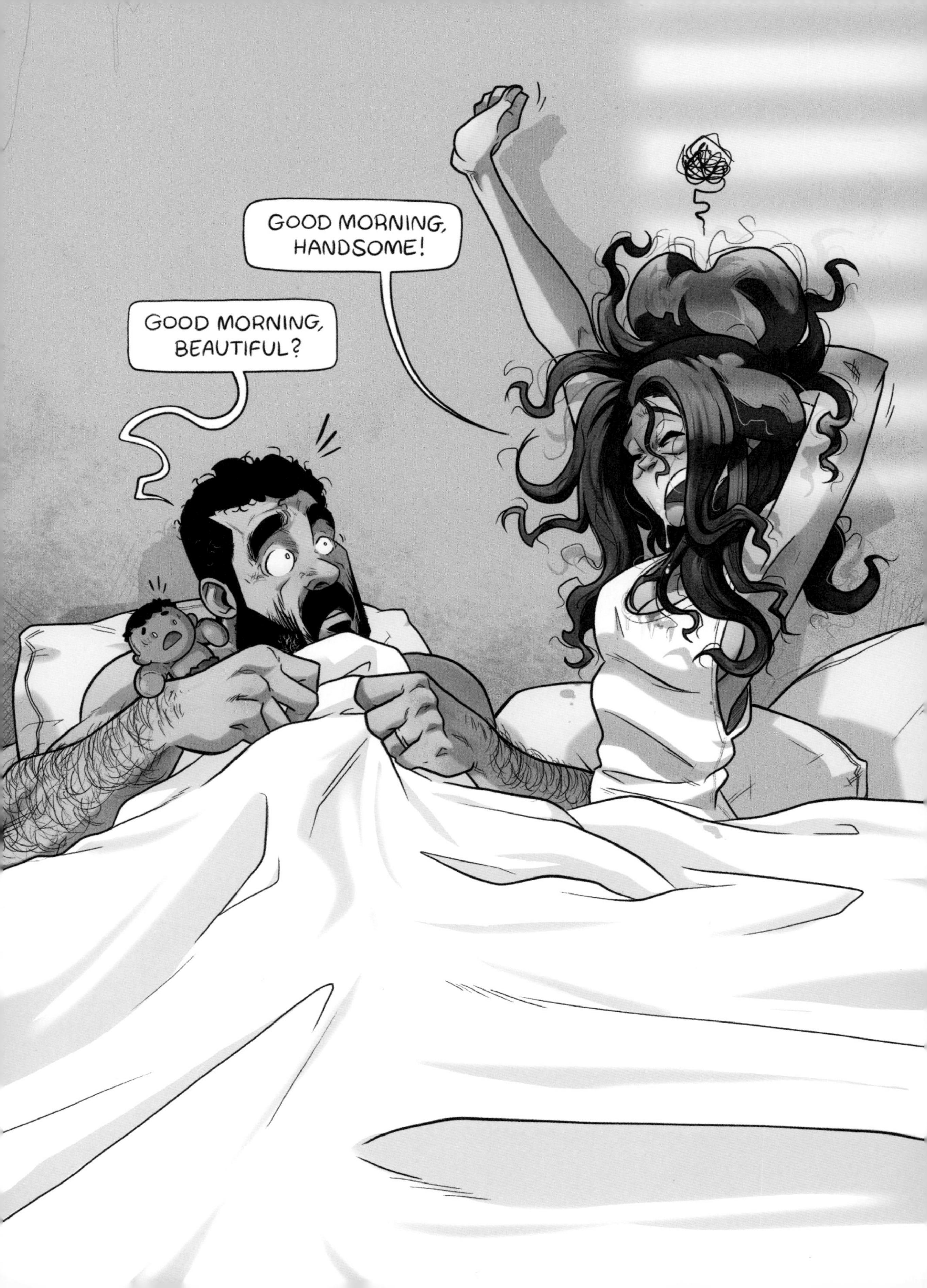
GOOD MORNING, HANDSOME!
GOOD MORNING, BEAUTIFUL?

83
I'M SORRY

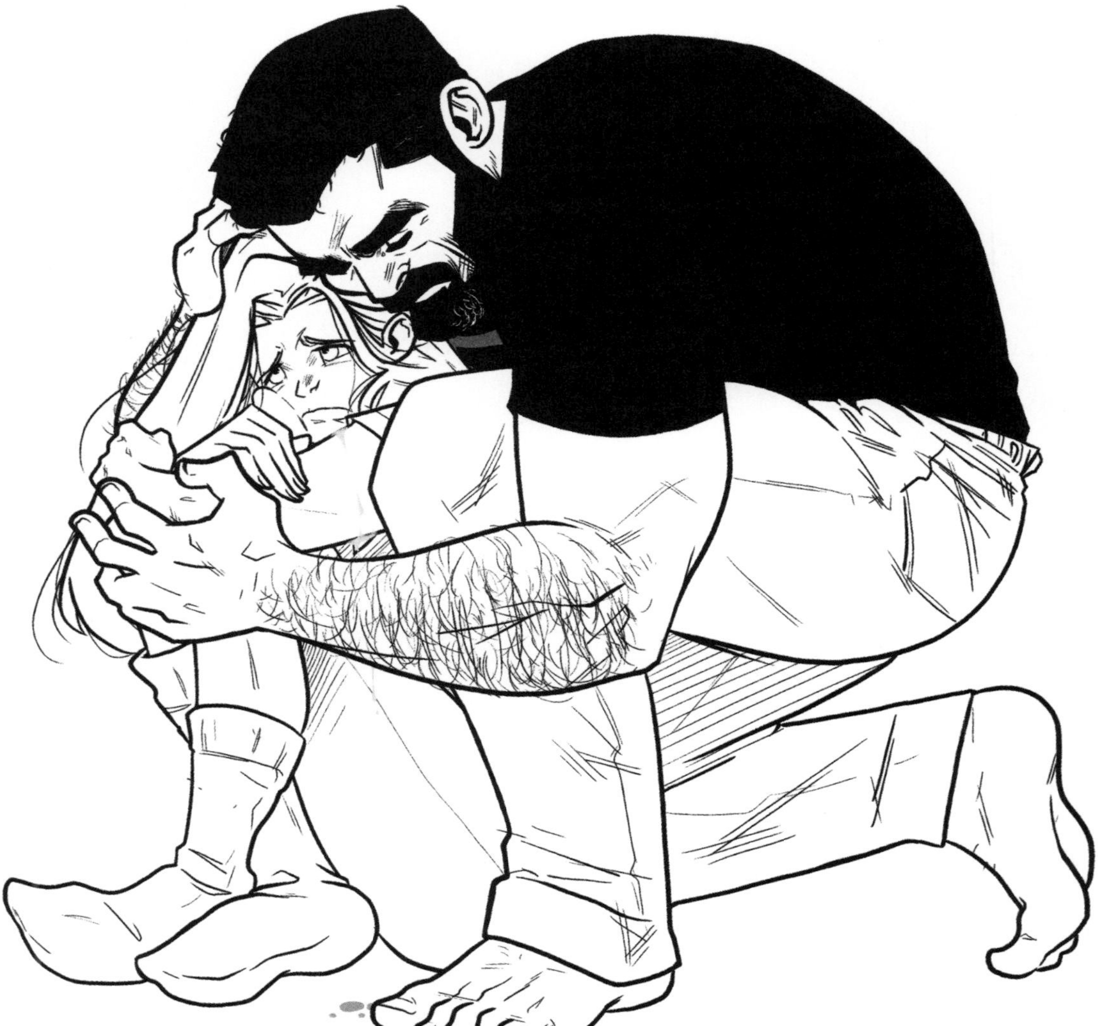

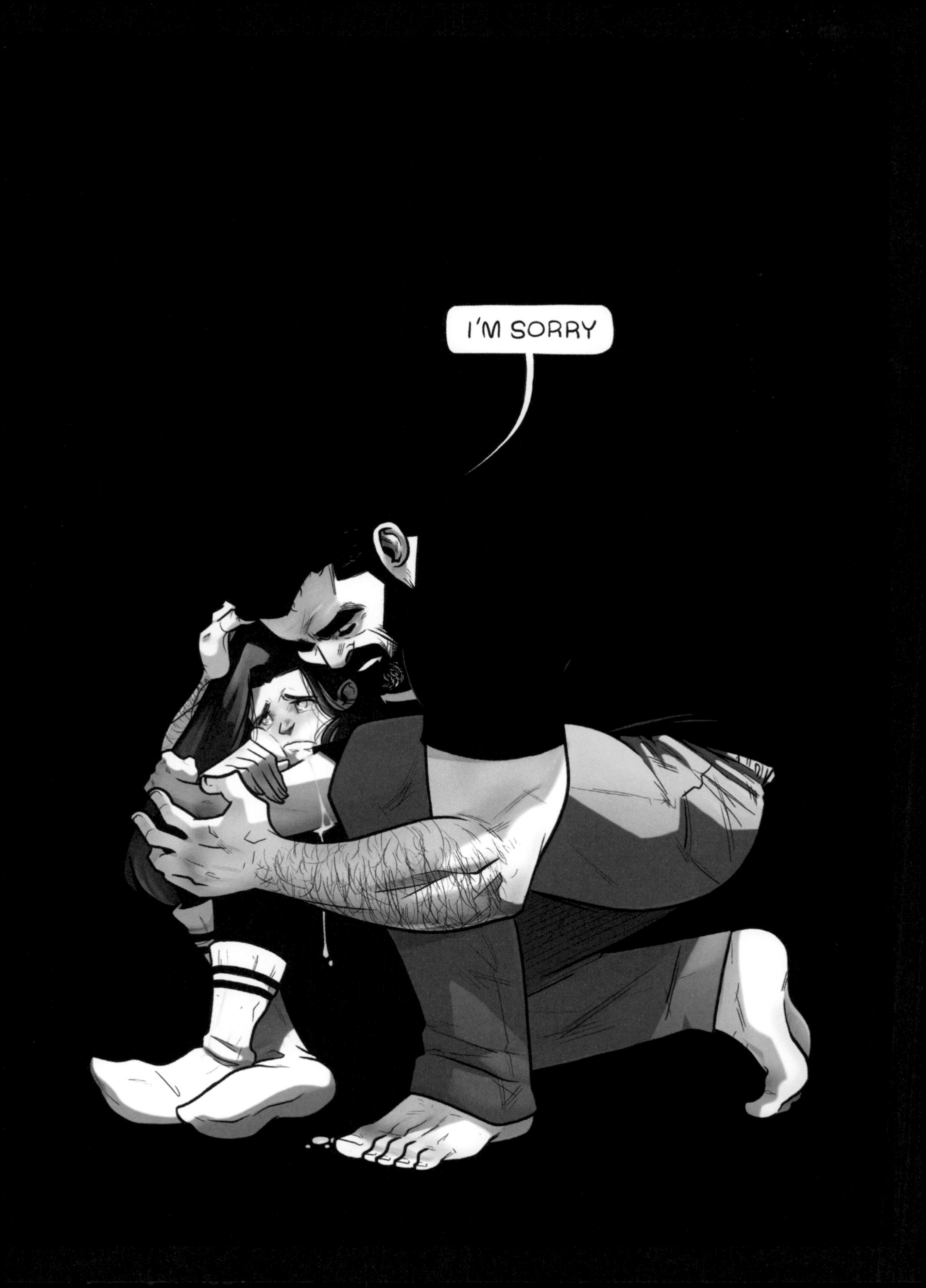
I'M SORRY

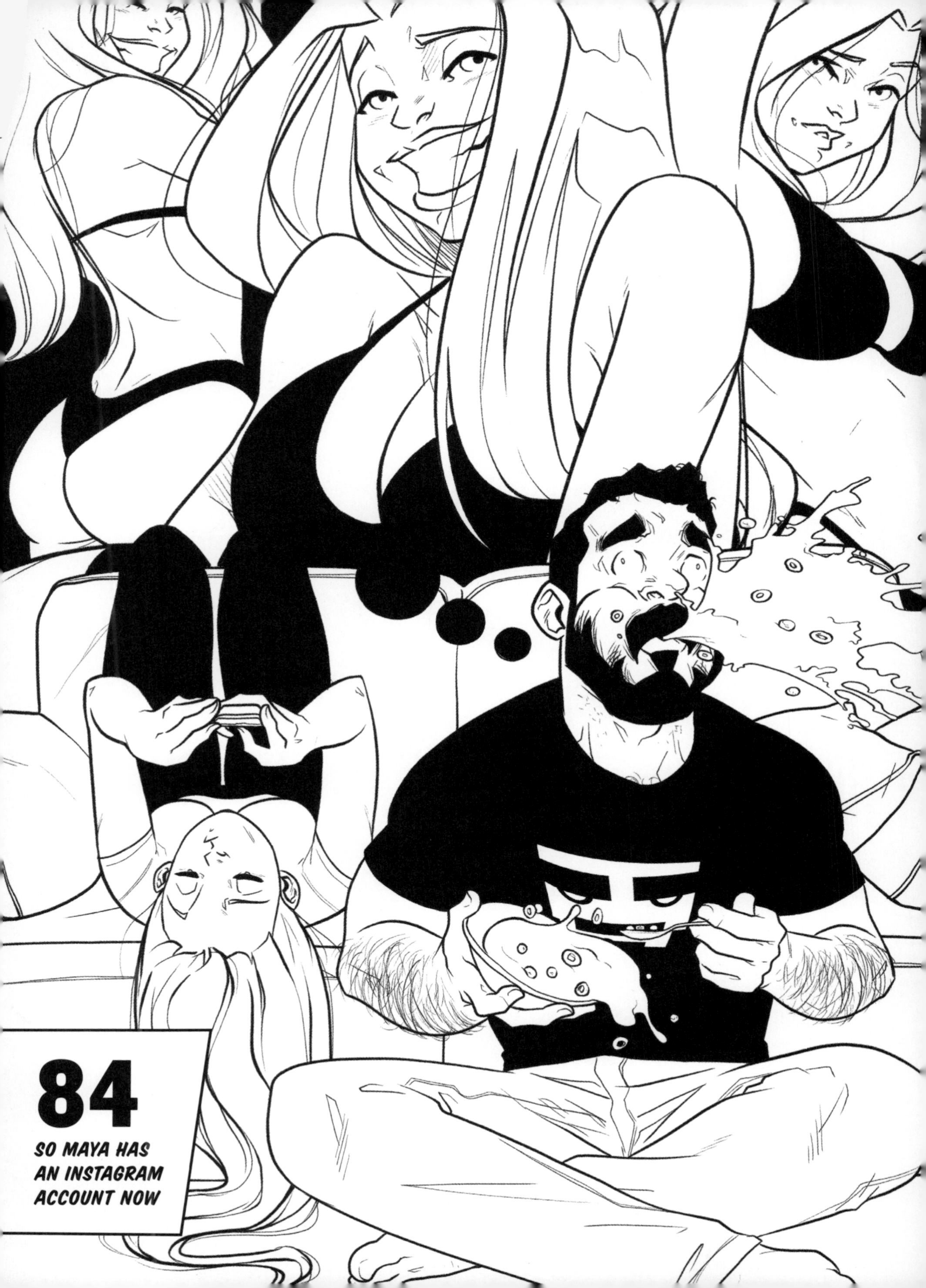

84

SO MAYA HAS AN INSTAGRAM ACCOUNT NOW

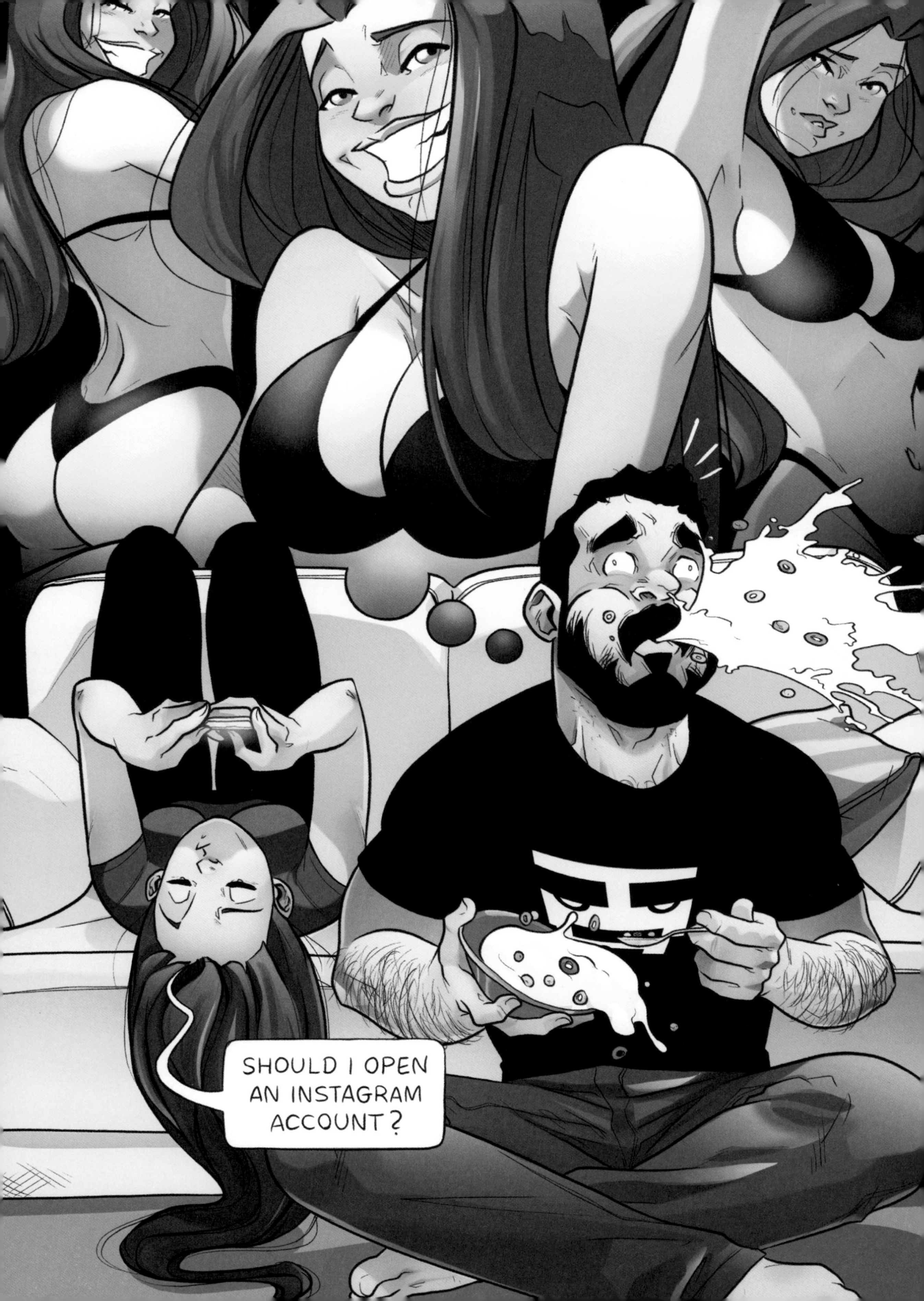
SHOULD I OPEN AN INSTAGRAM ACCOUNT?

85
DUCK KISS

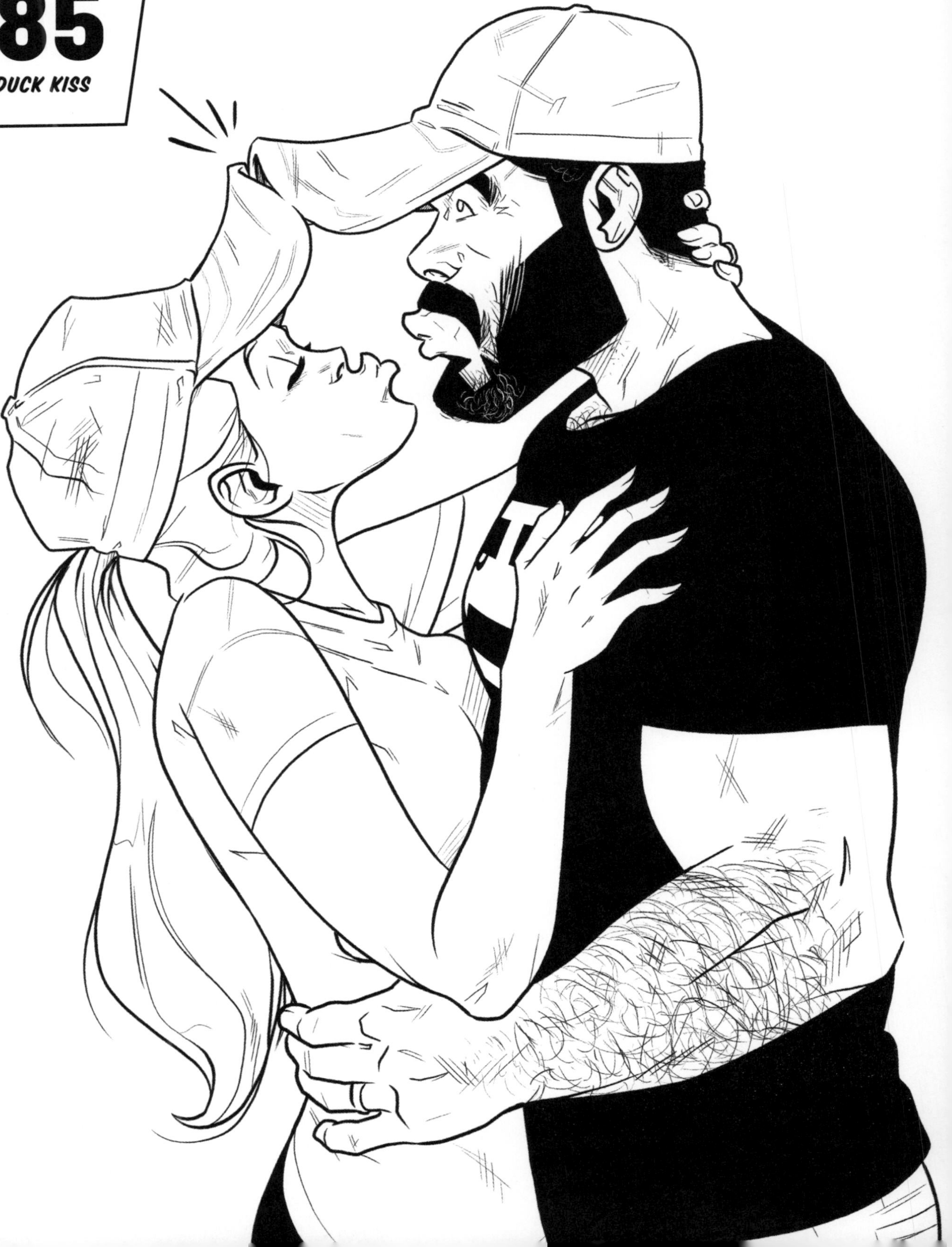

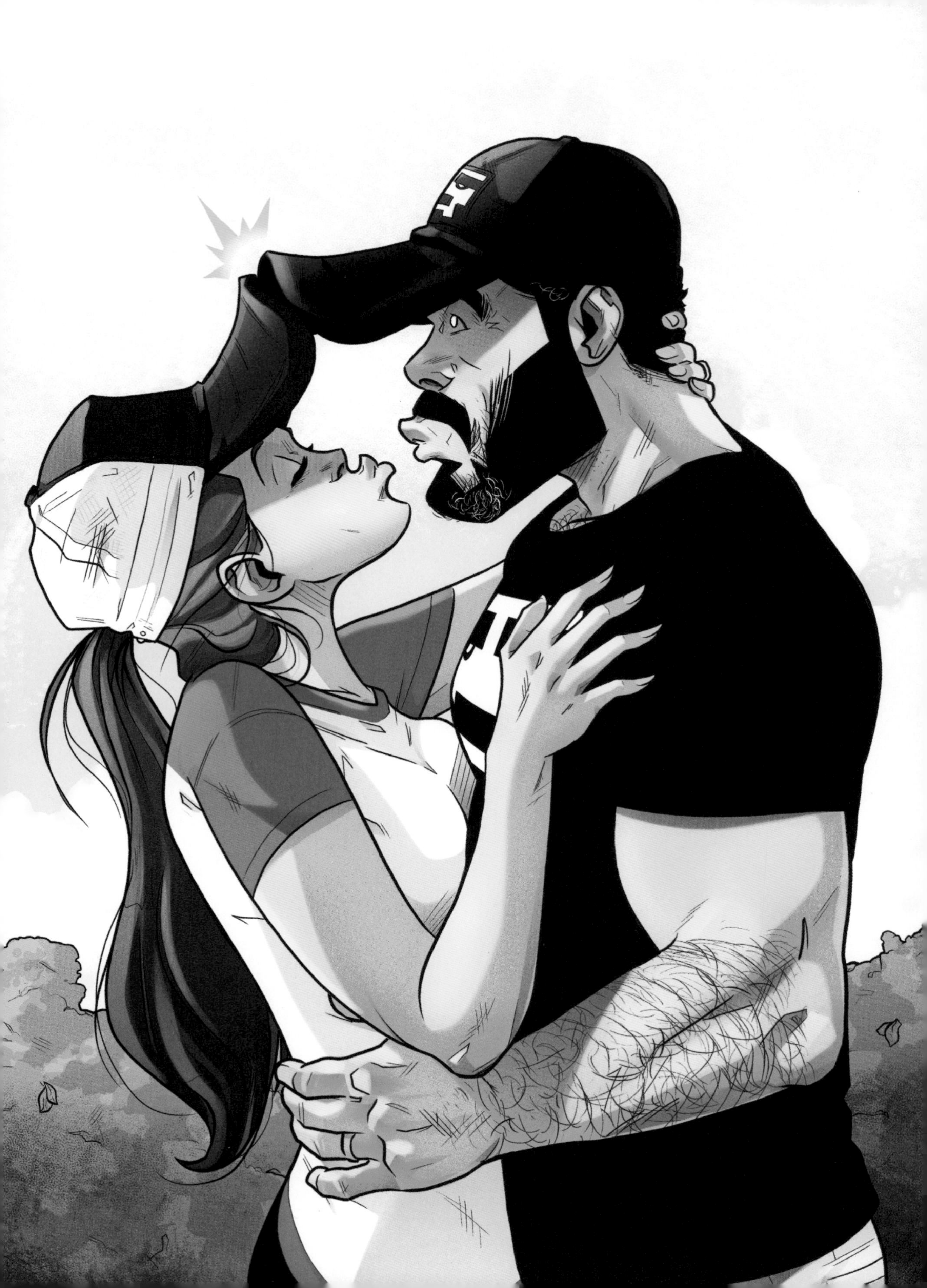

86

WORLD CUP

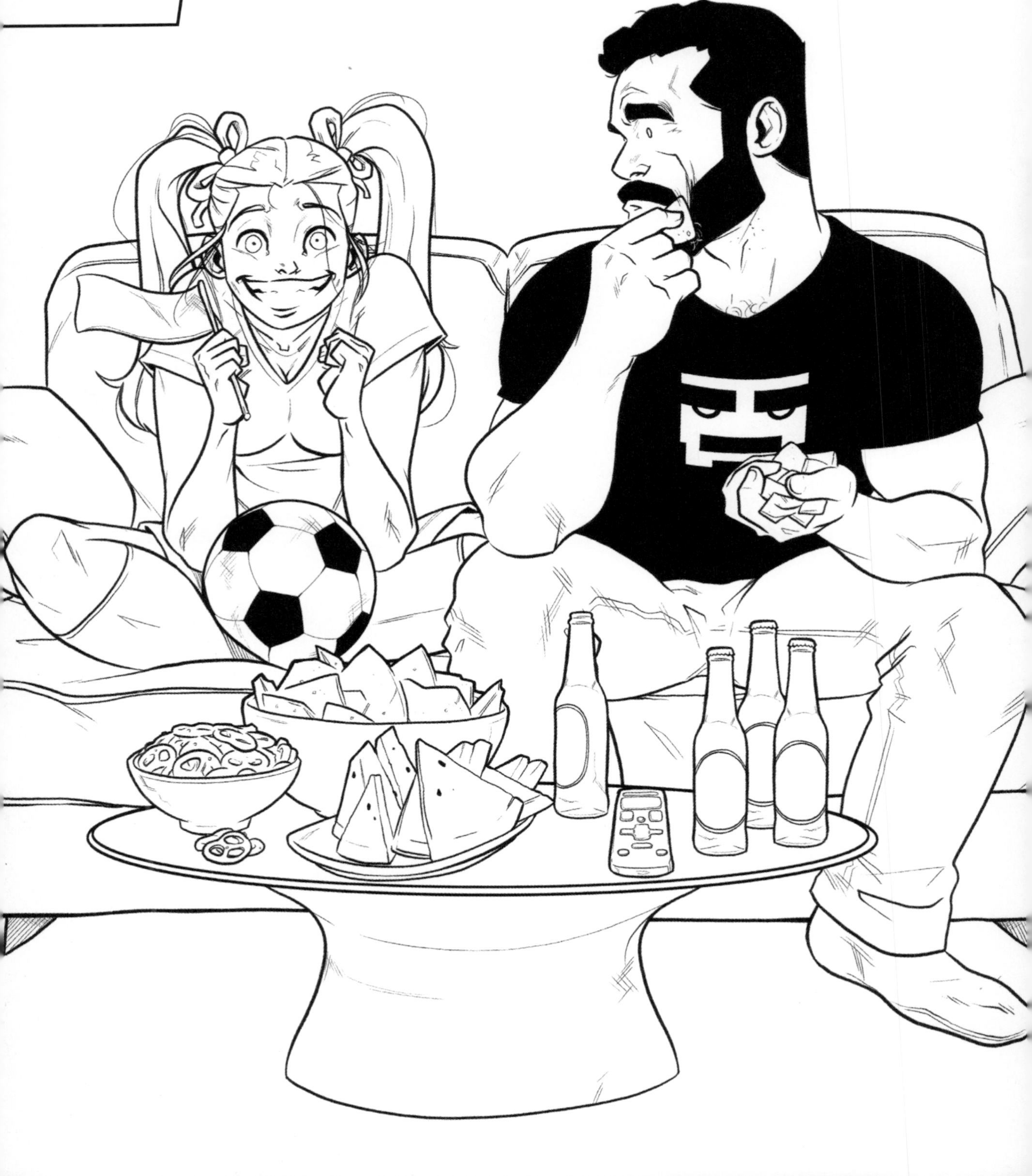

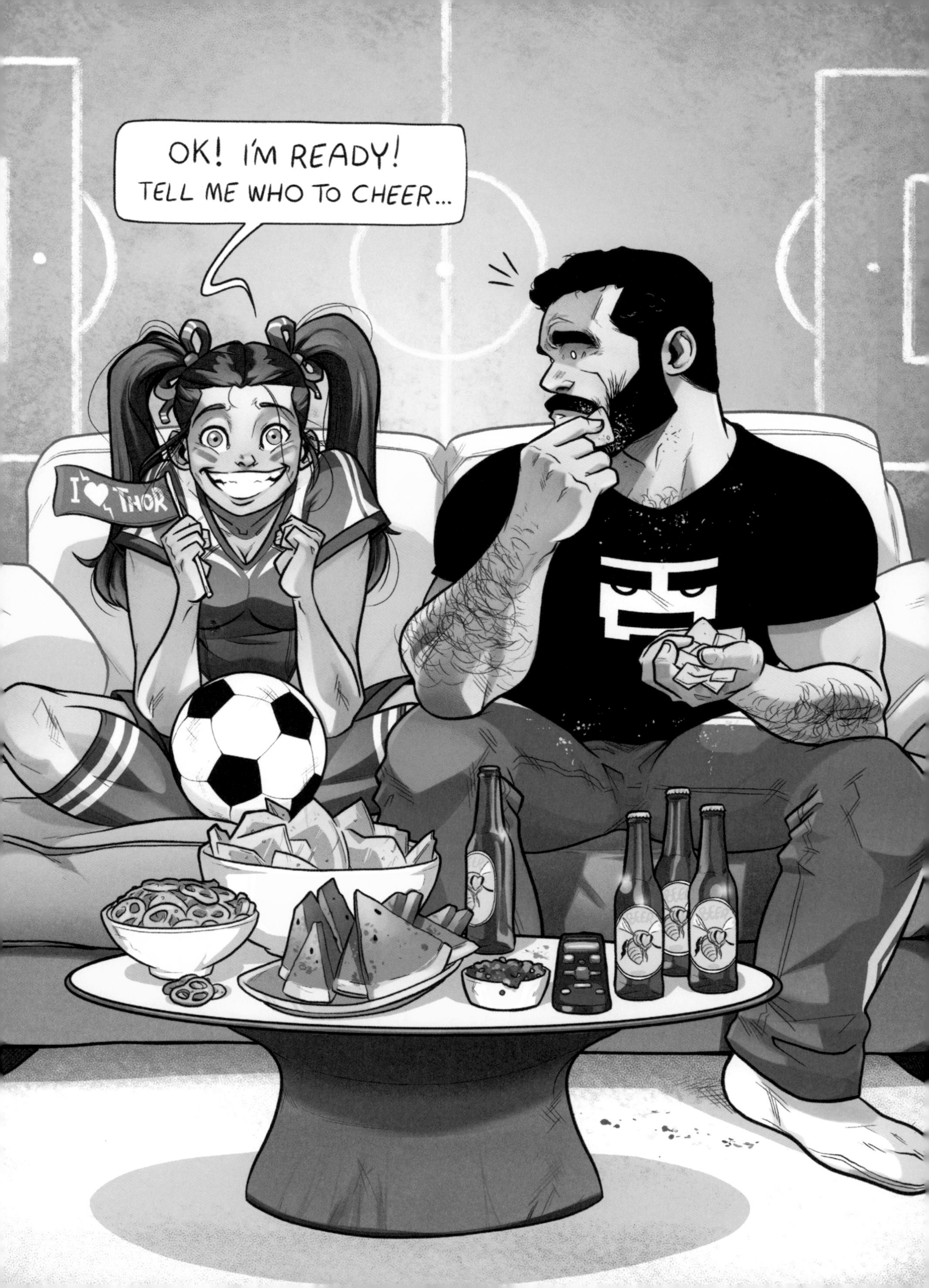
OK! I'M READY!
TELL ME WHO TO CHEER...
I ♥ THOR

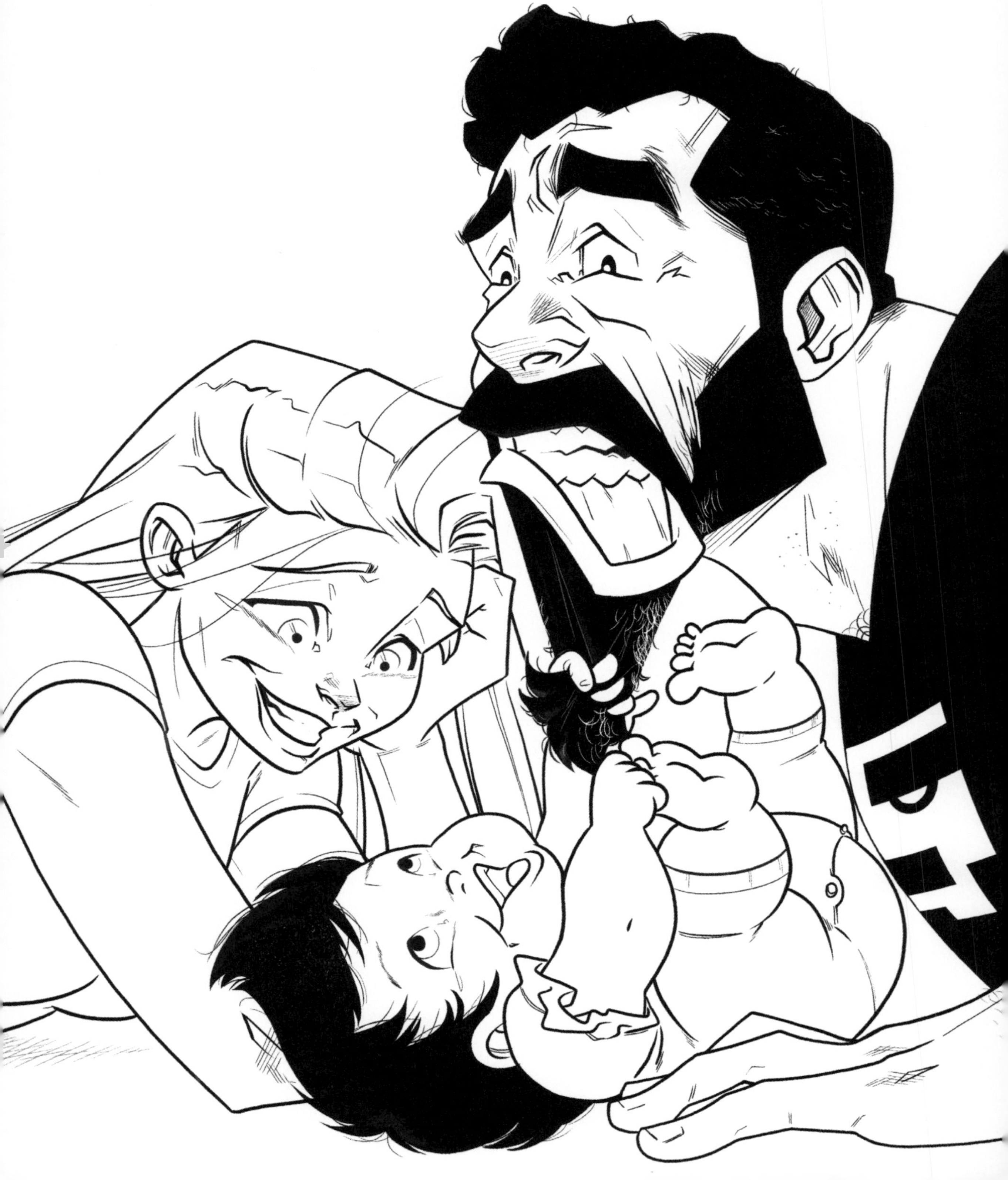

CHAPTER
THREE

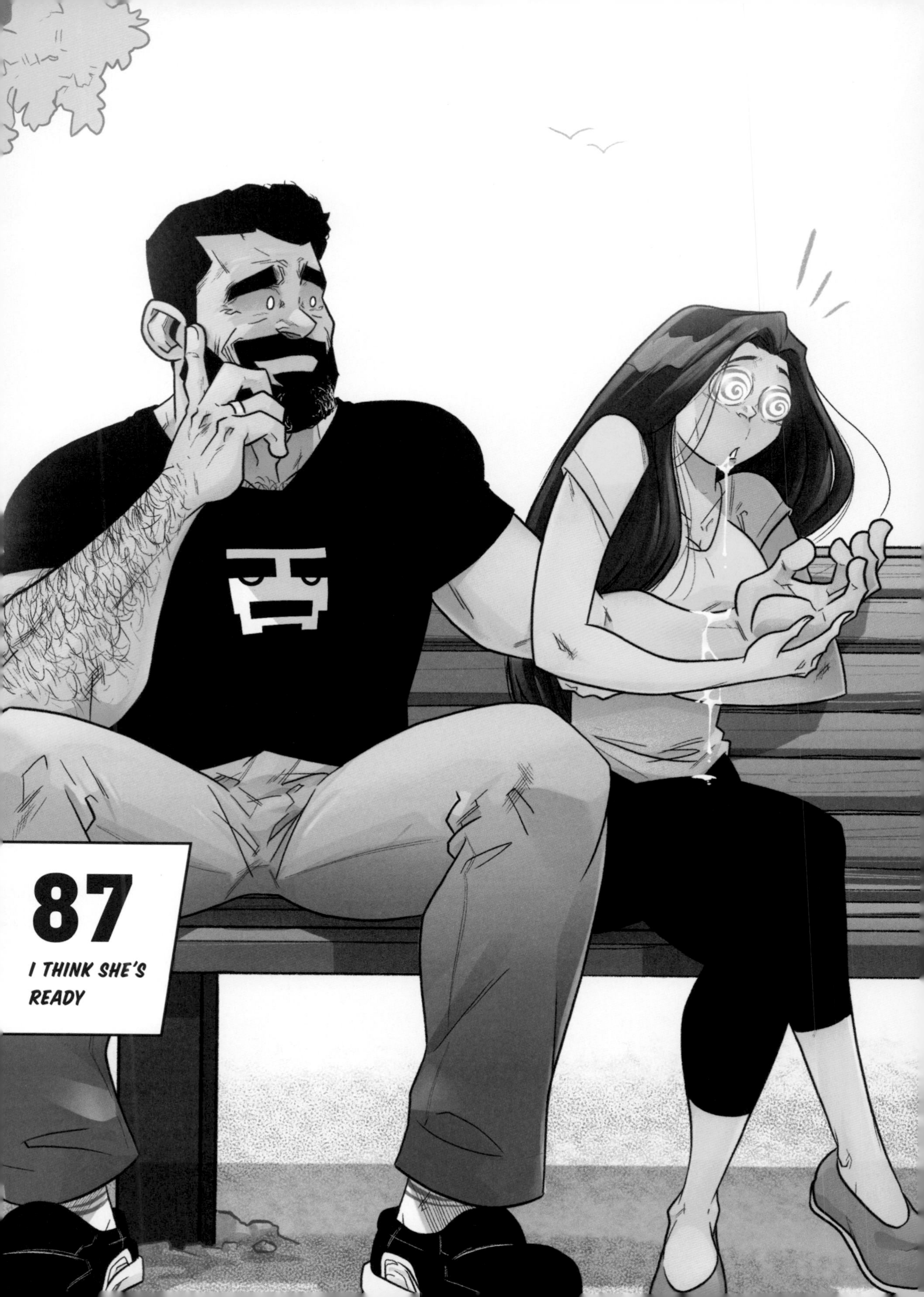

87

I THINK SHE'S READY

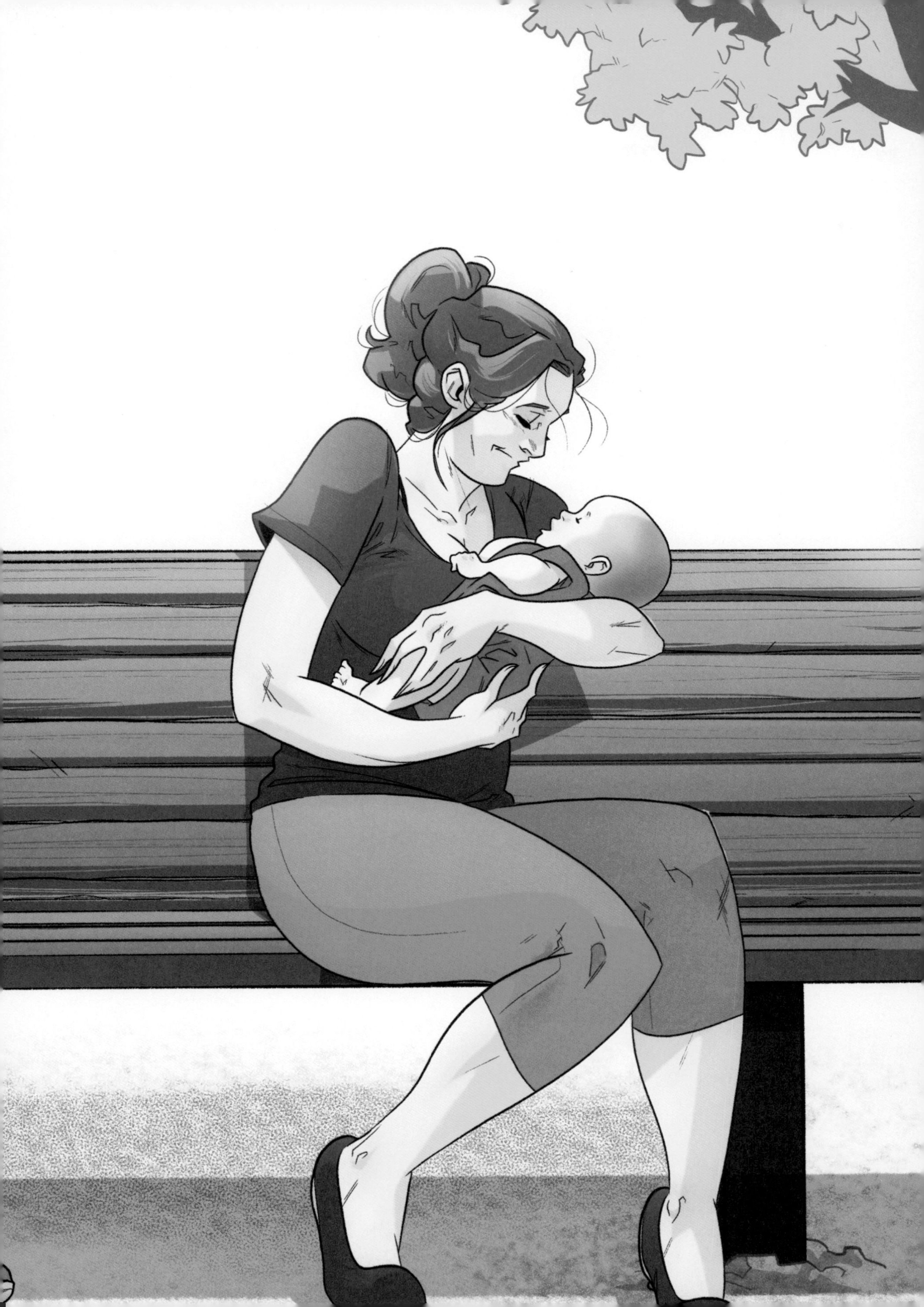

88

THE ART OF SEDUCTION

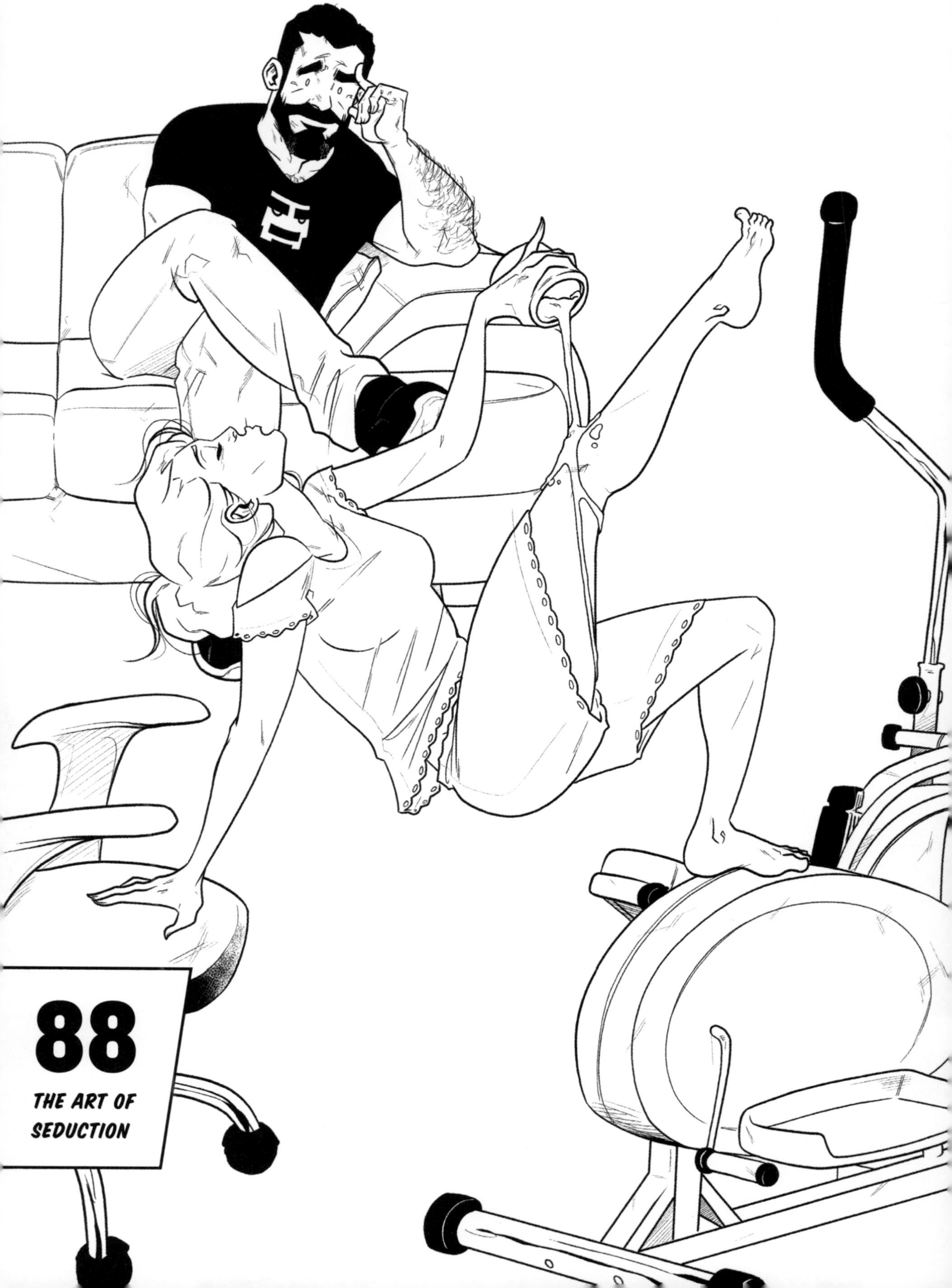

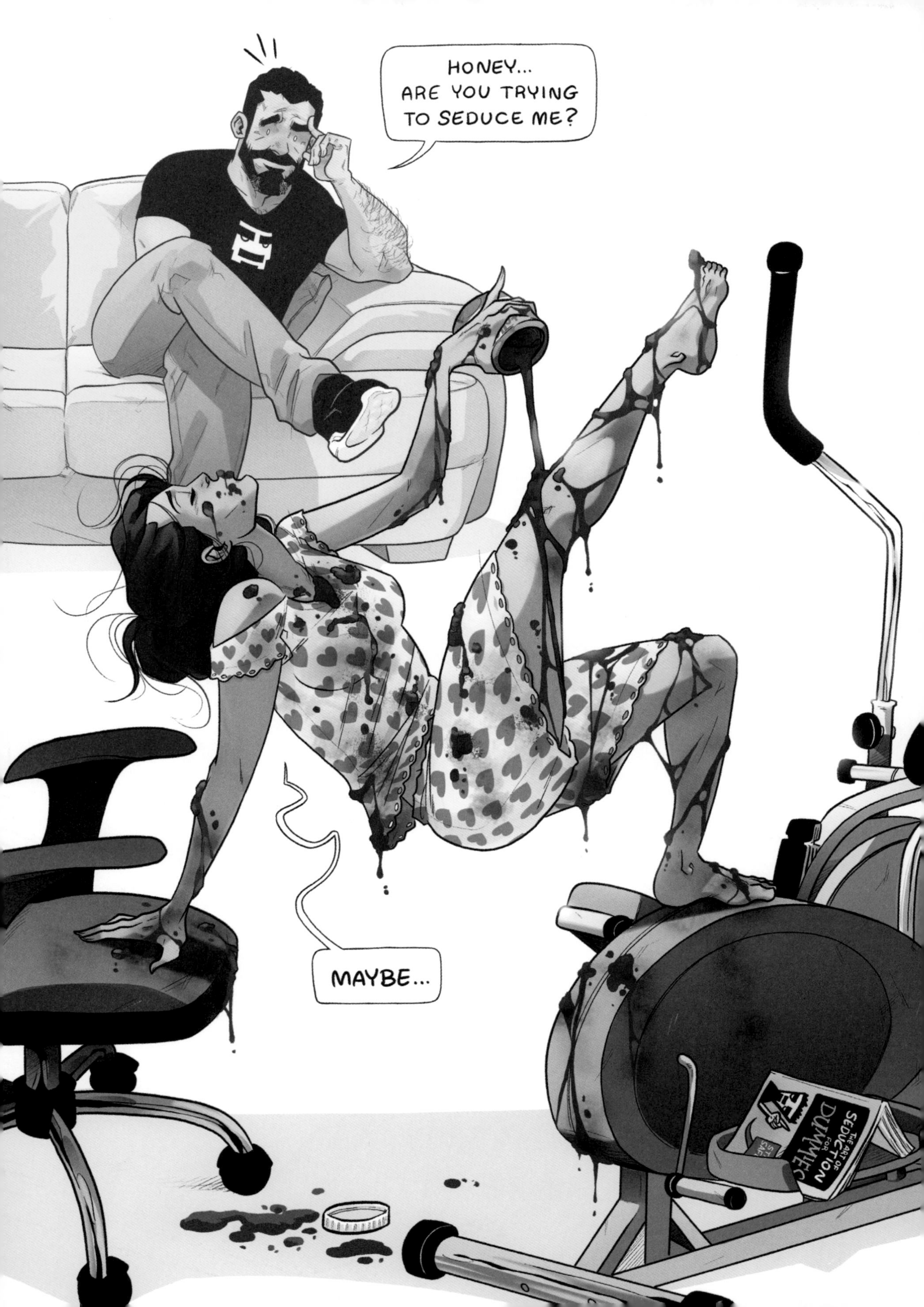
HONEY... ARE YOU TRYING TO SEDUCE ME?
MAYBE...

89

OPERATION OVULATION

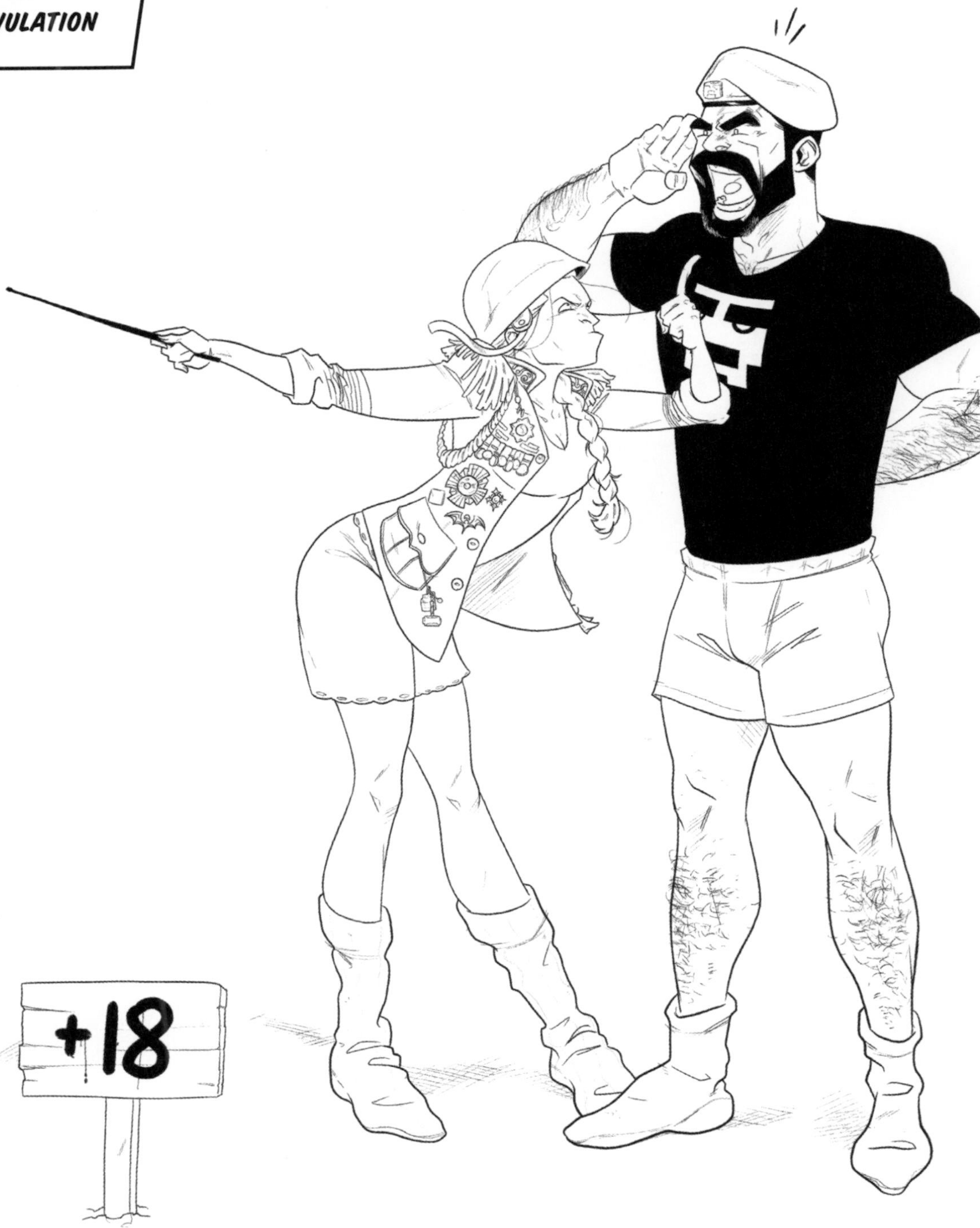
+18

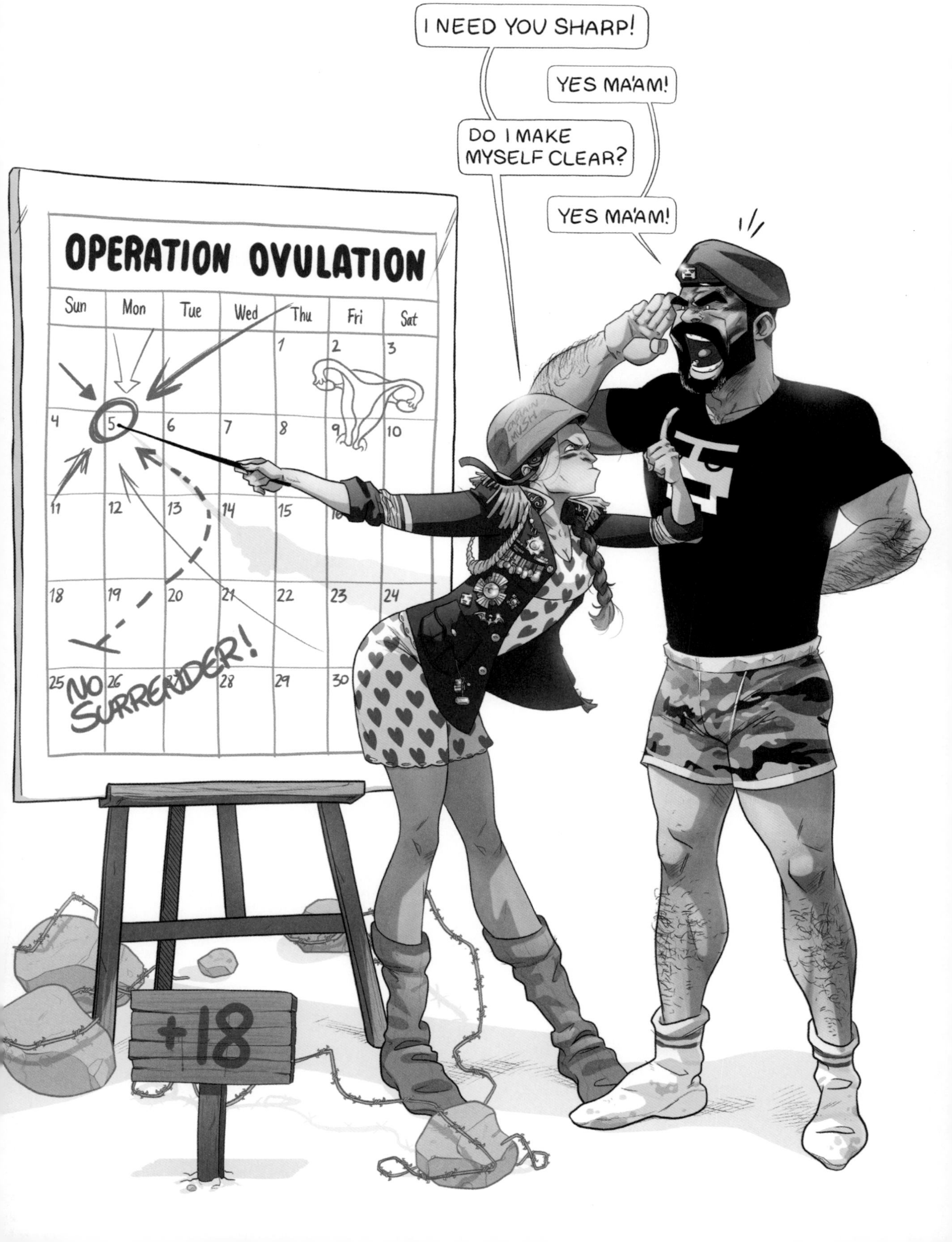
I NEED YOU SHARP!
YES MA'AM!
DO I MAKE MYSELF CLEAR?
YES MA'AM!
OPERATION OVULATION
Sun Mon Tue Wed Thu Fri Sat
NO SURRENDER!
CAPTAIN MUSH
+18

90

NO PAIN NO GAIN

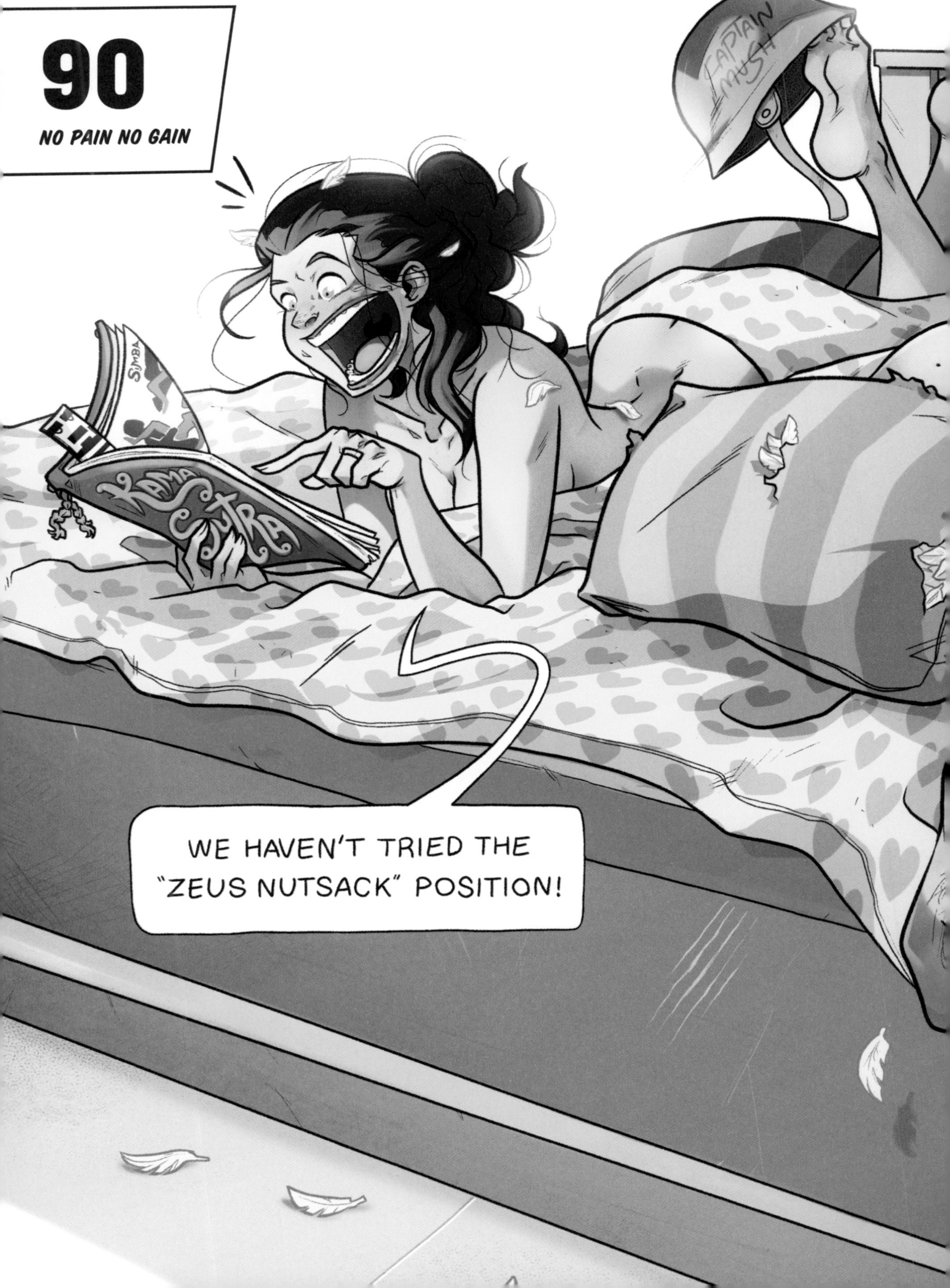
CAPTAIN MUSH
SIMBA
KAMA SUTRA
WE HAVEN'T TRIED THE "ZEUS NUTSACK" POSITION!

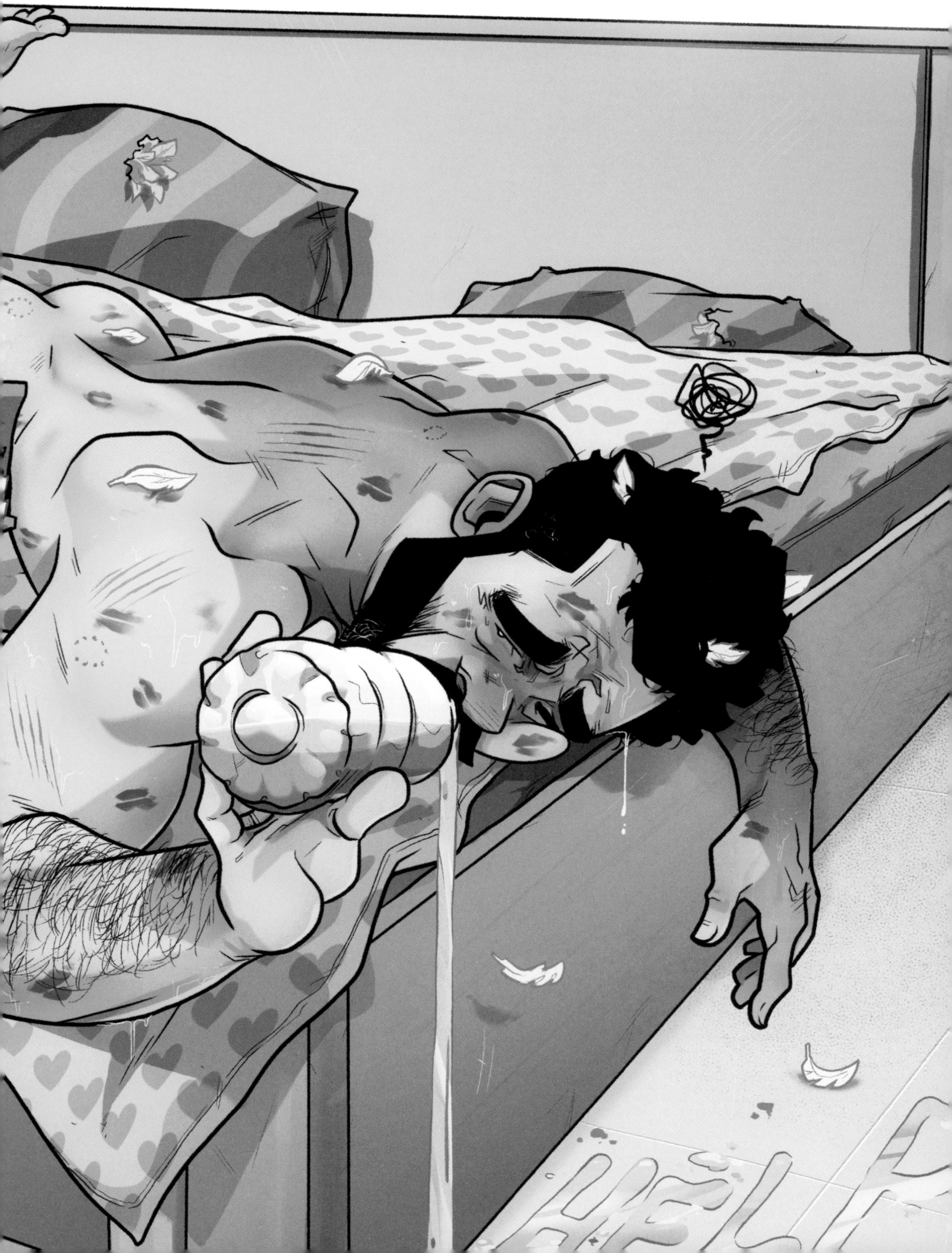
HELP

91

BABY POTION

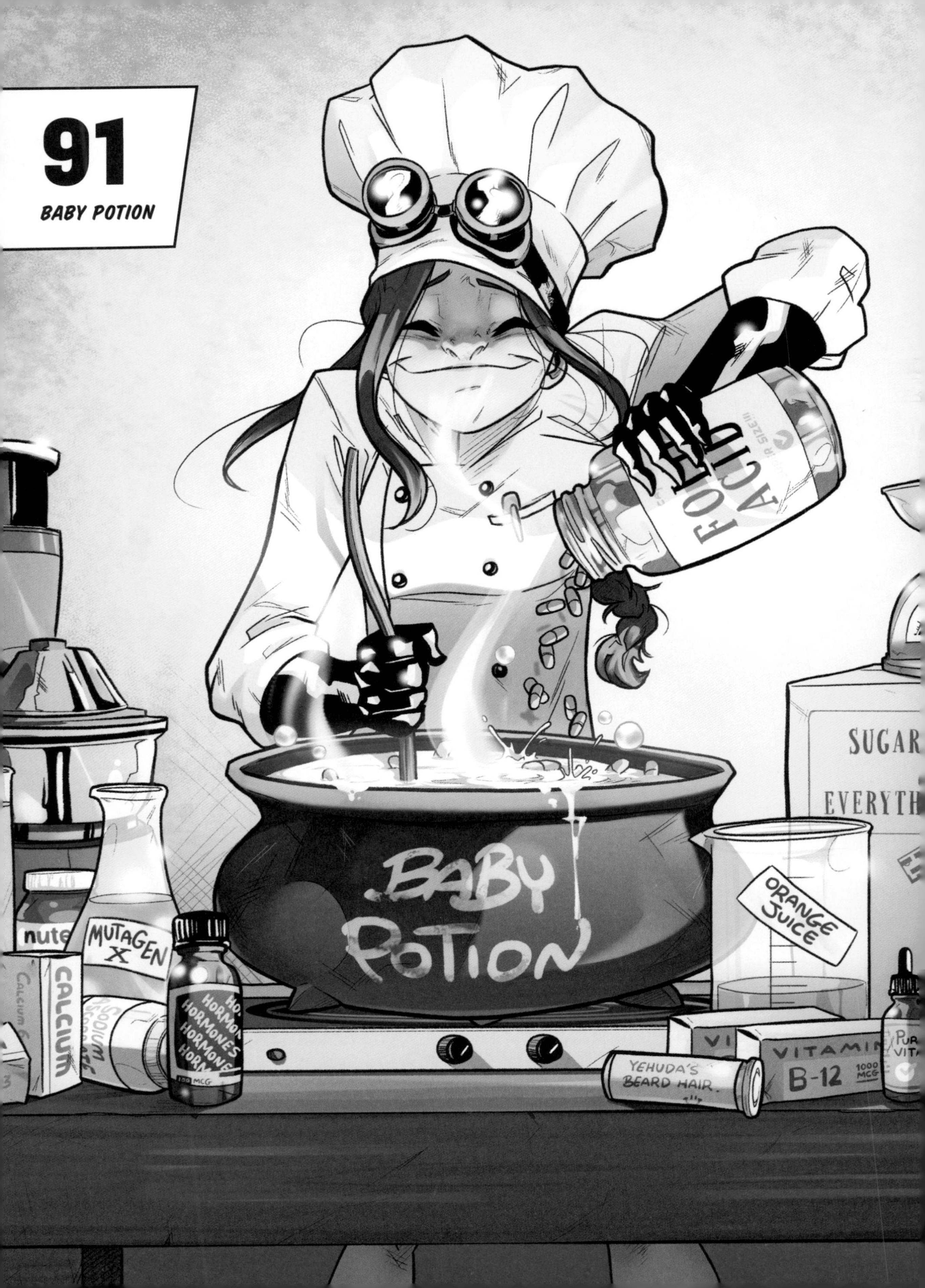
FOLIC ACID
SUGAR
EVERYTH
BABY POTION
ORANGE JUICE
nute
MUTAGEN X
CALCIUM
HORMONES
YEHUDA'S BEARD HAIR.
VITAMIN B-12 1000 MCG

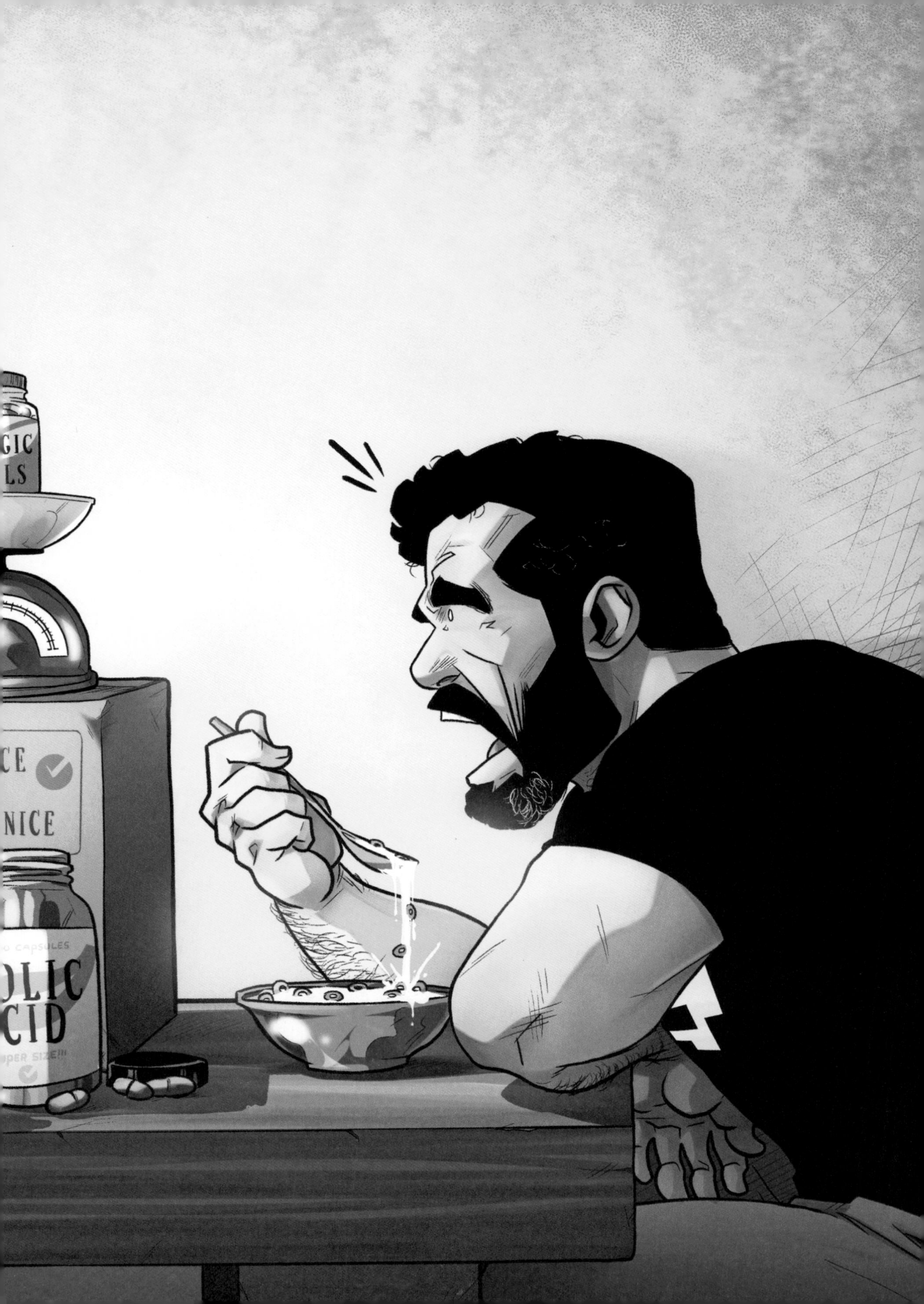
GIC
LS
CE
NICE
CAPSULES
OLIC
CID
UPER SIZE!!!

92

HUMAN MATTRESS

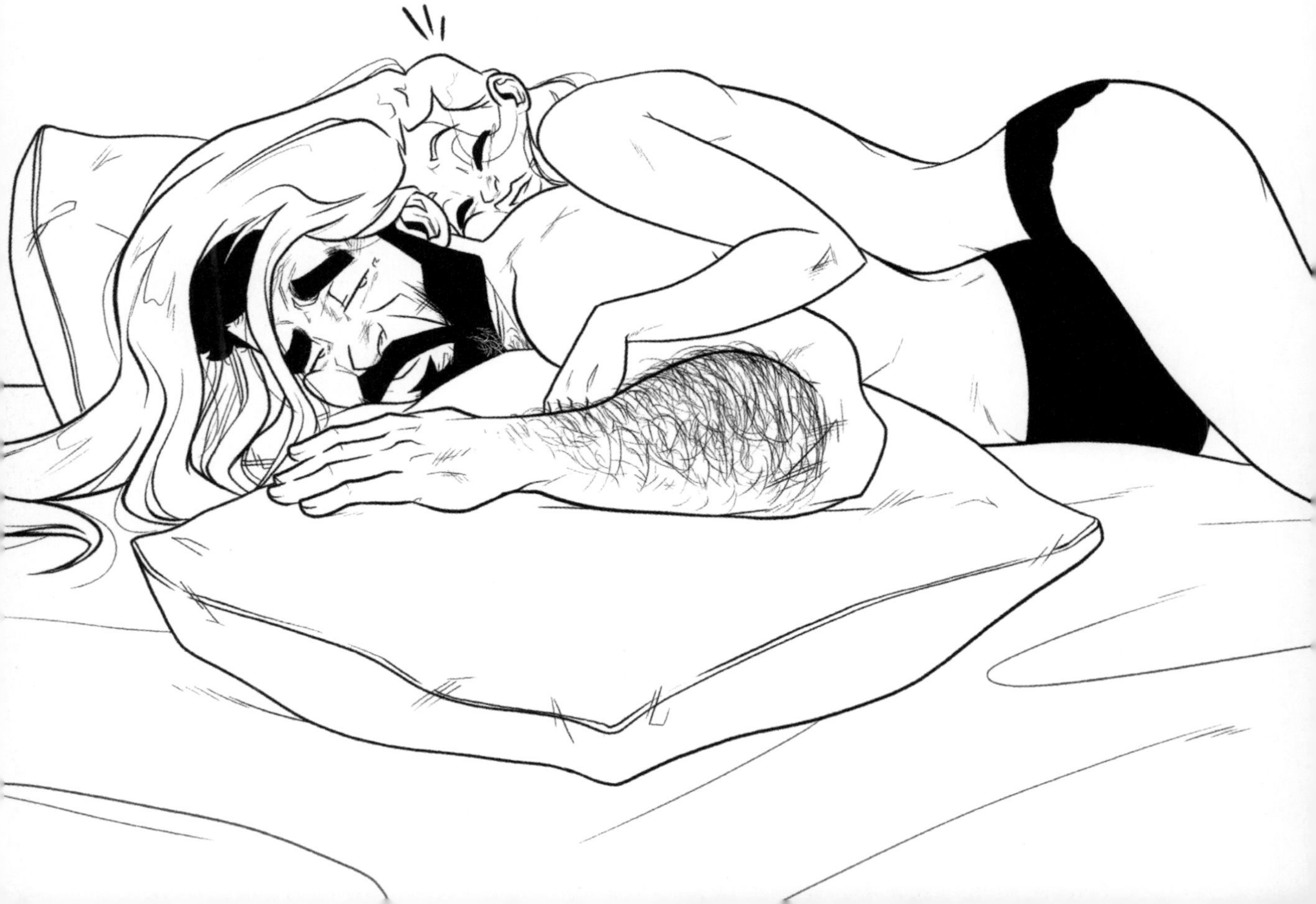

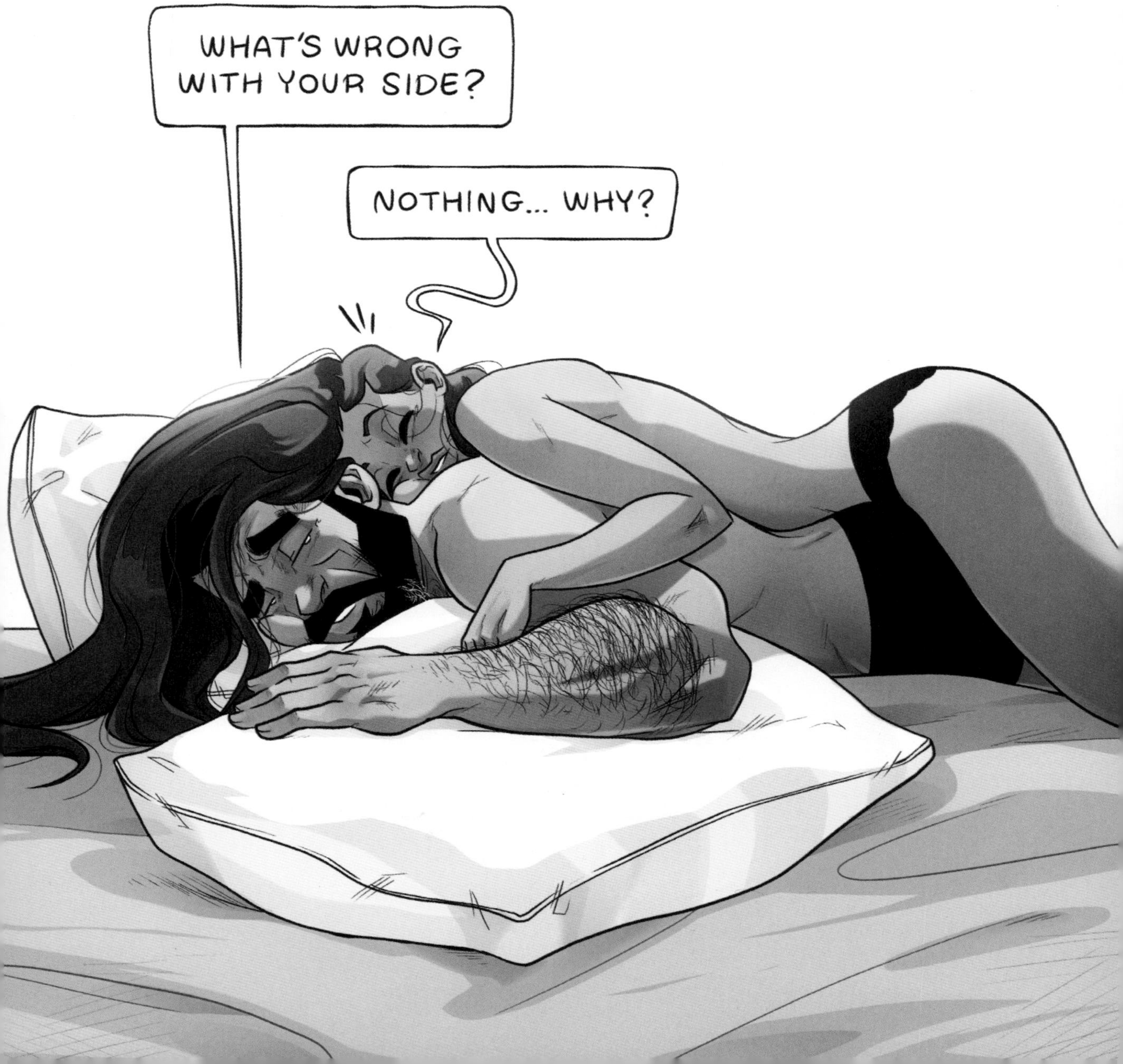
WHAT'S WRONG WITH YOUR SIDE?
NOTHING... WHY?

93

THE PERIOD

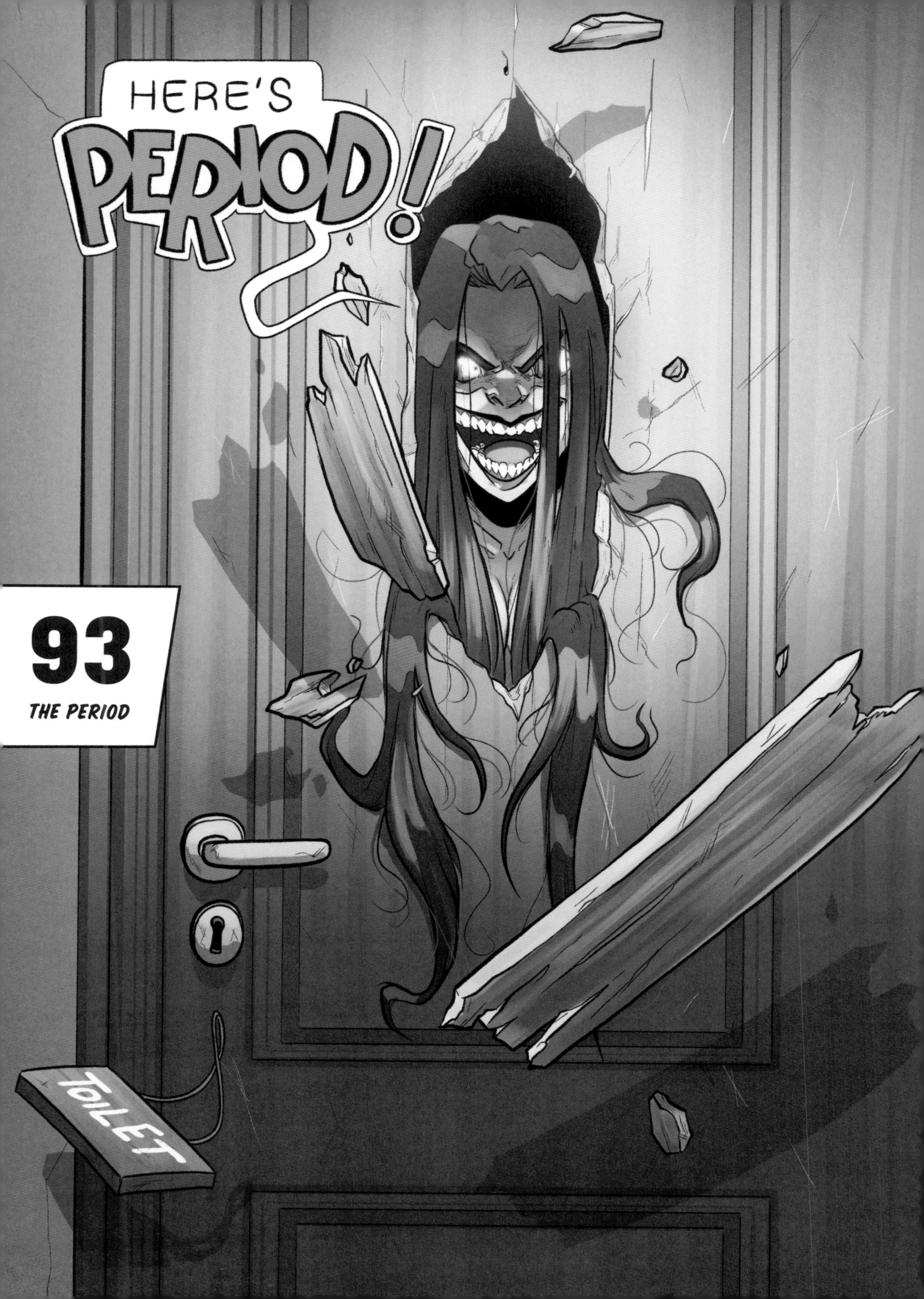
HERE'S PERIOD!
TOILET

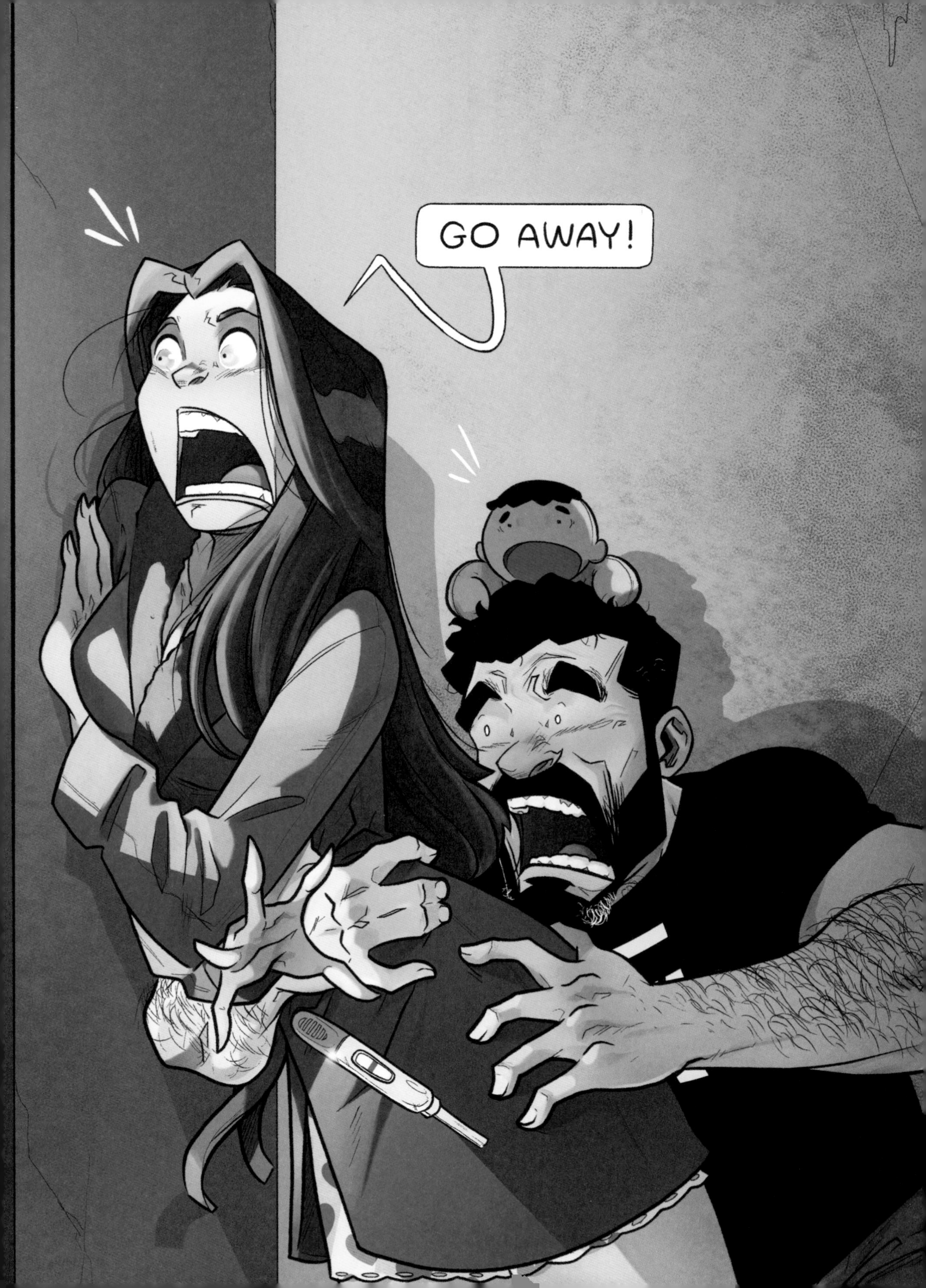
GO AWAY!

94

I'M A BIG BOY NOW!

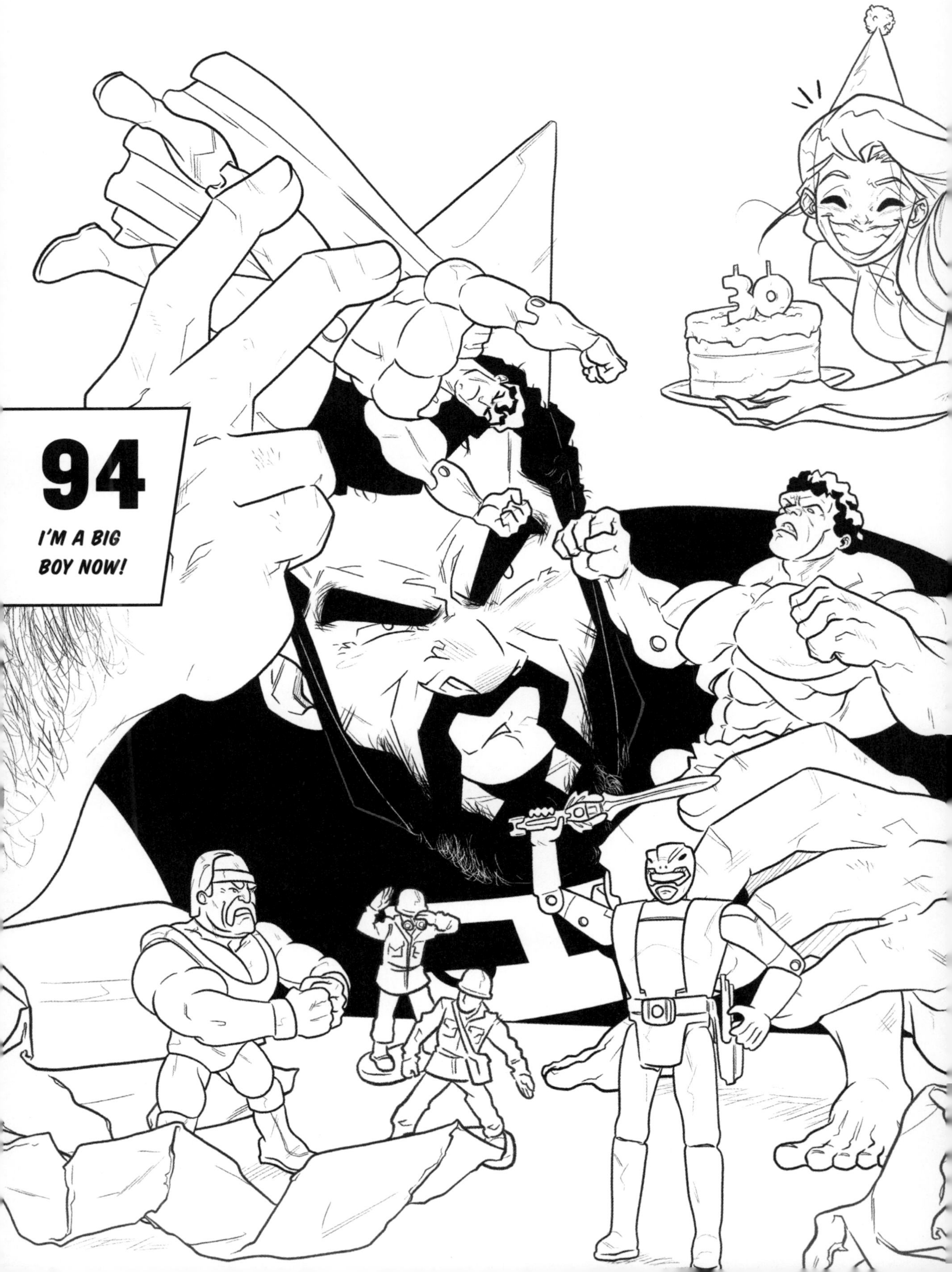

30

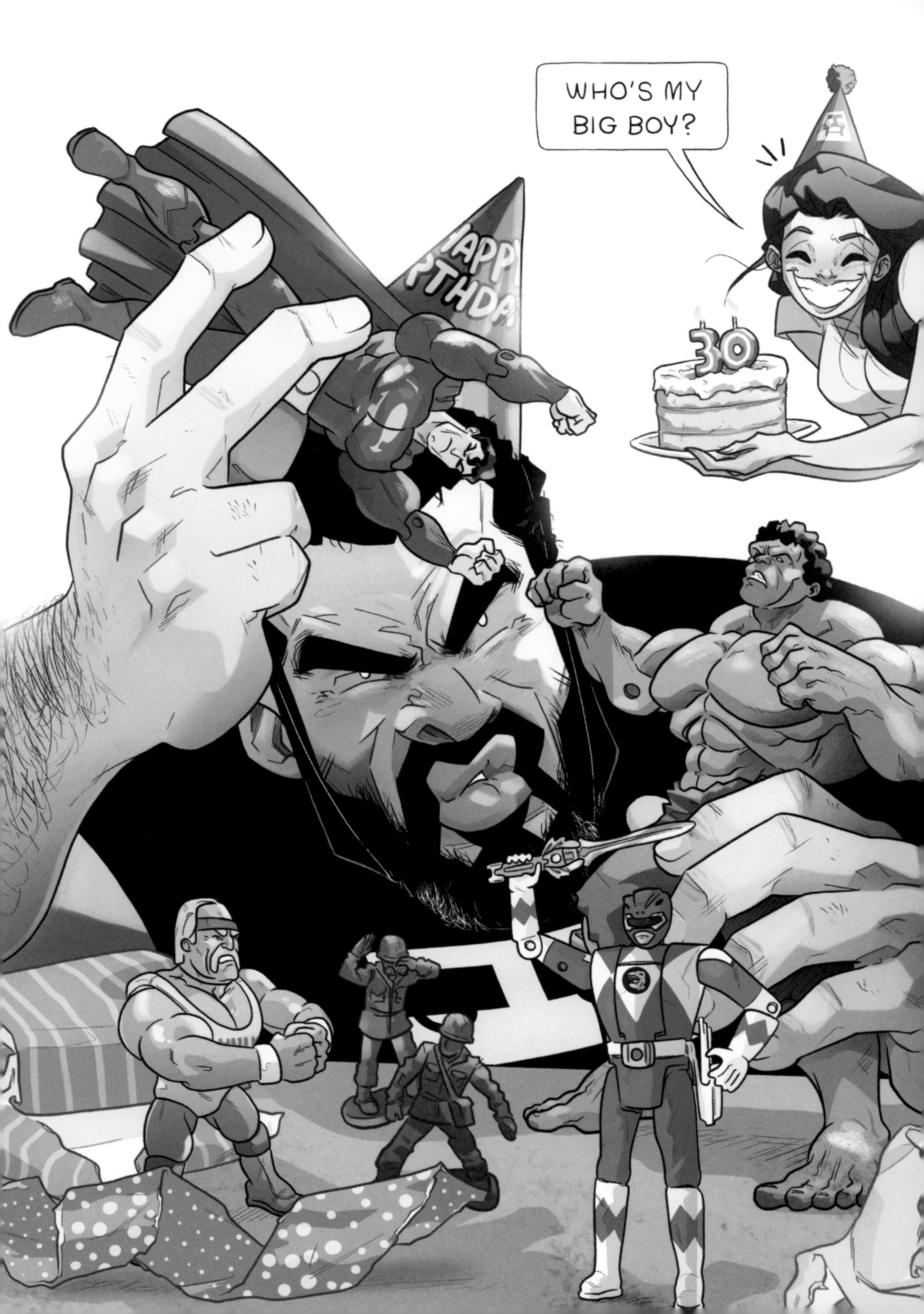
WHO'S MY BIG BOY?
HAPPY
RTHDA
30

95

LAUNDRY DAY

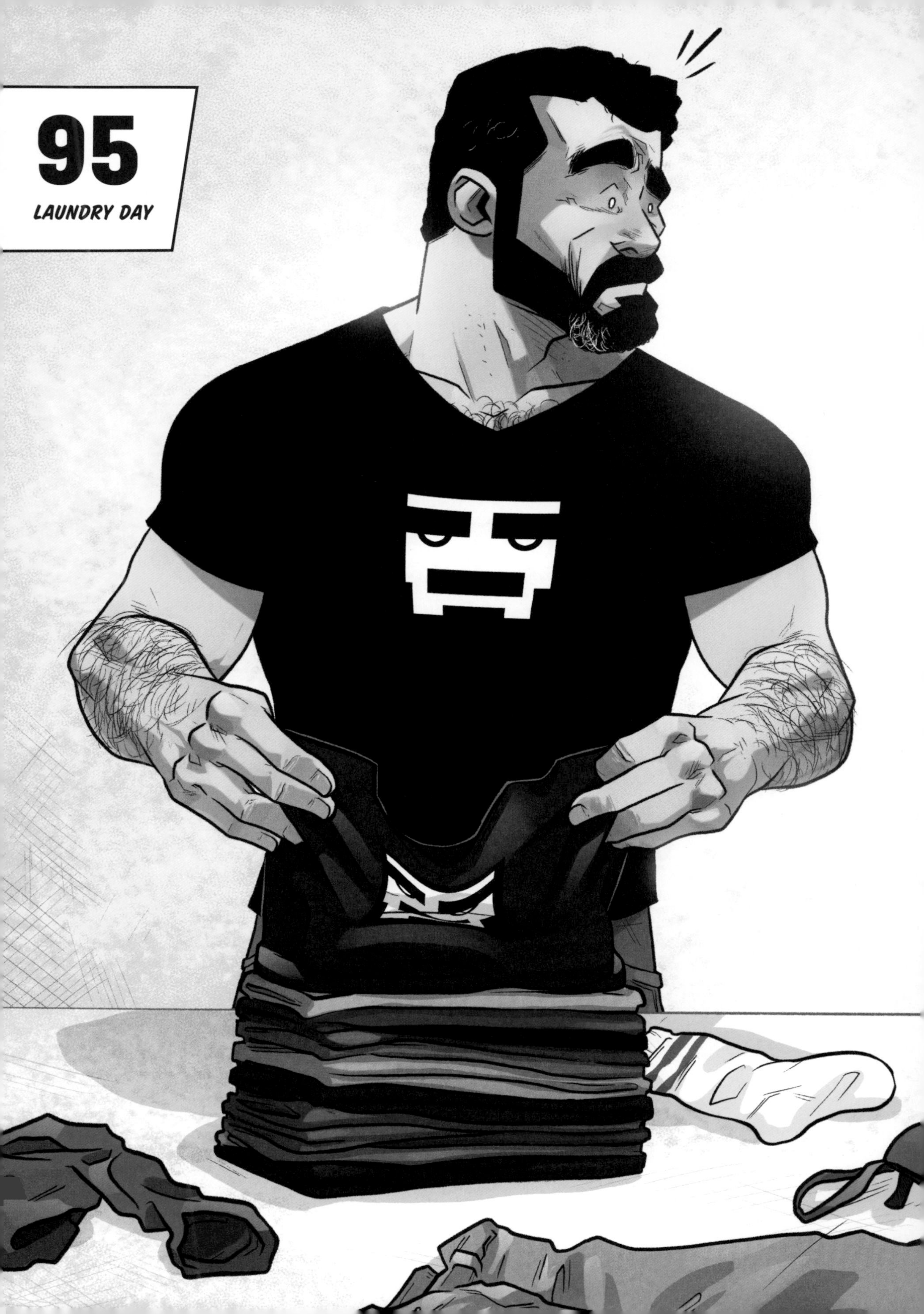

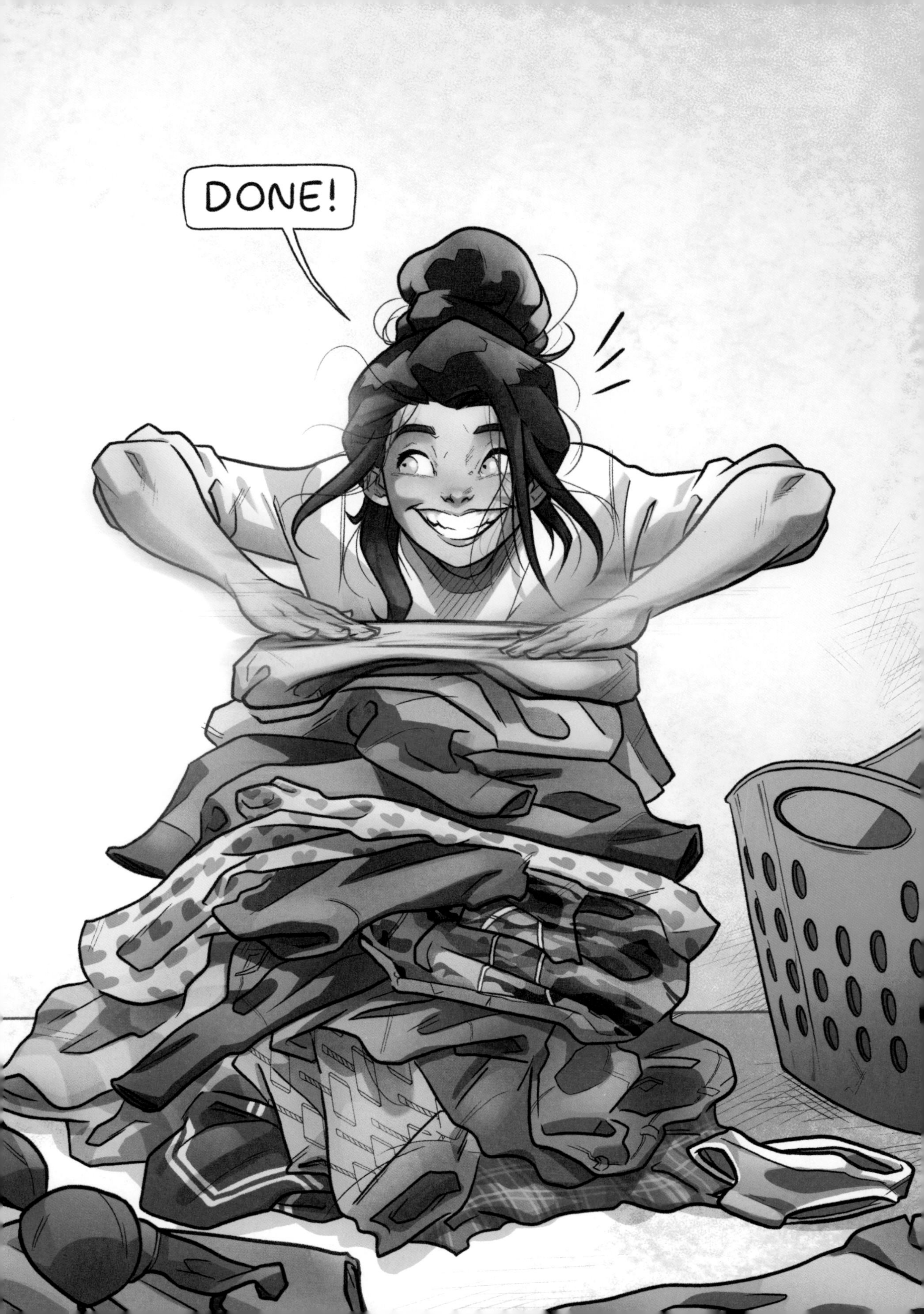
DONE!

96

BLACK FRIDAY

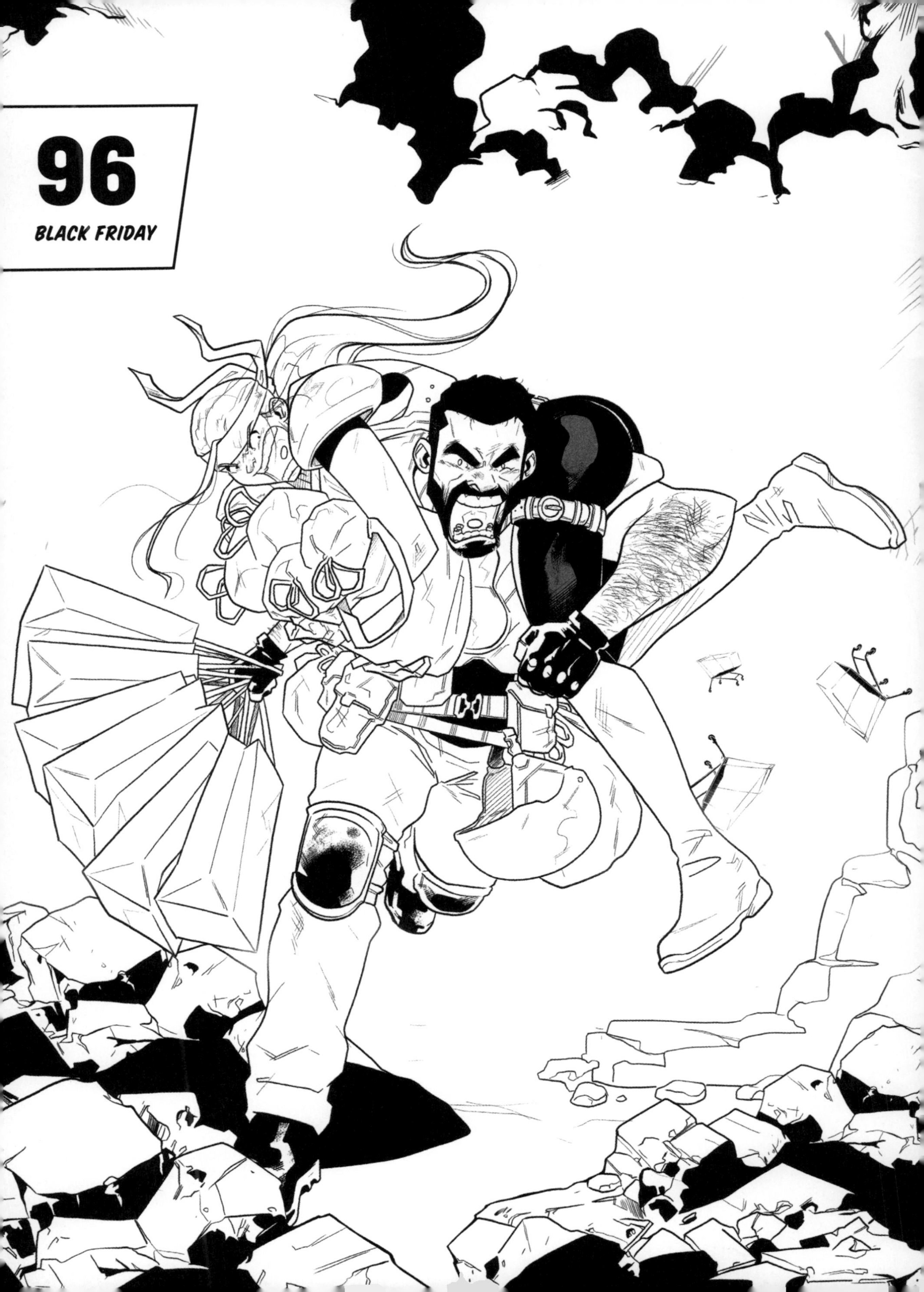

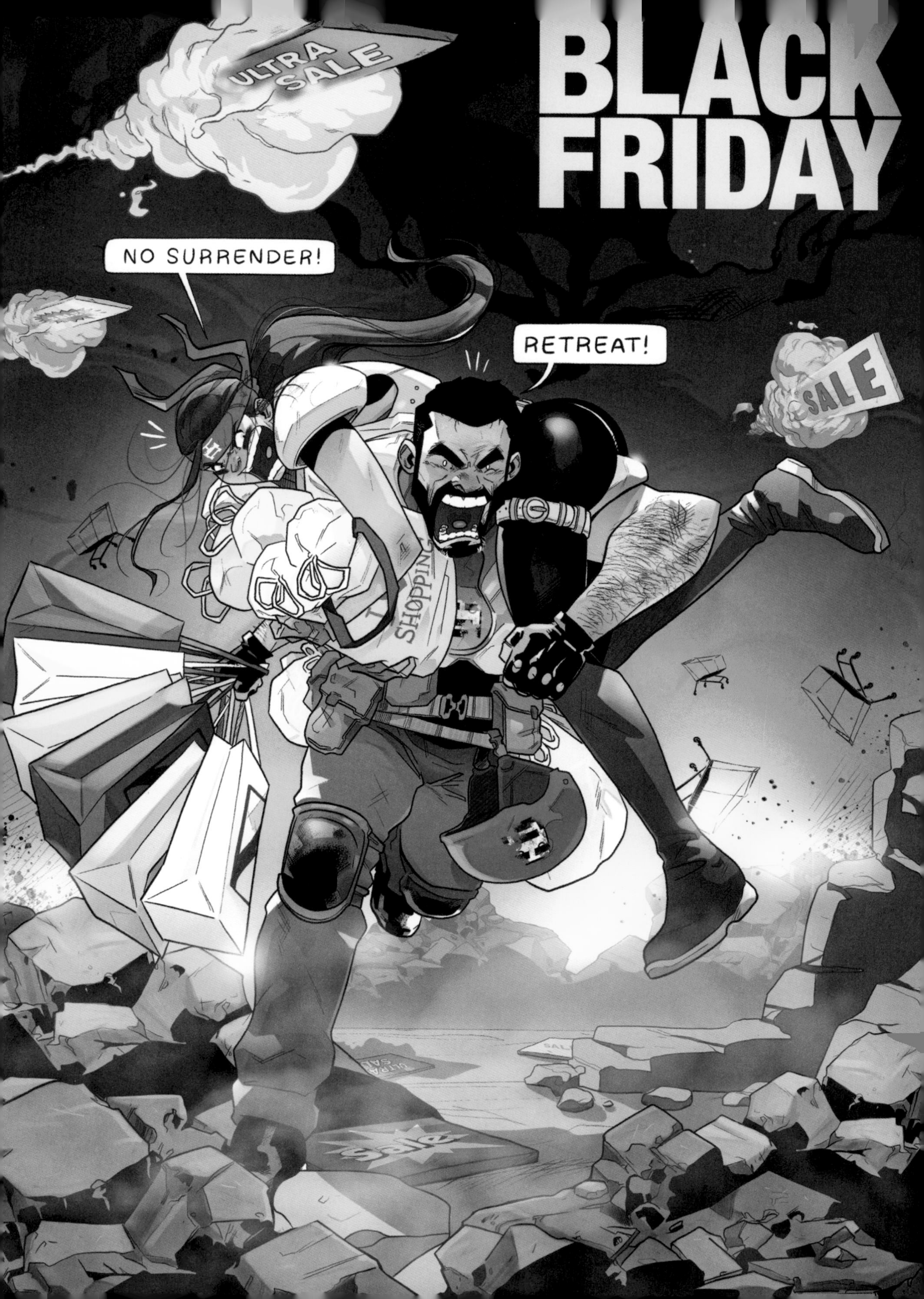

BLACK FRIDAY
ULTRA SALE
NO SURRENDER!
RETREAT!
SALE
SHOPPING
Sale

97

DRAMA QUEEN

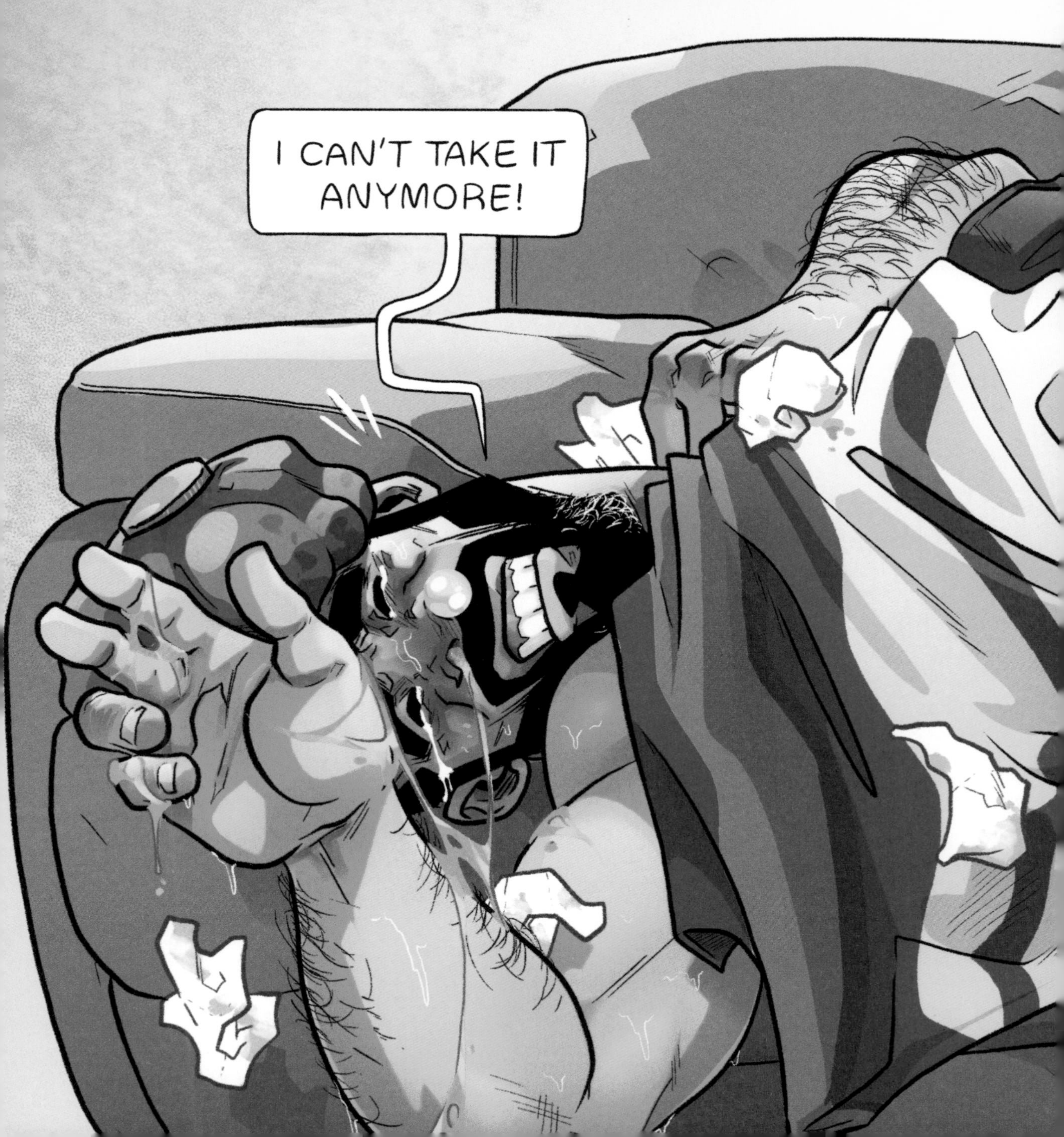
I CAN'T TAKE IT ANYMORE!

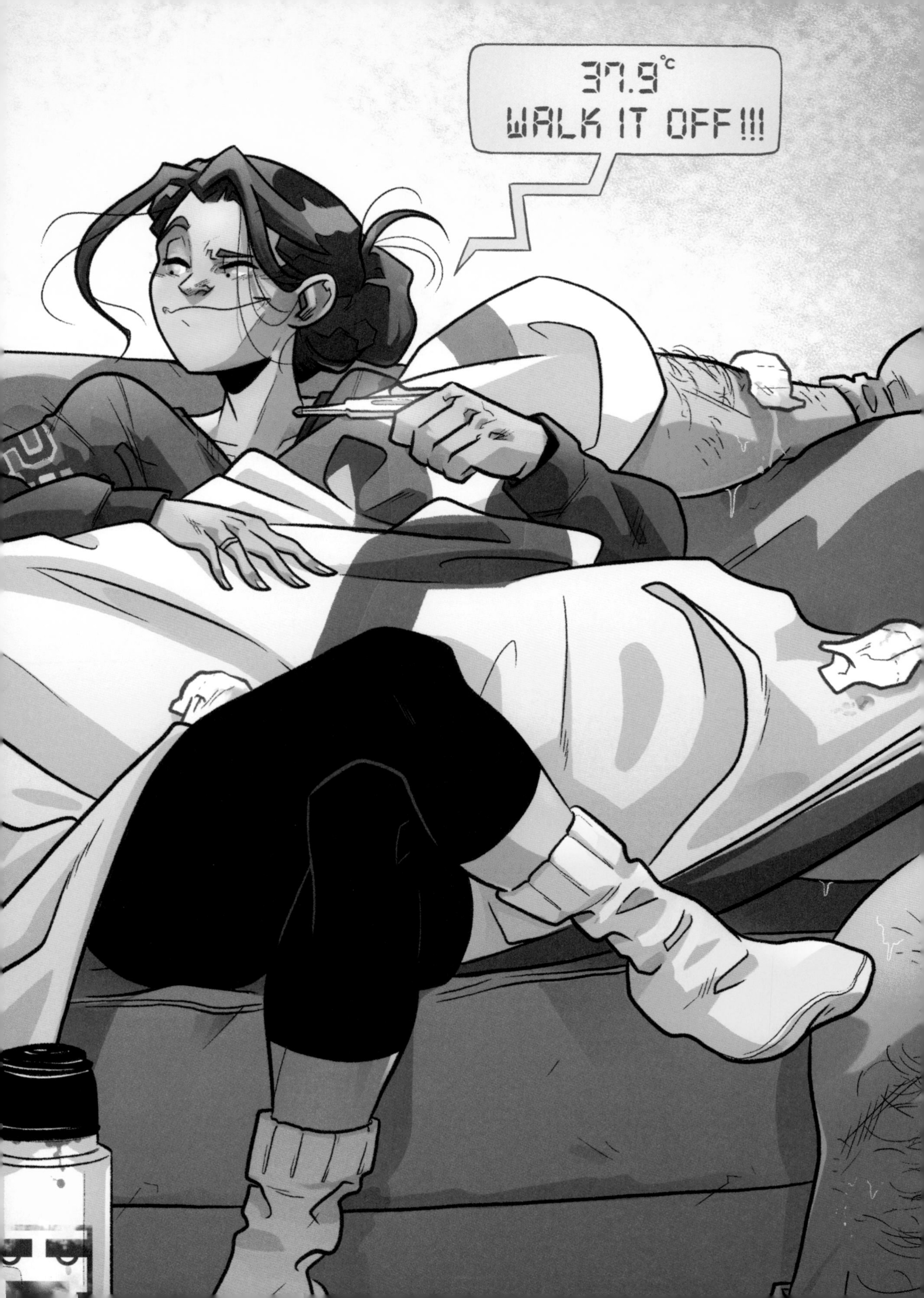
37.9°C
WALK IT OFF!!!!

98

WE HAVE A NEW WEBSITE!

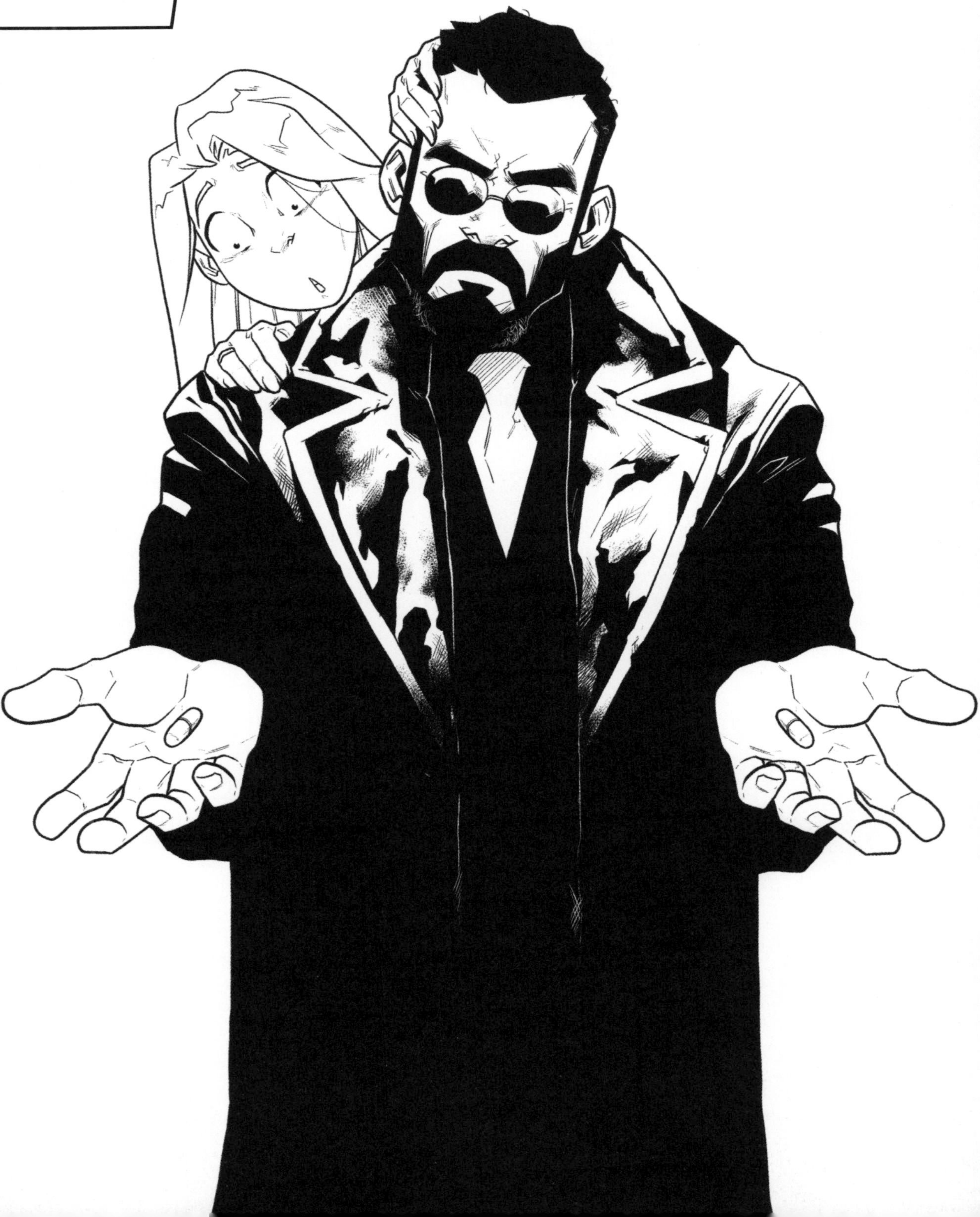

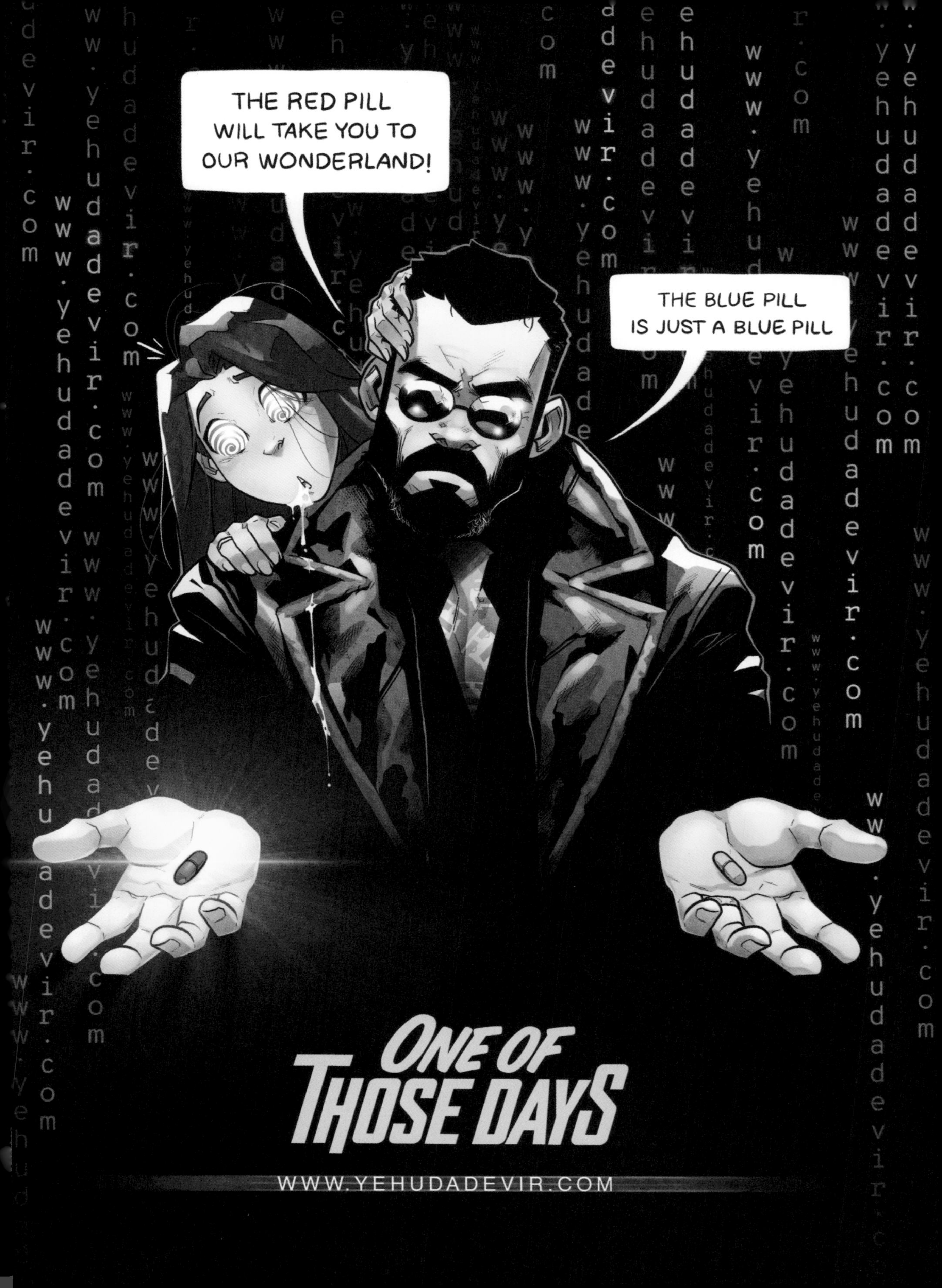
THE RED PILL WILL TAKE YOU TO OUR WONDERLAND!
THE BLUE PILL IS JUST A BLUE PILL
ONE OF THOSE DAYS
WWW.YEHUDADEVIR.COM

99

WE WERE MAID FOR EACH OTHER

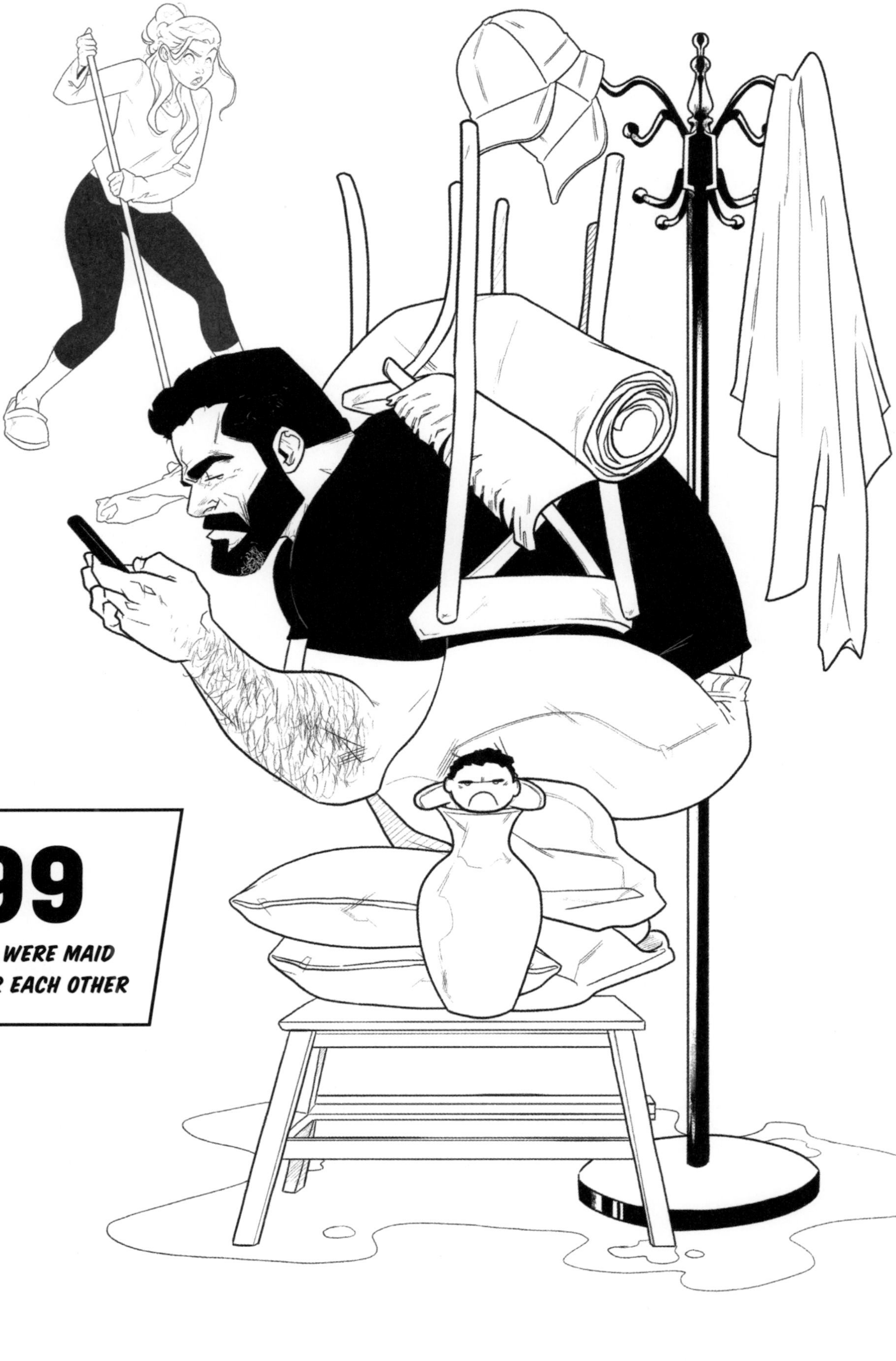

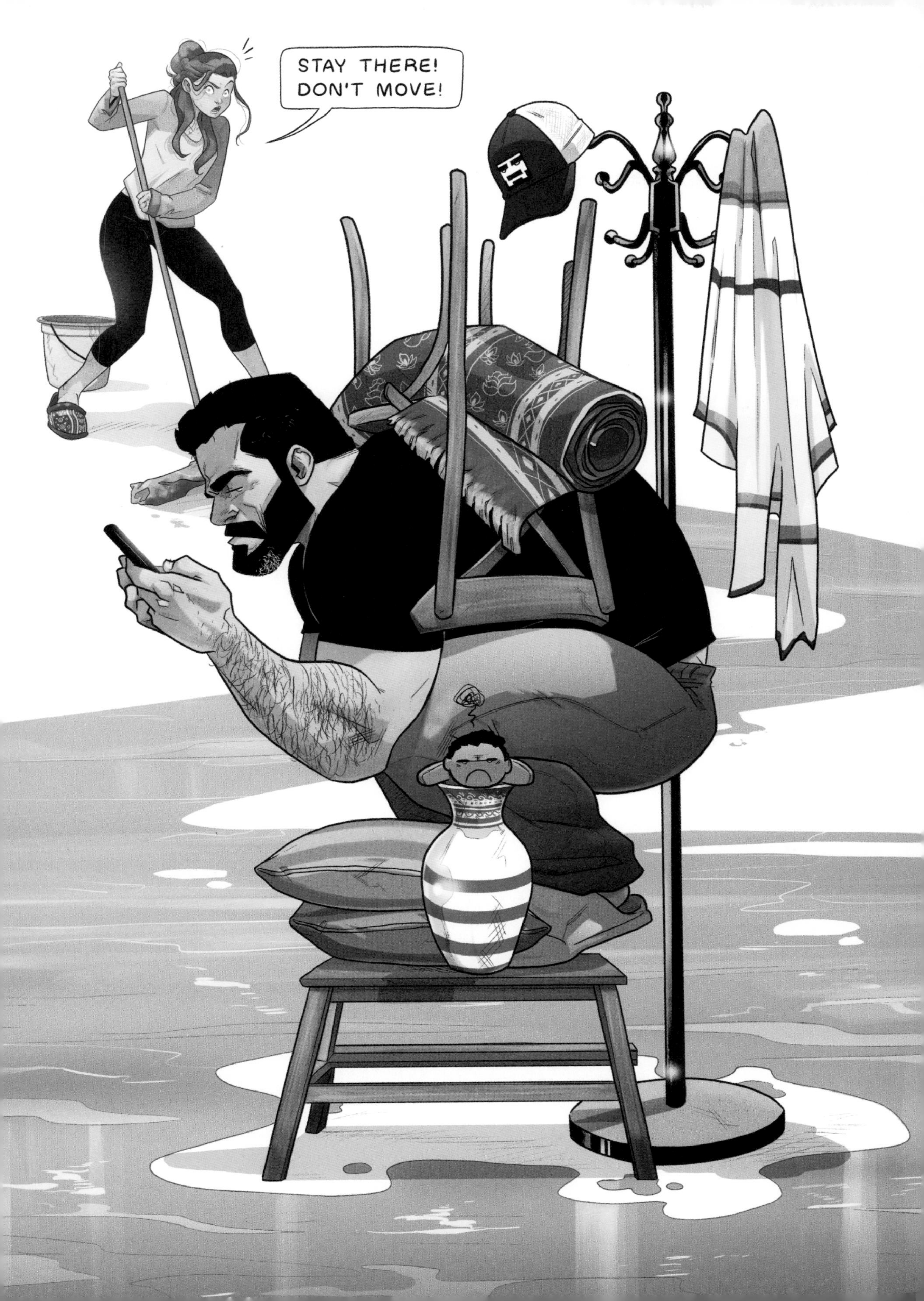
STAY THERE! DON'T MOVE!

100

WE'RE PREGNANT!

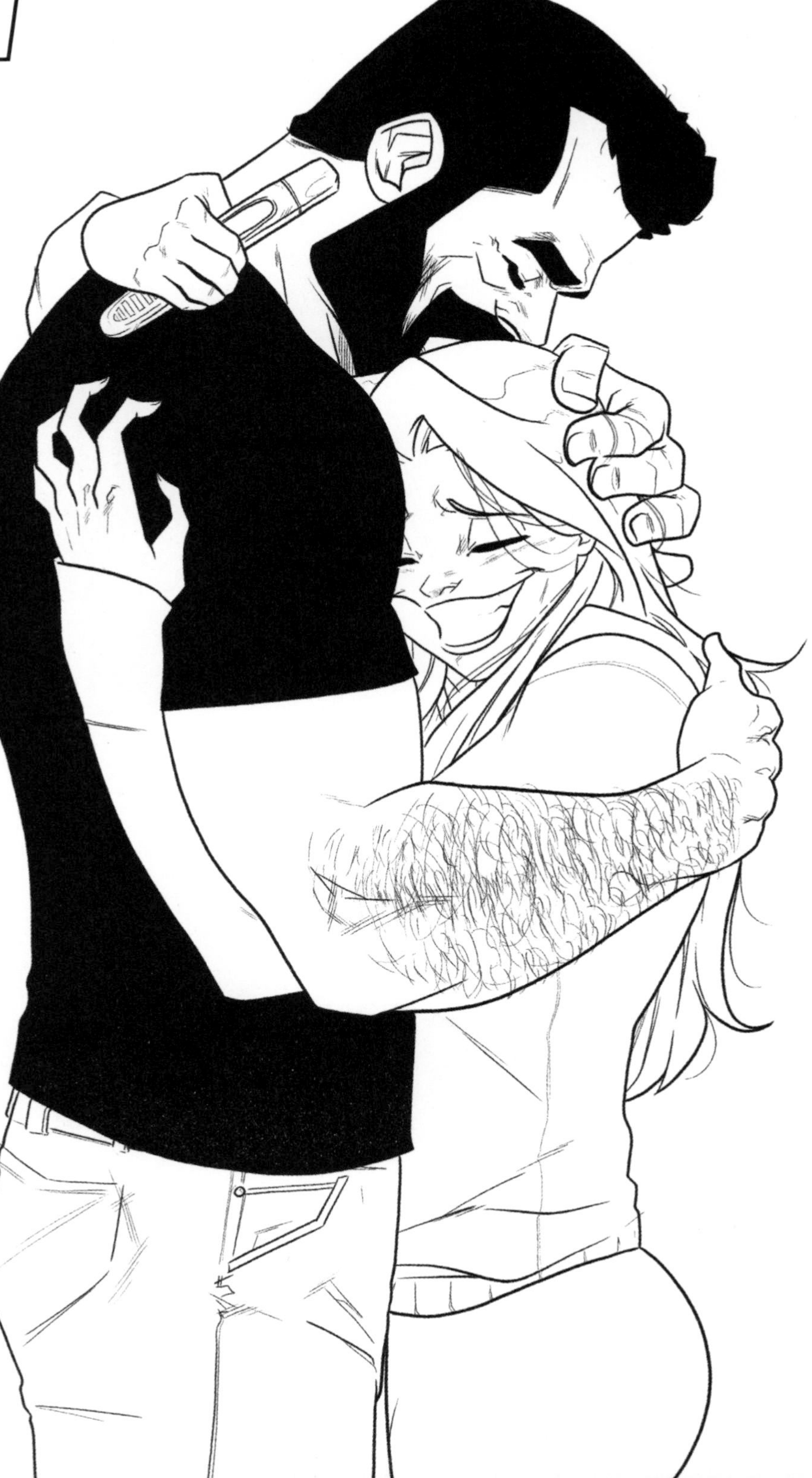

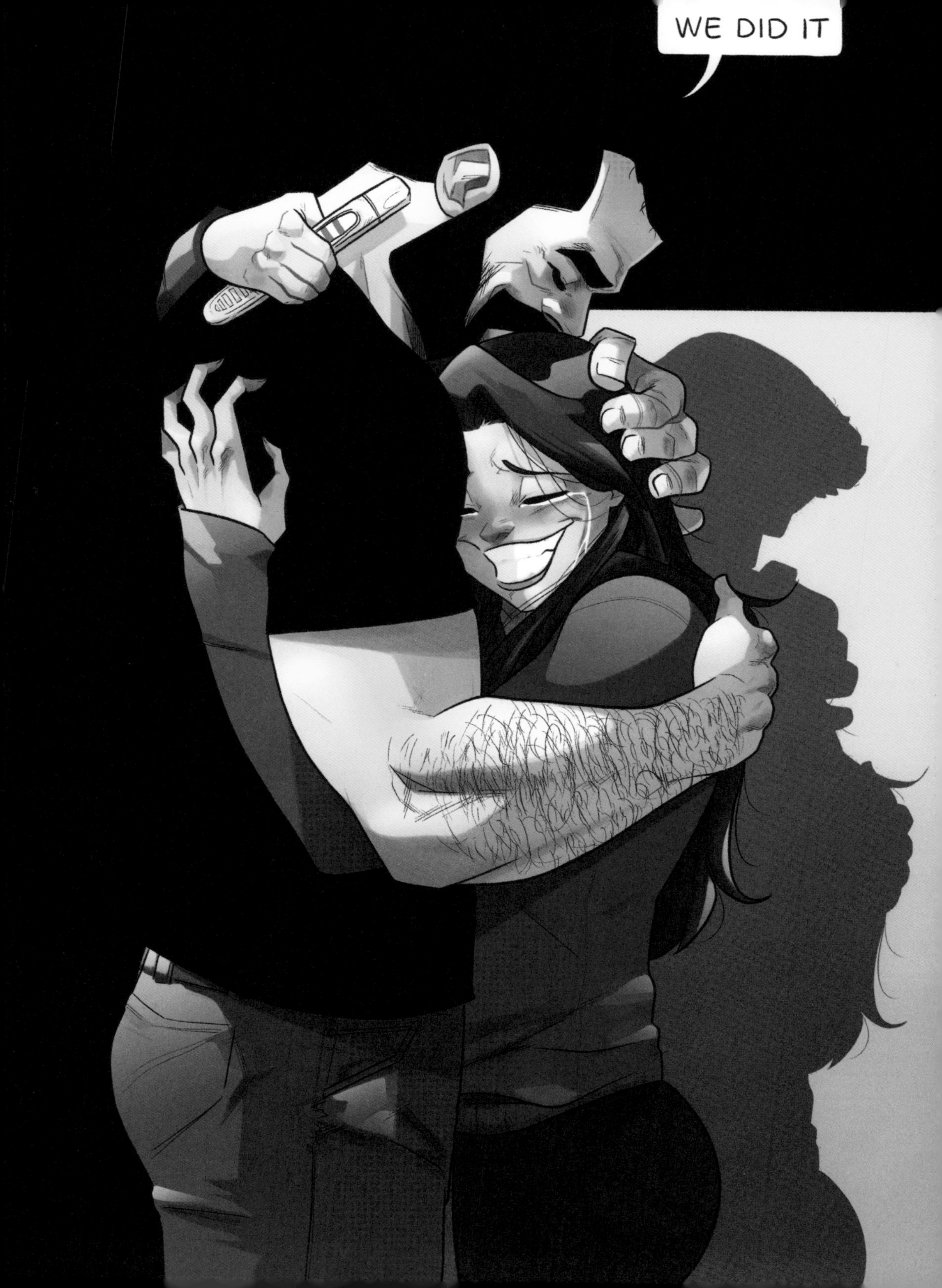
WE DID IT

101

MOVING TO THE COUNTRYSIDE

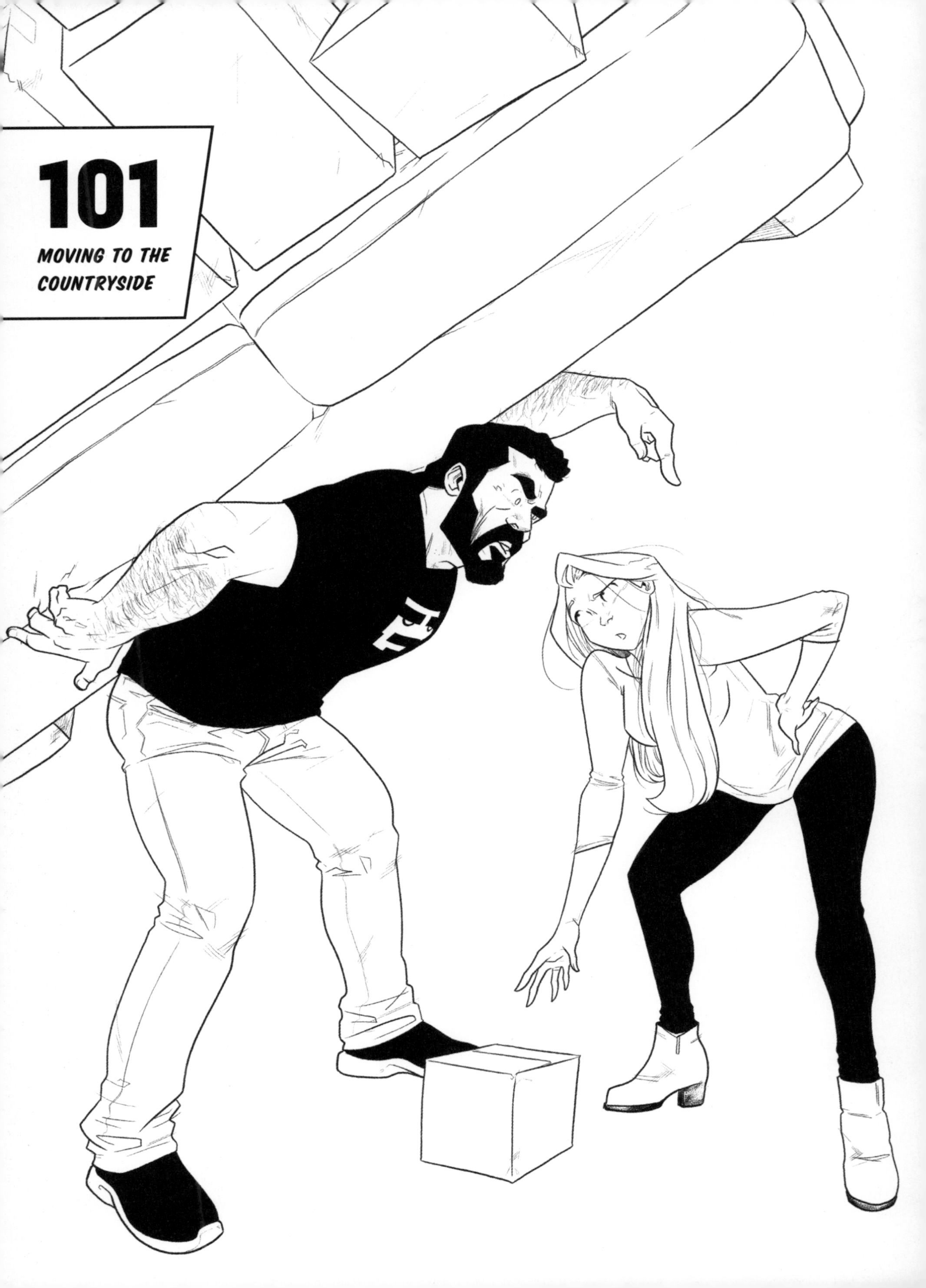

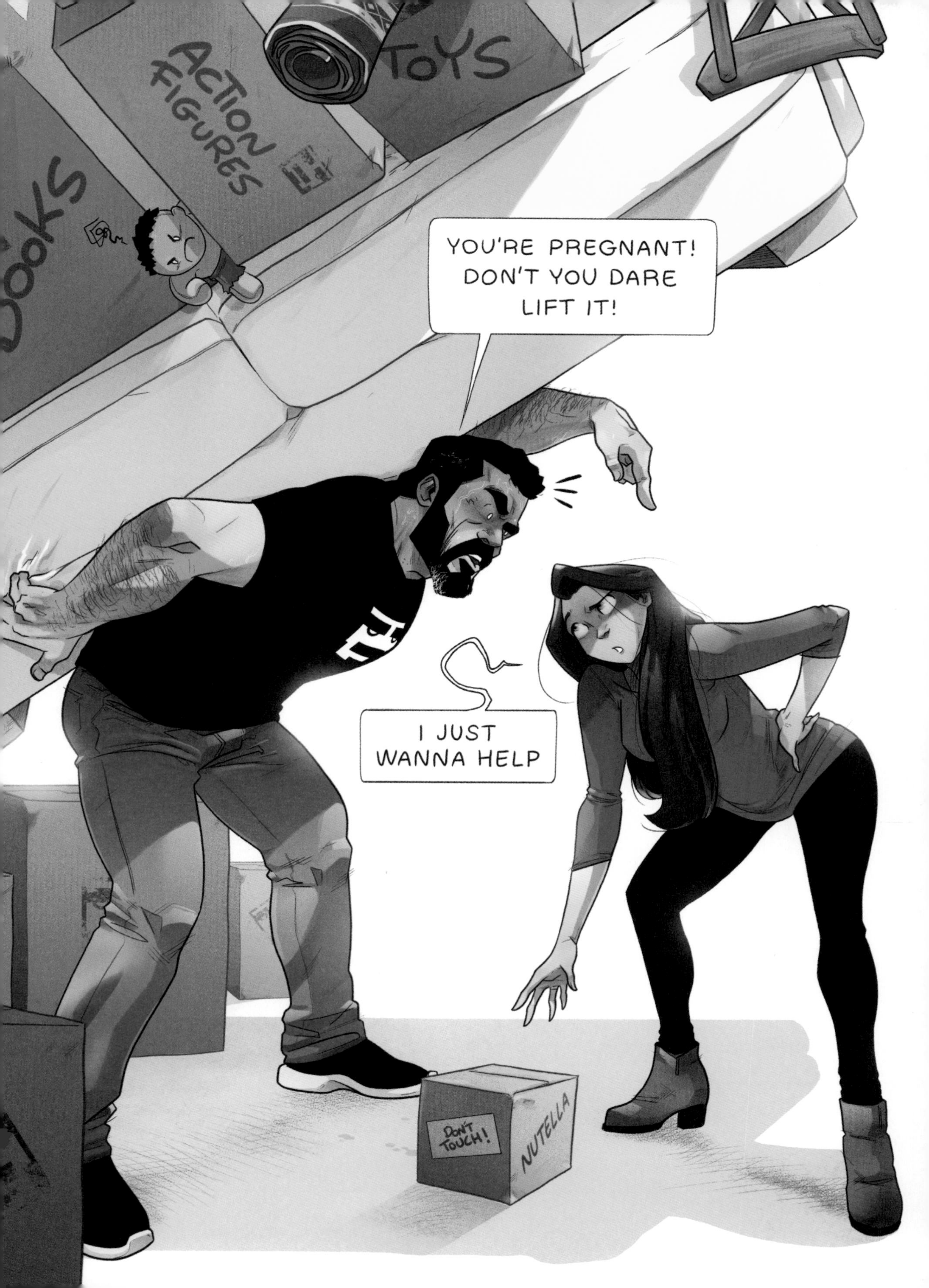
ACTION FIGURES
TOYS
BOOKS
YOU'RE PREGNANT! DON'T YOU DARE LIFT IT!
I JUST WANNA HELP
DON'T TOUCH!
NUTELLA

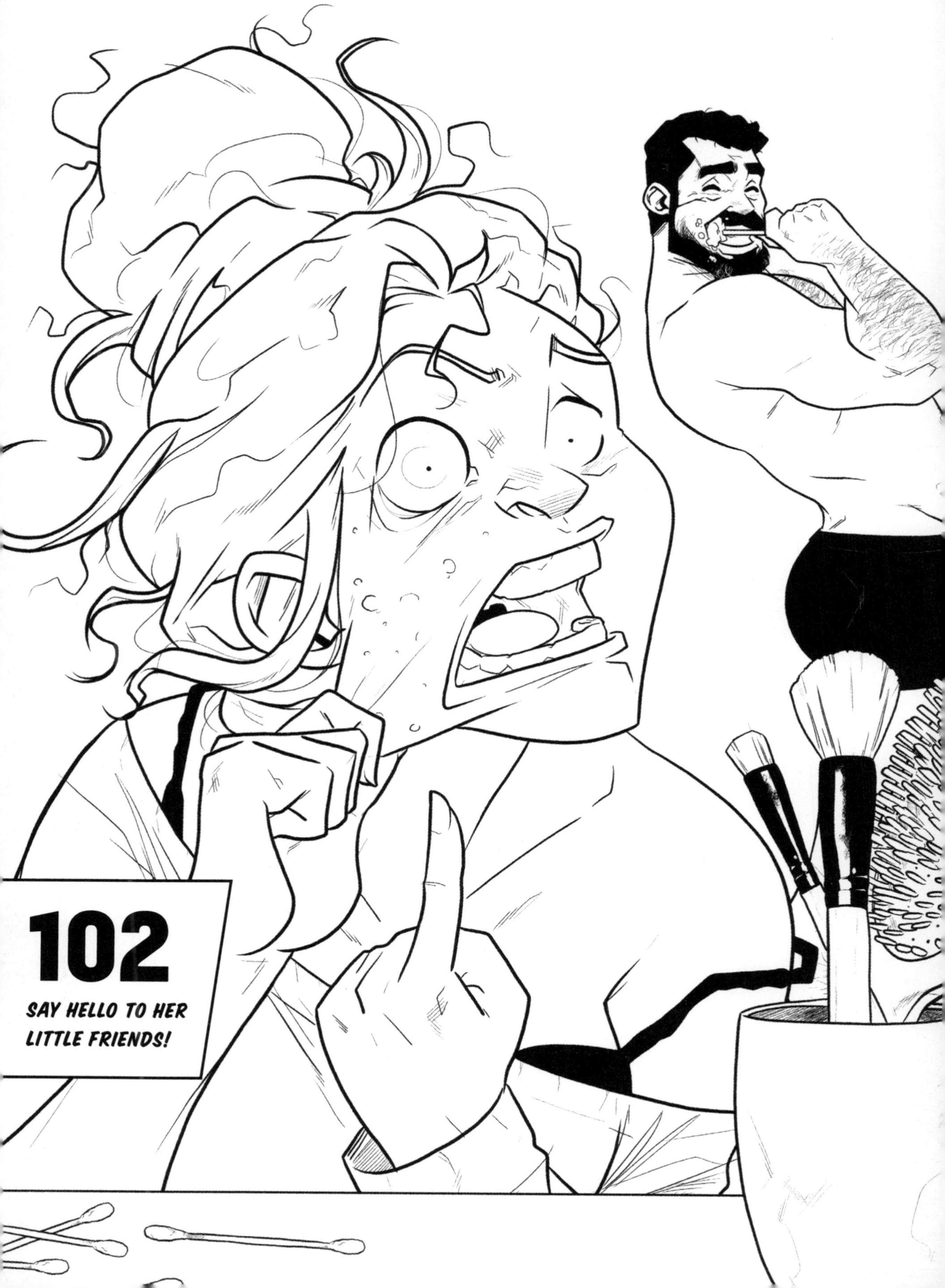

102

SAY HELLO TO HER LITTLE FRIENDS!

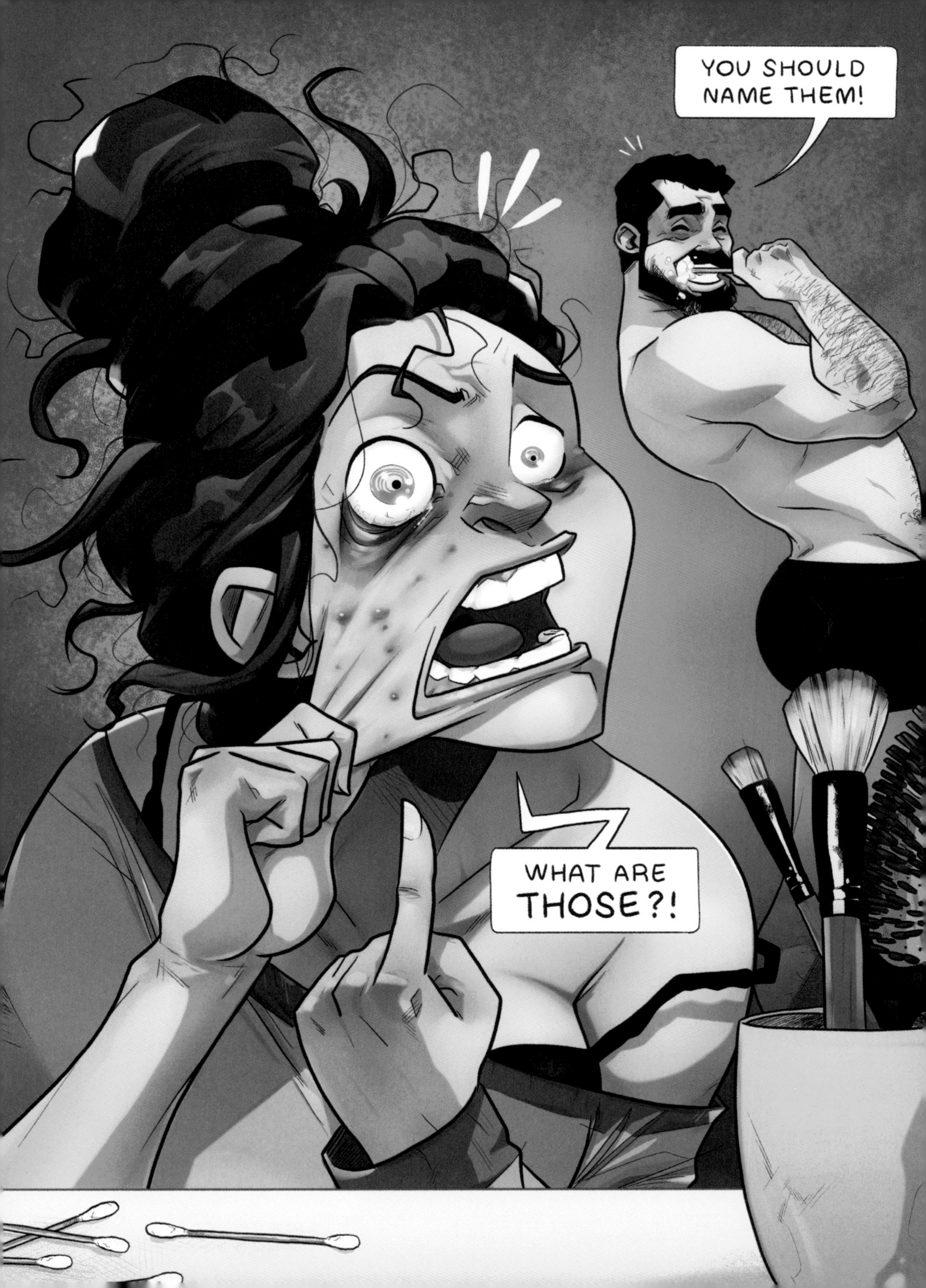
YOU SHOULD NAME THEM!
WHAT ARE THOSE?!

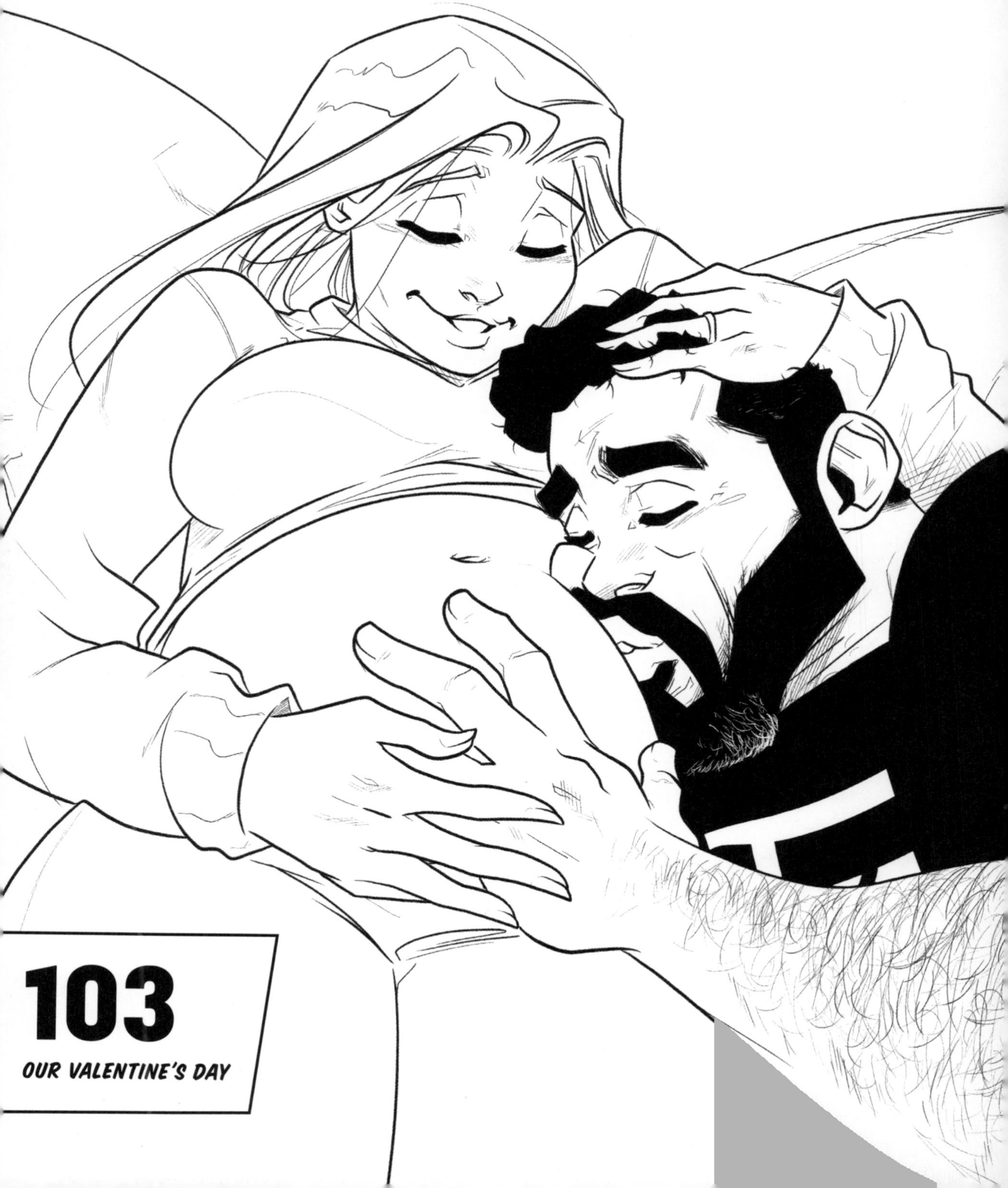

103

OUR VALENTINE'S DAY

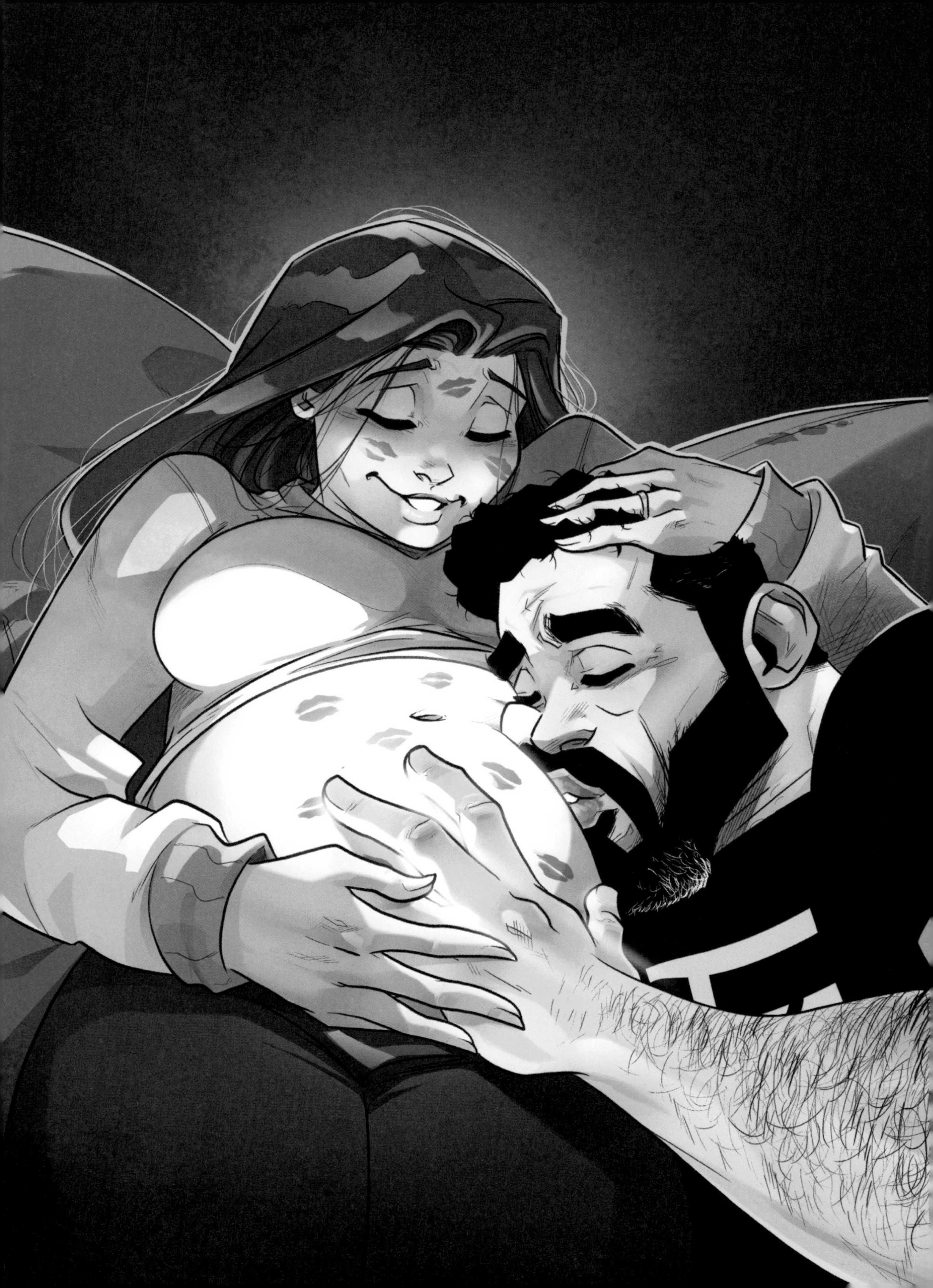

104

I BOUGHT HER A PHYSIO BALL

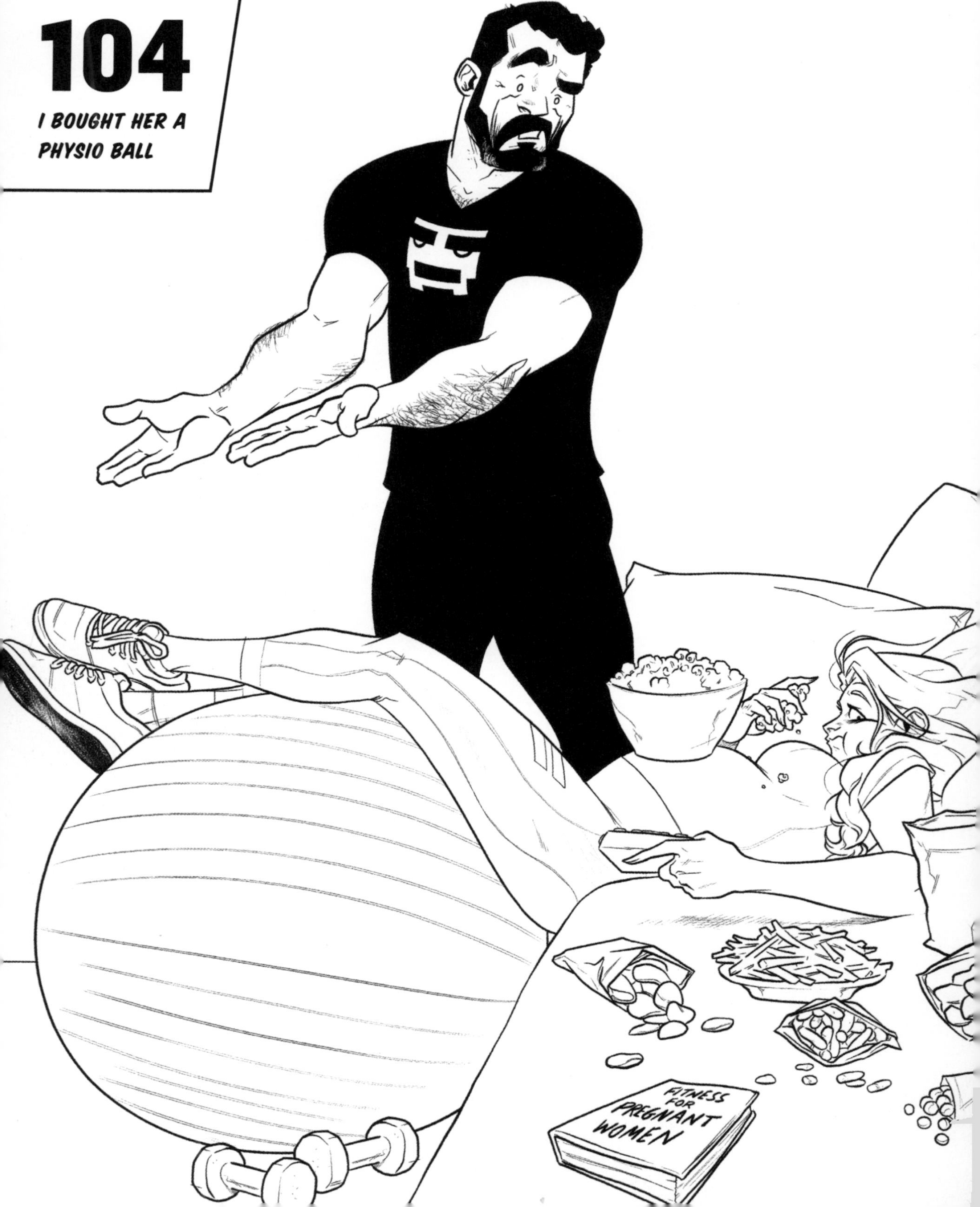
FITNESS FOR PREGNANT WOMEN

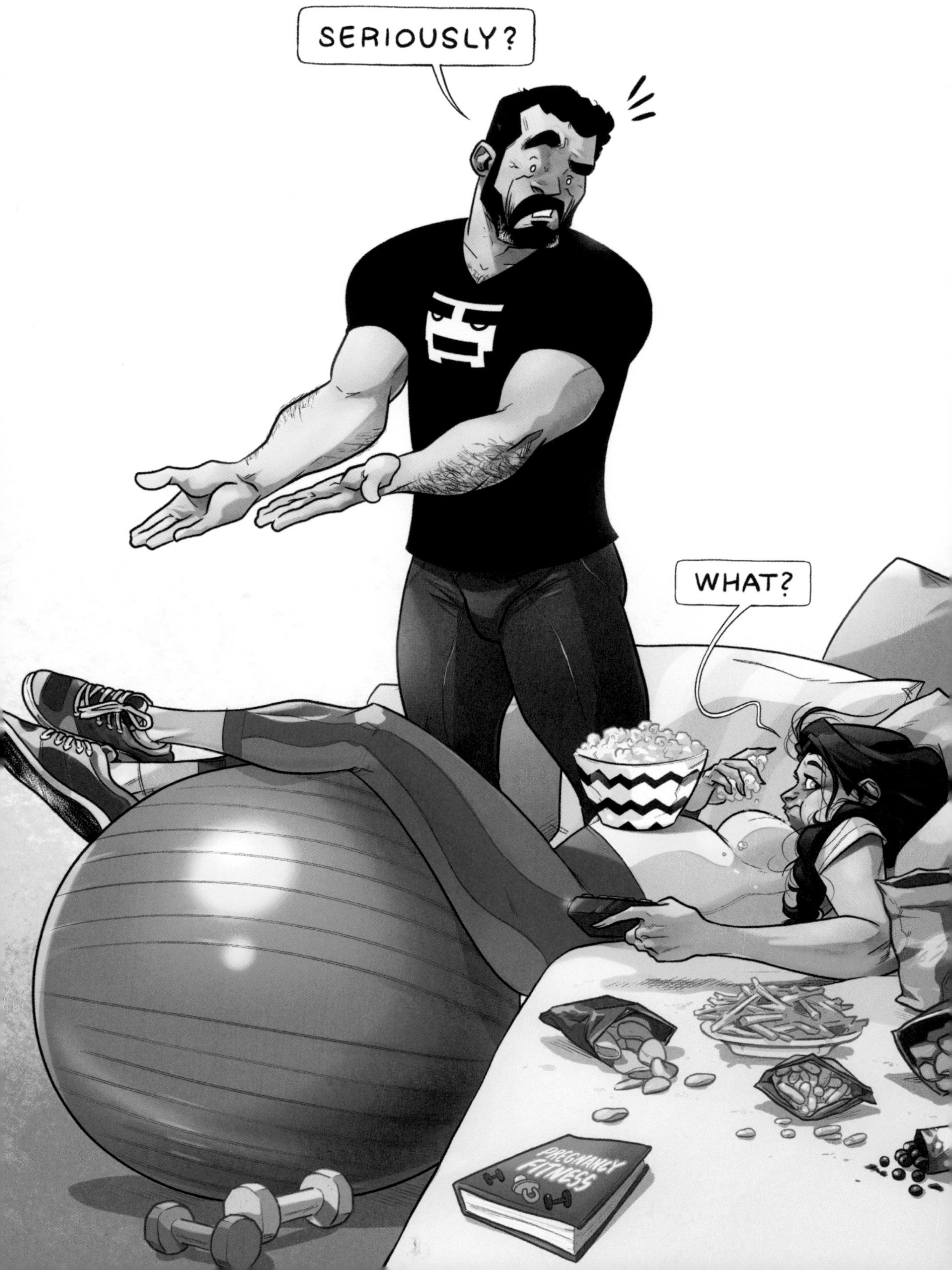
SERIOUSLY?
WHAT?
PREGNANCY FITNESS

105

BODY CHANGES

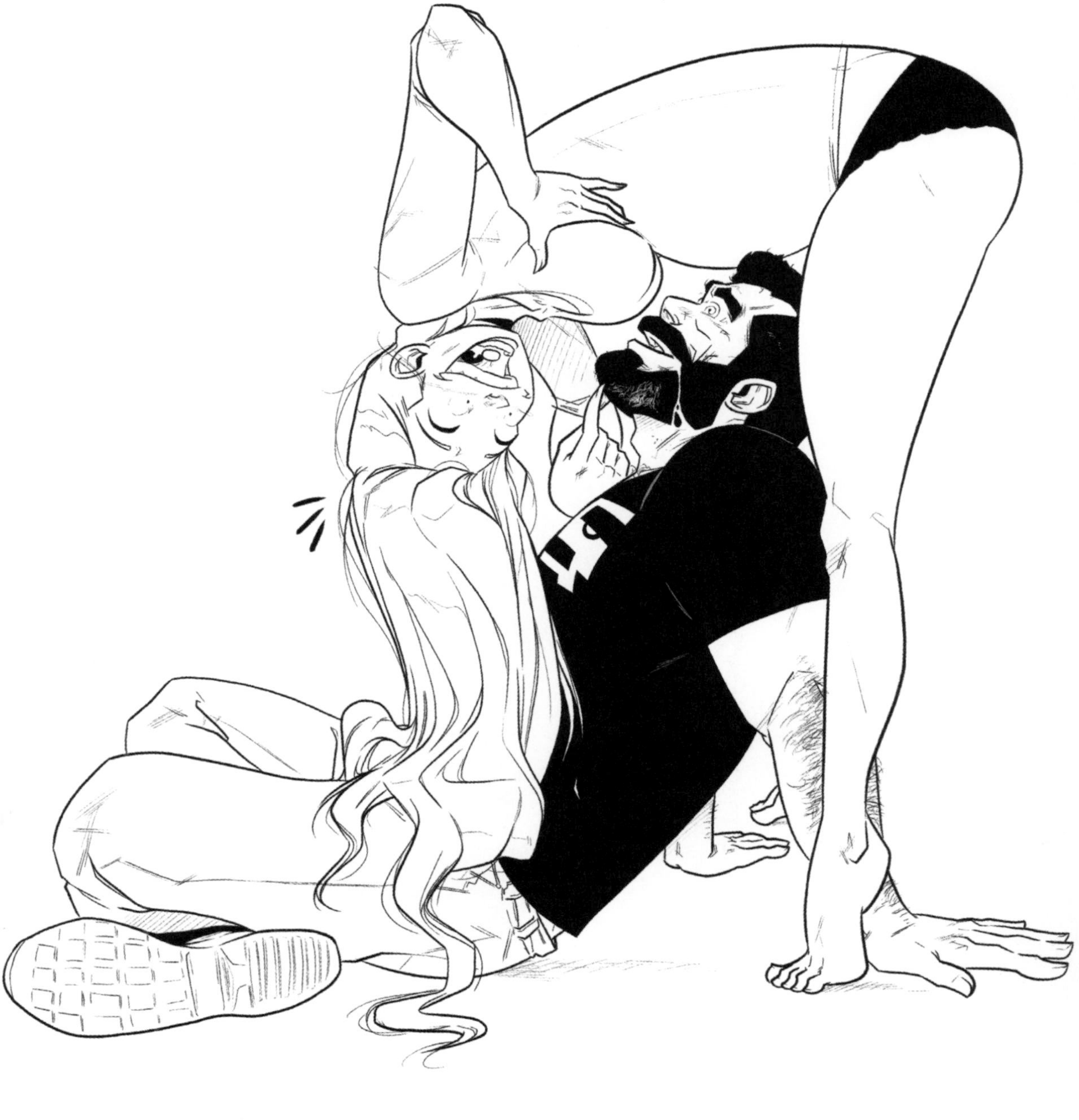

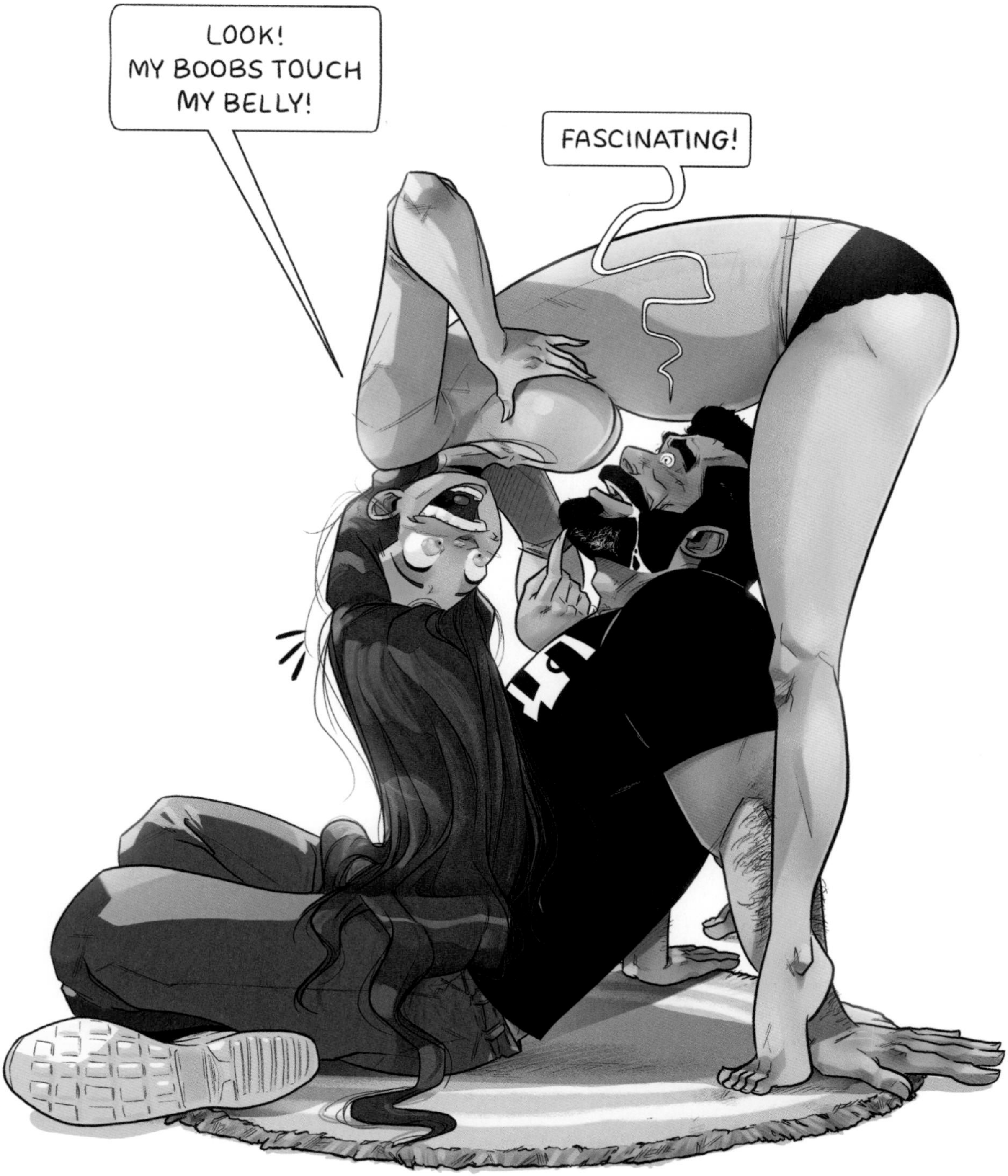
LOOK! MY BOOBS TOUCH MY BELLY!
FASCINATING!

106

SALT FACE

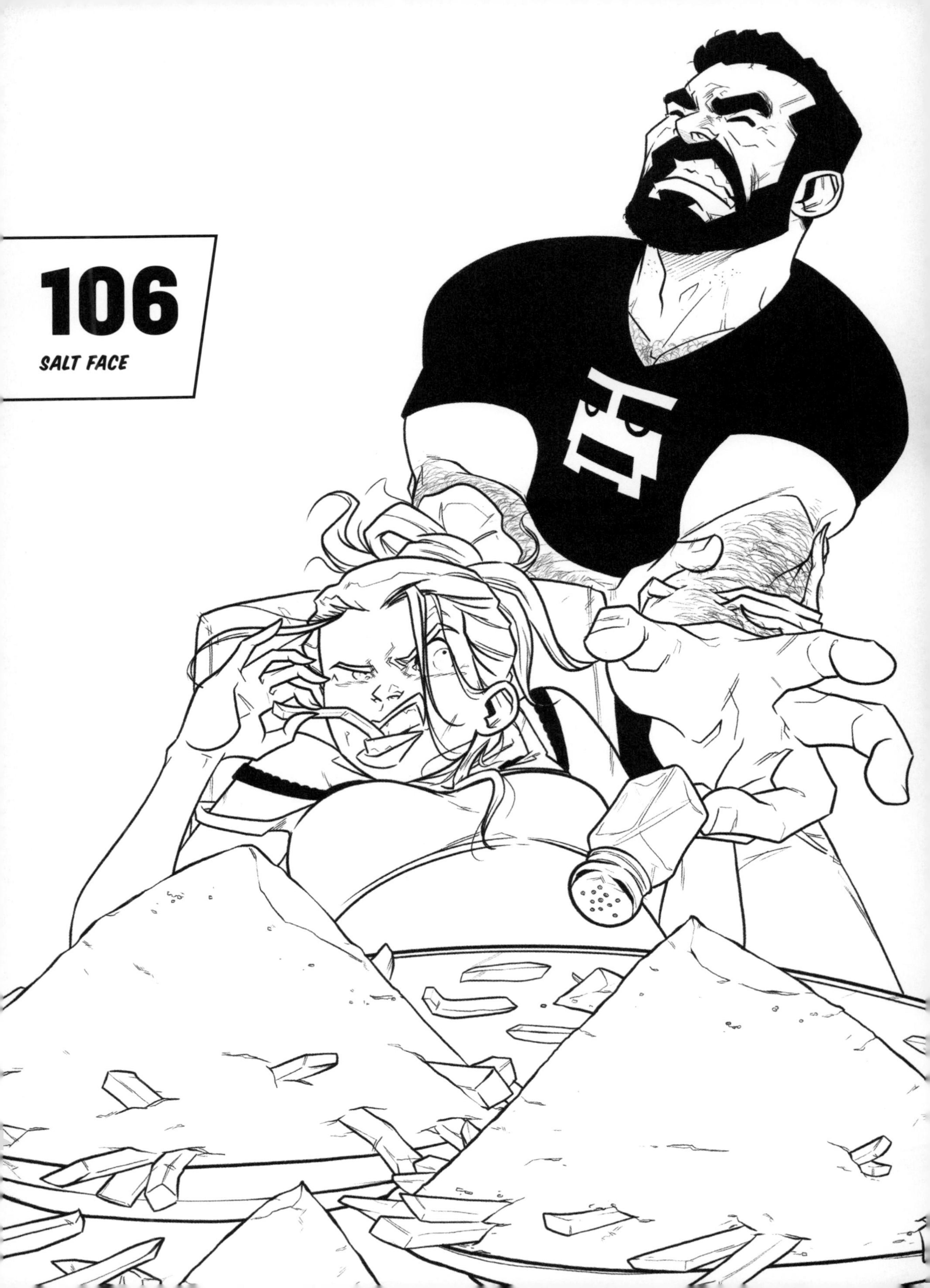

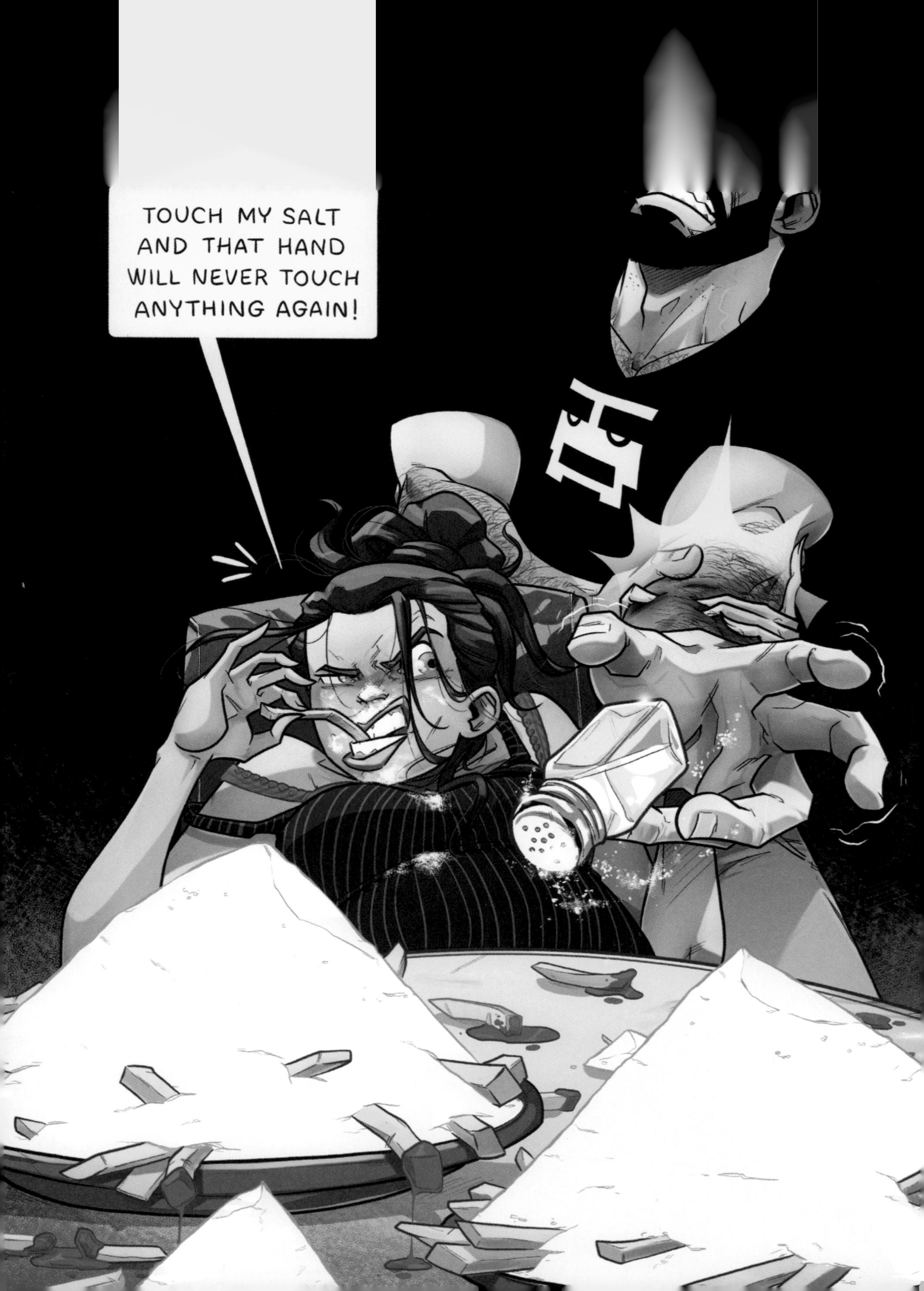
TOUCH MY SALT AND THAT HAND WILL NEVER TOUCH ANYTHING AGAIN!

107

THE FIRST KICK

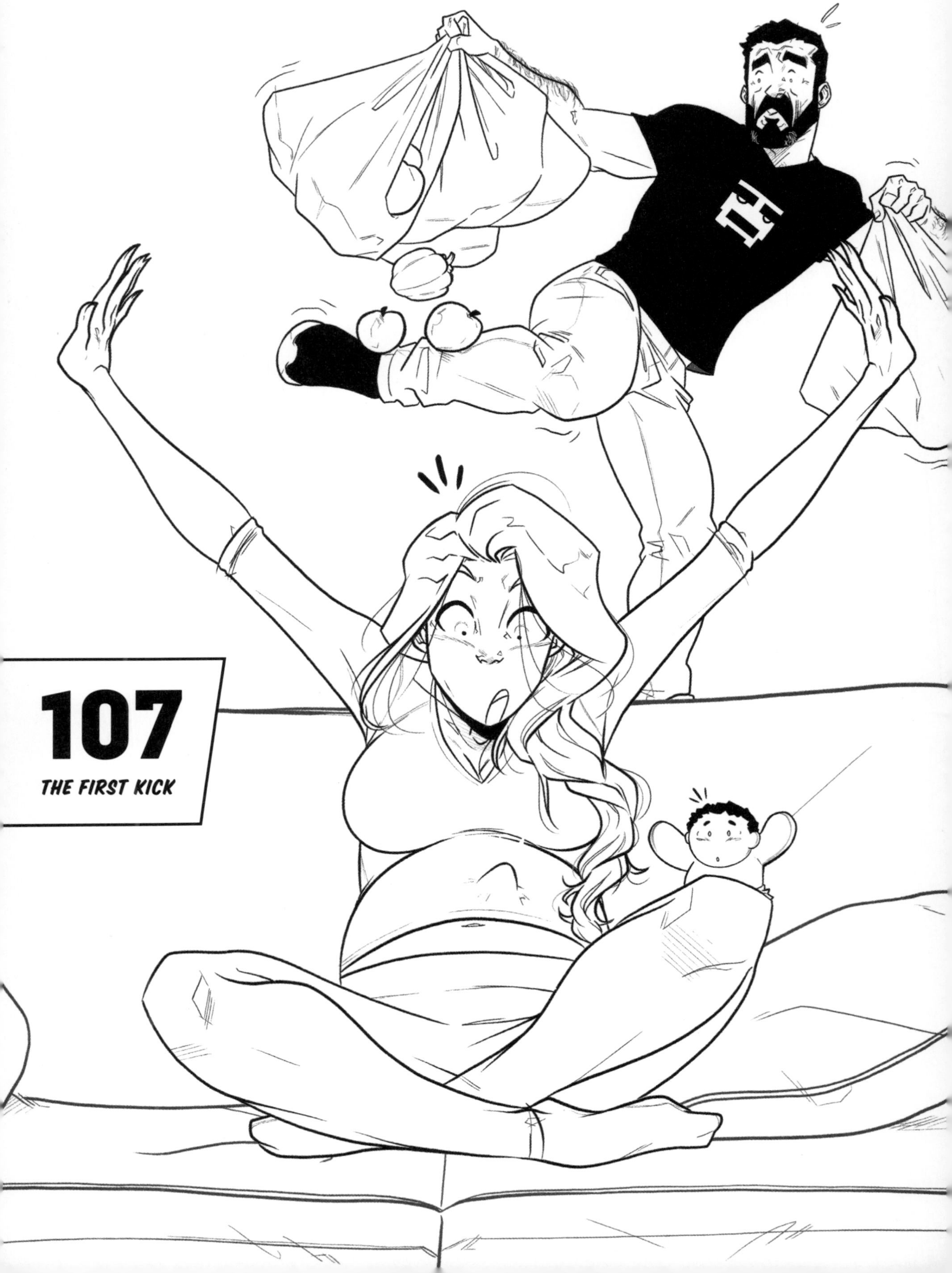

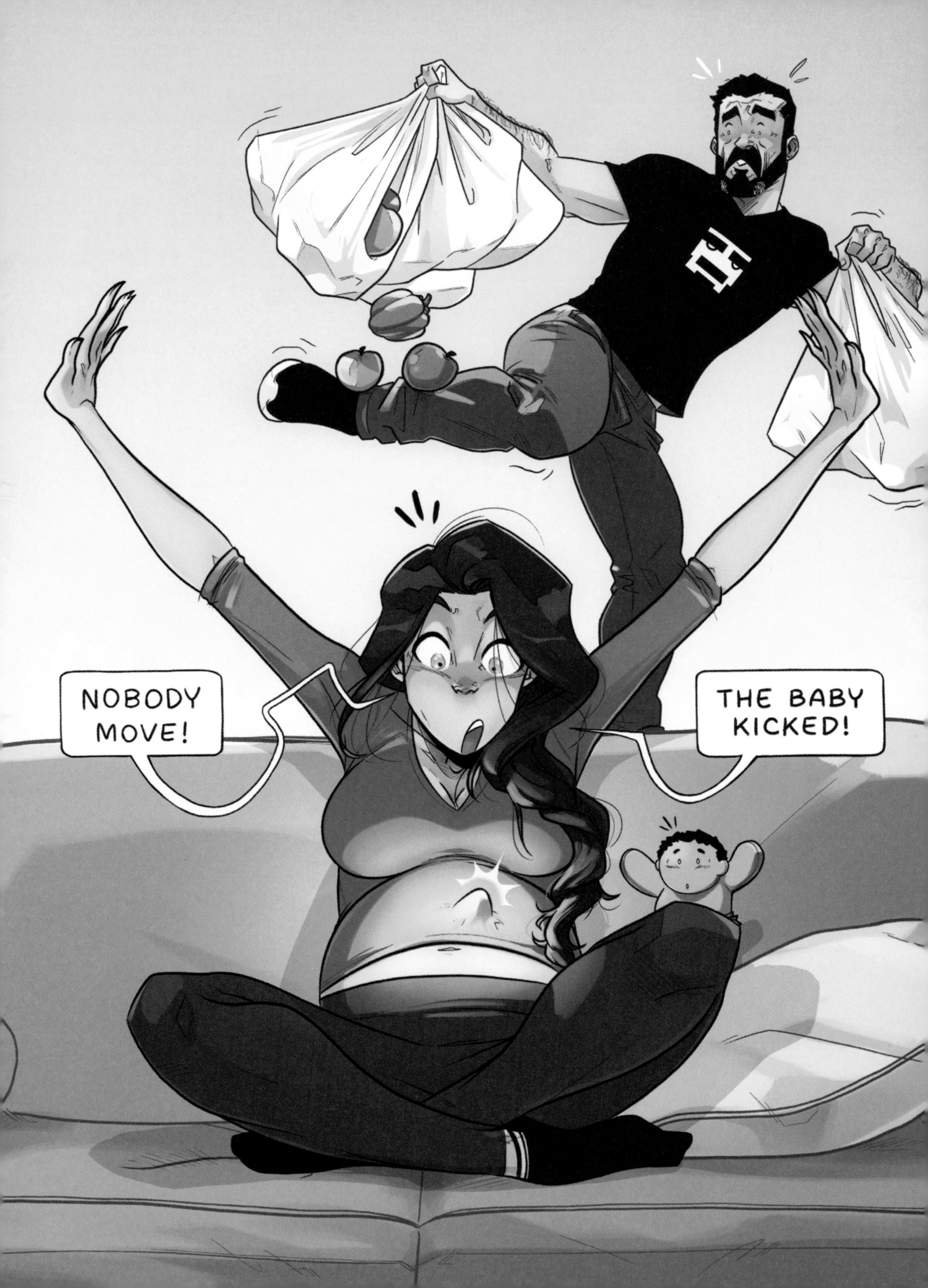
NOBODY MOVE!
THE BABY KICKED!

108

BELLY PILLOW

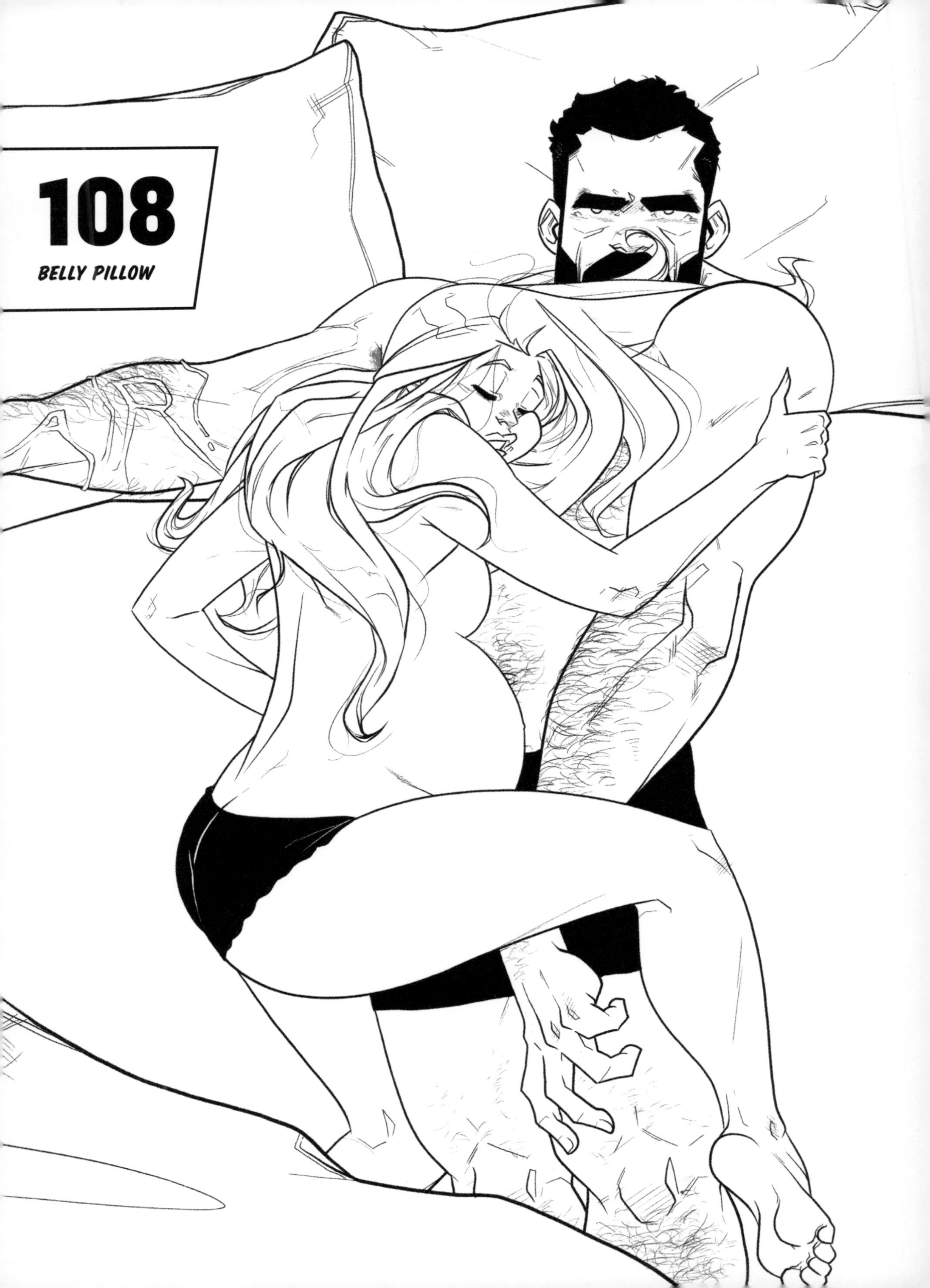

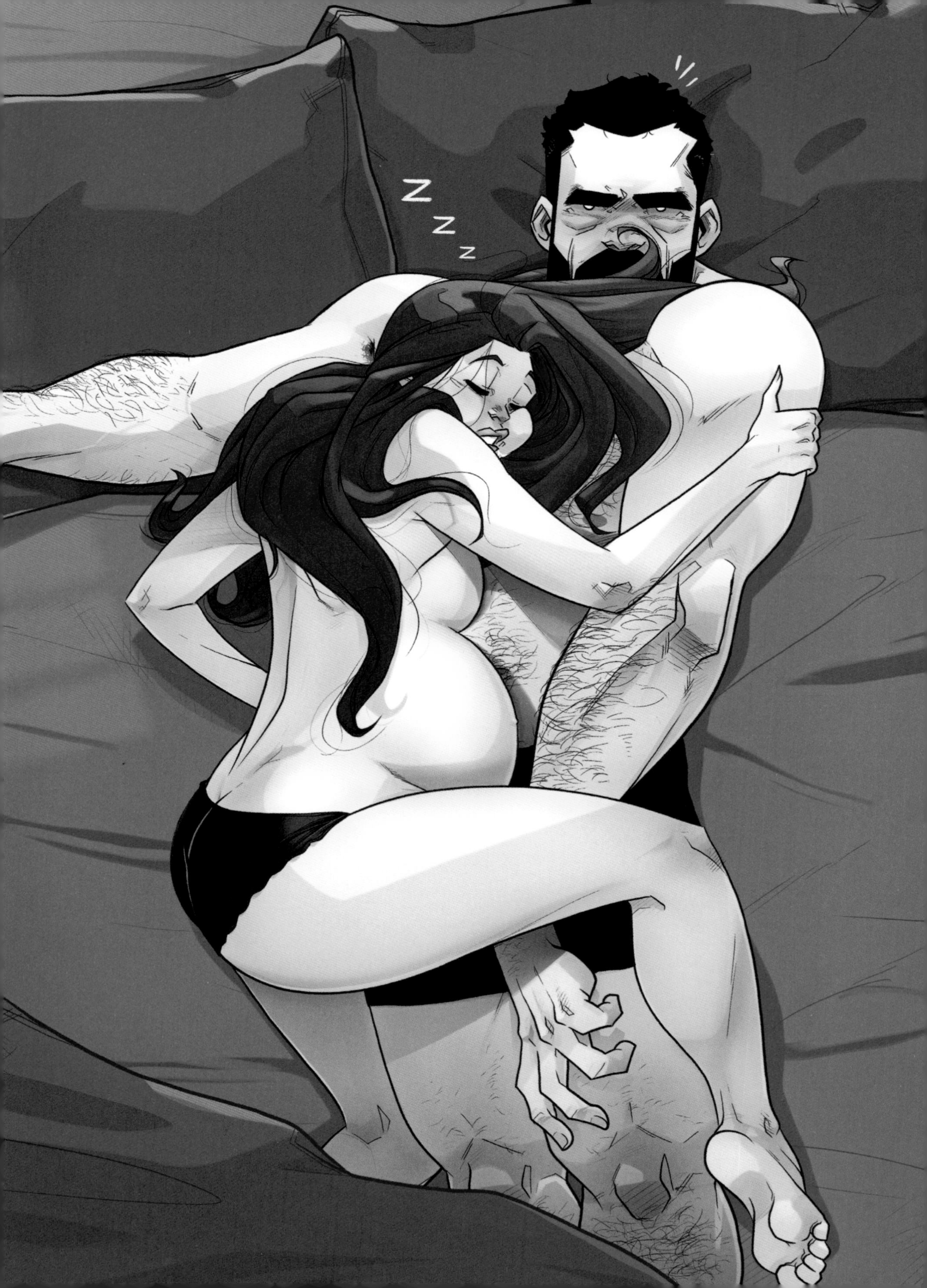
ZZZ

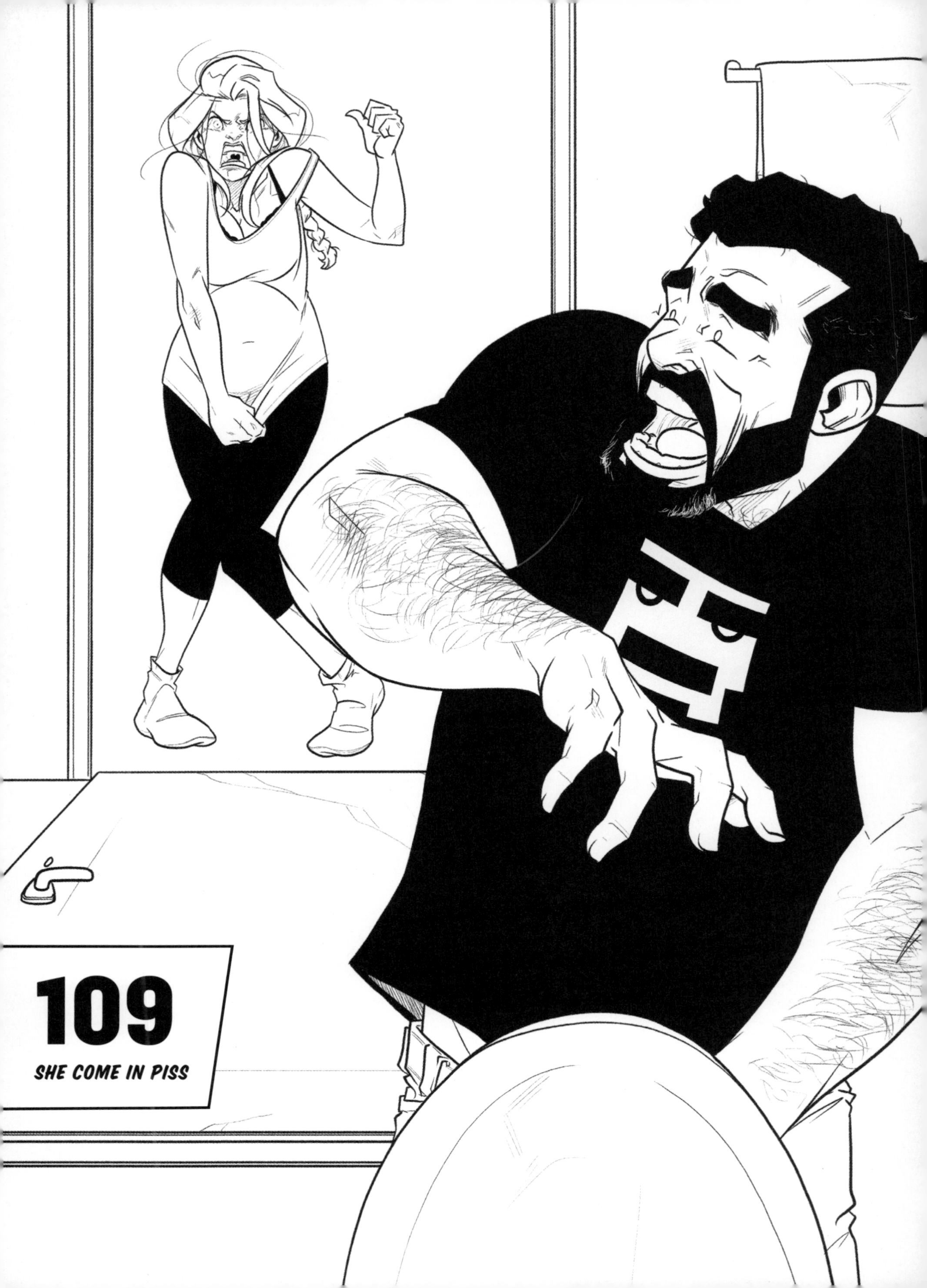
109
SHE COME IN PISS

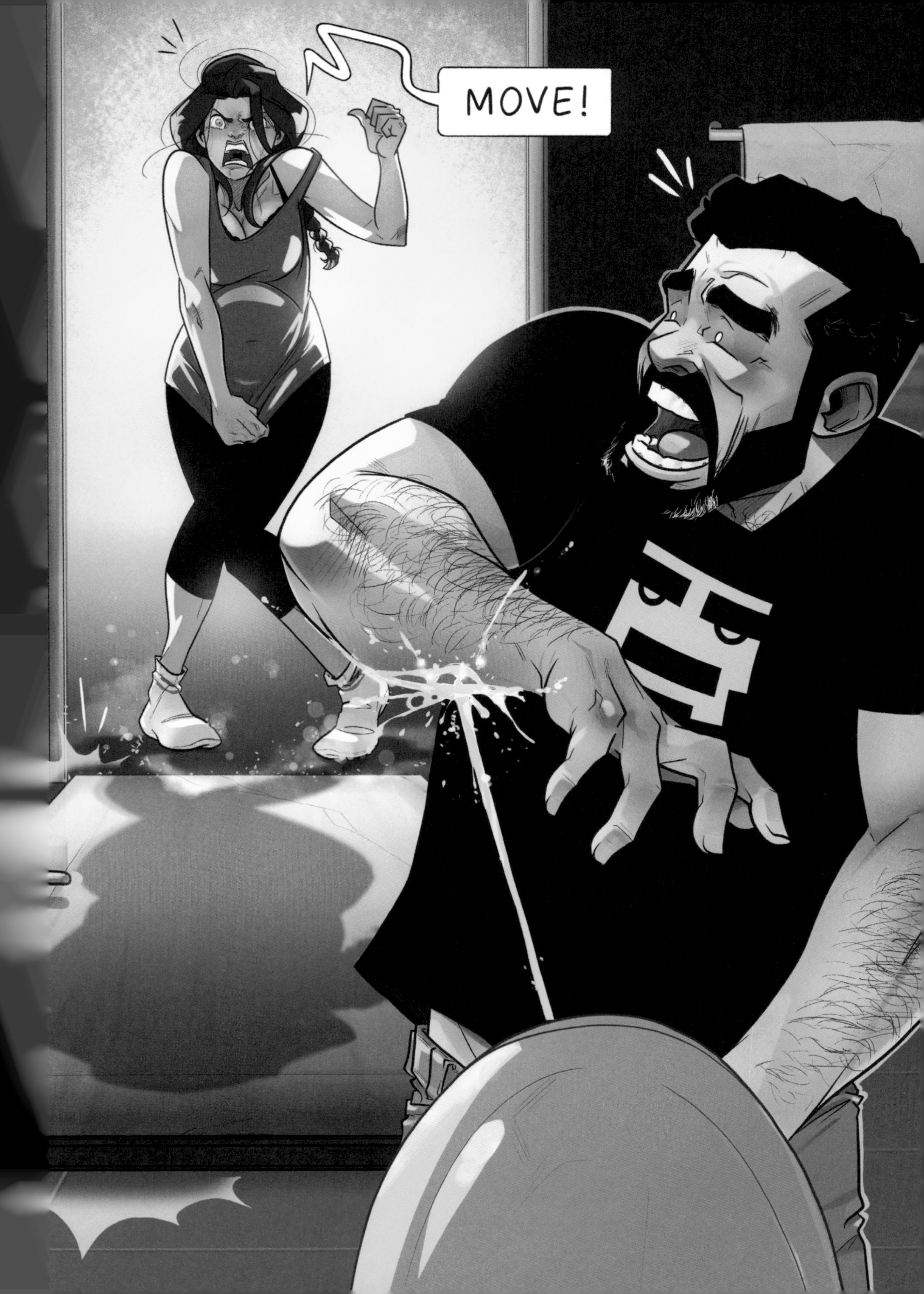
MOVE!

110

SO CLOSE AND YET SO FAR

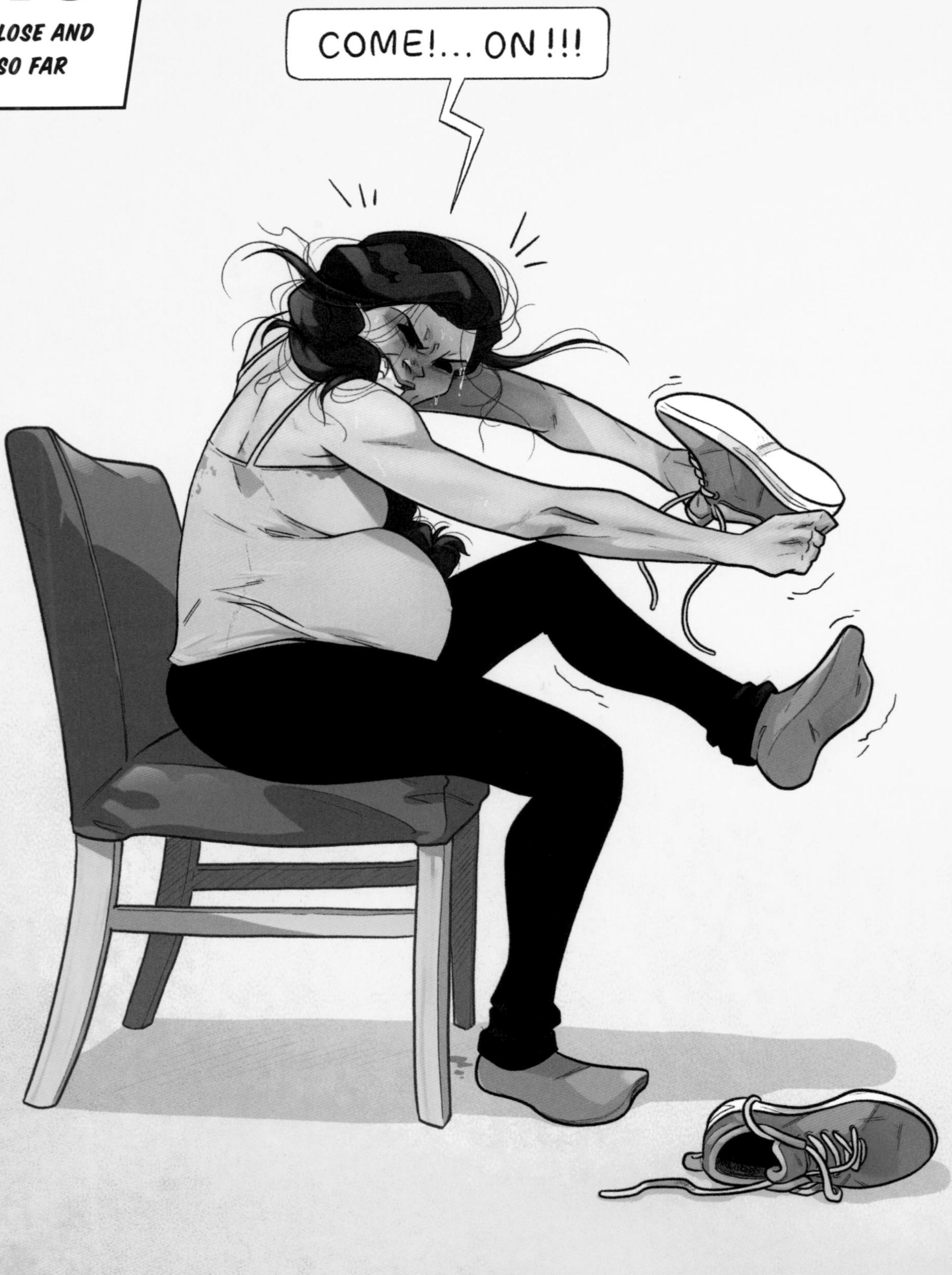
COME!... ON!!!

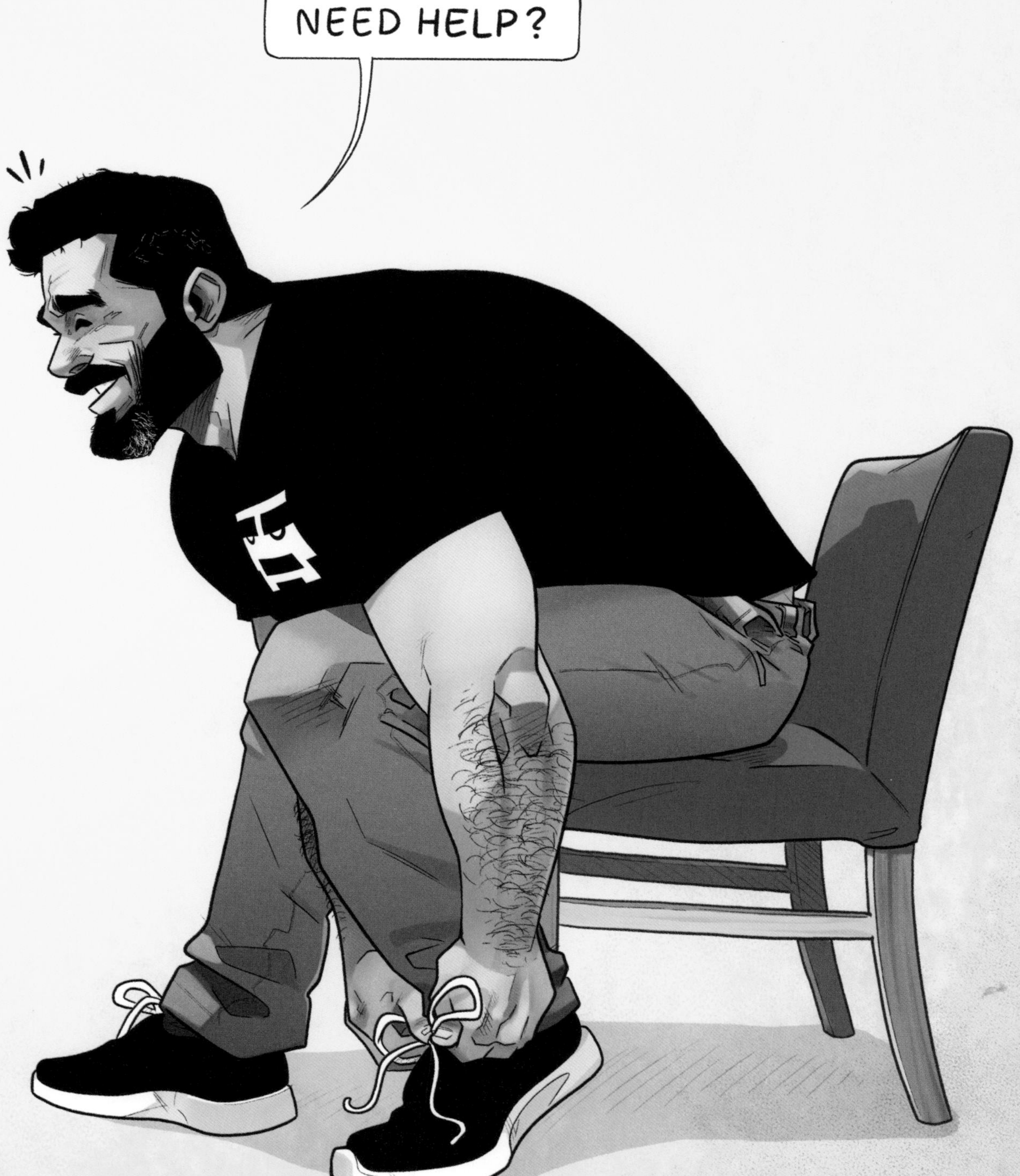
NEED HELP?

111

ALMOST THERE!

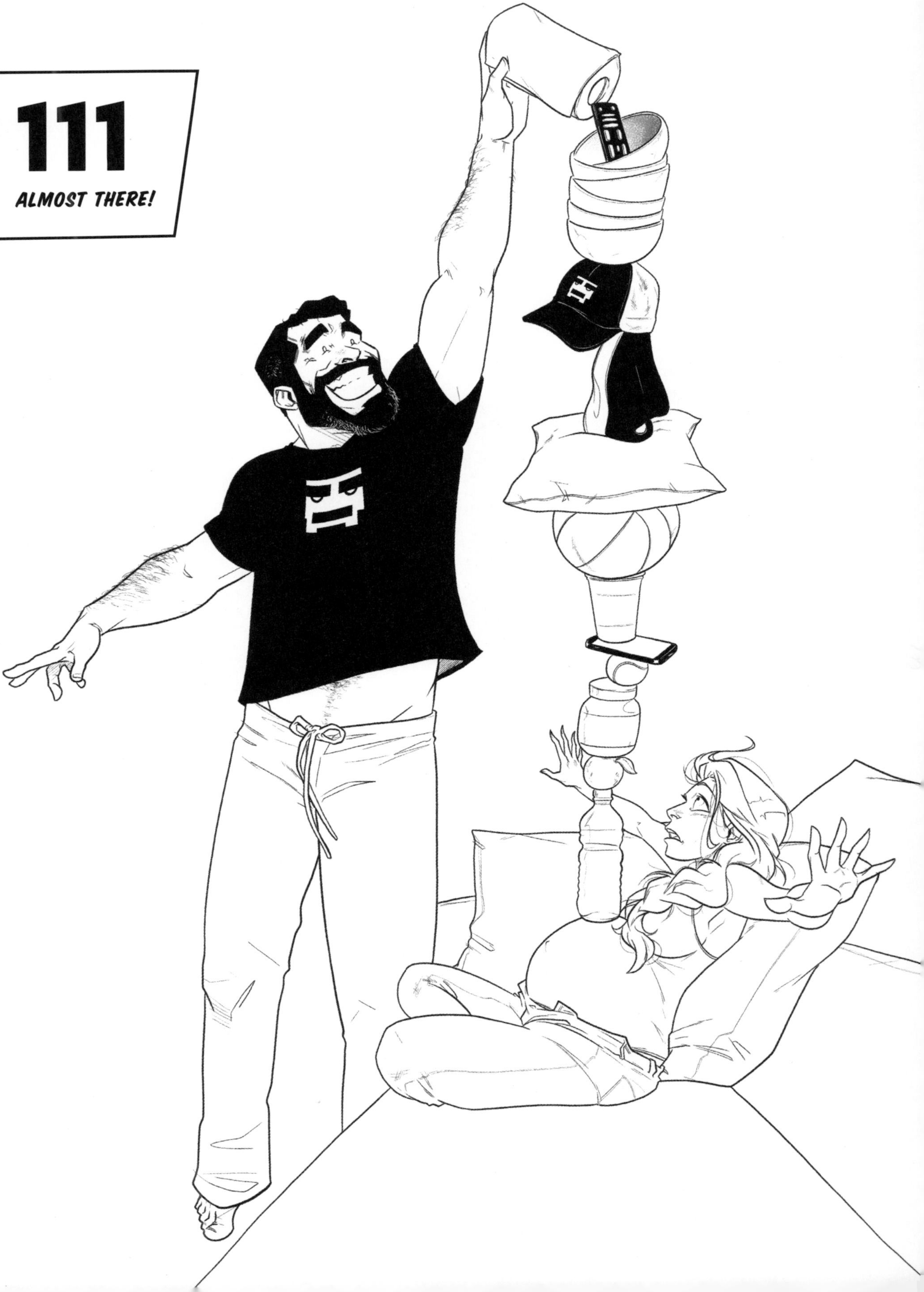

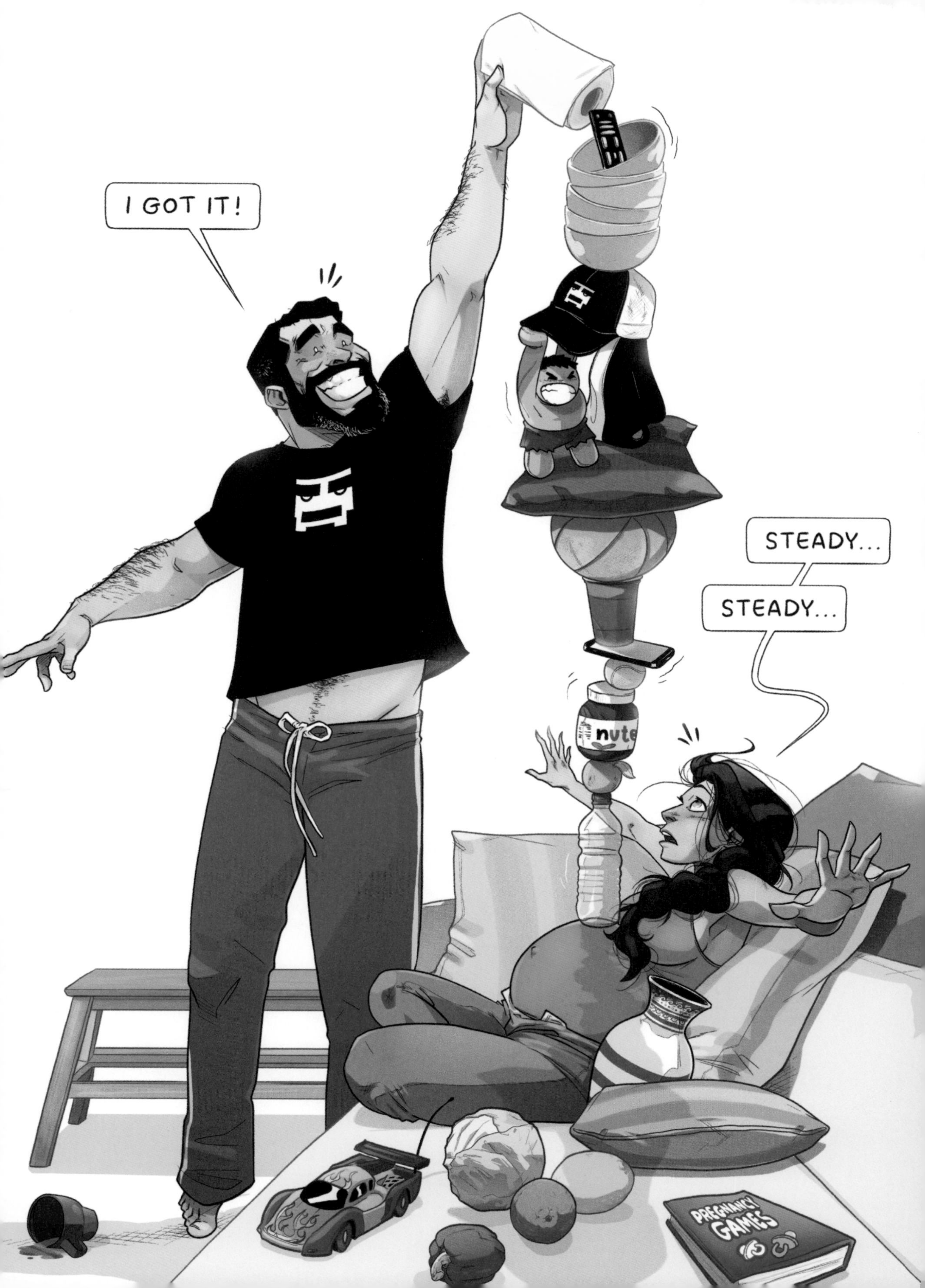

I GOT IT!
STEADY...
STEADY...
PREGNANCY GAMES

112
WATER BREAK

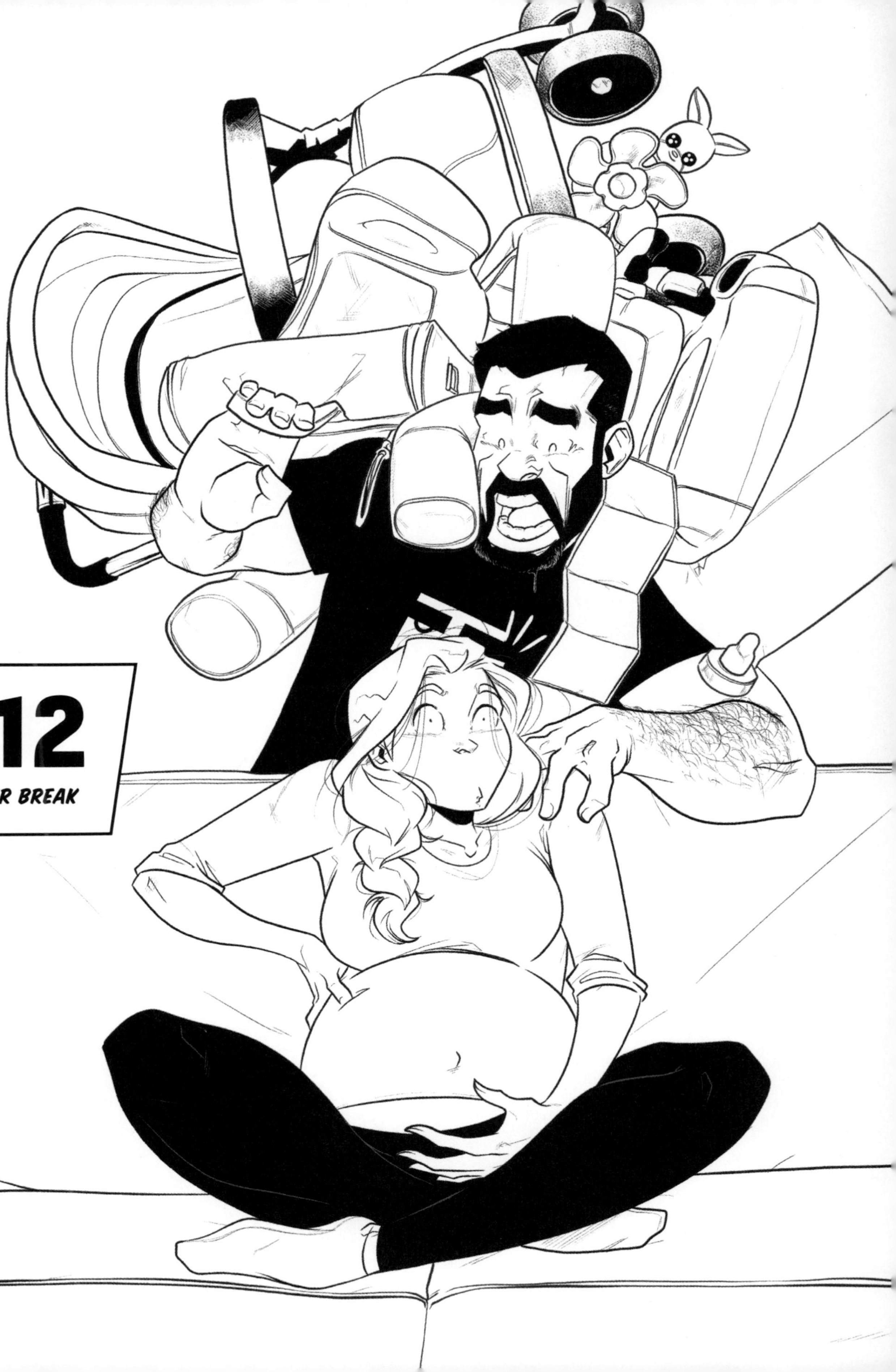

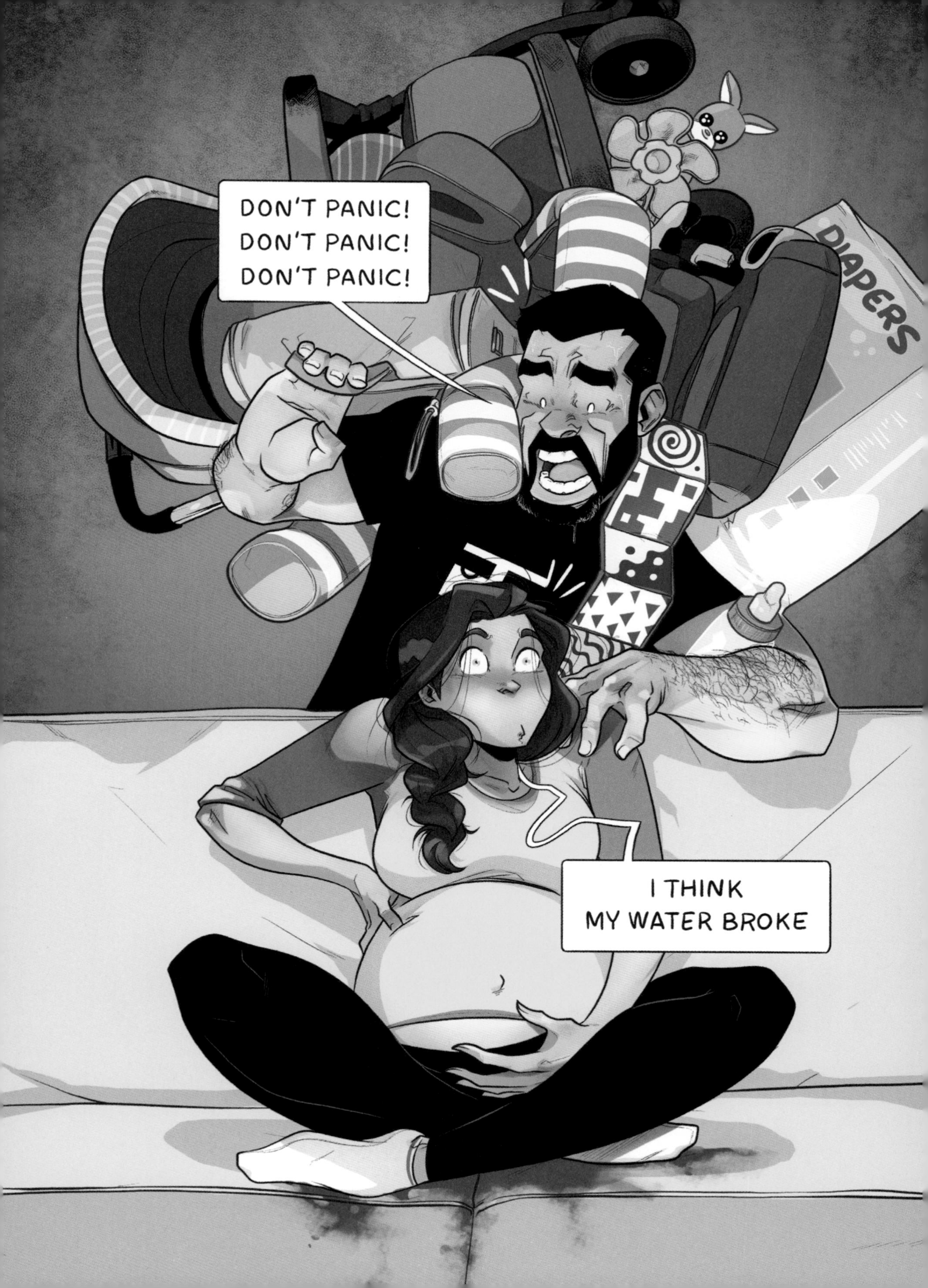
DON'T PANIC!
DON'T PANIC!
DON'T PANIC!
DIAPERS
I THINK
MY WATER BROKE

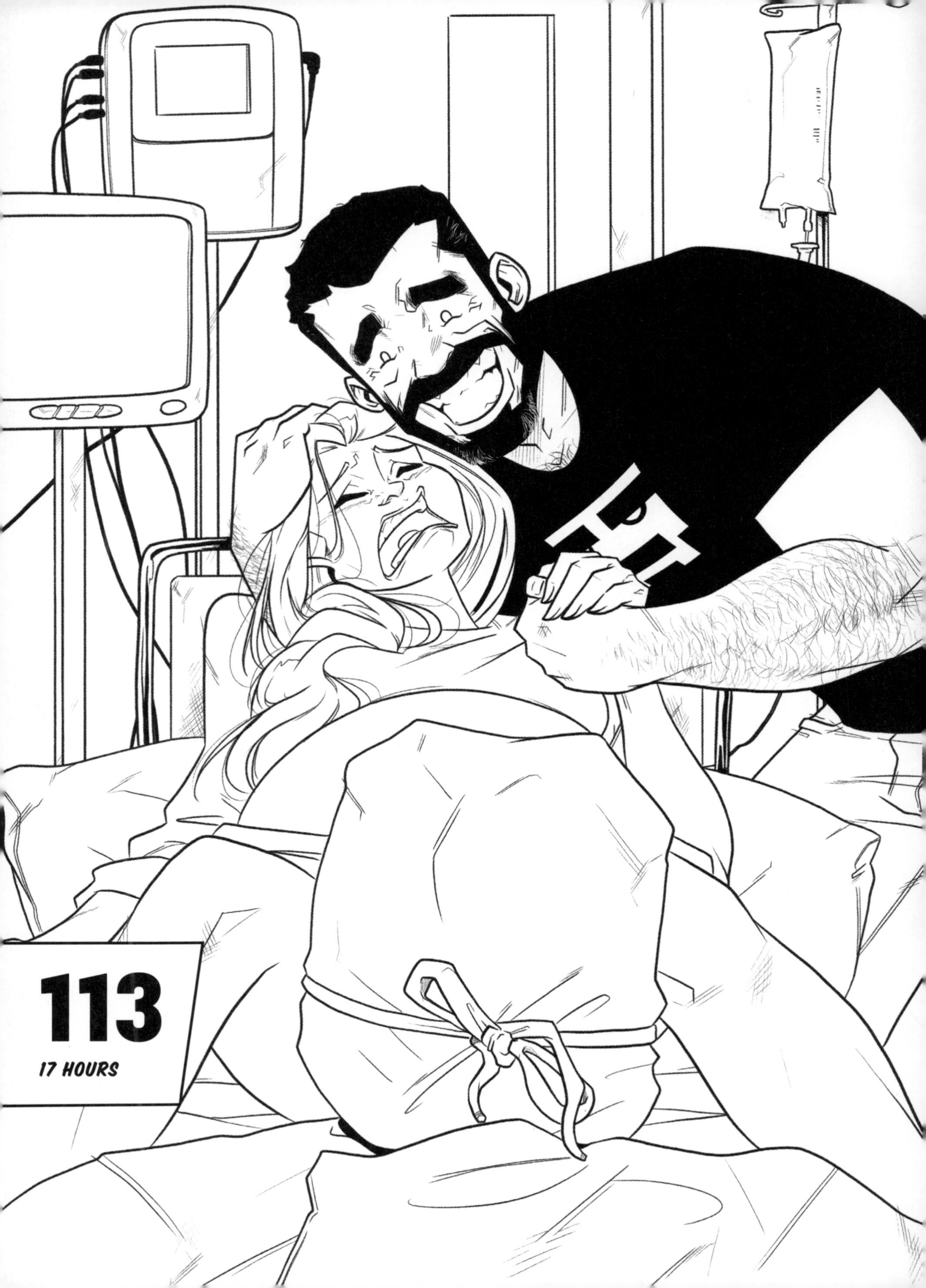
113
17 HOURS

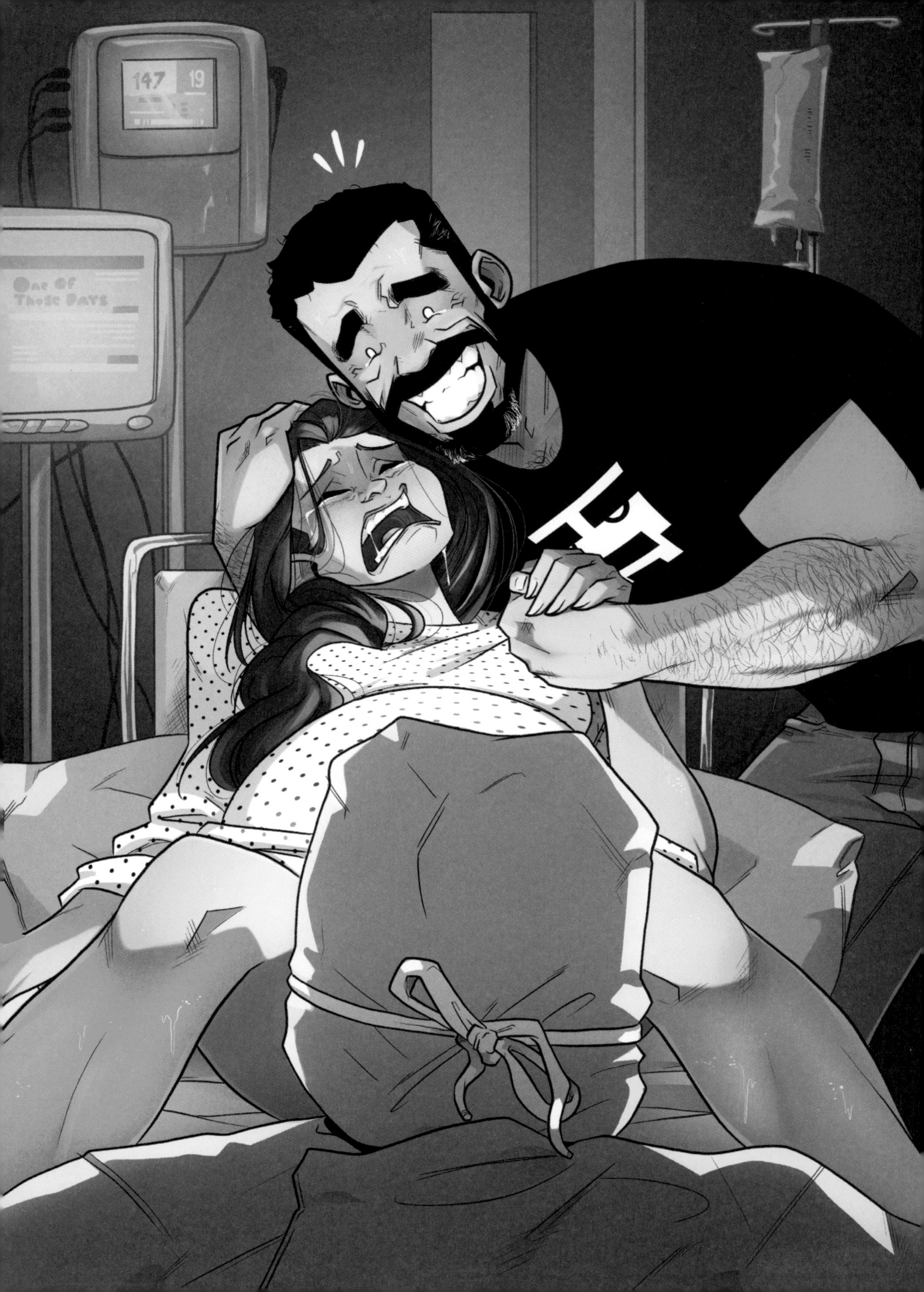
147
19
One Of Those Days

114

IT'S A GIRL!

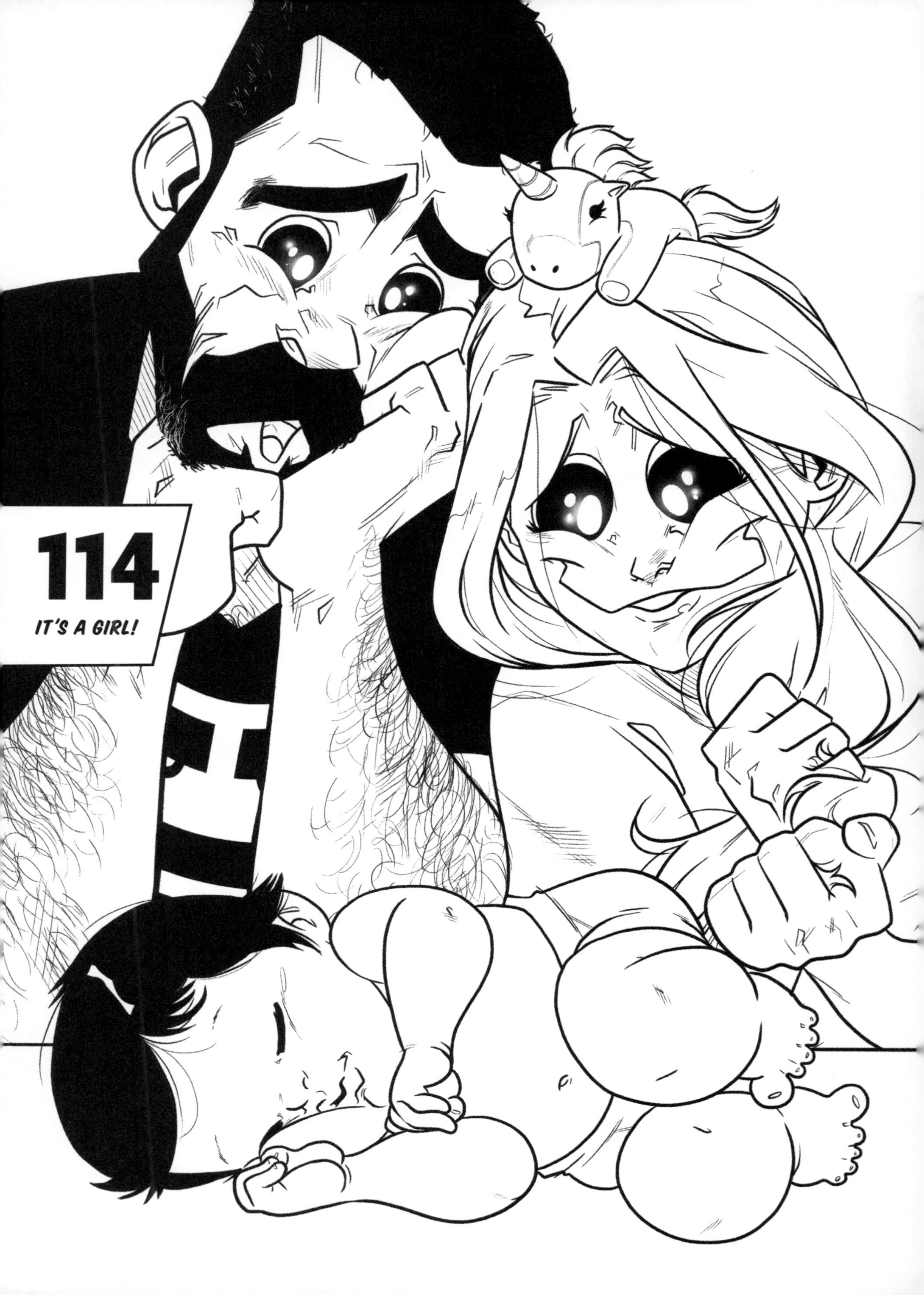

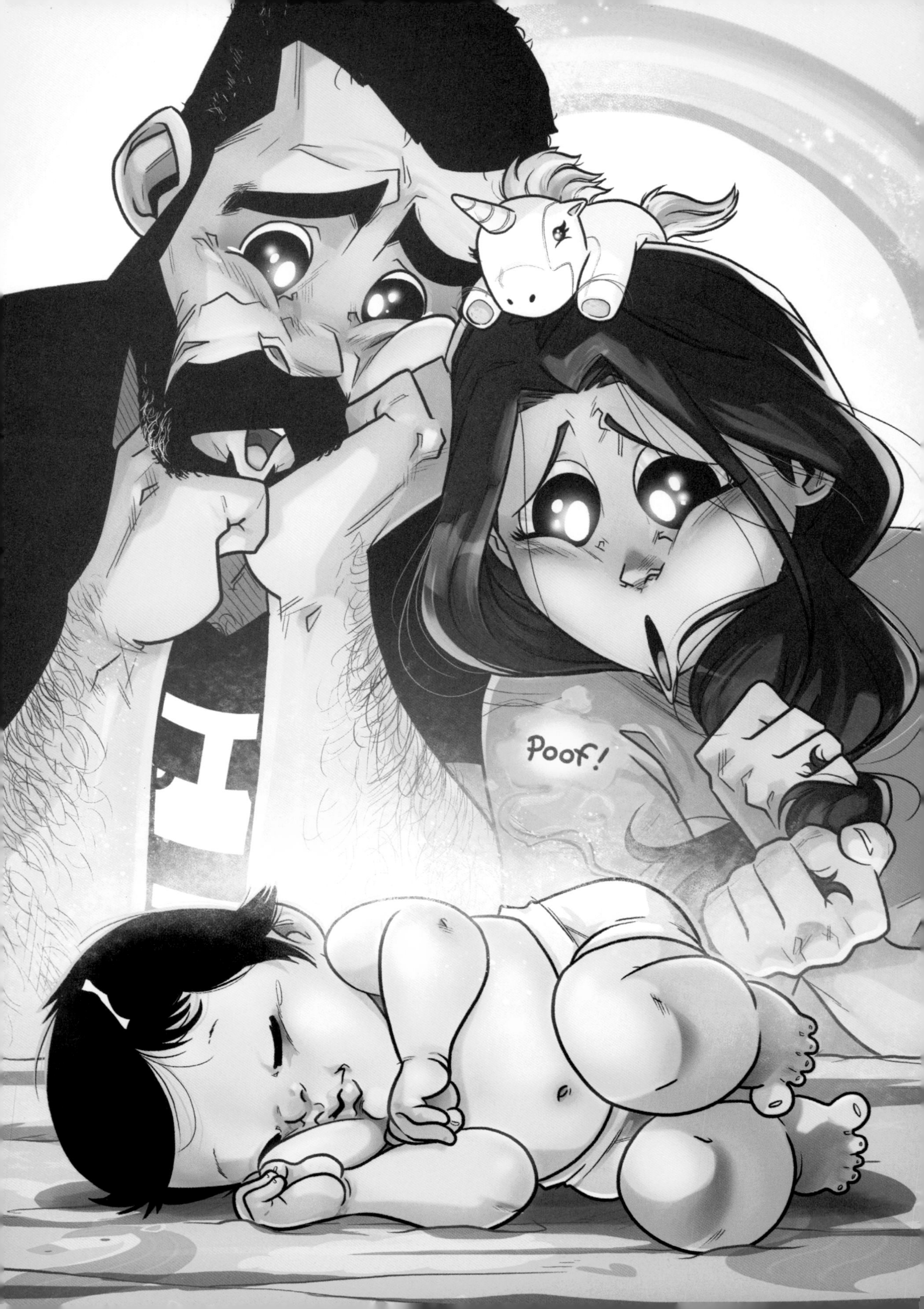
Poof!

115

SHIT HAPPENS!

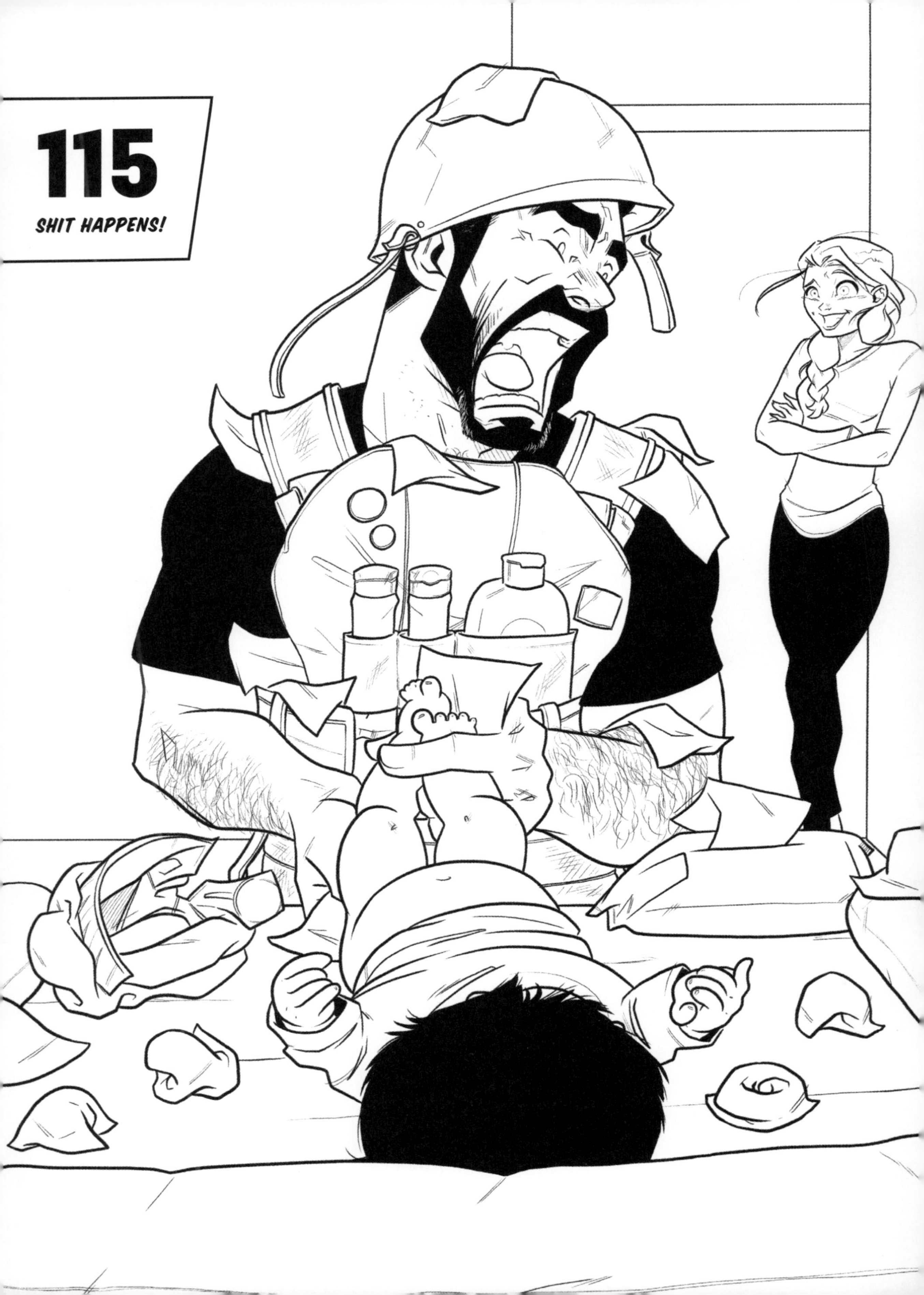

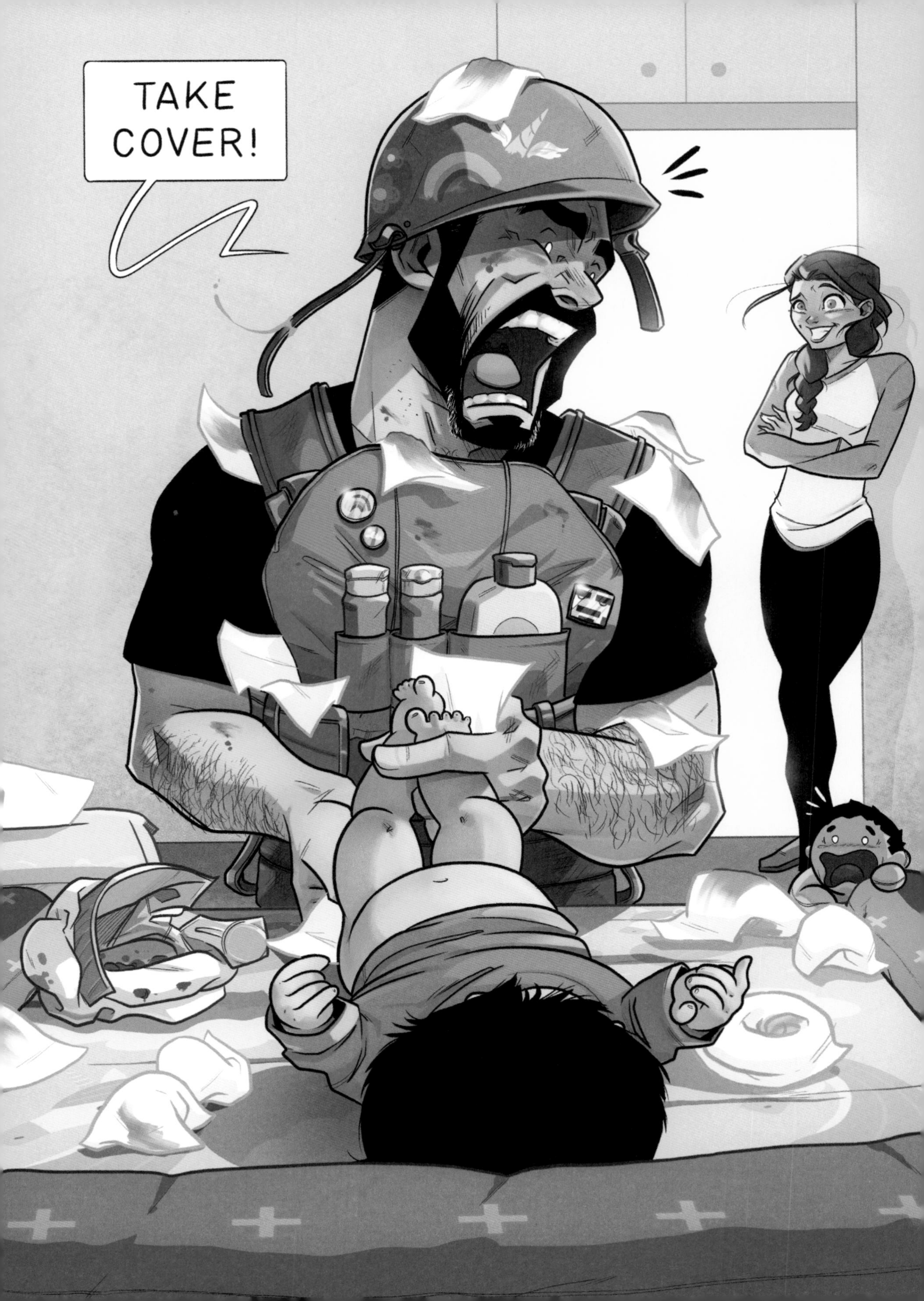
TAKE COVER!

116
THAT TOUCH

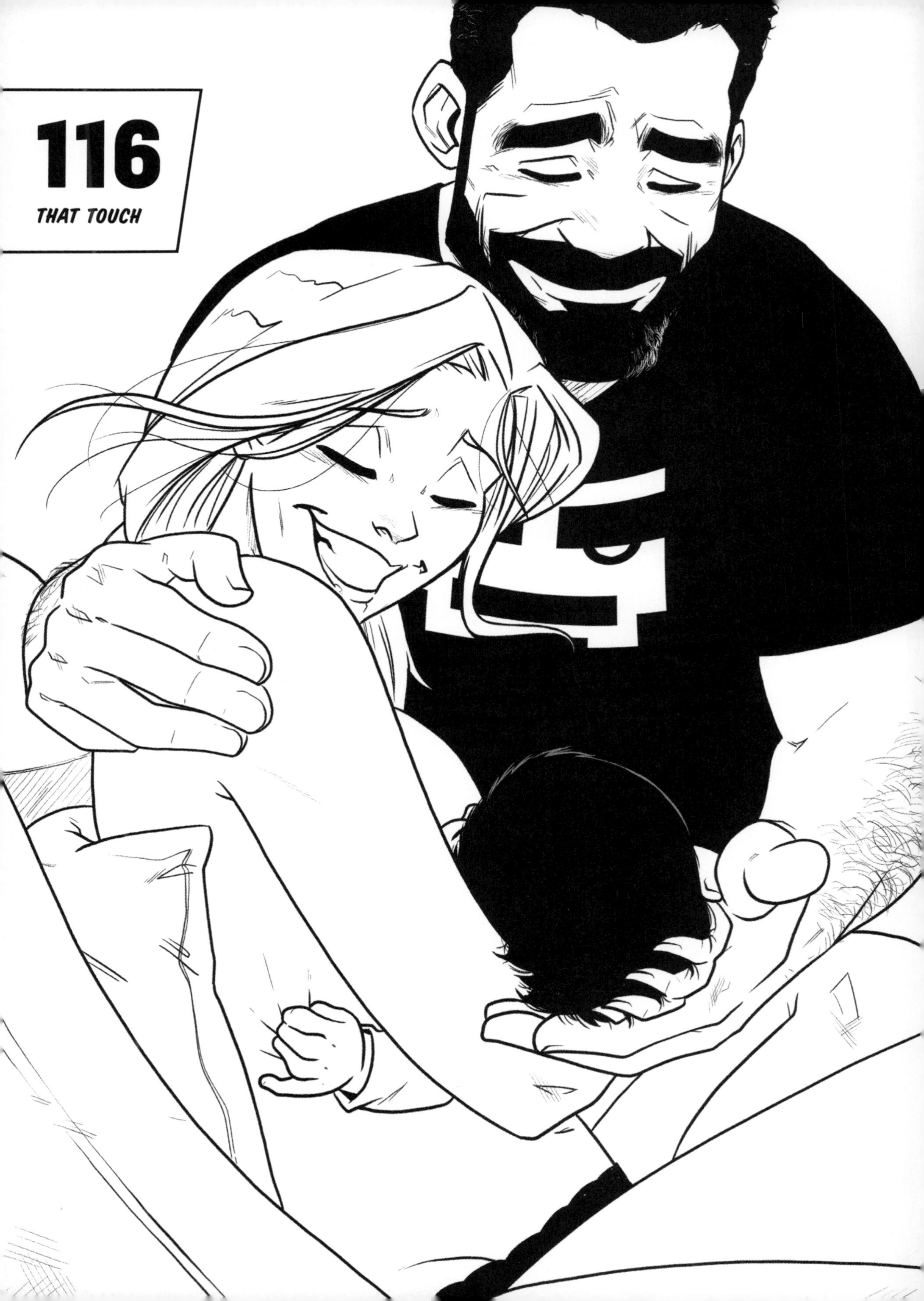

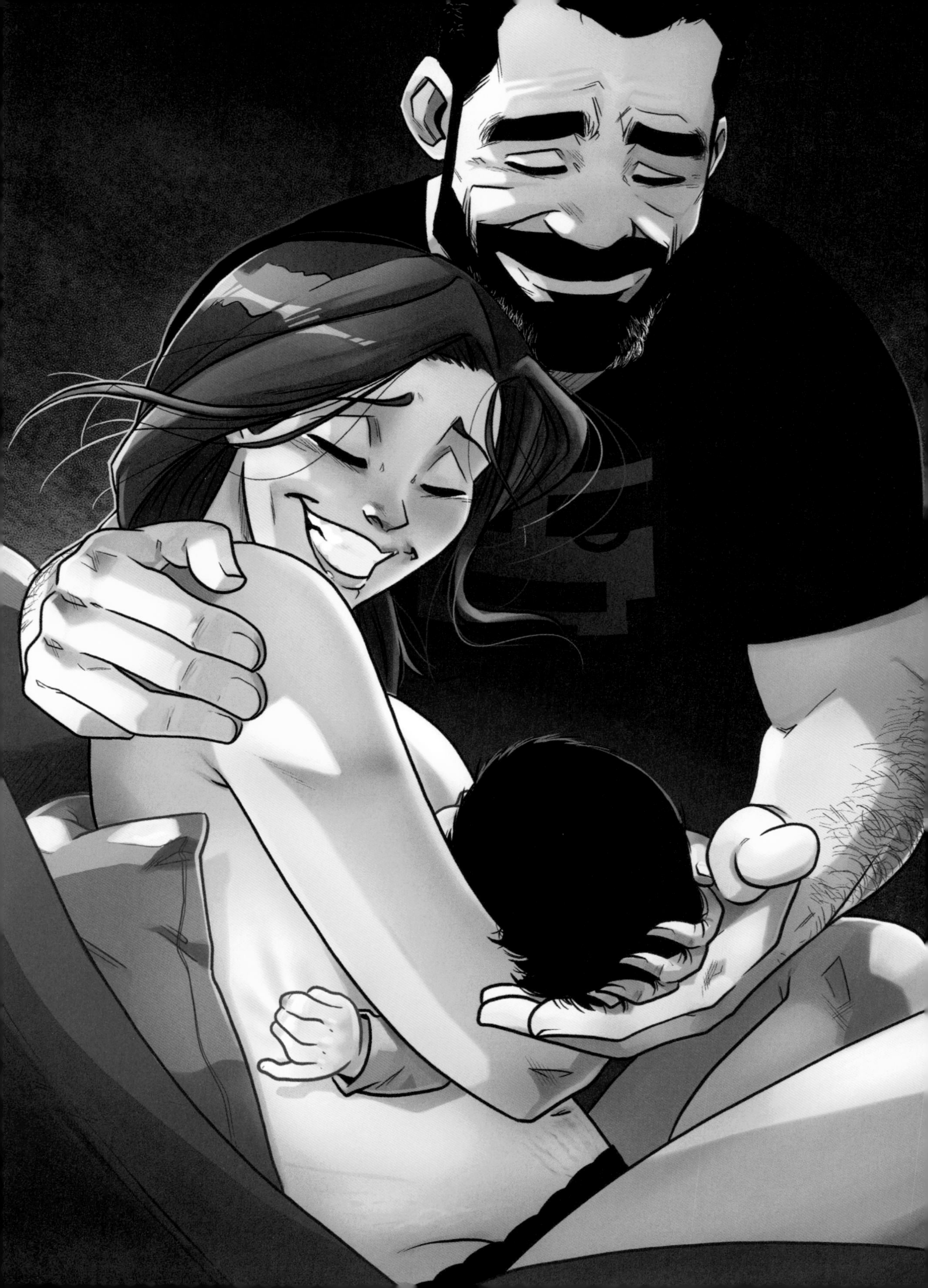

117

HAPPY BIRTHDAY, MOMMA

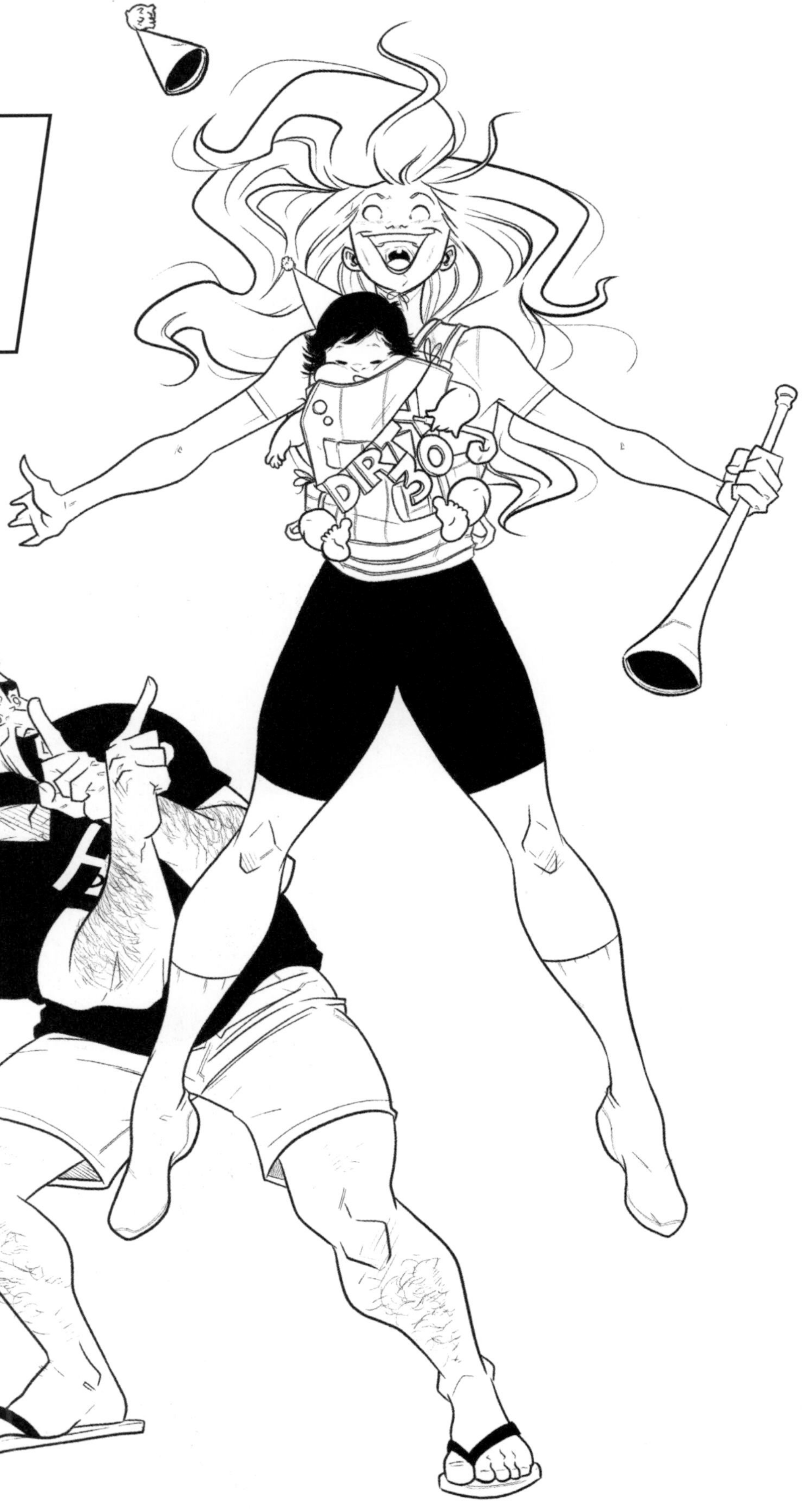

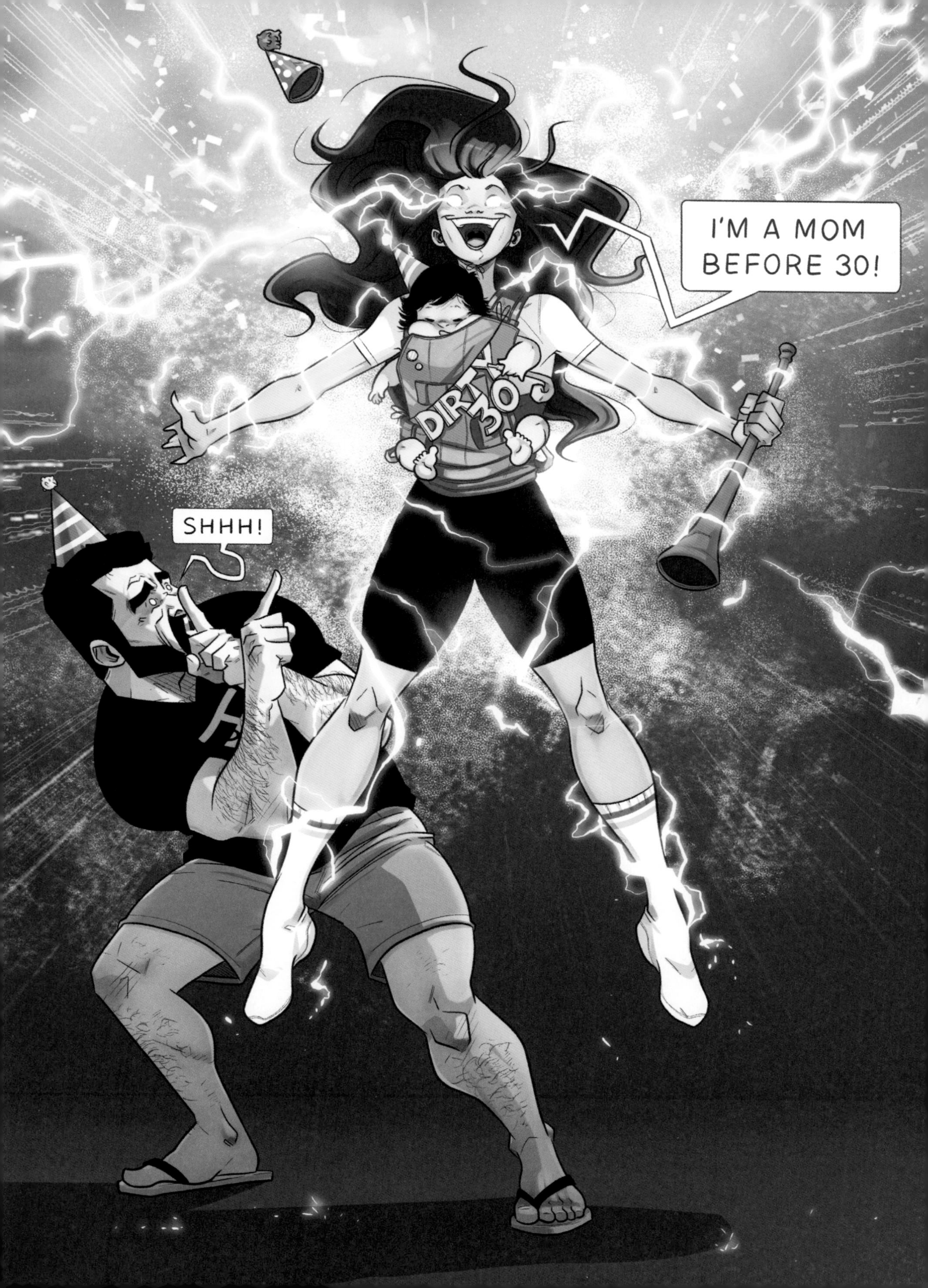
I'M A MOM BEFORE 30!
SHHH!

118

PLEASE GO TO SLEEP

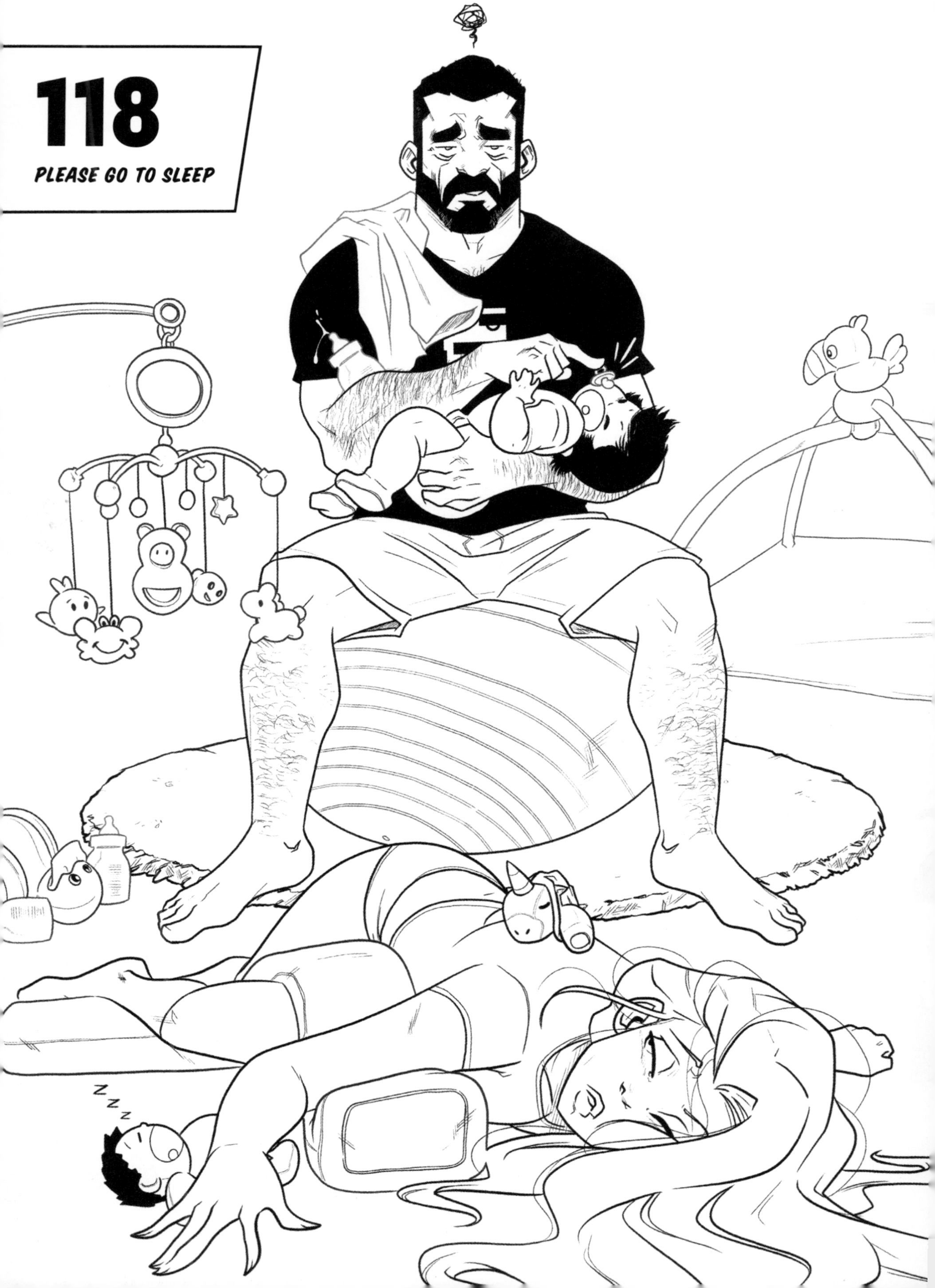
ZZZ

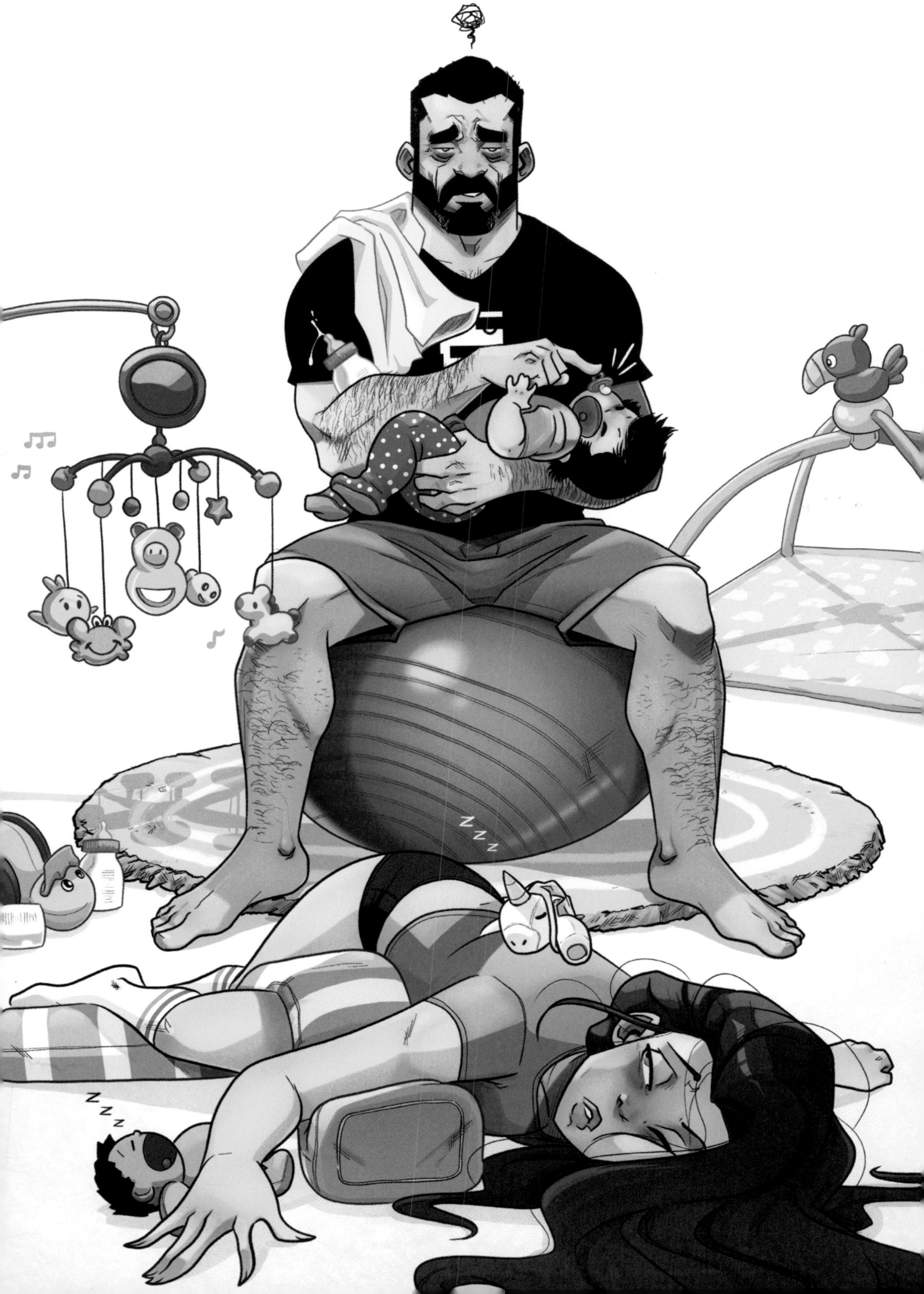

119

THE FIRST SHOWER

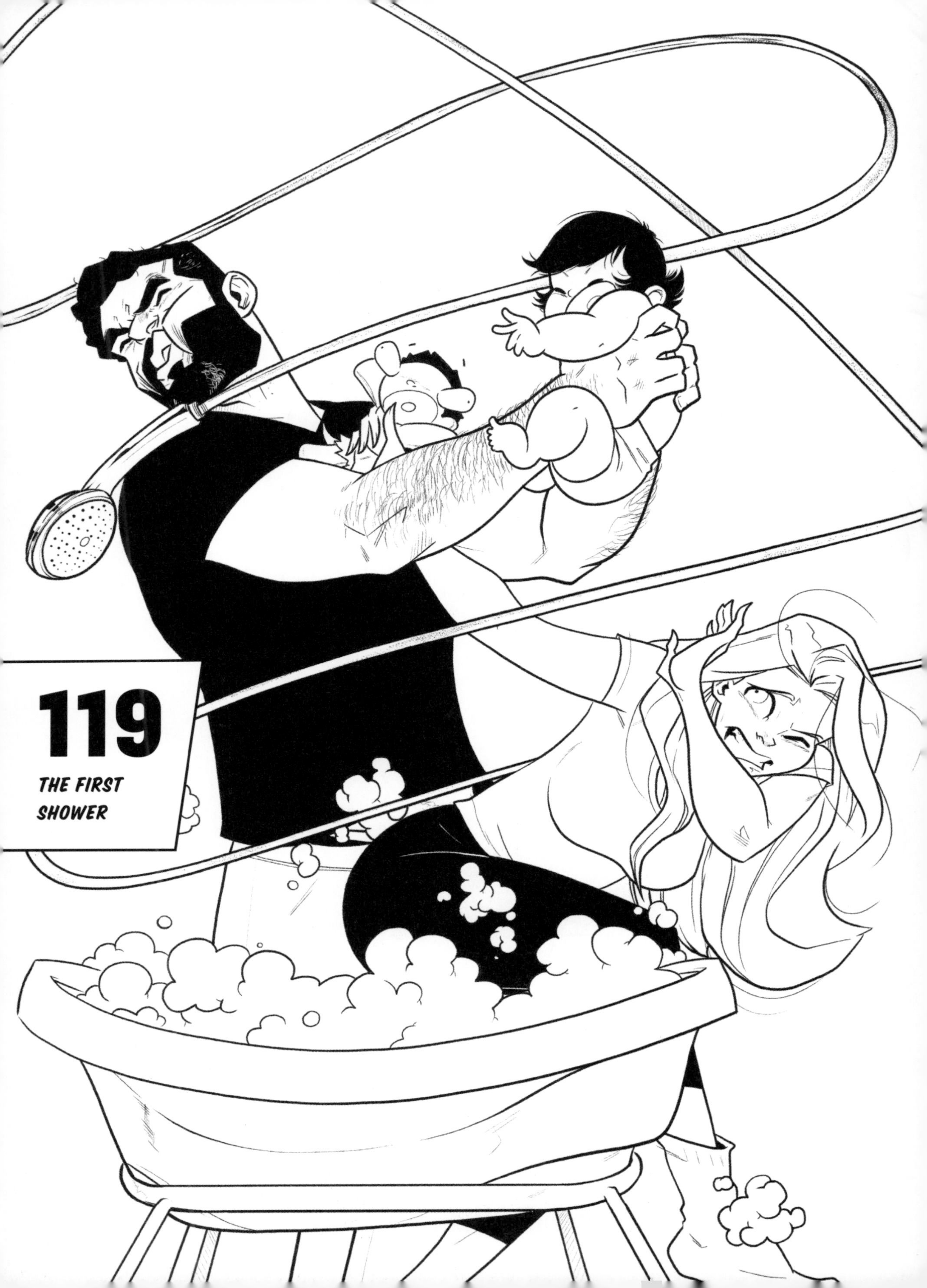

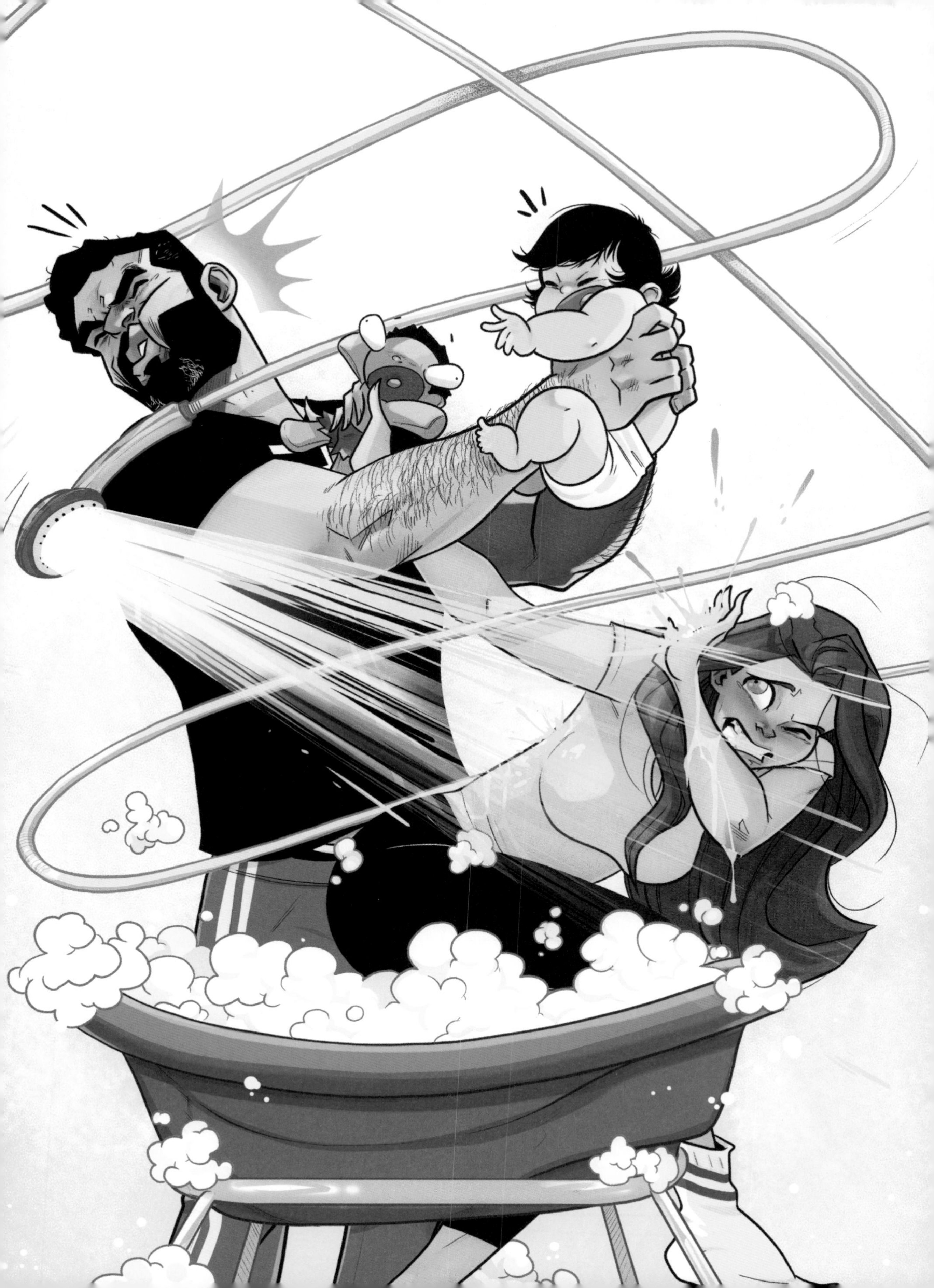

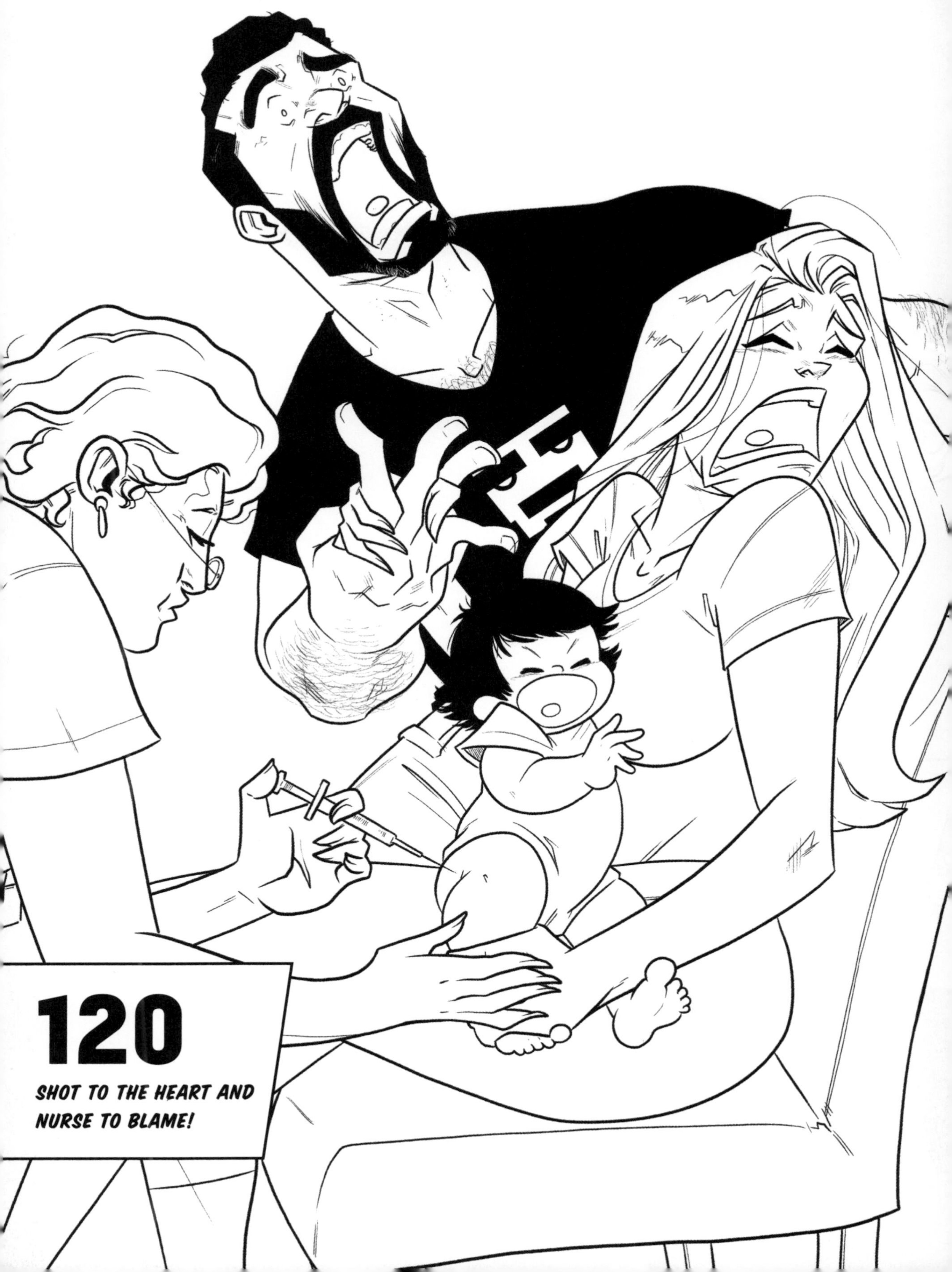

120

SHOT TO THE HEART AND NURSE TO BLAME!

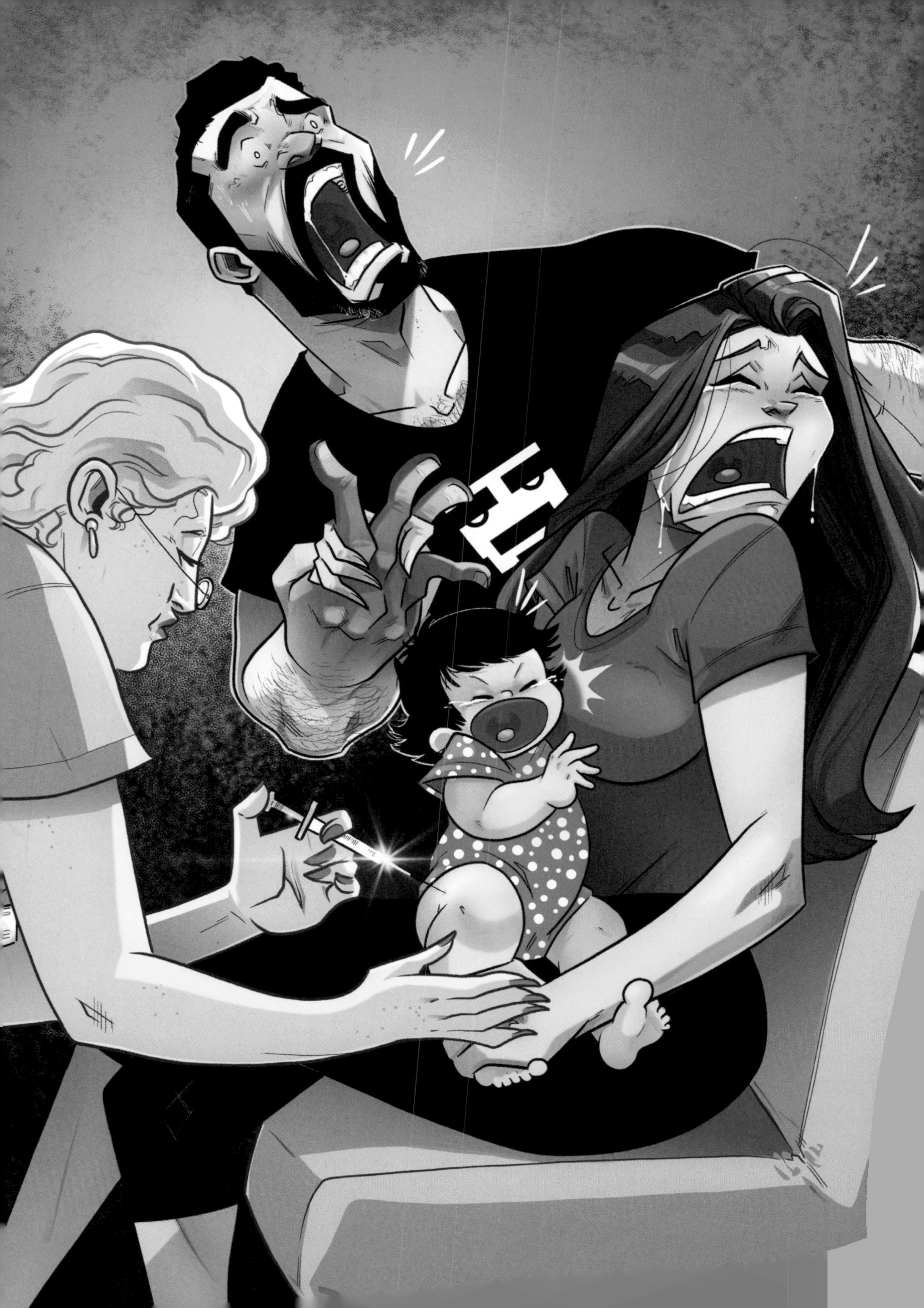

121

MOMMY FOR EVERYONE!

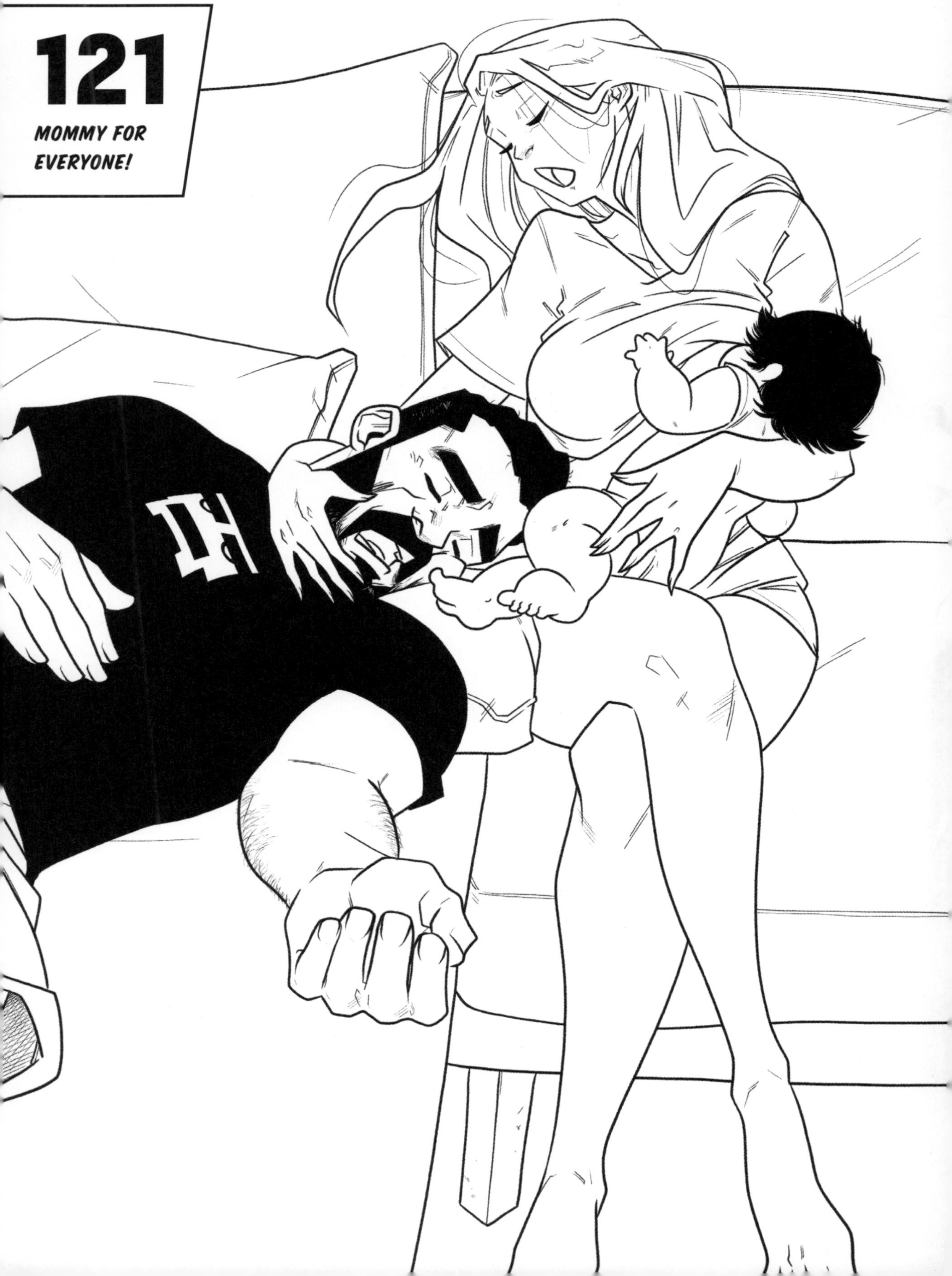

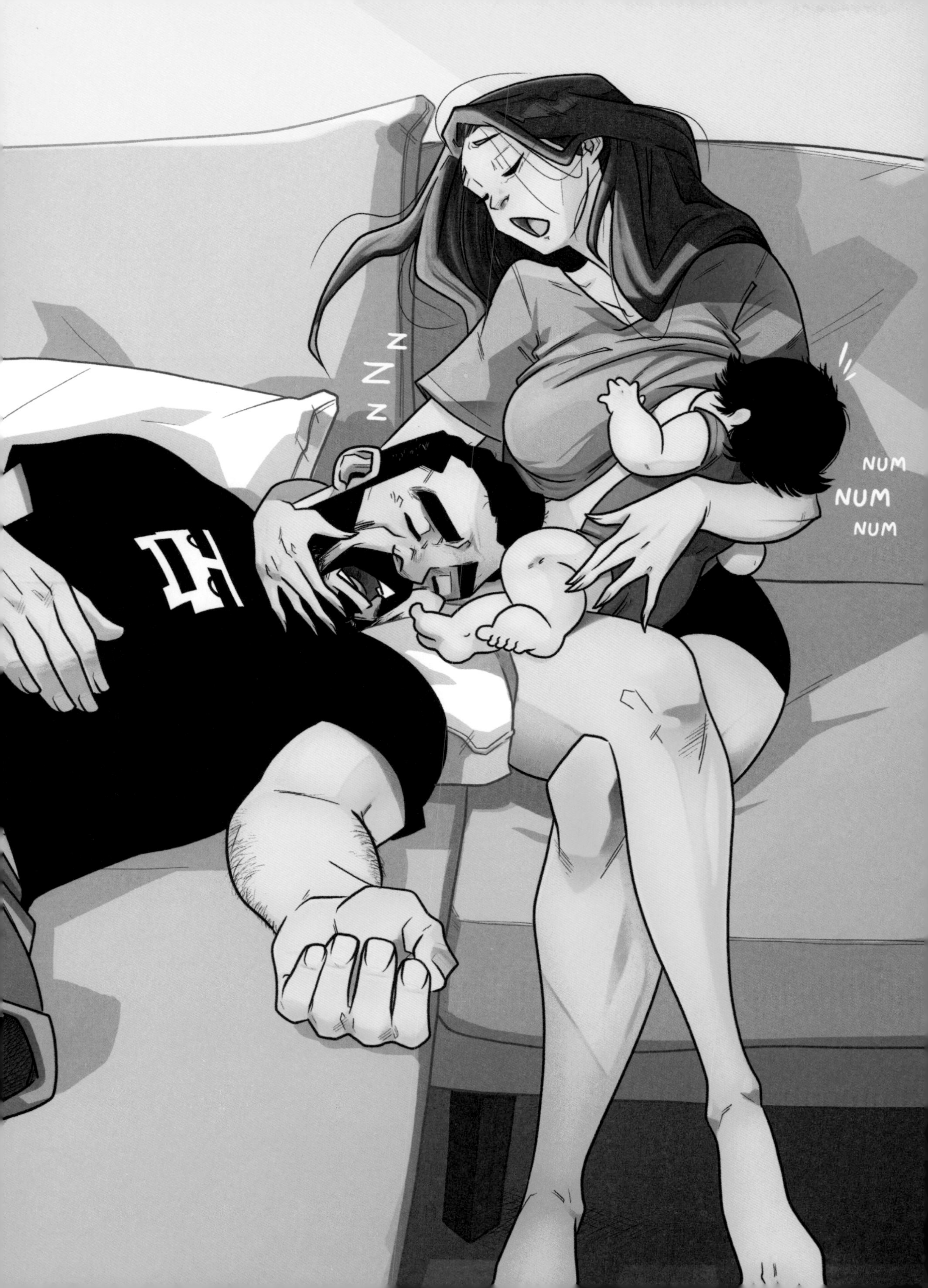
Z
Z
Z
NUM
NUM
NUM

122

ALL FOR ONE!

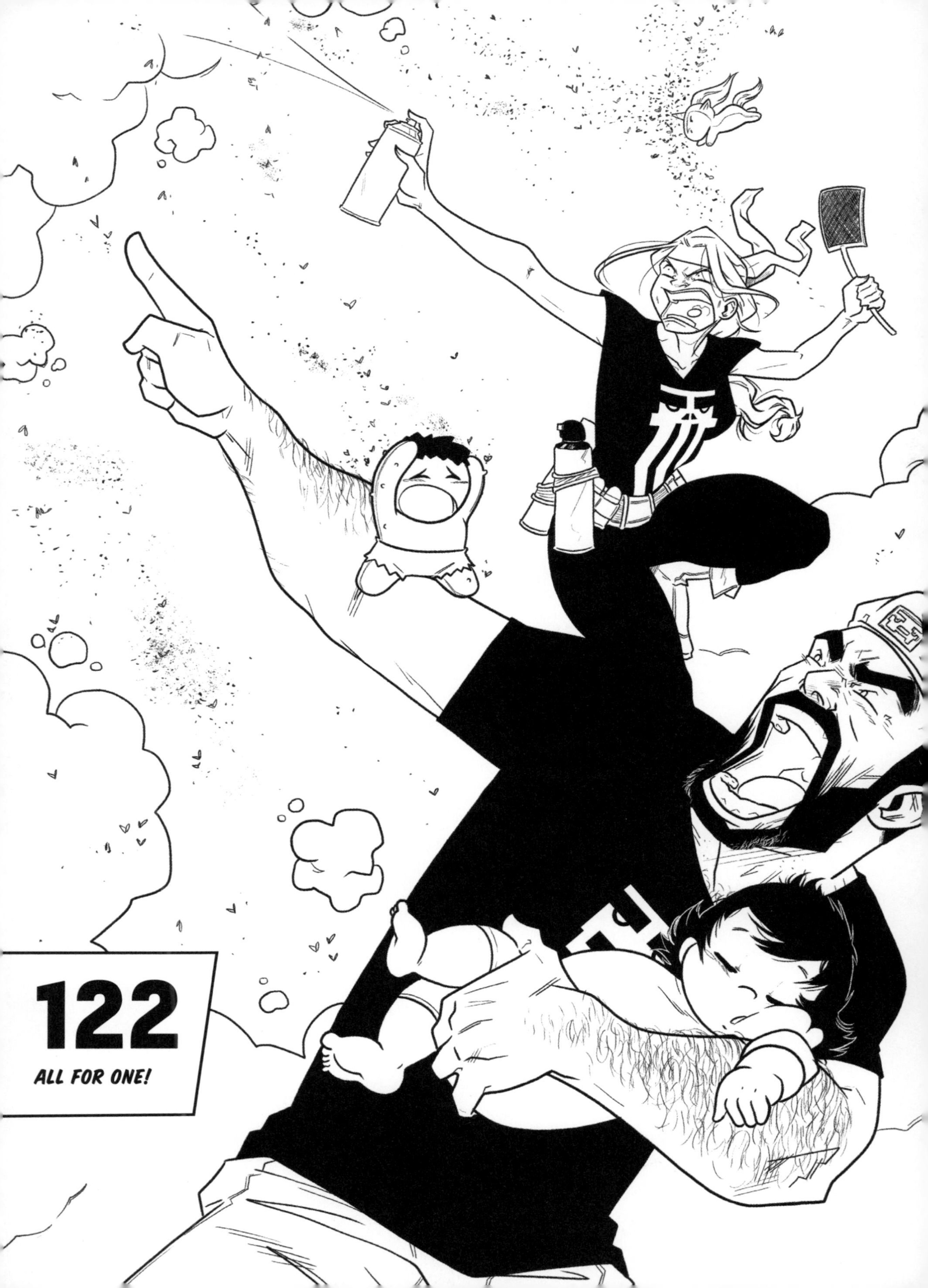

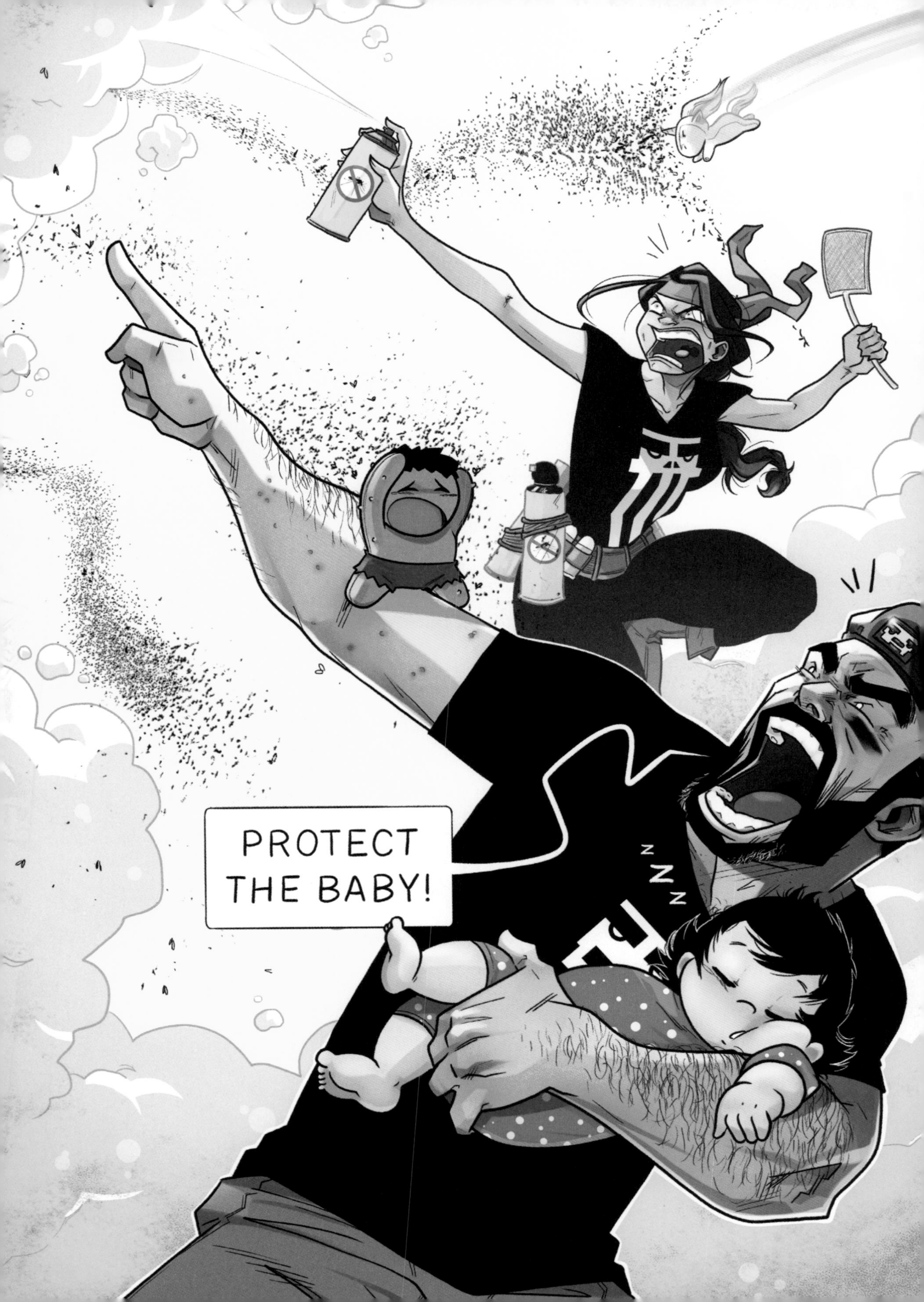
PROTECT THE BABY!

123

SAY CHEESE!

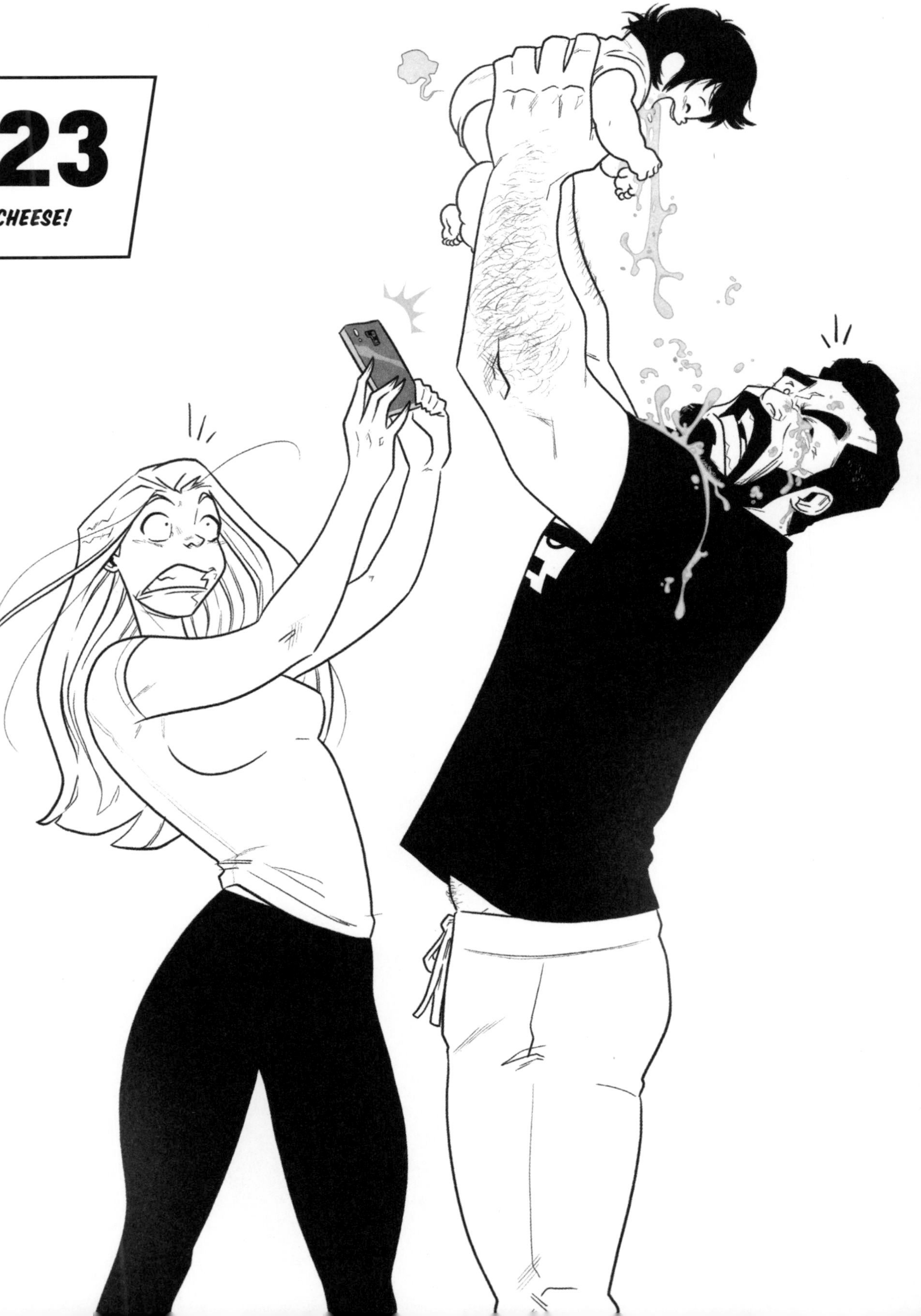

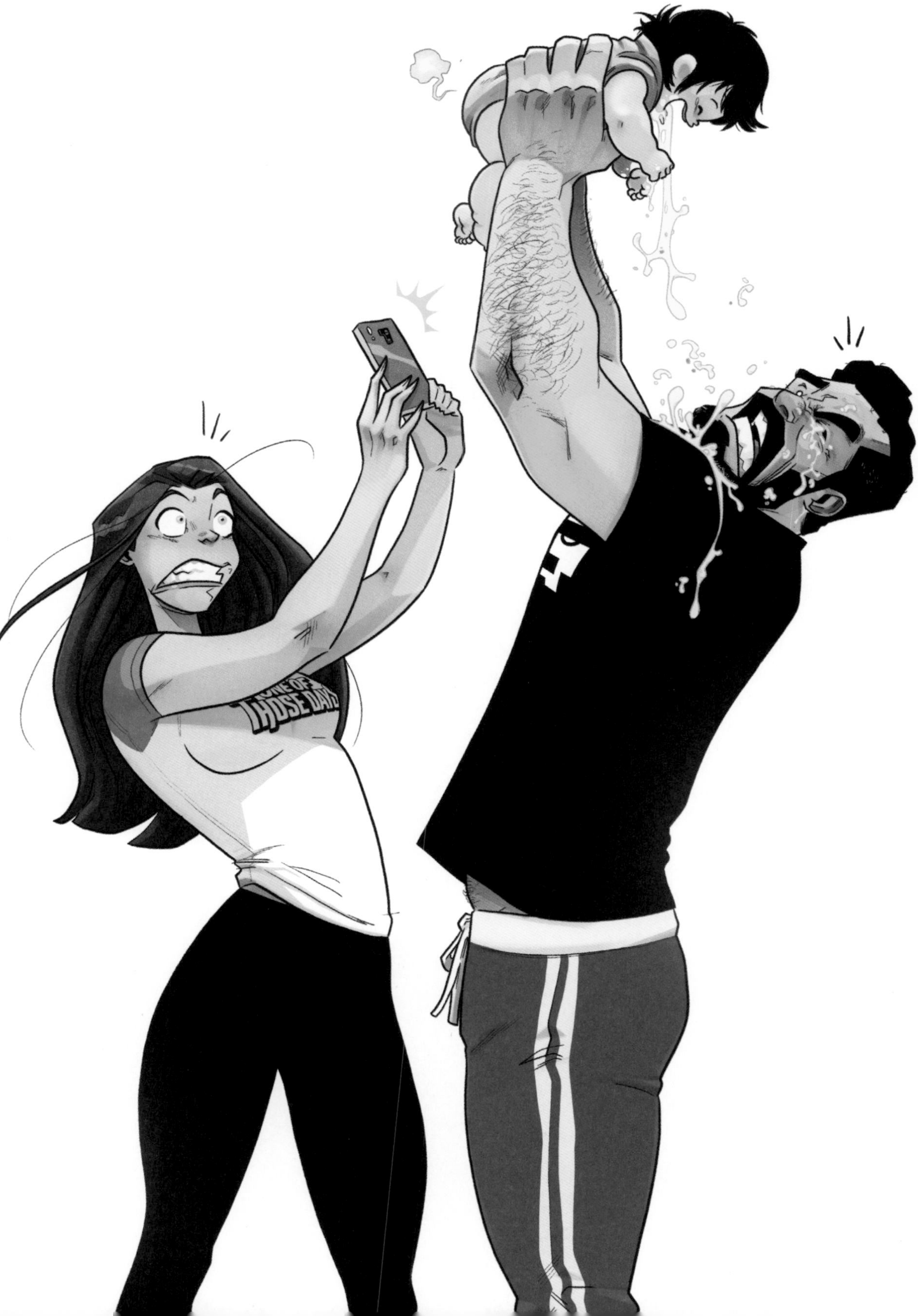

124

IT'S OKAY

IT'S OKAY WHEN SHE CRIES IN YOUR HANDS.
IT'S OKAY THAT SHE ONLY WANTS HER MOM.
IT'S OKAY THAT YOU CAN'T PUT HER TO SLEEP.
IT'S OKAY THAT YOU STILL DON'T UNDERSTAND
YOUR STATUS.
IT'S OKAY THAT YOU DON'T HAVE THAT
CONNECTION THAT EVERYBODY IS TALKING ABOUT.
IT'S OKAY THAT YOU STILL DON'T UNDERSTAND
YOUR JOB DEFINITION.
IT'S OKAY THAT YOU DON'T MAKE HER LAUGH.
IT'S OKAY THAT YOU'RE TIRED.
IT'S OKAY THAT YOU'RE ANGRY.
IT'S OKAY THAT THINGS DON'T WORK OUT FOR YOU.
IT'S OKAY TO ASK FOR A HUG.
IT'S OKAY TO SHARE WITH YOUR PARTNER EVERYTHING
YOU GO THROUGH, EVEN IF IT DOESN'T SEEM SO MANLY.
IT'S OKAY THAT YOUR LIFE HAS CHANGED.
IT'S OKAY THAT YOUR PLANS HAVE BEEN CANCELED.
IT'S OKAY THAT YOU HAVE NO TIME FOR ANYTHING.
IT'S OKAY TO FEEL WEAK.
IT'S OKAY TO BE MOODY.
IT'S OKAY TO FEEL LONELY.
IT'S OKAY TO ASK FOR HELP.
IT'S OKAY.

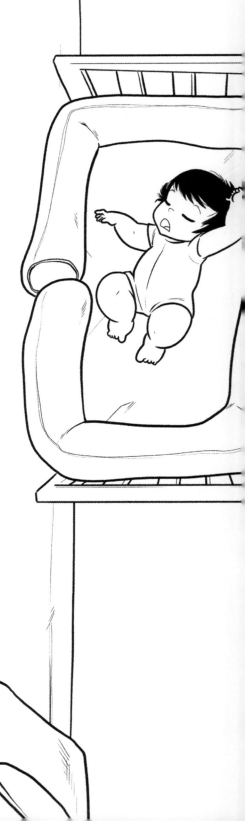

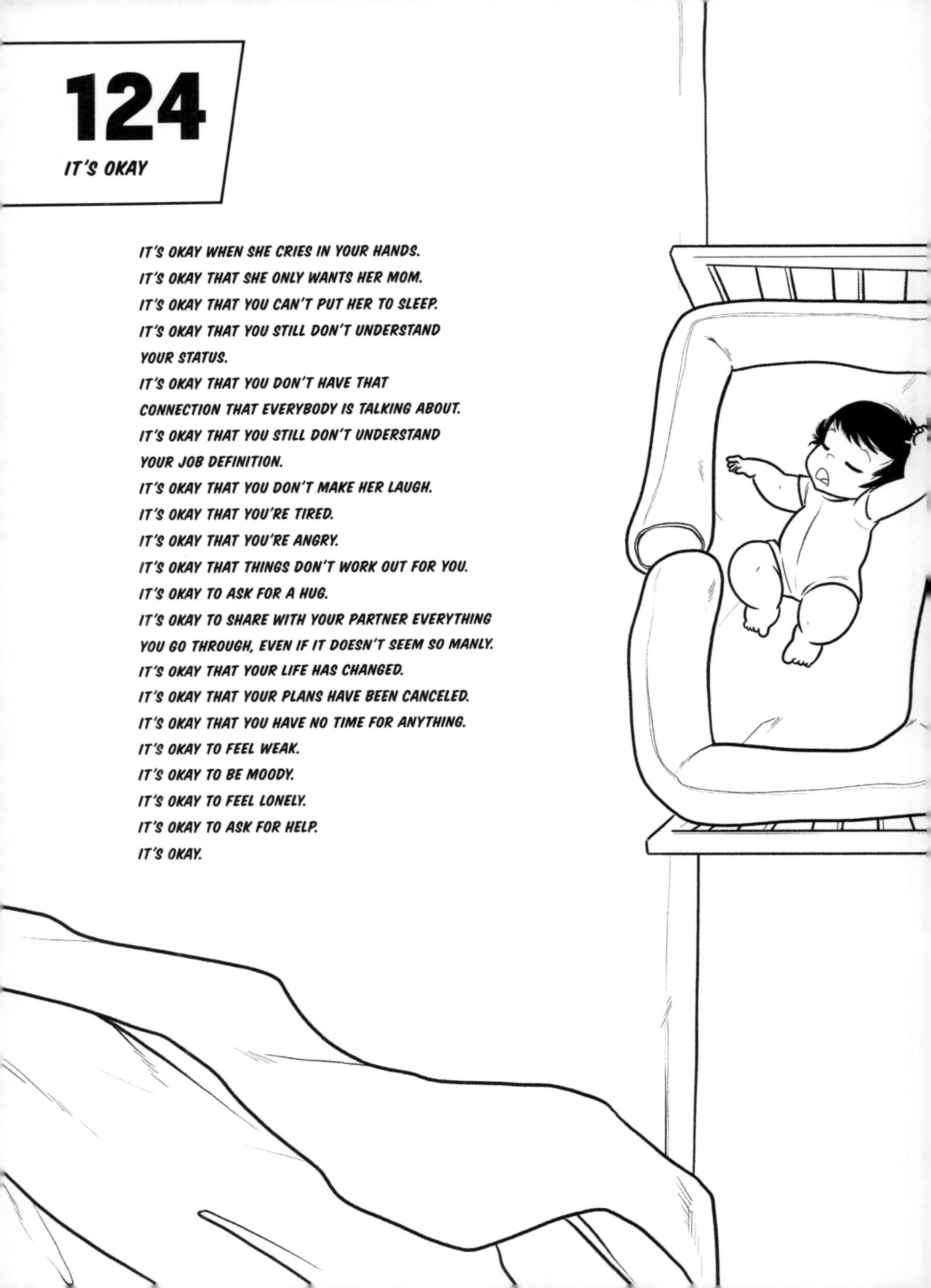

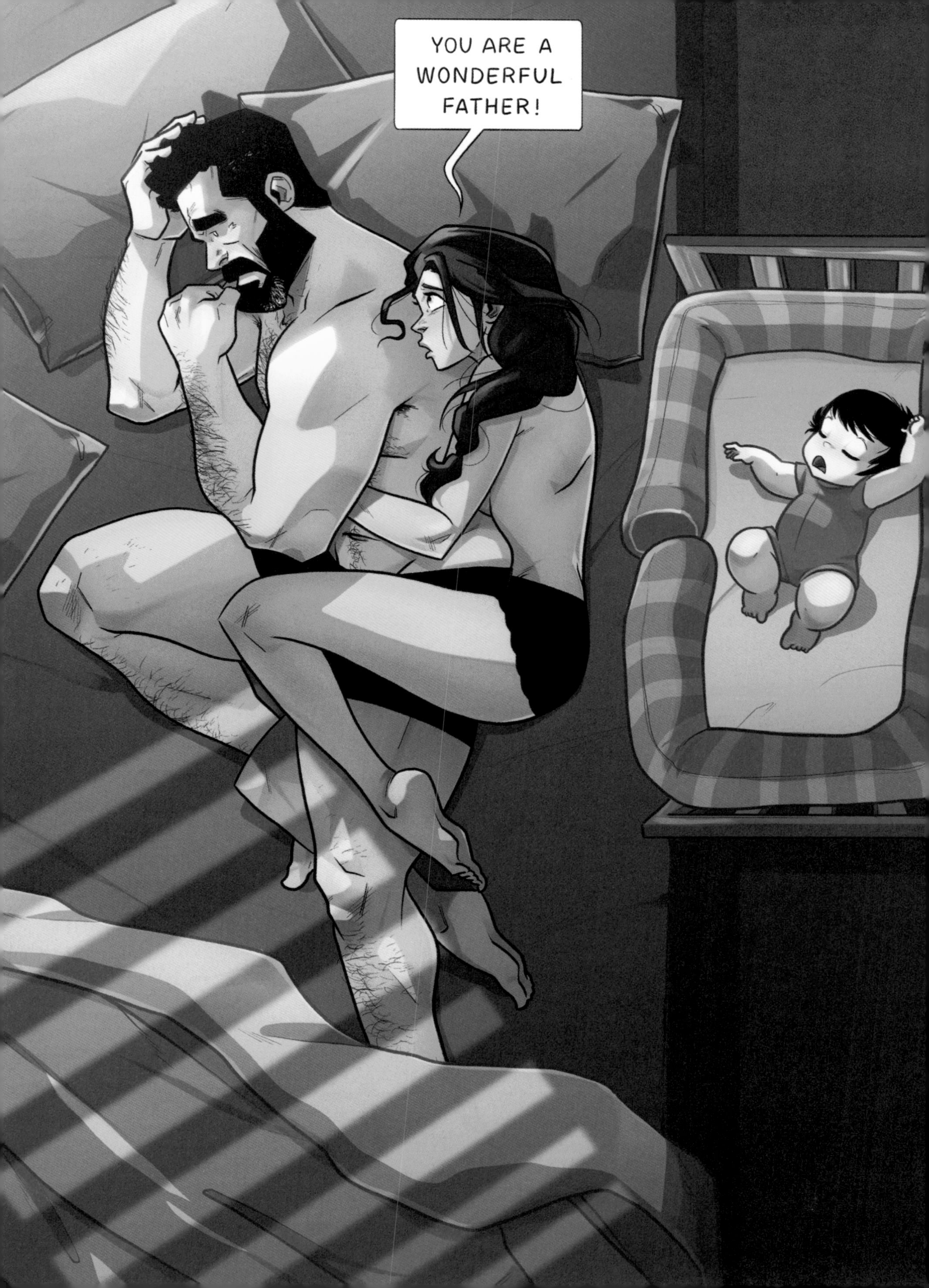
YOU ARE A WONDERFUL FATHER!

125

GOING OUT

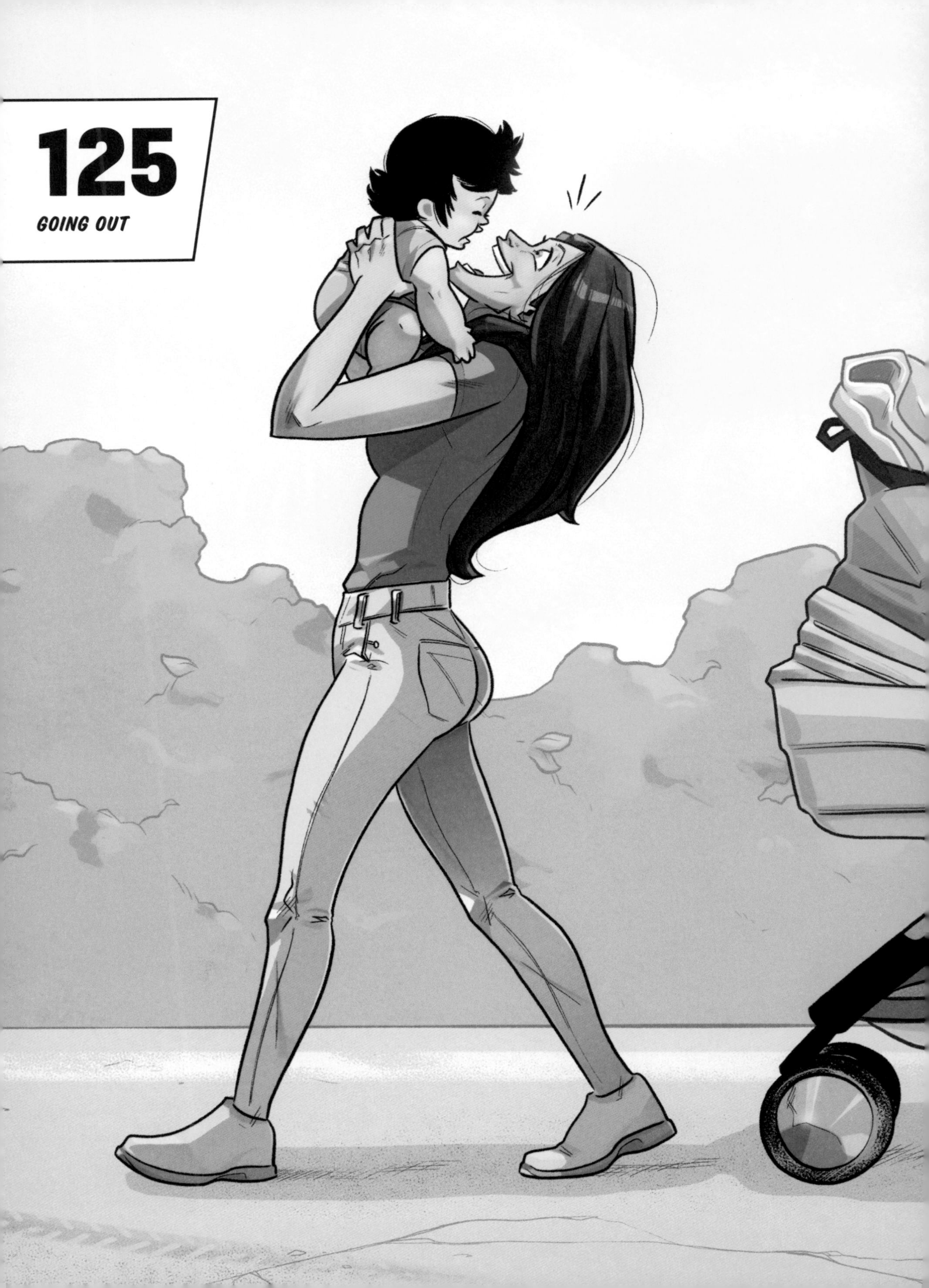

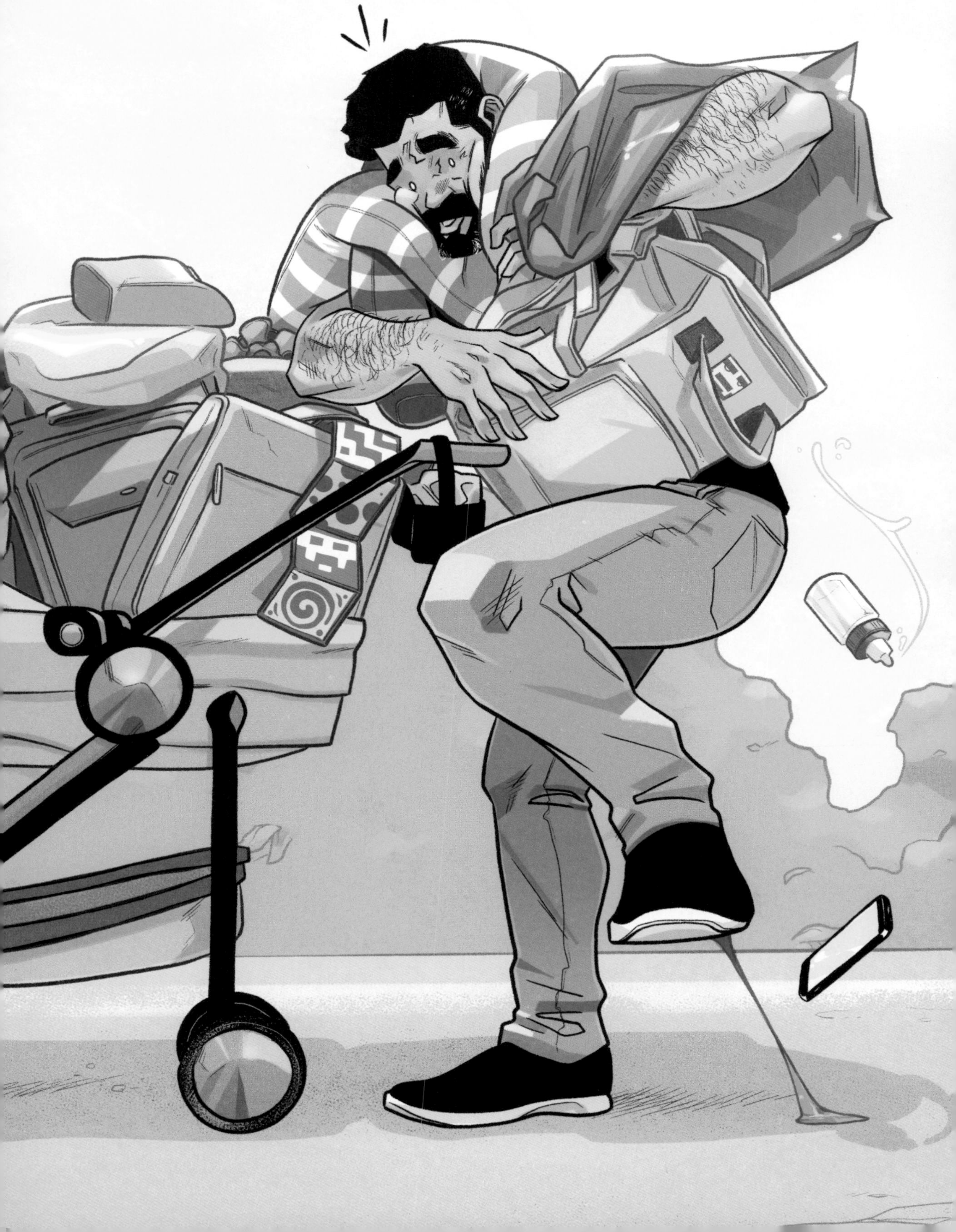

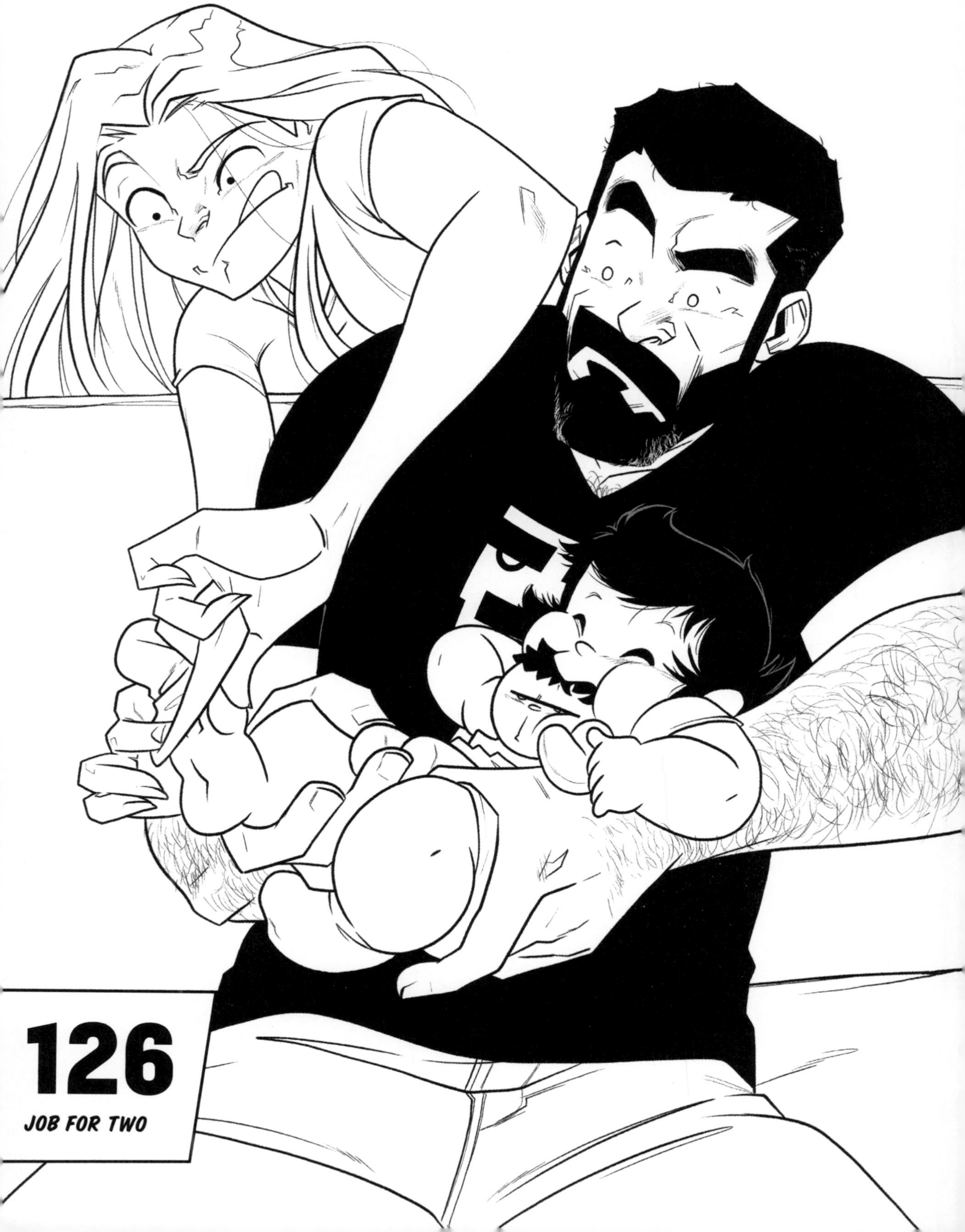

126

JOB FOR TWO

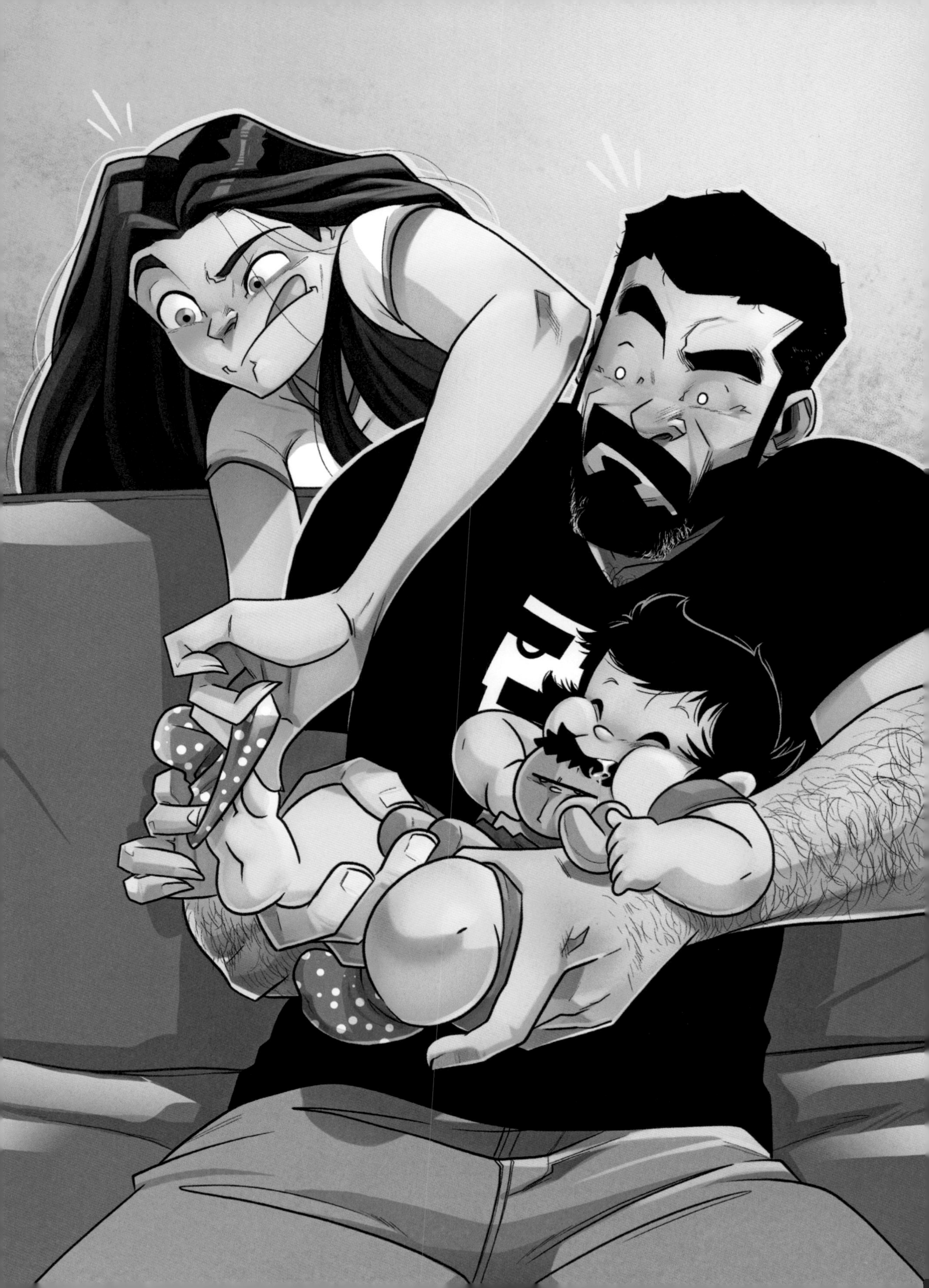

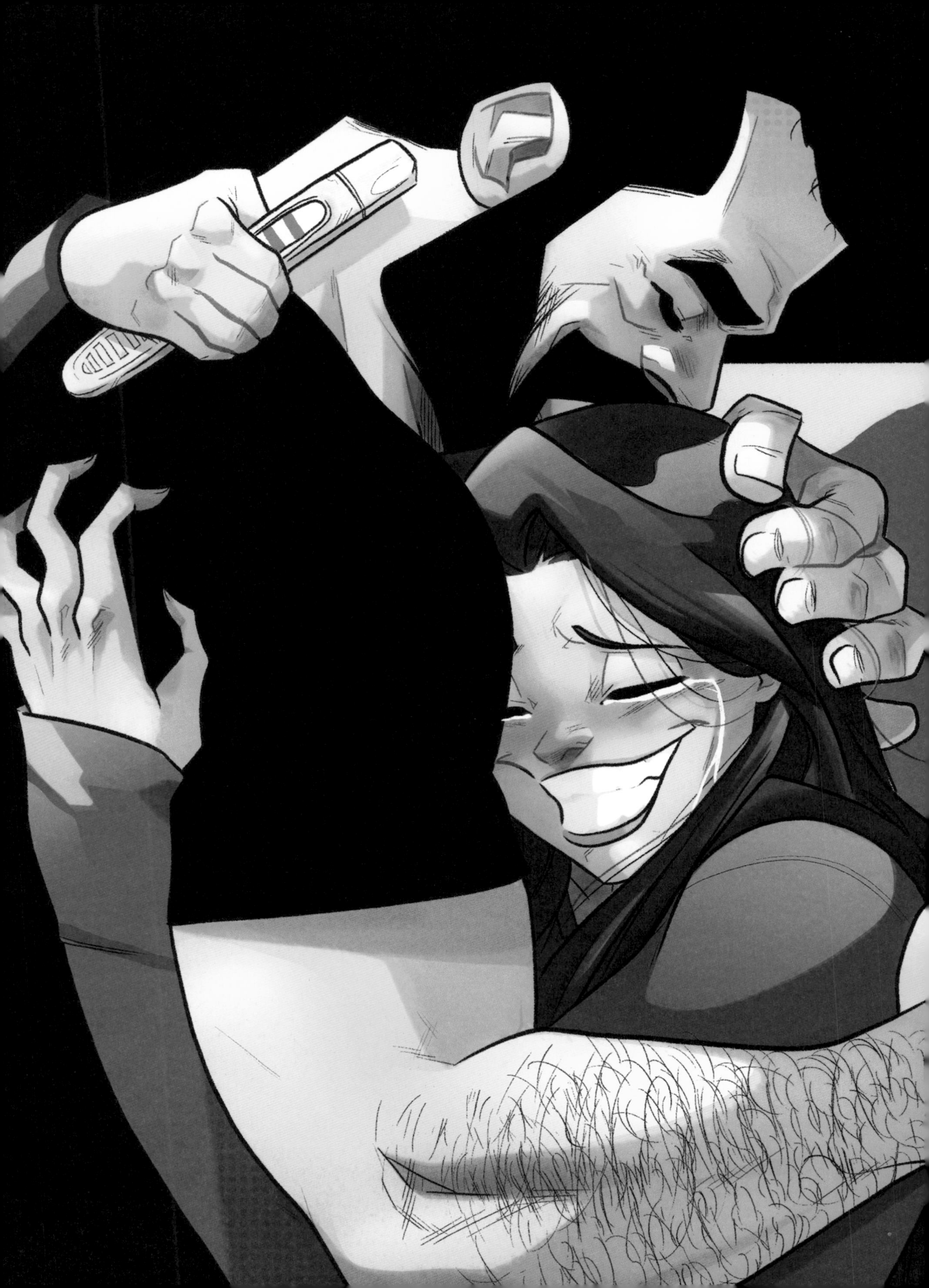

ABOUT THE AUTHORS

YEHUDA and MAYA DEVIR are married Israeli comic artists and the creators of the popular webcomic *One of Those Days*.

The hyperenergetic YEHUDA DEVIR "makes the ants look lazy," according to Maya. He discovered his love for drawing in infancy when he began painting on his bedroom walls, and was particularly influenced by the American comics and film industry.

MAYA DEVIR is a "goddess in a form of a woman who spreads joy wherever she goes," according to Yehuda. She is a realist artist and the *One of Those Days* art director, and she specializes in the art of teasing Yehuda.

The couple both studied visual communication at Bezalel Academy of Art and Design, Jerusalem. Today they live and work in their small, quiet apartment with their new baby girl, Ariel.

FOLLOW US ON

- yehudadevir.com
- @jude_devir, @maya_devir, @ariel_devir, @oneof_thosedays
- @Yehuda Devir
- Yehuda & Maya Devir
- @YehudaDevir
- Patreon.com/yehudadevir
- @judedevir

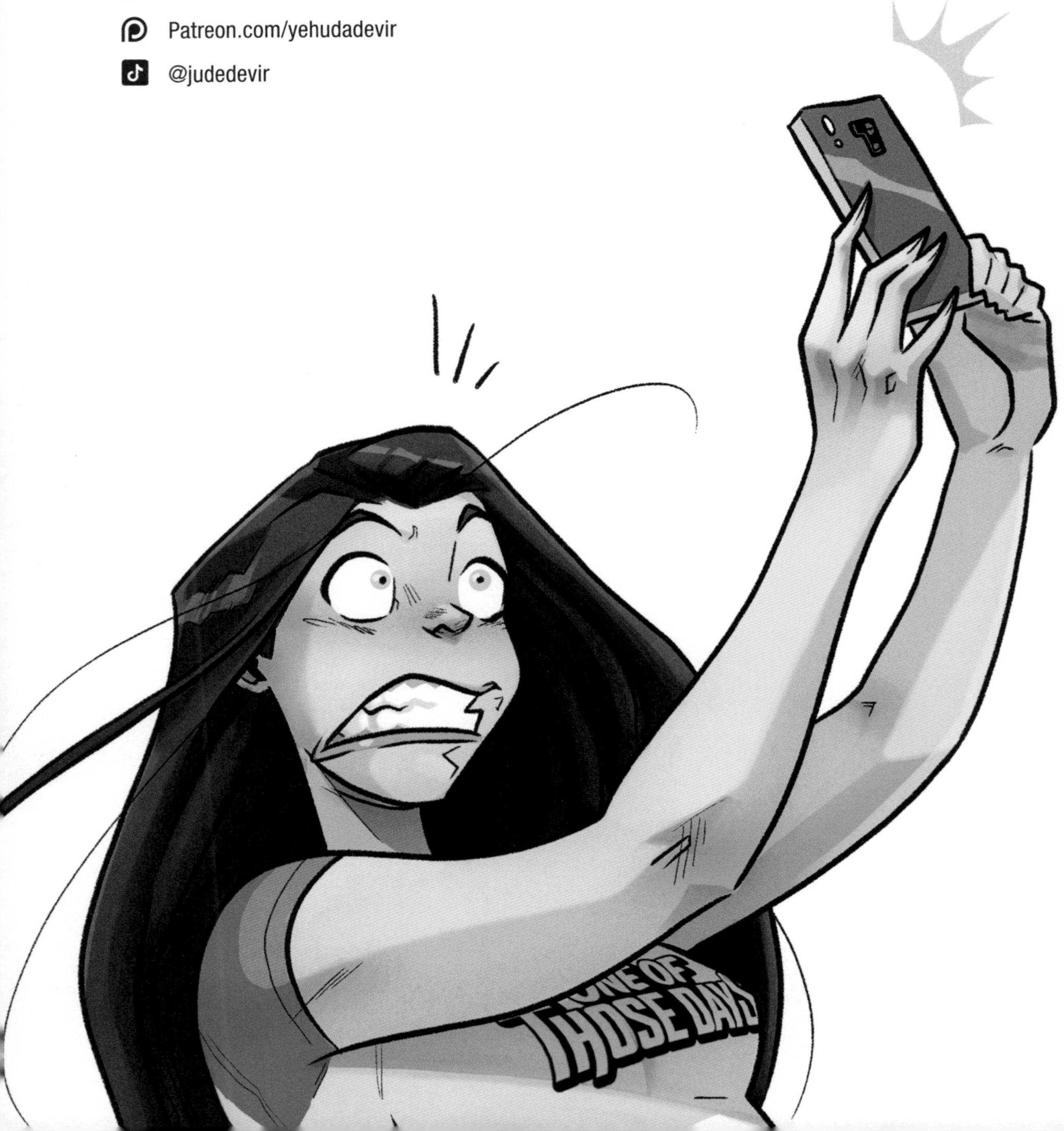

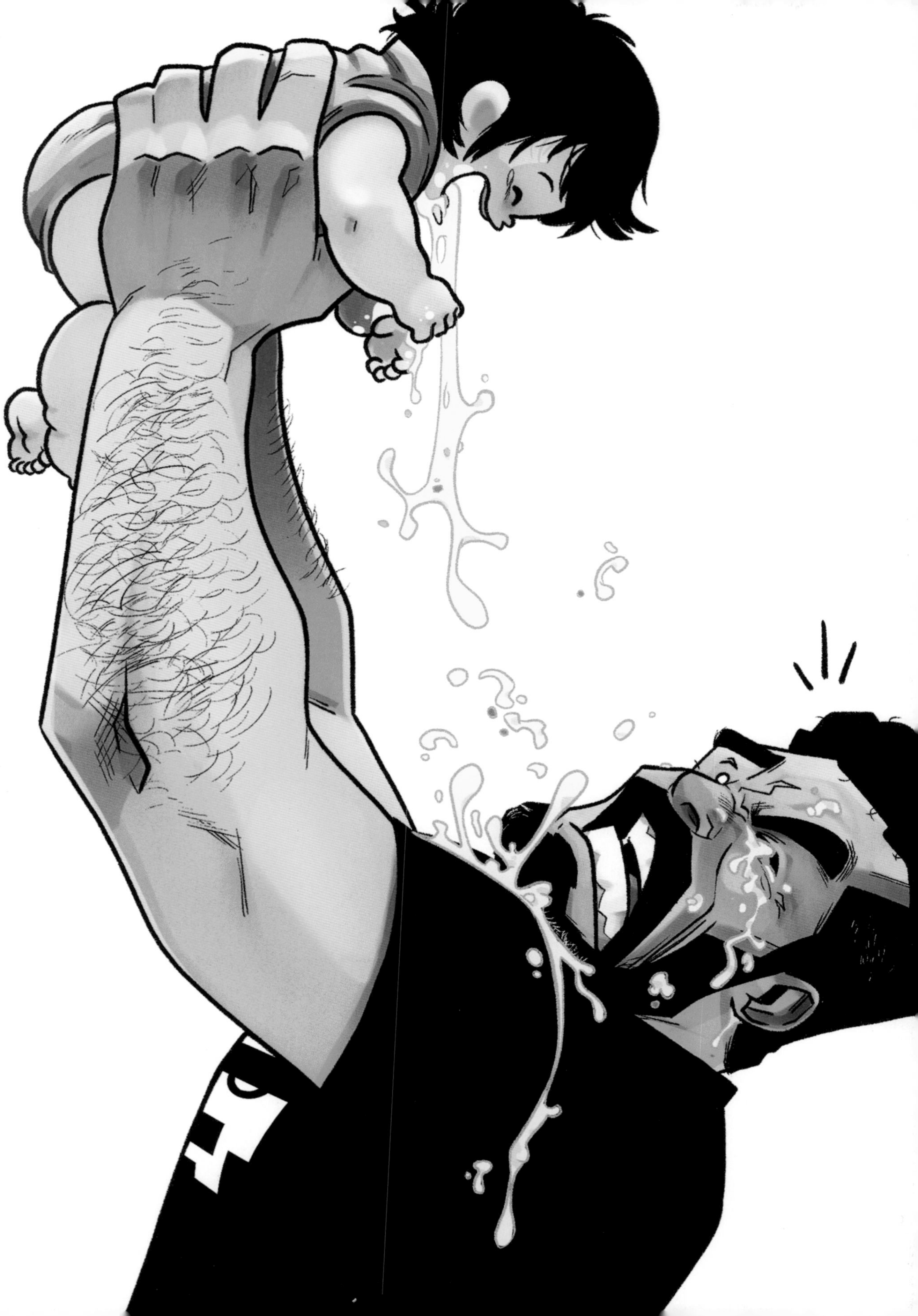

FOR ARIEL